India: The Emerging Giant

INDIA: THE EMERGING GIANT

Arvind Panagariya

2008

OXFORD

UNIVERSITY PRESS

Oxford University Press, Inc., publishes works that further
Oxford University's objective of excellence
in research, scholarship, and education.

Oxford New York

Auckland Cape Town Dar es Salaam Hong Kong Karachi
Kuala Lumpur Madrid Melbourne Mexico City Nairobi
New Delhi Shanghai Taipei Toronto

With offices in

Argentina Austria Brazil Chile Czech Republic France Greece
Guatemala Hungary Italy Japan Poland Portugal Singapore
South Korea Switzerland Thailand Turkey Ukraine Vietnam

Published by Oxford University Press, Inc.
198 Madison Avenue, New York, New York 10016
www.oup.com

Oxford is a registered trademark of Oxford University Press.

Library of Congress Cataloging-in-Publication Data

Panagariya, Arvind.
India : the emerging giant / Arvind Panagariya.
p. cm.
Includes bibliographical references and index.
ISBN 978-0-19-531503-5
1. India—Economic policy. 2. India—Economic conditions.
3. India—Commerce. I. Title.
HC435.3P36 2007
330.954'05—dc22 2007034153

3 5 7 9 8 6 4 2

Printed in the United States of America on acid-free paper

In Memory of
My Father

ACKNOWLEDGMENTS

"Take your time, but write a definite book on India." Those were the last words of advice from my father on a telephone call from Jaipur, my hometown. He passed away a week later, on New Year's Day, 2006. At 84, his enthusiasm to see his children (and grandchildren) excel was undiminished. He had lived his life by the same rule, distinguishing himself first as a top-class civil servant and then, after retirement, as an author of a dozen books, of which one was released by no less than Prime Minister Indira Gandhi.

In writing this book, I have benefited from the wisdom and generosity of many. But I owe by far the greatest debt to Jagdish Bhagwati, who has been a constant source of inspiration throughout my professional life. As a student in India, I read many of his prolific writings on international trade, development, and India. At the time, I scarcely imagined that one day I would have the honor to occupy a chair named after him. His 1970 book on India, jointly written with Padma Desai, is the best work in existence on the economic policies and their pitfalls in postindependence India. It also outlines a strategy of growth and poverty reduction that India would begin to implement only many years later. My thinking, as that of virtually every leading scholar of the Indian economy, is greatly influenced by this monumental work.

I also wish to thank T. N. Srinivasan, a great scholar of international trade and economic development, for helping me understand better many of the intricacies of the Indian economy. Numerous discussions with Vijay Kelkar during his tenure as India's executive director at the International Monetary Fund sparked my interest in aspects of the economy about which I had not thought before. This is particularly true of higher education. My longtime friends Govinda Rao and Rajesh Chadha have been most generous at all stages during this work. With their vast knowledge of the Indian economy, they have always been there to answer my questions, big and small.

As will be apparent from my extensive references, many of the ideas in the book originated in my monthly column in the *Economic Times*, India's leading financial daily. For this, my thanks go to Swaminathan S. Anklesaria Aiyar, who invited me to contribute to the *Economic Times*. I should also like to thank successive editors of the editorial page of the newspaper—Mythili Bhusnurmath, T. K. Arun, and Bodhisatva Ganguli—who provided me the opportunity to try out my ideas on more than a million of the newspaper's readers.

My task in writing this book was considerably simplified by the availability of extensive data on the Reserve Bank of India Web site. The Reserve Bank has done an excellent job of organizing the important data on the Indian economy and making them accessible to researchers. Its *Handbook of Statistics on Indian Economy*, updated every year in a timely fashion, proved especially useful. Also helpful were the tables accompanying the *Economic Survey*, published annually by the Ministry of Finance and posted on its Web site.

Among those who generously commented on earlier drafts of several of the book's chapters, my greatest debt is to Poonam Gupta, a former student of mine who is now an associate professor at the Delhi School of Economics. Whenever I needed a friendly but critical reader, I went to her. I am equally grateful to Deena Khatkhate for his willingness to read many of the chapters and to offer his sage advice. Also helpful at various stages of the work were discussions with or comments from Pranab Bardhan, Suman Bery, Angus Deaton, Pramod Deo, Shanta Devarajan, Ashok Gulati, Nandini Gupta, Rana Hasan, James Hanson, Kishore Gawande, Vijay Jagannathan, Vijay Joshi, Anjini Kochar, Ashok Kotwal, Pravin Krishna, R. D. Maheshwari, Deepak Mishra, Srijit Mishra, Devashish Mitra, Rakesh Mohan, Garry Pursell, Govinda Rao, Kavita Rao, Devesh Roy, Gunjan Sharma, N. K. Singh, Nirivikar Singh, Arun Shourie, S. Sriraman, Prem Vashishtha, Jessica Wallack, and Roberto Zagha.

I owe a great debt to Brian Desmond, my production editor at Oxford, and I am especially grateful to my editor, Terry Vaughn, and his assistant, Catherine Rae, who were there to answer my numerous queries from the submission of the manuscript to the final publication. Last but not least, I thank Yuko Ota for editing the Getty image to turn it into a beautiful book cover.

A large part of the credit for making this book happen goes to Amita, my wife. I could write the book because she did everything else. As a non-economist who regularly reads the *Economist*, *Financial Times,* and *Economic Times*, she also served as the sounding board for many of my ideas, especially those that were half-baked and shaky. This has helped keep many crazy ideas out of the book. Finally, I should mention our two boys, Ananth and Ajay, now young men with whom I love to chat leisurely, but have not been able to do so lately. With the book over, I can now catch up with them.

CONTENTS

Part V. The Government

PRIME MINISTERS OF INDIA

Prime Minister	Dates	Party	Coalition
Jawaharlal Nehru	August 15, 1947 to May 27, 1964	Indian National Congress	
Gulzari Lal Nanda	(Interim)	May 27, 1964 to June 9, 1964	Indian National Congress
Lal Bahadur Shastri	June 9, 1964 to January 11, 1966	Indian National Congress	
Gulzari Lal Nanda	(Interim)	January 11, 1966 to January 24, 1966	Indian National Congress
Indira Gandhi	January 24, 1966 to March 24, 1977	Indian National Congress	
Morarji Desai	March 24, 1977 to July 28, 1979	Indian National Congress (O)	Janata Party (minority)
Choudhary Charan Singh	July 28, 1979 to January 14, 1980	Bharatiya Lok Dal	Janata Party (minority)
Indira Gandhi	January 14, 1980 to October 31, 1984	Indian National Congress (I)	
Rajiv Gandhi	October 31, 1984 to December 2, 1989	Indian National Congress (I)	
Vishwanath Pratap Singh	December 2, 1989 to November 10, 1990	Janata Dal	National Front (minority)
Chandra Shekhar	November 10, 1990 to June 21, 1991	Samajwadi Janata Party (minority)	
P. V. Narasimha Rao	June 21, 1991 to May 16, 1996	Indian National Congress (I) (minority)	

Prime Minister	Dates	Party	Coalition
Atal Behari Vajpayee	May 16, 1996 to June 1, 1996	Bharatiya Janata Party (minority)	
H. D. Deve Gowda	June 1, 1996 to April 21, 1997	Janata Dal	United Front (minority)
Inder Kumar Gujral	April 21, 1997 to March 19, 1998	Janata Dal	United Front (minority)
Atal Bihari Vajpayee	March 19, 1998 to May 22, 2004	Bharatiya Janata Party	National Democratic Alliance
Dr. Manmohan Singh	May 22, 2004 to present	Indian National Congress	United Progressive Alliance (minority)

Note: "Party" refers to the party of affiliation of the Prime Minister. Where relevant, the column headed "coalition" names the coalition of the parties that ruled jointly. No entry in this column implies the party of the Prime Minister alone ruled. The entry "minority" indicates that the government lacked full majority in the Parliament and was supported by one or more parties from outside without direct participation in the government.

INTRODUCTION

India became independent on August 15, 1947. Under its visionary leader, Jawaharlal Nehru, it adopted a system of parliamentary democracy that remains intact today. Along with Costa Rica, Jamaica, and Sri Lanka, India is one of only four developing countries to have had democratically elected governments throughout the second half of the twentieth century and beyond. With 1.1 billion citizens, it is also by far the largest democracy in the world.

In 1951, India formally initiated its development program via the launch of the First Five-Year Plan. The United States, which was by then the undisputed leader of the free world, held high hopes from India. The consensus view in the United States was that whereas the East Asian countries, such as the Republic of Korea, were likely to turn into basket cases, India and Africa would quickly grow out of poverty. The U.S. enthusiasm was shared by the scholarly community, which flocked to study India as the model of economic development.

Yet, by 1980, the tables had been turned. In the early 1960s, the Republic of Korea decisively switched from an inward-looking, import-substitution industrialization strategy to a policy of aggressive outward orientation. The results were spectacular: Its per-capita gross domestic product (GDP) grew at an average annual rate of more than 6 percent during the 1960s and 1970s. In two decades, it virtually eliminated poverty as conventionally measured. In contrast, India turned progressively inward, embarked upon a major expansion of the public sector, and subjected the private sector to strict investment licensing. The result was an average annual growth in per-capita GDP of just a little above 1 percent per annum in the 1960s and 1970s. There was no change in the trend of the proportion of the population living below the official poverty line. Indeed, with the population growing more than 2 percent per annum, the absolute number of poor in the country rose.

But just as India was beginning to be viewed as a basket case (Fields, 1980, p. 204) with no hope for the vast numbers of its poor, it was beginning to prepare ground for another surprise: this time around, a pleasant one. Between the financial years 1965–66 (April 1, 1960, to March 31, 1961) and 1980–81, India's GDP, as distinct from per-capita GDP, had grown only 3.2 percent per annum. Starting in the early 1980s, the growth rate shifted up, averaging 4.8 percent between 1980–81 and 1987–88. The late 1980s saw another major shift, which pushed the average annual growth rate to 6.3 percent between 1988–89 and 2005–06. Indeed, since 2003–04, the economy has been growing at an average rate exceeding 8 percent. Unsurprisingly, the poverty ratio has been cut in half during this period, with a large reduction in the absolute number of the poor despite a growing population.

One casualty of India's poor performance during the 1960s and 1970s, in addition to its prickly relations with the United States, was the scholarship on the Indian economy. In the 1950s and early 1960s, the study of India carried a large premium for development economists, especially in the United States. But by the early 1970s, the premium had turned into a discount. I distinctly remember noting this change upon arrival at Princeton for my doctoral work in the mid-1970s. That observation led me to switch my own area of research from India to international trade theory.

The 1970s and subsequent decades produced only three major scholarly works on the Indian economy: Bhagwati and Desai (1970), Bhagwati and Srinivasan (1975), and Joshi and Little (1994). Of these, the Bhagwati and Desai (1970) contribution was the most comprehensive and also the most influential in the long run, while the latter two focused specifically on international trade and macroeconomic policies, respectively. Unfortunately, none of these works is recent enough to tell the story of India's turnaround since the 1980s or to interpret the prior experience in the light of the later. They also do not cover topics such as education, health, water supply, telecommunications, electricity, and transportation, all of them important areas of policy reform today.

Accordingly, in this book I offer an analytic account and interpretation of the major economic developments in postindependence India. I also provide a detailed discussion of where the policies currently stand and a road map of the future reforms necessary to accelerate and sustain growth. Furthermore, I cover the major scholarly and policy debates and controversies that have arisen in recent years in various areas of policy.

The prospects of a major turnaround in the fortunes of 1.1 billion people and the warming up of relations between India and the United States have led to a revival of interest in the study of the Indian economy among scholars around the world. In turn, this has led to a rapid accumulation of research on the economy. This research and its ready availability on the Internet have proved most helpful in completing this work, as the reference list at the end of the book will testify.

Fifty-five years is a long time, and India is a vast country. Therefore, even a long book such as this one cannot cover every important topic. Recognizing this limitation, I have chosen to focus almost exclusively on the national economy. India's 28 states and 7 union territories exhibit vast differences in policies and performance. Indeed, an argument can be made that the real action in India today has shifted to the states. Yet, with rare exceptions, I do not analyze the state-level policies. In the same vein, fiscal relations between the central government and the states constitute a critical area of study. But based on space considerations, I had to exclude it.

My approach in the book is to focus on the major areas of the national economy and analyze them in depth. I have carefully read the writings of other scholars within and outside India that I could access, done my own research, and then derived my conclusions. While many readers will undoubtedly disagree with many of my prescriptions, I hope the facts and analysis in the book will help them come to informed conclusions of their own.

The book is divided into five parts. Part I focuses on growth; part II, on poverty and inequality; part III, on macroeconomic policies; and parts IV and V, on microeconomic policies. Parts I and II are devoted to contemporary debates among scholars on growth, poverty, and inequality. They also offer my own view of how the economic policies have crucially influenced growth and poverty outcomes at various times since the 1950s. Parts III to V analyze the events and developments since the 1980s and the necessary future reforms in greater detail. The readers interested in the contemporary policies can choose to go directly to part III.

In the remainder of this introduction, I summarize some of the important themes of the book to give the reader the flavor of what follows. I begin with the title.

INDIA: THE EMERGING GIANT

A sure-fire way for an outsider to capture the attention of Indian audiences is to tell them that India is destined for stardom in the twenty-first century. If he can also argue that India's growth is more sustainable than that of China, and that it might even overtake the latter in the near future, the audiences may reward him with an instant celebrity status. This point was graphically illustrated by the thunderous reception the Indian press and politicians gave to the 2003 Goldman Sachs paper, "Dreaming with the BRICs: The Path to 2050." The paper, popularly known as the BRIC [Brazil, Russia, India, and China] Report, predicted that India's GDP growth rate between 2015 and 2050 would exceed that of all other major countries in the world, including China, and that its total income would reach almost 80 percent of that of the United States by 2050. The report became an instant object of adulation in India. Few readers stopped to think that such long-term predictions have no more validity than astrological predictions (though a wit might observe that astrological predictions have salience in India). Everyone also forgot that the predictions in the 1950s that India and Africa were destined to glory while East Asia was left in the dust had been turned on their heads in just three decades.

In the same vein, when the economists Tarun Khanna of Harvard and Yasheng Huang of MIT wrote in the July–August 2003 issue of *Foreign Policy* that India's reliance on homegrown entrepreneurship may enable it to catch up with and perhaps even overtake China, which depended on foreign investors, the Indian media rewarded them with instant celebrity status. The media did not even stop to consider that given the differences in the total income levels of the two countries in 2003, even if India sustained 8.5 percent per annum growth over the following 30 years, it could overtake China only if the latter grew only 5 percent over the same period! With China continuing to grow faster than India, the differences in the GDP as of 2007 are larger, not smaller.

The title of this book makes no claims to predictions of this nature. It is only intended to suggest that the changes in policy as well as performance in recent years make it likely that the current growth rate of 8 percent will be sustained for some time to come, and may even accelerate, provided India undertakes some key reforms. But I attempt no predictions of how long this high growth will be sustained. My prognosis is based on neither a numerically calibrated model nor some vague expectations, but instead on a number of changes that have already taken place. In particular:

- In real dollars, the GDP grew 13.8 percent per annum during 2003–04 to 2005–06. In 2006–07, this growth rate was even higher.
- Merchandise exports in current dollars were $18.1 billion in 1990–91 and doubled for the first time in 1999–2000. In the recent period, they doubled in just three years: from $52.7 billion in 2002–03 to $102.7 billion in 2005–06.
- Services exports doubled from $26.9 billion in 2003–04 to $60.6 billion in 2005–06.
- India is now far more integrated into the world economy than in 1990. The exports of goods and services as a proportion of the GDP rose from 7.2 percent in 1990–91 to 11.6 percent in 1999–2000, and shot up to 20.5 percent in 2005–06. The proportion of total trade to the GDP reached 43.1 percent in 2005–06.
- Total foreign investment rose from $6 billion in 2002–03 to $20.2 billion in 2005–06. And direct foreign investment, which stood at $7.8 billion in 2005–06, shot up to $16.4 billion in the first ten months of 2006–07.
- Remittances rose from $17.2 billion in 2002–03 to $24.6 billion in 2005–06.
- As of April 7, 2007, the foreign exchange reserves crossed the $200 billion mark.
- There has been a revolution in the telecommunications sector. For example, in 1990–91, India had approximately 5 million phone lines *in total*. Currently, India is adding more than 5 million phone lines *per month*.
- The sales of passenger vehicles rose from 707,000 in 2002–03 to 1.14 million in 2005–06. The total number of vehicles produced during 2003–06 exceeded the entire stock of registered vehicles in 1990–91.

Four factors can be noted in favor of continued rapid growth. First, the above developments have fundamentally altered the initial conditions of the economy. For example, India is now far better integrated into the world economy, which will enable it to take advantage of continued innovations around the world. Second, given the strength of the external sector and the large foreign exchange reserves, the prospects of a depreciation of the rupee are low. Indeed, by mid-April 2007, the currency had appreciated vis-à-vis the U.S. dollar by almost 6 percent relative to its level at the end of February 2007. This means that the GDP is likely to grow rapidly in dollar terms in the forthcoming years. Third, the impending demographic transition will raise the proportion of the working age population. When this fact is combined with the considerable liberalization that has taken place, the response of the economy to it, and the consensus in favor of continued liberalization, a further upward shift in the growth rate is highly probable. Finally, India can expect its savings rate to continue to increase. This is likely not only because the proportion of the working age population is expected to rise, but also because the contribution of corporate savings to total savings currently is low when compared to countries such as China. As the corporate sector in India grows larger, it is bound to help raise the overall savings rate.

GROWTH AND REFORMS

While most observers of the Indian economy now accept the view that reforms have been central to the turnaround of the Indian economy, a handful of skeptics remain. Therefore, in part I of this book, I offer a unified analytic narrative of the performance of the Indian economy since the 1950s and its relationship to the policies. The story is in fours phases, 1951–52 to 1964–65; 1965–66 to 1980–81; 1981–82 to 1987–88; and 1988–89 to 2005–06.

The first of these phases saw India's growth rate rise to 4.1 percent from less than 1 percent in the first half of the twentieth century. While the introduction of a coherent development strategy that included institution building by the government was central to this shift, contrary to the general impression, this phase was characterized by relatively liberal policies. The import regime remained quite free until a balance of payments crisis led to the introduction of foreign exchange budgeting in 1958. Even then, the impact of the budgeting was seriously felt only in the 1960s. Investment licenses were issued relatively freely during the 1950s, with the restrictive policy coming into play only after foreign exchange budgeting began to require restrictions on the imports of machinery. The direct foreign investment regime remained quite open until at least the mid-1960s. The pragmatic Prime Minister Nehru appreciated the need for both foreign capital and technology, and successfully overcame the demands for the ouster of multinationals by the Left parties.

The period from 1965–66 to 1980–81 turned out to be the darkest in the postindependence economic history of India. By the mid-1960s, foreign exchange budgeting had led to considerable tightening of imports as well as investment. But the government interventions did not end there. Prime Minister Indira Gandhi came to the helm in 1967 and decided to rely on a major shift toward state control as the means to seize control of the Congress Party. She nationalized the major banks, oil companies, and coal mines. She imposed tight restrictions on the operations of foreign companies and effectively forced the vast majority of them either to transform themselves into Indian companies or to leave the country. Mrs. Gandhi also restricted investments by large firms (defined to include all firms with assets exceeding $27 million in 1969) to a handful of core sectors. She introduced tight ceilings on urban landholdings and effectively outlawed layoffs of workers by firms with 100 or more employees under any circumstances. The result was that whereas the Republic of Korea saw the growth rate of its total income rise from 4 percent in the 1950s and early 1960s to the 8–9 percent range, India found its growth rate plummeting to 3.2 percent. Many of the restrictions introduced during this era proved politically difficult to undo later, and some of them continue to harm growth today.

By the middle of the 1970s, it was becoming clear that the strategy the government had chosen was not working. The average annual growth in the total income between 1965–66 and 1974–75 had been just 2.6 percent. With the population growing 2.3 percent per annum, this translated into a growth rate of per-capita income of just 0.3 percent. While the government understandably did not publicly acknowledge that it had gone too far in restricting industrial activity, it quietly began to ease up on the controls through administrative measures. These measures included capacity expansion, increase in the threshold level of investment below which no license was required, delicensing in selected sectors, and permission to change the product mix (broad-bending) within the existing authorized capacity. The measures were introduced between 1975 and 1979 and were expanded between 1979 and 1984. On the import front, open general licensing was introduced in 1977, and the list of items belonging to it was gradually expanded. The years 1985 to 1990 saw more substantial liberalization, including major depreciation of the rupee that led to a spurt in exports. This liberalization went hand in hand with expansionary fiscal policies and borrowing abroad. The growth rate moved up to 4.8 percent between 1981–82 and 1987–88.

The second half of the 1980s saw some acceleration of liberalization, as well as continued fiscal expansion, financed partially by external borrowing. The two facts combined to produce a major growth spurt of 7.6 percent per year between 1988–89 and 1990–91, but they also culminated in a balance of payments crisis. While the Persian Gulf War, which led to a large jump in oil prices, provided the immediate cause, the seeds of the crisis had been sown in the prior years. The growth rate in 1991–92 fell to 1.2 percent.

Luckily, Prime Minister Narasimha Rao, who came to the helm in June 1991, decided to set the house in order and appointed Dr. Manmohan Singh, an economist, as his finance minister. Abandoning the past approach of piecemeal reforms, Dr. Singh inaugurated an era of more systematic reforms. He quickly proceeded to dismantle licensing on machinery and raw material imports, lower industrial tariffs, open most industries to foreign investment, and end investment licensing. He also moved ahead with the reform of direct and indirect taxes, liberalization of the financial sector, and trimming of the fiscal deficit. Early steps were also taken to open telecommunications and domestic civil aviation to the private sector. These measures yielded the handsome growth rate of 7.1 percent between 1993–94 and 1996–97, and also placed the economy on a long-term growth trajectory of 6 percent.

The last two years of Prime Minister Rao's term in office and the following three years, which were characterized by a series of unstable coalition governments, saw the reform process slow down. To be sure, some progress was made, notably in the area of taxation via the 1997–98 budget of Finance Minister P. Chidambaram, but the slowdown was perceptible. In turn, the growth rate declined as well.

The reform process picked up in a major way once again under Prime Mister Atal Bihari Vajpayee, especially after the 1999 elections returned his National Democratic Alliance (NDA) with a clear parliamentary majority. Assured of a full five-year term, the Vajpayee government systematically moved to open the economy to foreign and domestic competition and to build the country's infrastructure. The import licensing on consumer goods, which the trade reform of 1991–92 had ubiquitously failed to remove, was ended. Tariff rates were brought down, with the top industrial tariff rate declining from 45 to 20 percent. There was a major reform of the indirect tax system and tax administration. The telecommunications sector was revolutionized through a series of very important reforms. The government introduced genuine privatization, with several public sector enterprises transferred into private hands. The insurance sector was opened to the private sector, with limited foreign investment permitted as well. The reform of the civil service pension system was also launched. On the macroeconomic front, most interest rates were liberalized, greater competition was introduced in the banking sector through more liberal entry of domestic and foreign private banks, and several external capital account transactions were freed up. The Urban Land Ceilings and Regulation Act of 1976 was repealed. The government successfully embarked upon a massive program of highway construction. A major step toward the reform of the power sector was taken through the Electricity Act of 2003. The government also amended the Companies Act of 1956 to introduce a genuine bankruptcy law, though its implementation has been stalled by challenges in the Supreme Court. The recent spurt in the growth rate owes much to these reforms.

The accomplishments in promoting the reforms notwithstanding, the NDA lost the elections in May 2004, paving the way for the Congress Party-led United Progressive Alliance (UPA) to take charge of the government. The UPA chose Dr. Manmohan Singh as prime minister. Despite his impeccable reform credentials, the reforms once again slowed down. In part, the Left Front parties, whose support has been crucial for the survival of the UPA government, have held Prime Minister Singh's hand back. But the resolve within the UPA to move the reforms forward has also been at best weak. The Congress Party president, Sonia Gandhi, has often shown sympathy for the views of the Left Front parties and has intervened on their behalf.

POVERTY, INEQUALITY, AND REFORMS

While the precise extent of poverty reduction will always remain in dispute, there is now general agreement that the reform era has seen substantial poverty reduction relative to the first three decades of development. Chapter 7 of this book discusses in detail this evidence and various controversies surrounding it. The chapter also offers a detailed analysis of the farmer suicides that have been much in the news in recent years.

The more interesting question concerns the role inequality should play in the choice of policies. There is no serious disagreement among analysts on the proposition that the policies that promote equality by reducing poverty are desirable. But differences emerge when we want to include equality in general among the central goals of policy. My own conclusion from the review of Indian economic history since the 1950s is that the focus on equality should be resisted since it can often end up harming the fight against poverty. Policies that promote both equity and growth may exist. But in practice, once equity is placed at the center of policymaking, politicians are unable to resist opting for those equity-oriented policies that hamper growth and, therefore, poverty alleviation.

The equity-driven policies often target the creators of wealth, who happen to be the most visible symbols of inequality. The policies promoted by Mrs. Gandhi between 1967 and 1977 offer ample evidence supporting this thesis. The confinement of large firms to a handful of core industries and the reservation of labor-intensive products exclusively for small-scale producers were driven by equity considerations. The same goes for nationalization of banks and oil companies, and for the Urban Land Ceilings and Regulation Act of 1976 and the ban placed on worker layoffs by firms with 100 or more workers. The choice of marginal income tax rates of 95 percent on even modest incomes during this period was also driven by equity considerations.

One subtle example from the current policy regime further illustrates the point. Along with electricity, high-quality roads connecting the rural areas to the national and state highways constitute the most important public good the government can supply to assist the rural poor in translating their entrepreneurial talents into effective income. After decades of poor-quality roads, India has now learned to build world-class roads. This is evidenced by the Golden Quadrilateral project that is nearly complete and by other national highway projects under way. A key factor behind this success has been the contracting out of road construction to top-class domestic and foreign companies. But the same success has not been achieved in building reliable rural roads, despite the allocation of vast sums of resources to them, most recently under the Bharat Nirman initiative. The reason is that equity considerations have led the government to parcel out the contracts for these roads in small projects of 10 to 50 million rupees each. Few world-class companies, whether domestic or foreign, bother to bid for such small projects. Moreover, the ability of the government to monitor a large number of very small projects is limited. The result is continued non-delivery or poor delivery of rural roads. While the policy promotes equity among road builders, it punishes the rural poor. Offering contracts for the construction of rural roads in an entire district or group of districts can readily bring the large firms into the game and connect the rural poor to the mainstream of the economy.

Tilting the policies in favor of smaller entrepreneurs and against large firms is one way to promote equity. The more conventional instrument is redistribution via tax expenditure policies. While the objective behind these policies in India has been to alleviate poverty, as opposed to promoting equity, in practice they have proved to be anti-poor and regressive. Big farmers in the richer states of Punjab, Haryan, and Andhra Pradesh have largely captured food subsidies in the form of high procurement prices. Fertilizer, irrigation, and electricity subsidies naturally go to larger farmers, since the more land you own, the more of these inputs you consume. Those who are truly poor own no land, and therefore cannot benefit from any of these subsidies except perhaps through low-priced food provided by the public distribution system. Even expenditures on health and education are substantially wasted on teachers and health workers, who frequently absent themselves from their posts. As much as 80 percent of the rural population currently relies on private providers for outpatient care. I discuss these issues in detail in part V of the book and argue that if the government genuinely wants to redistribute income in favor of the poor, it must switch massively to cash transfers and education vouchers. Given the recent technological innovations, such transfers can be made with minimal leakage and with recipients being the intended beneficiaries of the system.

THE POLITICAL ECONOMY OF POLICYMAKING

Although I do not devote a separate chapter to the political economy of policymaking in the book, the issue receives attention in several contexts, especially in chapters 3 and 5. Most authors analyze the political economy of policymaking in terms of interest group politics, as brilliantly expounded by my late former colleague Mancur Olson in his pioneering 1965 book *The Logic of Collective Action*.

An alternative approach emphasizes electoral politics with policies chosen to win the election. In the context of a two-candidate election with a single policy at issue, this approach boils down to the median voter model.

While both these approaches are relevant, they fail to emphasize one key element that has been important in India. Within the parliamentary democracy of the country, a determined leader at the top plays a decisive role in shaping the economic policies. The leader is constrained by the fact that he cannot promote a policy package that will result in the defeat of his party in a future election. But elections are almost always fought along multiple dimensions, including social and economic issues, law and order, military strength, and international diplomacy. Even within economic issues, a variety of policy packages can be envisaged. This fact gives the leader considerable latitude in the choice of economic policies. Indeed, insofar as the policies can be expected to improve the fate of the poor, they can improve the prospects of victory in future elections.

The immediate resistance to a specific policy reform can come from three sources: those within the ruling party, those within the opposition, and those adversely affected by the reform. These three entities may interact. For example, those expecting to be adversely impacted may take their grievance to their contacts within the ruling party or make a common cause with the opposition parties. Likewise, the opposition parties may see political advantage in joining hands with the losers under reforms and appearing with them in public protests against the proposed reforms.

A determined leader can often overcome the resistance from all three of these sources. Typically, those on the ruling side of the fence do not want to vote themselves out of power. Within the Indian parliamentary system, a negative vote on a proposed piece of legislation leads to the fall of the government. Therefore, even when some members of the ruling coalition are opposed to a policy change, they are unlikely to defeat it in the Parliament. For example, when the current UPA government proposed to raise the sectoral caps on foreign investment in telecommunications from 49 to 74 percent, and in civil aviation from 40 to 49 percent, the Left Front parties opposed it. But the government remained firm and carried the motion. The Left Front parties were not ready to vote themselves out of power by bringing the government down. Prime Minister Vajpayee often faced similar opposition from within his party, but he remained firm on pushing the reform agenda forward, even offering to resign if not permitted to pursue his policy agenda. He knew that the ruling coalition would not risk his departure, for fear that there was no other consensus candidate.

Internal opposition can block or substantially slow the reform if the distribution of power is such that the position of the leadership within the coalition is not secure. This was the case with the United Front governments between 1996 and 1998. They relied heavily on support from outside by the Congress Party, which was itself seeking power. Under such circumstances, the leadership is struggling for its survival on a day-to-day basis, and is unlikely to take any initiatives that may be opposed by supporters within or outside the government. This situation is to be distinguished from the one currently facing the UPA, in which its outside Left Front supporters have no prospects of capturing the leadership, and make most political gains by ensuring the survival of the government.

The resistance from the opposition parties by itself is less potent. They can make noises and vote against a measure proposed by the government, but they lack the votes to defeat the reform. For instance, the opposition brought charges of corruption in the privatization program the NDA government launched in the early 2000s, but the determined disinvestment minister, Arun Shourie, could push ahead with the agenda. It was only a Supreme Court ruling that eventually halted the privatization of government-owned oil companies. The opposition by itself is able to block only a reform requiring a constitutional amendment, for which a two-thirds majority is needed. The last time a government had such large majority was in 1989.

Much of the focus of the traditional political economy analysis is centered on the resistance provided by the adversely affected interest groups. But even here, a determined government is for the most part successful in carrying out its will. The immediate successor of Nehru, Prime Minister Lal Bahadur Shastri, was in power for only 20 months, yet he could fundamentally shift the policies away from heavy industry and toward agriculture because the Congress Party was firmly behind him. Indira Gandhi could nationalize major banks, general insurance companies, oil companies, and coal mines between the late 1960s and mid-1970s with relative ease. In 1980, she was able to nationalize a further six banks at the mere suggestion of the governor of the Reserve Bank of India. The Rao government could implement far-reaching reforms in the 1990s with relatively little opposition.

Even when the adversely affected interest groups mount vocal opposition through agitation in the public space and with the support of the opposition parties, time is on the side of the government. If the public sees the policy change as being in the national interest, agitators quickly lose its sympathy. This was graphically illustrated by the failure of the airport workers to block the privatization of Delhi and Mumbai airports in 2006. But even when a large section of the public views a policy change as detrimental to its interests, the free-rider problem works in favor of the government. The cost of the agitation falls disproportionately on those participating in it, but the benefits are diffused. Therefore, a determined and patient government can readily outlast the agitators. The failure of the public in 2006 to reverse the government's decision to extend caste-based quotas for admissions to private schools and colleges illustrates this point.

When the interests likely to lose from the reform are concentrated, they can provide effective opposition and either derail or slow down the reform. Under such circumstances, only a truly determined government with a reasonable degree of internal cohesion is able to move the process forward, and that only gradually. This is illustrated by the reforms experience in the telecommunications sector (chapter 17). The monopoly sector supplier of the telephone service in the public sector, the Department of Telecommunications (DoT), proved a formidable opponent to the reform. It tried to sabotage the process virtually at every step of the way, but the government persisted and eventually fully opened the sector. The experience in civil aviation was similar, although less extreme.

There are two qualifications to this analysis. First, the success of the central government in carrying out policy changes has been far more partial in areas that are substantially under the purview of the states. They include electricity, water, education, health, land, sales tax, rural and urban infrastructure, and, above all, agriculture. Even Nehru, who enjoyed near universal confidence of the public, had at best limited success in implementing the land reforms. Large landowners were locally powerful and successfully blocked the reform at the level of the state. Mrs. Gandhi, who at best faced limited opposition to the nationalization of banks, general insurance companies, and oil companies, failed when she tried to take over wholesale trade in wheat in 1973. Any reforms that depend on land acquisition have likewise been difficult. Many important states have continued to drag their feet on the repeal of state-level laws on rent control and urban land ceilings, despite considerable efforts by successive central governments. The issue of providing legal titles to property in both rural and urban areas has made little progress as well.

The second qualification applies to the reforms in the area of labor regulations. Most of the political parties have their affiliate labor unions. Because these unions serve as virtually guaranteed vote banks, no government has been able to place labor reform on its agenda. The Vajpayee government came closest to it when Finance Minister Yashwant Sinha announced his intention to reform two key labor laws in his 2001–02 budget. But in the end, it could not build consensus within the party to bring the matter to the Parliament floor. The current UPA government has explicitly ruled out this labor reform.

It is important to recognize that the prevailing ethos among policymakers, bureaucrats, the press, and the public places some limits on the policy change any government would propose. The greater the distance between a given policy change and the central tendency of the economic philosophy shared by the politicians, economic advisers, senior bureaucrats, and the press at any given time, the more reluctant is the government to propose that policy. Over time, the ethos itself may change, however. As policymakers and press learn from the experience of their own country and that of other countries, the central tendency of their economic philosophy shifts. For example, under the prevailing economic philosophy in the 1960s and 1970s, the reforms of the early 1990s would have been unthinkable. As a matter of record, the politicians, economic advisers, and bureaucrats of the time paid virtually no attention to Bhagwati and Desai (1970) and Bhagwati and Srinivasan (1975), who advocated pro-market reforms. But the dismal experience with three decades of license raj, experimentation with piecemeal liberalization in the 1980s, the demise of the Soviet Union, and the success of liberal policies in China shifted the central tendency of the economic philosophy among politicians and senior bureaucrats in India (see chapter 5). In turn, this shift made the reforms of the early 1990s possible. Symmetrically, given the central tendency of the current economic philosophy, few politicians want to be seen as hostile to reforms, and virtually no one dares advocate a return to the license raj. Therefore, even when the politicians hesitate to risk proposing new reforms, they broadly endorse what has been accomplished. This means the risk of significant policy reversals is minimal.

A final word concerns the slowdown in reforms under the current government. The UPA leadership attributed the ouster of the NDA in the May 2004 elections to the public sentiment that the NDA reforms had bypassed the rural poor. The adherence to this interpretation had the effect of weakening the resolve of the UPA government to introduce major new reforms. It did not matter that the available scientific evidence pointed to a steady decline in poverty in rural as well as urban areas following the reforms. Once the UPA publicly embraced the view that the reforms had not helped the poor, its ability to push the same reforms was greatly undercut.

There are least four facts that cast doubt on the interpretation of its election victory to which the UPA government chose to subscribe. First, the Congress Party, which leads the UPA, won 145 out of a total of 543 seats in the lower house of the Parliament and 26.5 percent of the popular vote. The Bhartiya Janata Party (BJP), which led the NDA, won 138 seats and 22.2 percent of the popular vote. Given that the elections are fought on multiple dimensions and that state-level politics is critical in determining the outcome in each state, these results can hardly be seen as either a strong endorsement or a categorical rejection of the reforms. Second, had the southern regional party DMK not switched sides prior to the elections, the NDA would have been the one to return with a majority in the Parliament. Third, as I have discussed elsewhere (Panagariya, 2004d), anti-incumbent sentiment at the state level better explains the election outcomes. Finally, if the UPA interpretation was correct, we should have observed the rural vote going consistently to the UPA and the urban vote to the NDA. No such divide in the voting pattern can be discerned.

ISSUES IN MACROECONOMICS

A stable macroeconomic environment is widely regarded as a necessary, though not sufficient, condition for sustained, rapid growth. Of course, stability does not necessarily imply efficiency. India has had a history of maintaining a relatively stable macroeconomic environment, but it has begun to pay attention to efficiency only recently.

Consider first the issue of stability. Though India has been subject to occasional macroeconomic crises, the latter have been mild and short-lived by the standards of virtually all other countries. Even the balance of payments crisis of 1991, which served as the trigger for major reforms, lasted for less than a year. Historically, the Consumer Price Index has risen more than 20 percent per annum only twice since the 1950s: 21 percent in 1973–74 and 27 percent in 1974–75. For the vast majority of the years, inflation has remained in the single digits. Insofar as it can be accurately measured, the unemployment rate in India has also been relatively stable.

This is not to suggest, however, that there are no serious reform issues relating to macroeconomic policies in India. My detailed discussion of macroeconomic policies since the 1980s in part III of the book reveals many distortions and vulnerabilities. An important immediate concern has been large public debt accompanied by large fiscal deficits. The debt currently exceeds 80 percent of the GDP. Until recently, the combined fiscal deficit of the central government and the state governments was nearly 10 percent of the GDP. As discussed in chapter 9, these two key vulnerabilities have led some analysts to suggest that India may face another macroeconomic crisis in the near future. Luckily, the fiscal deficit came down to approximately 6 percent of the GDP in 2006–07, and is predicted to decrease further in 2007–08.

On the international front, India has done reasonably well since the early 1990s. The Reserve Bank of India (RBI), India's central bank, has avoided large short-run fluctuations in the exchange rate but has allowed the rupee to steadily depreciate over the long run. This policy, along with steady inflows of foreign investment and remittances, has allowed the bank to accumulate large sums of foreign exchange that currently exceed $200 billion. When the RBI purchases the foreign exchange, it releases rupees into the economy and risks inflation. To counteract this, it has generally sold equivalent domestic securities in return for rupees, thus "sterilizing" the money supply.

The major policy question currently confronting India on the external front is whether it should embrace full capital account convertibility in the sense of allowing anyone wishing to convert any amount of rupees into other currencies, and vice versa, to do so without any questions asked. I discuss this issue in detail in chapter 10, and conclude against rushing into such convertibility. The bottom line is that the proven benefits of full capital account convertibility beyond direct and portfolio foreign investment are few, whereas the potential costs in case of a financial flow crisis are large.

The greatest challenge India faces in the area of macroeconomic policies concerns the financial markets. Financially intermediated savings in India remain low, indicating that the capital markets remain inefficient. In my discussion in chapter 11, I divide this market into three components: money and banking; capital markets; and insurance and pensions. Both insurance and pension funds represent savings that potentially can be used for productive investment through intermediation.

Since the 1980s, when India engaged in active financial repression, considerable progress has been made in freeing up the financial markets. With some exceptions, interest rates are now market-determined, and considerable progress has been made in bringing down nonperforming assets as a proportion of total bank assets. The easing of entry of private banks, both foreign and domestic, has resulted in increased competition and improved efficiency of banks across the board. Regulatory standards have also been raised over time.

While the overall financial health of the banking sector in India is quite good relative to that in many countries in Asia, including China, the sector remains dominated by inefficient public sector banks. Much of the empirical evidence I review shows that private banks outperform public sector banks. The relevance of social objectives, such as priority sector lending and rural bank branch expansion, has declined in recent years. And even if these objectives are to be pursued, regulatory mechanisms can be put in place to achieve them within the private ownership structure. In the past, private banks, when subject to binding priority sector lending targets, have delivered on them. For these and other reasons, I conclude in favor of phased privatization of banks. Of course, given the current state of play in privatization, this can be seen as only a distant goal.

Insofar as the capital market is concerned, India has made far greater progress in the equity market than in the bond market. Though there is a relatively large government bond market in existence, the corporate bond market remains thin. A top priority of the policy currently is the development of the latter. On the regulatory front, the Securities and Exchange Board of India (SEBI) was created in 1987 and awarded a statutory status in 1992.

Over the years, the investors, the firms, and the SEBI have all learned from experience in the equity market. The regulatory mechanism has evolved, and market forces now govern the prices of stocks and transactions in them. Trade in derivatives was introduced in 2000 and has grown exponentially since then. The foreign institutional investors are active players in the market. Private mutual funds have also emerged.

The insurance market was also opened to private entry. The Insurance Regulatory and Development Authority was set up as a statutory regulatory body in 1999. Simultaneously, the sector was opened to foreign investment with a sectoral cap of

26 percent. The liberalization has led to an increase in the insurance penetration ratio (proportion of premiums to the GDP) from less than 1 percent in 1990–91 and between 1 and 2 percent in the 1990s to 3.2 percent in 2004–05. In 2004–05, there were 12 private companies in life insurance and 8 in nonlife insurance. The share of private companies (including foreign partners) in the total premiums in the life insurance segment rose from 4.7 percent in 2003–04 to 9.3 percent in 2004–05. Further reforms must focus on relaxing the foreign investment cap and rules governing the investment of premiums in various instruments.

Pension funds constitute another potential major source of savings that markets can intermediate. But pension schemes are confined to the organized sector. The bulk of the population, being employed in the unorganized sector, remains uncovered by any pension schemes. Even within the organized sector, until recently civil servants were covered by an unfunded, defined benefits pension system that relied entirely on the government revenues. Starting January 1, 2004, a defined contributions system was introduced for newly hired employees, but this reform has remained incomplete since the government has been unable to put a statutory regulatory authority in place. As discussed in detail in chapter 11, the pension system remains in urgent need of reform. There is a particular urgency to introduce instruments that allow coverage to those employed in the informal sector.

TRANSFORMING INDIA

The ultimate development problem India faces is that of transforming its primarily rural, agrarian economy into a modern one. To be sure, the share of agriculture (excluding forestry and fishing) in the total output has been declining rapidly. It fell from 28.5 percent in 1990–91 to 16.5 percent in 2005–06. Nevertheless, the vast majority of the Indian population continues to live in rural areas and rely on farming as the principal source of income. Between the 1991 and 2001 censuses, the rural population fell from 79 percent to 77 percent. The corresponding change in the proportion of the population employed in farming was from 67 to 58 percent. Looking at the issue from a slightly different angle, even outside of agriculture, approximately 90 percent of the workforce remains employed in the informal, unorganized sector. Employment in the organized sector either has not grown or has grown very little.

The reasons for this slow structural transformation of the economy and the reforms necessary to accelerate it constitute the subject of part IV of the book. There are three chapters in this part, focusing on international trade, industry and services, and agriculture, respectively. My main thesis (originally stated in Panagariya, 2002a) is that the slow transformation of the economy to date is to be attributed to the slow growth of industry, especially manufacturing. The share of manufacturing in the total output in India has remained stagnant at 17 percent since 1990–91.

This stagnation is in turn to be attributed to the slow growth of the unskilled labor-intensive sectors, such as apparel, footwear, and toys, in which India has a comparative advantage. In the organized sector, goods and services that have grown rapidly in India are either capital- or skilled-labor-intensive. The former include steel, petroleum, auto parts, and automobiles, and the latter include software and pharmaceuticals. I argue that if the transformation is to be speeded up, India must remove the barriers to the growth of the sectors in which it has comparative advantage. I also argue that at least in the short run, the transformation can be aided by reforms in agriculture that better connect the farmers to the economic mainstream through direct access to urban markets in farm products, and development of food processing.

In the area of international trade, I suggest continued removal of tariffs and export subsidies; trade facilitation measures that reduce delays in the movement of goods that are particularly detrimental to apparel exports, which require timely delivery; creation of a flexible labor market regime in the special economic zones; reform of policies toward anti-dumping; reform of the rules on the use of traditional safeguard measures; and speedy conclusion of the Doha Round of trade negotiations (chapter 12). In the area of industry and services, I stress the urgent need for a variety of labor market reforms; speedy implementation of the new bankruptcy law put in place by the Companies (Second Amendment) Act of 2002; revival of genuine privatization; building of urban infrastructure; and the reform of higher education (chapter 13). In agriculture, I outline detailed product market and input market reforms (chapter 14). The former include substantial downsizing of the public distribution system; a single India-wide market in farm goods; repeal of the Essential Commodities Act that is still keeping the specter of price and distribution controls alive for many products; a rapid end to the government monopoly over marketing of agricultural produce; development of food processing; and contract farming. Likewise, input market reforms include issuance of proper ownership titles for land; improved access to rural credit; and an end to fertilizer, electricity, and water subsidies.

TELECOMMUNICATIONS: A TRIUMPH OF REFORMS

Perhaps the single most important success story of reforms is telecommunications (chapter 17). While no quantitative assessment to date has been attempted, it may be hypothesized that the high rate of growth in the services sector in recent years is due at least in part to the success achieved in this important sector. It is highly improbable that the massive expansion of telephones in service has not led to a major boost in productivity even in informal services sectors. Most Indians with limited education may not be able to use computers, but they are able to use the telephone effectively.

The success in the telecommunications sector, in the minds of many older Indians, is associated with Prime Minister Rajiv Gandhi. The reality, however, is that tele-density—the number of phone lines per 100 people—rose from 0.4 in 1984–85 to just 0.6 in 1989–90. Even as late as 1998–99, four years after cell phones had arrived in the country, tele-density remained low, at 2.8 percent, compared with more than 18 percent as of February 28, 2007.

The crucial step in bringing about the current telecommunications revolution was the New Telecom Policy (NTP) of 1999, which the government systematically implemented in the early 2000s. The DoT did its best to sabotage the reform every step of the way. But luckily, the prime minster's office took it upon itself to implement various components of the NTP. Among other things, the government separated the service provision and policymaking arms of the DoT, with the former turned into a corporate entity known as the Bharat Sanchar Nigam Limited (BSNL) in October 2000. In 2003, the government introduced a unified license that allowed its holder to provide wireless as well as wire-line service. In between, it made a number of changes in the regulatory regime.

On the surface, it would seem that the successful model of telecommunications reform could have been applied to electricity. But, as I explain in chapter 17, the two sectors are fundamentally different from each other, with electricity being far more complex to reform. The basic legal framework, in the form of the Electricity Act of 2003, has been put in place, and some partial success stories, such as those of the privatization of distribution in Delhi, are beginning to emerge. But most state governments remain ill-equipped to implement an independent regulatory regime. Moreover, with the financially weak state entities still the principal buyers of electricity, private entry into generation has been limited. Modernization of this sector is likely to take some years.

TRANSPORTATION: A MIXED RECORD

Within the transportation sector (chapter 18), success has been achieved in at least two major areas: national highway construction and domestic civil aviation. The major achievement with respect to national highways has been the near completion of the Golden Quadrilateral project, which involves widening the highways connecting the metropolitan cities of Delhi, Mumbai, Chennai, and Calcutta to four or more lanes. There has been a slowdown recently, but progress is being made toward the conversion of the north-south and east-west highways to four lanes as well. The contracts for more than 85 percent of this project have been awarded, and are being implemented. There are also plans to convert the highways connecting all state capitals and places of economic, commercial, and tourist importance to the national highways into four-lane highways.

In domestic civil aviation, a 1997 reform entirely freed entry into the airline industry. As a result, rising demand for domestic air service in the 2000s has been followed by the entry of several new airlines, including Spice Jet, GoAir, IndiGo, and Kingfisher. These airlines are competing against previously existing airlines including Jet, Sahara, Air Deccan, and Indian (previously Indian Airlines). The total number of air passengers carried domestically, which had grown relatively gradually in the 1990s from 8.1 million in 1991 to 13.3 million in 2000, shot up in the 2000s, reaching 22.7 million in 2005.

Progress has also been made in bringing the private sector into the construction of airports. Despite agitation by airport workers, the Delhi and Mumbai airports were placed under private management via public-private partnership (PPP) agreements in May 2006. Under the concession on the Delhi airport, the private partner is to complete enhanced facilities at the existing airport, including development of new terminals and runways, by March 2010. Two Greenfield (i.e., entirely new) international airports at Bangalore and Hyderabad are also under construction under the PPPs. Prospects for substantial improvement in infrastructure for international air travel look good.

Railways have seen some progress under the dynamic leadership of Railway Minister Lalu Prasad Yadav. While this is good news, I remain skeptical of the long-term prospects in this mode of transportation. The reason is that railways will remain in the public sector, so the leadership in the Railway Ministry will largely determine their fate. Unless a significant proportion of the railway operations are subject to commercial pressures, progress is unlikely to be sustained in the long run.

Two areas in which progress remains illusive to date are rural roads and urban infrastructure, including urban transportation. I have already mentioned a key factor accounting for the slow progress in building rural roads. The problem of urban infrastructure is even more complex (chapter 13). Rent control, restrictions on the sale of urban land on a competitive basis, laws governing the conversion of agricultural land into land usable for alternative purposes, laws governing land acquisition for public projects, and tight restrictions on the floor space permitted to be built in a given location have come together to make the urban infrastructure problem nearly intractable. The central government has launched the Jawaharlal Nehru National Urban Renewal Mission and has allocated substantial resources to improve urban infrastructure. But ultimately, the reform in this area depends on the state governments and city administrations. To date, only Delhi has made satisfactory progress in improving urban transportation. It has constructed wide roads and overpasses, and has developed a commuter rail system to relieve congestion. But the use of urban land remains highly inefficient even in Delhi.

PUBLIC DELIVERY OF SOCIAL SERVICES: A FAILED EXPERIMENT

Most economists advise against the entry of the government into manufacturing activities. But they do endorse the provision of social services such as education, health, and water by the government. Since the government in India has had significant presence even in manufacturing, its ubiquity in the social sector should be no surprise.

Unfortunately, however, as discussed in chapters 19 and 20, the government in India has utterly failed in the delivery of these services. In the health sector, despite considerable resources invested in the subcenters, primary health centers, and community health centers, 80 percent of outpatient care and more than 55 percent of inpatient care in both rural and urban areas is provided by the private sector. Absenteeism among government health workers is estimated at 40 percent.

A similar situation prevails in primary education. Private schools, even in rural areas, now account for 18 percent of the students enrolled. In the urban areas, the figure is much higher. More important, the quality of education in public schools is extremely poor. Studies show that even unrecognized private schools, with relatively low fees (approximately $3.00 per month) and much lower teacher salaries, impart better education than public sector schools. Teacher absenteeism in public schools is rampant. Higher education in India, tightly controlled by a central government body, the University Grants Commission, is a shambles. By some estimates, the total public expenditure on higher education is less than what affluent students now spend abroad to access better-quality higher education. Yet, the government persists in disallowing smooth entry to private universities.

My conclusion after the review of the available evidence is that the government needs to learn from its own experience in the infrastructure sector. For example, it was unable to build reliable roads as long as its own departments undertook the building activity. It was only after it handed the task to the private sector that reliable roads begin to emerge on a large scale. Likewise, the government needs to deploy the private sector more effectively in the provision of social services that generate substantial private benefits.

For outpatient care, the government should simply give cash transfers to the bottom 30 percent of the population and let them choose the provider. For inpatient care, it should provide free medical insurance (up to a limit) to the bottom 30 percent of the population, once again letting individuals choose between private and public facilities. For primary education, the government should use its resources to give education vouchers to the bottom 30 percent of the population, thereby giving the students in this group the same options as those with more affluent parents.

The higher education system in India needs a complete overhaul. Here the central government is the key player, so a reform is entirely possible. Unfortunately, the Education Ministry had the misfortune of being successively headed by persons with no interest whatsoever in reforming this important sector. I discuss in detail the problems ailing the system and possible solutions. Unfortunately, however, there is little reason to be optimistic that something will be done in the near future in this sector.

CONCLUDING REMARKS

Rather than summarize the summary of the book, let me conclude this introduction with three observations. First, as already noted, my paramount objective in writing this book is to provide the reader with an analytic account of India's economic successes and failures since the early 1950s, and their sources, in one place. While I have drawn my own conclusions from this account and wish most readers will agree with them, I also hope that those who disagree will learn enough from the book to draw their own informed conclusions.

Second, I have struggled hard to avoid jargon and to present the analysis in a language that an intelligent reader without a formal background in economics can follow. Nevertheless, the book represents a scholarly effort that makes extensive use of data to support its hypotheses. Therefore, readers without a background in economics may have to work through parts of the book with some patience. Part III, which deals with macroeconomic issues, is perhaps the most challenging, but even here there is nothing that an intelligent reader with some patience cannot follow.

Finally, the book has been written over a period of at least two years. Therefore, the terminal year of analysis may vary slightly across chapters. In some parts of the book, I have been able to update the information up to 2006–07, but in other parts the terminal year may be either 2003–04 or 2004–05. I hope readers will not find these differences too much of a distraction.

PART I

Growth and Economic Reforms

1

DISTINGUISHING FOUR PHASES

India has been growing at an average annual rate exceeding 6 percent since the late 1980s. During the four years spanning 2003–04 (April 1, 2003–March 31, 2004) to 2006–07, its growth rate reached 8.6 percent—a level close to that experienced by the East Asian miracle economies of the Republic of Korea and Taiwan during their peak years.[1] As the book goes to press, fears that the economy is overheating can be heard loudly, but virtually no one is predicting a significant slowdown in the growth rate in the forthcoming years.

The upward shift in the growth rate in the late 1980s came on the heels of extremely slow growth for more than three decades. India gained independence on August 15, 1947. It launched its development program formally in the year 1951–52 with the First Five-Year Plan.[2] Despite very high hopes around the world, especially among economists and official U.S. circles, the economy grew only 3.8 percent between 1951–52 and 1987–88. In contrast, and contrary to the consensus view at the time, the economy of the Republic of Korea took off in a major way, registering an average growth rate in excess of 8 percent in the 1960s and 1970s.

At least three features distinguish India's growth experience from that of virtually all other countries. First, its growth trajectory is virtually unique among developing countries. Unlike the miracle economies of East Asia and later Southeast Asia, it has not grown at superhigh rates of 8 to 10 percent per annum on a sustained basis. At the same time, unlike most countries in Africa and Latin America, it has not suffered periods of prolonged stagnation or decline. Even when macroeconomic crises have visited India, they have been short-lived, with the economy quickly returning to its trend growth rate.

Second, India had a substantial private sector and yet it consistently pursued near-autarkic trade policies alongside highly interventionist domestic policies for more than three decades. But subsequently, it turned to progressively outward-looking and market-friendly policies. Because both sets of policies have been pursued in a politically and macroeconomically stable environment, the contrasting results across these policy regimes offer obvious lessons for development strategies.

Finally, India is one of the four developing countries with effective democracy since the 1940s.[3] And among these four, its vastly larger population and extremely diverse electorate in terms of religion, caste, and ideology distinguish it. Unsurprisingly, it offers a political economy experience with liberalizing reforms that is quite different from that of countries, such as the Republic of Korea, Taiwan, Singapore, Hong and Kong, and the People's Republic of China, that have attained high rates of growth under authoritarian regimes.

Against this background, the present book is an attempt to understand India's experiments with various economic policies since the early-1950s, with particular focus on the economic reforms since the mid-1980s. Where appropriate, I contrast India's experience with that of other countries. Two specific comparisons carried out in detail are those with the Republic of Korea during approximately 1950 to 1980 (chapter 6) and with China during the 1980s and beyond (chapter 12). The book also offers recommendations for future reforms in different areas of the economy and their rationale. The range of topics covered is comprehensive, though by no means exhaustive.

In part I, I study the evolution of policies and growth outcomes as they have unfolded since the launch of the development process in 1951–52. In part II, I turn to issues of poverty and equality. In part III, I discuss macroeconomic policies and reforms. In part IV, I consider the major sectors of the economy, including trade, industry, agriculture, and services. Part V presents a dissection of the government sector, which includes taxation; subsidies and the civil service; economic services such as telecommunications, electricity, and transportation; and social services such as health, water supply and sanitation, and education. In each case, I consider the reforms undertaken to date and their impact, as well as further reforms that must be undertaken to accelerate and sustain growth. I also discuss the major debates that have occupied policy analysts in each area covered in the book.

The remainder of this chapter has two primary objectives: to offer an overview of India's growth experience since 1951–52 and to set the stage for its more detailed discussion in the remainder of part I. I distinguish four phases of growth, which I then discuss in greater detail in chapters 2 through 5. In chapter 6, the last chapter in part I, I compare the growth experiences of India and the Republic of Korea during approximately 1950 to 1980.

DISTINGUISHING FOUR PHASES

The first step in our investigation is a closer examination of the growth rates. Table 1.1 shows the annual growth rates of the real GDP (Gross Domestic Product) at factor cost in 1993–94 prices for the 54-year period spanning 1951–52 to 2004–05. Additionally, it reports the annual growth rates for the years 1999–2000 to 2006–07 at 1999–2000 prices. The latter are provided because the growth rates for 2005–06 and 2006–07 are available at only 1999–2000 prices.

The first important issue we must confront is how to divide the five and a half decades into a limited number of phases for an orderly discussion of the growth experience. Authors choose different phases based on their preferred criteria: some

TABLE 1.1: Annual Growth Rates of GDP (at factor cost): 1951–2007

Year	Growth Rate	Year	Growth Rate	Year	Growth Rate	Year	Growth Rate
At 1993–94 Prices						*At 1999–2000 Prices*	
1951–52	2.3	1969–70	6.5	1987–88	3.8	2000–01	4.4
1952–53	2.8	1970–71	5.0	1988–89	10.5	2001–02	5.8
1953–54	6.1	1971–72	1.0	1989–90	6.7	2002–03	3.8
1954–55	4.2	1972–73	−0.3	1990–91	5.6	2003–04P	8.5
1955–56	2.6	1973–74	4.6	1991–92	1.3	2004–05QE	7.5
1956–57	5.7	1974–75	1.2	1992–93	5.1	2005–06QE	9.0
1957–58	−1.2	1975–76	9.0	1993–94	5.9	2006–07AE	9.2
1958–59	7.6	1976–77	1.2	1994–95	7.3		
1959–60	2.2	1977–78	7.5	1995–96	7.3		
1960–61	7.1	1978–79	5.5	1996–97	7.8		
1961–62	3.1	1979–80	−5.2	1997–98	4.8		
1962–63	2.1	1980–81	7.2	1998–99	6.5		
1963–64	5.1	1981–82	6.0	1999–2000	6.1		
1964–65	7.6	1982–83	3.1	2000–01	4.4		
1965–66	−3.7	1983–84	7.7	2001–02	5.8		
1966–67	1.0	1984–85	4.3	2002–03P	4.0		
1967–68	8.1	1985–86	4.5	2003–04QE	8.5		
1968–69	2.6	1986–87	4.3	2004–05QE	6.9		

P, Provisional; QE, Quick Estimate; AE, Advance Estimate.

Source: Author's calculations, using the GDP date reported in the Reserve Bank of India, *Handbook of Statistics on Indian Economy* (2006, table 2, col. 2).

according to the Five-Year Plans, others according to the decades, and still others according to shifts in policy or sharpness of differences in the growth rates. As a quick glance at table 1.1 reveals, the growth rates fluctuate wildly across years. Therefore, the precise choice of the cutoff years has an important bearing on the overall picture we draw.

   In this book, I choose the cutoff points across various phases primarily on the basis of the sharpness of differences in the growth rates, tempered by the consideration that an important objective underlying this exercise is to unearth the connection between growth and economic policies. As I will argue below, this criterion leads me to distinguish the following four phases (see figure 1.1):

- Phase I, from 1951–52 to 1964–65 (or 1951–65 for short), with an annual growth rate of 4.1 percent,[4]
- Phase II, spanning 1965–81, with a growth rate of 3.2 percent,
- Phase III, covering 1981–88, with growth rate of 4.8 percent, and
- Phase IV, beginning in 1988–89 and continuing to date, with a growth rate during 1988–06 of 6.3 percent.[5]

At the outset, let me state that the phases I have distinguished are not based on differences in the growth rates that are statistically significant from one another. Indeed, in view of the relatively short time series we have, not all differences in the growth rates across phases can be expected to be simultaneously statistically significant.

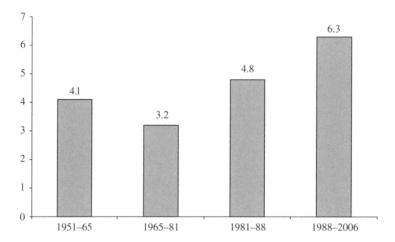

FIGURE I.I: Four Phases of Growth (percent)

This point is neatly illustrated in the careful work by Wallack (2003), who attempts to divide the years between 1951–52 and 2001–02 into periods with growth rates that are statistically significantly different from one another. She finds only a single statistically significant break point in the GDP and GNP (Gross National Product) series spanning the 51 years. She further finds that the dividing line between these two periods is extremely sensitive to small variations in the growth rates. Thus, for the GDP growth rate series, Wallack finds the single break point at the year 1980–81. But when she considers the growth rate series for the GNP, she finds the break point at 1987–88. Given that the GDP and GNP growth-rate series are virtually identical, the vast differences in the cutoff points in the two series indicate extreme sensitivity of the outcomes to small variations in the data.[6]

Based on Wallack's work, complete reliance on the statistical tests to arrive at a division of the 55-year period poses two problems for the purpose of this book. First, as already discussed, the cutoff point is not robust. Wallack herself recognizes this limitation when she states, "Although the evidence for the existence of a break is strong, the data are more ambiguous on its exact timing in the early and mid-1980s" (Wallack, 2003, p. 4314). Second, since Wallack finds only a single break point, reliance on the statistical technique would force us to divide the entire 55-year period into two parts. But this will be too broad a division to permit a nuanced narrative of the rich Indian experience.

While the reliance solely on statistical techniques to identify different phases of growth is thus problematic, I must still offer a plausible justification for the specific phases distinguished. In turn this requires a discussion of each of the three cutoff points. Therefore, consider first the dividing line between phases II and I. Coincidentally, statistical analysis does supports this division, in the sense that the trend growth rate during 1965–81 is statistically significantly different from that during 1951–65.[7]

But this is not the main reason for my choice of the two phases. Instead, the main reason derives from the dramatically superior performance of the East Asian countries such as the Republic of Korea and Taiwan during the years covered by phase II. Whereas these countries managed to transition from the 4 percent rate registered until the early 1960s into the 8 to 10 percent range in the following one and a half decades, India decelerated to approximately 3 percent. Thus, the counterfactual for phase II that we must explain is quite different from the one observed during phase I. Specifically, even though India faced the same global trading environment as the East Asian tigers, why did it stagnate while the latter transitioned from the modest growth rate of the 1950s and early 1960s into near-double-digit growth rates?

A secondary reason to draw a dividing line between 1951–65 and 1965–81 is that the latter period was characterized by profound change in economic policies. We will see in chapters 3 to 5 that the changes in phase II fundamentally altered the course of the Indian economy. They not only added to the woes originating in the external shocks during phase II but also had serious implications for the conduct of the policy in the subsequent phases. The bulk of the policy reforms undertaken since the mid-1980s and those still outstanding involve undoing what was done during phase II.

The dividing line between phases II and III is the least controversial. Virtually all analysts agree that the era of the so-called Hindu rate of growth ended in the late 1970s.[8] If we calculate growth rates before and after the late 1970s, regardless of the precise dividing line, acceleration in the growth rate is inescapable. What is controversial is the *extent* of acceleration in the early 1980s. And this controversy is rooted in the choice of the cutoff point between phases III and IV rather than phases II and III.[9]

Virtually all authors have chosen to divide the post-1980 period into two parts, with the dividing line at the beginning or end of 1991–92. The commonest practice is to divide the period into subperiods from 1981–82 to 1990–91 and from 1991–92 to the present. Some authors choose this division because they find it convenient to narrate the economic developments according to decades (1970s, 1980s, 1990s, etc.). From the viewpoint of assessing the economic performance, this is clearly nonsensical, since the division must be based on an *economic* criterion rather than the calendar. Others have chosen the same division on the ground that systematic reforms in India began in 1991. These latter argue that such a division allows them to compare the economy's performance in postreform years of the 1990s and beyond against the unreformed 1980s.

On the surface, this latter rationale seems compelling, but it is treacherous for two reasons. First, while the reforms did become systematic in 1991, they did not *begin* that year. As we will see in chapter 4, a piecemeal process of liberalization had already begun in the second half of the 1970s. This slow and halting process received considerable impetus under Prime Minister Rajiv Gandhi during the second half of the 1980s, especially 1985–86 and 1986–87. Therefore, a comparison between the 1980s and the 1990s is far from a clean comparison between the socialist India and the pro-market India. For that, we must compare the India of the 1960s and 1970s with the India of the 1990s and beyond. True, India was still a highly controlled economy in the 1980s, but the direction of movement during that decade was unambiguously toward greater liberalization. The controls introduced during the 1970s being extensive and the pace of liberalization in the 1980s piecemeal, India still looked highly controlled in 1991 when measured against a conventional market economy. Nevertheless, the change at the margin had been toward liberalization, and the policy regime in 1991 was significantly more liberal than in the late 1970s.

Second, and closely related to the first, as it happens, the three-year period from 1988–89 to 1990–91 was characterized by a hefty average annual growth rate of 7.6 percent. Therefore, the story of the 1980s is that India grew 4.8 percent per annum during 1981–88 (phase II) and 7.6 percent during 1988–91.[10] It is plain wrong to lump these two periods into one, obtain an average growth rate of 5.8 percent during 1981–91, and then claim that India had already shifted to the near 6 percent growth in the early 1980s, as many analysts implicitly or explicitly do (for example, Rodrik and Subramanian, 2005; Kelkar, 2004; and Kohli, 2006). To be sure, the growth rate shifted in the early 1980s, but only to the modest rate of 4.8 percent. The shift to the 6 percentplus rate did not take place until the late 1980s.

Therefore, in this book, I define phase III as covering the years 1981–88 and phase IV as covering 1988–2006. From the viewpoint of both growth and economic policies, it is 1988–2006, rather than 1981–91, that forms a self-contained, single period. This is explained below in brief, and expanded in much greater detail in chapters 2–5.

HAS INDIA ENTERED PHASE V?

There are indications that the trend growth rate in India may be shifting upward yet again.[11] During the latest four-year period, 2003–04 to 2006–07, the country's GDP at factor cost has grown at the impressive rate of 8.6 percent. While it is too early to tell conclusively whether this shift represents an especially strong upswing in the business cycle or a jump in the long-term trend growth rate, on balance, evidence favors the latter view.

Before I explain the reasoning behind this assertion, however, it is useful to consider the possibility of why the change may merely represent an upswing in the business cycle. Figure 1.2 divides the period 1990–2006 into four consecutive subperiods that are characterized by high and low growth rates. Specifically, the growth rate during 1990–93 was 4 percent. It rose to 7.1 percent during 1993–97 but fell to 5.2 percent during 1997–2003. Starting with 2003–04, the growth rate has risen once again, reaching the high average rate of 8.6 percent. It is not unreasonable to speculate that the rise is temporary this time around as well, and that the growth rate will likely drop yet again to 5 to 6 percent in a year or two.

While this possibility cannot be ruled out, evidence offers a more compelling case in favor of the alternative hypothesis that the growth rate will be sustained over a much longer period. The economy has produced some spectacular successes during 2003–06 that had not been witnessed before, successes that almost rival the performance of the Chinese economy.[12] In turn, these successes are bringing fundamental changes in the initial conditions that are likely to help the economy sustain the current growth rate.

Thus, consider first the GDP in current dollars at the market exchange rate. This is obtained by dividing the GDP at current consumer goods prices in rupees by the exchange rate. Because the GDP in current rupees has grown at extremely high rates

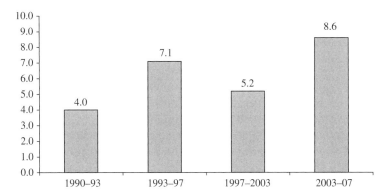

FIGURE 1.2: Business Cycle Effect or a Shift in the Trend Growth Rate? (GDP growth, percent)

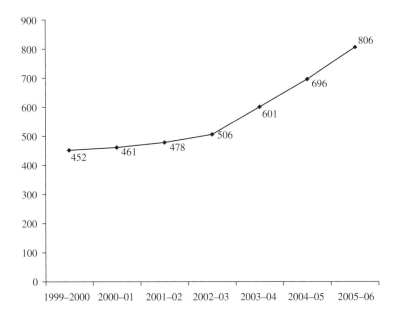

FIGURE 1.3: Dramatic 16.8 Percent per Annum Growth in the GDP at Current Dollars (in billions) between 2003–2004 and 2005–2006

and the value of the rupee in dollars has risen 9.3 percent during the three years following 2002–03, the GDP in current dollars has shown growth not seen before.[13] As figure 1.3 shows, the GDP rose from $506 billion in 2002–03 to $806 billion in 2005–06. This represents a 59 percent growth. The annual growth rate of the GDP in current dollars during 2003–06 turns out to be a whopping 16.8 percent. Allowing for 3 percent inflation in the United States, this works out to a 13.8 percent annual growth in real U.S. dollars. If this growth rate could be sustained, the GDP in India would come to exceed the 2005 U.S. GDP of $11.5 trillion in just 21 years!

While the likelihood of this outcome is nil, it remains true that given the stability of the rupee in terms of the dollar, the progress achieved in dollar terms so far will be largely preserved rather than reversed by a massive depreciation.

Several features of growth reinforce the picture brought out by the GDP in dollar terms during 2003–06. In particular, the following are some notable features:

- Exports grew dramatically during this period. For example, the *level* of merchandise exports in 1990–91 was $18.1 billion. In 2005–06, *growth* in exports over exports in 2004–05 exceeded this amount. Put another way, exports in 1990–91 doubled for the first time in 1999–2000. In the recent period, they doubled in just three years: from $52.7 billion in 2002–03 to $102.7 billion in 2005–06.
- Services exports doubled in just two years: from $26.9 billion in 2003–04 to $60.6 billion in 2005–06.
- India's share in world merchandise exports grew from 0.5 percent in 1990–91 to 0.7 percent in 1999–2000 and to 1.0 percent in 2005–06. In services exports, the share grew to a respectable 2.5 percent in 2005–06.
- These changes greatly increased the integration of India into the world economy. The exports of goods and services as a proportion of the GDP, which grew rather gradually from 7.2 percent in 1990–91 to 11.6 percent in 1999–2000, shot up to 20.5 percent in 2005–06. The proportion of total trade (exports plus imports of goods and services) to the GDP rose from 15.9 percent in 1990–91 to 25.2 percent in 1999–2000 and to 43.1 percent in 2005–06.
- The *total* foreign investment rose from $6 billion in 2002–03 to $20.2 billion in 2005–06, though the growth in direct foreign investment (DFI) from $5 billion to $7.8 billion over the same period was less impressive.
- Remittances increased from $17.2 billion in 2002–03 to $24.6 billion in 2005–06.
- If we add the remittances and foreign investment, the flow of foreign resources, at $44.8 billion, begins to look comparable to the DFI into China.
- In 1990–91, India had approximately 5 million phone lines *in total*. Currently, India is adding more than 5 million phone lines *per month*. By July 31, 2006 India had a total of 185 million phone lines.
- The total turnover of the automobile sector rose from $12.3 billion in 2002–03 to $19 billion in 2004–05. The sales of passenger vehicles rose from 707,000 in 2002–03 to 1.14 million in 2005–06. The total number of vehicles produced during 2003–06 exceeded the entire stock of registered vehicles in 1990–91.

Four factors may be identified that favor the hypothesis that the current growth represents a shift in the trend growth rather than a business cycle effect. First, the period 2003–06 saw India integrate into the world economy as in no prior period. The total trade in goods and services reached 43 percent of the GDP in the year 2005–06. Even merchandise trade to GDP ratio was a respectable 31 percent that year. Likewise, remittances and foreign investment together added up to almost $45 billion. These developments have fundamentally altered the initial conditions for future growth for good. Second, given the large stock of foreign exchange reserves of $165 billion on August 11, 2006, prospects of a large depreciation of the rupee are low. This means the expansion in the dollar value of the GDP achieved, will be sustained. Third, the savings and investment rates in India have been rising and can be expected to continue to rise in the near term. The savings rate rose from 29.7 percent of the GDP in 2003–04 to 32.4 percent in 2005–06. Gross investment during the same period rose from 28 percent to 33.8 percent of the GDP. While private corporate savings also rose from 4.7 percent of the GDP to 8.1 percent over this period, they are still very low compared to, for example, the corporate savings in China at 29 percent in 2005. Therefore, considerable scope for savings to rise in the future still remains. Finally, the last major spurt in growth India saw was between 1993–94 and 1996–97. During these years, the GDP grew a little more than 7 percent per annum. But the growth rate then plummeted to 4.8 percent in 1997–98. The current phase has so far shown no sign of slowing down. According to estimates available at the time of writing, revised estimates placed the growth in the GDP at factor cost in 2006–07 at 9.4 percent, which is slightly higher than the Advance Estimate shown in Table 1.1. In view of this positive outlook , I side with optimists (e.g., Kelkar, 2004) over skeptics (e.g., Acharya, 2004) in the debate on India's growth prospects.[14]

SECTORWISE GROWTH RATES AND THE COMPOSITION OF THE GDP

Let us next consider the growth rates of the major sectors of the economy: agriculture, industry, and services. These are shown in table 1.2 for the four phases identified above.[15] The table additionally shows the growth rate of manufacturing—the major component of industry.

As one would expect, agriculture grew slower than the GDP throughout the 55-year period, implying that the share of agriculture steadily declined. During 1965–81, when the GDP growth slowed down, it did so across all sectors. The largest drop was in industry: its growth rate fell from 6.7 percent in phase I to 4.0 percent. Much of this drop came from manufacturing, which grew at 6.6 percent during phase I but only 3.9 percent during phase II. During phase III, the growth rate in industry recovered substantially but not entirely. At 6.3 percent, it was still below

TABLE 1.2: Growth Rates of Sectoral GDP (at factor cost)

Period	Agriculture & Allied	Industries	Manufacturing	Services	GDP
1	*2*	*4*	*5*	*6*	*7*
1951–65	2.9	6.7	6.6	4.7	4.1
1965–81	2.1	4.0	3.9	4.3	3.2
1981–88	2.1	6.3	7.1	6.5	4.8
1988–2006	3.4	6.5	6.8	7.8	6.3

Note: Allied industries in the first category include forestry and fishing. Industry is defined as the sum of manufacturing, mining and quarrying, electricity, power, and water supply, and construction. All other output is included in services.

Source: Author's calculations, using the data on the components of the GDP reported in RBI, *Handbook of Statistics on Indian Economy* (2006, table 3).

the 6.7 percent rate achieved during the first phase. The sector that did the best was services, which grew at an unprecedented 6.5 percent rate.

In phase IV, all three sectors did better than in the previous two phases. If we take manufacturing by itself, in phase IV it grew at 6.8 percent, which is higher than in phase I but below that in phase III. The growth rate of services showed the biggest jump, rising to 7.8 percent. Indeed, as we will see immediately below, by phase IV, services had come to enjoy a very high weight in the GDP. Thus, the 7.8 percent growth in them made a very substantial contribution to the overall GDP growth of 6.3 percent during phase IV.

Further insight into the growth experience can be gained by examining the evolution of the shares of the three sectors in the GDP. Table 1.3 shows these shares for 1950–51 and the last year of each phase: 1964–65, 1980–81, 1987–88, and 2004–05.[16] Consistent with the experience of the other countries, growth has been accompanied by a steady decline in the share of agriculture in the GDP: It fell from 57 percent in 1950–51 to 21 percent in 2004–05. But in contrast to the experience of the other countries, the bulk of the growth in GDP share has been in services rather than industry. Over the entire period, the share of the industry grew from 15 percent to 27 percent. Much of this expansion took place in the earlier phases of growth. Remarkably, in phase IV, the fastest-growth phase, the share grew only one percentage point, from 26 percent to 27 percent. The share of services, on the other hand, grew from 28 percent to 52 percent over the 54-year period. During phase IV alone, this share rose from 41 percent to 52 percent. Figure 1.4 shows the changes in the structure of the GDP between 1980–81 and 2004–05.

This pattern of growth itself poses a major puzzle for economists: Why is it that the liberalization has not been accompanied by much faster industrial growth, as has been the case, for example, in China since the 1990s, and why is it that the services sector has managed to grow much more rapidly? Considerable research is required to answer this question definitively, but some tentative answers may be given.

Very likely, the lack of pickup in the growth rate of industry is related to continuing restrictions facing labor-intensive products. Until recently, the reservation of the vast majority of the labor-intensive products for small-scale enterprises kept large firms from entering their production despite the removal of licensing. This restriction has been relaxed since the late 1990s through a gradual trimming of the small-scale-industries reservation list and entry by large-scale firms into products still on the reservation list, provided they export the bulk of their output. Nevertheless, labor market inflexibilities, including the absence of rights to hire and fire workers, remain a major disincentive for the entry of large-scale firms into sectors such as apparel, toys, footwear, sports goods, and other light manufactures that China exports in large volumes. In contrast, capital-intensive industries, such as automobile and auto parts, and skilled-labor-intensive industries, such as pharmaceuticals, have done well, but they began with a low base. Their impact on the overall industrial growth will begin to be felt only after a few years.

Services, on the other hand, are not subject to the labor market inflexibilities. The bulk of the labor laws were enacted to protect the rights of labor working in factories and do not apply to service sector workers with any force. Moreover, services either employ white-collar skilled workers or operate in the informal sector. In either case, restrictions imposed by labor laws are limited. Specifically, employers

TABLE 1.3: The Composition of GDP (percent)

Year	Agriculture & Allied	Industries	Manufacturing	Services
1950–51	57	15	9	28
1964–65	49	21	12	31
1980–81	40	24	14	36
1987–88	33	26	16	41
2004–05	21	27	17	52

Note: Sectors are defined as in the note to table 1.2.

Source: Author's calculations, using the data on the components of the GDP reported in RBI, *Handbook of Statistics on Indian Economy* (2006, table 3).

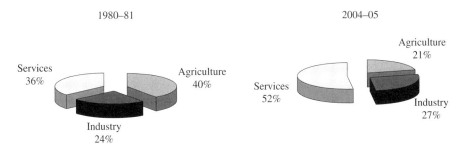

FIGURE 1.4: Sectoral Composition of Output, 1980–81 and 2004–05

keep the right to hire and fire. This has allowed the services sector firms to operate relatively more efficiently and respond flexibly to the reforms in other areas. The expansion of telecommunications and information technology industries has been clearly facilitated by this factor.

Additionally, industrial expansion at the higher rate during phases III and IV, relative to phase II, generated higher incomes that have in turn led to increased demand for tourism, construction, household work, wholesale and retail trade, and repair services. For example, as automobile ownership expands, the demand for drivers and auto mechanics rises. Likewise, as more individuals own TVs, refrigerators, and cell phones, the demand for retail and repair shops rises. The wages in the services sector being entirely flexible, it is able to respond to demand shifts with much greater ease than industry can.

LINKING GROWTH TO POLICIES

The key question confronting us is how closely we can link the performance during the four phases to the policies. The general practice in the literature addressing this question has been to compute the growth rate of total factor productivity and to explore the link between it and the policies. In the following chapters, I will deviate from this practice and focus directly on the link between growth rates and the policies. There are two reasons for this choice. First, employment data are notoriously unreliable in an economy such as India, which suffers from substantial disguised unemployment. Data on capital used to study productivity are also relatively poorly measured in India.[17] Therefore, productivity estimates at the aggregate GDP level must be taken with some grains of salt. On the other hand, productivity studies of the organized industry that use more reliable data on employment and capital accumulation have failed to reach a firm conclusion (Panagariya, 2004b).

Second, at least some of the changes in the employment of labor and the accumulation of capital must be attributed to the change in policy. For instance, suppose the policy change involves a gradual adjustment in the minimum wage from its excessively high level to the market-clearing level. This gradual adjustment will be reflected in an upward shift in the growth rate of employment and GDP. In the Indian context, policies that promote growth are likely to lower underemployment of the labor force. If employment is properly measured, this contribution of the policies will be wrongly attributed to the growth in labor input rather than to good policies. Likewise, better policies promising higher rates of return may change the incentives to save, and thus impact capital accumulation. In sum, good policies need not work through the total factor productivity growth alone.

In chapters 2–5, I will successively discuss the policies during phases I–IV and link them to the growth performance. Here I summarize the essential story developed in greater detail in these chapters. In phase I, India grew at 4.1 percent per year, which was a big jump over the 1 percent or less annual growth achieved during the first 50 years of the twentieth century and an even bigger jump over a negative growth rate during the preceding two decades. Because this shift took place with the active participation of the state, some market skeptics have gone on to celebrate it as a triumph of socialism (Nayyar, 2006). The fact of the matter, however, is that the shift took place in an essentially liberal policy environment. Foreign investment policy remained remarkably liberal throughout this period. Trade and investment licensing policies were also liberal until almost the end of the 1950s. Though trade policy began turning restrictive in mid-1958 with the introduction of foreign exchange budgeting, increased inflow of foreign resources and expansionary fiscal policies allowed India to maintain the high growth rate achieved in the 1950s until a macroeconomic crisis brought the economy to a halt in the mid-1960s.

Phase II saw socialism strike with vengeance. During 1967–76, legislations and rules were introduced to limit the scope of activity of the big business houses and foreign firms to a very small subset of products. Labor-intensive products came to be increasingly reserved exclusively for production by small-scale enterprises. Major banks, insurance companies, the oil industry, and coal mines were nationalized. Distribution and price controls were expanded considerably as well. Simultaneously, the economy was struck by a number of external shocks, including two wars with Pakistan, two oil price shocks, several droughts, and a considerable decline in the inflow of foreign financial resources. The policy changes and shocks together brought the growth rate crashing down to 2.6 percent during 1965–75. A spike in the growth rate to 9.4 percent in 1975–76 helped recover the incomes to some degree, but even so the growth rate during 1965–81 remained 3.2 percent. This was in contrast to the spectacular growth achieved by the more open economies of the Republic of Korea and Taiwan during the same period. Indeed, many African and Latin American economies also performed better than India during this period.

Toward the end of phase II, some piecemeal liberalization had already begun. This process continued into the 1980s as the economy entered phase III. The process received a major impetus in the mid-1980s when Rajiv Gandhi took the reins of the nation following the assassination of his mother, Indira Gandhi. All key areas—including trade, industrial licensing, distribution and price controls, the financial sector, foreign investment, and tax policy—were subject to some liberalization. The policy changes played a crucial role in edging the growth rate up to 4.8 percent in phase III.[18]

The liberalization process continued into the beginning of phase IV. The accumulated effect of this and prior liberalization, accompanied by a very substantial flow of foreign financial resources and fiscal expansion, pushed the growth rate during 1988–91 to 7.6 percent. But the policies of borrowing abroad and fiscal profligacy were unsustainable, and culminated in a macroeconomic crisis. In turn, the crisis opened the door to more systematic reforms that not only quickly returned the economy to the higher growth rate but also helped sustain it.

Four key features of the Indian policy that have been common to all four phases help explain why India never experienced complete stagnation or decline. First, with the exception of brief occasional episodes, India has maintained a stable macroeconomic environment. Double-digit inflation has been a feature of the Indian experience only on a handful of the occasions. Likewise, large devaluations have been rare despite prolonged periods of overvaluation of the domestic currency. This feature greatly distinguishes India from Latin America, which has had a history of repeated episodes of hyperinflation and balance of payments, capital flow, and debt crises.

Second, the policy changes in India have been gradual and largely predictable. Within the complex democratic setup of India, even relatively modest policy changes are usually preceded by the appointment of committees or commissions and extensive discussions. The process is, of course, often used by vested interests, including politicians and bureaucrats, to substantially delay or even block the necessary change. In turn this contributes to low productivity.[19] At the same time, however, it insulates the system from unexpected shifts in policy. When a change is actually made, it is rarely unanticipated.

Third, politically, India has exhibited remarkable stability. Apart from the brief episode of the emergency rule from June 26, 1975, to March 21, 1977, it has been governed entirely democratically. Even when coalition politics has led to the turnover of the government in less than five years, the transition has happened smoothly, without major shifts in policies. And despite the presence of a multitude of ethnic groups, castes, and tribes, India has not had the kind of social and political strife that has been witnessed in many parts of Africa and even Europe. Despite many flaws, a vibrant press, an extensive network of nongovernmental organizations, and a sound judicial system have ensured that the rights granted in the constitution and legal contracts are enforced.

Finally, India has generally exhibited the capacity to implement the policies adopted by the government. In practice, this has meant that once a policy is adopted, the necessary institutions and mechanisms to implement it are put in place. This applies to the good as well as the bad policies. To be sure, the endemic corruption has often led to distortions in the implementation, but this is different from the adoption of policies without the intention to implement them at all. Again, this feature distinguishes India from Africa, where policies got adopted under pressure from the International Monetary Fund and the World Bank, but were not implemented because the countries lacked administrative capacity and will, and never created the necessary institutions.

These four features have given the Indian system a certain predictability, and thus have encouraged savings and investment. The details of the policy regime within the broad framework provided by the above four features have nevertheless been a constraint on the efficiency with which resources get used, as well as the magnitude of savings and investment. The precise policy regime partially explains why India exhibited elephant- rather than tiger-like growth for a considerable part of its development history.

THE GREAT GROWTH DEBATE

I have already hinted at the ongoing debate between reform skeptics and reform advocates on the importance of liberalization by India in stimulating and sustaining growth. We may now consider it in greater detail.[20] The origins of the debate are to be found in a paper by DeLong (2003, chap. 7, p. 186). To quote him:

> What are the sources of India's recent acceleration in economic growth?
> Conventional wisdom traces them to policy reforms at the start of the 1990s.... Yet the aggregate growth data tells us that the acceleration of economic growth began earlier, in the early or mid-1980s, long before the exchange crisis of 1991 and the shift of the government of Narasimha Rao and Manmohan Singh toward neoliberal economic reforms.

DeLong (2003, p. 186) continues:

> Thus apparently the policy changes in the mid- and late-1980s under the last governments of the Nehru dynasty were sufficient to start the acceleration of growth, small as those policy reforms appear in retrospect. Would they have just produced a short-lived flash in the pan—a decade or so of fast growth followed by a slowdown—in the absence of the further reforms of the 1990s? My hunch is that the answer is "yes." In the absence of the second wave of reforms in the 1990s, it is unlikely that the rapid growth of the second half of the 1980s could be sustained. But hard evidence to support such a strong counterfactual judgment is lacking.

This account does not deny either the contribution of the 1980s liberalization to faster growth or the role of the 1990s reforms to sustain it. Toward the end, it only expresses discomfort with the absence of incontrovertible evidence establishing the positive role of the second wave of reforms in sustaining rapid growth. Thus, few reform advocates would find Delong's account unsettling. Therefore, it is left to Rodrik (2003) to turn DeLong's healthy skepticism into serious doubts. In his editor's introduction to the volume containing DeLong's paper, Rodrik (2003) interprets the latter as follows:

> How much reform did it take for India to leave behind its "Hindu rate of growth" of 3 percent a year? J. Bradford DeLong shows that the conventional account of India, which emphasizes the liberalizing reforms of the early 1990s as the turning point, is

wrong in many ways. He documents that growth took off not in the 1990s, but in the 1980s. What seems to have set off growth were some relatively minor reforms. Under Rajiv Gandhi, the government made some tentative moves to encourage capital-goods imports, relax industrial regulations, and rationalize the tax system. The consequence was an economic boom incommensurate with the modesty of the reforms. Furthermore, DeLong's back-of-the-envelope calculations suggest that the significantly more ambitious reforms of the 1990s actually had a smaller impact on India's long-run growth path. DeLong speculates that the change in official attitudes in the 1980s, towards encouraging rather than discouraging entrepreneurial activities and integration into the world economy, and a belief that the rules of the economic game had changed for good, may have had a bigger impact on growth than any specific policy reforms.

Rodrik thus effectively argues that liberalizing reforms, especially those undertaken in the 1990s, failed to make a significant contribution to India's growth. In Panagariya (2004a), I question Rodrik's assertions along three lines. First, the claim that growth in the 1990s was no higher than in the 1980s carries a fallacy of aggregation. As previously noted, the acceleration in the early 1980s was modest, with the bulk of the 1980s growth back loaded. Once we take out the years 1988–91, growth in the remaining years falls below 5 percent, which is significantly lower than the 1990s growth and closer to what had been achieved in phase I. The modest reforms of the early 1980s yielded only a modest shift in the growth rate.

Second, superhigh growth of 7.6 percent per annum during 1988–91 was preceded by significant reforms, especially in the years 1985–86 and 1986–87. But in addition, this growth (as well as that during 1981–88) was driven by fiscal expansion and external borrowing that were not sustainable. Unsurprisingly, the surge ended in a macroeconomic crisis in June 1991.

Finally, absent 1990s reforms, it is difficult to imagine that India would have resumed high growth and sustained it in the way it has done. Admittedly, we do not have "hard evidence" supporting the counterfactual judgment that absent the 1990s reforms, the growth process would have lost steam, but we do know that the option to continue indefinitely with the expansionary fiscal policy and external borrowing that partially drove the 1980s growth was not available within the inward-looking policy framework: This much is proved by the fact of the macroeconomic crisis of June 1991. Subsequent experience reinforces this point: During the 1990s and 2000s, India has been able to sustain large fiscal deficits and debt much longer due to an outward-oriented economy that has generated a large stock of foreign exchange reserves.

Reform skeptics have refused to confront the reality that the shift in the growth rate in the early 1980s was only a modest one, however. Instead, they have continued to lump the years 1988–91 with the remainder of the 1980s, and maintain that the acceleration to the 1990s level had already taken place at the beginning of the 1980s. Specifically, Rodrik and Subramanian (2005) argue that an "attitudinal change" on the part of the government in favor of private business around 1980, rather than liberalizing reforms, resulted in a permanent shift in the growth rate. They claim that "pro-business" policies that favor incumbent producers, rather than "pro-market" policies that promote new entrants and aim to benefit consumers, account for the once-for-all shift in the growth rate that took place in the early 1980s.

Few thoughtful economists accept this view, however. Specifically, Srinivasan (2005) provides a scathing critique that opens as follows:

> This is a disappointing paper. It sees a mystery and fails to convince through analysis why it does. Had the authors been familiar with Indian economic literature, they might not have written it! The literature has not only noted the growth acceleration in the 1980s but has also questioned its sustainability on the grounds of its possibly being debt-led and fueled by employment and real wage expansion in the public sector.

As a starting point for the critique of Rodrik and Subramanian, observe that the claim of no acceleration in the growth rate following the reforms has been greatly undercut by the superhigh growth rate achieved during 2003–07. Surely, this growth cannot be attributed to whatever mysterious "attitudinal change" triggered the modest shift in the early 1980s. It would be chutzpah to argue that the reforms of the late 1990s and early 2000s were irrelevant to this acceleration in growth.

Any residual claims of nonacceleration of growth in the wake of the reforms can be laid to rest by looking at the evidence from yet another angle. Thus, suppose we accept the preferred classification of DeLong, and Rodrik and Subramanian, and lump the years 1988–91 with the remaining years in the 1980s. As I have argued elsewhere (Panagariya, 2004a), business cycle considerations then dictate the cutoff point at the end of 1991–92 rather than 1990–91. This leads us to define phases III and IV as corresponding to the periods 1981–92 and 1992–2006, respectively. Given this division, the growth rates in phases III and IV turn out to be 5.2 and 6.3 percent, respectively. The conclusion that the growth rate accelerated in the wake of the liberal reforms is inescapable.

But let us set aside the quibble about growth acceleration and turn to the distinction between "pro-business" and "pro-market" reforms made by Rodrik and Subramanian. For all intents and purposes, this is a spurious distinction: "Pro-business" and pro-market reforms do not form mutually exclusive sets. Instead, policies that enhance the efficiency and profitability of the incumbent firms—the so-called pro-business policies—are an integral part of the neoliberal, pro-market reform packages, India's economy at the end of the 1970s was so tightly controlled that liberalization on almost any front was guaranteed to enhance efficiency, and would have been recommended by reform-oriented economists.

Moreover, it was the prevailing political economy of reforms rather than any clever realization that "pro-business" policy change would yield large and lasting payoffs that accounts for a partial focus of the policy change on the incumbent firms. In the 1980s, politicians were still afraid of being seen as turning away from socialism. Therefore, they preferred small policy changes to large ones and surreptitious ones to overt ones. Accordingly, they chose to go for the reforms that could be introduced strictly within the existing policy framework rather than those involving a change in the framework itself.[21] Unsurprisingly, the reforms prominently included capacity expansion by the existing firms, regularization of capacity that had been created surreptitiously, broad bending of products under the existing authorized capacity, and better access to imported raw materials.[22]

But even granting Rodrik and Subramanian their spurious distinction between pro-business and pro-market reforms, they are factually wrong in asserting that the early reforms did not include easing the entry of new firms. As long as entry barriers could be lowered within the existing policy framework, the government included them in the reform packages. As I will discuss in greater detail in chapter 4, at least four policy measures easing the entry of new firms during the 1980s fitted the bill.

First, the government delicensed several sectors. By 1990, these sectors accounted for as much as 23.6 percent of the value added in manufacturing (Sharma, 2006, p. 12). Second, the threshold level of investment in land, building, and machinery below which a license was not required was raised from 10 million rupees to 30 million rupees in 1978, to 50 million rupees in 1981, and to 150 million rupees in 1989–90. Third, the list of industries open to the big business houses was enlarged considerably in the early 1980s. This meant big business houses could now enter many sectors from which they were previously excluded. Finally, the threshold level of assets defining big business houses was revised upward. This change led to the exclusion of many firms from the definition of big business houses and paved the way for their entry into many sectors previously closed to them.

As regards the observation that the 1980s trade reform did not liberalize consumer goods, we must recall that the same was also true of the 1990s trade reform. Throughout the 1990s, India maintained strict import licensing on consumer goods, and eventually gave it up only as a result of a successful challenge to the policy by the United States in the World Trade Organization (WTO). On this score, we might argue that the 1990s reforms were also pro-business! But more seriously, the focus of earlier trade reform on raw materials and machinery was rooted not in the government's desire to favor the incumbent firms, but in the fear that opening the consumer goods imports would lead to a balance of payments crisis. Additionally, a lobby favoring consumer goods imports was absent. Therefore, in the end, the liberalization of consumer goods required external pressure via the WTO.

Recently, Kohli (2006) has added yet another note of skepticism toward the reforms. While his critique also relies on the pro-market and pro-business terminology, he defines them differently than Rodrik and Subramanian. He defines "pro-market" strategy as one that allows free play to markets to achieve efficient allocation of resources and promotes competition. As for "pro-business" strategy, it is viewed as one that has "developed more via real world experience, especially from the rapid growth successes of some East Asian economies."

But this distinction also reflects confusion, since outward orientation, timely depreciation to avoid overvaluation of the domestic currency, labor market flexibilities, and license-free entry of new businesses and expansion of the existing ones, advocated by pro-market economists, were all integral parts of the "real world experience" of the fast-growing economies of East Asia. It is not altogether clear how being pro-business is inconsistent with free play of markets. Giving monopoly of entire sectors (iron and steel, telecommunications equipment) to the government, as India did during the 1960s and 1970s, cannot be characterized as pro-business. Likewise, creating private sector oligopolies through licensing (Ambassador and Fiat cars) may favor specific businesses but is not truly pro-business.

A final and, indeed, most puzzling attack on India's reforms has come from Nayyar (2006), who concludes that it was the socialist rather than pro-market policies that yielded the most important structural change in India. He backs up this conclusion with the observation that the shift from less than 1 percent growth during the first half of the twentieth century to the 3 to 4 percent rate during 1951–80 was proportionately much larger than any shift subsequent to 1980. But as Khatkhate (2006, p.2204) rightly observes, "A comparison of the structural change in 1951–80 with the pre-independence decades is both fatuous and facetious." He goes on to elaborate:

> During the latter [pre-independence] period there was no autonomous economic policy geared to the interests of a nation. The objective functions were different. It was a colonial policy, addressing the interests of the home country. Any policy, statist or otherwise, with India's interests at the center, would have achieved better results than under a colonial regime. The real question is whether the statist policies were superior to other alternatives but this question can never be answered for want of counterfactual evidence.

Concrete evidence supporting the hypothesis advanced by Khatkhate can be found in Maddison (1971), who offers a detailed discussion of the reasons for the acceleration of India's economic growth since independence. The first reason he offers is as follows:

> With the departure of the colonial administration the emphasis of bureaucratic action has been switched from law and order to development, and bigger taxes have been levied to pay for the expansion of government services. From 1950 to 1969, government current expenditure on development rose from 2.2 percent to 6.5 percent of national income, and the proportion of labor force working in administration doubled. The biggest expansion has been in areas related to production. In rural areas, there are now 80,000 government employees whereas in British times there were only 2,000. In the field of research and development there are now 62,000 scientists and technicians in government employ. Universities and technical schools have greatly increased in number.... The government itself has entered industry on a large scale. Private industry has received help from new development banks, agriculture has benefited from a vast expansion of government-sponsored co-operative credit. (Maddison, 1971, pp. 76–77)

Maddison also points to the upward shift in population growth from 0.8 percent in the prewar era to 2.4 percent per year subsequently, and to vastly improved technological opportunities in the postwar years as additional reasons for the acceleration in growth. The ultimate conclusion Maddison (1971, p. 78) reaches, however, is this:

> Although India's post-war growth is much better than it was under colonial rule, and is a legitimate source of national pride, we must also remember that acceleration in growth is a world-wide phenomenon. It has happened to almost every country. To judge the effectiveness of policy, we must therefore make international as well as historical comparisons. In fact, India's post-war performance is well below average for developing countries (though not as much below as it was in pre-war years).

Maddison goes on to explore the hypothesis that the poor ranking of India in the international comparisons may simply be due to its poor growth potential in the first place. But after a systematic examination of various factors determining the growth potential, he rejects this hypothesis. Among the reasons why India did not achieve its true potential, he points to the poor performance of heavy industry: "The product mix was wrong, and the state enterprises were badly run. This investment has produced small economic benefits in relation to the effort. In each of the years 1966 to 1969 these enterprises taken as a whole have made losses" (Maddison, 1971

p. 82). He also notes that the overvaluation of the exchange rate made it necessary to impose tight physical controls on the allocation of imports, which severely limited the growth of exports. "An attempt has been made to produce everything that is physically possible to produce in India. Hence the potential gains from international specialization have been lost" (Maddison, 1971, p. 82).

More recent developments reinforce the conclusions of Khatkhate and Maddison. Abandonment of the heavy industry approach through greater reliance on the market, a realistic exchange rate, and trade liberalization have helped India shift to and sustain a substantially higher growth rate. The recent acceleration to 8 percent growth and the prospects that the economy may have already entered phase V lend further support to the view that market-friendly reforms are crucial to raising the living standards in India.

CONCLUSION

In this chapter, I have argued that if our objective is to understand the link between policies and growth performance of the Indian economy, it is most appropriate to divide the 55-year period from 1951–52 to 2005–06 into four phases: 1951–52 to 1964–65; 1965–66 to 1980–81; 1981–82 to 1987–88; and 1988–89 to 2005–06. Annual growth rates during these four phases have been 4.1, 3.2, 4.8, and 6.3 percent, respectively. I have provided an outline of the link between the performance of the economy in each phase and the policies pursued during it. In the next four chapters, I will explore this link in greater detail.

I have also examined critically the debate on the recent shift in the growth rate and the role played by economic reforms in stimulating and sustaining it. I have argued that the modest reforms of the early 1980s led to only a modest shift in the growth rate, and that subsequent reforms were critical to sustaining the higher growth rate. I have questioned the spurious distinctions between pro-business and pro-market reforms made by Rodrik and Subramanian (2005), on the one hand, and Kohli (2006), on the other. Additionally, I have argued that even if one accepts these distinctions, many of the reforms of the 1980s were aimed at easing the entry of new firms and were, thus, pro-market within the Rodrik-Subramanian terminology rather than just pro-business.

Finally, I have forcefully countered the view offered by Nayyar (2006) that socialist policies are to be credited with greatest structural transformation of India because the jump in the growth rate during 1951–80 over the pre-independence period was much bigger than that in the 1980s or later. The argument I have developed, following Maddison's important work, is that the success of the policies must be judged not by what was actually achieved in comparison to a prior period, but by the difference between what was possible and what was actually achieved. Once this is done, India is judged to have fared much more poorly during 1951–80 than subsequently.

2

PHASE I (1951–65): TAKEOFF UNDER
A LIBERAL REGIME

Most analysts, including those critical of India's controlled regime, broadly approve of the economic policies and performance during the 1950s. Differences between the advocates of pro-market and state-driven development strategy relate principally to the period beginning in the early 1960s when the Republic of Korea successfully switched from import-substitution policies to outward-oriented policies and India did not. For example, in their monumental work, Bhagwati and Desai (1970) are highly critical of the policy regime in existence in the late 1960s. Nevertheless, they write approvingly of India's performance during the first three plans:

> The overall performance, in terms of absolute and *per capita* incomes, of the [first] three Plans is on the whole quite respectable, even though inadequate to India's needs in view of her desperately low level of initial income and standard of living. (p. 64)

Coming from a position that is far more sympathetic to the state-driven interventionist strategy of development, Raj (1965, p. 2) provides an even more upbeat view of the Indian performance:[1]

> The rate of growth that has been achieved in India since 1950–51 is 2 to 3 times as high as the rate recorded earlier under British administration. As a result, the percentage increase in the national income in the last thirteen years has been higher than the percentage increase in India realized over the entire preceding half a century. Japan is generally believed to be [a] country which grew rapidly in the latter part of the 19th and first quarter of the 20th century; yet the rate of growth of national income in Japan was slightly less than 3 percent per annum in the period 1893–1912 and did not go up to more than 4 percent per annum even in the following decade. Judged by criteria such as these growth rates achieved in India in the last decade and a half is certainly a matter of some satisfaction.

India's GDP grew at nearly 4 percent per annum during the first two Five-Year Plans, spanning 1951–56 and 1956–61, respectively. During the first four years of the Third Five-Year Plan (1961–66), the growth rate averaged even higher, at 4.5 percent.[2] Allowing for the population growth of 2.1 percent, India thus grew 2.0 percent per annum on a per capita basis during 1951–65. Though admittedly below true potential (Maddison, 1971), this performance was superior to India's own prior performance during any historical period for which systematic data are available.

At the sectoral level, the effort at industrialization was seemingly successful, with industry growing at rates between 5.9 and 10.9 percent during 11 of the 14 years of phase I (table 2.1). Agriculture performed better during the First and Second Plans than the first four years of the Third Plan. Services, on the other hand, showed some acceleration during the Third Plan. Their improved performance is the principal reason for the slightly higher growth during the first four years of the Third Plan over the First and Second Plans.

India launched its development program with the First Five-Year Plan (1951–56) in 1951–52, under what was a relatively liberal policy regime. While the Industrial Policy Resolution (IPR), 1948 envisaged an expanded role for the public sector and also opened the door to licensing of private investment in certain sectors, the policy regime remained liberal until a balance of payments crisis led to the adoption of foreign exchange budgeting in mid-1958. By the early 1960s, the foreign exchange budgeting had the effect of making both trade and investment licensing regimes highly restrictive. Remarkably, however, the rules governing foreign investment and the operation of multinationals remained quite liberal throughout phase I. Starting in 1961–62, attempts were made to promote exports through subsidies and import

TABLE 2.1: Sectoral Growth Rates (1951–65)

Year	Agriculture, Forestry, & Fishing	Industry	Manufacturing	Services	GDP
1951–52	1.5	5.3	3.2	2.7	2.4
1952–53	3.2	0.4	3.5	3.1	2.7
1953–54	7.7	5.9	7.7	3.0	6.1
1954–55	2.9	8.1	7.0	4.8	4.2
1955–56	−0.9	10.2	7.8	5.1	2.5
1956–57	5.4	8.4	7.5	4.9	5.8
1957–58	−4.5	−0.3	3.9	3.8	−1.5
1958–59	10.1	6.7	5.0	4.3	7.8
1959–60	−1.0	6.9	6.8	5.1	2.1
1960–61	6.7	10.9	8.3	5.9	7.2
1961–62	0.1	7.1	8.5	5.5	2.9
1962–63	−2.0	6.9	7.3	5.8	2.0
1963–64	2.3	9.9	9.5	6.1	5.0
1964–65	9.2	6.8	6.9	5.9	7.7
1951–65	2.9	6.7	6.6	4.7	4.1

Note: Allied activities in the first category include forestry and fishing. Industry is defined as the sum of manufacturing, mining and quarrying, electricity, power, and water supply. All other output is included in services. The GDP obtained by adding its components is slightly different from that reported in the official GDP series. This fact accounts for the slight difference between annual GDP growth rates reported in this table and in table 1.1.

Source: Author's calculations, using the Central Statistical Organization data.

entitlement schemes, but they were relatively modest, so that a strong overall anti-trade bias in the regime remained. Toward the end of phase I, stagnation in agriculture, rising external debt, and fiscal deficits began to sow the seeds of a crisis that turned into reality at the beginning of phase II. [3]

THE 1950s: AN ERA OF LIBERAL TRADE AND FOREIGN INVESTMENT POLICIES

Students of Indian economic policies have often failed to appreciate that despite interventionist domestic policies, India had a relatively liberal trade and foreign investment regime in the 1950s.[4] This liberalism owed much to the benign neglect of trade policy and active defense of an open foreign investment policy by Prime Minister Nehru. Below, I first discuss the dominant role played by the latter in the design of the development strategy in general, and of external trade and investment policies in particular. I then offer evidence supporting the observation that trade policy during the 1950s was quite open. I conclude the section with a detailed consideration of the relatively open foreign investment policy regime during the 1950s.

Nehru's Vision of Economic Independence and Trade Policy

Prime Minister Nehru was an intellectual, a visionary, and a leader who enjoyed near universal confidence of the Indian public. Following the launch of the First Plan, the only direct challenge to his authority within the Congress Party came from the conservative-minded Purshottam Das Tandon, who became the president of the party against Nehru's wishes in 1950. But Nehru overcame that opposition, wrested the presidency of the party from Tandon in September 1951, and established himself firmly in control of the party. Throughout the remainder of his life, Nehru's authority remained unchallenged even though he relinquished the Congress Party presidency in 1954.

Unsurprisingly, Nehru's vision of building a socialistic society with particular emphasis on the development of heavy industry, on the one hand, and small-scale, cottage industry, on the other, played a central role in the determination of the policies and institutions put in place during the 1950s. As chairman of the Planning Commission, Nehru played a direct and proactive role in policymaking. He regularly advised the Planning Commission on all broad issues of strategy. Deviations from his vision occurred at the state level in areas where the Constitution gave states power to legislate and make policies concurrently with the center, but these were not on a scale large enough to distort the outcome significantly at the national level.[5]

Much of the economic policy debate that took place in India in the 1950s centered on the wisdom of promoting heavy industry and on the size of the Second Five-Year Plan. Trade policy in particular was not debated extensively. The key element in Nehru's thinking on trade policy was that India needed to be independent of the world markets. He saw this independence as essential to maintaining political independence. While this thinking ruled out active pursuit of outward-oriented strategy, it did not automatically imply a protectionist import policy. While Nehru did want domestic production to eventually replace imports, there are no statements in his writings or speeches to suggest that he wanted to achieve this by erecting import barriers. Instead, his vision was more consistent with interventions in production via direct public sector participation and licensing of private sector investment to progressively realign the domestic production basket with the consumption basket (including capital and intermediate goods necessary for production).

As early as 1938, the Congress Party had taken the initiative to appoint the National Planning Committee with representation from a variety of constituencies under the chairmanship of Nehru, in order to evolve the development strategy once independence was achieved. Describing the proceedings of the committee in *The Discovery of India*, Nehru (1946, p. 403) offers the following thoughts on trade policy:

> The objective for the country as a whole was the attainment, as far as possible, of national self-sufficiency. International trade was certainly not excluded, but we were anxious to avoid being drawn into the whirlpool of economic imperialism. We wanted neither to be victims of an imperialist power nor to develop such tendencies ourselves. The first charge on the country's produce should be to meet the domestic needs of food, raw materials, and manufactured goods. Surplus production would not be dumped abroad but be used for exchange of such commodities as we might require. To base our national economy on export markets might lead to conflicts with other nations and to sudden upsets when those markets were closed to us.

In his excellent work on the evolution of planning and economic policies in India since independence, Nayar (1972, pp. 113–40) offers a systematic documentation of the prominence Nehru gave to "economic independence" in his speeches. Nehru would invariably refer to it as the key objective of his advocacy of heavy industry. For example, at the National Development Council meeting on November 9, 1954, he (Nehru, n.d., p. 18) acknowledged that heavy industry would make a minimal contribution to employment, but added, "And yet it is essential for us to have many industries, for we cannot build up a sound economy and be independent of other countries without developing a good number of heavy industries." Previously, in a speech delivered in Hindi in March 1953, at the Federation of Indian Chamber of Commerce and Industry (FICCI), he had stated:[6]

> One thing is clear to me: that if we do not develop heavy industry here, then we either eliminate all modern things such as railways, airplanes and guns, as these things cannot be manufactured in small-scale industry, or else import them. But to import them from abroad is to be the slaves of foreign countries. Whenever these countries wished they could stop sending these things, bringing our work to a halt; we would thus remain slaves.

Recommendations by Mahalanobis (1955) for the formulation of the Second Five-Year Plan in the Planning Commission echo Nehru's view. He states, "One important aim is to make India independent, as quickly as possible, of foreign imports of producer goods so that the accumulation of capital would not be hampered by difficulties in securing support supplies of essential producer goods from other countries." A working paper underlying these recommendations, titled "The Second Five Year Plan: A Tentative Framework," articulates the same theme slightly differently: "It is only by developing basic industries that a secure foundation for capital formation can be laid and the country made more and more independent of imports of critically needed plant and equipment."[7]

The argument, common in the import substitution industrialization literature, that imports must be kept out so that domestic producers of like products may flourish, was essentially absent from these writings and statements. Instead, the objective was seen as promoting a production structure through planning and industrialization that would eliminate the needs for imports, and free the country from the threat of closure of the world markets. Against this background, it is not surprising that an active policy of raising trade barriers did not accompany the initial launch of industrialization, which principally relied on planning, public investment in heavy industry, and licensing of private sector investment.

A Liberal Trade Policy Regime

Though tariffs in India were first introduced in the 1920s, in response to demands by the domestic textile and steel industries, direct import controls appeared later, during the Second World War. Motivated by the need to conserve foreign exchange and shipping for the war, the British government introduced them in March 1940. Initially, the controls applied only to consumer goods, but by January 1942 they were extended to all imports. The principle of essentiality, whereby imports were permitted only if judged essential, was also evolved during this period. The restrictions nevertheless remained qualitative rather than quantitative—no explicit limits on specific imports were set. Indeed, imports from the Sterling Area were regulated according to shipping availability, not balance of payments considerations.[8]

According to Bhagwati and Desai (1970, p. 282), during 1945 and 1946, the scope of open general licensing (OGL) was considerably widened and "extended comprehensively to the Sterling Area countries."[9] During the war, India had accumulated substantial sterling balances that could be drawn down to import goods from the Sterling Area countries. Though the British government imposed restrictions on the rates at which these balances could be drawn down, it did not enforce them rigidly. This allowed the OGL regime with respect to the Sterling Area countries to be more liberal than with respect to hard currency countries. Since the pound sterling was not yet convertible into hard currencies, however, the balances could not be used to import goods from non-Sterling Area countries.

The late 1940s saw the import policy oscillate between liberalization and tightening of controls, principally according to the availability of the hard currency reserves and sterling balances. Sometime around 1948, the Finance Ministry introduced foreign exchange budgeting, which subjected direct imports by each ministry and the imports permitted to the private sector by the chief controller of imports and exports for each half year to separate limits on the use of hard currency and pounds sterling.[10]

The manner in which this budgeting was introduced offers important insight into the policymaking power of even relatively junior bureaucrats in India. Upon review of weekly figures on foreign exchange reserves, the joint secretary in charge of international finance in the Ministry of Finance at the time, B. K. Nehru, concluded that the rate at which foreign exchange was being drawn down was well beyond what was good for the country. He initially offered proposals for the introduction of foreign exchange budgeting to the finance secretary. But when the latter took no action, Nehru issued the necessary order under his own authority. In his autobiography, Nehru (1997, p. 214) triumphantly describes the impact of the order in the following words:

> All the spending ministries sent in their demands as did the Chief Controller of Imports and Exports through the Ministry of Commerce. Mr. B. K. Nehru, the junior-most Joint Secretary in the Government of India, sent for the representatives of each of the ministries, cut down their demands to what he thought was the right figure, discussed his demands with the Chief Controller of Imports and Exports, G. R. Kamat, and issued orders. No Ministry could any longer import anything without the sanctions of the Ministry of Finance.

In August 1949, B. K. Nehru left the Finance Ministry to serve as the executive director for India at the World Bank. Soon after, an order issued in the name of the finance minister discontinued the foreign exchange budgeting, paving the way for a relatively liberal trade regime in the 1950s.[11] According to Bhagwati and Desai (1970, p. 282), the period of the First Five-Year Plan (1951–52 to 1955–56) was one of "'progressive liberalization,' especially towards the end." But there are several pieces of evidence indicating that the trade regime was open during much of the 1950s.

First, after India's maiden election in 1952, Prime Minister Nehru appointed a new cabinet with technocrat C. D. Deshmukh as the finance minister and Congress Party stalwart and close confidant T. T. Krishnamachari (popularly known as "TTK") as the commerce minister. B. K. Nehru, who returned to the Finance Ministry in 1954, offers a detailed account of how affairs were being run during this period on the trade and foreign exchange front. According to this account, TTK was keen to expand investment and the economy, and would not let fears of the depletion of foreign exchange reserves get in the way of imports. To quote him (Nehru, 1997, p. 261):

> T. T. Krishnamachari, a most dynamic minister and a most powerful character dominated the economic scene. He was the Commerce Minister but in practice it was he and not the Finance Minister who was in charge of economic policy....TTK wanted the economy to develop and develop fast; for this purpose, he wanted to import and import here and now anything and everything that was not being produced in India. The only opposition he could have faced was from the Minister of Finance. But Deshmukh, who was Finance Minister, having no political clout, seems to have either not opposed at all or yielded far too easily to the pressure that emanated from further east in the North Block.

Second, consumer goods imports, including items such as cutlery, hardware, and electrical goods and apparatus, were an integral part of the import basket in the mid-1950s.[12] The Third Five-Year Plan (Planning Commission, 1961, chap. 8, para. 1) reports that 32 percent of the total imports in the First Plan and 23 percent in the Second Plan were accounted for by consumer goods. Only a small proportion of these imports were food grains; the latter acquired significance only in the mid-1960s.[13] In view of the fact that developing countries usually singled out imports of nonfood consumer goods for prohibition in the early years of development, even the presence of the imports of household consumer goods is indicative of a relatively relaxed trade regime.

Third, during the 1950s, "established importers" who were licensed to import goods for sale to other buyers were allowed to operate relatively freely. Typically, they were also the importers of consumer goods, whereas actual user licenses were issued to producers and almost always were for the imports of machinery and raw materials. Established importers accounted for almost one third of the import licenses in value terms until at least 1957–58. By the early 1960s, this share had dropped to one tenth, with actual user licenses gaining most in importance.

Finally, table 2.2 reports the ratio of merchandise exports and imports to the GDP at market prices from 1950–51 to 1966–67.[14] The important point to note is that until at least 1957–58, imports as a proportion of the GDP exhibit no signs of a declining trend. And in 1957–58, the ratio was 7.8 percent, which is comparable to the same ratio in South Korea at the time. Only after 1957–58 did the ratio steadily decline, falling to 5.1 percent in 1964–65.

According to the account provided by B. K. Nehru (1997), the policy of benign neglect on the trade policy front continued until the end of 1957. He returned to the Ministry of Finance in the spring of 1954. He writes (Nehru, 1997, p. 260): "On taking charge of my old office, the first thing I asked for was the Foreign Exchange budget. I was told there was none, the practice had been given up soon after I left [in 1949] under the orders of the minister." Seven pages later (pp. 267–68) Nehru states: "The complacency about our foreign exchange position, which I did not share, was short-lived. The outstanding orders of imports which we had so liberally placed were starting to come in and being paid for.... At first the weekly fall in the reserves was relatively small, later it started to increase and later yet the rate of fall became alarming. The situation was pointed out to the Finance Minister by me several times in written notes suggesting that action should be taken but the notes never came back."

TABLE 2.2: Merchandise Exports and Imports as Proportions of the GDP at Market Prices: 1950–67

Year	Exports/GDP	Imports/GDP
1950–51	6.1	6.1
1951–52	6.8	8.4
1952–53	5.6	6.8
1953–54	4.7	5.4
1954–55	5.6	6.6
1955–56	5.6	7.1
1956–57	4.7	6.5
1957–58	4.2	7.8
1958–59	3.9	6.1
1959–60	4.1	6.1
1960–61	3.7	6.5
1961–62	3.6	6.0
1962–63	3.5	5.8
1963–64	3.5	5.4
1964–65	3.1	5.1
1965–66	2.9	5.1
1966–67	3.7	6.6

Source: Author's calculations, using import and export data in Government of India, Finance Ministry, *Economic Survey* (2005–06, table 7.1), and GDP at current market prices in RBI, *Handbook of Statistics on the Indian Economy* (2006, table 1, col. 7).

In 1956, TTK replaced C. D. Deshmukh as the finance minister, and in 1957 he promoted Nehru to secretary, Department of Economic Affairs. By this time, Nehru (1997, p. 279) was even more alarmed by the rapid "hemorrhage in our foreign exchange resources. The reserves were by now beginning to get so low that there was a danger of our not being able to meet our obligations." Without any discussion of the available policy options, including possibly devaluation of the rupee, to combat the shortage of foreign exchange, Nehru once again took matters into his own hands and reintroduced the foreign exchange budgeting.[15] "Once again, I had to take the initiative and re-establish the whole control mechanism through the foreign exchange budget that I had invented nine years earlier."

The first foreign exchange budget was presented in the middle of 1958, by which time Morarji Desai had become the finance minister.[16] This was the beginning of India's turn to a much more restrictive trade- and investment-licensing regime. Though initially an effort was made to maintain liberalism by mobilizing external assistance to the tune of $995 million, imports as a proportion of the GDP began to slide down, and reached barely 5.1 percent in 1964–65. The adoption of the allocative mechanism for foreign exchange also led to the tightening of investment licensing: If a large investor needed to import machinery or raw material that exceeded the foreign exchange quota available to the relevant agency, the investment license would be denied in the first place.[17]

An Open Foreign Investment Regime

Whereas the attitude of the political leadership toward trade policy during the 1950s was one of benign neglect, which allowed a determined bureaucrat such as B. K. Nehru to play a decisive role in its formulation, Prime Minister Nehru himself played an active role in the making of foreign investment policy. In the postindependence era, both private sector and left-wing parties were outright hostile to future foreign investments in the country, and advocated using the sterling balances to buy out existing foreign investments. The Indian National Congress broadly shared this hostility, advocating the elimination of existing foreign capital from the "key industries." Indeed, the Industrial Policy Resolution (IPR), 1948 incorporated these sentiments. The sole paragraph in the resolution dealing with foreign investment, paragraph 10, read as follows:

> The Government of India agree with the view of the Industries Conference that, while it should be recognized that participation of foreign capital and enterprise, particularly as regards industrial technique and knowledge, will be of value to the rapid industrialization of the country, it is necessary that the conditions under which they may participate in Indian industry should be carefully regulated in the national interest. Suitable legislation will be introduced for this purpose. Such legislation will provide for the scrutiny and approval by the Central Government of every individual case of participation [of] foreign capital and management in industry. It will provide that, as a rule, the major interest in ownership, and effective control, should always be in Indian hands; but power will be taken to deal with exceptional cases in a manner calculated to serve the national interest. In all cases, however, the training of suitable Indian personnel for the purpose of eventually replacing foreign experts will be insisted upon.

The only concession the IPR, 1948 indirectly made was that it guaranteed that the government would not nationalize any business holdings. This guarantee also ruled out the takeover of any foreign firms by the government for the following ten years.

Despite the generally hostile environment, Prime Minister Nehru saw a clear need for foreign investment in India. He seized the initiative from the opponents and incorporated none of the restrictive provisions mentioned in paragraph 10 of the IPR in the Foreign Investment Policy Statement he delivered to the Parliament in April 1949. In the statement, Nehru accorded "national treatment" to the existing foreign interests and thus ended any discrimination in favor of domestic enterprises. The statement provided that the government would encourage new foreign capital by framing "policies to enable foreign capital investment on terms and conditions that are mutually advantageous." It permitted the remittances of profits and dividends of foreign companies abroad. It noted that although majority ownership by Indians was preferred, "Government will not object to foreign capital having control of a concern for a limited period, if it is found to be in the national interest." The government fully implemented these measures in the 1949–50 budget. It also provided depreciation allowances and income tax exemption to a wide range of foreign companies. In the 1949–50 budget, the government also abolished the capital gains tax, and in the 1950–51 budget, it reduced the business profit tax, personal income tax, and supertax as applied to foreign companies and their employees.[18]

Despite opposition, the government actually liberalized this policy further in the first few years of planning. In 1957, the government gave a number of concessions to foreign firms, including reduced wealth tax and tax exemption to foreign personnel. In the 1959 and 1961 budgets, the government lowered taxes on corporate income and royalties of foreign firms. India also signed agreements to avoid double taxation, in order to lower the tax burden of foreign investors. (The major source countries included the United States, Sweden, Denmark, West Germany, and Japan.) In 1961, the government established the Indian Investment Center, with offices in the major sources of private foreign capital to disseminate information and advice on the profitability of investing in India to foreign investors.

Relying on the contributions by Kidron (1965) and others, Kumar (1994) notes that the government recognized the foreign exchange bottlenecks in achieving the targets of the Third Five-Year plan and in 1961 issued a list of industries in which foreign investment was to be welcomed. The list included some of the most profitable industries into which the public sector had been moving rapidly: heavy electrical equipment, fertilizers, and synthetic rubber. The government also appointed an officer on special duty in the Ministry of Commerce and Industry to guide foreign investors on investment opportunities. The government welcomed local majority ownership but did not insist upon it. Indeed, the government approval process treated the proposals with foreign financial collaboration with special favor.

According to Kidron (1965), the Western multinationals had been lukewarm to India in the early 1950s and did not show much interest except in investing in oil refineries. In the period following 1957, substantial foreign investment came into a variety of industries including what might have been regarded as "nonessential" items. Kidron estimates that during the period 1957–63, as many as 45 percent of approvals of new capital issues involved foreign investment, as opposed to only 34 percent during 1951–63. According to the Hathi Committee (1975), this was the time during which most foreign drug firms set up manufacturing subsidiaries in the country.

The findings of a census survey by the Reserve Bank of India (1969), reported by Bhagwati and Desai (1970, chap. 11), throw further light on the extent of foreign capital participation and foreign technical collaboration agreements until March 31, 1964. The survey covered a total of 827 private sector companies with foreign participation of some kind. Of these, 591 had equity participation (with 262 having majority foreign holdings), while the remaining 236 had only technical collaboration agreements. Of the 591 firms with equity participation, 351 also had technical collaboration agreements. Separately, Kurien (1966) estimates that the share of foreign-controlled enterprises in the net worth of the private corporate sector rose from 35.8 percent in 1948 to 40.4 percent in 1960. Estimates by other investigators, summarized in Kumar (1994, pp. 50–52), reinforce this trend.

A RESTRICTIVE INDUSTRIAL POLICY REGIME

Policies toward industry were considerably more restrictive than those toward trade and foreign investment. But even in this area, as long as the economy was free of foreign exchange budgeting, the policy regime did not restrict private initiative in a major way. The regime began to tighten after the foreign exchange budgeting was put in place, becoming very restrictive by the mid-1960s. But even so, it remained less restrictive than what was to come in phase II.

There are three key elements of the industrial policy as it evolved in phase I: (1) dominant role of the public sector in the development of heavy industry; (2) regulation of private sector investment through licensing; and (3) distribution and price controls. Before I describe each of these elements of the policy in detail, let us briefly consider the rationale behind them, as seen by the policymakers themselves at the time.

The Mahalanobis model, on which the Second Five-Year Plan formally rested, is often credited with providing the intellectual basis for the development strategy based on the promotion of heavy industry.[19] But in reality, the decision followed directly from the self-sufficiency objective that guided much of Nehru's thinking on economic policy. Nehru wanted India to be independent of foreign markets in a relatively short period of time. This meant the development of the machinery sector so that future investments would not have to depend on external sources of supply.

The next question was who should build the heavy industry sector. The national independence objective meant that the country could not rely on foreign firms even if they were willing to invest in this sector—which they were not, in any case. It was also recognized that the resources of Indian private firms were too meager to allow them to fulfill the task. This left the public sector as the only viable option.

The leadership also felt that the heavy industry sector would be unable to generate adequate employment opportunities. Therefore, it was decided to leave the production of consumer goods to the household sector. This option also sat well with the Gandhian groups, who had substantial political clout immediately following independence. On the policy front, this required investment licensing that would guide large-scale private investment.

A final plank of the industrial policy pertains to the distribution and pricing of products. The government was to have the power to allocate the output of certain commodities at prices below what the market would fetch. According to Bhagwati and Desai (1970), the policy was motivated by considerations of equity, ensuring an adequate supply of inputs to "priority" sectors, and holding the line on inflation.

In retrospect, this policy framework had two glaring flaws despite the appearance of considerable coherence. First, it greatly underestimated the benefits of foreign trade via specialization in products of comparative advantage; exploitation of scale economies; transfer of technology embodied in goods; and enhanced competition. Had the policymakers fully appreciated the cost of opting out of the world markets, they would not have insisted on self-sufficiency as the central objective.

Second, in choosing to extend its role to manufacturing as well as distribution and pricing of goods, the leadership greatly overestimated the ability of the government to efficiently perform a wide variety of functions. As long as the economy was small, it was possible for the government to coordinate its various parts. For example, the First Five-Year Plan was merely a collection of a few projects that the government could oversee with its limited capacity. But as the economy grew larger and more complex in its structure, the diseconomies of management grew exponentially. If the government had understood that its ability to reproduce decentralized decisions of the market in a complex economy was very limited, it would have relied more heavily on market-based instruments to achieve the desired allocation of resources, regardless of whether it chose to participate in the world markets or not.

Against this background, let us now consider the key regulations governing the role of the public sector; investment licensing; and distribution and price controls.

Role of the Public Sector

The Industrial Policy Resolution (IPR), 1948 envisaged a mixed economy in which the public and private sectors would function side by side. It divided the industries into four categories:

1. Industries that were to be state monopolies. These were limited to atomic energy, arms and ammunitions, and railways.
2. Basic industries in which the state would have the exclusive right to new investments, though it could invite private sector cooperation if it was in the national interest. Six industries were included in this category: iron and steel, shipbuilding, mineral oils, coal, aircraft production, and telecommunications equipment (excluding radio receivers).
3. Industries of national importance that the state might regulate and license in consultation with the state governments. Eighteen industries were in this category.
4. All other industries that would be open to the private sector without constraints.

The resolution envisaged, however, that the state would increasingly participate in the last two categories of industries as well. As noted in the previous section, it reassured foreign investors and the domestic business community that their holdings would not be nationalized for the next ten years. This meant that any existing private companies, even those in category (2), would continue to operate without the fear of being nationalized for the following ten years. Indeed, the resolution promised facilities for the efficient working and "reasonable" expansion of these companies during this period.

Moreover, despite the explicit objective of a mixed economy in the IPR, 1948, the First Five-Year Plan did not set any targets for the allocation of investment between public and private sectors. Indeed, it took a very pragmatic view on the matter, noting (First Five-Year Plan, p. 422): "The scope and need for development are so great that it is best for the public sector to develop those industries in which private enterprise is unable or unwilling to put up the resources required and run the risk involved, leaving the rest of the field free for private enterprise." Thus, until the Second Five-Year Plan was launched, the operating principle was to let the private sector operate where it could.

The Industrial Policy Resolution, 1956 replaced the IPR, 1948. The likely motivation behind the introduction of the new resolution was that the government wanted the industrial policy to explicitly incorporate the objectives set forth in the Indian Constitution that had come into effect in 1950. It probably also wanted the resolution to adopt the socialistic pattern of society as the guiding principle of social and economic policy, as accepted by the Parliament in December 1954. While the IPR, 1956 did not fundamentally alter the provisions of the preceding IPR, it expanded the scope of the public sector and did not repeat the guarantee against nationalization.

The IPR, 1956 created three categories of industries. In the first, listed in schedule A, the state was to have the exclusive right of new investment. But the resolution allowed the existing private firms in the industries of schedule A to operate and expand in the future. In addition, the state reserved the right to seek the cooperation of the private firms in these industries if such cooperation was in the national interest.[20] Schedule A consisted of all nine industries in categories (1) and (2) of the IPR, 1948, plus eight others that included some heavy industries, mining sectors, and air transport. Thus, the schedule consisted of 17 industries in all. Since the industries in category (1) of the IPR, 1948 had previously been state monopolies without any private participation whatsoever, they could remain state monopolies under the IPR, 1956 unless the government chose to ask the private sector to cooperate with it.

Industries in the second category, numbering 12, were listed in schedule B. These industries principally included minerals and aluminum and other nonferrous metals not included in schedule A, machine tools, basic intermediate products required by chemical industries, antibiotics and other essential drugs, fertilizers, synthetic rubber, and road and sea transport. Schedule B industries were to be open to the private sector, but the state would increasingly establish new undertakings in them.

The remaining industries were included in the third category. These were to be developed principally through the initiative and enterprise of the private sector. The state reserved the right to enter these industries as well.

The essential similarity between the 1948 and 1956 legislations notwithstanding, the second half of the 1950s saw a clear shift in favor of the public sector. The impetus for the shift came largely from the Second Five-Year Plan, which made the promotion of heavy industry the centerpiece of India's development strategy. Inso-far as the private sector lacked resources to enter heavy industry or was forbidden entry, the shift necessarily resulted in the government's assuming an increased role in economic activity.

The share of the public sector in total investment in the First Five-Year Plan was 46 percent. The Second Plan set the explicit goal of raising this share to 61 percent. But because private sector investment greatly exceeded the projection, it fell well short (54 percent) of the target in proportionate terms, despite substantially achiev-ing the objective in absolute terms. The Third Plan sought to push the share to 64 percent, but once again fell short, at approximately 50 percent.

These facts notwithstanding, by the end of the period, a sizable public sector had emerged in the economy. On average, a quarter of the public investment went to organized industry and mining, with the rest taken by transport and communica-tion, irrigation, power, agriculture, village and small industries, and other services, including education.

Regulation of Private Sector Production and Investment

The second area of domestic policy concerns the regulation of private sector investment and production. The implementing legislation to regulate these activi-ties was the Industries (Development and Regulation) Act (IDRA), 1951, enacted within the broader context of the IPR, 1948. The IDRA sought to regulate indus-trial investments and production according to the Plan priorities, encourage "small" enterprises, achieve regional balance in industrial development, spell out the cir-cumstances under which the government could take over private firms' management and control, and regulate distribution and prices of products.

The provisions of IDRA applied to the industries included in its only schedule, schedule I, and called the "scheduled industries" throughout the legislation. The act introduced the concept of "industrial undertaking," defined as any undertaking "pertaining to a scheduled industry carried on in one or more factories." In turn, a "factory" was defined as any premises within which a manufacturing process was carried on, either with the aid of power and by at least 50 workers, or without the aid of power and by at least 100 workers. The registration and licensing provisions of the act applied to all "industrial undertakings," that is, the firms in the scheduled industries that met the criteria for a factory.

These provisions clearly meant that industries not included in schedule I and undertakings with fewer than 50 workers using power or fewer than 100 workers and not using power were exempt from licensing. Yet, the practice of licensing sug-gests otherwise. By default, all undertakings in all industries came to be subject to licensing unless given an explicit exemption.[21] Interpreting the product categories listed in schedule I broadly, licensing authorities would fit virtually any narrowly defined product into one of them. The exemption based on fewer than 100 workers if not using power and 50 workers if using power finds little mention in any of the subsequent industrial policy statements or press notes.

The IDRA required all industrial undertakings in the scheduled industries to register with the central government. It further stipulated that no new industrial undertakings or capacity expansion in the existing industrial undertakings in the scheduled industries was permitted without prior license. A license minimally spec-ified the product and its maximum quantity. In addition, the act gave the central government the right to specify the minimum scale of the plant and the location of production. The act further empowered the central government to exempt a subset of industrial undertakings, selected on the basis of their small size as measured by employment or investment, from some or all provisions of the act.

Apart from registration and licensing, the IDRA had three main provisions. First, it empowered the central government to specify criteria along certain dimensions that the small-scale and ancillary industrial undertakings would have to satisfy to be eligible for supportive measures, exemptions, or favorable treatment that the cen-tral government might decide to provide. The criteria for qualification were to be stated in terms of investment in plant and machinery or in land, building, plant, and machinery; the number of employees; the quality and cost of the product; for-eign exchange required for import of plant or machinery; and other relevant factors that might be prescribed.[22] Second, the act empowered the central government to assume direct management or control of industrial undertakings under certain cir-cumstances. Finally, the act empowered the central government to control the prices and distribution of specified scheduled industries or undertakings.

It is thus clear that the IDRA, 1951 gave the central government potentially very broad powers to regulate private sector industry. It is important to remember, however, that these were *potential* powers, so that the actual degree of regulation depended on the strictness with which the government chose to exercise the licens-ing authority and other powers given to it by the act. For instance, the government could choose to issue licenses on demand and for broad categories of products listed in schedule I. Alternatively, it could choose a high rejection rate, take a long time to make decisions, issue the license for narrowly defined products within the broad categories in schedule I, and even stipulate whether or not the licensee would be entitled to import machinery and raw materials, and whether and in what proportion foreign investment would be permitted.

Several related sources indicate that until the end of the Second Plan, the licens-ing regime was relatively liberal. First, Sengupta (1985), who offers a detailed account of how the licensing regime operated until the mid-1980s, identifies the years until the mid-1960s as relatively liberal, with 1951–58 being the most lib-eral. Marathe (1989, pp. 50–51), who served in senior positions in the Ministry of Industry from the mid-1960s to the mid-1980s and has produced a comprehensive account of industrial policy in India, takes a similar view:

> The licensing mechanism as well as the release of foreign exchange for imports of equipment were relatively uncomplicated in the first few years after the Industries (Development and Regulation) Act, 1951 came into force.... The clearance of foreign exchange for imports of raw materials [and] capital goods was also relatively easy till foreign exchange difficulties began to surface by 1958. As a result there was relatively little criticism of the working of the licensing regulatory system in the early years.
>
> The situation, however, changed when, on the one hand, the demands on the licens-ing system in the form of applications for new undertakings, substantial expansion and manufacturing [of] new articles, all of which required prior approval, began to increase. For instance, the total number of applications examined by the Licens-ing Committee increased from 1300 in 1956 to approximately 1900 by 1961 and to

approximately 2500 by 1966. Correspondingly, the number of requests entertained by the Capital Goods Committee for foreign exchange also increased significantly. The sheer administrative burden involved as well as the growing shortage of foreign exchange and domestic resources began to reflect itself in a chorus of criticisms directed against the licensing system.[23]

Later in the book, Marathe points out that once foreign exchange budgeting had been put in place, it became necessary to define the product for which a license was to be issued sufficiently narrowly (rather than in terms of the broad categories of schedule I), so that the director general of technical development could determine its machinery and raw material import requirements.[24] To quote Marathe (1989, p. 84) once again:

> For instance, in order to certify the essentiality of imports, the technical authorities needed a detailed description of the product being manufactured or proposed to be manufactured and give clearance from an indigenous angle. Thus, it was not enough to issue a license for an intending manufacturer to produce, say, machine tools or to permit him to import capital goods after taking into account his proposed productive capacity; but it became necessary to grant him a license, say, for a grinding machine or multi-spindle lathe. The reason for this was that unless the product description was sufficiently detailed, the Director General of Technical Development was not in a position to approve the import requirements of components or raw materials and also determine whether or not the particular type of equipment or intermediate or final product was domestically available.

According to Sengupta (1985), while licenses were issued liberally during the 1950s, the instrument was nevertheless deployed to achieve diversification along various dimensions. For example, to achieve product diversification, licenses were issued liberally for the chemical and engineering industries, which were still in their infancy. In contrast, the policy was stricter with respect to the cotton textiles industry, which was more developed. Likewise, to achieve geographical diversification of the basic industries, licenses for their expansion were given with ease for locations in the western, northern, and southern states in preference to the eastern states, where they were initially concentrated. Further, the government sought to broaden the entrepreneurial base by issuing licenses to entrepreneurs in industries in which they had not previously operated.[25] It also encouraged competition between large business houses and between the latter and foreign firms.[26]

The experience during the First and Second Plans provides some indirect evidence supporting the diversification hypothesis. Table 2.3 summarizes the growth achieved during the First and Second Plans in some of the key industrial sectors. Taking the output in the year 1950–51 as 100, it shows that iron and steel, machinery, and chemicals showed rapid growth, while cotton textiles grew more slowly. Of the sectors listed, the machinery sector grew most rapidly.[27]

The second piece of evidence supporting the hypothesis that the licensing regime was relatively liberal in the initial years is that despite the philosophical shift toward giving a central role to the public sector in the Second Plan, the private sector was not constrained through a repressive licensing policy insofar as overall investment was concerned. Recall that the Plan had set the objective of raising the share of public investment in total investment from 46 percent in the First Plan to 60 percent. But it could raise the share to only 54 percent, principally because private sector

TABLE 2.3: Index of Industrial Production (1950–51 = 100)

Group	1955–56	1960–61
General index	139	194
Cotton textiles	128	133
Iron and steel	122	238
Machinery (all types)	192	503
Chemicals	179	288

Source: Planning Commission, *Third Five-Year Plan* (1961, para. 16).

investment grew far more rapidly than anticipated. Thus, in his discussion of the prospects for the organized private sector during the Third Plan period, John Lewis (1962, pp. 208–09) attributes the 1957–58 balance of payments crisis to the surprisingly buoyant performance of the private sector:

> As we saw earlier, the vigor of the private sector's appetite for growth, catching the planners by surprise, precipitated a foreign-exchange crisis and so injected some serious discontinuities into the phasing of the overall expansion. But one net effect of the episode was substantially to increase the government's appreciation of the private sector's capacity for making and implementing expansion decisions.

More interestingly, later in the chapter, Lewis identifies four problems the organized private sector might face in the near future: inadequate financing; management's relations with organized industrial labor; inefficiencies resulting from production behind import barriers; and economic concentration. Remarkably, licensing as an area of concern does not find a place on this list. On one hand, one may attribute this omission to Lewis's generally sympathetic attitude toward the development approach adopted by India. But on the other hand, and more likely, at the time Lewis wrote, licensing had simply not emerged as a major bottleneck in the growth of private industry.[28]

Finally, consider table 2.4, which reports the target output, existing capacity, licensed capacity, and actual output for a number of commodities during the Second and Third Plans in columns 4, 5, 6, and 7, respectively. In the crucial last column, the table gives the extent to which the licensed production capacity exceeded the difference between the targeted capacity and the initial output. If there is enough demand for the product and licensing is enforced strictly in accordance with the target, we should expect the entry in this last column to be zero. A positive number would suggest that licensing is freer than dictated by the Plan targets. A negative number, on the other hand, may suggest either an overly restrictive enforcement of licensing or the absence of sufficient demand for the product

The total number of items shown in table 2.4 is 27. In the Second Plan, licensed production capacity for 22 of these items exceeded the difference between the targeted production capacity and that in existence at the beginning of the Plan. In the vast majority of these cases, the authorized license exceeds the shortfall by a considerable margin, suggesting that licenses may have been issued on demand. For four of the remaining five products, actual output during the plan exceeded the targeted capacity, presumably because entrepreneurs chose to produce them on a scale that did not

TABLE 2.4: A Relaxed Licensing Regime in the Second Plan

Industry	Unit	Plan Period	Production Target	Production Capacity Beginning	Production Capacity Licensed	Production Actually Achieved	Licensed Minus Shortfall in Targeted Capacity
(1)	(2)	(3)	(4)	(5)	(6)	(7)	(8) = (6)−[(4)−(5)]
Commercial vehicles, cars, and jeeps	units	II	57,000	29,000	28,000	52,675	0
Motorcycles/scooters, and 3-wheelers	units	III	100,000	56,700	39,500	70,736	−3,800
		II	11,000	1,500	36,000	25,490	26,500
Fans	units	III	50,000	26,000	28,500	48,859	4,500
		II	900,000	401,700	117,750	1,058,151	−380,550
		III	2,500,000	871,750	97,200	1,358,300	−1,531,050
Sugar mill machinery	Rs. lakhs	II	200	negligible	1407	466.55	1,207
		III	11,400	1,160	149	808.09	−10,091
Cement mill machinery	Rs. lakhs	II	250	negligible	900	90.79	650
		III	450	110	1,300	490.88	960
Boilers (private sector)	Rs. lakhs	II	not included	negligible	691	101.18	691
		III	2,500	370	289	529.42	−1,841
Steel castings	tons	II	not included	15,600	139,130	29,000	139,130
		III	200,000	54,620	431,112	59,626	285,732
Steel forgings	tons	II	not included	41,340	126,320	35,000	126,320
		III	200,000	84,240	345,910	67,800	230,150
Bicycles	units	II	1,250,000	760,000	753,000	1,307,000	263,000
		III	2,500,000	1,117,500	—	1,570,550	−2,500,000
Sewing machines	units	II	300,000	46,500	323,500	297,300	70,000
		III	850,000	267,400	85,500	430,040	−497,100
Agricultural tractors	units	II	—	—	9,000	92	9,000
		III	10,000	negligible	21,000	5,714	11,000
Diesel engines	units	II	20,500	40,000	49,449	43,408	68,949
		III	66,000	47,700	8,546	93,100	−9,754

38

	units						
Power-driven pumps	units	II	86,000	69,000	95,806	94,689	78,806
		III	150,000	128,000	48,420	261,676	26,420
Cement	mil. metric tons	II	n.a.	4.9	6.5	32.48	7
		III	15	9.3	4.3	47.16	−1
Particle board	mil. sq. ft.	II	not included	6	195.55	0.7	195.55
		III	n.a.		13,773	8.1	13,773
Sulfuric acid	tons	II	470,000	242,000	1,316,214	367,731	1,088,214
		III	1,500,000	580,630	2,152,360	663,622	1,232,990
Phosphatic fertilizers	tons	II	120,000	35,000	477,624	52,441	392,624
		III	400,000	52,441	493,820	121,666	146,261
Automobile tires	mil. units	II	2.3	1.05	1.89	1.546	1
		III	3.85	1.46	1.74	2.533	−1
Bicycle tires	mil. units	II	20	6.87	8.28	11.14	−5
		III	20	15.11	3.78	18.45	−1
Acetic acid	metric tons	II	—	3,109	7,576	3,258	7,576
		III	28,000	3,589	5,137	8,231	−19,274
Synthetic detergent	metric tons	II	—	—	7,200	1,654	7,200
		III	20,000	7,200	16,200	8,408	3,400
Pesticides: BHC	metric tons	II	2,500	2,500	4,100	3,891	4,100
		III	15,000	3,900	3,600	7,441	−7,500
Pesticides: DDT	metric tons	II	2,800	700	2,640	2,838	540
		III	2,800	2,800	—	2,745	
Refractories	mil. metric tons	II	0.8	0.44	1.6	0.55	1
		III	1–5	0.82	0.8	0.7	0
Biscuits	mil. metric tons	II	15,000	33,750	n.a.	23,700	
		III	40,000	30,528	4,550	44,049	−4,922
Confectionery	mil. metric tons	II	10,000	40,600	n.a.	17,000	27,440
		III	25,000	51,840	600	25,889	
Infant milk food	mil. metric tons	II	no target	—	4,898	—	4,898
		III	6,000	4,000	6,000	5,281	4,000

Source: Bhagwati and Desai (1970, table 12.1). I have deleted (a) similar information for the First Plan because it is very incomplete, and (b) the data on installed capacity during each Plan, which is not especially relevant for my purpose. The last column in the above table is my addition and is derived from columns 4, 5, and 6. The original source of table 12.1 in Bhagwati and Desai is *Ninth Report of the Estimates Committee (1967–68) on Industrial Licensing* (New Delhi; Lok Sabha Secretariat, July 1967; app. IV, pp. 309–24). The Ministry of Industrial Development and Company Affairs supplied data to the Estimates Committee.

require a license. It is only in the case of commercial vehicles, cars, and Jeeps that the licensed capacity was exactly equal to the shortfall between the targeted and existing capacity, and the actual output during the Plan was less than the targeted output.

In comparison to the Second Plan, the picture in the Third Plan is far less compelling. In 13 out of 27 items, the licensed capacity falls short of the difference between the target output and initial production capacity. In many cases, the shortfall is quite substantial. As just noted, this shortfall may have resulted from a lack of demand by the entrepreneurs for production capacity. But when viewed in the context of the widespread complaints of delays and difficulties in obtaining licenses, it more likely reflects tightening the hold of the system.

It can be hypothesized that until the end of the Second Plan, the economy was still relatively small and simple, and the top bureaucracy, efficient and honest. This would mean that the bureaucracy could make decisions on the applications for licenses relatively expeditiously. Moreover, according to some of the discussion in the Third Plan to which Lewis (1962, p. 207–08) alludes, the government's attitude toward the private sector was still flexible and pragmatic rather than rigid.[29] It was only during the 1960s, when the economy in general and the industrial sector in particular became more complex and the objectives sought to be achieved through licensing multiplied, that the administration of licensing turned progressively more chaotic, arbitrary, and subject to lobbying and corruption. In turn, these developments gave big business houses with deep pockets a major advantage over the smaller entrepreneurs. For example, their ability to wait in the face of delays was greater than that of the smaller entrepreneurs. They also had more resources to bribe the officials and buy off the politicians to secure a license for themselves or block the one sought by a potential competitor. Unsurprisingly, the big business houses were the ones to flourish most during these years, which opened the door for a socialist backlash under Indira Gandhi in the years to come.

Judging by the number of official studies as well, widespread dissatisfaction with the operation and efficiency of investment licensing seems to be a post-1950s phenomenon. Thus, one comes across few official reports pointing to licensing as a critical factor facing industrial efficiency and growth during the 1950s. But starting around 1964, a host of official reports came out that expressed dissatisfaction with one or another aspects of the system. Among the most commonly cited reports are the Report of the Monopolies Enquiry Commission headed by K. C. Dasgupta (1965), the Swaminathan Committee Report (1964), the Report of the R. K. Hazari Committee on Industrial Planning and Licensing Policy (1967), the Ninth Report of the Committee on Industrial Licensing by the Lok Sabha Secretariat (1967), and the Industrial Licensing Policy Enquiry Committee (1969), headed by S. Dutt.[30] Unfortunately, as we shall see in the next chapter, these reports did not lead to liberalization of licensing; instead, they focused on the concentration of economic power and led to the restraining of larger firms and business houses.

Distribution and Price Controls

The third and final area of controls in industry was distribution and prices.[31] As with import controls, powers for the control of distribution and prices of industrial products had existed during the Second World War, under the Defense of India Rules.

As already noted, in the postindependence era, the same powers for the "scheduled industries" were included in the IDRA, 1951. In areas not covered by the IDRA, most notably agriculture, the government acquired these powers through the Essential Commodities Act, 1955.

While distribution and price controls existed throughout phase I, their incidence grew considerably in the 1960s. Recall that until the import policy was relatively liberal, at least in the case of tradable goods, the need for these controls was not acute. But as import controls became tighter and the production structure more diversified, the government saw greater need for these controls to ensure adequate supply of critical inputs to key sectors at reasonable prices. The list of commodities subject to the controls at one time or another during phase I was long, and included iron and steel, nonferrous metals, coal, fertilizers, cotton textiles, paper, sugar, motorcars, scooters, commercial vehicles, ethyl alcohol, molasses, cement, drugs and medicines, kerosene and petroleum products, bicycles, tires and tubes, natural rubber, vegetable oil, soap, and matches.

As previously noted, the distribution and price controls had three objectives: to ensure allocation of an adequate supply of inputs to "priority" sectors at "reasonable" prices; to ensure "equity" in distribution; and to control "inflationary" pressures. For example, iron and steel were subject to both distribution and price controls to make this important input available to priority sectors at reasonable prices. Cement control was prompted by similar considerations. Cars were allotted to consumers at controlled prices according to a queuing system to ensure equity, and coal prices were regulated to control inflation.

AGRICULTURE

Given Nehru's focus on industry, agriculture did not receive a high priority during this period. This was particularly true after the heavy industry strategy was launched at the beginning of the Second Five-Year Plan. In the First Five-Year Plan, 15.1 percent of the total Plan outlay was allocated to agriculture and community development, and 16.3 percent to irrigation (Second Five-Year Plan, chap. 3, para. 2). In the Second Five-Year Plan, these allocations were reduced to 11 and 9 percent, respectively. In the Third Five-Year Plan, the allocation to agriculture rose slightly, to 14 percent, but that to irrigation remained 9 percent of the total outlay (Third Five-Year Plan, chap. 5, table 2).

Strategy in agriculture mainly relied on what is called the institutional model, though it did contain some elements of the technocratic model.[32] On the institutional side, the strategy placed emphasis on land reforms and farm and service cooperatives, while on the technocratic front, it included irrigation and, given Nehru's general enthusiasm for science and technology, research and extension. To some degree, even the emphasis on irrigation was a by-product of Nehru's desire to boost the output of power—an important input for the development of heavy industry—that involved building a number of mega hydroelectric power projects. Altogether absent from the "technocratic" part of the strategy was a role for chemical fertilizers and price incentives. High yielding varieties of seeds, also a part of the "technocratic" model, had not yet appeared on the scene.

In hindsight, a particularly important missing element in the strategy was the role for price incentives. This was not a coincidence, because the prevailing wisdom at the time was that farmers were unresponsive to prices. Systematic studies showing the positive response of farmers to increased prices began to come only in the 1960s. Nehru himself did not consider the profit motive to be a key factor driving farmers' behavior, and even when he accepted its importance, he leaned against it on normative grounds, arguing that he did not want to "encourage acquisitiveness beyond a certain measure."[33]

An important piece of policy legislation relating to agriculture enacted during phase I was the Essential Commodities Act, 1955. This act gave the central government wide powers to control production, supply, distribution, and purchase and sales prices of essential commodities. On the price front, the purpose of this legislation was to place a price ceiling on commodities of essential consumption, and thus discouraged rather than encouraged production. Though the list of commodities to which the legislation applies has been trimmed in recent years, it still remains operative.

Insofar as the effectiveness of agricultural policy during phase I is concerned, land reforms were slow and drawn out, and achieved at best very partial success. While revenue-collecting landlords (*zamindars*) were eliminated in the first round of the reforms, progress on land ceilings, land redistribution, and tenancy reform was limited. Very little land was actually redistributed, with holders of large pieces of land transferring parts of their holdings to their relatives before land ceiling laws were enacted by the states. Tenancy laws remain fuzzy and poorly implemented. This is particularly true for the sharecroppers and subtenants, whose rights remain ill-defined to date. The cooperative movement from which Nehru had hoped so much was an outright failure. The main success was in irrigation, especially during the First Five-Year Plan, when several of the river valley projects were successfully launched and completed.

Progress in agriculture during this period can be measured by growth in food grain output in relation to the area cultivated. This is shown in figure 2.1. Food grains output rose satisfactorily during the first half of the 1950s, stagnated briefly, and then grew steadily again toward the end of the 1950s. But throughout the first half of the 1960s, except in 1964–65, output stagnated once again. The stagnation during the 1960s had important economic and political implications that we will consider in the next chapter. For now, note that the increase in output closely followed the expansion of the cultivated area.[34] As table 2.5 further shows, yield per hectare followed only a modest upward trend. Moreover, the proportion of area irrigated hardly expanded. The efforts at increased irrigation only kept up with the expansion of the total area cultivated.

SUMMARY AND CONCLUSIONS: LINKING POLICIES TO GROWTH

In the early 1950s, India began with a relatively liberal regime. Despite some expansion of interventionist polices through the public sector participation, licensing, and import and export controls, the regime remained relatively liberal in phase I,

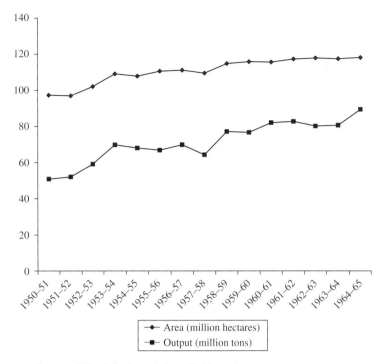

FIGURE 2.1: Output of Food Grain and Area Cultivated

especially in the 1950s. Though the balance of payments crisis in 1957–58 led to the introduction of foreign exchange budgeting in mid-1958, it tightened only gradually.

The foreign investment regime was liberal and was progressively liberalized throughout the period. The problem on this front was on the supply side: In the early 1950s, few foreign companies wanted to enter the Indian market. This changed subsequently, however, with substantial foreign capital and technology coming into the country.

On the investment licensing front, the period during the First Plan was virtually unconstrained. Some tightening began with the Second Five-Year Plan and its emphasis on heavy industry and the public sector. But even then, the private sector had relatively free play, with licenses issued far in excess of the shortfall in the targeted capacity. In the absence of foreign exchange budgeting until mid-1958, the shortage of foreign exchange played no role in licensing decisions. Even after the budgeting was introduced, a sharp increase in foreign aid and loans initially moderated its impact on investment licensing.

A critical question is why the growth rate during the first four years of the Third Plan did not fall in the face of rising interventionism resulting from both import and investment licensing. There are three complementary answers to this question. First, the tightening of policy itself was gradual and, moreover, its impact on the growth rate was felt with lag. We will see this to be the case more generally later. For example, even when the policy regime was liberalized in the mid-1980s, the impact on the growth rate was experienced with lag in the late 1980s. And once again,

TABLE 2.5: Food Grain Output, Area Cultivated, and Area Irrigated

Year	Area (million hectares)	Output (million metric tons)	Yield (kg./hectare)	Percent under Irrigation
1950–51	97.32	50.82	522	18.1
1951–52	96.96	51.99	536	18.4
1952–53	102.09	59.2	580	18.1
1953–54	109.07	69.82	640	18.1
1954–55	107.86	68.03	631	18.4
1955–56	110.56	66.85	605	18.5
1956–57	111.14	69.86	629	18.2
1957–58	109.48	64.31	587	19.3
1958–59	114.76	77.14	672	18.7
1959–60	115.82	76.67	662	18.8
1960–61	115.58	82.02	710	19.1
1961–62	117.23	82.71	706	19.1
1962–63	117.84	80.15	680	19.8
1963–64	117.42	80.64	687	19.8
1964–65	118.11	89.36	757	20.2

Source: *Agricultural Statistics at a Glance* (New Delhi: Ministry of Agriculture, Government of India, August 2004, table 4.5(a)).

the liberalization in the 1990s and early 2000s was reflected in the acceleration of growth between 2003–04 and 2005–06.

Second, continuously rising investment rates helped sustain the growth rate. Investment as a proportion of the GDP rose from 9.7 percent in 1954–55, to 12.1 percent in 1959–60, and to 14.1 percent in 1964–65. While the initial increases were largely due to the increase in the savings rate, the increases in the 1960s were principally due to the inflow of foreign funds.

Finally, growth during the first four years of the Third Plan was also fueled by expansionary fiscal policies. This is partially supported by the observation that the years 1960–65 were characterized by an upward shift in the growth rate in services, which were able to respond more rapidly to the pull provided by the expansion of demand. I will document the extent and the sources of the fiscal expansion in greater detail in the next chapter. Here it suffices to note that such expansion was not sustainable over a long period of time and, indeed, culminated in a macroeconomic crisis during 1965–67.

In concluding this chapter, let us revisit the question of why India was able to shift its growth rate from less than 1 percent in the first half of the twentieth century to 4.1 percent in the first 14 years of the postindependence era, and also to address the question of whether the chosen policies served India well. In addition to what has been said in the previous chapter in the context of the "great growth debate," let me make five points.

First, at independence, India inherited a largely honest and efficient bureaucracy and judiciary, strong political leadership under Nehru, and a vibrant entrepreneurial class. While corruption and inefficiency eventually crept into the system, at least during the 1950s the top rung of the bureaucracy and judiciary functioned efficiently and relatively free of corruption. Nehru and the Congress Party also provided political stability within a democratic setup. Necessary investments were made during this period in infrastructure, with irrigation, power, transport, and communication accounting for approximately half of the total public expenditures in both the Second and Third Five-Year Plans. All these factors provided a facilitating environment to entrepreneurs even though some of the benefits were eroded by the controls that became particularly onerous toward the end of the period.

Second, the task of planning is by nature less onerous at the early stages of development since the economy is not hugely complex and the number of projects to be overseen is small. Under such circumstances, a small number of competent decision-makers can solve the coordination failure problems. The system can respond to the shortages that appear in one part of the economy by moving resources from where they are plentiful. But as the economy grows large and complex, diseconomies of large organization set in, and the task of coordination becomes harder. As we have seen, and will see further in the next chapter, this was already beginning to happen in the 1960s, with the government having to introduce increasingly complex and distortionary regulations to control the economic activity and the size of the firms.

Third, while the general direction of the policy was toward increased controls, especially after mid-1958, since the policies and the necessary institutions were still being put in place, the implementation of controls was not as vigorous in the earlier years as in the later years. I noted above that the policy regime during the First and Second Plans was relatively liberal. During that period, there was even plenty of scope to expand into the labor-intensive industries, since the private sector accounted for more than half of the investment in industry. Although the scope of licensing kept expanding until it had covered virtually all industries by the mid-1960s, licenses were issued relatively freely (Sengupta, 1985).

Fourth, and extremely important, since the foreign investment regime was still relatively open, and the domestic machinery sector still in its infancy, machinery imports were less likely to be denied. This meant that entrepreneurs were able to access the benefits of the innovations embodied in foreign machinery and management with relative ease. Insofar as foreign collaborators were bringing the investments in as machinery, the foreign exchange constraint was not binding. Complementing this was the fact that the world economy itself was experiencing rapid growth in incomes and productivity during this period. Easy entry of foreign capital allowed India to take advantage of this technical change.

Finally, from the late 1950s to the mid-1960s, growth was partially sustained by borrowing abroad and expansionary fiscal policies at home to boost public investment. But this was an unsustainable strategy and carried the seeds of a crisis. Unsurprisingly, two consecutive droughts in 1965–66 and 1966–67 were sufficient to break the camel's back, and India was thrown into an explicit crisis.

Regarding the question of whether the chosen policies served India well, the answer is broadly in the affirmative. The policies helped catalyze growth without scuttling private initiative. Licensing was limited to specific industries, and licenses were issued relatively freely. Foreign investment policy was broadly liberal, and even imports of consumer goods were permitted with ease until the 1957–58 balance of payments crisis.

India's single most important mistake was to ignore the critical importance of international trade for a poor, developing country. Rather than turn to outward-oriented policies that exploited the export potential in labor-intensive products, as Korea did starting in the early 1960s, India pushed import substitution deeper and deeper into a diverse set of goods including machinery. Moreover, an ever-tightening licensing policy subsequently scuttled domestic competition as well, and therefore the efficiency effects such competition brings. As we will see in the next chapter, this road was to lead India into a crisis followed by a long period of stagnation in per-capita income.

3

PHASE II (1965–81): SOCIALISM STRIKES WITH A VENGEANCE

The years 1965–75 saw the average GDP growth rate of India plummet to just 2.6 percent from 4.1 percent during 1951–65. With population growing at 2.3 percent per annum, this meant a per-capita income growth of just 0.3 percent—a virtual standstill in the average living standards. Because the growth rate spiked to 9.4 percent in 1975–76, the addition of this year brings the average GDP and per-capita GDP growth rates over 1965–76 (and also over 1965–81) up to 3.2 and 0.9 percent, respectively. This is still low compared to what had been achieved during the preceding one and a half decades, and considerably lower than what the Republic of Korea managed to achieve over the same period.

Table 3.1 shows the sectoral growth rates during phase II. Though growth rates across all sectors fell during this phase in comparison to phase I, by far the sharpest decline was in industry. Industrial growth fell from 6.7 percent in phase I to just 3.6 percent in phase II. Interestingly, the spurt in the growth rate in services during the last five years of phase I subsided, with the growth rate returning to that achieved during the first nine years of phase I. As noted in the previous chapter, the spurt in services was to some degree the result of expansionary policies, and could not be sustained.

The decline in the overall growth rate is explained by external shocks, reduced flow of external resources, and further tightening of controls that followed the failed attempt at liberalization in the early part of phase II. External shocks included two consecutive drought years during 1965–67; a war with Pakistan in 1965 that came on the heels of a war with China in 1962; another war with Pakistan in 1971, which was preceded by a huge influx of refugees and culminated in the creation of Bangladesh; two further consecutive droughts in 1971–72 and 1972–73; and the oil price shock in October 1973, which contributed to a nearly 40 percent deterioration in India's terms of trade over 1972–76. The decline in the growth rate in agriculture is to be attributed largely to droughts that more than offset the positive

TABLE 3.1: Annual Growth Rates of GDP (at factor cost), 1965–81

Year	Agriculture, Forestry & Fishing	Industry	Manufacturing	Services	GDP
1965–66	−11.0	3.8	0.9	2.8	−3.7
1966–67	−1.4	3.3	0.8	3.1	1.1
1967–68	14.9	3.1	0.4	3.9	8.5
1968–69	−0.2	5.0	5.5	4.6	2.5
1969–70	6.4	7.8	10.7	5.2	6.3
1970–71	7.1	1.0	2.3	4.9	5.0
1971–72	−1.9	2.7	3.3	3.6	0.9
1972–73	−5.0	3.7	3.9	3.0	−0.5
1973–74	7.2	1.1	4.4	3.3	4.5
1974–75	−1.5	1.6	2.9	4.5	1.2
1975–76	12.9	6.6	2.1	6.8	9.4
1976–77	−5.8	8.7	8.8	4.6	0.9
1977–78	10.0	6.9	6.2	5.0	7.5
1978–79	2.3	7.6	12.4	6.7	5.1
1979–80	−12.8	−3.1	−3.2	2.2	−5.2
1980–81	12.9	4.7	0.2	4.5	7.7
1965–81	2.1	4.0	3.9	4.3	3.2

Note: Allied activities in the first category include forestry and fishing. Industry is defined as the sum of manufacturing, mining and quarrying, electricity, power, and water supply. All other output is included in services. The GDP obtained by adding the components is slightly different from that reported in the official GDP series. This fact accounts for the slight difference between annual GDP growth rates reported in this table and in table 1.1.

Source: Author's calculations, using the Central Statistical Organization data.

contribution of the Green Revolution, which bore fruits in phase III. The slow-down in industry must be attributed largely to its strangulation by highly restrictive policies in all spheres, though the slowdown in agriculture and oil price shocks also contributed to it.

The period began with a crisis-cum-liberalization episode, but the liberalization could not be sustained. In the aftermath, not only did the old controls quickly return, but much more restrictive and complex new regulations were piled on top of them. These latter included extra regulations applicable to large enterprises through the Monopolies and Restrictive Trade Practices Act, 1969; severe restrictions on foreign investment through the Foreign Exchange Regulations Act, 1973; further tightening of the licensing regime; the small-scale industries reservation; and the nationalization of banks, insurance firms, and the coal and oil industries.

I begin with a brief discussion of the political developments that influenced the evolution of the economic policy in phase II. This is followed by a discussion of the liberalization attempt and the reasons why it could not be sustained. The bulk of the chapter is then devoted to the discussion of the new, elaborate controls in virtually all areas. I deliberately leave out some liberalization that began in the second half of the 1970s because it better fits the theme of the next chapter, and in any case had at best a limited impact on growth during phase II. I conclude the chapter with an analysis of why the performance during phase II was poorer than in any other period.

THE POLITICAL CONTEXT

Nehru died in May 1964, and Lal Bahadur Shastri succeeded him as the prime minister. Shastri was keener on agriculture than on heavy industry, and successfully brought it to the center of the policy agenda. Against much opposition from the Left parties, he laid the foundation of the Green Revolution. He also created some of the key institutions in agriculture (see below). But his tenure was cut short by his untimely death in January 1966, immediately after he signed a peace accord with Pakistan in Tashkent, Uzbekistan, presumably under pressure from the Soviet Union.

Indira Gandhi, Nehru's daughter, succeeded Shastri and served as India's prime minister until her assassination on October 31, 1984, except between March 24, 1977, and January 14, 1980. In the latter period, a motley collection of parties, united principally by their opposition to Mrs. Gandhi, ruled. It expended much of its energy squabbling over perks of high offices and attempting to prosecute Mrs. Gandhi and her younger son, Sanjay Gandhi. Minor policy changes in the trade regime during this period resulted from bureaucratic initiative and political default rather than the initiatives taken by the leadership.

Mrs. Gandhi's relationship with the United States, on the one hand, and the bosses within the Congress Party, on the other, played a crucial role in influencing her policy choices in the early years of her rule. Therefore, I briefly examine each of these relationships in turn, followed by a discussion of the events leading to the emergency rule and the dominant role Mrs. Gandhi played in driving the policy agenda.

Mrs. Gandhi's Relationship with the United States

An important external factor influencing the policy changes made by India during phase II was its testy relationship with the United States. On the one hand, India resented being equated to Pakistan by the United States despite its democratic status, while on the other hand, President Lyndon Johnson found India's refusal to lend diplomatic support for the Vietnam War irksome. India's extreme dependence on food imports from the United States under its Public Law 480 food aid program allowed Johnson to turn excessively intrusive, which made matters worse.

During the first four years of the Third Five-Year Plan, India imported 25.4 million tons of food grain.[1] The following two years, 1965–66 and 1966–67, India faced drought, which necessitated the imports of another 19 million tons of food grains.[2] A substantial part of these imports came under the PL 480 aid program. Johnson kept India on what he called "ship to mouth" existence by subjecting these shipments to constant threats of suspension. Recognizing that the U.S. shipments were the only escape from famine for India, he also intruded into domestic policy issues, playing a critical role in forcing the ill-fated devaluation of the rupee in June 1966 (see below).

These machinations added to the suspicion and anger that India already harbored toward the United States. Political scientist Stephen Cohen (2000) describes the outcome in these stark terms: "The Indian response to these policies was deep anger, as Indira Gandhi and much of the Indian public felt that Indian sovereignty was under attack by a bullying America. Since America was then deeply enmeshed in Vietnam, many Indians came to see the policy not as well-meaning but the behavior of a bully, and one that had Asian blood on its hands at that."[3]

Following the devaluation of the rupee, Mrs. Gandhi and much of the Indian public came to the conclusion that the donors had failed to fulfill their end of the bargain. India had devalued the rupee in June 1966 at the recommendation the World Bank, made on behalf of the Aid India Consortium (of which the United States was the most influential member).[4] According to those involved in the negotiations on the Indian side, the World Bank and the United States had made oral promises that the former would provide India $900 million per annum in nonproject aid for several years.[5] But, ostensibly under pressure from President Johnson, the promised aid dramatically fell after one year. Moreover, the Indian public viewed devaluation as an unqualified failure. Mrs. Gandhi personally suffered from the episode: Though the Congress Party returned to power at the center in the 1967 elections, its majority was much reduced. More important, it lost elections for the first time in seven states. The entire experience strengthened the socialist convictions of Mrs. Gandhi and reinforced the sentiment that the United States was not a reliably ally. She became more determined than ever not to count on U.S. aid and support in the future.

Split in the Congress Party and Further Shift to the Left

In parallel with these international events, domestic political developments had pitted Mrs. Gandhi against the "Syndicate" that dominated the organizational wing of the Congress Party and wanted to rule India in her name. In contrast to her left-of-center policy agenda, they favored the dilution of planning; a reduced role for the public sector; and greater reliance on private enterprise and foreign capital. Mrs. Gandhi blamed the poor showing in the general elections in February 1967 on the Syndicate, and used the occasion to advocate a shift farther to the left and pushed a major left-of-center Ten-Point Program through the Congress Working Committee.

The Ten-Point Program promised wide-ranging policy changes, including nationalization of banks and general insurance companies; ceilings on urban property and income; curbs on business monopolies and concentration of economic power; public distribution of food grains; rapid implementation of land reforms; provision of house sites to the rural poor; and abolition of princely privileges. Recognizing the popularity of this agenda, the Syndicate's Morarji Desai, whom Mrs. Gandhi had been compelled to appoint as her finance minister, shelved his own convictions and accepted the idea that the government must seize "social control" of the banks. With the assistance of the Reserve Bank of India (RBI) governor, L. K. Jha, an appointee of Mrs. Gandhi's, he even embarked upon a program of channeling bank lending to "priority sectors" such as agriculture and small-scale industries, though within the existing ownership structure. Mrs. Gandhi initially went along with these changes but did not publicly renounce the alternative of nationalization.

In 1969, the death of President Zakir Hussain, and ensuing differences on the choice of the Congress Party candidate for a successor, brought the power struggle between Mrs. Gandhi and the Syndicate into the open. At this point, Mrs. Gandhi seized the initiative, relieved Desai of the Finance portfolio, announced the nationalization of the largest banks, and went on to portray the latter as a friend of big business. Soon after, the party split into the new Congress and the Old Congress, with the former being identified as the traditional Indian National Congress or simply the Congress, and the latter as Congress (O).[6] Mrs. Gandhi nominated her own Congress candidate against the one nominated by Congress (O). Her candidate won, which placed her in firm control of the government. From then on, Mrs. Gandhi systematically proceeded to implement her socialist agenda. In the short run, this made her very popular with the electorate and delivered a landslide victory in the parliamentary elections in March 1971. She won 351 out of 525 seats in the lower house of the Parliament. These seats gave her the two-thirds majority required for the amendment of the Constitution.

In India's war with Pakistan in December 1971, the United States sided with Pakistan, and the Soviet Union with India. This experience led Mrs. Gandhi to move farther away from the United States and sign the 20-year peace treaty with the Soviet Union. The shift also had serious implications for the economic policy: Domestically, it strengthened Mrs. Gandhi's resolve to press ahead with the socialist agenda (see below), and internationally, it redirected India's meager foreign trade toward the Soviet Bloc countries through a series of bilateral, barter-trade agreements.

Economic Failure Culminating in the Emergency Rule

Mrs. Gandhi's popularity was short-lived, however. The droughts in 1971–72 and 1972–73 and the first oil price shock brought high inflation alongside economic stagnation. Controlled in the extreme, the economy simply failed to adjust to the shocks. Though Mrs. Gandhi argued that inflation was a worldwide phenomenon and that external shocks, rather than her policies, were at the heart of India's misfortunes, the public did not offer her a sympathetic ear. Instead, this time around, the opposition parties regained some of their lost ground. They were further helped in their endeavor by a June 1975 Allahabad High Court ruling that held Mrs. Gandhi guilty of fraud in her March 1971 election. The court ordered her removed from the Parliament.

Although Mrs. Gandhi appealed the decision, the opposition organized mass rallies, strikes, and protests calling for her resignation. Rather than oblige, she declared a state of internal emergency on June 26, 1975. For reasons that remain unclear, Mrs. Gandhi decided to call for fresh elections in January 1977. The elections were held in March 1977. Widespread dissatisfaction with the emergency rule resulted in her defeat, with the Janata Party coalition, led by Congress (O), coming to power. For the first time in history, independent India had a non-Congress government. Morarji Desai served as prime minister from March 1977 to July 1979, and Charan Singh succeeded him from July 1979 to January 1980. The three-year Janata rule was undistinguished, with continuous bickering among the coalition members. In the end, the coalition failed to serve its full term and was forced to call for new elections. In January 1980, Mrs. Gandhi returned to power after a resounding victory in the elections.[7] She remained prime minister until her assassination in May 1984. Her son Rajiv succeeded her immediately and remained prime minister until December 1, 1989.

A Note on the Political Economy of Policymaking

We saw in the last chapter that Nehru had enjoyed near universal approval and confidence of the public, so that his vision essentially determined the course of the economic policy during phase I. Though Shastri and Mrs. Gandhi did not enjoy the same degree of public approval and support, they continued to have a dominant influence on the policies adopted during their respective reigns. In less than two years, Shastri was able to turn agriculture into the highest priority item on the policy agenda. Likewise, driven by her socialist policy agenda, Mrs. Gandhi substantially transferred the control of the commanding heights of not just industry but also of finance to the government within a few years of coming to power.

The experience during phase II shows that within the parliamentary democracy of India, a determined leader has the decisive role in shaping the economic policies. In principle, the prospect of defeat in reaction to unpopular policies places some limit on the policy change a leader can bring about. But in practice, since the elections are fought along multiple dimensions including social, economic, military, and political initiatives, the leader retains considerable flexibility in pushing his or her economic policy agenda.

In the short run, the immediate opposition to a specific policy proposal comes from two sources: opposition from within the ruling party and resistance by the opposition parties, including agitation in the public domain. If the leader enjoys the confidence of the membership of the ruling party, as was the case with Shastri and also Mrs. Gandhi once she had ousted the Syndicate from the Congress Party, the opposition from the former source is rendered irrelevant. But even when this is not the case, the dissenting members are severely constrained from voting against the specific policy proposal of the government in the Parliament. This is because a negative vote by a majority within India's parliamentary system leads to the downfall of the government.

As regards resistance from the opposition parties, including agitation in the public space, in most cases time is on the side of the government. If the public at large sees the policy change as being in the overall national interest, those agitating against it quickly lose public sympathy. This was graphically demonstrated by the failure of the airport workers in blocking the privatization of Delhi and Mumbai airports in 2006. But even when a policy change is viewed as leading to adverse effects by a wide spectrum of the population, the free rider problem in organizing dissent places agitators at a disadvantage. The cost of organizing the agitation falls disproportionately on those participating in it, but the benefits from forcing the government's hand accrue to nonparticipants as well. A determined and patient government can readily tire the agitators. This was demonstrated by the failure of the public to reverse the government's decision to extend caste-based quotas in private schools and colleges in 2006.

The experience with the introduction of the Green Revolution, discussed below in detail, illustrates many of these points. As prime minister, both Shastri and Mrs. Gandhi supported the measures required to launch the revolution. But they faced considerable opposition from within the cabinet, Parliament and the public. Nevertheless, with a committed minister of food and agriculture leading the charge, they successfully overcame the opposition at all levels.

The case of bank nationalization by Mrs. Gandhi also testifies to the decisive role a determined leader can play within the Indian democracy. When Mrs. Gandhi came to power, it was widely believed that commercial banks effectively excluded farmers and small entrepreneurs from their lending operations, and that the government needed to do something to improve the access of these groups to credit. This objective could have been achieved either through regulation within the existing ownership structure or through nationalization. In the end, Mrs. Gandhi alone made the choice between these two alternatives.

Though initially Mrs. Gandhi opted for the regulatory route that was favored by Finance Minister Morarji Desai, who came from the rival groups within the Congress Party, narrow political considerations led her to eventually opt for nationalization. Counting on the support of the Members of Parliament from the Congress Party, she could entirely ignore the rival groups within her own party. She wrested control of the Finance Ministry from Desai and declared her intention to nationalize the banks in the public interest.

In his memoir, I. G. Patel (2002, p. 135), who served as the economic secretary in the Finance Ministry at the time the banks were nationalized, offers an interesting account of the decision-making process:

> It was, I think, later in July 1969 that I was sent for once again. No one else was present. Without any fanfare, she asked me whether banking was under my charge. On my telling her it was, she simply said, "For political reasons, it has been decided to nationalize the banks. You have to prepare within 24 hours the bill, a note for the Cabinet and a speech for me to make to the nation on the radio tomorrow evening. Can you do it and make sure there is no leak?" There was no pretence that this was not a political decision, and the message was clear that no argument from me was required. I assured her that we will keep to the timetable and keep the secret. I summoned courage, however, to make two suggestions: to leave the foreign banks alone, and nationalize only the major ones. The former was intended to avoid sharp reaction abroad; and the latter because the purpose would be served by taking only the major banks and leaving the scores of small banks alone. She immediately agreed and added that she could trust the details to me.

Thus, the prime minister could take the decision for a policy change of far-reaching importance purely on narrowly defined political considerations and almost entirely on her own. Those directly and immediately affected by the policy change—bank owners, bank employees, and customers—had virtually no say in the matter. Even the important details of the policy, such as which banks to nationalize and which ones to leave out, were left to senior bureaucrats. Patel (2002, p. 136) underlines this in a later paragraph: "I drafted the Cabinet paper and the speech for Mrs. Gandhi and they [RBI Governor L. K. Jha and an RBI officer, R. K. Seshadri] prepared a draft bill. Fourteen banks were selected for nationalization as between them they accounted for some 85 to 90 percent of the deposits."

Later in 1980, when Mrs. Gandhi returned to power with a two-thirds majority in the Parliament, a second set of banks was nationalized. This change was once again imposed from the top and without any consultation whatsoever with those directly affected. Patel (2002, pp. 165–66), who was now the governor of the RBI and claims the credit for persuading Mrs. Gandhi to bring yet more banks into the fold of the public sector, describes the events leading to the policy as follows:

> Such is the irony of life that one of the first steps I had to recommend to Mrs. Gandhi was that she should nationalize another swathe [*sic*] of private banks. The Reserve Bank had the responsibility to supervise private banks and to ensure their compliance with social control norms as well as with law. Several small private banks had now grown to respectable size and it was not easy to control their activities in practice. Some of them, like the Punjab and Sind Bank and the Vijaya Bank, had become the personal fiefdoms of individuals who disregarded all rules and advice with impunity. They, with their shady dealings, were offering unfair competition to the nationalized banks. I decided that the only practical way to tackle the problem was to nationalize the banks which had now reached the cut-off point of the 1969 Act. Mrs. Gandhi readily accepted the advice—going against her promise of no new wave of nationalization, strictly speaking. But it must be said that she had no appetite for nationalization now and that this particular initiative for the second phase of bank nationalization came entirely from me.

One area in which the argument made in this section loses validity is agriculture. There are numerous examples of the central government failing to carry out reforms in this sector despite a determined effort. In part, the reforms were not carried out because agriculture is a state subject under the constitution. This fact automatically limits the power of the central government except in matters, such as the Green Revolution, that it could centrally orchestrate with the help of one or two states (see below). But in matters such as land reform, the central government has been far less successful because the reforms had to be carried out at the level of the states, where those adversely affected by the reform were politically powerful.

Equally important, with the spread of industrialization, on the one hand, and the success of the Green Revolution, on the other, powerful farm leaders with national stature began to emerge in the 1970s. These leaders successfully brought the farm interests from states to the center. Varshney (1995, p. 81) makes this point forcefully in his important work on urban-rural struggle in India:

> By the end of the 1970s, a new agrarian force had emerged in national politics. On the one hand, this force was dramatically represented in the personality and ideology of Chaudhary Charan Singh, one of the most powerful peasant leaders in postindependence India, who came to occupy important ministerial positions in the central government and brought his peasant-based party into the uppermost state of the power structure. On the other hand, new ideologies of rural political mobilization began to take root. Agricultural prices increasingly came to replace land reform as the major element in agrarian unrest. This was a development with major political implications, because land reforms had mobilized only the classes against the landlords, never the rural sector as a whole.

Not only has the central government had limited success in pushing the desired policies in agriculture; there are also numerous instances of the farmers successfully pushing their desired policies from below. For example, in 1973, a determined Mrs. Gandhi decided to nationalize the wholesale trade in wheat, on the ground that she wanted to eliminate speculation and guarantee the supply of wheat to consumers at reasonable prices. But the attempt failed miserably, and the government had to reverse its decision. Likewise, farmers came to exert considerable influence on the support and procurement prices set by the central government in the 1970s and 1980s (Varshney 1995, chap. 4). As will see later in the book, even in the postreform era, the government's efforts to end the fertilizer and power subsidies to farmers have had limited success.

THE CRISIS AND THE FAILED LIBERALIZATION
EPISODE (1965–67)

Against this brief historical and political background, let us now consider the evolution of domestic economic policies in phase II. In this section, I focus on the macroeconomic crisis that visited the economy at the beginning of the period.

Recognizing the tight foreign exchange situation in the early 1960s, the government had begun to introduce measures to stimulate exports. These measures included fiscal incentives and import entitlements for exporters.[8] Expansionary fiscal policies also led the government to raise the tariff duties, thus, converting the quota rents (i.e., excess of domestic price over the world price) associated with imports into government revenue. In the process, the government also undertook some rationalization of the tariff structure. In 1965–66, it replaced a complex set of tariffs with five rates—15, 35, 40, 60, and 100 percent—topped by a 10 percent across-the-board regulatory duty (Bhagwati and Srinivasan, 1975).

By the early 1960s, evidence of dissatisfaction with the working of the licensing system had begun to accumulate. This led the government to appoint a number of committees to recommend changes. The objective behind setting up these committees was never to dismantle or drastically limit the scope of licensing. Instead, the government sought changes on the margin that would help reduce the administrative burden of the various departments and speed up the decision-making process.

The recommendations by the second Swaminathan Committee on Industries Development Procedures led to delicensing of 11 industries in May 1966.[9] The government cited two criteria for its choice of the industries: They should not require substantial use of foreign exchange for the imports of intermediate inputs and should not pose a threat to the small and cottage industries. The government expanded the list of delicensed items by two in July 1966 and another 29 in November 1966, bringing the total to 42. In addition, two important industries were freed from distribution and price controls—cement in January 1966 and iron and steel (in a phased manner) in May 1967.

Prior to these measures, the government had raised the limit on fixed assets in land, building, and machinery below which new undertakings were exempt from licensing, from 1 million to 2.5 million rupees. In addition, capacity expansion limit without a license was raised from 10 to 25 percent of the registered capacity. Finally, the limit on diversification beyond the specific products for which the unit had been licensed was raised from 10 to 25 percent of the capacity.

Many of these developments took place alongside a macroeconomic crisis, however.[10] While the failure in agriculture was the most important cause of the crisis, borrowing abroad and expansionary fiscal policies played a role as well. Agricultural production had been virtually flat from 1960–61 to 1963–64. The year 1964–65 yielded a bumper crop, but it was immediately followed by drought and debacle for two consecutive years. During these latter years, industry also went into a deep recession, with industrial growth declining to below 4 percent from rates that ranged from 7 to 11 percent in the preceding five years.

In terms of the government budget, public fixed investment rose at the rapid rate of 11.2 percent a year from 1961–62 to 1965–66, reaching an unprecedented 9.6 percent of the GDP. Government consumption (wage bill plus supplies) rose from 6.5 to 8.9 percent of the GDP over the same period. As a response to the war with China in 1962, defense expenditure (not included in government consumption) doubled from 2 to 4 percent of the GDP between 1960–61 and 1963–64. The consolidated government fiscal deficit went up from 5.6 percent of the GDP in 1960–61 to 6.7 percent in 1965–66.

The 1960s saw foreign borrowing on the rise as well (Bhagwati and Desai, 1970, chap. 10). Loans from abroad (as distinct from grants and PL 480/665 assistance) rose steadily from 1.4 percent of the GDP in 1960–61 to 2.4 percent in 1965–66. The resulting debt was beginning to build up the principal and interest payments, which reached 21 percent of the export earnings in 1966–67 and as much as 28 percent in 1967–68.

The one-time jump in agricultural output in 1964–65 could not contain the inflationary pressure resulting from the stagnant output during the previous four years. The wholesale price index (WPI) rose 11 percent, and food prices 20 percent, in 1964–65. In the following three years, food grain price inflation continued unabated at 6, 18, and 20 percent per annum, respectively.

By September 1964, the Aid India Consortium had become alarmed at the stagnation in agriculture and what it saw as a brewing crisis. Therefore, it appointed a mission headed by Bernard Bell, under the auspices of the World Bank, to study the situation and make policy recommendations. The Bell mission gave its final report to the World Bank president in August 1965. Its major concern was the low level of foreign exchange reserves and, therefore, "maintenance" imports including agricultural products and fertilizer. It made two major policy recommendations: a shift away from heavy industry and toward agriculture, and devaluation of the rupee accompanied by an end to licensing on the bulk of intermediate inputs (but not consumer goods and machinery) and export subsidies. The Bell mission also recommended substantial nonproject aid for maintenance imports until the reform secured the necessary improvement. According to Joshi and Little (1994), the understanding of the government of India was that $900 million would to be provided annually for several years.

In June 1966, the government adopted these changes, devaluing the rupee 36.5 percent, from 21 cents to 13.33 cents (or, equivalently, revaluing the dollar 57.6 percent, from 4.76 to 7.5 rupees per dollar). The devaluation was accompanied by decreased import protection, increased export taxes, and decreased export subsidies. Fifty-nine "priority" industries, accounting for 80 percent of the output in the organized sector, were given the freedom to import their intermediate inputs, though the necessity to secure licenses and restrictions on the sources of imports were continued (Bhagwati and Desai, 1970, p. 483). Various export subsidy schemes, including the import entitlement schemes, were withdrawn.

Unfortunately, this liberalization experiment was destined to fail for at least three reasons. First, the program had not been launched out of a strong conviction for liberal, market-friendly policies. Virtually no constituency within the government was pushing for an outward-oriented, pro-market policy regime. The earlier measures to delicense some products had resulted largely from a desire to reduce the administrative burden on the relevant bodies that were unable to process the licensing applications in a timely fashion. There was little appreciation by the policymakers that licensing itself was the problem, and there surely was no road map for continuing to move in the pro-market direction. The criterion applied by the Swaminathan Committee for delicensing was that the products should not require foreign exchange—a clear indication that there was no plan to end licensing for products using imported inputs and machinery. And insofar as the devaluation package was concerned, it was clearly seen as having been imposed from outside, its acceptance dictated by a shortage of foreign exchange for even "maintenance" imports. Unless the liberalization turned out to be an unmitigated success, it was unlikely to be sustained.

Second, on the import side, the timing of the liberalization worked against the success of the program. The liberalization and rupee devaluation coincided with two successive crop failures in 1965–66 and 1966–67 (see table 3.1). Given India's relatively closed economy, the crop failures triggered an industrial recession, and therefore a slackening in industrial demand. In turn, this made the abandonment of the "domestic availability" criterion for import licenses politically hard to sell. Soon after the announcement of the liberalization, the Commerce Ministry came under attack for issuing import licenses when the products were domestically available. As Bhagwati and Desai (1970, pp. 485–86) rightly note:

> In a very real sense, therefore, the timing of import liberalization was not ideal, in retrospect: a burgeoning economy would have increased the chances of making an effective dent in the practice of granting automatic protection to every activity. On the other hand, it was quite naïve to expect the industrialists...to agree to switch over to an efficient system involving international competition....In this, the pressure groups were often in the company of disinterested politicians (such as Finance Minister Morarji Desai) whose thinking had been conditioned by the planning philosophy of the earlier period: that anything that could be produced and supplied from domestic capacity must automatically be precluded from imports. It was thus obvious that getting away from the backlog of the earlier economic philosophy was a Herculean task.

Finally, on the export side, in the public perception the rupee devaluation itself failed to deliver the promised response. Partially, this was because the import liberalization, export taxes, and export subsidy reductions reversed some of the appreciation of the dollar. On the import side, reduced protection meant the rupee price of imports rose less than the nominal revaluation of the dollar. Symmetrically, on the export side, the removal of the subsidies and imposition of export taxes meant that the rupee price received for exports did not rise by the full extent of revaluation of the dollar. According to the calculations by Bhagwati and Srinivasan (1975), once we take the trade policy measures into account, the dollar was revalued 21.6 percent for exports and 42.3 percent for imports instead of the 57.6 percent across-the-board nominal revaluation. Additionally, if we take the inflation following the revaluation into account, the real revaluation of the dollar was even less. These facts already meant that the potential export response would be muted.

In the short run, the crop failure and recession also had an adverse impact on the export response. The industrial activity suffered in general, impacting exports adversely as well. Exports of jute and cotton manufactures, tea, oil cakes, tobacco, and pepper declined. The adverse effect was presumably reinforced by the announcements of the Commerce Ministry, immediately following the devaluation package, that it was going to reintroduce the export subsidies, which it did in a phased manner starting in August 1966. The rational response by exporters to such an announcement would be to restrict exports until the subsidies were in place.

Bhagwati and Srinivasan (1975, chap. 9) present a quantitative analysis of the devaluation and reject the view, expressed by many at the time, that exports were priceinelastic, so that devaluation was the wrong prescription to solve the foreign exchange problem in the first place. Their analysis implies that absent devaluation, the export performance would have been worse than what was observed. Nevertheless, the overall outcome was a decline in exports in both 1966–67 and 1967–68. Politically, this was sufficient to persuade an already skeptical and suspicious public (and policymakers) that the devaluation was a failure.

The outcome of these factors was that liberalization could not be sustained. On the import side, the principle of "domestic availability" remained more or less in place. By 1970–71, the import controls had returned with full force, becoming as stringent as they had ever been (Joshi and Little 1994, p. 83). The export subsidies, applying selectively and at different rates to different products, made a comeback even faster. They now included cash subsidies, import replenishments, supply of indigenous materials to exporters at international prices, and drawbacks of excise and custom duties on inputs used in exports.

Cash subsidies were introduced in August 1966 on most engineering goods and chemicals, and their scope was considerably expanded by the end of 1967. Import replenishments, also introduced in August 1966, operated like the predevaluation import entitlement scheme, except that they were limited to the supposed import content of the exports. Given the scarcity premiums on the replenishments, they, too, had an element of export subsidy. The provision of iron and steel at international prices became widespread in May 1967, while the drawback had existed prior to devaluation and was continued. According to Bhagwati and Srinivasan (1975, table 7.1), the combined export subsidy as a result of these measures on some selected items—including engineering goods, chemicals, plastics, and other "new" products (sports goods, paper products, and processed foods) was anywhere between 50 and 90 percent on the effective ad valorem basis.

Agriculture registered a hefty growth of almost 15 percent in 1967–68 (see table 3.1), which led to a substantial reduction in cereal imports, and hence a favorable balance of payments. With a lag, growth in the WPI, which had been 13.9 and 11.6 percent in 1966–67 and 1967–68, respectively, came down to 1.2 percent in 1968–69. Thus, by the end of 1967–68, the crisis and the liberalization attempt were over.

STRANGULATION OF INDUSTRY

With the liberalization episode over, new controls on industry followed from multiple directions: a new layer of regulations aimed at the large firms under the Monopolies and Restrictive Trade Practices (MRTP) Act, 1969; increasingly tighter restrictions on foreign investment and foreign firms, culminating in the Foreign Exchange Regulation Act (FERA), 1973; the introduction of the policy reserving certain products for small-scale enterprises in 1967; and further tightening of the licensing regulations through the Industrial Licensing Policy, 1970 and press notes on industrial policy dated February 2 and 19, 1973.

Regulation of Big Business Houses

By 1963, dissatisfaction with the working of the licensing system had begun to attract the attention of the government. Unsurprisingly, the resulting debate at the official levels focused not on the impact licensing was having on economic efficiency and growth, but on the complaints by bureaucrats about the absence of clear guidelines for the grant or denial of licenses, delays in decision-making due to the large volume of applications, and the exploitation of the licensing system by the big business houses to concentrate economic power in their hands. The government set up a number of committees to suggest improvements in the system in order to address these problems. The committees included the Monopolies Enquiry Commission (1964); the two Swaminathan committees (reporting in 1964 and 1966); the R. K. Hazari Committee on Industrial Planning and Licensing Policy (1967); the Administrative Reforms Commission (1968); and the S. Dutt Industrial Licensing Committee (1969).

The Monopolies Enquiry Commission had concluded that licensing restricted the entry of smaller firms and led to increased concentration of economic power. The Hazari Committee report noted that the system allowed influential groups to foreclose the licensing capacity. The Dutt Committee came down particularly heavily on the big business houses, arguing that they had successfully used the licensing system to concentrate economic power in their hands. It also echoed the Hazari Committee in noting that these houses had monopolized the licensed capacity in many cases, through multiple applications in different names.

The Dutt Committee report effectively set the stage for the enactment of the MRTP Act, 1969, which gave the government sweeping powers to regulate big business houses. The act introduced several new regulations applying to the so-called MRTP companies, which included (1) undertakings with gross assets of 200 million rupees or more, (2) interconnected undertakings with gross assets of 200 million rupees or more, (3) dominant undertakings (defined as having fixed assets of 10 million rupees or more and market share of 33 percent or more), and (4) interconnected dominant undertakings (defined the same way as dominant undertakings).[11]

As we will see below, the Industrial Licensing Policy 1970 and press notes dated February 2 and February 19, 1973, restricted new production activity of the MRTP companies to a very narrow set of industries that came to be known as the appendix I industries. In addition to the usual licensing procedures for these industries, the firms were subject to an additional, separate approval from the central government for all cases of new undertakings, substantial expansion, mergers, amalgamations, and takeovers under the MRTP Act, 1969. The act allowed the government to give approval to an investment activity only if it would not lead to further concentration and would positively promote the public interest. The act also gave the government the right to grant exemptions from its provisions in the interest of national priorities such as defense needs, market requirements, efficiency, regional growth, and economies of scale.

Regulation of Foreign Investment

According to Kumar (1994, pp. 22–29), who has carefully studied the evolution of foreign investment policies in India, liberalization of the policy toward foreign capital lasted until the mid-1960s. The crisis during 1965–67 inevitably drew the government's attention to foreign exchange outflows resulting from remittances of dividends, profits, and royalties, and led it to introduce restrictions on foreign investment and technology imports. The basic recommendations for the changes came from the Mudaliar Committee on Foreign Collaborations (1966).

The general impression among analysts is that the foreign investment regime in India became repressive only after the introduction of the Foreign Exchange Regulation Act, 1973. The reality, however, is that severe restrictions came to be imposed in 1968 with the setting up of the Foreign Investment Board (FIB) at the recommendation of the Mudaliar Committee. The FIB was given authority to make decisions on all projects involving foreign collaboration with total investment no larger than 20 million rupees ($2.66 million) or foreign equity share no higher than 40 percent. Decisions on all projects involving total investment of more than 20 million rupees or foreign equity share of more than 40 percent were to be made by the cabinet. The change sent a clear signal that projects involving foreign collaboration with total investment exceeding 20 million rupees or foreign equity share exceeding 40 percent would have to pass tougher scrutiny, and had an immediate adverse effect on the appetite of entrepreneurs to seek approval for such projects.

But this was not all. To further discourage imports of technology and investment, the government issued specific lists of products in which foreign investment and technology imports were to be permitted or denied. Three such lists were announced: (1) products in which no foreign collaboration would be permitted; (2) those in which technical collaboration, but not foreign investment, would be permitted; and (3) those in which both foreign investment and technical collaboration would be permitted. According to Desai (1994, p. 43), the last of these lists included only two types of products: those whose production was proving to be difficult to set up and those for which there was only one producer, generally a foreign firm, with no competitor. For many products, it was to be determined at the time of the application whether a competitor existed or not. For technical collaborations, the government specified the maximum royalty payments, which generally did not exceed 5 percent. The term of the collaboration was also reduced from 10 to 5 years.

Starting in February 1972, the government began to use the permission for capacity expansion as an instrument of diluting the stake of foreign investors with majority shares. It made such permissions subject to the condition that the expansion would be financed through additional equity, to be issued to Indian nationals.[12] Subsequently, as we will see below, the 1973 industrial policy decisions were to restrict foreign firms with more than 40 percent share in investment quite dramatically.

While these measures had already begun to choke off the inflow of foreign investment and technology, the Foreign Exchange Regulation Act (FERA), 1973 administered the final blow to them. Under the Companies Act, 1956, an undertaking whose parent office is incorporated abroad is treated as a branch of a foreign company.[13] FERA required all nonbank foreign branches and companies incorporated in India that had foreign equity share in excess of 40 percent to obtain permission from the RBI to continue business in India. The RBI granted this permission, provided the foreign branches and companies diluted the foreign equity share to 40 percent or less. They were then also granted "national treatment," meaning that they enjoyed the same rights as Indian companies. For example, they no longer required RBI approval for sale or purchase of real property, borrowing or lending, and the use of trademarks.[14]

Nonbank branches or companies that did not dilute their foreign equity share to 40 percent, and also did not fall under the exceptions to be described shortly, had to wind up their business. Two sets of exceptions to the 40 percent limit on foreign equity share were granted. First, the guidelines for the implementation of FERA, issued in December 1973, provided that a company could retain foreign equity share up to 74 percent under one of the following conditions:

(a) It manufactured one or more products in the core sector listed in appendix I of the press note on industrial policy issued on February 2, 1973 (see below);
(b) It engaged in manufacturing and exported 60 percent or more of its output;
(c) It used sophisticated technology;
(d) It grew tea;[15]
(e) It engaged in trade and developed skills or infrastructure (e.g., distribution networks) not available indigenously and contributed significantly to exports; or
(f) It was a foreign branch of an airline or shipping company (permitted under reciprocal arrangements).

The second exception to the 40 percent limit on foreign equity share was granted under the 1976 amplification of the implementation guidelines. They provided that a maximum of 51 percent of foreign equity in a company would be allowed, provided:

(a) It exported 40 percent of its production; or
(b) At least 60 percent of its output was in the core sector (appendix I) and it exported 10 percent of its total output.

Companies that took one of the above exceptions and chose not to dilute foreign equity to 40 percent or less were not given "national treatment." Instead, they fell into a category that came to be called "FERA companies," and were subject to FERA discipline as well as many restrictions applied to the MRTP companies. Section 29(1) of FERA, 1973 forbade these companies from carrying on any activity of a trading, commercial, or industrial nature other than the one for which they had obtained permission of the Reserve Bank of India under section 28. Section 29(1) forbade FERA companies from acquiring wholly or partially, or from buying shares in, undertakings in India that were carrying on trade, commerce, or industrial activity.

FERA led the vast majority of foreign companies operating in India outside of airline, shipping, and banking sectors to incorporate under the Companies Act, 1956. The change had a particularly profound effect on the tea plantation industry, which had been dominated by 114 British tea companies. In the wake of FERA, 45 companies incorporated in India and, having up to 74 percent foreign equity, took over the business of these British companies. Multinational companies that operated branches for the purpose of monitoring investment opportunities, but did not manufacture anything, had no simple way of lowering foreign equity to 40 percent and had to wind up their operations.

According to a study by Johan Martinusson (1987), as reported by Desai (1994, pp. 46–47), by December 31, 1982, 895 companies had applied to RBI under section 29 of FERA, 1973. RBI granted approval to 248 companies without dilution of foreign equity (105 of them already had 40 percent or less foreign equity) and to 361 companies after dilution. The latter group included as many as 245 companies that diluted their foreign equity share to 40 percent or less. RBI rejected the applications of 97 companies and directed them to wind up operations or eliminate nonresident status. Another 14 companies decided to wind up operations despite being granted permission. As many as 18 companies were either nationalized or merged with other companies.

Approval of foreign collaborations slowed down considerably in the post-FERA period. Kumar (1994, p. 44) states this succinctly:

> The gradual liberalization of policy in the early post-Independence period in the wake of the economic crisis of the late 1950s resulted in an almost five-fold increase in the number of collaborations approved per year—from 50 during the period 1948–1958 to 297 during 1959–1966. Since foreign exchange was a major constraint during the period, a high (over 36 percent) proportion of the collaborations approved were with financial participation. The restrictive posture adopted by the government during the 1967–1979 period brought down the average number of approvals to 242. The squeeze on foreign financial collaborations was far more drastic, bringing their proportion down from 36.36 percent during the period 1959–1966 to just 16.11 percent during 1967–1979.

Tightening of the Licensing Regime

Alongside the MRTP Act, 1969 and FERA, 1973, the government introduced several measures aimed at limiting the scope of foreign and large domestic firms and "rationalizing" the system. [16] The changes were introduced in two steps: the basic framework was introduced in the Industrial Licensing Policy dated February 18, 1970, and additional modifications were made through the press notes dated February 2, 1973, and February 19, 1973.

The Industrial Licensing Policy of February 18, 1970, was wide-ranging and therefore is worthy of detailed consideration. The following are its main provisions:

1. The policy introduced a list of nine "core" industries that were seen as basic, critical, and strategic products industries in which detailed industry plans were prepared and essential inputs were provided on a priority basis.[17] It also deemed all new investments of over 50 million rupees as part of the "heavy

investment sector." The "larger industrial houses," defined as those with fixed assets of 350 million rupees or more, and foreign firms were confined to investing in these (core and heavy) sectors.[18]

2. The policy raised the exemption limit on licenses for new undertakings, and also provided for substantial expansion of existing capacity, from 2.5 million rupees to l0 million rupees in investment in fixed assets (land, building, and machinery). Registered or licensed industrial undertakings having fixed assets not exceeding 50 million rupees were permitted to take advantage of this exemption, provided the value of fixed assets after substantial expansion did not exceed 50 million rupees. This provision automatically excluded undertakings with 50 million rupees or more in fixed assets (and therefore the larger business houses) from taking advantage of the exemption. The policy also excluded foreign firms and dominant undertakings from eligibility. The exemption was also denied, regardless of the size of the applicant, if the new undertaking or capacity expansion required foreign exchange for machinery imports in excess of the smaller of 1 million rupees or 10 percent of the proposed investment. In a similar vein, firms could not avail themselves of the exemption if the proposed output expansion would require more than a marginal amount of foreign exchange in raw material imports.

3. For undertakings with investments ranging from 10 to 50 million rupees, license applications of parties other than those belonging to the larger industrial houses and foreign firms were to be given special consideration. Unless foreign exchange implications necessitated careful scrutiny, licenses for these undertakings were to be issued liberally.

4. The policy continued the existing policy of reservation for industries in the small-scale sector and stipulated that such reservation would be extended from time to time. In agro-industries, particularly undertakings processing sugarcane, jute, and other agricultural commodities, preference was to be given to licensing applications from the cooperative sector.

5. In May, July, and November 1966, the government had announced three lists containing a total of 41 industries that were delicensed. The basis on which the industries were chosen was that they did not require imports of capital goods or raw materials. With the exemption limit for licensing having been raised to 10 million rupees and the restriction on the imports of capital and raw materials applying to the exemption, the 1970 policy brought these industries back into the licensing ambit.

6. The past provision of diversification allowing the manufacture of new articles up to 25 percent of the licensed capacity was continued, but foreign firms and domestic firms with 50 million rupees or more in fixed assets were excluded from this provision. Likewise, the expansion of output up to 25 percent of the licensed capacity in the line of manufacture for which the undertaking was licensed was continued. Both provisions were subject to the condition that they not lead to increased foreign exchange requirements. Further, the expansion of output was not to require installation of additional machinery and equipment.

7. The policy gave some role to the expansion of exports. The larger industrial houses and foreign firms were permitted to operate outside the core and heavy

investment sectors, provided they undertook to export at least 60 percent of the additional output within three years. Units other than small-scale units were also to be permitted in the small-scale sector, provided they undertook to export 75 percent of the additional output within three years.

Two press notes issued by the Ministry of Industry in 1973 further tightened the scope of larger undertakings. The note dated February 2, 1973, consolidated the core and heavy investment sectors into 19 industries listed in its appendix I. In turn, the note dated February 19, 1973, restricted future investments of all MRTP companies (large and dominant undertakings, interconnected or otherwise) and foreign firms to appendix I industries. As under previous rules, participation by these firms in other industries was permitted only if production was predominantly for export.

The two press notes together also excluded all MRTP and foreign firms, and existing undertakings with 50 million rupees or more in fixed assets, from the licensing exemption otherwise granted on investments up to 10 million rupees in fixed assets. Additionally, the press note dated February 19, 1973, introduced three schedules of products—schedules I, II, and IV—to which the licensing exemption was not applicable.[19] Schedule I contained industries reserved for small-scale units; schedule II, industries specified in schedule A of IPR, 1956, and therefore reserved for the public sector; and schedule IV contained industries subject to special regulations. Over time, schedule IV expanded to contain 78 items in April 1982.

As discussed above, Mrs. Gandhi ushered in the emergency rule in June 1975; it lasted until January 1977. During this period, she introduced a few minor liberalizing policy changes that will be discussed in detail in the next chapter. In March 1977, the Janata Party—a coalition of disparate parties—came to power. On December 23, 1977, the new government issued a new Industrial Policy Statement. The principal distinguishing feature of this statement was its greater emphasis on the small-scale units, and it is discussed in the following subsection. As for large business houses, it stipulated that they should rely mainly on their internal financial resources for new investments. The only other significant change made during the Janata Party rule was the increase in the licensing exemption limit on investment in fixed assets from 10 million rupees to 30 million rupees in 1978.

The Small-Scale Industries Reservation

The government introduced the small-scale industries (SSI) reservation policy in April 1967 by creating a list of items that would henceforth be reserved for production exclusively by small-scale units. In turn, small-scale units were defined within the context of IDRA, 1951 as undertakings with investment of 0.75 million rupees or less in plant and machinery. Once an item was placed on the SSI list, no new medium or large enterprises were permitted to enter, and the production capacity of the existing medium and large enterprises was frozen. According to Mohan (2006), "The rationale used for the selection of items to be reserved is not available in any official documents. The only criterion mentioned in such documents is the ability of the small scale sector to manufacture such an item." Mohan notes, however, that the bulk of the items on the list are labor-intensive products in which India would have a comparative advantage. The list began with 47 items but expanded steadily to 177 items by February 1974, and 504 items by April 1978.[20] The last expansion, which added as many as 324 new items, was the direct result of the major shift toward small-scale units envisaged in the Industrial Policy Statement of December 23, 1977. Items such as clothing, knitted textiles, shoes, leather products, sports goods, toys, stationery, office products, furniture, simple electrical appliances, and simple extruded plastic products, which have been among the major export items of successful labor-abundant countries such as the Republic of Korea, Taiwan, and China at one time or another, have been on this list for the better part of the last several decades.

A Brief Assessment of the Industrial Policy Measures

Successive official committees that reviewed the licensing system from the mid-to-late 1960s had complained that the licensing process had become arbitrary and unpredictable; the policy gave no specific direction on the criteria for the award of licenses. The committees had also complained that the system had led to the concentration of economic power in big industrial houses. This assessment coincided with (and in some cases may indeed have been heavily influenced by) Mrs. Gandhi's embrace of socialism as a way to win back the popular support the Congress Party had lost in the 1967 election. The result was the adoption of a set of policy measures that favored small enterprises to the point of complete exclusion of other enterprises from the manufacture of the vast majority of labor-intensive products. Even in capital-intensive products, clear preference was given to small and medium enterprises, with large enterprises restricted exclusively to a small number of appendix I industries. Thus, some of the most capable entrepreneurs from the technical as well as financial standpoint were excluded from the vast majority of the industries.

The restrictions on foreign investment introduced through the creation of the two-track approval process and exclusionary product lists, initially in 1968 and via FERA, 1973 later, drastically cut the inflows of foreign investment and technology. Such major multinationals as IBM and Coca-Cola wound up their operations and left India. Efficiency in production as well as product quality suffered greatly.

The stifling impact of these regulations began to be recognized in the second half of the 1970s. This recognition led to some relaxation of the licensing policy. I will discuss the specific measures undertaken as a part of this deregulation in the next chapter.

FOREIGN TRADE

In the discussion of the liberalization episode, I have already noted that by 1970–71, import controls and export subsidies had returned with full force. Import licensing covered all imports, and the foreign exchange control was applied with stringency. Every six months, an import policy with a list of products that could be imported was issued. With rare exceptions, consumer goods were entirely excluded from the list. For each listed product, the policy identified the users of inputs that could import it and the proportion of their requirement (measured by production capacity) allowed to be imported. The list also named the sponsoring agency that would have to certify the "essentiality" and perhaps the domestic nonavailability of the product. The availability of foreign exchange played a crucial role in determining the severity with which the policy was implemented.

Starting in 1976, the import control system was reorganized, and some piece-meal liberalization began. Along with industrial deregulation, I will discuss this liberalization in the next chapter. Here, let me describe briefly the evolution of exports and imports. Table 3.2 shows the evolution of merchandise exports and imports as proportions of the GDP. It is evident that these ratios had essentially bottomed out by the early 1970s. In 1971–72, the exports-to-GDP ratio was 3.3 and the imports-to-GDP ratio, 3.7 percent.

During the 1970s, exports grew very rapidly: 18 percent in nominal dollars over 1971–76 and 13 percent during 1976–81. The rapid growth is to be attributed largely to the real depreciation of the rupee. Recall that the rupee had been substantially devalued in nominal terms in 1966, and export subsidies had been introduced soon after. In December 1971, taking advantage of the demise of the Bretton Woods adjustable peg system, India decided to link the rupee to the pound sterling rather than the U.S. dollar.[21] This policy continued until September 1975, when the rupee was repegged to a basket of undisclosed currencies. The pound sterling depreciated during the first half of the 1970s, which allowed the rupee to depreciate against currencies other than the pound sterling. According to Joshi and Little (1994, p. 122), the fall in the effective nominal exchange rate from 1972 to mid-September 1975 more than offset the high domestic inflation, allowing a real effective devaluation of the rupee by 10 percent. Fortuitously, the switch in the peg to an undisclosed basket of currencies in September 1975 did not arrest continued real depreciation because

TABLE 3.2: Merchandise Exports and Imports as Proportions of the GDP at Market Prices, 1965–81

Year	Exports/GDP	Imports/GDP
1965–66	2.9	5.1
1966–67	3.7	6.6
1967–68	3.3	5.5
1968–69	3.5	4.9
1969–70	3.3	3.7
1970–71	3.4	3.6
1971–72	3.3	3.7
1972–73	3.7	3.5
1973–74	3.8	4.5
1974–75	4.3	5.8
1975–76	4.8	6.3
1976–77	5.7	5.7
1977–78	5.3	5.9
1978–79	5.2	6.2
1979–80	5.3	7.6
1980–81	4.7	8.7

Source: Author's calculations, using import and export data in Ministry of Finance, *Economic Survey* (2005–06, table 7.1), and GDP at market prices in RBI, *Handbook of Statistics on the Indian Economy* (2006, table 1, col. 7).

by then, domestic inflation had turned negative. That meant a constant nominal exchange rate still allowed the rupee to depreciate in real terms.

Because the initial exports were tiny, this rapid growth still did not result in a large absolute increase in the exports. Consequently, even in 1979–80 the exports-to-GDP ratio was only 5.3 percent. The story was not especially different on the import side. Here, increased remittances from workers who migrated temporarily to the Middle East in the wake of the oil price rise and external borrowing allowed the total imports to grow faster, with the imports-to-GDP ratio rising to 8.7 percent in 1980–81.

FACTOR MARKET REGULATIONS: LABOR AND LAND

Labor market regulations had begun to turn unfriendly to growth even in phase I. Lewis (1962) succinctly states this in his discussion of the outlook for the organized private sector.[22] He includes the existing labor legislations and labor market processes among four key problems facing the organized sector of industry. Referring to the demands by organized labor for higher levels and rates of increase in compensation than were justified by the level and rate of growth of productivity, Lewis (1962, pp. 226–27) wrote:

> Manufacturers who occupy a protected quasi-monopoly position in a market whose consistent expansion is practically assured are not disposed to resist such demands very strongly and may not appear to be seriously injured by them. However, in the process, receipts that should be reinvested may be diverted into personal incomes and—what is far more serious—India's capacity to export at competitive prices may be gravely undermined. Equally serious is the fact that labor's elaborate protections, particularly in a period when some entrepreneurs have not yet fully embraced an expansionist view of the future, may deter private manufacturers from pressing production to the limits of their capacity.

The march toward socialism in phase II continued in the area of labor legislation as well, culminating in the introduction of a key amendment to the Industrial Disputes Act (IDA), 1947 that made it virtually impossible for the larger firms to lay off or retrench workers. The amendment was introduced in 1976 through the addition of chapter V.B to IDA. The chapter defined an establishment to include factories, mines, and plantations, and provided that establishments with 300 workers or more must get prior permission from the appropriate government authority (generally the government of the state where the establishment was located) to retrench one or more workers. Given political pressures, the authority never gave such permission. Because the provision also applied to any establishments seeking to shut down, it made the exit of firms nearly impossible. In 1982, the limit on the establishments subject to the provision was revised downward to just 100 workers.

The near absolute protection from layoff and retrenchment provided by the amended IDA, 1947 had a hugely detrimental impact on worker efficiency, and therefore on the effective labor costs in phase III and beyond. Labor strikes became endemic, with the owners of large establishments unable to resist the escalating wage demands of the unions. This situation increasingly drove entrepreneurs away from labor-intensive, and toward capital-intensive, industries. In addition, for any given industry, they chose the most capital-intensive technology in order to stay out of the ambit of chapter V.B of IDA. Firms that did have to employ labor looked for ways to rely on contract labor, which did not have the protection provided by the IDA.

New regulations were also introduced in the land market. In conformity with the Ten-Point Program, the government passed the Urban Land (Ceiling and Regulation) Act (ULCRA) in 1976. It fixed a ceiling on how much vacant urban land could be acquired and held in an urban agglomeration by an individual, a family, a firm, a company, or an association or body of individuals, whether incorporated or not. This ceiling varied from 500 to 2000 square meters, with the lower limit applying to the great cities. Holders of excess vacant land had to either surrender that land to the competent authority appointed under the act for a small compensation, or develop it only for specified purposes.

The ostensible objective behind the act was to prevent the concentration of urban land in the hands of a few individuals or firms and to end profiteering from land speculation. The ceilings were further justified by appeal to the existence of similar ceilings on the holdings of agricultural land. In practice, the act led to a serious shortage of land in urban areas. Few holders of land were willing to hand over their holdings to the government for a fraction of its market value. They therefore resorted to the loopholes in the law and bribery to retain their possession. As recently as 2002, the Tenth Five-Year Plan (Planning Commission, 2002) reported only 19,020 hectares of urban land had been acquired under ULCRA. The resulting shortage, which was further exacerbated by the existing rent control laws, sent urban land prices sky high. During the 1990s, land prices in Bombay ended up higher than anywhere else in the world, including Tokyo. Worse yet, the ULCRA provisions became an extra barrier to the exit of failed firms. Proceeds from the sale of land held by these firms could potentially be used to satisfy claimants on the firm, including workers. However, ULCRA forbade such sales.

NATIONALIZATION OF BANKS

The period under consideration was also remarkable for the changes it brought to the banking industry.[23] Because I have not introduced this subject so far, I begin here with some historical background. This is followed by the major policy changes introduced during phase II.

India's central bank, the Reserve Bank of India (RBI), was created through the RBI Act, 1934 and commenced operation on April 1, 1935. It was originally set up as a shareholders' bank, but was nationalized in 1949. In the postindependence era, the RBI was given broad regulatory authority over commercial banks in India. It also played an important role, especially starting in the 1960s, in building India's financial infrastructure by helping set up institutions such as the Deposit Insurance and Credit Guarantee Corporation of India, the Unit Trust of India, the Industrial Development Bank of India, and the National Bank of Agriculture and Rural Development.

The first major state-owned commercial bank in India was the State Bank of India (SBI). Though the origins of the SBI went back to the Bank of Calcutta, which was set up in 1806, its immediate precursor was the Imperial Bank of India.[24] The

Imperial Bank of India was created in 1921 by merging the Bank of Bengal, Bank of Bombay, and Bank of Madras with their 70 branches. The Imperial Bank played the triple role of a commercial bank, a bankers' bank, and a banker to the government. In 1935, when the RBI was created, the Imperial Bank ceded the function of banker to the government to the RBI, and was gradually converted into a purely commercial bank. At independence, the Imperial Bank had 172 branches and more than 200 suboffices around the country.

In the immediate postindependence era, the operations of the commercial banks, including the Imperial Bank, had been confined to the urban areas. Therefore, after rural development was identified as a priority in the First Five-Year Plan, the need was felt for a financial institution that would operate in rural areas. Toward that end, on the recommendation of the All-India Rural Credit Survey Committee, an act was passed in the Parliament in May 1955 to constitute the State Bank of India by taking over the Imperial Bank of India. In one stroke, the act brought a quarter of the resources of the Indian banking system under the direct control of the state. Later, the Parliament passed the State Bank of India (Subsidiary Banks) Act, 1959, under which the SBI took over eight former state-associated banks in the former princely states as its subsidiaries.

In 1969, there were 79 scheduled and 16 unscheduled commercial banks in India.[25] The SBI was by far the largest bank, accounting for 31 percent of the scheduled bank branches. But the government held the view that the banking sector as whole primarily served the industrial and urban areas at the expense of agriculture and rural areas. For example, rural areas accounted for three fourths of the total population but only one fifth of the bank branches. The government also felt that the banks ignored small entrepreneurs and concentrated lending on big corporations that were the owners of the banks in many cases. Frequent bank failures were also a concern.

Many of these concerns could have been addressed without nationalization, and some progress in this direction was indeed being made. But, as described earlier, the power struggle between Mrs. Gandhi and the Syndicate led the former to opt for nationalization of the major private banks. This was accomplished through the Banking Companies (Acquisition and Transfer of Undertakings) Act, 1969, which nationalized all banks whose nationwide deposits exceeded 500 million rupees. This criterion brought an additional 14 banks, and 54 percent of the bank branches, into the public sector.[26] Taking the SBI branches into account, 84 percent of the bank branches were now in the public sector. With only 16 percent of the branches, the remaining 58 scheduled and 16 unscheduled banks were relatively small. An amendment of the Banking Companies Act in 1980 brought another six of the largest private banks into the public sector.

The government was able to promote its goal of bringing formal banking to the rural areas rather quickly. The proportion of the bank branches in the rural areas jumped to 35 percent in 1972 from 22 percent in 1969. The density of bank branches also rose: The population per branch declined from 64,000 in 1969 to 29,000 in 1976 and 19,000 in 1981. Rural branches, whose deposits were backed by an implicit government guarantee, had a great success in mobilizing rural savings. Rural bank deposits as a proportion of total deposits rose from 3 percent in 1969 to 9 percent in 1976 and 13 percent in 1981. Rural credit expanded at the same pace proportionately, but less so absolutely: from 2 percent in 1969 to 6 percent in 1976 and 11 percent in

1981. Priority sector lending also received a boost, per the government's objectives: It rose from 14 percent of the total lending by scheduled banks to 25 percent in 1976 and 36 percent in 1981.

These observations indicate that bank nationalization was successful. But this is questionable at two levels. First, we must ask whether the objectives set by the government were themselves economically sensible. Second, even if we answer this question in the affirmative, we must ask whether these objectives could have been achieved at a lower cost, using instruments other than nationalization. The objectives of expanding branches with total disregard for commercial viability, and priority sector lending without concern for loan recovery, are surely questionable. But even accepting them as desirable objectives, less costly instruments must be explored. I will return to these and related critical issues in chapter 11, which is devoted to financial sector reforms.

NATIONALIZATION OF INSURANCE

The origins of the life insurance industry in India can be traced back to the Oriental Life Insurance Company, which began operations in 1818 and was soon followed by others.[27] Initially, the companies insured the lives of Europeans only. When they did start insuring the lives of Indians, they charged them an extra 20 percent or more in premiums. The first company to insure Indians at "fair value" was the Bombay Mutual Life Assurance Society, beginning in 1871.

The first general insurance company to operate in India was the Triton Insurance Company, established in 1850.[28] This was a British-owned and -operated company. The Indian Mercantile Insurance Company, Ltd., established in Bombay in 1907, was the first indigenous general insurance company. The Insurance Act, 1912 provided the first legislation aimed at regulating the insurance companies. By 1938, more than 100 insurance companies were operating, but the industry was plagued by fraud. The Insurance Act, 1938 was passed to give order to the industry; it also brought other fundamental changes, including the creation of an insurance wing in the Ministry of Finance.

The next major development in the insurance sector was the Life Insurance Corporation Act, 1956. Passed under the leadership of Finance Minister C. D. Deshmukh, the act nationalized life insurance in India. In 1956, 170 insurance companies—154 Indian and 16 foreign—and 75 provident societies actively issued life insurance policies, and their operations were concentrated mainly in Bombay, Delhi, Calcutta, and Madras. Three factors motivated the government's decision to nationalize life insurance: (1) private companies limited their operations to the major cities, and there were no prospects of their offering life insurance in the rural areas; (2) the government felt it was better positioned to channel the savings so generated into development; and (3) bankruptcies of life insurance companies had reached epidemic proportions: at the time of nationalization, 25 companies were already bankrupt and another 25 were on the verge of bankruptcy.

As noted earlier, nationalization of general insurance was an objective in the Ten-Point Program of Prime Minister Indira Gandhi, adopted by the Congress Working Committee in 1967. This objective was achieved through the General Insurance

Business (Nationalization) Act, 1972. The act set up the General Insurance Corporation (GIC) as a holding company with four subsidiaries: New India, Oriental, United India, and National Insurance (NOUN). The original intent was that these companies would compete with one another in the market. But in reality, the GIC functioned as a monopoly.

Given the chaos that existed in the general insurance sector at the time, the immediate impact of nationalization was probably positive. It increased customers' confidence and protected their interests. Nevertheless, the long-run implications were less positive. As was true of the commercial banks, the insurance bureaucracy had become infected by huge inefficiencies. Branches were expanded without regard to efficiency; by the 1990s, almost a quarter of the GIC branches were unviable. I will return to this subject later in chapter 11 in the context of financial sector reforms.

AGRICULTURE: THE GREEN REVOLUTION AND RELATED DEVELOPMENTS

By far the most important positive development during phase II was the successful launch of the Green Revolution.[29] There is no doubt that in its absence, the debacle in agriculture during phase II would have been much worse, and agricultural growth in subsequent phases much slower.

As noted earlier, Shastri, who succeeded Nehru as prime minister in 1964, had been warmer to agriculture and cooler to heavy industry than Nehru. He appointed C. Subramaniam, the minister of steel, mines, and industry under Nehru, as the minister of food and agriculture. Mrs. Gandhi, who succeeded Shastri after the latter's untimely death in January 1966, retained Subramaniam as the minister of food and agriculture.

Even during the first four years of the Third Five-Year Plan, which preceded the drought years, India's dependence on food imports had steadily risen (see table 3.3). Because progressively inward-looking policies had made the foreign exchange situation generally precarious, the rising demand for imports also translated into increased dependence on food aid from the United States. The Indian leadership found that dependence and the accompanying intrusiveness of the U.S. policy toward India so painful that at one time Prime Minister Shastri called upon all Indians to miss one meal each week. Under these circumstances, achieving a quantum jump in the production of food grains naturally became the highest priority. The real question was how best to achieve this objective.

Subramaniam came to the helm at this critical juncture. Fortuitously, around the same time, Ralph Cummings of the Rockefeller Foundation had been attempting to introduce new high yielding varieties (HYVs) of wheat from Mexico with the support of the Ford Foundation. As part of an experiment, HYV seed had been distributed to the Indian Agricultural Research Institute (IARI) in New Delhi, the Punjab Agricultural University at Ludhiana, and the Pantnagar University in Pantnagar and almost twice the traditional yields had been reaped. But there was little progress in propagating these seeds. Cummings brought the studies based on his experiments to the attention of Subramaniam. In turn, Subramaniam had the studies reviewed by the panel of scientists he had constituted from the IARI for the purpose

TABLE 3.3: Food Grain Availability, 1961–81

Year	Net Production	Net Imports	Public Procurement	Public Distribution	Net Availability*
1961	72	3.5	0.5	4	75.7
1962	72.1	3.6	0.5	4.4	76.1
1963	70.3	4.5	0.8	5.2	74.9
1964	70.6	6.3	1.4	8.7	78.1
1965	78.2	7.4	4	10.1	84.6
1966	63.3	10.3	4	14.1	73.5
1967	65	8.7	4.5	13.2	73.9
1968	83.2	5.7	6.8	10.2	86.8
1969	82.3	3.8	6.4	9.4	85.6
1970	87.1	3.6	6.7	8.8	89.5
1971	94.9	2.0	8.9	7.8	94.3
1972	92.0	−0.5	7.7	10.5	96.2
1973	84.9	3.6	8.4	11.4	88.8
1974	91.6	5.2	5.7	10.8	97.1
1975	87.4	7.5	9.6	11.3	89.3
1976	105.9	6.9	12.9	9.2	102.1
1977	97.3	0.1	10.0	11.7	99.0
1978	110.6	−0.6	11.1	10.2	110.3
1979	115.4	−0.2	13.9	11.7	114.9
1980	96.0	−0.3	11.2	15.0	101.8
1981	113.9	0.7	13.0	13.0	114.3

*Net availability = net production + net imports – accumulation of government stocks.

Production data relate to the agricultural year just finished. For example, 1961 figures relate to 1960–61. Public procurement and distribution data relate to calendar years. Net production is gross production minus 12.5 percent for seed and waste.

Source: Joshi and Little (1994, tables 4.9 and 5.11), who cite Government of India, Ministry of Finance, *Economic Survey* (various issues).

of devising solutions to the problem of raising agricultural productivity. The panel was not unanimous in its opinion, but Subramaniam was persuaded, and decided in favor of the new technology.

The implementation of the new policy faced enormous opposition from within the cabinet, Parliament, and the public. Subramaniam needed foreign exchange to import the new seeds and financial resources to assure the farmers that the government would compensate them for any losses incurred as a consequence of the adoption of the new seeds. But he lacked support for the new policy from Finance Minister T. T. Krishnamachari. The Left parties were also up in arms, partially because they feared the new technology would have adverse income distribution effects, but also because they saw an American hand in the new policy.[30] Many economists also opposed the change. Over a thousand demonstrations took place around the country to protest the new policy.

But Subramaniam, who enjoyed the confidence of both Shastri and Mrs. Gandhi, worked diligently to persuade various constituencies. Among other things, he converted five acres of lawns and playgrounds that came with his bungalow into a demonstration farm of high yielding varieties of seeds. That experiment proved highly successful, leading his cabinet colleagues to capitulate.

In 1966, India imported 18,000 tons of Mexican seed. In addition, there existed 5,000 tons of seed within India, which had been multiplied from 250 tons imported in 1965. Based on his assessment of land quality, climate, and entrepreneurship, Subramaniam chose to distribute this seed in Punjab (now divided into Punjab and Haryana) and western Uttar Pradesh. The results were spectacular, with the experiment turning into what quickly came to be called the "Green Revolution." In 1967–68, India produced 17 million tons of wheat, compared with the previous record high of 12 million tons.

The success quickly quelled all remaining opposition to the new policy. Gradually, the policy was extended geographically as well as to other crops, including rice, maize, millet, and sorghum. While India still suffered from food shortages during the consecutive drought years of 1971–72 and 1972–73, by the late 1970s food grain production had expanded sufficiently to make the country self-sufficient.

The success of the Green Revolution may not be immediately apparent from growth rate comparisons of agriculture, since the agricultural growth rate in phase II, at 2.1 percent, was distinctly below the growth rate of 2.9 percent in phase I (table 1.3). But this comparison is misleading because agriculture includes items other than food grains. If we compute the growth rates of food grain production alone from the production levels shown in table 3.3, the average growth rate during 1966–81 (4.7 percent) substantially exceeded the average growth rate of 2.2 percent during 1961–65.[31] Moreover, the breakthrough must be evaluated not just against the prior period's performance, but also against the counterfactual that would have been observed absent the Green Revolution. It is not inconceivable that absent the Green Revolution, agricultural growth could have fallen below even the level achieved in the first half of the 1960s.

On the other hand, this success is not altogether without potential criticism. For example, we must ask whether the focus on heavy industry starting with the Second Five-year Plan resulted in the neglect of agriculture and actually set back the Green Revolution by several years. The signs of stagnation in agriculture were loud and clear for some years, with the problem recognized at home as well as abroad. Yet, action was slow, and absent the change in leadership that brought Shastri, with his greater sympathy for agriculture, to the helm, the neglect would have continued. More important, had the economy been more open and export-oriented, it would not have required severe restrictions on the imports of farm machinery, fertilizer, and equipment that substantially delayed the spread of the Green Revolution.

Alongside the developments surrounding the Green Revolution, the Shastri government had also moved to build up India's institutional infrastructure in agriculture. The Agricultural Price Commission (APC), the Food Corporation of India (FCI), and the National Dairy Development Board (NDDB) were all established in 1965.[32] The APC was to set the minimum support prices for various commodities in order to assure remunerative prices to farmers even in the face of a bumper crop that might lead to depressed prices in the market. The FCI was to carry out price support operations, distribute food grain throughout the country for the Public Distribution System, and maintain satisfactory levels of buffer stocks of food grains. The government created the NDDB to promote milk production by small producers at the grassroots level. On the research front, Subramaniam strengthened the Indian Council of Agricultural Research (ICAR), which, along

with the Punjab Agricultural University, played an important role in the indigenization of the HYV seeds.

The FCI quickly became a major player in the procurement and distribution of
food grains. This is readily seen from table 3.3, which shows the rising volumes of
procurement and public distribution after the FCI was established. India faced a
food crisis yet again during 1971–73, due to crop failure and gross upward bias in
the forecasts of food grain output. But by the late 1970s the Green Revolution had
spread sufficiently, and the FCI had built sufficient buffer stocks, that India did not
face food shortages again.

But over time, the FCI turned into an extremely large, corrupt, and inefficient
bureaucracy and a source of inordinate waste of public resources. Political pressures
resulted in very high procurement prices, leading to very large volumes of procurement and, therefore, very large food stocks. The latter reached levels that were far in
excess of the buffer necessary to meet any conceivable food shortage, and were even
beyond the storage capacity of the FCI. The public distribution system became a way
of guaranteeing above-market prices to typically rich farmers in Punjab, Haryana,
and Andhra Pradesh, with only a small fraction of the FCI sales at the subsidized
prices actually reaching the poor. I will return to this subject in chapter 16.

SAVINGS AND INVESTMENT

In addition to the Green Revolution, an important achievement of phase II was the
steady rise in the savings rate. Gross savings climbed from 12–13 percent in the first
half of the 1960s to 18–19 percent by the mid-1970s and to 21–22 percent by the late
1970s. While an increase in income was the key factor behind the increase, greater
access to banks probably played a role as well. The latter is partially confirmed by
the rising rate of private financial savings, though there was also a very substantial
increase in household physical savings (from 4.9 percent of the GDP in 1964–65 to
9.8 percent in 1980–81).

The rapid increase in the savings rate helped in two ways. First, it more than
made up for the sharp decline in the inflow of foreign financial resources during this
period. Second, it prevented an even sharper decline in the growth rate that would
have resulted from the external shocks and inefficiencies generated by the policy
changes during this period.

All of the growth in private investment was concentrated in the household sector, however. This investment as a percentage of the GDP rose from 4.9 percent
in 1964–65 to 9.7 percent in 1980–81. Investment as a percentage of the GDP in
the corporate sector actually fell from 3.6 percent to 2.5 percent of the GDP over
the same period. Thus, the wholesale discrimination against the corporate sector
introduced during this period had a significant adverse impact on the growth of
investment in this sector. The decline took place despite a rise in financially intermediated household savings from 2.9 percent of the GDP in 1964–65 to 6.3 percent
in 1980–81.

Though the government absorbed much of the increase in household financial
savings, public investment did not rise correspondingly. Indeed, after peaking at
8.5 percent of the GDP in 1965–66, it fell to 5.6 percent by 1969–70. It recovered

steadily thereafter, but remained below the previous peak until 1974–75. The burden of this decline in the share fell disproportionately on infrastructure, especially railways and power. According to Acharya et al. (2003), the share of infrastructure in total public investment declined from 36 percent in the first half of the 1960s to 29 percent between 1966–67 and 1975–76. Put differently, infrastructure investment, which had grown at an annual rate of almost 17 percent in the first half of the 1960s, decelerated to just 2 percent per annum during 1966–76. Public investment recovered in the second half of the 1970s and reached between 9 and 10 percent of the GDP in the late 1970s.

CONCLUSIONS

In concluding this chapter, I focus on two issues: the role of policy as opposed to external shock in explaining the sharp decline in the growth rate during phase II, and the consequences for growth and poverty of excessive focus on equity.

The Growth Debacle and Its Connection to the Policies

I have already noted that the economic performance during 1965–81 was worse than during any other period of the five and a half decades under analysis. To be sure, external shocks greatly contributed to the poor performance. During the second half of the 1960s, the droughts in 1965–66 and 1966–67 contributed in a major way to the decline in agricultural output, which in turn contributed to the industrial recession in 1966–67 and 1967–68. India also had to fight a war against Pakistan in September 1965, which was preceded by the 1962 India-China war, putting further strain on the country's meager resources.

This history was repeated in the first half of the 1970s with four major shocks hitting the economy. First, there was a dramatic decline in foreign aid. In 1966–67, foreign savings had reached 3.1 percent of the GDP. They fell to 2.4 and 1 percent of the GDP, respectively, in the following two years, and never rose above the 1 percent mark in the 1970s. Second, India was once again involved in a war with Pakistan that culminated in the creation of Bangladesh in December 1971. But the war was preceded by the inflow of as many as eight to ten million refugees who had to be provided shelter and food. The war also resulted in approximately one million prisoners of war, and the burden of their upkeep fell on the country. Third, almost simultaneously, there was drought that lasted for the years 1971–72 and 1972–73. With the agricultural growth rate at –5 percent, the impact of the drought was particularly severe in the latter year.[33] Finally, oil prices rose sharply from 1972–73 to 1975–76. These shocks contributed significantly to the prolonged stagnation in industry coupled with the escalation of inflation. Thus, India suffered the stagflation that afflicted much of the world economy during these years.

Indeed, it is tempting to argue that since the growth rate in phase II fell short of that in phase I by barely a percentage point, and the economy faced several very severe exogenous shocks, the repressive policies of the period did not have a serious detrimental impact on growth. This, I believe, is the wrong conclusion to draw, for at least five reasons.

First, during the period that shocks dominated, the growth rate did decline more substantially. During the drought era, 1965–73, agricultural growth fell to just 1.1 percent. In the drought-cum-oil-price-shock era, 1965–75, industrial growth fell to 3.3 percent. During the subperiod 1970–75, industrial growth fell to a mere 2 percent. Because services growth was impacted less sharply by the shocks, the decline in the overall GDP was less sharp. But even the average GDP growth during 1965–73 fell to 2.5 percent.

Second, during 1965–75, the world economy as a whole grew rapidly, generating growth opportunities for the developing countries. Though I do not subscribe to this view, according to some development economists, this was the golden age of growth for developing countries.[34] To be sure, more developing countries from Asia, Africa, and Latin America grew rapidly during this period than in the 1980s and 1990s. By being relatively closed, India missed out on the opportunities that the rapidly growing world economy had created during 1965–75.

Third, if we go by the experience of countries such as Taiwan and the Republic of Korea, which switched to outward-oriented strategies after brief phases of import substitution, the benchmark growth rate for our comparison should be in the 7–9 percent range rather than that achieved in phase I by India. India had as vibrant an entrepreneurial class as any other country in Asia. This is testified to by the growth of the textiles and steel industries under British rule without protection and, indeed, a variety of obstacles placed by the British in the way of Indian entrepreneurs. India had as good a chance as Korea and Taiwan to launch itself into a higher growth orbit under a better policy regime. India's own experience since the 1980s demonstrates this fact. Seen this way, and recognizing that at least the oil price shock impacted the East Asian economies even more, since India was largely able to offset the high oil prices by the substantial worker remittances that directly resulted from the price hike, one is forced to conclude that the repressive policies compromised growth more than marginally.

Fourth, with the savings and investment rates having gone up substantially, the decline in the growth rate points to a decline in productivity. As we will see in the next chapter, by the end of the 1970s, several official and expert committees had begun to point to the adverse effects of the policy regime on productivity in industry. In agriculture, productivity had begun to turn around as a result of the adoption of new seed varieties and technology, but this had been accompanied by increasing support prices and fertilizer and other input subsidies that were leading to the crowding out of investment in infrastructure.

Finally, the tightening of controls introduced during phase II had a large detrimental effect on growth in the longer run. The policies put in place during this period created institutions and vested interests in both private and public sectors that made the subsequent liberalization that much more difficult. In turn, these institutions and interests delayed the launch of the Indian economy into the growth orbit of 8 to 10 percent. For example, privatization of banks and the public sector units remains a major challenge for the government even after more than two decades of economic reforms. I have also mentioned the waste of public resources by the FCI, whose downsizing has remained off- limits to date. The reform of the IDA, 1947 is viewed with such hostility by labor unions that the United Progressive Alliance (UPA), which came to power in 2004, committed itself to not touching this piece of legislation. Prior to the UPA government, its predecessor, the National Democratic Alliance, had made a valiant effort to introduce legislation to amend the IDA, 1947, but was unsuccessful even after the bill had been considerably diluted from its original form. The removal of the restrictions on the sale of urban land placed by the ULCRA, 1976 has been taking a long time, with some states still dragging their feet. The bottom line is that the regime put in place during phase II had a major detrimental effect on the prospects for future growth.

Focus on Equity Leading to Harmful Effects on Poverty Alleviation

The key objective behind the myriad interventions introduced by Mrs. Gandhi during the first 11 years of her rule was to achieve an equitable distribution of income and wealth. In pursuing this objective she introduced policies that effectively killed the incentive to create wealth at various levels. For example, the fear that the expansion of big business houses would lead to concentration of wealth caused their exclusion from all but a handful of highly capital-intensive "core" sectors. It was entirely forgotten that by expanding economic activity in a broader set of products, these business houses would generate employment for the poor.

Likewise, the small-scale-industries (SSI) reservation excluded all but tiny firms from entering the manufacturing of virtually all labor-intensive products. With no large firms allowed to manufacture these products, India excluded itself from the world market for them. The SSI enterprises had at most limited ability to deliver high-quality products on time to customers in the world market. The vast majority of them ended up specializing in low-quality products meant for domestic customers, who were in turn denied access to world-class products through autarkic policies. The low-quality products of the SSI enterprises could generate only low-wage jobs.

The laws guaranteeing virtually unlimited rights to workers in the organized sector and placing a tight ceiling on the sale of urban land were also motivated by equity considerations. If entrepreneurs were guaranteed the domestic market through trade restrictions and investment licensing, workers had to be guaranteed the same protection. The result was that even after the protection of entrepreneurs had been ended in the 1990s, protection of labor remained in place, scuttling the growth of labor-intensive industry in the organized sector. Likewise, the restriction on profiting from the sales of land led those in possession of urban land to keep it off the market even if it was entirely unused, and hence unproductive.

Thus, equity-driven policies were also largely anti-growth, and insofar as growth is the most powerful instrument of poverty reduction (see chapter 7), they were also anti-poor. The lesson from the Indian experience during phase II is that a prudent government is better advised to focus on poverty alleviation directly rather than through equality of income and wealth. The focus on equity invariably results in the adoption of policies that discourage wealth creation and have an adverse impact on the poor. The goal of equity itself is likely to be served better if the policy focuses on poverty alleviation. I will return to this theme more frontally in chapter 8.

4

PHASE III (1981–88): LIBERALIZATION BY STEALTH

As discussed in detail in the previous chapter, by the time the first oil price crisis hit the world economy, Mrs. Gandhi had implemented the key components of the Ten-Point Program. All major banks, insurance companies, oil companies, and coal mines had been nationalized. With some exceptions, foreign companies were in the process of being brought under the purview of FERA, 1973, which required most of them to lower foreign equity to 40 percent and to register in India as Indian companies.[1] Activity of big business houses and large enterprises was subject to tight controls and confined to a narrow range of industries. A number of products came to be reserved for manufacture exclusively by small-scale enterprises. Licensing reigned supreme in virtually all industries. Entry and expansion of firms came to be governed by a series of lists subject to a complex web of rules. The most important of these lists were the following:[2]

1. Schedule A of the Industrial Policy Resolution (IPR), 1956 listed industries reserved for the public sector, though the state reserved the right to invite the private sector to cooperate if it saw such cooperation as in the national interest.
2. Schedule B of the IPR, 1956 listed industries in which state enterprises were to acquire the dominant role.
3. Schedule I of the Industries (Development and Regulation) Act (IDRA), 1951, which was virtually all-inclusive and subjected all investments in fixed assets in excess of 10 million rupees to licensing.
4. Appendix I of the press note on industrial policy dated February 2, 1973 listed industries open to the MRTP and foreign companies, provided they were not reserved for the public sector and small-scale units, or subject to special regulations. Outside of this very narrow list, the MRTP and foreign companies were normally not permitted new undertakings or expansion of existing capacity.

5. Schedule IV of the press note dated February 19, 1973, listed industries in which diversification and substantial expansion were disallowed regardless of the firm's size.

6. Schedule I of the same note listed industries reserved for small-scale units.

In international trade, all imports were subject to licensing and strict foreign exchange control. Import restrictions interacted with the investment licensing in a fundamental way: If investment required machinery or raw material imports, clearance would be required from licensing as well as import authorities. Consumer goods other than those imported by the canalizing agencies of the government were banned.

As noted in the previous chapter, industrial performance during the first half of the 1970s was dismal. The sector grew only 2 percent per annum during 1970–75. This performance led some in official circles to begin advocating the relaxation of controls after the first oil price crisis. As a result, the second half of the 1970s saw some piecemeal deregulation of industry. Likewise, steps were taken to streamline the import licensing procedures. The process gained momentum in the 1980s, especially after Rajiv Gandhi became the prime minister. Politicians remained fearful, however, that the public might equate the relaxation of controls to the renunciation of socialistic goals. As a result, the liberalization during this period was done quietly, as if by stealth.[3]

THE POLITICAL CONTEXT

By 1975, Mrs. Gandhi had pushed her policy agenda as far to the left as she could. The failure of the attempt to nationalize the wholesale wheat trade in 1973 defined the limits of how far she could push. Poor industrial performance in the first half of the 1970s and India's largest ever increases in the Consumer Price Index for industrial workers—21 percent in 1973–74 and 27 percent in 1974–75—further demonstrated that the strategy she had chosen was not working. True, these were the days of the oil crisis and the birth of stagflation, but the episode also revealed the inability of the economy to adjust to external shocks.

As discussed in the previous chapter, the Allahabad High Court verdict declaring Mrs. Gandhi's election to the Parliament as fraudulent came in June 1975. Agitation by the opposition parties to force her to resign culminated in the declaration of a state of emergency. During the emergency rule, which lasted for 19 months, an attempt was made to bring the derailed economy back on track. As a part of this effort, the government tried to relax some constraints on the margin to allow better use of the production capacity. Elections held in March 1977 brought a non-Congress Party coalition government at the national level for the first time. But continued squabbles among the coalition partners precluded major policy changes, and the policy was run largely by bureaucrats. In the end, the coalition fell apart before completing its five-year term, and fresh elections were called in January 1980.

The elections returned Mrs. Gandhi to power with a two-thirds majority in the Parliament. This time around she was a changed prime minister, more pragmatic and less dogmatic. She had no socialist agenda to push. Indeed, as we saw in the previous chapter, the only significant step in this direction was the nationalization of six more banks, the initiative for which came from RBI Governor I. G. Patel. The available evidence suggests that within broadly defined parameters, Mrs. Gandhi listened to her advisers and gave them space within limits.

This is illustrated by the $6 billion loan India sought and got from the IMF in the early 1980s. According to Chaudhry, Kelkar, and Yadav (2004), soon after Mrs. Gandhi returned to power, senior officials "formulated a strategy of 'homegrown conditionality,' whereby the various aspects of economic reforms would be initiated by domestic policymakers prior to the onset of a crisis and then presented to international financial institutions." They first informally ascertained from the IMF leadership that it would support such a loan, and then approached Mrs. Gandhi. The officials argued that the approach they suggested would avoid a repeat of the events of 1966 and preserve India's independence, since the conditions were all derived from the Sixth Five-Year Plan (spanning 1980–81 to 1984–85). Mrs. Gandhi gave a go-ahead.

Toward the end of her last term, Mrs. Gandhi was preoccupied with the militant Sikh separatist movement in Punjab. In June 1984, she ordered the Indian Army to enter the Golden Temple, one of the holiest shrines of the Sikhs, where a group of militant Sikhs was fortified. Thousands of innocent Sikh pilgrims died in the operation, angering the Sikh community at large. In retaliation, two of Mrs. Gandhi's own guards assassinated her on October 31, 1984.

Rajiv Gandhi, Mrs. Gandhi's older son, succeeded her. In the elections that followed soon after, he won a resounding victory with a three-fourths majority in the Parliament. He was India's first modern prime minister who had mostly grown up in an independent India. He was freer of the socialist baggage and less fearful of being subject to dependence on the world markets than his predecessors. He came to power with aspirations of launching India into the twenty-first century. Unsurprisingly, he implemented a program of economic liberalization and introduced many important reforms in the first two years of his rule. He also improved relations with the United States. Unfortunately, however, in the later years of his term he was enmeshed in defending himself against corruption charges that were never proved. He was also hurt politically by the military intervention, at the urging of Sri Lanka's government, against the Tamil insurgency in Sri Lanka. The Indian Army suffered heavy casualties at the hands of the Tamil guerrillas and was eventually withdrawn by V. P. Singh, who succeeded Gandhi as prime minister in 1989.

DEREGULATION OF INDUSTRY

Three phases of industrial deregulation, each more significant than the preceding one, can be identified. The first set of measures was taken during 1975–79, the second set during 1979–84, and the final set during 1985–89. The large majority of the steps during the first period were taken in 1975 and 1976, and can be summarized as follows:[4]

- Under *diversification* provisions, firms in several engineering industries were permitted to change the mix of products within the existing capacity. This was an early attempt at "broad-bending," which received much greater impetus under Rajiv Gandhi. But because the firms were not permitted to install new machinery to achieve the desired adjustment, the measure could have only limited impact.

- *Recognition of capacity* over and above the licensed capacity on the basis of such considerations as modernization, export performance, increased efficiency, and rationalization of shifts. The underlying idea was to reward the firms that exported or were able to increase output through modernization, increased efficiency, or rationalization of shifts. Once again, the actual impact of the measure was limited by side conditions. If the product had been moved to the SSI list, no capacity recognition was permitted. In the case of modernization-based capacity recognition, firms were not permitted to increase the use of foreign exchange, which ruled out machinery or raw material imports to achieve modernization. In the case of capacity recognition based on efficiency improvement, no new machinery, either foreign or domestic, could be installed. The MRTP and FERA companies were denied recourse to the provision altogether. These limitations meant that the provision principally resulted in the formal recognition of the capacity surreptitiously created in the previous years.

- Automatic capacity *expansion* up to 25 percent of the licensed capacity in 15 selected engineering industries and for establishing new capacity on the basis of "commercial" utilization of results of research and development (R&D) in other industries. The side conditions in the case of engineering industries ruled out the SSI products and dominant firms, disallowed borrowing from financial institutions, and stipulated that if the capacity expansion required the import of machinery, a corresponding export requirement would be specified. Under the R&D provision, if the research leading to the improved technology was in-house, the MRTP and FERA companies were confined to capacity expansion in the core (appendix I) industries. If the research was not in-house, it had to come from approved laboratories, and the firms undertaking the capacity expansion could not be dominant undertakings or large business houses.

- 24 sectors were delicensed, subject to the condition that no import of machinery or raw material or foreign collaboration would be required. MRTP and FERA firms were excluded from taking advantage of the provision. Likewise, products subject to the SSI reservations were off-limits.

- The asset limit on plant and machinery in the small-scale enterprise was raised from 0.75 million to 1 million rupees.

- The *exemption limit* on investment in fixed assets for capacity expansion by existing undertakings or establishment of production capacity by new undertakings was raised from 10 million to 30 million rupees in 1978. As per the press note of February 19, 1973, the MRTP and FERA companies were not permitted to avail themselves of this provision.

The second oil price shock in 1979 almost coincided with the return of Mrs. Gandhi as prime minister in January 1980. Gandhi quickly moved to set the tone for industrial policy through the Industrial Policy Statement of July 1980. This statement carried forward the piecemeal retreat, begun in 1975, from the highly restrictive regime that she had herself put in place. While the policy changes announced in the wake of the 1980 statement bore some resemblance to those announced in 1975 and 1976, they went much farther than the latter. Schemes for capacity expansion and licensing exemption were more generous and wide-ranging, and imposed fewer restrictions in terms of new investment, machinery imports, and foreign exchange. The main measures were as follows:

- *Regularization* of capacity in excess of licensed levels in 34 key industries, and the exclusion of production for export in the calculation of the licensed capacity. Because this scheme related to regularization of capacity that had come to exist, unlike some other schemes discussed below, it did not permit installation of new machinery. The scheme was extended to nondominant MRTP and FERA firms.

- Extension of the scheme for automatic capacity *expansion* up to 25 percent of the licensed capacity from the 15 engineering industries to appendix I industries in 1980, and to 45 other new industries in 1982. The 1975 provision that the expansion be undertaken without borrowing from financial institutions was withdrawn. On the other hand, an amendment of the MRTP Act in August 1982 added the MRTP clearance requirement for capacity expansion not just to the dominant but to the nondominant MRTP firms as well.

- Most important, under the reendorsement of capacity scheme (April 1982), if actual production of an enterprise exceeded licensed capacity by 25 percent in any year, the enterprise was granted a one-third increase in its existing licensed capacity.[5] In the next year, the firm became eligible for reendorsement once again if its production exceeded its new licensed capacity by 25 percent. Firms were permitted to install the necessary equipment and allowed to import it under open general licensing (OGL) for the expansion of capacity up to 25 percent in any single year. Because the scheme permitted capacity expansion every year and allowed the installation of new machinery, whether domestic or imported, it was far more attractive than the automatic growth scheme, which was limited to one-time expansion of 25 percent. As usual, the provision did not apply to the SSI products and dominant firms, but was available to MRTP and FERA companies within appendix I industries.

- Enlargement of the scope for new investment activity by the MRTP and FERA companies through (1) enlargement of appendix I (October 1984), (2) identification of nine industries of national importance that were freed of the MRTP clearance, (3) special incentives for investment in backward areas with no industrial activity, and (4) 100 percent export production units.

- Enhancement of the investment limits for exemption from industrial licensing from 30 million to 50 million rupees (1981). Machinery imports of 4 million rupees were permitted, and there was no restriction on raw material imports other than those imposed by the import regime. As usual, SSI products and MRTP and FERA companies were excluded.

- In March 1984, private sector participation was introduced in the manufacture of telecommunications equipment, which was otherwise reserved for the public sector under schedule A of IPR (1956).

- In 1980, the asset limit on plant and machinery in the small-scale enterprises was raised from 1 million to 2 million rupees.

The second round of liberalizing measures went some way toward relaxing the restraints faced by private industry. Three measures deserve particular emphasis. First, the exemption limit on licensing went from 10 million rupees in 1973 to 50 million rupees in 1981. The restraints on the import of machinery and raw materials originally applied to this exemption were also considerably relaxed. Second, several avenues for the expansion of capacity in existing firms were opened. Of major importance was the reendorsement facility that had a dynamic element in it such that the capacity could be expanded every year. This provision allowed both machinery and raw material imports, and was available to the nondominant MRTP and FERA firms in appendix I industries. Finally, considerable progress was also made toward allowing the MRTP companies into additional industries through the expansion of appendix I. Combined with trade liberalization (described later), these measures probably made a significant contribution to industrial growth.

Industrial licensing reforms received a major boost under Rajiv Gandhi, who succeeded his mother in 1984. Among the steps taken under him were the following:[6]

- Broadbending for licensing purposes, which allowed firms to switch between similar production lines, such as trucks and cars, rather than be confined to narrowly defined products, was introduced in January 1986 in 28 industry groups.[7] Given the common design and production facilities for many related products, the flexibility in the product mix could be expected to allow fuller use of the capacity. The provision was significantly expanded in subsequent years and led to increased flexibility in many industries. As usual, the MRTP and FERA firms were excluded from this provision.
- In 1986, firms that reached 80 percent capacity utilization in any of the five years preceding 1985 were assured authorization to expand capacity up to 133 percent of the maximum capacity utilization reached in those years. The MRTP and FERA firms were excluded from this provision.
- To relax the licensing and capacity constraints on the larger firms, in 1985–86 the asset limit above which firms were subject to the MRTP regulations was raised from 200 million rupees to 1 billion rupees. As a result, as many as 90 out of 180 large business houses registered under the MRTP Act were freed from restrictions on growth in established product lines (World Bank, 1985, p. 13, para. 1.19). The requirement of MRTP clearance for 27 industries was waived. MRTP firms in a number of industries were exempt from industrial licensing provided they were located 100 kilometers from large cities. MRTP firms that were so defined because they were "dominant" were allowed to avail themselves of the general delicensing measures in sectors in which they were not dominant. These measures significantly enhanced the freedom of large firms (with assets exceeding 1 billion rupees) to enter new product areas.
- 30 industries and 82 pharmaceutical products were delicensed in or after 1985.
- The ceiling on asset size in plant and machinery of small-scale enterprises was raised from 2 million to 3.5 million rupees in 1985. Around the same time, the excise tax exemption based on the volume of sales became subject to a gradual phaseout. Previously, the exemption was ended abruptly when sales reached 0.75 million rupees and encouraged firms to stay even smaller than the SSI limit would allow. Under the new regime, the exemption was phased out

gradually until sales reached 7.5 million rupees, when it ended entirely. The list of products reserved for small-scale enterprises was also trimmed.

• Price and distribution controls on cement and aluminum were entirely abolished. Decontrol in cement eliminated the black market, and through expanded production brought the free market price down to the controlled levels within a short time. New entrants intensified competition, which led to improvements in quality along with the decline in price.

The ultimate effect of these liberalizing reforms was seen in the higher industrial growth (see table 4.1), which rose to 6.3 percent in phase III, compared with

TABLE 4.1: Sectoral Growth Rates (1961–88)

Year	Agriculture, Forestry, & Fisheries	Industry	Manufacturing	Services	GDP
1981–82	5.3	8.0	8.0	5.4	6.0
1982–83	0.7	3.7	6.6	6.7	3.1
1983–84	9.6	8.1	10.1	5.5	7.7
1984–85	1.5	5.8	6.6	6.3	4.3
1985–86	0.7	4.8	3.9	7.9	4.5
1986–87	0.6	6.9	7.0	7.4	4.3
1987–88	1.3	6.6	7.3	6.5	3.8
1981–88	2.1	6.3	7.1	6.3	4.8

Source: Author's calculations, using the Central Statistical Organization data. The GDP obtained by adding its components is slightly different from that reported in the official GDP series, which accounts for the small differences between annual GDP growth rates reported in this table and in table 1.1.

TABLE 4.2: License Applications by the MRTP Firms and Their Approval in the First Year

	1981	1982	1983	1984	1985	1986
	Absolute Numbers					
Substantial expansion						
Total under consideration	215	204	197	234	190	99
Approved during year	73	71	42	79	89	30
Rejected during year	31	26	45	28	27	11
New undertakings						
Total under consideration	295	304	281	342	456	399
Approved during year	70	89	48	52	195	129
Rejected during year	44	57	57	50	75	84
	As % of Total					
Substantial expansion						
Approved during year	34.0	34.8	21.3	33.8	46.8	30.3
Rejected during year	14.4	12.7	22.8	12.0	14.2	11.1
New undertakings						
Approved during year	23.7	29.3	17.1	15.2	42.8	32.3
Rejected during year	14.9	18.8	20.3	14.6	16.4	21.1

Source: World Bank (1987, table 3.1). Derived from the *Annual Reports* of the Department of Company Affairs.

4.0 percent in phase II. Somewhat more direct evidence of the impact of the liberalization can be seen in the increased rates of application for new undertakings by the MRTP firms and their approval. Table 4.2 reports this information. In particular, it shows the total number of applications for capacity expansion and new undertakings by the MRTP firms and the number of approvals and rejections within one year. Four features of this table are worth noting. First, applications for new undertakings by the MRTP firms show an upward trend until 1985, reflecting the opening up of new sectors to them through the expansion of appendix I. In 1986, the number of applications drops, reflecting the increased asset limit defining the MRTP firms, from 200 million to 1 billion rupees, which led to a substantial cut in the total number of MRTP firms. Second, the process of approval for new undertakings was speeded up during the period under consideration. The rate of decision in the first year rose from 38.6 percent in 1981 to 53.4 percent in 1986. Third, the approval rate for new undertakings in the first year also saw an upward shift, with the rate rising from 23.7 percent in 1981 to 32.3 percent in 1986. Finally, a similar trend was not observed for applications for substantial expansion of capacity. This fact suggests that the implementation of the policy in products where the MRTP firms already had a presence probably did not shift.

TRADE LIBERALIZATION

Let us next turn to the reforms in international trade.[8] It is useful to divide this discussion into three parts: direct import controls, tariffs, and export restrictions.

Direct Import Controls

Until 1976, an import policy was issued every six months in the form of the so-called Red Book. The main part of the policy was a long list of importable products with restrictions stated for each product regarding who could import it, up to what proportion of the need as measured by production capacity, which varieties, and, sometimes, from which source. For each import, the sponsoring authority was also identified. For some products, the conditions were too complicated to be stated in the main list, and these were relegated to an appendix.

We saw in the last chapter (table 3.2) that the severity of the import controls was reflected in the ratio of imports to GDP, which dropped to just 3.5 percent in 1972–73. The ratio is even lower if we exclude oil and food grain imports, which would indicate extremely limited room for the imports of raw materials and machinery. The impact on the pattern of industrialization and efficiency was visible. Pursell (1992, pp. 433–34) offers a vivid description of the costs to the economy:

> During this period, import-substitution policies were followed with little or no regard to costs. They resulted in an extremely diverse industrial structure and high degree of self-sufficiency, but many industries had high production costs. In addition, there was a general problem of poor quality and technological backwardness, which beset even low-cost sectors with comparative advantage such as the textiles, garments, leather goods, many light industries, and primary industries such as cotton.

Pursell (p. 434) continues:

> Although import substitution reduced imports of substitute products, this was replaced by increased demand for imported capital equipment and technology and for raw materials not domestically produced or in insufficient quantities. During the 1960s and the first half of the 1970s, the former demand was suppressed by extensive import substitution in the capital goods industries and attempts to indigenize R&D. By about 1976, however, the resulting obsolescence of the capital stock and technology of many industries was becoming apparent, and a steady liberalization of imports of capital equipment and of technology started soon after.

The first step toward liberalization was the rationalization of the licensing regime in 1978–79, based on the 1978 report of the P. C. Alexander Committee. The Alexander Committee strongly recommended that products not produced domestically be freed from licensing through inclusion in the open general licensing (OGL) list that had been revived in 1976. Using this change as the anchor, it recommended replacing the long list of imports and the accompanying conditions, issued biannually, with a policy that would divide imports into banned, restricted, and OGL lists. Goods in the first category would be banned altogether, and those in the second category would require a license. Products in the third category would not require a license in principle, though they would be subject to the actual user (but not the domestic availability) condition. The inclusion of an item on the OGL list would signify that it was not domestically available and would therefore be presumed to satisfy the domestic availability condition. Imports of all other goods would continue to be subject to this condition and would require certification from a government-designated "sponsoring" agency.

This general framework was adopted in 1978–79 and remained in place with some modifications until the major reforms in the 1990s. For implementation purposes, products were divided into consumer, capital, and intermediate goods. The only consumer goods imports permitted were those judged essential by the government. These were assigned exclusively to a governmental "canalizing" agency. All other consumer goods imports fell in the banned category.

Capital goods fell into either the restricted or the OGL category. Licenses were required for the restricted category, whereas the items on the OGL list could be imported without a license, provided the importer was the actual user of the import and the expansion of productive capacity resulting from the import was compatible with the capacity approved by the licensing authority. If an item was not on the OGL list, a license was usually required even if it was not on the restricted list.

Intermediate goods were divided into banned, restricted, limited permissible, and OGL categories, with the severity of restrictions declining in that order.[9] The OGL items did not require a license but were subject to the "actual user" and other conditions. Licenses were required for the items on the limited permissible list, but they were issued with relative ease. Licenses for items on the restricted list were issued very selectively, and items on the banned list were off-limits. By 1985, the banned list had been reduced to just two items: animal fats and oils, and animal rennet. Thus, only the restricted, limited permissible, and OGL lists were of practical significance.

As in the past, imports of several items remained the exclusive monopoly of the government through the "canalizing agencies." For example, crude oil and petroleum products were canalized through the Indian Oil Corporation; iron and steel, nonferrous metals, and fertilizers through the Minerals and Metals Trading Corporation; edible oils, natural rubber, newsprint, cement, and sugar through the State Trading Corporation; scrap metal through the Metal Scrap Trading Corporation; cereals through the Food Corporation of India (FCI); and cotton through the Cotton Corporation of India. The canalized items were entirely off-limits to private importers, whether they were actual users or not. In 1987, there were 16 canalizing agencies in existence.

At least three features of the industrial and technology policies served as non-tariff barriers to imports. First, under the so-called Phased Manufacturing Program (PMP) accompanying the license, a firm agreed to progressive indigenization of the product. This involved replacing the imported components with domestically sourced ones produced in-house or by other Indian firms. To ensure compliance, the firm was required to obtain certification from the sponsoring authority that the inputs it sought to import were not included on the list of products it agreed to source locally under the PMP. The certification was required even if the products in question were on the OGL list.

Second, the Capital Goods Committee cleared all applications for industrial licenses for new or expanded capacity. The committee could reject applications that in its view involved excessive foreign exchange outlay. Alternatively, it could require local sourcing of particular machinery and equipment items even though the latter might be on the OGL list.

Finally, the technology import policy protected the capital goods industries. Under the policy, applications for technology imports were reviewed for their foreign exchange requirements for the payment of royalties and license fees. Insofar as the technology was embodied in capital goods, denial of an application on grounds of the unavailability of foreign exchange resulted in the denial of imports, and hence protection for the domestic industry.

Within this set of constraints and general framework, trade liberalization proceeded along several fronts. First, the share of the canalized imports declined. Between 1980–81 and 1986–87, the share of canalized imports in total imports fell from a hefty 67 percent to 27 percent. Over the same period, canalized non-POL (petroleum, oil, and lubricants) imports as a proportion of total non-POL imports declined from 44 percent to 11 percent. While the government did take steps to decanalize some items—21 in 1985 and 26 in 1988—much of the decline in the volume of the canalized imports was due to factors other than decanalization. Pursell (1992) points to three such factors: (1) increased domestic crude oil production and the decline in the world prices of crude oil and petroleum products in the 1980s led to a decline in the POL imports; (2) the success of the Green Revolution led to the disappearance of grain imports, and cotton imports fell for other reasons; and (3) there was a large decline during the 1980s (until 1987) in the international prices of some of the other principal canalized imports, especially fertilizers, edible oils, nonferrous metals, and iron and steel.

Second, the OGL list was steadily expanded. Having disappeared earlier, this list was reintroduced in 1976 with 79 capital goods items on it. The number of capital goods items included in the OGL list expanded steadily, reaching 1007 in April 1987, 1170 in April 1988, and 1329 in April 1990 (Pursell 1992). In parallel, intermediate inputs were also placed on the OGL list, and their number expanded steadily over the years. Based on the best available information, this number had reached 620 by April 1987, and increased to 949 in April 1988 (World Bank, 1988, para. 2.59). According to Pursell (1992, p. 441), "Imports that were neither canalized nor subject to licensing (presumably mainly OGL imports) increased from about 5 percent in 1980–81 to about 30 percent in 1987–88." The inclusion of an item on the OGL list was usually accompanied by an "exemption," which amounted to a tariff reduction on that item. In almost all cases, the items on the list were machinery or raw materials for which no substitutes were produced at home. Thus their contribution to increased productivity was likely to be significant.

It is evident that simply counting the number of items on the OGL list gives no clear indication of the degree of liberalization of the trade regime. The problem is compounded by the fact that as import substitution proceeded, a broad product group got disaggregated into more finely defined items, with some items ending up on the restricted or banned lists and some on the OGL list. This fact sometimes made both the OGL and the non-OGL lists longer, as pointed out by Desai (1994). Nonetheless, as the World Bank (1987, p. 89, para. 4.25) notes, "Most informed commentaries on the trends in import policies agree that some loosening of raw material controls has occurred in each year beginning with the 1977/78 policy, except in 1980/81 when controls were tightened."

Third, several export incentives were introduced or expanded, which helped increase imports directly when they were tied to exports, and indirectly by relaxing the foreign exchange constraint. Replenishment (REP) licenses, which were given to exporters and could be freely traded on the market, directly helped relax the constraints on some imports. Exporters were given REP licenses in amounts that were approximately twice their import needs, and thus provided a source of input imports for goods sold in the domestic market. The key distinguishing feature of the REP licenses was that they allowed the holder to import items on the restricted list (and therefore those outside of the OGL or canalized list) and that had domestic import-competing counterparts. The list of the items that could be imported under the REP licenses was expanded, increasing their liberalizing impact. As exports increased, the volume of these imports followed suit. This factor became particularly important during 1985–90, when exports expanded rapidly.

Finally, and perhaps most important, the setting of the exchange rate at a realistic level reduced the bias against traded goods relative to nontraded goods. It helped expand exports, which in turn relaxed the restrictive effect of the foreign exchange constraint on imports. According to the charts provided by Pursell (1992), the import-weighted real exchange rates depreciated steadily by as much as 30 percent between 1974–75 and 1978–79. Symmetrically, the export-weighted real exchange rate depreciated by 27 percent over the same period. Interestingly, this was also a period of rapid export expansion (see below) and foreign exchange reserves accumulation that paved the way for import liberalization. The real exchange rate appreciated marginally in the following two years, stayed more or less unchanged until 1984–85, and depreciated steadily thereafter. Joshi and Little (1994) attribute a considerable part of the successful export expansion during the second half of the 1980s to the real exchange rate management.

Tariffs

The period under consideration was characterized by steep tariff escalation, especially after 1984–85. An indicator of this escalation is the change in tariff revenue as a percent of imports, which rose from 27 percent in 1977–78 to 62 percent in 1987–88. The objective behind the tariff escalation was to convert the large quota rent (i.e., the excess of the domestic price over the world price) associated with imports into government revenue. By all accounts, the rise in the tariffs did not have an extra protective effect beyond import licensing. Indeed, when products were moved to the OGL list, typically the government also introduced the "tariff exemption," which amounted to a lower applied duty than the statutory one.

Relying exclusively on the tariff rates as indicators of the level of protection, some analysts erroneously conclude from the rising tariffs that protection during this period was rising. The World Bank (1987, p. 100, para. 4.45) explains the error underlying such a conclusion:

> Although the rising average level of tariffs since 1978 has been accompanied by a steady increase in products under OGL, it should not be interpreted as an upward adjustment of tariffs on imports freed from licensing, in order to maintain protection of competing domestic industries. As mentioned before, most items (especially machinery) moved to the OGL lists were not produced in India, and these also were the products to which many of the tariff reductions were applied, the purpose being to reduce their costs and encourage the modernization and development of the industries which use them. The great majority of products on which tariff levels increased were not on OGL and were and remain protected by import licensing controls.

The customs duty included a basic duty and an auxiliary duty. According to Pursell (1992), the simple average of the basic and auxiliary duties in 1986 was 137.6 percent, with 59 percent of all tariffs in the 120–140 percent range, 8.5 percent exceeding 200 percent, and only 2.4 percent less than 60 percent.

Export Incentives and Restrictions

Many exports were subject to licensing. Objectives behind the controls included keeping domestic prices low, using market power to improve the terms of trade, and the promotion of exports of high-value-added products using the licensed items as inputs. Exports of certain items were also canalized. Nevertheless, the main thrust of the export policies being promotion rather than restriction of exports, the scope of export licensing and canalization was relatively limited.

On the incentives side, three schemes were most crucial: REP licenses, duty drawback, and the Cash Compensatory Scheme (CCS) (Pursell 1992). REP licenses allowed the exporter to import some of the non-OGL raw materials and components on the restricted, limited permissible, and canalized lists. The license holder would pay normal customs duties, which would then be refunded through the duty drawback scheme. In addition, the CCS compensated the exporter for other domestic taxes, such as sales taxes. The CCS involved the largest single direct budgetary outlay in support of exports during the mid- to late 1980s.

The export-import policy listed the products whose exports were entitled to the REP license along with the foreign exchange value of the entitlement as a percent of the value of the exports. The export-import policy also listed the inputs that could be imported under the REP license. The exporter was free to sell the REP license on the open market. Until the mid-1980s, the rent on such licenses being high, they commanded a hefty price. But after 1984–85, the rents declined sharply due to increased custom duties, import liberalization, and real depreciation of the rupee

One problem exporters faced was that due to high customs duties, they tied up substantial financial resources until they received the duty drawback. Several schemes existed to alleviate this problem, among which the most important one was the Advance Licensing Scheme, under which specified materials could be imported duty-free on the basis of export orders. The schemes were not widely used, however, until 1988, due to safeguards applied to check the diversion of imported inputs to the domestic market.

During 1985–86 and 1986–87, the government took several measures to promote exports, including the following (World Bank, 1987, p. 12, para. 1.30):

- A passbook scheme for duty-free imports for exporters, which broadened the coverage of the existing Advance Licensing Scheme.
- Increase in the business income tax deduction to 4 percent of net foreign exchange realization plus 50 percent (raised to 100 percent in 1988) of the remaining profits from exports.
- Reduction in the interest rate on export credit from 12 percent to 9.5 percent.
- Faster processing of export credit and duty drawbacks.
- Upward revision of the rates of the Cash Compensatory Scheme (CCS) for offsetting internal taxes.
- International Price Reimbursement Scheme for raw materials for all major export sectors (i.e., exporters were effectively offered international prices on internationally traded goods even when such inputs were purchased domestically).
- Permission to retain 5–10 percent of foreign exchange receipts for export promotion.
- Duty-free capital goods imports for exporters in "thrust" (i.e., targeted) industries.
- Full remission of excise duties and domestic taxes.
- Remission of 20 percent of interest charges on Industrial Development Bank of India (IDBI) loans for firms exporting over 25 percent of output.

Finally, India also employed export processing zones (EPZs) and bonded manufacturing (100 percent export-oriented units or EOU) schemes to promote exports. The first EPZ appeared in the early 1960s, the second in the early 1970s, and the next four in the 1980s. The EOU schemes were introduced in 1981. While neither of these schemes operated effectively due to heavy customs and regulatory controls, the host of measures described above went some way toward correcting the anti-export bias that had existed due to heavy import protection.

The Impact of Liberalization

Liberalization, though piecemeal and limited in scope, had a definite impact on imports. Pursell (1992, p. 441) states this succinctly and emphatically: "The available data on imports and import licensing are incomplete, out of date, and often inconsistent. Nevertheless, whichever way they are manipulated, they confirm very substantial and steady import liberalization that occurred after 1977–78 and during [the]1980s." He goes on to note that imports outside of canalization and licensing (i.e., those mainly on the OGL) increased from 5 percent of total imports in 1980–81 to 30 percent in 1987–88. The share of non-POL imports in the remaining imports increased from 8 percent to 37 percent over the same period.

Quite apart from this compositional change, there was considerable expansion of the level of imports during the 1970s and the second half of the 1980s. Increased growth in exports due to the steady depreciation of the real exchange rate and remittances from the overseas workers in the Middle East had begun to relax the balance of payments constraint during the first half of the 1970s, leading to the expansion of non-oil imports at the annual rate of 17.8 percent. This rapid expansion continued during the second half of the 1970s, with non-oil imports registering an impressive 15 percent annual growth rate over the period 1970–79. In contrast, in the subsequent five years, when the real exchange rate appreciated slightly and the income growth slowed down, non-oil imports expanded only 7.1 percent per annum. During 1985–90, they grew 12.3 percent. Thus, liberalized licensing rules flexibly accommodated the increased demand for imports during the fast growth periods.

Alternatively, the impact of the movement in the real exchange rate and related policy changes can be seen in the changes in the merchandise imports-to-GDP ratio. Table 4.3 shows non-oil imports as a proportion of GDP. This ratio had bottomed

TABLE 4.3: Merchandise Exports and Imports as Proportions of the GDP

Year	Exports/GDP (%)	Non-Oil Imports/GDP (%)	Imports/GDP (%)
1	*2*	*3*	*4*
1972–73	3.7	3.1	3.5
1977–78	5.3	4.4	5.9
1978–79	5.2	4.7	6.2
1979–80	5.3	4.9	7.6
1980–81	4.7	5.1	8.7
1981–82	4.6	5.0	8.1
1982–83	4.7	4.6	7.6
1983–84	4.5	5.0	7.2
1984–85	4.8	4.8	7.0
1985–86	3.9	5.3	7.1
1986–87	4.0	5.6	6.5
1987–88	4.4	5.1	6.3
1988–89	4.8	5.7	6.7
1989–90	5.7	6.0	7.3

Source: Author's calculations, using trade data from Table 135 and GDP at market prices from Table 1 (column 7) in RBI, *Handbook of Statistics on the Indian Economy* (2006).

out at 3.1 percent in 1972–73. It rose steadily during the rest of the 1970s, reaching 5.1 percent in 1980–81. During the first half of the 1980s, the ratio either fell or stagnated. This was the period during which the real exchange rate appreciated slightly in real terms and the foreign exchange constraint became tighter once again. The scenario shifted favorably again in the second half of the 1980s with the non-oil imports-to-GDP ratio rising during most years.

FOREIGN INVESTMENT AND TECHNOLOGY IMPORTS

For purposes of foreign investment, the FERA regime remained largely intact during this period, though there was some relaxation of attitude toward export-oriented units. The change was more pronounced toward technology imports, since technological obsolescence was an important concern during the period. The July 1980 Industrial Policy Statement had provided that "Companies which have well established R&D organization, and have demonstrated their ability to absorb, adapt and disseminate modern technology will be permitted to import such technology as will increase their efficiency and cost-effectiveness." The statement also provided that "In [a] case where a larger production base would increase the competitiveness of Indian Industry abroad, Government will consider favorably the induction of advanced technology." According to Kumar (1994), starting in November 1980, policy guidelines were issued to streamline foreign collaboration approvals. The government delegated the power to approve foreign collaborations involving up to 5 million rupees in foreign exchange and not involving foreign equity participation to the administrative ministries. In January 1987, this limit was raised to 10 million rupees. At this time, the government also relaxed the rules on the payment of royalties and lump-sum technical payments. On foreign equity, exceptions to the 40 percent ceiling were allowed more liberally. In 1986, the government decided to allow foreign equity even in existing Indian companies employing superior technology.

None of these *policy* changes was profound. Yet, the implementation of the existing policies seemed to have been relaxed substantially more than the change in the policy. This is reflected in the substantial jump in the rate of approvals of proposals involving foreign collaborations. Kumar (1994, p. 45) summarizes the evidence as follows:

> The considerable liberalization of policy in the 1980s caused the average number of approvals [of foreign collaboration] per year to increase from 242 during the period 1967–79 to 744 during 1980–88. The increase in the number of financial collaborations per year was even sharper, their proportion in the total approvals increasing from 16.1 percent to 22.8 percent. The average value of foreign investment approved per year increased by over 17 times, from Rs. 53.62 million to Rs. 930.84 million.

OTHER REFORMS

Piecemeal reforms were introduced during this period in virtually all areas. This will become clear when I discuss the policies in several individual sectors of the economy later in the book. Here I mention just four: distribution and price controls, taxation, telecommunications, and education. Price and distribution controls on cement and aluminum were entirely abolished. Decontrol of cement eliminated the black market and, through expanded production, brought the free market price down to the controlled levels within a short time. New entrants intensified competition, which led to improvements in quality along with the decline in the price.

In the taxation area, there was a major reform of the tax system. The multipoint excise duties were converted into a modified value-added (MODVAT) tax, which enabled manufacturers to deduct excise taxes paid on domestically produced inputs and countervailing duties paid on imported inputs from their excise obligations on output. By 1990, MODVAT came to cover all subsectors of manufacturing except petroleum products, textiles, and tobacco. This change significantly reduced the taxation of inputs and the associated distortion. I will have more to say about these reforms in the context of tax reforms later in the book.

In telecommunications, the early reform involved its separation from the Post and Telegraph Department and the creation of the Department of Telecommunication in 1985. Rajiv Gandhi also ended the government monopoly on the manufacture of telecommunications equipment, and allowed the private sector into it in the mid-1980s. He also opened the first technology park in Bangalore and liberalized imports of electronic equipment. These measures helped accelerate the expansion of the telephone network to some degree in the second half of the 1980s. These reforms are discussed in greater detail in chapter 17.

In the area of education, the National Policy on Education was announced in May 1986. (The previous education policy had been formulated in 1968.) It provided for a large-scale, nonformal education centers program "for school drop-outs, for children from habitations without schools, working children, and girls who cannot attend whole-day schools" (National Policy on Education, 1986, para. 5.8). It emphasized bridging inequality in education by devoting greater attention to the education of women, scheduled castes and tribes, the handicapped, and other minorities. The policy also proposed numerous changes in higher education, especially emphasizing management and technical education. I will return to these issues in the chapter on education.

CONCLUSION

Some scholars have argued that India grew almost as rapidly in the 1980s as in the 1990s, and since liberalization started only in 1991, any positive contribution of liberalization to India's growth is in doubt. To be sure, growth rates during 1981–91 and 1991–2001, at 5.6 percent and 5.8 percent, do look comparable and the major liberalizing reform did take place in 1991, giving this view some prima facie validity.

I have argued, however, that a careful look at the data and policy changes contradicts both the growth experience and the policy regime as described by these scholars. Though the aggregate growth during 1981–91 was 5.6 percent, growth during 1981–88 was only 4.8 percent. It is only beginning with 1988–89 that the growth rate shifted significantly, with the average during 1988–91 jumping to 7.6 percent. It is the inclusion of these three years with the remaining seven during the 1980s that makes the overall 1980s growth look similar to that in the 1990s. But if we are going to try explaining the shift in the growth rate, it is not just misleading but plain wrong to draw the line in 1981–82.

The discussion in this chapter has focused on seeking an explanation of the shift in the growth rate from 3.2 percent during 1965–81 to 4.8 percent during 1981–88. Once we recognize that the Indian economy had already achieved the growth rate of 4.1 percent during 1951–65, and that the policy measures introduced during 1965–81 (with the exception of some minor liberalizing steps during 1975–78) had effectively scuttled Indian industry, it is reasonably plausible that the progressive, albeit piece-meal, liberalization in trade and industry during 1981–89 described in this chapter helped the economy return to the original rate of growth with a small bonus.

Admittedly, I have done no quantification of the effects of liberalization. Nor have I done even the lesser exercise of linking the liberalization measures to the actual expansion of specific industries. Instead, I have relied on the correlation between the higher growth and liberalization, and economic theory. In this context, it is impor-tant to remember that according to economic theory, if the initial distortion is large, as was the case in India at the end of the 1970s, even small liberalization bestows large gains. Moreover, when restrictions are quantitative, liberalization on any front is welfare-enhancing (Krishna and Panagariya, 2001).

This said, there is clearly need for further empirical work to better connect the liberalization to industrial growth. Insofar as the precise information on the nature of liberalization by industry is available in the notifications issued by the ministries of Industry and Commerce, and data on investment, output, and other variable are available, at the minimum the connection between the policy changes and growth of specific industries can in principle be studied. Sharma (2006) has made some progress in this direction.

5

PHASE IV (1988–2006): TRIUMPH OF LIBERALIZATION

Phase IV began with an unprecedented growth spurt that ended in a balance of payments crisis. The response to the crisis was a major liberalization on both the domestic and the external fronts. The economy was successfully stabilized, and growth at the higher rate resumed within a short period. The higher growth has been maintained to date, and prospects are good that with some key reforms it can be raised further.

Though the necessity to borrow from the International Monetary Fund (IMF) and World Bank had subjected the initial liberalization package to the conditionality of these institutions, the proposed reforms were essentially domestic in origin. The crisis and the conditionality did speed up the initial liberalization, but the measures essentially reflected the consensus that had emerged among the Indian policymakers. Contrary to the assertions by many, the influence of the IMF and the World Bank was confined to the first set of actions. After the World Bank structural adjustment loan (SAL) of December 1991, which concluded in December 1992, the government of India was back in the driving seat. From then on, it was the World Bank that needed India rather than the opposite. It wanted to maintain the appearance of being involved in India's liberalization process, and therefore continued to lend money. For example, the trade and investment liberalization loan that followed the SAL was an entirely opportunistic move on the part of the Bank and came without conditions.[1]

Experimentation with piecemeal reforms in the 1980s had demonstrated to the policymakers that liberalization could yield improved performance. They also learned that contrary to long-standing fears, liberalization was politically feasible as long as it was packaged as necessary for the good of the common man. More important, the fall of the Soviet Union and the spectacular success of outward-oriented policies in China, a country that was even more populous than India, greatly undermined the view that India could steer itself out of poverty through investment and import controls. In the past, politicians, bureaucrats, and policy analysts in India would smugly dismiss the successes of outward-oriented policies in Singapore, Hong Kong, South Korea, and Taiwan on the ground that these countries were too small to be relevant to India. But the same could not be said of China.

THE POLITICAL CONTEXT

Every government since the end of Rajiv Gandhi's term in December 1989 has either been formed by a coalition of parties or survived through support of one or more parties that did not join the coalition but nevertheless supported it. Gandhi's immediate successor was his former finance (and later defense) minister, V. P. Singh. Having fallen out of favor with Gandhi, Singh had been expelled from the Congress Party in 1989. Taking a faction of Congress members with him, he joined hands with the Lok Dal and one of the major factions of the Janata Party (which had ruled during 1977–80) to form the Janata Dal. In the election Gandhi's Congress Party failed to get a majority. This allowed the Janata Dal and a group of smaller parties to form the National Front coalition. Supported from outside by the Bharatiya Janata Party (BJP), the National Front formed the government and Singh came to the helm as prime minster. As finance minister in Gandhi's cabinet, Singh had been responsible for the liberalization and reforms during 1985–86 and 1986–87. He continued on this path, but internal politics of the National Front brought him down in November 1990. This deprived him of the opportunity to implement the industrial policy of 1990, a major step toward liberalization (see below).

Chandra Sekhar, who had once been a confidant and ardent supporter of Mrs. Gandhi but was now a member of the National Front, succeeded Singh. He, too, failed to hold the coalition together for long, however. His government fell in March 1991 and fresh elections were called. However, he was allowed to stay in charge of the caretaker government until the elections had been held.

During the election campaign, on May 21, 1991, Rajiv Gandhi was assassinated. The resulting public sympathy probably helped the Congress Party win enough seats in the Parliament to form a minority government with the support of the Left Front parties. P. Narasimha Rao was elected as the leader of the Congress Parliamentary Party and became the prime minister in June 1991.

The macroeconomic crisis of 1991 had been under way during the elections. This presented Rao with the opportunity to undertake major reforms. He clearly rose to the occasion. He appointed a technocrat, Dr. Manmohan Singh, as the finance minister, and himself held the Ministry of Industry. As industry minister, Rao announced the industrial policy of 1991, which put an end to licensing except in 18 sectors and opened the door to foreign investment much wider. As finance minster, Singh took the lead to end import licensing on capital goods and intermediate inputs, and to correct the overvaluation of the exchange rate, a key element in the liberalization strategy. He then proceeded to cut the tariff rates, with the top rate falling from 355 percent to 110 percent in 1991–92 and to 65 percent in 1994–95. Singh also introduced important financial sector reforms.

Big reforms of the 1990s got done principally during the first three years of the Rao government. Progress slowed down considerably in the last two years of his term. But the government had introduced enough liberalizing measures to set the economy on the course to sustaining approximately 6 percent growth on a long-term basis. Indeed, during 1993–97, the economy grew at the rate of 7.1 percent. But this economic performance proved insufficient to counter the negative effects of a 10 percent hike in the Consumer Price Index during 1994–95 and 1995–96 and the corruption scandals that beset his administration. The Congress Party lost the 1996 election.

In the following three years, India had a series of short-lived governments. The election yielded a hung Parliament. The BJP, having won the most seats, was invited to form the government. Atal Bihari Vajpayee became the prime minister but failed to muster a majority of votes in the Parliament. He resigned in less than three weeks. The Congress Party and the Communist Party of India (Marxist) agreed to support from outside a new coalition of seven parties known as the United Front. The dominant party in the United Front was the Janata Dal. Deve Gowda of the Janata Dal became the prime minister on June 1, 1996, but was in office less than a year due to differences with the Congress Party leadership. Inder Kumar Gujral, also of the Janata Dal, succeeded as a compromise candidate on April 21, 1997, but he, too, lasted less than a year. Fresh elections were called.

Vajpayee returned as prime minister on March 19, 1998, heading the National Democratic Alliance (NDA), a coalition of several parties led by the BJP. But a year later, one member of the coalition withdrew support and the government fell. Because no other party or coalition of parties could muster a majority, elections were called once again, with Vajpayee serving as the caretaker prime minister.

This time around, the election produced a clearer mandate in favor of the NDA, and Vajpayee formed a government on October 13, 1999. This government proved stable and served its full five-year term. The Vajpayee government proceeded to carry forward the reform agenda in a number of directions, including international trade, foreign investment, insurance, telecommunications, electricity, roads, privatization, and education. In terms of the reach of the reforms, this period matched the first three years of the Rao government. The shift in the growth rate from 6 percent to more than 8 percent during 2003–07 must be attributed largely to these reforms.

The May 2004 election produced a surprise, however. Anti-incumbent voting at the state level resulted in a loss of mandate for the NDA government (Panagariya, 2004d). The NDA also suffered on account of the coalition politics, most notably from the switch in allegiance by the Dravida Munnetra Kazhagam (DMK), which had 16 members of Parliament, from the NDA to the United Progressive Alliance (UPA) that came to power. On May 22, 2004, Dr. Manmohan Singh formed the government on behalf of the UPA, whose largest member is the Congress Party. The UPA is a minority coalition, however, and relies on the outside support of the Left Front parties.

The UPA leadership read the election mandate as a signal that reforms had failed to serve the poor well. As Bhagwati and Panagariya (2004) argued, this was inconsistent with the massive anti-incumbency element in the election outcomes. They argued instead that it was the revolution of rising expectations that led the voters in both rural and urban areas to throw out those ruling in favor of the alternative.[2] Nevertheless, the view the UPA leadership embraced and the need for the support of the Left Front parties for survival has had the unfortunate effect of slowing the reform.

The National Common Minimum Program it drew up effectively abandoned privatization and explicitly ruled out a key labor market reform necessary to stimulate labor-intensive manufacturing in the organized sector.

A remarkable feature of Phase IV (1988–2006), however, is that despite eight different prime ministers, from Rajiv Gandhi to Manmohan Singh, leading coalitions consisting of parties from far Left to far Right, the reform process kept moving forward. Differences among the prime ministers and parties were at best in terms of speed and emphasis. Even during 1996–99, when the governments were short-lived, Finance Minister P. Chidambaram managed to present a highly reformist budget for the year 1997–98. Likewise, even as it was losing the majority in the Parliament, the Vajpayee government managed to announce the landmark new telecom policy of March 1999. The reason for this steady progress lay in the consensus that had been building below the surface in the second half of the 1980s. While no politician wanted to overtly announce the failure of the inward-looking, anti-market policies, everyone now saw it, and some who were bold enough to at least quietly try a change of direction encountered relatively little resistance. In the next section, I offer evidence in support of the hypothesis that the consensus had shifted in favor of pro-market and outward-oriented policies in the late 1980s.

THE SHIFTING CONSENSUS

The consensus in favor of the controlled regime among politicians and bureaucrats was beginning to break during the second half of the 1980s. This is graphically illustrated by the discussion of ongoing liberalizing reforms under Rajiv Gandhi and their advocacy by none other than I. G. Patel, who had loyally served successive governments of Mrs. Gandhi and of Morarji Desai and others with little reservation expressed for the controlled regime. And, as the governor of the Reserve Bank of India, he had been the prime mover behind the second nationalization of banks as late as 1980.

In his Kingsley Martin Memorial Lecture, delivered in Cambridge, Patel (1987) approvingly described the reforms introduced by Rajiv Gandhi in the preceding one and a half years as the "New Economic Policy." He first made the point that the consensus in the policy circles within India had shifted considerably away from the controlled regime:

> There has been, I think, a general perception in India for quite some time that change is needed at least in these two respects—to reverse the trend towards increasing inefficiency and to make the anti-poverty programs more effective. Not everyone had, or indeed has, the same remedy to prescribe. But the diagnosis has been more uniform than what most people realize or might care to admit. Even those of us who had actively promoted the earlier policies of the 'fifties and the early 'sixties have come to realize for some time now that we had underestimated the long-term deleterious effects of controls and had not appreciated sufficiently the potential for a self-serving alliance between political leaders and civil servants on the one hand and captains of industry or the large farmers who have sufficient clout both socially and financially on the other. This diagnosis, I believe, is largely shared by critics from the Left as well. (p. 215)

Patel (1987, p. 215) went on to add:

> You will, therefore, not be surprised when I say that I have been generally enthusiastic about the turn that Rajiv Gandhi has been trying to give to Indian economic policy. At any rate, I subscribe to the view that Indian industry must be subjected increasingly to the forces of competition, both internal and international, if it is to become more efficient and that this requires that it be made increasingly free from the shackles of industrial licensing, import control and other forms of control such as price control or controls exercised ostensibly to overcome regional imbalance or monopoly and restrictive practices or that peculiarly Indian invention, viz, concentration of economic power.

The consensus that Patel spoke of had moved considerably more toward increased outward and inward competition by the end of the 1980s, and had been finding expression in liberalizing policy measures discussed in the last chapter. The little-known Industrial Policy Statement, 1990, provides compelling evidence of the considerable political acceptance that internal and external liberalization had gained at least a year before the balance of payments crisis. To be sure, not being certain how the electorate might react, the politicians were still afraid to announce their conversion openly. But they were sufficiently convinced of the need for change to move forward to open the markets in larger steps than had been the case in the past.

In view of the general lack of awareness of the Industrial Policy Statement, 1990, among scholars of the Indian economy, I reproduce it as appendix 1 and will also discuss it in greater detail in this chapter. For now, let me note that Prime Minister V. P. Singh, who announced the policy statement on May 31, 1990, lost his mandate in the Parliament on November 10, 1990, before he had a chance to implement it.[3] Prime Minister Chandra Sekhar succeeded him, but his government proved equally fragile due to internal feuds, and fell in March 1991.[4]

Given that politicians were still wary that the opposition parties would readily label any relaxation of controls as favoring the rich and big businesses, the policy statement begins with the usual populist rhetoric about the need for changes that would promote employment, rural industry, and the small-scale sector.[5] To give substance to this assertion, it promises to expand the SSI reservation list and to improve access to credit and technology for the SSI units. But once this lip service is paid to small entrepreneurs, virtually all of the policy changes the statement proposes are conventional reforms that found a place in the package adopted by the Narsimha Rao government a year later.

The following are the major changes that the Industrial Policy Statement, 1990 proposed:

- The investment ceiling in plant and machinery for small-scale industries (fixed in 1985) would be raised from 3.5 million rupees to 6.0 million rupees.
- All new units, up to an investment of 250 million rupees in fixed assets in non-backward areas, and 750 million rupees in backward areas, would be exempt from the requirement of obtaining a license.
- For the import of capital goods, the entrepreneur would be entitled to import up to a landed value of 30 percent of the total value of plant and machinery required for the unit.

- Imports of raw materials and components would be permitted up to a landed value of 30 percent of the ex-factory value of annual production. The ex-factory value of production would exclude the excise duty on the item of production. Raw materials and components on OGL would not be included within this 30 percent limit. In respect of transfer of technology, if import of technology was considered necessary by the entrepreneur, he could conclude an agreement with the collaborator, without obtaining any clearance from the government, provided that royalty payment did not exceed 5 percent on domestic sales and 8 percent on exports
- Keeping in view the need to attract an effective inflow of technology, investment up to 40 percent of equity would automatically be allowed.
- The deregulation suggested above would cover all cases of expansion and would not be restricted to new units.
- 100 percent export-oriented units and units to be set up in export-processing zones would be delicensed up to an investment limit of 750 million rupees.
- Units set up by MRTP and FERA companies would be covered by the procedures set out above, but they would continue to need clearances under the provisions and regulations of these two acts.

One way to appreciate the significance of these proposals is to recall that just five years earlier, an undertaking or interconnected undertakings with 200 million rupees in fixed assets would have been placed among the MRTP firms and excluded from investing outside of appendix I industries. In contrast, the 1990 statement proposed complete abolition of licensing for units investing 250 million rupees or less. Likewise, the changes guaranteeing machinery imports worth 30 percent of total investment and raw material imports worth 30 percent of output, valued at producer prices regardless of the entrepreneur's export status, would have gone considerable distance toward the 1991–92 trade reform that was confined to delicensing of imports of capital goods and intermediate inputs, and entirely excluded consumer goods.

GROWTH SPURT AND THE BALANCE OF PAYMENTS CRISIS

During the fiscal years spanning 1988–91, GDP at factor costs grew at rates of 10.5, 6.7, and 5.6 percent, respectively. The average of these rates was 7.6 percent, a rate not previously recorded over any continuous three-year period in Indian history. Growth was spread across all sectors: 7 percent in agriculture, 9.1 percent in industry, and 7.1 percent in services.

The explanation for agricultural growth is relatively simple: Despite continuous spread of the use of the high yielding varieties of seeds and the steady expansion of the use of tractors and fertilizers, this sector had grown at the average rate of just 0.1 percent in the preceding four years (1984–88). The sector was ripe to catch up as soon as Mother Nature got kind. Therefore, my main task is to explain higher growth rates in industry and services. Here we have two complementary explanations: liberalization, and expansionary fiscal policy combined with foreign borrowing. The second of these factors inevitably carried the seeds of a crisis that became a reality in 1991.

But let us consider first the role of liberalization. Since the mid-1950s, both good and bad policy changes in India have produced results with a lag. The liberalization measures in trade and industry undertaken during the Rajiv Gandhi era were no exception. Because the process of liberalization had continued during 1988–91 without significant reversals, entrepreneurs could be confident that the elbow room they had been given would not be withdrawn. For example, in 1989–90, the exemption limit on license-free investment in fixed assets for new undertakings or expansion of existing capacity was raised from 50 million rupees to 150 million rupees for investment in nonbackward areas and to 500 million rupees in backward areas. This was a threefold increase in the exemption limit. Viewed another way, only four years earlier, the total investment of 200 million rupees in fixed assets would have qualified an undertaking as an MRTP undertaking and confined it to investment in appendix I industries.

Likewise, on the external front, the expansion of OGL continued. For example, 329 intermediates, raw materials, and components were added in April 1988 and another 82 in April 1990. A major effort was also made to make the environment export-friendly. Machinery and equipment for export-oriented industries were generally placed on the OGL list. All exporters were entitled to tradable replenishment licenses that allowed them to import any item on the limited permissible and canalized lists, up to specific percentages of the value of exports. The government also exempted the imports of restricted capital goods by exporters from the domestic availability clearance requirement. In 1988, the deduction of profits on export sales from taxable income was raised from 50 to 100 percent. Finally, as discussed in the previous chapter, the real exchange rate was allowed to depreciate in order to make exports more attractive to entrepreneurs.

The impact of the more liberal policy regime can also be seen from the outcome variables. Thus, according to the Government of India (*Economic Survey*, table 1.5), gross fixed private investment as a proportion of GDP steadily rose from 10.2 percent in 1986–87 to 11.5 percent in 1987–88, 12 percent in 1988–89, and 13.9 percent in 1990–91. On the external front, the merchandise imports-to-GDP ratio rose from 6.3 percent in 1987–88 to 7.6 percent in 1990–91.

Some may argue that rising imports may simply reflect rising incomes rather than any liberalization. But this argument has two limitations. First, even if imports rise because incomes rise, they need not rise as a *proportion* of the GDP. Second, and more important, if the trade regime is held tightly controlled, the rising demand for imports in response to income increases need not translate into an actual rise unless the policy regime allows such response to be accommodated. Conversely, either rising exports or expanded capital account inflows from abroad must provide the necessary foreign exchange to allow imports to expand. Both of them depend on policy choices.

Complementing liberalization in stimulating growth were borrowing abroad and fiscal expansion. Throughout the 1980s, India ran large current account deficits. The deficit became particularly large during the second half of the decade. From 1980–81 to 1984–85, it ranged between 1.3 and 1.9 percent of the GDP. In 1985–86, it jumped to 2.4 percent, fell back to 2 percent in 1987–88, and then shot up to 3.1 percent in 1988–89, 2.6 percent in 1989–90, and 3.4 percent in 1990–91.

While foreign borrowing reflected in these current account deficits made a positive contribution to growth by allowing domestic investment to exceed domestic savings, it also led to a rapid accumulation of foreign debt, which rose from $20.6 billion in 1980–81 to $64.4 billion in 1989–90 (Joshi and Little, 1994, p. 186). The accumulation was especially rapid during the second half of the decade, with net long-term borrowing rising from the annual average of $1.9 billion during 1980–81 to 1984–85 to $3.5 billion from 1985–86 to 1989–90. The external debt to GDP ratio rose from 17.7 percent in 1984–85 to 24.5 percent in 1989–90. Over the same period, the debt service ratio rose from 18 percent to 27 percent.

The growth in debt was accompanied by a rapid deterioration in the "quality" of debt between 1984–85 and 1989–90. "Other" capital flows, and errors and omissions, turned from a large negative figure in the first half of the decade into a positive figure, indicating an increase in short-term borrowing in the latter period. The share of private borrowers in the total long-term debt increased from 28 percent to 41 percent. The share of nonconcessional debt rose from 42 percent to 54 percent. The average maturity of debt declined from 27 years to 20 years. Thus, while external debt was helping the economy grow, it was also moving it steadily toward a crash.

A similar story was evolving on the internal front. While external borrowing helped relieve some supply-side constraints, rising current domestic public expenditures provided the stimulus to demand, particularly in the services sector. Srinivasan and Tendulkar (2003) assign much of the credit for the growth during the 1980s to this demand-side factor. Defense spending, interest payments, subsidies, and the higher wages following the implementation of the Fourth Pay Commission recommendations fueled these expenditures. Table 5.1, which reproduces table 7.5 in Joshi and Little (1994), documents the magnitude of the expansion of current government expenditures at the central and state levels combined during the second half of the 1980s. During the first half of the 1980s, these expenditures averaged 18.6 percent of the GDP. In the second half, they rose to an average of 23 percent,

TABLE 5.1: Fiscal Indicators: 1980–81 to 1989–90 (as percent of GDP)

	Average 1980–81 to 1984–85	1985–86	1986–87	1987–88	1988–89	1989–90	1990–91	Average 1985–86 to 1989–90
Revenue	18.1	19.5	20	20.1	19.6	20.9	19.5	20
Current expenditure	18.6	21.4	22.6	23.1	22.7	24.8	23.9	23
Defense	2.7	3.3	3.8	4	3.8	3.6	—	3.7
Interest	2.6	3.3	3.6	4	4.2	4.6	4.8	3.9
Subsidies*	2.6	3.3	3.4	3.5	3.6	4.2	—	3.6
Capital expenditure	7.5	7.4	8.3	7	6.3	6.5	6	7.1
Total expenditure	26.1	28.8	30.9	30.1	29	31.3	29.9	30.1
Fiscal deficit	8	9.3	10.9	10	9.4	10.4	10.4	10.1

*CSO Estimates.

Source: Joshi and Little (1994, table 7.5).

with the bulk of the expansion coming from defense, interest payments, and subsidies, whose average rose from 7.9 percent to 11.2 percent of the GDP.

As with external borrowing, high current expenditures proved unsustainable. They manifested themselves in extremely large fiscal deficits. As table 5.1 shows, combined fiscal deficits at the central and state levels, which averaged 8 percent in the first half of the 1980s, went up to 10.1 percent in the second half. Continued deficits of this magnitude led to a buildup of very substantial public debt with interest payments accounting for a large proportion of the government revenues. They also inevitably fed into the current account deficits, which kept rising steadily until they reached 3.4 percent of the GDP in 1990–91. The eventual outcome of these developments was the June 1991 crisis.

The final blow was administered by the decline in the stock of foreign exchange reserves. From an average of 4.6 months' worth of imports during 1984–87, the reserves fell to 3.9 months' worth of imports in 1987–88. The trend continued with a drop in the reserves to 2.5 months' worth of imports in 1988–89, 2 months in 1989–90, and just one month in 1990–91 (Joshi and Little, 1994, table 7.10). In June 1991, with confidence in the ability of the government to service its external debt completely lost, the crisis reached the doorstep of the country with the downgrading of its credit rating and loss of access to the world financial markets.

The resolution of the crisis took the form of the International Monetary Fund (IMF) entering the scene with a program in July 1991 and the World Bank following with a structural adjustment loan (SAL). The IMF program and the World Bank SAL initiated a process of liberalization that has continued to move forward at a gradual pace until today. In the intervening years, the policy regime and the economy have been considerably transformed, with the growth rate stabilized at approximately 6 percent per annum and possibly shifting to 8 percent recently. In the following section, I discuss the liberalization that has taken place in industry and trade.

TRIUMPH OF LIBERALIZATION: THE NEW INDUSTRIAL POLICY

The preceding discussion and that in the previous chapter should leave little doubt that the old regime was in retreat. Thus the liberalization measures in 1991–92 may be viewed as a continuation of the process that had begun as early as 1975. But one key difference sets the 1991–92 liberalization apart from the piecemeal measures preceding it: Whereas the prior liberalization had been undertaken within the essential framework of investment, import licensing, and price and distribution controls, the 1991 reform abandoned that framework and moved some way toward replacing it with the market mechanism. Although the fears of political backlash still compelled Finance Minister Manmohan Singh to represent the reforms as the continuation of the past policies, the actual measures represented complete renunciation of the old policy framework and brought liberalization out in the open.[6]

Thus, in a single stroke, the statement of industrial policy dated July 24, 1991, did away with investment licensing and myriad entry restrictions on the MRTP firms. It also ended public sector monopoly in many sectors and initiated a policy of automatic approval for foreign direct investment up to 51 percent.

On licensing, the new policy explicitly stated, "Industrial licensing will henceforth be abolished for all industries, except those specified, irrespective of levels of investment." Thus, rather than follow the path of gradually raising the limit on investment in fixed assets without license until such limit became nonbinding, the new policy simply abolished licensing subject to a negative list. The policy listed 18 industries in annex II that remained subject to licensing. True to the commitment in the policy that "Government's policy will be continuity with change," annex II was trimmed in the subsequent years until it was left with only five sectors justified on health, safety, or environmental grounds: (a) arms and ammunition, explosives, and allied items of defense equipment, defense aircraft, and warships; (b) atomic substances; (c) narcotics and psychotropic substances and hazardous chemicals; (d) distillation and brewing of alcoholic drinks; and (e) cigarettes/cigars and manufactured tobacco substitutes.

The new policy also limited the public sector monopoly to eight sectors selected on security and strategic grounds, and listed in annex I. All other sectors were opened to the private sector. In subsequent years, annex I has been trimmed, with only railway transportation and atomic energy remaining on it. Entry to the private sector has been given even in the manufacture of defense equipment.

The new policy also did away with entry restrictions on MRTP firms. Again, the policy was notable for its unequivocal renunciation of the past approach:

> The pre-entry scrutiny of investment decisions by so called MRTP companies will no longer be required. Instead, emphasis will be on controlling and regulating monopolistic, restrictive and unfair trade practices rather than making it necessary for the monopoly house to obtain prior approval of Central Government for expansion, establishment of new undertakings, merger, amalgamation and takeover and appointment of certain directors. The MRTP Act will be restructured. The provisions relating to merger, amalgamation, and takeover will also be repealed. Similarly, the provisions regarding restrictions on acquisition of and transfer of shares will be appropriately incorporated in the Companies Act.

These changes are now in place.

In the area of foreign investment, the policy statement abolished the threshold of 40 percent on foreign equity investment. The concept of automatic approval was introduced whereby the Reserve Bank of India was empowered to approve equity investment up to 51 percent in the 34 "priority" industries traditionally called "appendix I" industries and now listed in annex III of the new policy. In subsequent years, this policy was considerably liberalized, with automatic approval made available to almost all industries except those subject to public sector monopoly and industrial licensing. I will describe the current DFI regime in greater detail in the section on trade liberalization below. Nevertheless, I note here that within the context of the new industrial policy, successive governments have steadily opened the Indian economy to foreign investors. Currently, the system operates on a negative list approach such that unless the official DFI policy explicitly spells out specific restrictions, no restriction applies. The current regime prohibits DFI in only four sectors: retail trading (except single-brand product retailing), atomic energy, the lottery business, and betting and other forms of gambling. A handful of additional sectors are subject to specified caps and DFI in the sectors reserved for small-scale products is limited to 24 percent.

On foreign technology agreements, the policy introduced automatic permission in high priority industries (annex III) up to a lump-sum payment of 10 million rupees, and 5 percent royalties for domestic sales and 8 percent for exports, subject to total payment of 8 percent of sales over a ten-year period from the date of the agreement or seven years from commencement of production. Subsequently, the policy was extended to other industries.

TRADE LIBERALIZATION

Starting with the July 1991 budget, there was a clear switch in trade policy in favor of a more outward-oriented regime. The trade liberalization program initiated in the budget was comprehensive, though there were hiccups subsequently, with the pace remaining gradual. In the following, I divide the discussion into measures aimed at liberalizing trade in goods and those liberalizing trade in services.

Merchandise Trade Liberalization

The July 1991 reforms did away with import licensing on all but a handful of inter-mediate inputs and capital goods items. But consumer goods, accounting for approx-imately 30 percent of the tariff lines, remained under licensing. It was only after a successful challenge by India's trading partners in the Dispute Settlement Body of the World Trade Organization (WTO) that these goods were freed of licensing a decade later, starting April 1, 2001. Today, except for a handful of goods disallowed on environmental, health, and safety grounds and a few others, including fertilizer, cereals, edible oils, and petroleum products that remain canalized, all goods can be imported without a license or other restrictions. As per the Uruguay Round (UR) Agreement on Agriculture, all border measures on agricultural goods have been replaced by tariffs.

As noted earlier, tariff rates in India had been raised substantially during the 1980s to turn quota rents into tariff revenue. In 1990–91, the highest tariff rate stood at 355 percent; the simple average of all tariff rates at 113 percent; and the import-weighted average of tariff rates at 87 percent (WTO, 1998). With the removal of licensing, these tariff rates became effective restrictions on imports. Therefore, a major task of the reforms in the 1990s and beyond has been to lower tariffs.

Tariff reductions have been confined to nonagricultural industrial goods, how-ever. Therefore, the liberalization described immediately below applies strictly to these goods. The reduction in tariffs has been accomplished through a gradual compression of the top tariff rates with a simultaneous rationalization of the tariff structure through a reduction in the number of tariff bands. The top rate fell to 85 percent in 1993–94 and to 50 percent in 1995–96. Though there were some reversals along the way in the form of special duties and through unification of two successive rates, such as 10 percent and 15 percent, to the higher rate (15 percent), the trend has been toward liberalization. Prior to the latest elections in May 2004, Finance Minister Jaswant Singh had announced reduction of the top tariff rate from 25 to 20 percent and the elimination of the special additional duty that could be as much as 4 percent. The succeeding government did not reverse these changes. Indeed, it lowered the top tariff rate to 15 percent in 2005–06, 12.5 percent in 2006–07, and 10 percent in 2007–08. There remain exceptions to this rule, however. For example, the customs duty on automobiles remains in the neighborhood of 100 percent. Likewise, several textile items remain subject to duties exceeding 10 percent. Nevertheless, the decline in customs duties is pronounced: Customs revenue as a proportion of merchandise imports was only 4.9 percent in 2005–06.

In agriculture, India took the same essential approach as the OECD countries, and chose excessively high tariff bindings ranging from 100 to 300 percent to replace border measures under the UR Agreement on Agriculture. For agricultural products including skimmed milk powder, rice, corn, wheat, and millet, India had traditionally zero or very low bound rates. These were renegotiated under GATT, article XXXVIII, in December 1999 in return for concessions on other products.[7] According to the WTO (2002, table III.1), India's average bound rate in agriculture is 115.2 percent. In comparison, the applied most favored nation tariff rate was 35.1 percent in 1997–98 and 41.7 percent in 2001–02.

As described earlier, traditionally India had restricted exports of several commodities. As a part of its liberalization policy, the government began to reduce the number of products subject to export controls in 1989–90. But prior to the July 1991 reforms, exports of 439 items were still subject to controls, including (in declining order of severity) prohibition (185 items), licensing (55 items), quantitative ceilings (38 items), canalization (49 items), and prespecified terms and conditions (112 items). The March 1992 export-import policy reduced the number of items subject to controls to 296, with prohibited items reduced to 16. The process continued subsequently, so that export prohibitions currently apply to a small number of items on health, environmental, or moral grounds; export restrictions are maintained mainly on cattle, camels, fertilizers, cereals, peanut oil, and pulses.

The lifting of exchange controls and elimination of overvaluation of the rupee that had served as additional barriers against the traded goods sector also accompanied the 1990s reforms. As a part of the 1991 reform, the government devalued the rupee by 18 percent against the dollar, from 21.2 rupees to 25.8 rupees per dollar. In February 1992, a dual exchange rate system was introduced, which allowed exporters to sell 60 percent of their foreign exchange in the free market and 40 percent to the government at the lower official price. Importers were authorized to purchase foreign exchange in the open market at the higher price, effectively ending the exchange control. Within a year of establishing this market exchange rate, the official exchange rate was unified with it. Starting in February 1994, many current account transactions, including all current business transactions, education, medical expenses, and foreign travel were permitted at the market exchange rate. These steps culminated in India's accepting the IMF article VIII obligations on August 20, 1994, which made the rupee officially convertible on the current account. In recent years, bolstered by the accumulation of a large stock of foreign exchange reserves ($189 billion in February 2007), India has freed up many capital account transactions. Two provisions are of special significance: (1) residents can remit up to $25,000 abroad every year; and (2) firms can borrow freely abroad as long as the maturity of the loan is five years or more.

Trade in Services and Foreign Investment

Since 1991, India has carried out a substantial liberalization of trade in services via freeing up foreign investment. Traditionally, services sectors have been subject to heavy government intervention. Public sector presence has been conspicuous in the key sectors of insurance, banking, and telecommunications. Nevertheless, considerable progress has been made toward opening the door wider to private sector participation, including foreign investors.

The current foreign investment regime in India operates on "negative list philosophy," meaning that unless there are specific restrictions spelled out in the foreign direct investment (FDI) policy, up to 100 percent foreign investment, subject to the sectoral rules and regulations, is permitted under the automatic route.[8] Four exceptions apply to 100 percent foreign investment under the automatic route:

- In four sectors, FDI is prohibited outright: retail trading (except single-brand product retailing), atomic energy, the lottery business, and betting and other forms of gambling.
- Foreign equity share in excess of 24 percent in the manufacturing of items reserved for the small-scale sector requires prior government approval.
- Prior government approval is required when the foreign investor has an existing joint venture or technology transfer/trademark agreement in the same field.
- The FDI policy lists 28 sectors (some of which are divided into subsectors for purposes of different rules) that are subject to sector-specific policies and sectoral caps on foreign investment that may or may not go up to 100 percent.

With respect to the last item, the following sectoral caps apply:

- 20 percent on FM radio (FDI plus portfolio investment by foreign institutional investors).
- 26 percent on uplinking a news and current affairs TV channel; defense production; insurance; public sector refineries; air transport services (100 percent for nonresident Indians); and publishing of newspapers and periodicals dealing with news and current affairs.
- 49 percent on asset reconstruction companies; three broadcasting subsectors including a cable network; and companies investing in infrastructure and services except telecommunications.
- 51 percent on single-brand retailing.
- 74 or 100 percent on all others, including banking, nonbanking finance companies (approved activities); telecommunications; manufacture of telecom equipment; trading, construction, airports, power, petroleum and natural gas, coal and lignite mining; tea; coffee and rubber processing; and special economic zones.

Taken as a whole, India now has a foreign investment policy that is approximately as open as that of China. Even in the retail sector, back-door entry has been permitted recently whereby foreign retail companies such as Wal-Mart can supply supermarkets owned by Indian companies. This leaves electronic and print media as the main sector subject to tight foreign investment caps.

LIBERALIZATION IN OTHER SECTORS

While I have focused on industrial delicensing, trade, and foreign investment above, the reforms during the 1990s and later have gone far beyond these sectors. I discuss these reforms at length in parts III to V of the book. For completeness, let me note here that India has made remarkable progress in reforming the policy regime in areas such as taxation, the financial sector, telecommunications, electricity, the airline industry, and national highway construction. Some success has also been achieved in privatization under the NDA government, but the process has slowed down considerably under the current UPA government. While these reforms have been introduced, India has maintained a relatively stable macroeconomic environment. Some vulnerability has arisen from large deficits for prolonged periods, leading to a high level of public debt, but lately some progress has been made on this front as well.

Success in the electricity sector, airports, rural roads, and urban infrastructure has fallen far short of that achieved in the other sectors, but policy initiatives that promise future success have been introduced. The greatest failure to date has been in the social services sector, where the government has utterly failed to deliver the services. Health, water supply and sanitation, and education are the areas requiring innovative new approaches.

CONCLUDING REMARKS

Phase IV has been characterized by an acceleration of growth in the GDP, foreign trade, and foreign investment. At the aggregate level, the growth rate during 1988–2006 was 6.3 percent, compared with 4.8 percent during 1981–88. During the period from 2003–04 to 2005–07, the country's GDP at factor cost grew at the impressive rate of 8.6 percent.

Opening the economy to the world markets and subjecting it to greater market discipline has been at the heart of the success India has achieved to date. While the reforms under Rajiv Gandhi gave rise to the growth spurt in the late 1980s, it was the systematic reforms of the early 1990s that helped accelerate the growth rate to 7.1 percent during 1993–97 and then sustain it at the 6 percent level over a longer period of time. In turn, the substantial reforms in several key sectors under the NDA government helped shift the growth rate to 8.6 percent during 2003–04 to 2005–06.

Growth in trade has been an integral part of India's growth story. To put the matter dramatically, merchandise exports in 1990–91 were $18.1 billion. In 2005–06, *growth* in exports over the preceding year exceeded this amount. The acceleration in the growth of trade in recent years has been spectacular. Exports took nine years to double from their level in 1990–91. In the recent period, they doubled in one-third of that time: from $52.7 billion in 2002–03 to $102.7 billion in 2005–06. Services exports more than doubled from $26.9 billion in 2003–04 to $60.6 billion in 2005–06.

India's share in world merchandise exports grew from 0.5 percent in 1990–91 to 0.7 percent in 1999–2000 and to 1.0 percent in 2005–06. In services exports, the share grew to a respectable 2.5 percent in 2005–06. These changes have greatly increased the integration of India into the world economy. The exports of goods and services as a proportion of the GDP, which grew rather gradually from 7.2 percent in 1990–91 to 11.6 percent in 1999–2000, shot up to 20.5 percent in 2005–06. The proportion of total trade (exports plus imports of goods and services) to the GDP rose from 15.9 percent in 1990–91 to 25.2 percent in 1999–2000, and then to 43.1 percent in 2005–06.

6

A TALE OF TWO COUNTRIES

India and the Republic of Korea

In the 1950s, India had been widely perceived as a rising star among the developing countries and was the darling of virtually all development economists. But by mid-1960, its economy had begun to exhibit clear signs of fatigue, and by 1980 it came to be regarded as an unqualified failure. In the interim, it also dropped off the research agenda of development economists—few of them could expect to make a career for themselves studying India.

In contrast, in the 1950s, South Korea was seen as a basket case, sustained by massive doses of U.S. aid. Even excluding the military aid, the U.S. economic aid comfortably exceeded 10 percent of the Korean GNP in the 1950s. But aid peaked in 1957, and by the early 1960s Korea could no longer count on it to sustain what was a relatively low rate of investment. Nevertheless, by the mid-1960s, Korea had turned itself around and achieved an unprecedented near-double-digit growth rate. And by the mid-1980s, it had acquired the status of an upper-middle-income country.[1] In 1996, it was invited to join the Organization for Economic Cooperation and Development (OECD), a club consisting mainly of rich countries.[2]

In this chapter, I briefly review the Korean experience to bring out the sharp contrast between its performance and policies and those of India. There is an ongoing debate among economists on what accounts for the spectacular growth of Korea. While the dominant view among economists is that Korea owes its phenomenal success to orthodox outward-oriented and market-friendly policies, a small group of "revisionist" economists attributes it to industrial targeting, protectionism, and interventionism. As we will see, regardless of the school to which one subscribes, there is no disputing the fact that Korea was miles away from the autarkic and wholesale interventionist policies that India pursued starting in the early 1960s.

A BRIEF HISTORY OF THE KOREAN MIRACLE

Japan occupied the Korean Peninsula from 1910 to 1945. The end of the Japanese rule in 1945 was accompanied by a de facto partition of the peninsula, with the United States supporting South Korea and the Soviet Union backing North Korea. In 1948, Syngman Rhee, a Princeton Ph.D. and longtime exile in the United States, became the president of South Korea. Rhee essentially used economic policies including the allocation of aid goods, import licenses, and government contracts to gain and maintain political support. A highly overvalued exchange rate, very tight foreign exchange rationing, a large current account deficit (financed principally by U.S. foreign aid), and a high degree of protection through tariffs as well as quantitative barriers characterized the Korean economy during the 1950s. There is general agreement that this was a period of import-substitution industrialization. Rhee ruled Korea until a student protest in April 1960 ousted him.

Unsurprisingly, economic performance of South Korea during this period was not particularly impressive by the standards of what was to come, and especially after we take into account the fact that aid flows financed the bulk of the imports and investment. Excluding the period covering the war with North Korea (1950–53), the growth rate in South Korea in the 1950s averaged 4 percent.[3] While this is comparable to the growth rate in India during the 1950s, aid flows into India were far smaller.

Moreover, the performance of the Korean economy during the preceding three decades had been an order of magnitude superior to that of India. Cha (2004, p. 288) places the annual growth rate of per-capita real consumption in Korea during the period 1911–40 at 2.3 percent, which is well above the rate of growth of the *total* GDP of less than 1 percent in India during the same period.[4] Cha further observes (p. 289) that

> contrary to the popular claim of South Korea growing out of the ashes left by the Korean War (1950–53), it seems undeniable that the South Korean economy rose on the shoulders of the colonial achievement, which included physical and human capital as well as key institutions such as property rights and markets.

Following the student-led revolution in April 1960 that ousted Rhee, Chang Myon was elected prime minister of South Korea. But his tenure was short-lived, with General Park Chung Hee abruptly terminating it in a coup d'état on May 6, 1961. Park's central objective upon assuming power was to beat North Korea in the race for economic prosperity. At the time, North Korea, whose per-capita income was estimated to be double that of South Korea, seemed to be winning the race.[5] Park quickly moved to introduce a series of economic reforms (to be described below) and to create institutions necessary to implement these reforms that placed South Korea on an exceptionally high growth trajectory.

Korea's annual per-capita GDP at current prices was barely $79 in 1960. But it rose to $248 in 1970, $1632 in 1980, and $5199 in 1989 (Harvie and Lee, 2003, table 1). In 1960, Korea started with a real per-capita income below that of Haiti, which is currently classified as a least developed country by the United Nations, and comfortably crossed the upper-middle-income level by the late 1980s.[6] As table 6.1,

TABLE 6.1: Annual Growth Rates of GNP and Average Real Wage in Korea

			Annual Percentage Change in			
Year	GNP	Average Real Wage	Year	GNP	Average Real Wage
1960	2.3	−14.1	1977	10.7	23.7
1961	4.2	4.8	1978	11	20.2
1962	3.5	1	1979	7	10.3
1963	9.1	−5.4	1980	−4.8	−6
1964	9.6	−6	1981	6.6	−1.2
1965	5.8	4.3	1982	5.4	7.5
1966	12.7	6.2	1983	11.9	8.8
1967	6.6	11.3	1984	8.4	5.8
1968	11.3	16.5	1985	5.4	7.4
1969	13.8	22.2	1986	11.7	6.4
1970	7.6	9.8	1987	13	8.6
1971	9.1	2.7	1988	12.4	12.5
1972	5.3	2.2	1989	6.8	19.4
1973	14	14.9	1990	9.3	11.6
1974	8.5	11	1963–73	9.5	7.2
1975	6.8	1.7	1974–82	7.2	9.6
1976	13.4	19.4	1983–90	9.9	10.1

Note: The changes in the average real wages are obtained by subtracting the change in the Consumer Price Index from the average nominal wage. The wage during 1960–70 relates to manufacturing wages.

Source: Economic Planning Board, *Major Statistics of the Korean Economy* (various issues). As cited in Yoo (1997, table 1), from which this table is excerpted.

based on Yoo (1997, table 1), shows, the Korean economy took off in 1963 and went on to register average growth rates of real GNP of 9.5 percent during 1963–73, 7.2 percent during 1974–82, and 9.9 percent during 1983–90.[7]

During these years of rapid growth, the Korean economy also underwent a dramatic structural transformation, with shares of agriculture in GDP and employment declining and those of manufacturing rising sharply. Table 6.2, excerpted from Yoo (1997), captures this transformation. The share of agriculture, forestry, and fisheries in the Korean GDP fell from 37 percent in 1960 to 26 percent in 1970, to 15 percent in 1980, and to 9 percent in 1990. While the share of industry in general rose, the most dramatic gains were made by manufacturing, which rose from 14 percent in 1960 to 21 percent in 1970 and to 31 percent in 1980.[8] In an economy that had been growing 8 percent per year overall, the sharp rise in the share of manufacturing during 1960–80 implies a very rapid expansion of manufacturing in absolute terms. According to Yoo (1997, p. 8), manufacturing growth averaged a hefty 16 percent during the 1960s and 1970s.

These changes in sectoral output shares were reflected in the employment shares. According to table 6.2, the employment share of manufacturing rose from 9.4 percent in 1965 to 22 percent in 1980 and to 27 percent in 1990. The share of agriculture, forestry, and fisheries declined from 58.6 percent to 18.3 percent of the total employment between 1965 and 1990. This shift in employment was accompanied

TABLE 6.2: Sectoral Shares in the GDP and Employment in Korea

Year	Agriculture Forestry & Fisheries	Mining	Manufacturing	Other
A. Gross Domestic Product by Sector (as percent of GDP)				
1960	36.9	2.1	13.6	47.4
1965	38.7	1.8	17.7	41.8
1970	25.8	1.3	21	51.9
1975	24.9	1.4	26.6	47.1
1980	15.1	1.4	30.6	52.9
1985	13.9	1.5	29.2	55.3
1990	9.1	0.5	29.2	61.2
B. Employment by Sector (as percent of total employment)				
1960	68.3	0.3	1.5	29.9
1965	58.6	0.9	9.4	31.1
1970	50.4	1.1	13.1	35.4
1975	45.7	0.5	18.6	35.2
1980	34	0.9	21.6	43.5
1985	24.9	1	23.4	50.7
1990	18.3	0.4	26.9	54.4

Source: Economic Planning Board, *Major Statistics of Korean Economy* (various issues), and Bank of Korea, *Economic Statistics Yearbook 1962*. As cited by Yoo (1997, table 2), from which this table is taken.

by substantial increases in wages—approximately 7 to 8 percent annually during 1961–81. Thus, Korea was entirely transformed from a primarily agricultural to a primarily industrial nation, and from a basket case of sorts to an upper-middle-income economy, in a matter of 30 years.

THE CENTRALITY OF TRADE OPENNESS IN KOREA'S TRANSFORMATION

Most experts, including many who view industrial targeting as an important key to Korea's success, consider outward orientation as the single most important element in Korea's development strategy.[9] But this view is not universally shared. In particular, following the lead of Amsdan (1989) and Wade (1990), Rodrik (1995) argues that Korea grew rapidly during the 1960s and 1970s because its government "managed to engineer a significant increase in the private return to capital" by "subsidizing and coordinating investment decisions." In his story, the expansion of trade was merely a passive outcome of the process unleashed by this expansion of investment: New investments required machinery that had to be imported, and increased imports necessitated increased exports.

For starters, we can question the basic premise underlying this description of the Korean experience. During 1961–80, Korea's exports of goods and services grew at an annual rate of 23.7 percent in real terms. Even though Korea began at a relatively low exports to GDP ratio of 5.3 percent in 1961, by 1980 that ratio had reached

33.1 percent.[10] This dramatic growth in exports, which came in large part after 1965, had to be the outcome of an active policy change rather than a passive response to the government-coordinated investment boom. More important, the dramatic growth in exports had to be a significant stimulus to the economy at the margin. The efficiency gains that accrue from competing against the most efficient producers in the world and from accessing state-of-the-art technology via imports of new products and machinery had to be of primary importance.

Westphal and Kim (1982), who provided one of the first careful and comprehensive analyses of the Korean experience and take a favorable view of the infant industry protection and industrial targeting, assign a central role to activist trade policy in stimulating growth in Korea. Consider the following statement from the concluding section of their study (p. 271):

> The growth of manufactured exports over the fifteen years from 1960 to 1975 contributed to Korea's industrial development in various ways. Export expansion was directly responsible for more than one quarter of the growth of manufactured output and for an even larger fraction of the increase in manufactured [sic] employment. In turn, the manufacturing sector has accounted for almost 40 percent of the growth in both GNP and employment. These figures understate the contribution of export growth. They do not reflect the backward linkages to domestically produced intermediate inputs, the multiplier effect resulting from increased consumption and investment resulting from additional income earned, or the increase in economic efficiency that results from exporting in accordance with a country's comparative advantage.

Thus, Westphal and Kim turn the Rodrik story almost on its head, partially attributing the growth in investment itself to export growth and the income increase stimulated by it. Subsequently, in his review article in the *Journal of Economic Perspectives* titled "Industrial Policy in an Export-Propelled Economy: Lessons from South Korea's Experience," Westphal (1990) notes:

> Korea's industrial performance owes a great deal to the government's promotional policies toward exports and to its initiatives in targeting industries for development. If nothing else, policies toward exports have created an atmosphere—rare in the Third World—in which businessmen could be certain that the economic system would respond to and subsequently reward their efforts aimed at expanding and upgrading exports.

In the view of Westphal, exports were not a passive response to the import demand generated by the investment boom, but one of the "propellers" of the investment activity itself.

That exports were central to the economic transformation also follows from the fact that the changes in their sectoral distribution mirrored the changes in the sectoral distribution of output and employment. This is shown in table 6.3, abstracted from Yoo (1997, table 3). In 1962, labor-intensive light manufactures (SITC categories 6 and 8) such as clothing, footwear, travel goods, textiles, leather goods, and simple fabricated metals accounted for only 15 percent of the total exports, which amounted to a low $55 million. On the other hand, primary products (SITC categories 0, 1, 2, and 4) accounted for three-fourths of the total exports. But the labor-intensive light manufactures accounted for much of the expansion of exports in the remainder of the 1960s, with their share in total exports rising to a hefty 69 percent in 1970. In

TABLE 6.3: Total Korean Exports and Imports, and Their Composition (percent)

SITC Category	1962	1965	1970	1975	1980	1985	1990
Exports							
0 & 1	40.2	16.6	9.5	13.2	7.3	4.2	3.3
2 & 4	35.4	21.2	12	2.8	2	1	1.5
3	5	1.1	1	2.2	0.3	3.1	1.1
5	1.8	0.2	1.4	1.3	4.3	3.1	3.9
6 & 8	14.8	57.6	68.6	65.2	65.6	50.9	50.7
7	2.6	3.1	7.4	15	20.3	37.6	39.3
Total ($ million)	55	175	835	5,081	17,505	30,283	65,016
Imports							
0 & 1	11.6	13.7	16.2	13.2	8.5	4.7	4.9
2 & 4	22.2	24.5	21.2	16.1	16.8	12.9	12.6
3	7.3	6.7	6.9	19.1	29.9	23.6	15.8
5	22.4	22.3	8.3	10.7	8.1	9	10.6
6 & 8	19.8	16.8	17.8	14.2	14.1	15.4	21.2
7	16.5	15.9	29.7	26.5	22.4	34.2	34.3
Total ($ million)	422	463	1,984	7,274	22,292	31,136	69,844
Trade Balance							
Total ($ million)	−367	−288	−1,149	−2,193	−4,787	−853	−4,828
As % of imports	−87.0	−62.2	−57.9	−30.1	−21.5	−2.7	−6.9

Note: The SITC categories are defined as follows: 0, Food & Live Animals; 1, Beverages; 2, Inedible Crude Materials; 3, Mineral Fuels, Lubricants; 4, Animal & Vegetable Oils; 5, Chemicals; 6, Classified Manufactured Goods; 7, Machinery; 8, Miscellaneous Manufactures.

Source: Yoo (1997, table 3).

the 1970s, partially as a result of a policy shift, machinery exports grew more rapidly, so that by 1980, the share of light manufactures declined slightly to 66 percent of total exports and that of machinery rose to 20 percent. This means that by 1980, manufactures other than chemicals had come to account for more than 85 percent of Korea's exports.

It is important to note here that the outward orientation story of Korea is not a mercantilist one whereby the country pushed exports for their own sake. At least at the aggregate level, Korea was as much open to imports as it was keen to push exports. Throughout the period covered in table 6.3, Korea ran a trade deficit, meaning its imports exceeded its exports. In the second half of the 1960s, this deficit accounted for more than half of Korea's imports. In turn, the deficit was largely accounted for by external borrowing. Compositionally, imports were not concentrated in just machinery (SITC category 7), as the Rodrik story would imply. Instead, they included large volumes of inedible crude materials and oils as well as light manufactures.

But suppose we grant Rodrik the point that it was the successful coordination of the investment decisions by the government that triggered Korea's growth. Does this diminish the importance of outward-oriented trade policies that Korea pursued? In other words, what would have happened if Korea had chosen to continue to raise trade barriers and moved deeper into import substitution by attempting to produce all of the machinery on its own to undertake the investments?

The answer to this question is provided by India, which had been pursuing the strategy of ever deepening import substitution at the same time that Korea was switching to a more outward-oriented strategy. As we have seen in the previous chapters, India definitely tried to solve the investment coordination problem through explicit investment planning from the 1950s onward. Public interventions in India were surely successful, with the total investment as a proportion of the GDP rising from 15.7 percent in 1960–61 to 22.7 percent in 1980–81. Public investment consistently accounted for more than a third of this investment.

Through macroeconomic stability, policy credibility, and legal institutions capable of enforcing contracts, India was successful in pushing its GDP growth rate from less than 1 percent during the first half of the twentieth century to the 3–4 percent range during 1950–80. But it came nowhere near the ultra-high growth rates experienced by Korea during the 1960s and 1970s principally because it opted for an increasingly protectionist trade policy regime with nearly all imports coming under strict licensing by the early 1970s. By the mid-1970s, India's trade regime had become so repressive that imports (other than oil and cereals) had fallen from the already low level of 7 percent of GDP in 1957–58 to 3 percent in 1975–76.

Whereas Korea recognized the importance of competing against the world's most efficient producers and the need for importing state-of-the-art machinery from abroad, India chose to hide behind a steel wall of protection, manufacturing its own machinery (and steel!). Thus, Rodrik's assertion that outward orientation of the Korean economy was merely the result of the increase in the demand for imported capital goods misses the important point that ultimately such openness was the result of a conscious policy choice. Had Korea chosen to take the same path as India and opted for autarkic policies to block the flow of international trade, its miraculous growth would have been choked despite its presumed success in coordinating the investment decisions.

Differences between the experiences of Korea and India during the 1960s and 1970s are to be seen not just in terms of the outcome variables, such as growth in trade and GDP, but also in terms of policies and policy changes. Whereas Korea consciously moved away from import substitution to an outward-oriented trade regime relatively early in the game, India became progressively protectionist. In the case of Korea, it is once again instructive to quote Westphal and Kim (1982, p. 214):

> Until the early 1960s, Korea followed a protectionist strategy of import substitution for non-durable consumer goods. Once import substitution could go no further in these areas, the government had to decide whether to continue with an inward-looking strategy but shift to import substitution for intermediate and durable goods, or whether to adopt an outward-looking strategy providing equal incentive to exports and import substitution. On the whole, it opted for the latter.

As previously noted, the 1950s, which began with the Korean War, had been characterized by inward-looking import-substitution industrialization. The exchange rate was highly overvalued, leading to a large excess of imports over exports each year. Foreign exchange controls were widely practiced, finished consumer goods were subject to high tariffs, and the government relied progressively on quantitative import controls. The main incentive to exporters was the sale of foreign exchange in the free market.

In 1957, the U.S. aid peaked, and steadily declined thereafter. Therefore, when Park assumed the reins of power, one of his key concerns was to look for alternative sources of foreign exchange. It was decided that further import substitution into consumer durables, machinery, and intermediate inputs used in them was not a viable option because of the small size of the domestic market and the large capital requirements it entailed. An export-oriented strategy was the only viable option. The strategy also sat well with the international financial institutions, which Korea hoped to enlist as a source of finance in the face of declining U.S. assistance.

Several measures were taken to boost exports in the first half of the 1960s. The Korean won was devalued from 65 won per U.S. dollar to 130 won per dollar in 1961 and again to 256 won per dollar in 1964. Profits on exports were taxed at only half the regular rate from 1962 to 1973. Up to 1975, accelerated depreciation was allowed for assets used in exports. Tariff and indirect domestic tax exemptions on inputs used in exports were also allowed. Exporters were given automatic access to bank credit at highly preferential rates. In the mid-1960s, the margin of preference over the market rate was as much as 20 percentage points.[11]

Korean policymakers recognized that if the protection level was kept high, producers would continue to have greater incentive to sell their products in the domestic rather than the export market. This led them to undertake import liberalization as well. Korea joined the GATT in 1967. It also replaced its positive list of imports allowed without a license by a negative list. Protection on the manufacturing sector declined substantially during this period.

In 1962, Korea set up an export targeting system. Export targets were agreed between the government and the firms. A failure to meet the targets resulted in heavy administrative sanctions. But in the vast majority of the cases, exports exceeded the targets by a wide margin, so that targets turned out to be nonbinding. Because large firms were at an advantage in meeting the quality and timely delivery standards in the world markets, the emphasis on exports led to their greater expansion. The government reinforced this advantage by giving the larger firms greater preference in credit.[12]

As discussed in chapter 3, trade policy in India during the 1960s and 1970s bore a sharp contrast to this Korean approach. To recapitulate, India started with a relatively open trade regime in 1950 and did not begin turning inward until a foreign exchange crisis in 1957–58. Tariffs were low; quantitative import restrictions, though present on account of having been inherited from the Second World War, were not onerous; and, foreign exchange reserves being comfortable, there was no evidence of foreign exchange controls being practiced. But following the crisis, foreign exchange budgeting was introduced, which led to progressive tightening of imports as well as industrial licensing. This process continued until 1966, though some export subsidization schemes were introduced in 1962 and expanded subsequently to partially offset the discrimination against exports.

According to Bhagwati and Srinivasan (1975, p. 46), the effective export exchange rate was uniformly less than the effective import exchange rate across industries. This was partially redressed, starting in 1962, through export subsidization schemes, but the change did not go far enough. One of the important side effects of the requirement that domestically produced inputs be used when available was that exportable items had to be manufactured with inferior inputs and capital equipment.

In turn, this had a detrimental effect on product quality and placed exporters at considerable disadvantage in the highly competitive world markets.

During 1966–68, India went through a brief liberalization episode. In June 1966, the rupee was devalued by 57.5 percent, from 4.7 rupees to 7.5 rupees per dollar. The devaluation was accompanied by some liberalization of import licensing, cuts in import tariffs, and export subsidies. Because the devaluation turned into a serious political liability (in part due to the widespread impression that the World Bank had forced it), the process of liberalization was quickly reversed. By 1969–70, the liberalization had been largely reversed, with the import premium back to 30 to 50 percent. Almost all liberalizing initiatives were reversed and import controls were tightened. This regime was consolidated and strengthened in subsequent years, and remained more or less intact until the beginning of a period of phased liberalization in the late 1970s.

To sum up, then, both Korea and India started with import substitution policies. India intervened at least as much as Korea—perhaps more—to boost investment, and was even successful in it. But after a short phase that was limited to the production of nondurable consumer goods and their inputs, Korea shifted to an export-oriented policy. India, on the other hand, continued to go deeper into import substitution, extending it to consumer durables, raw materials, and machinery. The policies had vastly different outcomes. GDP and trade in Korea grew at astronomical rates, while those in India grew at barely visible rates.

HEAVY AND CHEMICAL INDUSTRY DRIVE (1973–79)

In the early 1970s, Korea decided to move away from industry-neutral policies to a policy of selective targeting of heavy and chemical industries (HCI). The policy was initiated with a presidential announcement in January 1973 and ended with the announcement of the Comprehensive Stabilization Program in April 1979. The HCI drive aimed to develop industries that were seen as strategic and included steel, nonferrous metals, automobiles, shipbuilding, heavy machinery, and industrial electronics.

Origins of the Shift and Policy Instruments

At least three factors contributed to the switch in the policy. First, in 1971, the United States cut its forces in Korea by a third. The Korean government saw this move as the first phase of a full military withdrawal, and felt the need to develop certain strategic industries for defense purposes. Second, throughout the 1960s and early 1970s, Korea had experienced large and rising absolute trade deficits. Though exports had grown faster than imports, imports had grown from a much larger base, so the trade deficit kept rising. One element in the HCI drive was to contain this trade deficit by slowing the growth of imports. Finally, Korean policymakers felt that rising competition from other East Asian countries in light manufacturing and a growing protectionist sentiment in the developed countries against labor-intensive exports necessitated a shift into other sectors.[13]

The most important instrument deployed to stimulate the targeted industries was directed bank credit at low and sometimes negative real interest rates. The government directed the commercial banks that were largely state-owned to make loans to the favored industries and projects. According to Harvie and Lee (2003, p. 271), almost 60 percent of the bank loans and 75 percent of the manufacturing investment went to the targeted sectors over the course of the HCI drive. A substantial part of the investment was financed by external borrowing, which led to the expansion of foreign debt from 25 percent of the GNP in 1970 to 49 percent in 1980.

Other policy instruments deployed to promote the targeted industries included tax and trade policy concessions (Yoo, 1997, p. 6). The tax concessions included tax holidays, accelerated depreciation, and temporary tax credits for investment. The government also introduced a number of laws to accommodate these concessions. On the trade policy front, there was some reversal of the liberalization that had begun in the mid-1960s. In particular, some products were put back on the negative list and therefore were subject to approval for imports.

Why Revisionists Are Wrong

While the Korean economy grew at respectable rates during the HCI drive, the conclusion that this growth vindicates interventionism and casts doubt on the efficacy of pro-market, outward-oriented policies, drawn by the revisionists, is to be questioned for at least four reasons. First and foremost, when compared with the Indian interventionism, the Korean HCI drive was highly selective and largely relied on the market-based instruments. For the most part, the state did not get into manufacturing activity directly. Nor did it use licensing to regulate and restrict entry and investment in the sectors that were not selected for promotion. Instead, it relied on subsidies in the form of cheaper credit and tax breaks, which have natural limits on account of fiscal constraints. Moreover, the firms successful in taking advantage of the subsidies were among the more efficient, since the less efficient ones could not operate profitably even with the subsidy, and therefore never entered the production activity. This was unlike the interventions in India that vested the power to make decisions regarding entry and investment in the hands of bureaucrats, frequently on the basis of criteria unrelated to efficiency. And once a firm was granted license to operate, as much protection as was necessary to allow it to operate profitably was provided. Therefore, the scope for damage under the Korean policy regime was considerably less than in India.

Second and related to the first point, during 1963–73, real wages in Korea had grown rapidly, its savings rate had shot up, and education levels having risen, the labor force was substantially more skilled. All these factors had shifted the country's comparative advantage away from light manufacturing and toward skilled-labor and capital-intensive industries that were now being targeted. This meant that some shift toward the targeted industries would have taken place even in the absence of the interventionist policies. Viewed this way, in broad terms the targeting policies pushed resource allocation in the same direction that the market would have, except that it pushed faster and farther.[14]

Third, by the time Korea turned to the HCI drive, it had already sustained 9.5 percent annual growth of GNP for ten years, relying principally on industry-neutral export-oriented policies.[15] By 1973, Korea had established a generally open trade policy regime. Though some reversal did happen during the HCI drive and the real exchange rate appreciated, by the then prevailing standards Korea was still a low protection country. Moreover, the existence of an environment in which the success of entrepreneurs in the export market remained the litmus test, the firms benefiting from targeting had to become competitive in the world markets relatively quickly. This was almost entirely the opposite of the situation in India, where the licensing regime required firms to turn the product progressively indigenous by producing more and more components domestically, with virtually automatic protection granted from foreign competition against all components and final products. That the Korean firms did acquire a certain degree of competitiveness in the world markets is illustrated by the fact that the share of machinery exports (SITC category 7 in table 6.3) in Korea's total exports rose from 7 percent in 1970 to 20 percent in 1980, and that of chemicals (SITC category 5) rose from 1 percent to 4 percent over the same period.

Finally, as many observers (for example, Little, 1996; Bhagwati, 1999) have persuasively argued, at the margin, interventionism did damage the Korean economy.[16] The damage took the form of reduced growth, poorer export performance, and macroeconomic instability. The effect on growth was felt with a lag, with the GNP registering just 3.5 percent growth during 1979–82. Lest this seem too short a period and one that was characterized by political, natural, and external shocks (see below), the essential story is unchanged when we focus on the longer pre- and post-HCI periods. Thus, the average annual growth rate during 1963–73, at 9.5 percent, was more than two percentage points higher than that during 1974–82, at 7.2 percent. On the margin, targeting did shave more than two percentage points off the growth rate annually.

Little (1996) further points out that the performance of interventionist Korea fell short of other less interventionist countries, such as Hong Kong, Singapore, and Taiwan, which also relied on an outward-oriented strategy. It is useful here to quote Little (1996, p. 12):[17]

> [The revisionists] do not question the proposition that industrial policy was successful [because government leadership fixed some market failure or another]. To quote Wade (1990, pp. 305–06):
>
> ...the balance of presumption must be that government industrial policies, including sectoral ones, helped more than hindered. To argue otherwise is to suppose that that economic performance would have been still more exceptional with less intervention which is simply less plausible than the converse.
>
> Since the less interventionist Hong Kong, Singapore, and Taiwan grew faster than Korea, it is unclear why Wade thinks it simply less plausible that less intervention would have been better, given also the widespread failure of government industrial policies elsewhere. I find it simply more plausible that Korea grew fast despite its industrial policies, than because of them.

Yoo (1997, p. 10) offers further evidence supporting the view advanced by Little and casting doubt on the success of the HCI drive. He points out that real export growth of Korea started to decelerate sharply in 1977, to the point that real export volume fell in absolute terms in 1979. More important, he finds that Korea's performance in the OECD markets deteriorated relative to that of Taiwan, which was at approximately the same stage of development as Korea and shared many of the latter's economic characteristics, including scarcity of natural resources and outward-oriented strategy of development. Specifically, Yoo finds that Korea's share in the OECD manufactures imports fell in 1979 and 1980, whereas that of Taiwan continued to rise. When Yoo decomposes manufactures into light and heavy industry manufactures, he finds the decline originated in the declining share of light manufactures, which suffered on account of the targeting of heavy industry manufactures. What is interesting is that insofar as exports are concerned, favored sectors failed to compensate for the weaker performance in disfavored sectors.

The HCI drive also contributed to macroeconomic instability. As already noted, the investment expansion in the targeted industries had relied heavily on external borrowing, with the debt rising from 25 percent of GNP to 49 percent. In addition, the Korean construction companies profited hugely from the construction boom in the Middle East following the first oil price shock. They invested these profits in land in Korea, leading to a boom in land prices. The government also held the nominal exchange rate fixed to limit the domestic currency liabilities of these firms.[18] In the absence of an effective sterilization policy, the inflow of foreign money led to rapid monetary expansion and fueled inflation. As can be seen from table 6.1, the second half of the 1970s was characterized by a very rapid rise in the Consumer and Wholesale Price Indexes, accompanied by an even more rapid rise in wages. With the nominal exchange rate fixed, these changes implied substantial real appreciation of the domestic currency and a deterioration of export performance to the point that real export growth turned negative in 1979.[19]

STABILIZATION AND MORE LIBERALIZATION IN THE 1980s

The government announced the Comprehensive Stabilization Program on April 17, 1979. It effectively ended the HCI drive and provided for tighter fiscal and monetary management in the short run and liberalization in the long run. But President Park was assassinated in October 1979, leaving the country in a political turmoil. Prime Minister Choi Kyu Hwa became acting president but was replaced by General Chun Doo Hwan, under martial law, in May 1980. Alongside the political uncertainty created by these events, the second oil price crisis and a major crop failure resulting from a cold spell in the summer of 1980 added to the economic woes of the country. The Consumer Price Index rose 28.7 percent in 1980.

Chun was inaugurated as president in March 1981, and quickly embarked upon a program of economic stabilization and liberalization. A key element in the policy was to return the economy to a neutral regime, as had been the case until the early 1970s. Having been held at 484 won per dollar since 1974, the domestic currency was devalued to 660 won per dollar in 1980. In the following years, the government let the won depreciate in small increments, with the exchange rate successively changing to 701, 749, 796, 827, and 890 won per dollar in the following five years.[20] Other stabilization measures were taken that helped bring inflation down to the levels experienced in the second half of the 1960s and the early 1970s.

The 1980s also saw trade and financial liberalization in Korea. While there had been some minimal trade liberalization in 1979, the process stalled partially due to the balance of payments difficulties in the early 1980s. In 1983, the Tariff Reform

Committee was set up, which outlined a phased program of import liberalization. The recommendations of this committee resulted in a reduction in the average nominal tariff rate from 24 percent in 1983 to 19 percent in 1988 and 11 percent in 1990. Many of the tariff exemptions for the strategic industries were withdrawn in 1984. U.S. pressure played an important role in this import liberalization.

The promotion of strategic industries through preferential credit and tax treatment came to an end in the early 1980s. Preferential interest rates that had been applicable to strategic industries and exporters were officially abolished in June 1982. The list of industries classified as strategic was trimmed, and the concessions now took the form of tax breaks on technology development. The 1980s saw a major drive for upgrading of technology, principally through the instrumentality of research and development by private firms. One policy instrument deployed for this purpose was the liberalization of the foreign direct investment (FDI) regime. In 1980, Korea liberalized regulations to facilitate FDI as a means of upgrading technology. In 1984, it switched from a positive list to a negative list approach, meaning that the sectors not included on the negative list were now open to FDI.

Finally, starting in the early 1980s, Korea undertook substantial financial sector liberalization. The measures included privatization of commercial banks, unrestricted entry of nonbank financial institutions, relaxation of directed credit, abolition of preferential interest rates for strategic or export industries, the introduction of new financial instruments, and the opening of the financial sector to FDI. While the government continued to exert controls over the sector in a variety of forms, there is no denying that the direction was toward liberalization and greater autonomy. The outcome was a rapid growth of the sector, with total credit rising from 68 percent of the GNP in 1980 to 94 percent in 1984.

Overall growth in the 1980s returned to the pre-HCI levels. The GNP grew at the rate of 9.1 percent during 1981–90. If we exclude the first two years from this period, which were characterized by relatively low growth rates due to the lagged effect of the HCI years, the growth rate during 1983–90 jumps to 9.9 percent. This higher growth rate over the HCI years reinforces the conclusion, drawn earlier, that the targeting had a negative, not a positive, effect on the margin.

SAVINGS AND INVESTMENT

So far I have said nothing about savings and investment. As one would expect, the superior performance of Korea took place in the presence of substantially higher savings and investment ratios than in India. This is shown in table 6.4. Korea began with an extremely low savings rate, the bulk of its investment financed through aid. For instance, during the first three years of the 1960s, its savings rate was below 4 percent, while investment ranged between 11 and 13 percent. On the average, Korea had received $280 million per year in economic aid and another $220 million per year in military aid between 1956 and 1962 (Lim 2000, p. 13). Given that the nominal GDP of Korea in 1962 was only $2.3 billion (Harvie and Lee, 2003, table 1), economic aid alone averaged more than 12 percent of the nominal GDP during this period. Comparing this figure to the investment rates in the years 1960–62 in table 6.4, on average, economic aid may have slightly exceeded total investment!

TABLE 6.4: Savings and Investment Ratios

	India*		Korea*	
	Savings	Investment	Savings	Investment
1960–61	11.6	12.7	0.8	10.9
1961–62	11.7	13.4	2.8	13.2
1962–63	12.7	13.8	3.3	12.8
1963–64	12.3	14.2	8.7	18.1
1964–65	11.9	14.1	8.7	14.0
1965–66	14	15.1	7.4	15.0
1966–67	14	14.9	11.8	21.6
1967–68	11.9	14	11.4	21.9
1968–69	12.2	14	15.1	25.9
1969–70	14.3	14	18.8	28.8
1970–71	14.6	14	16.2	24.6
1971–72	15.1	14.7	14.5	25.1
1972–73	14.6	15.3	15.7	20.9
1973–74	16.8	14	21.4	24.7
1974–75	16	14.4	19.3	31.8
1975–76	17.2	16.2	16.9	27.5
1976–77	19.4	17.3	22.2	25.7
1977–78	19.8	17.2	25.4	27.7
1978–79	21.5	17.4	27.3	31.9
1979–80	20.1	17.9	26.5	36.0
1980–81	18.9	18.5	20.8	32.1
1981–82	18.6	18.9	20.5	30.3
1982–83	18.3	19.2	20.9	28.6
1983–84	17.6	18.8	25.3	29.9
1984–85	18.8	19.6	27.9	31.9
1985–86	19.5	20.6	28.6	31.1

*In the case of India, the year shown is its fiscal year. In the case of Korea, a year such as 1960–61 refers to the calendar year 1960.

Source: Ministry of Finance, *Economic Survey* (2002–03) for India, and Bank of Korea for Korea. As cited in Harvie and Lee (2003, table 1) from which the data are excerpted.

In comparison, India's savings rates closely tracked its investment rate during this period, and the latter closely tracked the Korea investment rates.

But once Korea switched to an outward-oriented strategy, its savings and investment rates began to climb rapidly. The investment rate rose to 25 percent in 1970 and to 32 percent in 1978, then stayed there with some fluctuations. By 1985, the savings rate had climbed to 28–29 percent. India also experienced a rise in its savings and investment rates, but it was at a much slower pace and far more modest. The investment rate rose to 14–15 percent in the mid-1960s and stayed there until the mid-1970s. In the mid-1970s, the rate began to rise again, reaching approximately 20 percent in the mid-1980s.

Krugman (1994) and others have agued that there is nothing special or miraculous about the high growth rates in East Asia, including South Korea: They all resulted from very high investment rates, which in turn resulted from high savings rates. The argument is based on productivity analysis that shows that the growth in the factors of production is able to explain virtually all of the observed growth in the

GDP, with productivity growth being negligible. If one were to accept this position at face value, the differences between the performances of India and Korea could also be attributed to the differences between their investment, and hence their savings, rates.

But Bhagwati (1999) has rightly pointed out that even if we explain the miracle of high growth in terms of factor accumulation, there still remains a miracle of high investment to be explained. He goes on to hypothesize that the outward-oriented strategy adopted by the countries in East Asia provided substantial inducement to invest through access to the large world markets. In contrast, the import substitution (IS) strategy adopted by India impaired rapid capital accumulation by limiting the demand to the domestic market, whose growth was limited principally by the relatively low agricultural growth. To quote Bhagwati (1999, p. 17 in the Web version):

> The elimination of the "bias against exports," and indeed a net (if mild) excess of the effective rate for exports over the effective exchange rate for imports (signifying the relative profitability of the foreign over the home market), ensured that the world markets were profitable to aim for, assuring in turn that the inducement to invest was no longer constrained by the growth of domestic market as in the IS strategy.

To the hypothesis provided by Bhagwati, we may add that as an empirical matter, the savings rates are positively related to incomes, at least up to a point. As we have seen in the previous chapters, savings rates in India have risen progressively with increases in incomes. The same has been true of Korea and other East Asian economies. Indeed, the more rapid growth in Korea, starting from approximately the same initial per-capita income as India, produced higher savings rates as well.

CONCLUSION

The growth rate in India during what I have called phase I (4.1 percent) was not markedly different from that of Korea during the same time period. But there are two reasons why the performance of the Indian economy during this period can be regarded as superior to that of Korea. First, during the Japanese occupation (1910–45), Korea had already achieved the growth rate of 4 percent. Thus, the performance of the economy during the 1950s and early 1960s showed no significant improvement over what had been achieved and sustained in the preceding four decades. India, on the other hand, had grown less than 1 percent per annum during the first half of the twentieth century. Thus, its growth rate of 4.1 percent represented a marked improvement over what had been achieved earlier. Second, in relation to its GNP, Korea received massive foreign aid during this period. Economic aid alone exceeded 10 percent of its GNP throughout. India, on the other hand, relied mostly on its domestic savings. It was only toward the late 1950s that aid poured in, in significant amounts, but even then it never exceeded 2 to 3 percent of the GDP.

But the tables clearly got turned as India entered phase II. Korea made a decisive turn toward outward-oriented policies that were also neutral across industries, and managed to accelerate the growth rate to 9.5 percent during 1963–73. India, on the other hand, made a halfhearted attempt at liberalization in the early-to-mid-1960s, abandoned it, and turned progressively more inward and interventionist. The outcome was a drop in the growth rate during 1965–81 to 3.2 percent. Though Korea also pursued a more interventionist policy of industrial targeting during 1973–79, it did so in a relatively open trading environment and largely relied on market-based instruments. As a result, it was still able to grow at 7.2 percent during 1974–82.

The experience during phase III was quite similar: India finally began to turn away from inward-oriented, interventionist policies, albeit very gradually, and found its growth rate returning to what it had achieved in phase I. Since the change was from a very high level of intervention, growth rose to only 4.8 percent in phase III (1981–88). Korea also abandoned industrial targeting, and introduced further liberalization with expected results: The growth rate returned to the 9 percent-plus level.

In concluding, it may be emphasized that the revisionists have greatly overstated the role of interventionism in Korea. The truth is that even during the peak of interventionist policies during 1973–79, the trade regime in Korea was quite open by the standards of the time. This meant that even the firms in the targeted sectors were subject to the discipline of the world markets. Moreover, interventions on behalf of the targeted sectors were generally market-based. All this was in stark contrast to India, where the trade regime came close to being autarkic and allocation was done by bureaucratic decision throughout the licensing regime.

PART II

Poverty, Inequality, and Economic Reforms

7

DECLINING POVERTY
The Human Face of Reforms

After a careful review of the available evidence, Gary Fields (1980, p. 204) described the state of poverty in India in 1980 in the following stark terms:

> India is a miserably poor country. Per-capita yearly income is under $100. Of the Indian people, 45 percent receive incomes below $50 per year and 90 percent below $150. Of the total number of absolutely poor in the world (according to the AID data in Table 1.1), more than half are Indian. During the 1960s, per capita private consumer expenditure grew by less than ½ percent per annum. India's poverty problem is so acute and her resources so limited that it is debatable whether any internal policy change short of a major administrative overhaul and radical redirection of effort might be expected to improve things substantially.

Though the piecemeal changes in the policy that would soon prove Fields wrong were already under way when he offered this diagnosis and prognosis, his gloom was not without foundation. It had been three long decades since India had launched its development program, but it was yet to register significant sustained reduction in poverty. All evidence pointed to persistent and high proportions of the poor in the population.

But as the 1980s unfolded, India began to emerge out of the slow growth it had experienced, especially in phase II. And as the growth rate shifted upward, poverty began to decline as well. The process continued through the 1990s, with the proportion of the poor in the population cut approximately in half between the late 1970s and 2000. As we will see later in this chapter, precise numbers on poverty remain controversial and crucially depend on the data and methodology used to derive them. But the broad conclusion that poverty has declined substantially since the early 1980s is irrefutable.

Unemployment almost always has salience in the policy debates. Yet its measurement with any degree of accuracy is difficult in a country such as India. Almost 90 percent of its labor force is employed in either agriculture or the informal sector. Work in these sectors is associated with disguised unemployment, which is harder to measure than open unemployment.[1] Therefore, any evidence on unemployment in India must be taken with a grain of salt. In my judgment, a more fruitful avenue is to study the pressures in the labor market as reflected in wages, an issue I consider in greater detail than unemployment in this chapter. Also important are the human development indexes such as infant mortality, life expectancy, and literacy rates. I consider them briefly toward the end of the chapter as well.

A particularly disturbing development in recent years has been a rise in the suicide rates among male farmers. Because this increase has coincided with the deepening of economic reforms, some observers have attributed it to this. I review the systematic scholarly studies of the causes of farm suicides and conclude that the evidence does not support this link. But more work is required to fully understand the causes of the acceleration to arrive at policy measures necessary to arrest and reverse the phenomenon.

An issue of concern to some scholars recently has been that even though poverty has declined with reforms, increased openness to trade by itself may have moved it in the opposite direction. But the latest work of Hasan, Mitra, and Ural (2007) points in the opposite direction, showing that the effect of openness in India has been to lower rather than to increase poverty. Later in the chapter, I will review this debate in careful detail. Here, I begin with a conceptual discussion of the relationship among openness, growth, and poverty alleviation.

OPENNESS, GROWTH, AND POVERTY ALLEVIATION

Though the link among openness, growth, and poverty alleviation is disputed by some, most economists believe that trade openness alleviates poverty both directly and through faster economic growth. The direct effect works through at least two channels. First, we have what trade economists call the Stolper-Samuelson effect. Labor-abundant economies have a comparative advantage in labor-intensive goods. Hence, these are the goods they export. Protection makes the import-competing goods more attractive to produce. In turn, this pushes down the demand for labor and, hence, wages. Removal of trade barriers reverses this process and increases the price of labor-intensive goods and, hence, wages. In India, this effect was strong, with labor-intensive sectors miserably failing to emerge as dynamic exporters. Second, typically, protectionist policies discriminate against agriculture, which employs the bulk of the poor. Liberalization removes this discrimination and is thus likely to benefit the poor. This effect was perhaps not very strong in the past, partially because the policies aimed at the Green Revolution, including price supports, partially offset the bias arising out of the trade policy, but also because the world market in agriculture did not offer huge opportunities in the 1950s and 1960s. But with the current move toward ending protection and subsidies in agriculture worldwide, the end to any bias against exportable agricultural products in trade policy offers an additional route to poverty alleviation.

The indirect effect, which works through growth, is much more powerful. It works through at least three channels. First, growth leads to what Jagdish Bhagwati

(1988) calls the active "pull-up" effect rather than what skeptics call the passive "trickle-down" effect. I have documented (Panagariya, 2004e) that economies that have managed to push the per-capita growth rate to 3 percent or more on a sustained basis have almost always managed to lower the proportion of those living below a specified poverty line. Such economies rapidly absorb the poor into gainful employment and out of marginal jobs. Rising rural and urban wages in India during the 1980s and 1990s offer evidence of the rising demand for labor outstripping supply. Second, rapidly growing economies generate vast fiscal resources that allow governments to undertake targeted antipoverty programs. The Employment Guarantee Scheme introduced in India in 2005 was clearly an example of growth yielding the necessary revenues for poverty alleviation programs. In contrast, stagnant economies rob the government of its ability to fight poverty through such programs. Finally, growth that helps raise incomes of poor families also improves their ability to access public services such as education and health care. Even if the government builds schools and offers free education, however, poor families may fail to take advantage of it because children must work to help the family earn two square meals a day.

One may argue that ultimately, the question of whether trade openness helps or hurts the poor is an empirical question. This is certainly valid, and I will return to the available empirical evidence from India later in this chapter. While this evidence is supportive of the view articulated above, it is important to note that establishing causation conclusively in econometric work is often very difficult, so that economic argumentation offers a useful complement.

PHASES I AND II: THREE DECADES OF GOOD INTENTIONS BUT POOR PERFORMANCE

It is sometimes asserted that since the mid-1950s, developing countries have placed undue emphasis on growth and neglected poverty alleviation. This is definitely not true of India. Poverty alleviation was always the central goal of the policy in India, with growth viewed as a means rather than an end in itself. While evidence for this can be found even in many pre-independence documents, the First Five-Year Plan perhaps offers a good starting point.[2] In the fourth paragraph, the plan states:

> The urge to economic and social change under present conditions comes from the fact of poverty and of inequalities in income, wealth, and opportunity. The elimination of poverty cannot, obviously, be achieved merely by redistributing existing wealth. Nor can a program aiming only at raising production remove existing inequalities. The two have to be considered together; only a simultaneous advance along both these lines can create the conditions in which the community can put forth its best efforts for promoting development.

By the time the Second Five-Year Plan was formulated, the Parliament had adopted explicit legislation aimed at promoting a "socialistic pattern" of society in the country. In chapter 2, the plan listed four key objectives: "sizeable increase in national income so as to raise the level of living in the country"; "rapid industrialization with particular emphasis on the development of basic and heavy industries";

"a large expansion of employment opportunities"; and "reduction of inequalities in income and wealth and a more even distribution of economic power." Thus, both growth and equity remained at the center of the plan.

Subsequently, Pant (1962), a member of the Planning Commission, prepared a 15-year plan (1961–76) that aimed at providing a "minimum level of living" for all Indians. The plan had two essential planks.[3] First, by appeal to the cross-section data available then, it concluded that the income distribution was relatively stable across different income levels: "[I]n countries at very different levels of development and with varying socio-political environments, the distribution of incomes follows a remarkably similar pattern, especially in respect of the proportion of incomes earned by the lowest three or four deciles of the population." Therefore, the plan advocated adopting growth as the key to alleviating poverty and recommended 7 percent annual growth.[4] Second, the plan identified 20 percent of the population as consisting of groups that were at best loosely integrated with the growing sectors of the economy. It recognized that growth would fail to perceptibly improve the lot of these groups. For them, the plan advocated the need for social safety nets and more targeted action.

While 7 percent annual growth was never adopted as a target, the concern for poverty and equity remained central to virtually all of the major policy documents issued by the government, including the Third, Fourth, and Fifth Five-Year Plans. Indeed, some of the key policies were adopted precisely with a view to promoting smaller entrepreneurs, curbing the concentration of economic power, and expanding employment opportunities. Preoccupation with growth and a lack of concern for the poor was, thus, not at the center of the failure of India to achieve substantial reduction in poverty until the 1980s. As I will discuss later, ironically, the key source of the failure was the preoccupation with equity and the confusion that the pursuit of equity is equivalent to the pursuit of poverty reduction that led to the adoption of policies that were both anti-growth and anti-poor.

India has had a long tradition of the study of poverty. The National Sample Survey (NSS), which generates the distribution of household expenditures at the state and national levels and in rural and urban areas, has been conducted regularly since 1950.[5] While this continuity allows us to study the evolution of poverty over a long period of time, the estimates have several well-known limitations. First, they are subject to the usual sampling and nonsampling errors, including those due to non-responses or biased responses. Second, the sample sizes and their duration have varied over time. The duration has ranged from as short as four months to a full year. The sample size has varied from fewer than 3000 to more than 100,000. Third, because many rounds are in the field for less than a year, seasonal variations can influence the responses and estimates. Likewise, because surveys are staggered within each round, different individuals register their responses at different times in a year. Fourth, the choice of the price index used to translate the poverty line from one year into another can greatly influence the poverty ratio. Fifth, the reference period for household consumption expenditures varies across items within the same round and sometimes may vary for the same commodities across rounds. Finally, estimates of per-capita expenditure in the NSS vary considerably from those generated by the National Accounts Surveys (NAS) and diverged considerably during the 1990s. As we will see later, the last three factors are at the heart of the controversies on poverty numbers in recent years.

Notwithstanding these limitations of the estimates, there is consensus among economists who have studied poverty in India that there was no significant reduction in poverty during at least the first 25 years of development. Table 7.1, which is drawn from Datt (1998, table 1, and 1999, table 1), supports this conclusion. The table reports the population below the official poverty line in rural and urban India and in the country as a whole. The poverty line underlying these calculations is 49 rupees per capita per month for rural India and 57 rupees per capita per month for urban India, at October 1973 to June 1974 all-India rural and urban prices, respectively.[6] An expert group appointed by the Planning Commission (1993) set these poverty lines.[7]

TABLE 7.1: The Rural, Urban, and National Poverty Ratios

NSS Round	Survey Period	Year	Head Count Index		
			Rural	Urban	National
3	Aug 51–Nov 52	1951–52	47.37	35.46	45.31
5	Dec 52–Mar 53	1952–53	48.21	40.14	46.80
7	Oct 53–Mar 54	1953–54	61.29	49.92	59.30
8	Jul 54–Mar 55	1954–55	64.24	46.19	61.07
10	Oct 55–May 56	1955–56	48.34	43.15	47.43
11	Aug 56–Feb 57	1956–57	58.86	51.45	57.55
13	Sept 57–May 58	1957–58	55.16	47.75	53.84
14	Jul 58–June 59	1958–59	53.26	44.76	51.75
15	Jul 59–Jun 60	1959–60	50.89	49.17	50.58
16	Jul 60–Aug 61	1960–61	45.40	44.65	45.27
17	Sept 61–Jul 62	1961–62	47.20	43.55	46.54
18	Feb 63–Jan 64	1963–64	48.53	44.83	47.85
19	Jul 64–Jun 65	1964–65	53.66	48.78	52.75
20	Jul 65–Jun 66	1965–66	57.60	52.90	56.71
21	Jul 66–Jun 67	1966–67	64.30	52.24	62.00
22	Jul 67–Jun 68	1967–68	63.67	52.91	61.60
23	Jul 68–Jun 69	1968–69	59.00	49.29	57.11
24	Jul 69–Jun70	1969–70	57.61	47.16	55.56
25	Jul 70–Jun 71	1970–71	54.84	44.98	52.88
27	Oct 72–Sept 73	1972–73	55.36	45.67	53.37
28	Oct 73–Jun 74	1973–74	55.72	47.96	54.00
32	Jul 77–Jun 78	1977–78	50.6	40.5	48.36
38	Jan 83–Dec 83	1983–84	45.31	35.65	43.00
42	Jul 86–Jun 87	1986–87	38.81	34.29	37.69
43	Jul 87–Jun 88	1987–88	39.23	36.2	38.47
44	Jul 88–Jun 89	1988–89	39.06	36.6	38.44
45	Jul 89–Jun 90	1989–90	34.3	33.4	34.07
46	Jul 90–Jun 91	1990–91	36.43	32.76	35.49
47	Jul 91–Dec 91	1991–92	37.42	33.23	36.34
48	Jan 92–Dec 92	1992–93	43.47	33.73	40.93
50	Jul 93–Jun 94	1993–94	36.66	30.51	35.04
51	July 94–June 95	1994–95	39.75	33.50	38.40
52	July 95–June 96	1995–95	37.46	28.04	35.00
53	Jan 97–Dec 97	1996–97	35.69	29.99	34.40

Sources: Datt (1998, table 1) for estimates until 1993–94; Datt (1999) for the last three years.

Starting in 1950, the NSS was conducted at least once a year until 1973–74. Starting in 1973–74, the government decided to replace the annual surveys with quinquennial (i.e., once every five years) surveys with very large samples.[8] Therefore, with some exceptions, table 7.1 reports the poverty ratio annually until 1973–74 and then at intervals of four or five years.[9]

The key message conveyed by table 7.1 is that the poverty ratio at the national level fluctuated during 1951–78 between 45.27 percent in 1960–61 and 62 percent in 1966–67, but did not show a clear trend. The absence of a trend is explicitly seen in figures 7.1 and 7.2, which place the national annual poverty ratios on bar graphs separating the years from 1951–52 to 1961–62 and those from 1963–64 to 1973–74.[10] The figures also insert the exponential trend lines for each of these periods. Trend growth rate in the poverty ratio turns out to be −0.2 percent per year during the first period and 1.34 percent during the second period. That is to say, the poverty ratio exhibited a slightly declining trend during 1951–62 and a slightly rising trend during 1963–74. The period 1951–74, taken as a whole, shows a slightly rising trend. Table 7.1 further shows the poverty ratio declining from 54 percent in 1973–74 to 48.4 percent in 1977–78, but it cannot be taken as a definite sign of a declining trend. It is only when we move into the 1980s that we begin to see a declining trend in the ratio. These conclusions hold true when we consider rural and urban poverty ratios separately.

The fundamental cause of the failure to achieve a reduction in the proportion of the poor in the total population during this period was, of course, slow growth. With the population growing at more than 2 percent per year, per-capita income grew at just a little above 1 percent during this period. While sustained growth in per-capita income at 3 percent or more almost always delivers poverty reduction, growth rates of 1 to 2 percent may or may not lead to such an outcome. At these low growth rates,

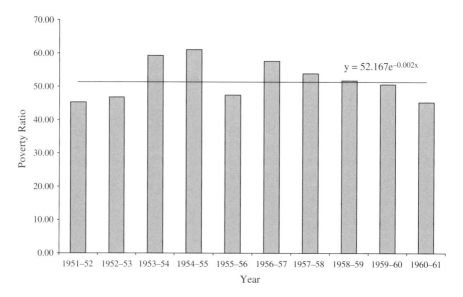

FIGURE 7.1: Poverty Trend: 1951–62

the pull-up effect may be too weak to pull a larger proportion of the poor at the margin than their average proportion in the population into gainful employment.

But there are perhaps two additional interrelated reasons why poverty did not decline with modestly rising incomes during the first three decades. First, the path to industrialization that India chose failed to produce rapid growth of labor-intensive industry, which could have generated well-paid jobs for the poor. Even before India had successfully completed the first stage of import substitution, which encourages the production of light manufacturing, such as clothing and footwear, and of the intermediate inputs used in them, it moved into heavy industry. In the subsequent years, it exhibited near obsession with diversification of production. Any product that could potentially be produced in the country was given automatic protection from imports. Likewise, under the Phased Manufacturing Program, firms were required to progressively replace the imported components with domestically sourced ones produced in-house or by other Indian firms. These policies led to a movement of the economy into industries that were farther and farther away from India's comparative advantage and were generally capital-intensive.

Second, the 15-year plan presented by Pant (1962) had laid out a clear strategy of rapid growth complemented by expenditures targeted at the bottom 20 percent of the population as the way to attack poverty. But, in practice, the government confused poverty alleviation with equity, and rather than target expenditures at the poor, it chose to control the incomes at the top. Thus, starting in the early 1970s, the expansion of big business houses was confined to a short list of relatively capital-intensive sectors in appendix I of the Industrial Policy Decision of 1973. The key mistake here was that poverty alleviation did not depend so much on who owned capital, or even how diversified the ownership was, but on whether profits were plowed back to boost the capital stock and whether such capital stock generated a large number

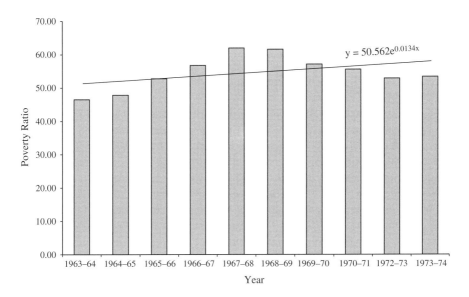

FIGURE 7.2: Poverty Trend: 1963–74

of jobs attractive to those employed in agriculture or informal services. Simultaneously, at the other extreme, the government went on to create a labor-rights regime in the organized sector that resulted in a very high cost of labor. In turn, this led larger firms to enter the production of capital-intensive heavy-industry products rather than labor-intensive light-industry products. It also led them to opt for more capital-intensive techniques of production on the average.

Reservation of the most labor-intensive products exclusively for production by small-scale units further stunted the growth of export-based, large-scale, labor-intensive industry that could have generated employment for the masses. Small enterprises had at best limited capacity to meet the quality standards required in the world market at competitive prices.

PHASES III AND IV: LIBERALIZING REFORMS AND SIGNIFICANT DECLINE IN POVERTY

As we have already discussed, phase III, spanning 1981–88, saw the growth rate rise to 4.8 percent from 3.2 percent in phase II. Fortuitously, this shift in the growth rate also coincided with a break in the poverty trend. As shown in table 7.1, the poverty ratio at the national level fell from 48.4 percent in 1977–78 to 43 percent in 1983–84, and to 38.5 percent in 1987–88. The same qualitative conclusion of declining poverty after 1977–78 applies if we consider the rural and urban poverty ratios separately. The estimates for all three of these years are based on the quinquennial thick samples, and are therefore likely to be more precise, ceteris paribus, than the estimates based on the annual, thin samples. Moreover, they are more directly comparable to one another than the estimates based on thin and thick samples. Broadly, there is no serious controversy in the literature on the proposition that phase III saw a decline in the poverty trend.

But phase IV is a different story. Here several controversies have arisen. Many of these controversies have evolved and progressed as successive NSS data have been collected and have become available to researchers. To carefully explain various twists and turns of the debate, a chronological approach turns out to be most convenient.

The initial controversy arose from the thin surveys following the 1993–94 thick survey. As table 7.1, shows, the national poverty ratio fell from 38.5 percent in 1987–88 to 35 percent in 1993–94, rose in 1994–95, but fell back to the 1993–94 level in the subsequent two years. This same trend applied to rural and urban poverty considered separately. Furthermore, Deaton and Drèze (2002, p. 3728) report that the 54th round, which was in the field during the first six months of 1998, yielded estimates similar to those in 1993–94.

This pattern in the poverty ratio led some reform skeptics to conclude that liberalizing reforms had not been good for the poor. At one level, this claim could be countered by arguing that thin surveys are not entirely reliable, and surely not comparable to the thick surveys. But even if one accepts the results at face value, in my personal view the conclusion is unwarranted since the poverty reduction in the 1980s, especially that between 1987–88 and 1993–94, was itself the result of a move toward more, not less, liberal policies. If we are looking for comparison with truly socialist decades, we must compare phase II to phases III and IV. The growth rate had shifted from 3.2 percent in phase II (1965–81) to 4.8 percent in phase III (1981–88). The growth rate during 1988–94, at 5.8 percent, was even higher. These shifts had much to do with economic liberalization that began on a piecemeal basis in the late 1970s, accelerated in the second half of the 1980s, and became much more systematic after the major reform package in 1991. Without the shift to the higher growth rates, it is inconceivable that a substantial decline in poverty could have been achieved during the 1980s and early 1990s.

Nevertheless, since many advocates of reforms (wrongly) embrace the view that reforms began in 1991, the apparent lack of decline in the poverty ratio in the second half of the 1990s posed a formidable challenge for them. A key explanation offered for the absence of a decline in poverty in the NSS data was that reported expenditures in the surveys were biased downward, with the bias rising over time. Thus, for example, the mean per-capita expenditure in the 54th round was approximately the same as in the 50th round, implying zero growth in the mean per-capita expenditure. But with per-capita GDP at factor cost growing more than 4 percent per year over the same period and no significant shift in the savings rate, such stagnation in the mean per-capita expenditure would be highly improbable. I will return to this issue in greater detail below.

While this debate was in progress, however, the results of the 55th (quinquennial) round of the NSS, conducted in 1999–2000, became available. These results showed a sharp decline in poverty over the previous quinquennial round conducted in 1993–94, thereby reversing the conclusions of the thin rounds. This is shown in table 7.2, which presents the official Government of India poverty estimates, published for all years for which the thick quinquennial survey is done. At the rural, urban, and national levels, these estimates exhibit a clear declining trend that applies to the last set of years as well.[11] Figure 7.3 shows this trend graphically. A comparison of figures 7.1 and 7.2 with figure 7.3 shows the dramatic difference between the first three decades and subsequent ones.

According to the estimates in table 7.2, poverty ratios fell more—in absolute percentage points as well as proportionately—between 1993–94 and 1999–2000 than between 1987–88 and 1993–94. The decline in rural poverty was from 37.1 to 26.8 percent, and in urban poverty from 32.9 to 24.1 percent between 1993–94 and 1999–2000. In comparison, the decline was considerably less between 1987–88 and 1993–94 in each of the sectors.

TABLE 7.2: Official Poverty Estimates (quinquennial surveys)

Year	Poverty Ratio (%)			Number of Poor (million)		
	Rural	Urban	Combined	Rural	Urban	Combined
1973–74	56.4	49	54.9	261.3	60	321.3
1977–78	53.1	45.2	51.3	264.3	64.6	328.9
1983	45.7	40.8	44.5	252	70.9	322.9
1987–88	39.1	38.2	38.9	231.9	75.2	307.1
1993–94	37.3	32.4	36	244	76.3	320.3
1999–2000	27.1	23.6	26.1	193.2	67.1	260.3

Source: Planning Commission, *Tenth Five-Year Plan* (2002).

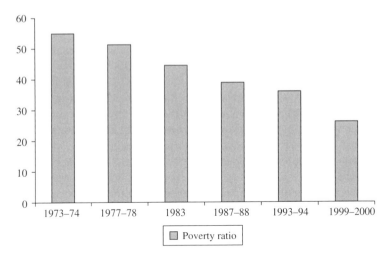

FIGURE 7.3: Poverty Decline under Liberalizing Reforms

Being uniformly based on quinquennial surveys, this evidence would seem to settle the debate. Unfortunately, however, as reform skeptics (Sen, 2000) were quick to point out, a critical change in the sample design introduced in the 55th round makes the calculations based on it noncomparable to those based on the earlier rounds, including the 50th round, conducted in 1993–94. The change relates to the recall period in the administration of the questionnaires.

Traditionally, the NSS had given a "30-day recall" questionnaire to all respondents. After the 50th round, however, the National Sample Survey Organization (NSSO), which is responsible for conducting the NSS, introduced an additional experimental questionnaire that used different recall periods for different goods. This questionnaire used a seven-day recall period for food, paan (betel leaf stuffed with betel nuts and condiments), and tobacco; a one-year recall period for infrequently purchased items, including clothing, footwear, durable goods, and educational and institutional medical expenditures; and the traditional 30-day recall period for the remainder of the goods. Prior to 1999–2000, the traditional "30-days only" recall and the newly introduced experimental questionnaire were administered to distinct and independent samples of households. The two questionnaires produced two independent sets of expenditure estimates. The estimated total expenditure based on the traditional questionnaire was consistently lower than that based on the experimental one, with the ratio of the two expenditures relatively stable across surveys.

In 1999–2000, the NSSO decided to administer the two questionnaires to the same sample of households. This resulted in a reconciliation of the two expenditure estimates probably near the level in the experimental questionnaire, because the investigator and the respondent sought consistency across two sets of responses and considered the seven-day recall period more reliable than the 30-day one. Therefore, in comparison to the sample design applied to the 50th round, the new sample design led to an upward bias in expenditures and a downward bias in poverty estimates.

Correcting for the Differences in the Sample Design

In response to the criticism, researchers proceeded along two alternative but comparable lines. Sundaram and Tendulkar (2003a, 2003b) adjusted the estimates for the 50th round to make them comparable to those obtained from the 55th round. Deaton and Drèze (2002) did the opposite. While I begin by briefly outlining the Sundaram and Tendulkar approach, I devote much of this section to the Deaton and Drèze approach and their estimates. The preference is dictated principally by the consideration that Deaton and Drèze build further on their corrected estimates by correcting for price index-related errors that make the official poverty lines for different states, across rural and urban areas and over time, noncomparable. Sen and Himanshu (2004) point to a potential problem with the correction done for the change in the sample design by Deaton and Drèze, but it is uncertain precisely how much it impacts their estimate.[12]

Taking first the corrected estimates obtained by Sundaram and Tendulkar (2003a), observe that the NSSO conducted an employment-unemployment survey (EUS) alongside the consumer expenditure survey (CES). The EUS includes a separate, albeit limited, consumer expenditure component. Sundaram and Tendulkar begin by noting that the consumer expenditure survey in the 1999–2000 EUS relies exclusively on the traditional 30-day reporting period. While the coverage in the EUS is less extensive than in the CES, they find that for questions with comparable coverage, the mean expenditures in the EUS are typically close to those in the 30-day questionnaire in the CES. They conclude that, therefore, the responses to the questions in the 30-day questionnaire in the 1999–2000 CES were not contaminated by the simultaneous administration of the seven-day questionnaire for the same questions.

This leaves the revised treatment of low frequency items that were subject to a 30-day reporting period in the 50th round but to a one-year reporting period in the 55th round as the only source of incomparability. The argument here is that a one-year reporting period results in the reporting of larger expenditures on these items by the poor, which pushes some of them above the poverty line. Sundaram and Tendulkar note that the 50th round contained both 30-day and one-year reporting periods for the low frequency items. This allows them to recalculate the 50th round poverty ratio using the one-year reporting period, thus making the 50th and 55th round estimates roughly comparable.

The original calculations by Sundaram and Tendulkar (2003a) yielded reductions in the poverty ratio that were approximately three-fourths of the official estimates. Sen and Himanshu (2004a, 2004b) pointed out an inadvertent, albeit important, error in these calculations, however, which led Sundaram and Tendulkar (2003b) to revise their estimates. In this latter work, they concluded that while the necessary correction reduces the magnitude of poverty reduction, the annual percentage reduction in poverty between the 50th and 55th rounds continues to be larger than that during the preceding ten years.

Deaton and Drèze (2002) take a somewhat different approach to the sample design problem.[13] As noted above, the experimental questionnaire uses the seven-day or one-year reporting period for only a subset of the commodities. There remain a subset of commodities (including fuels, light, and noninstitutional medical care) and large categories of miscellaneous goods, however, for which the reporting period is 30 days. For these commodities, there can be no bias arising from differences in the reporting period between the traditional and experimental questionnaires. Moreover, the expenditure on them turns out to be highly correlated with the total expenditure. Therefore, the expenditure on these comparably surveyed goods can be used to estimate the total expenditure and, hence, poverty.

The validity of this procedure requires two assumptions. First, expenditures on the goods for which the recall period is unchanged are not affected by changes in the questionnaire elsewhere in the survey. Second, the relationship between expenditures on these goods and the total expenditure in 1999–2000 is the same as in 1993–94. The validity of this latter assumption can be verified using the annual thin surveys that are uncontaminated by the differences in the recall periods for the two questionnaires. Deaton and Drèze observe that the check suggests the procedure works reasonably well.[14]

The rows labeled "step 1" in table 7.3 show the adjusted estimates of rural and urban poverty after this correction is applied to the expenditure data. Table 7.3 also presents uncorrected, official estimates. Since the correction applies only to 1999–2000 estimates, official and "step 1" estimates for 1987–88 and 1993–94 are identical. The correction raises the estimate of rural poverty in 1999–2000 from 26.8 to 30.0 percent and that of urban poverty from 24.1 to 24.7 percent. Revised estimates

TABLE 7.3: Deaton and Drèze Poverty Estimates; 1987–2000

	1987–88	1993–94	1999–2000
Rural			
Official estimates	39.4	37.1	26.8
Percent point reduction over the preceding round		2.3	10.3
Percent reduction over the preceding round		5.8	27.8
Adjusted estimates			
Step 1: Adjusting for questionnaire design change	39.4	37.1	30.0
Percent point reduction over the preceding round		2.3	7.1
Percent reduction over the preceding round		5.8	19.1
Step 2: Revising the poverty lines	39.4	33.0	26.3
Percent point reduction over the preceding round		6.4	6.7
Percent reduction over the preceding round		16.2	20.3
Urban			
Official estimates	39.1	32.9	24.1
Percent point reduction over the preceding round		6.2	8.8
Percent reduction over the preceding round		15.9	26.7
Adjusted estimates			
Step 1: Adjusting for questionnaire design change	39.1	32.9	24.7
Percent point reduction over the preceding round		6.2	8.2
Percent reduction over the preceding round		15.9	24.9
Step 2: Revising the poverty lines	22.5	17.8	12.0
Percent point reduction over the preceding round		4.7	5.8
Percent reduction over the preceding round		20.9	32.6

Source: Deaton and Drèze (2002, table 1a), supplemented by the author's calculations.

are higher than official ones, but they remain considerably lower than the corresponding estimates for 1993–94. The percentage point and proportionate declines in each sector between 1993–94 and 1999–2000 also remain larger than those between 1987–88 and 1993–94.

Getting the Poverty Lines Right

In the methodology used to compute official estimates at the national level, the Planning Commission begins with separate national rural and urban poverty lines and adjusts them for price movements over time in each sector, using approximate price indexes such as the Wholesale Price Index or the Consumer Price Index for Agricultural Laborers (CPIAL). An important limitation of these indexes is that they rely on fixed and outdated weights. For example, the CPIAL uses a large weight of 0.78 for food that has not been changed for decades. Evidence suggests that the consumption patterns have been changing over time and that the proportion of expenditure on food has declined, even for the poor, from this high figure. The use of these price indexes has led to some results that seem prima facie problematic. Thus, official urban poverty lines in Andhra Pradesh and Karnataka have been approximately 70 percent higher than their rural counterparts, with the result that the official urban poverty ratio in these states turns out to be higher than the corresponding rural poverty ratio. At the other extreme, in Assam, the rural poverty line is higher than its urban counterpart, leading to the result that Assam has one of the highest rural poverty ratios, but one of the lowest urban poverty ratios, across states.

To alleviate this problem and obtain an internally consistent set of poverty lines, Deaton and Drèze begin with the single official all-India rural poverty line of 115.70 rupees per person per month in 1987–88. They then calculate alternative price indexes, using the information in the consumer expenditure surveys themselves. In the surveys, consumers report expenditures on and quantities of 170 commodities purchased. This allows the calculation of the price paid for each of the commodities. In turn the information on prices based on literally millions of purchases allows Deaton and Drèze to calculate superlative indexes, such as the Tornqvist Price Index, that allow for substitution across commodities in response to a price change.

Deaton and Drèze obtain the national urban poverty line for 1987–88 by multiplying the 115.70 rupees per month per person rural poverty line by the urban, relative to the rural Tornqvist Price Index. They obtain rural and urban poverty lines for 1993–94 by multiplying the 1987–88 poverty lines by the corresponding Tornqvist Price Index in 1993–94 relative to that in 1987–88. Rural and urban poverty lines for 1999–2000 are obtained analogously. They then apply each of these poverty lines to the relevant sample to obtain revised estimates of rural and urban poverty ratios in 1987–88, 1993–94, and 1999–2000.

The combined effect of recall period and price index corrections on the poverty estimates associated with the three quinquennial rounds are shown in the line labeled "step 2" in table 7.3. The rural poverty line in 1987–88, from which all other poverty lines are calculated, is the same in step 2 as in step 1. Therefore, step 2 correction contributes no change in the estimated rural poverty in 1987–88. All other estimates in step 2 are lower than those in step 1. There are two reasons for this pattern. First, by accepting the Deaton and Drèze rural and urban price indexes as true measures of differences between rural and urban price levels, the true urban poverty line was much lower than the official urban poverty line in 1987–88. This fact leads to a substantially lower urban poverty estimate in 1987–88 in step 2 than in step 1. Second, Tornqvist Price indexes, applied by Deaton and Drèze, rise less sharply than the price indexes implicit in the official poverty lines. This leads to lower poverty lines in 1993–94 and 1999–2000.

The final estimates in table 7.3 show a uniformly declining pattern for both rural and urban poverty. In addition, the acceleration in the decline in poverty in the second period that characterized the official estimates remains valid. Thus, no matter how one looks at the data, a substantial decline and an accelerating pattern in the 1990s cannot be denied.

Expenditure Growth: The NAS versus the NSS

Let us briefly return to the issue of the slow growth of expenditures in the NSS data. I mentioned earlier that the mean per-capita expenditure in the 54th round shows virtually no change over that in the 50th round. This does not square with the fact that according to the National Accounts Survey (NAS) conducted by the Central Statistical Organization (CSO), per-capita GDP grew nearly 4 percent annually during this same period.

More directly, it is possible to obtain per-capita expenditure from the NAS and check the NSS mean per-capita expenditure against it. Systematic comparisons show that the ratio of mean per-capita expenditure obtained from the NSS to that obtained from the NAS is less than unity, and declines rapidly during the 1990s. According to a chart in Srinivasan (1999), this ratio was 0.67 in 1987–88, fell to 0.55 in 1993–94, and to 0.5 in 1998–99. Both the NAS and the NSS are subject to a variety of sampling and nonsampling errors. Yet, the vast and rising differences between the expenditure estimates obtained from the two sources are not easily explained. One possible explanation is that the NSS estimate consists of household expenditures only, whereas NAS estimates include additional items, such as expenditures incurred by nonprofit organizations, imputed rent on owner-occupied housing, and net interest earned by financial intermediaries. According to a cross-validation study by the National Accounts Department, the last two of these items account for 22 percent of the levels of differences between NAS and NSS estimates (Sundaram and Tendulkar, 2002). But this is far from sufficient to account for the full and rising gap over time between the two estimates.

The differences between the NSS and NAS mean per-capita expenditures pose an important dilemma for researchers. If we take the view that the NSS estimate represents true per-capita expenditure, we are forced to conclude that the 6 percent GDP growth in India during the late 1980s and 1990s is a myth. On the other hand, if we take the view that the NAS estimates better capture the reality, in all likelihood we are overstating the number of the poor at any given poverty line.

Few economists are willing to take the view that the slow growth in the mean per-capita expenditure in the data generated by the NSS represents true growth in India during the period under consideration. This then raises the question of whether we need to revise the poverty estimates based on the NSS data. Bhalla (2002) answers this question emphatically in the affirmative, taking the position that while the NSS data correctly represent the distribution of expenditures across different income groups, the NAS estimate accurately represents the mean per-capita expenditure. Therefore, he shifts the entire distribution of the expenditures generated by the NSS to the right by the difference between the NSS and NAS mean per-capita expenditures, and recalculates the poverty ratio. Unsurprisingly, the large upward shift in the expenditure of each income group implies fewer poor individuals for a given poverty line. Moreover, since the difference between the NAS and NSS mean per-capita expenditures is larger for later years, the rightward shift in the distribution is also larger for the later years. The adjustment reinforces the acceleration in poverty reduction in the second half of the 1990s. Bhalla's poverty estimates turn out to be substantially lower than the official estimates, as well as those of Deaton and Drèze.

The approach taken by Bhalla has not received wide acceptance, however. One problem with it is that Bhalla does not provide a sound basis for accepting the distribution generated by the NSS but rejecting its mean value. His approach effectively assumes that the NAS estimate represents the true mean per-capita expenditure, and that the error in the NSS-generated expenditures is uniformly distributed over different income groups. But this need not be true. For example, what if the lower mean in the NSS surveys resulted exclusively from the underreporting of expenditures by individuals above the poverty line? In that case, despite incorrect mean per-capita expenditure, the unadjusted distribution would yield the correct estimate of the poverty ratio. While it is reasonable to assume that expenditures are understated for all classes of individuals, and therefore the poverty ratio is lower than that computed on the basis of unadjusted distribution ("step 1" estimates of Deaton and Drèze), the extent of this understatement depends on the extent to which different groups underreport expenditures.

For example, according to a careful comparison of the components of the aggregate expenditures in 1993–94 by Sundaram and Tendulkar (2001), item groups that account for a very large proportion of the aggregate discrepancy between NAS and NSS estimates have a much smaller budget share in the consumption basket of the bottom 30 percent of the rural and urban populations. Symmetrically, for item groups that together account for over 75 percent of the consumption of the bottom 30 percent, the divergence between the NAS and NSS estimates is "much smaller than on the average for all item groups and negative in some cases."[15]

The problem posed by the increasing difference between the NSS and NAS mean per-capita expenditures over time is somewhat alleviated in "step 2" estimates of Deaton and Drèze. Recall that the price indexes used by them rise less sharply than those implicit in the official poverty estimates. This means the real expenditures rise more sharply under the Deaton and Drèze approach than under the official approach. Specifically, the adjusted ("step 2") per-capita expenditure obtained by Deaton and Drèze grows 2 percent annually between 1993–94 and 1999–2000. Nevertheless, insofar as the correction still falls short of fully bridging the gap between the NAS and NSS mean per-capita expenditures, their estimates of poverty reduction should be taken as the lower bound on the actual poverty reduction.

Postscript: The 61st Round

The 61st round of the NSS, relating to the year 2004–05, has been completed. This round conducted a thick survey and closely tracked the sampling design of the 1993–94 survey. Therefore, its results are comparable to the latter. No estimates derived from these data by independent researchers are available, but the Planning Commission (2006) has reported the aggregate countrywide poverty ratio computed from them. Accordingly, the poverty ratio in 2004–05 was 27.8 percent. Recalling the ratio of 36 percent in 1993–94, this represents a reduction of 8.2 percentage points. Stated differently, the poverty ratio fell 22.8 percent over 11 years. This compares favorably to the 19.1 percent reduction in the ratio that took place between 1983 and 1993–94. Thus, even if one insists that the period 1983–94 represented a "pre-reform" period, poverty reduction in the post-reform period is at least comparable. Of course, if we calculate the poverty lines in an internally consistent manner, as in step 2 of Deaton and Drèze, the post-reform era would look even more superior. Some correction for the progressive understatement of the expenditures of the poor in the NSS data would work in the same direction.

TRADE AND POVERTY ONCE AGAIN

The debate as reviewed above focuses only on the question of whether poverty in India declined after 1993–94, and if so, whether the decline was at an accelerated pace. As I have argued earlier, this debate sheds little light on whether economic reforms speeded up poverty reduction. The reduction in poverty, at least during the second (if not the first) half of the 1980s partially resulted from economic reforms of the Rajiv Gandhi era. No doubt direct antipoverty programs also contributed to the reduction, but they could not have been sustained without economic reforms, as was demonstrated by the 1991 crisis.

In a recent paper, Topolova (2005) takes a different approach to the question by studying the causal link between poverty reduction and trade liberalization, using the district as the unit of analysis. She measures the openness of a district by the weighted average of tariffs, such that the tariff in each sector is weighted by that sector's share in the total employment in the district. The higher this weighted average tariff, the less open the district. Topolova then calculates the poverty ratio at the level of the district using the NSS data, and studies its relationship to the weighted average tariff. Using the "difference-in-difference" approach currently popular with applied econometricians, she finds that "rural districts where industries more exposed to trade liberalization were concentrated experienced a slower progress in poverty reduction." She further concludes that "compared to a rural district experiencing no change in tariffs, a district experiencing the mean level of tariff changes [reduction] saw a 2 percentage points increase in poverty incidence and a 0.6 percentage points increase in poverty depth. This setback represents about 15 percent of India's progress in poverty reduction over the 1990s."

A casual reader is almost sure to conclude from these statements that trade openness has had a detrimental effect on poverty reduction in India. But the "difference-in-difference" approach does not allow us to infer anything about the effect of tariff reduction on overall poverty. All that Topolova's results imply is that, *assuming* increased openness led to reduced poverty overall, the reduction was smaller in the districts where tariffs fell more. Or, alternatively, *assuming* increased openness led to increased poverty overall, the increase was larger in the districts where tariffs fell more.

Once we understand this, the results obtained by Topolova are hardly surprising. To explain in the simplest terms, take the extreme case in which a district produces either export goods or import goods, but not both. As measured, protection in this example is concentrated in the districts producing import goods (since the tariffs on exports are zero). When the tariffs are lowered, resources are temporarily rendered unemployed in the districts specializing in import goods, while profitability rises in the districts specializing in export goods. Immediately, poverty rises in the former district types and falls in the latter district types. The net effect is ambiguous, but is likely to be positive once resources begin to be reallocated from districts specializing in imports to those specializing in exports.

While any inference that increased openness resulted in increased poverty in India is, thus, unwarranted from the study by Topolova, an important recent paper by Hasan, Mitra, and Ural (2007) raises serious methodological questions about it as well. The criticisms have substantive implications: Once corrections are made, Topolova's results turn on their head. Of the several problems Hasan et al. point out, I note only three.

First, Topolova entirely ignores the fact that during the period of her analysis, consumer goods were subject to strict licensing. Therefore, tariff rates carried little information on the degree of protection enjoyed by these goods. To measure protection correctly, one must take the nontariff barriers into account.

Second, the measure of average tariff in a district used by Topolova suffers from a serious flaw. She assigns zero tariffs to nontraded goods. That is to say, in calculating the average tariff in the district, the employment share of nontraded goods is multiplied by zero. But goods may be nontraded precisely because tariffs and border barriers on their trade are prohibitively high. Ceteris paribus, Topolova's procedure effectively understates protection in districts intensive in the production of nontraded goods.

Finally, the unit of analysis chosen by Topolova—the district—raises a serious sampling problem. According to the sampling strategy employed to collect the NSS data, samples at the level of the district, especially in the urban areas, are often not random. Moreover, sometimes district boundaries are redefined across surveys, which makes the analysis involving data over time problematic.

Hasan et al. avoid these problems by including nontariff barriers in their index of protection, avoiding the use of nontraded sectors in the construction of the protection index and conducting the analysis at the state and regional levels. These and other corrections lead the authors to very different conclusions. To quote them:

> Our results are different from Topolova's. In no case do we find reductions in trade protection to have worsened poverty at the state or region level. Instead, we find that states whose workers are on average more exposed to foreign competition tend to have lower rural, urban and overall poverty rates (and poverty gaps), and this beneficial effect of greater trade openness is more pronounced in states that have more flexible labor market institutions.

In terms of economic reasoning, the findings of Hasan et al. (2007) suggest that productivity gains from greater exposure to trade shield the workers against adverse short-run employment effects that Topolova's results would imply. Instead, increased efficiency allows the states with greater exposure to trade to offer better employment and wage prospects. The qualifications regarding the effect of trade liberalization on the overall effect on poverty applicable to the analysis based on the "difference-in-difference" approach would seem to apply to Hasan et al. as well.

EMPLOYMENT GROWTH AND UNEMPLOYMENT

Reform critics argue that post-reforms growth has been characterized by a slow-down in job creation and increased unemployment rates (Gupta, 2002a, 2002b). The National Rural Employment Guarantee Act of 2005, which guarantees 100 days' worth of work to every rural household at the minimum wage, is also a response to the perception by the UPA government that growth has failed to generate adequate employment opportunities for the rural poor. The claims and perceptions are once again based on the comparison of the 1980s with the 1990s. As I have already argued, such comparisons contaminate the assessment of the relative efficacy of pro-market reforms. If we desire an uncontaminated comparison with the socialist era policies, we must go farther back, to the 1970s and 1960s.

One argument made by reform skeptics is that the annual rate of growth of employment declined in the 1990s in comparison to that in the 1980s. Specifically, this rate was 2.1 percent between 1983 and 1993–94, but only 1.6 percent between 1993–94 and 1999–2000. It turns out, however, that this trend has been reversed in the most recent thick employment-unemployment survey: The growth rate of employment between 1999–2000 and 2004–05 was 2.5 percent. Taking the full eleven-year period from 1993–94 to 2004–05 together, employment growth was virtually the same as in the preceding ten years.

Turning to unemployment, we must first introduce its various measures available for India. In conducting its surveys, the NSSO employs three different definitions of unemployment:

- The "usual" status measure designates a person unemployed if he or she is looking for a job and was unemployed for the major part of the preceding 365 days. There are two usual status measures: one designates a person unemployed on the basis of whether he is unemployed on account of only the principal activity, and the other on the basis of whether he is unemployed on account of the principal *and* subsidiary activities. To avoid confusion, I follow most researchers in reporting the usual status unemployment estimates based on the principal activity alone in table 7.4 below.
- The "weekly" status measure designates an individual unemployed if he or she has worked less than one hour in the preceding seven days. In other words, an individual employed for one or more hours on any one of the preceding seven days is considered employed.
- The "daily" status measure is more complex and intended to better capture the employment status in informal employment. It collects information on the

TABLE 7.4: Unemployment Rates According to Various Measures

Round	Year	Male			Female		
		Usual (principal)	Weekly	Daily	Usual (principal)	Weekly	Daily
Rural							
61	2004–05	2.1	3.8	8	3.1	4.2	8.7
55	1999–2000	2.1	3.9	7.2	1.5	3.7	7
50	1993–94	2	3.1	5.6	1.3	2.9	5.6
43	1987–88	2.8	4.2	4.6	3.5	4.4	6.7
38	1983	2.1	3.7	7.5	1.4	4.3	9
32	1977–78	2.2	3.6	7.1	5.5	4.1	9.2
27	1972–73		3	6.8		5.5	11.2
Urban							
61	2004–05	4.4	5.2	7.5	9.1	9	11.6
55	1999–2000	4.8	5.6	7.3	7.1	7.3	9.4
50	1993–94	5.4	5.2	6.7	8.3	7.9	10.4
43	1987–88	6.1	6.6	8.8	8.5	9.2	12
38	1983	5.9	6.7	9.2	6.9	7.5	11
32	1977–78	6.5	7.1	9.4	17.8	10.9	14.5
27	1972–73		6	8		9.2	13.7

Note: "Usual" measures unemployment based on the work status during the preceding 365 days; "weekly" measures it according to the status in the preceding seven days; and "daily" divides each of the preceding seven days into equal halves and records status for each of the 14 half days.

Source: National Sample Survey Organization, *Employment and Unemployment Situation in India, 2004–05*, Part I (2006).

preceding seven days, dividing each day into halves. A person working for four hours any day is considered as employed for the entire day. A person employed for one hour in any half day is considered employed for that half day.

Table 7.4 presents detailed estimates of unemployment in the rural and urban areas for male and female populations separately, using the three measures discussed above for all thick surveys. Four observations can be made. First, regardless of the measure, the unemployment rate is uniformly higher in the urban areas than in the rural areas. Second, the unemployment rates among female workers are uniformly higher than among male workers. Third, some of the highest unemployment rates were observed in 1977–78 and 1987–88. Finally, unemployment rates in the 1990s and beyond have been generally lower than in 1987–88 and have varied within a narrow range. Given the relatively high margin of error in these estimates noted by the NSSO (2006, p. 153, para. 6.1.1.1), no firm inference on their evolution over time can be drawn. The most we can say is that unemployment rates in the 1990s were no higher than in 1987–88.

AGRICULTURAL WAGES

We can look for further evidence on poverty alleviation through wages. As Deaton and Drèze (2002) point out, there are two justifications for wage movements serving as indicators of changes in the level of poverty. First, as long as wages are deter-mined on the labor supply curve, which is true if the labor market is competitive at least on the supply side, they reflect the workers' opportunity cost of employ-ment. The acceptance of a lower wage than before reflects increased desperation and deprivation. Likewise, the demands for higher wages along the supply curve imply increased reservation wage (i.e., the wage below which workers would not work at the margin) on the part of the workers, and therefore improved opportunities. Second, statistically, agricultural wages and rural poverty are highly correlated. As real agricultural wages rise, rural poverty falls. Therefore, increasing real wages in agriculture serves as an independent indicator of declining poverty.

Annual wages on a continuous basis are available in India in agriculture only. There are two series available that span approximately 30 years. The most commonly used series is Agricultural Wages in India (AWI), published by the Ministry of Agriculture. It gives nominal wages by district for the agricultural year, which runs from July to June, and is available for the period spanning 1960–61 to 1999–2000. The nationwide mean wage can be determined by averaging district wages weighted by the number of agricultural laborers. In turn, nominal wages can be converted into real wages by applying the CPIAL.

The second wage series comes from Cost of Cultivation of Principal Crops in India (COC). This series is available from 1971–72 onward, with 1999–2000 being the last year for which data are available. The COC survey has details on the crops cultivated, the wage bill in nominal terms, and the quantity of labor used. Once again, CPIAL is used to convert nominal wages into real wages.

Bhalla and Das (2006, appendix table) provide the real wages from AWI and COC series for the years 1971–2000. Using these data, we can calculate the growth in real wages during 1972–81, 1981–88, and 1988–2000, periods that approximately correspond to phases II, III, and IV, respectively. The results of these calculations are shown in table 7.5. Wage movements based on the COC survey exhibit a pattern fully consistent with our growth story: Wage growth, at 0.3 percent per year, is tiny during phase II but rises to 3.1 percent during phase III and further accelerates to 3.5 percent during phase IV.

The pattern is somewhat different, however, if we rely on the AWI series. According to this series, the growth rate of real agricultural wages was nil dur-ing 1972–81, shot up to 5.4 percent during 1981–88, and came down to 2.0 percent during 1988–2000. In other words, the growth rate in wages decelerated in phase

TABLE 7.5: Growth in Agricultural Wages

Period	AWI	COC
1971–81	0.02	0.26
1981–88	5.36	3.08
1988–2004	1.96	3.51

Source: Author's calculations, using wage data in Bhalla and Das (2006, appendix table). The Agricultural Wages in India (AWI) and Cost of Crops (COC) wage series are published by the Department of Agriculture, Government of India.

IV. The reasons for this divergence between the AWI and COC series are not clear. Nor do we have reason to prefer one series to the other.

The NSSO employment-unemployment surveys provide yet one more source of information on wages. The strength of this source is that it covers both agricultural and nonagricultural wages; the weakness is that it is limited to the years corresponding to quinquennial rounds. Even among these surveys, the data for 1987–88 exhibit anomalies that render them unusable for the purpose at hand. Therefore, we are left with wage data at three points in time: 1983–84, 1993–94, and 1999–2000. Using them, Bhalla and Das (2006, table 20) calculate the annual growth rates of both urban and rural wages between 1993–94 and 1999–2000, and between 1983 and 1993–94. Both sets of wages exhibit an accelerating pattern. Thus, with the exception of the AWI series, evidence on wages supports the direct evidence of an accelerating pattern of declining poverty derived from consumption expenditure surveys.

SOCIAL AND HUMAN DEVELOPMENT INDICATORS

Next, we may briefly consider other social and human development indicators. Two important points are worthy of mention at the outset. First, as in other countries of the world, progress on many of these indicators was made even during phases I and II, when the poverty ratio trend was more or less static. India started with very low values of most of these indicators, so that even 1 to 2 percent annual growth, coupled with modest spending on medical care, health, and education, yielded improvements. Medical advances further added to these gains. Second, as these indicators improve, additional progress at the margin is likely to become more difficult. When infant mortality is 150 per 1000 live births, a 10 percent reduction in it is likely to involve less effort than when it is 50. Therefore, we should not make too much of a slowdown in progress over time unless the slowdown is especially pronounced and dramatic.

Data on social and human indicators on a long-term basis are scarce. Tables 7.6–7.8 present the main ones I have been able to find. Child labor has declined steadily since 1960, with some acceleration during the 1990s and beyond. The same holds true for mortality among females. Infant mortality and mortality under five years

TABLE 7.6: Social/Human Development Indicators: Child Labor and Mortality Rates

Indicator	1960	1970	1980	1990	2000	2004
Labor force, children 10–14 (% of age group)	30.1	25.5	21.4	16.7	12.1	10.2
Mortality rate, adult females (per 1,000 female adults)	407.3	352.7	278.9	241.4	191.0	
Mortality rate, adult males (per 1,000 male adults)	397.9	324.4	261.5	236.5	250.0	
Mortality rate, infants (per 1,000 live births)	146.0	127.0	113.0	84.0	68.0	
Mortality rate, children under 5 (per 1,000)	242.0	202.0	173.0	123.0	94.0	

Source: World Bank, 2005d, World Development Indicators, Washington, DC.

TABLE 7.7: Social/Human Development Indicators: Education and Life Expectancy

	1990		2002	
Education and Life Expectancy	Female	Male	Female	Male
Gross pre-primary school enrollment ratio	3	4	34	34
Gross primary school enrollment ratio	84	110	104	111
Gross secondary school enrollment ratio	33	55	47	58
Gross tertiary school enrollment ratio	4	8	10	14
Pupils starting grade 1 who reach grade 5*	55	61	59	59
Literacy rate (15 yrs. or over)†	36	62	48	73
Literacy rate (15–24 yrs.) †	54	73	68	84
Life expectancy at birth (years) ††	59	59	63	60

*Starting year relates to 1993 and terminal year to 1999.

†Terminal year data relate to 2000–04.

††Terminal year is 2003.

Source: Asian Development Bank, *Key Indicators* (2005).

TABLE 7.8: Social/Human Development Indicators: Gender Gap

	1990	2000	2002
Ratio of girls to boys at education level			
Primary	0.76	0.83	0.94
Secondary	0.60	0.71	0.80
Tertiary	0.54	0.68	0.68
Share of women in wage employment in nonagricultural sectors	12.7	16.6	17.5

Source: Asian Development Bank, *Key Indicators* (2005).

have both declined throughout, but the decline slowed during the 1990s. Male mortality is the big exception, having actually risen in 2000 over that in 1990.

Tables 7.7 and 7.8 present indicators of progress in education, life expectancy, and the gender gap during the 1990s. According to these tables, considerable progress has been made in raising the education levels and eliminating the gender gap since 1990. For example, literacy rates have gone up across the board. Among other education indicators, those relating to the female population have shown especially impressive progress. The gross primary school enrollment ratio for females rose from 84 in 1990 to 104 in 2002.[16] Table 7.8 reveals that women have gained proportionately over men in education at all levels. Their share in wage employment in nonagricultural sectors has also gone up. Progress has been less impressive for the male population. Specifically, life expectancy for males is now below that for females.

FARMER SUICIDES

A final issue related to poverty is the upsurge in suicides among male farmers. Many politicians, columnists, and NGOs have expressed fears that this phenomenon reflects shrinking economic opportunities and increased distress among farmers even as economic reforms bring good fortune to many others. This is a sensitive subject that, nevertheless, requires dispassionate analysis. Some excellent work on the subject has been done, but much more is required for a better understanding of why the suicide rates have gone up in some pockets of a handful of the states.

Trends in Suicides

Mishra (2006a, 2007) offers comprehensive data on suicides in India. Using the data in the annual publication *Accidental Deaths and Suicides in India,* brought out by the National Crime Records Bureau of the Ministry of Home Affairs, he constructs a time series of suicides across states for male and female populations. In turn, the National Crime Records Bureau compiles its data painstakingly from the police records. An anomaly in the data is an extremely high suicide mortality rate (SMR) per 100,000 population for male farmers in Pondicherry relative to other states. These rates also show very high variance over time. The rate rose from 292 in 1997 to the peak of 2066 in 2000, and fell back to 247 in 2003. The second highest SMR among male farmers is in Kerala, which stood at 139 in 1995, 185 in 2000, and 298 in 2003. These rates are an order of magnitude smaller and less dispersed than those for Pondicherry. But even they are excessively high when compared to the rates in other high-suicide states. These anomalies suggest that the data must be taken with some grain of salt, though they probably convey the broad picture accurately.

The longest available time series on suicides ranges from 1975 to 2001 and relates to the entire population. Specifically, it does not separate suicide rates for farmers. Mishra (2006a) reports this series for male and female populations by states and for India as a whole. He calculates that the age-adjusted SMR, defined as the ratio of deaths from suicide per 100,000 population of those aged five years or more, grew 2.4 percent per annum for males and 2.3 percent per annum for females between 1975 and 2001.

Therefore, the first point to note is that the suicide rates among males and females in the general population have been rising since the data became available. A natural candidate for the explanation of this phenomenon is the weakening of the family support structure following the breakup of the joint family system and the lack of emergence of alternative social support systems. It may be further hypothesized that the breakup of the joint family and the emergence of unitary families in the rural areas is of more recent origin and may have contributed to the recent increase in farmer suicides relative to nonfarmer suicides.

The natural question at this point is whether the suicide rates among male farmers are higher than those in the general population. Separate data on male farmer and nonfarmer suicides for all states and the country as a whole are available for only ten years: 1995 to 2004. Figure 7.4 shows these rates at the all-India level. The data do show a rising trend in the SMR among male farmers, while that among nonfarmers has stabilized around 13.5. In 2004, the latest year for which data are available, the SMR among male farmers (19.2) was considerably higher than that for nonfarmers (13.4).

A look at the disaggregated data across states further reveals that the higher SMR among male farmers is driven by extra-high SMR in some large states. Four

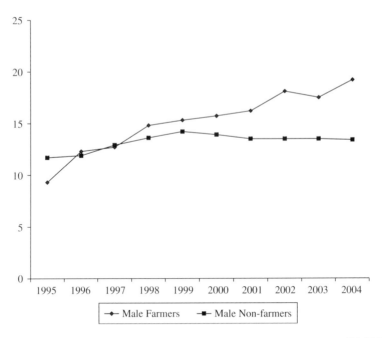

FIGURE 7.4: Suicide Mortality Rates for Male Farmers and Non-Farmers (per 100,000)

states—Andhra Pradesh, Karnataka, Kerala, and Maharashtra—account for more than half of the suicide mortality among farmers. Undivided Madhya Pradesh and Tamil Nadu account for another quarter of the suicide mortality.[17] Even within these states, suicide mortality concentrates in specific regions, such as northeastern Maharashtra and northern Karnataka. On the other hand, in Orissa, Rajasthan, Punjab, Haryana, and undivided Uttar Pradesh, the SMR among male farmers has been predominantly in the single digits and below the SMR among nonfarmers. Even in the relatively poor state of Bihar, the rates have been well below the national average and below the corresponding rate in the state for the nonfarmer male population.

Causes of Farmer Suicides

High and rising suicide rates among farmers have led to considerable speculation that reforms are to blame for them. But there is no systematic study to date that establishes this connection. Virtually all studies analyze the phenomenon at a point in time in a specific state, and look into the causes of suicide within the sample considered. Occasionally, the studies speculate about the changing environment over time, but do not connect this change to rising rates of suicide over time. One of the many difficulties in forging a link between reforms and increased farmer suicides is that the upsurge has been observed only in specific regions of a handful of the states. We have relatively rich states, such as Punjab and Haryana, as well as poorer states, such as Rajasthan, Orissa, and Bihar, where male farmer suicide rates show either decline or no trend.

TABLE 7.9: Reasons for Suicide

Reason	Percent
Habits like drinking, gambling, overspending	20.35
Failure of crops	16.81
Other reasons (e.g., chit fund)	15.04
Family problems with spouse or others	13.27
Chronic illness	9.73
Marriage of daughters	5.31
Political affiliation	4.42
Property disputes	2.65
Debt burden	2.65
Price crash	2.65
Borrowing beyond paying capacity (e.g., house construction)	2.65
Loss in nonagricultural activities	1.77
Failure of bore wells	0.88

Note: Reasons were given by close relatives and friends. There are multiple reasons for suicides. Not even one case was given only one reason.

Source: Deshpande (2002, table 15).

Unsurprisingly, careful studies rarely find a single cause of suicide. Deshpande (2002), who studies farmer suicides in Karnataka, makes this point forcefully. He analyzes 99 suicide cases in greater detail, both qualitatively, through extensive interviews with the friends and relatives of the victims, and quantitatively, in terms of variables such as debt, assets, crop pattern, and the cost of cultivation. In his qualitative analysis, Deshpande does not find a single case in which one reason accounts for the fateful event. On the average, each case has three to four reasons.

Using the frequency with which each cause is listed by friends and relatives of victims in his sample, Deshpande calculates the overall percentage of times each cause gets listed. His compilation is reproduced in table 7.9. Surprisingly, farm-related reasons get cited only approximately 25 percent of the time as reasons for suicide. Even more surprisingly, as Deshpande (2002, p. 2608) states, "Debt burden and the price crash, which have been quite commonly referred [to] as important factors by the media and public personalities, happens to score 6 per cent probability of being one of the prominent reasons for suicides along with other reasons." Admittedly, some of the reasons are interconnected—for example, crop failure and marriage of a daughter have obvious possible connections to debt—but the overall picture emerging from table 7.9 is quite different from that played up in the media. Traditional factors such as addiction to alcohol and gambling; chronic illness; family problems with spouse; and property disputes continue to be major factors in suicides.

To be sure, studies do consistently show greater debt burden and greater reliance on the informal sources of credit (e.g., the traditional moneylender and traders who sell inputs such as seeds on credit, at ultra-high interest rates) among the victims than the control group. Mishra (2006b) studied 111 suicide cases from 2004 and January 2005 in Maharashtra against a control group. He found that purely in terms of volume, the total outstanding debt of the victims was on average 3.7 times that of the individuals in the control group. Victims also had 72 percent of the outstanding debt from informal sources, against only 38 percent in the control group. This pattern is repeated in the cases studied by Deshpande (2002, table 12).

While the presence of high debt burden and dependence on the informal market for credit among the victims is thus confirmed, the findings of Deshpande (2002) cast doubt on them as leading factors explaining farmer suicides. By itself, debt gets mentioned as a cause less than 3 percent of the time by the friends and relatives of the victims. To some degree, high debt among the victims may reflect their inherently risk-taking nature. Deshpande finds this to be the case in the related context of the choice of crops. To quote him (Deshpande, 2002, p. 2605):

> One clear difference that emerges between the control group and the victims' families is that the latter group preferred to venture into new crops, cash crops and leaned more towards market orientation. This is an indicator of the basic entrepreneurial characteristic of the victims; however, they could not reach their expected goals due to various constraints.

Policy Response

The existing studies do not systematically connect the dramatic rise in farmer suicides in certain regions to the reforms. In each case, there are multiple causes of suicide, but evidence does not connect these causes to the reforms. Mishra (2007) argues plausibly that farmer distress has been on the rise, but he does not connect the increase to the reforms. One hypothesis is that, on the one hand, the rising incomes have sensitized even poorer farmers to the need for educating children and providing health care, and on the other hand, the breakup of the joint family has left them without moral and financial support in the face of a crisis. But even this hypothesis cannot explain why the suicide rates should sharply rise in some regions but not others.

Seeking to slow the reforms on account of the rise in suicides when no connection between the two can be found in the data would only deprive the vast majority of the population of the benefits of the reforms without bringing relief to potential suicide victims. Instead, the response must focus directly on the causes of suicides as revealed by the studies. This may include better access to credit and other inputs. The extension service's providing information on how to go about experimenting with a new crop and publicizing the names of traders who are known to provide substandard inputs can also help. Steps may be taken to discourage the bundling of credit and input sales, since this is often accompanied by the sales of substandard inputs that lead to crop failures and to the buildup of debt. Improved crop insurance can help protect farmers against crop failures. Likewise, the provision of free health insurance in case of hospitalization for those below the poverty line may help many farmers avoid accumulating large debts in case of serious illness (see chapter 19).

In addition, it is important to begin building social support networks at the level of the village. Unitary families are beginning to be the norm even in the villages now. This has resulted in the erosion of both moral and financial support from the extended family that had existed in the past. NGOs can play an especially important role in mobilizing village communities to create such networks.

CONCLUSIONS

The claim by some that the comparison between poverty reductions achieved from 1987–88 to 1993–94 and from 1993–94 to 1999–2000 shows that liberal reforms have failed the poor is wrong for two reasons. First, liberalizing reforms that helped induce 5.8 percent growth during 1988–94 surely played an important role in poverty reduction during this period. Second, the available evidence does not support the claim of the skeptics that poverty reduction decelerated between 1993–94 and 1999–2000 relative to that between 1987–88 and 1993–94. This conclusion is reinforced by the results of the 61st NSS round, which is strictly comparable in sample design to the 1993–94 round.

This conclusion is valid even when we consider step 1 estimates of Deaton and Drèze. But once we allow for two additional important factors, the room for dispute disappears altogether. Step 2 estimates of Deaton and Drèze that hold the poverty line over time and across rural and urban areas consistently fixed in real terms show a decline in poverty in the second period that is even sharper than that shown in the official calculations for 1990–2000. Even step 2 estimates take no account whatsoever of the fact that the NAS data show a far more rapid expansion of per-capita consumption than the NSS data. Even if the population below the poverty line accounts for only a small fraction of this discrepancy in mean per-capita expenditures from the two sources, the reduction in poverty would be larger than in step 2 estimates of Deaton and Drèze.

More starkly, however, if we want a true comparison between the impact of the old and new policies, we must compare the first three decades (1951–81) with the subsequent two (1981–2000). As I have already noted, liberalizing reforms had been adopted both in the 1980s and in the 1990s, so that the acceleration in poverty reduction, or lack thereof, between these two decades sheds at best limited light on the power of the reforms. If this comparison is done, the evidence becomes much more dramatic: Virtually no poverty reduction was achieved under the old policies, while the poverty ratio has been cut in half during the period of liberalizing reforms.

In this chapter, I have also reviewed evidence on unemployment and wages. Claims by some that reforms have produced jobless growth have been proved wrong by the most recent evidence based on the 2004–05 Employment-Unemployment Survey. Unemployment data show relatively little movement to provide a signal one way or the other. Movements in the wages and social and human development indexes reinforce the direct evidence on poverty reduction flowing from the expenditure surveys.

Finally, I have briefly discussed the phenomenon of suicides among male farmers that has been much in the news lately. An examination of the available data shows that the rise in farmer suicides has been concentrated in some specific pockets of a handful of states. In many states—rich and poor—there is no discernible pattern. There are also wide differences in the suicide rates among male farmers across states. These facts cast doubt on the widespread claims that reforms are at the heart of the surge in farmer suicides. A review of some of the key studies of the suicides reveals no such link, either. One key study (Deshpande, 2002) emphasizes that on the average there are three to four reasons for every suicide, and none results from a single factor. Therefore, the right course for the government is not to move away from the reforms but to take measures that will reduce distress among the farmers. These include improved access to credit, prohibiting the bundling of input sales and credit, improved crop and health insurance, and building of social networks to which individuals in distress can turn for help in case of personal crises.

8

INEQUALITY
A Lesser Problem

Critics of liberalization express much concern at increased inequality in India in the 1990s. While some advocates of reforms question the validity of the finding that inequality has gone up, I will argue in this chapter that even accepting the evidence offered by the critics at face value, from the policy perspective, preoccupation with inequality is largely a diversion. I begin with a discussion of various forms of inequality.

FORMS OF INEQUALITY

In the Indian context, inequality may be analyzed from at least five different perspectives. First, we may consider the national income distribution. Even as accelerated growth improves the status of all, including the poor, it may be accompanied by proportionately larger increases in the incomes of the rich. Because the large majority of the Indian population lives in the rural areas and the income distribution there behaves very differently from that in the urban areas, researchers typically also study the rural and urban inequalities separately at the national level. Second, growth may be concentrated geographically and may increase regional disparities. This form of inequality in India is studied at the state level and refers to the distribution of the mean incomes across states. Third, benefits of growth may accrue disproportionately to the urban population, with a concomitant increase in urban-rural inequality. Here we compare the mean rural and urban incomes. Fourth, growth may benefit workers in the organized—mainly public—sector more than those in the unorganized sector. The increase in this form of inequality would be reflected in the increasing ratio of the wages in the organized and unorganized sectors. Finally, growth may be accompanied by a faster increase in the wages of the skilled than of the unskilled. We can classify the last two forms of inequality as wage inequality. There is no reason for the two indicators to move in the same direction, of course.

It is a simple matter to see that an increase in one form of inequality may be accompanied by a decrease in another form of inequality. For example, urban-rural inequality may rise, but if within-sector inequality in urban and rural areas declines sufficiently, overall national inequality may decline. Likewise, faster growth in some states than in others may raise per-capita-income inequality across states, but increased equality within states may offset this effect when it comes to national income distribution. More subtly, even if within-state inequality is unchanged, if one or two populous but poor states grow rapidly, several poor states with small populations grow slowly or decline, and the richer states grow at rates matching the national average, across-states inequality may rise while the national-level inequality falls. Finally, the ratio of skilled to unskilled wages in industry may rise, but large increases in farm income may still improve the overall income distribution.

In what follows, I offer a detailed discussion of inequality from three perspectives: national income distribution, including rural and urban inequality; regional imbalance; and urban-rural inequality. I have already discussed rural and urban wage movements in the context of poverty above. While rising urban and skilled wages have raised concerns, systematic evidence on them remains to be collected. For these reasons, I do not consider wage inequality in this chapter.

INEQUALITY AT THE NATIONAL LEVEL

The discussion of national inequality may be divided into two sections: empirical evidence and the case for addressing inequality through specific policy measures.

Empirical Evidence

Deaton and Drèze (2002) provide calculations for rural, urban, and all-India inequality, both with and without their step 1 correction.[1] They use two indexes of inequality: difference between the logarithms of arithmetic and geometric means of expenditures, and the variance of logarithm of per-capita expenditures across households. The larger the value of either index, the greater is inequality. Their calculations are reported in table 8.1.

In the absence of their step 1 correction, rural inequality declines according to both indexes, while urban inequality rises from 0.19 to 0.20 according to the first index and remains unchanged according to the second index. When the step 1 correction is applied, rural inequality is unchanged according to the first index and rises from 0.23 to 0.24 according to the second index. The correction raises urban inequality according to both indexes. Thus, only urban inequality shows clear signs of increase, according to the calculations by Deaton and Drèze. At the all-India level, without step 1 correction, inequality is unchanged according to the second index and rises from 0.17 to 0.18 according to the first index. With the step 1 correction, the increase is larger.

The overall thrust of this evidence is that rural inequality remained unchanged or fell slightly during 1994–2000, while urban inequality rose noticeably. But if we

TABLE 8.1: Indexes of Inequality

Index	50th Round	55th Round	55th Round with Step 1 Correction
Rural			
Log AM-log GM	0.14	0.11	0.14
Variance of logs of incomes	0.23	0.21	0.24
Urban			
Log AM-log GM	0.19	0.20	0.21
Variance of logs of incomes	0.34	0.34	0.37
All-India			
Log AM-log GM	0.17	0.18	0.19
Variance of logs of incomes	0.29	0.29	0.32

Source: Deaton and Drèze (2002).

additionally factor in the substantial reduction in urban poverty, the rise in inequality would not seem to be especially alarming—the growth engine has done an excellent job of pulling the poor into gainful employment. Deaton and Drèze (2002, p. 3740) nevertheless take an almost ominous view of the change in the following words: "To sum up, except for the absence of clear evidence of rising intra-rural inequality within states, we find strong indications of a pervasive increase in economic inequality in the nineties. This is a new development in the Indian economy: until 1993–94, the all-India Gini coefficients of per capita consumer expenditure in rural and urban areas were fairly stable." They go on to calculate that if growth between 1993–94 and 1999–2000 had been distribution neutral, all-India poverty reduction would have been approximately 1.7 percentage points higher.

The Dubious Case for Equity Driven Policies

Even taking the strong conclusion of Deaton and Drèze on the rise in inequality at face value, any policy implications of decompositions such as these must be drawn very carefully. The implicit message of the decomposition exercise is that countries like India must actively pursue policies aimed at the reduction of inequality. But this can be risky, in that such an approach may undermine the poverty reduction objective.

Policies aimed at tackling inequality can be broadly divided into two categories: tax and expenditure polices that redistribute, rather than create, income from the higher-income groups to lower-income groups, and policies that do not use resources but improve the ability of lower-income groups to profit from the economy and its growth. Policies such as progressive income taxation, the employment guarantee scheme, and subsidies on food and fertilizer fall in the first category, while affirmative action involving reservation of jobs and slots in educational institutions for certain disadvantaged sections of the society fall in the second category.

While there is some role for redistributive policies that directly target the poor, I am deeply skeptical of the case for assigning such policies a central role in the quest for poverty reduction or deploying them to address inequality beyond what is required to fight poverty. There are at least three reasons for this skepticism. First, in principle, increased equality can have a direct adverse impact on poverty if redistribution of income from a few individuals to many leads to increased conspicuous consumption and reduced philanthropy. Bhagwati (2004, pp. 66–67) puts the matter succinctly:

> If a thousand people become millionaires, the inequality is less than if Bill Gates gets to make a billion all by himself. But the thousand millionaires, with only a million each, will likely buy expensive vacations, BMWs, houses in the Hamptons, and toys at FAO Schwarz. In contrast, Gates will not be able to spend his billion even if he were to buy a European castle a day, and the unconscionable wealth would likely propel him, as in fact it has, to spend the bulk of the money on social good.

Second, policies aimed at the reduction of income inequality may also have an adverse effect on growth, and therefore on poverty. Ultimately, growth and income distribution are determined simultaneously, so that a shift in the policies to push income distribution toward greater equality also impacts growth. The empirical evidence on whether policies that promote greater equality also lead to faster growth is at best mixed.[2]

Finally and most important, while it is not difficult to identify policies that promote equity and growth simultaneously, once equity and fairness are turned into explicit goals of the policy, populism among the political leadership and the ability of the lobbies to capture the policies often leads to the adoption of precisely those policies that are detrimental to growth. It is here that the World Bank (2005a) makes a major error of judgment in the *World Development Report 2006: Equity and Development.* Arguing that there are many policies that promote growth while promoting greater equity, it tries to put equity at the center of policymaking.

No country offers a better illustration of the perverse outcome of putting equity at the center stage of policy than India. It was the desire to establish a socialistic pattern of society that led Indian policymakers to assign a dominant role to the public sector in industry. The same desire also contributed to the control of the private sector through industrial licensing. And when the liberal foreign investment policy and relatively relaxed investment and import licensing regime in the 1950s led to rapid growth of private industry and the emergence of several large industrial houses, it was once again the concern for equality, captured in the memorable phrase *Garibi Hatao*, coined and popularized by Prime Minister Indira Gandhi, that led to the erection of the massive regulatory structure that even 20 years of reforms have not been able to demolish entirely.

To cap the concentration of economic power in industry, Mrs. Gandhi confined all future investments by business houses having investments in land, buildings, and machinery in excess of 200 million rupees ($27 million) to a narrow list of 19 "core" industries. At the other extreme, she reserved many labor-intensive products for production exclusively by small-scale units, entities with investment in machinery and plant not exceeding 750,000 rupees ($100,000). Considerations that large banks did not adequately lend to the smaller enterprises or open rural branches led Mrs. Gandhi to nationalize them. She also restricted foreign equity in an enterprise to 40 percent. Undertakings with 100 or more workers were denied the right to fire employees. The acquisition of vacant land in the great cities by households and firms was limited to just 500 square meters. Marginal income tax rates on even modest incomes were set at 95 percent. Concerned that intermediaries in the grain market were depriving farmers of their rightful price, Mrs. Gandhi also tried to nationalize the wholesale grain trade, but had to reverse course midway due to a massive disruption in the market.

Luckily, there was one area in which the calls for equality got trumped by the "national" interest: the Green Revolution. The Left parties and their sympathizers had been vehemently opposed to the introduction of the high yielding varieties of seeds for fear they would benefit the richer farmers, and the decline in the price resulting from higher yields would impoverish the less well-to-do farmers. Luckily, the heavy-handed and intrusive approach of President Lyndon Johnson toward India strengthened the hand of those seeking self-sufficiency in food at the national level.

More recently, some of the reforms in India have become hostage to the capture resulting from the pursuit of equity and fairness. To counter the exclusionary attitudes and correct the past discrimination, the Indian Constitution mandated reservation of fixed proportions of the slots in public educational institutions and public sector jobs for groups of castes and tribes listed in a schedule, and hence called the "scheduled castes and tribes." The payoff to this policy in terms of increased opportunity for the poor has been limited: The castes and tribes within the reserved categories that happened to have better opportunities to begin with managed to capture the lion's share of the reserved slots. Moreover, in due course, other caste groups with lesser claims to discrimination but greater political clout also sought and got reservation.

At the same time, the proliferation of reservation has had a detrimental impact on the economic reforms, and hence on growth potential. Today, privatization of public sector enterprises has been partially stalled because there is no provision for caste-based reservation in the private sector. Rather than privatize, the government has chosen to partially disinvest, which keeps the enterprises in the public sector and preserves the reservation. Likewise, the appearance of private universities in India has been an anathema, partially because the reservation policy could not be applied to private educational institutions not aided by the government.

It was only after the Indian policymakers gave up their obsession with fighting the concentration of economic power that industry was returned to the healthier growth achieved in phase I. In the 1980s, the change came largely surreptitiously, through an increase in the maximum limit on investment permitted without a license, a hike in the asset limit defining the MRTP firms, and selective delicensing of industries. In the 1990s, the change became more overt with an end to licensing and MRTP regulations, and the opening up to foreign investors.

REGIONAL INEQUALITY

Once again, let us consider the empirical evidence and its implications for policy in turn.

Empirical Evidence

Though the increase in regional inequality remains subject to considerable debate among scholars, the bottom line is that if we go by per-capita incomes across states, inequality has definitely gone up. Shetty (2003, table 6) reports the Gini coefficient for real per-capita gross state domestic product (GSDP) for all states as well as for the 16 major states between 1980–81 and 2000–01. The coefficient shows a steadily rising trend throughout the period, its value for all states rising from 0.209 in 1980–81 to 0.217 in 1987–88, 0.237 in 1993–94 and 0.292 in 2000–01. The rise is even sharper for the 16 major states.

Many researchers have attempted to address the issue of regional inequality in terms of convergence and divergence of per-capita state incomes. Singh, Bhandari, Chen, and Khare (2003) review the evidence based on studies by these researchers. The question these studies ask is whether per-capita GSDP has grown faster, on the average, in the states that initially had lower per-capita GSDP, thus leading to a convergence of per-capita GSDPs across states. While conclusions vary according to the time period chosen and whether the regressions test for conditional or unconditional convergence, the weight of the evidence from this literature favors divergence, which is consistent with the conclusion based on the rising Gini coefficient.[3]

N. Singh and Srinivasan (2002) argue, however, that per-capita GSDP is only one measure of welfare, and that inequality can also be analyzed in terms of other indicators. They then consider the National Human Development Index (HDI), published by the Planning Commission, which takes into account eight variables: per-capita expenditure, head count poverty ratio, literacy rate, a formal education enrollment index, infant mortality rate, life expectancy, access to safe water, and access to housing constructed with relatively permanent materials. Singh and Srinivasan find that the movements in this index offer no evidence of rising interstate inequality in the 1990s. The unweighted standard deviation of the index across 14 major states falls marginally from 0.075 in 1991 to 0.072 in 2001, but due to the rise in the average value of the index across states, the coefficient of variation falls substantially, from 0.185 to 0.155, over the same period. Singh, Bhandari, Chen, and Khare (2003) have gone on to apply the convergence analysis, using the Planning Commission's HDI, and have found evidence in favor of convergence.

Why the Case for Policy Intervention Is Weak

Insofar as the policymakers and analysts have a tendency to focus more centrally on the GDP rather than the HDI, the popular view remains that interstate inequality has gone up and that something needs to be done about it. As in the case of national inequality discussed above, the case for such intervention is weak. At least five points can be made in this regard.

First, in considering the interventions, the critical question we must ask is whether increasing inequality across states is the result of richer states getting richer and poor states getting poorer, or of all states growing fast but richer states growing faster.[4] If the latter, in all likelihood the poor are benefiting everywhere, and that is likely to cushion the political fallout from increased inequality across states. In such a situation, before one rushes to take measures aimed at correcting inequality, one must consider the harmful effects such measures might have on growth across all states. For example, it is not inconceivable that such measures might have an adverse effect on the growth rates in the richer states, which may in turn have an adverse effect on the growth rates in the poorer states as well.

Table 8.2, which shows the growth rates pf per-capita net state domestic product in various states for various time periods, sheds some light on the question at hand.[5] The first time period (1981–88) in the table coincides with phase III, and the second (1988–94) and third (1994–2004), taken together, with phase IV. It can be seen that growth rates in phase IV are higher than those achieved in phase III for the vast majority of the states. By and large, growth has benefited all states, and the increase in interstate inequality has resulted from the richer states growing faster than the poorer states, rather than poorer states stagnating.

In a comparison of 16 large states on the basis of per-capita gross state domestic product, Shetty (2003) identifies Assam, Madhya Pradesh, Uttar Pradesh, Orissa,

TABLE 8.2: Growth in Per-Capita Net State Domestic Product

State/Union Territory	1981–88	1988–94	1994–2004
Andhra Pradesh	2.9	5.2	4.4
Arunachal Pradesh	5.4	7.0	0.4
Assam	2.0	1.3	1.3
Bihar	2.1	−0.3	2.8
Goa*	1.8	8.1	6.3
Gujarat	0.7	8.3	5.8
Haryana	2.1	4.7	3.6
Himachal*	1.4	3.9	4.7
Jammu & Kashmir†	−1.6	2.9	1.8
Karnataka*	3.0	4.5	4.7
Kerala	−0.2	6.0	4.3
Madhya Pradesh	1.2	3.3	2.7
Maharashtra	1.9	7.2	2.9
Manipur	2.4	2.0	4.3
Meghalaya*	1.3	2.3	3.9
Orissa	0.9	2.8	2.9
Punjab	3.6	2.8	2.2
Rajasthan	1.3	6.7	3.6
Tamil Nadu	3.1	5.6	4.2
Tripura†	1.1	4.4	8.2
Uttar Pradesh*	1.7	2.2	1.2
West Bengal*	2.0	3.0	5.5
Andaman & Nicobar†	0.6	3.0	0.6
Delhi*	3.2	3.9	5.0
Pondicherry	1.1	−0.9	9.9

*Growth rate for the last period is over 1994–2003.

†Growth rate for the last period is over 1994–2002.

Growth rates for 1981–88 and 1988–94 are based on the product measured at 1980–81 prices, and for 1994–2004, on product measured at 1993–94 prices.

Source: Author's calculations, using data in RBI (2005a, table 9).

Rajasthan, and Bihar as the bottom six states during 1980–2001, regardless of the choice of the year. Orissa and Bihar, in that order, remain at the bottom of this group throughout. Rajasthan begins third from the bottom in the early 1980s but reaches the top within the group in the early 1990s and stays there. Madhya Pradesh begins at the top within the group but drops to the second position in the early 1990s and stays there.

According to table 8.2, among the six bottom states, only Assam saw a clear decline in its growth rate in phase IV over phase III. Among the remaining five, Rajasthan, Madhya Pradesh, and Orissa saw a clear and significant rise in the growth rates of per-capita net domestic product in phase IV. Bihar saw a sharp decline from 2.1 percent during phase III to –0.3 percent during 1988–94, but recovered to 2.8 percent during the longer phase of 1994–2004. Uttar Pradesh had the opposite fate: Its growth rate rose from 1.7 percent in phase III to 2.2 percent during 1988–94, but fell to 1.2 percent during 1994–2004.

The second reason why the case for intervention to directly address the issue of regional inequality is weak is that insofar as this inequality reflects slower progress in poverty alleviation in the poorer states, an attack on poverty would automatically attack regional inequality. Any national program that seriously aims to alleviate poverty must automatically focus on the four poorest states as measured by per-capita state incomes: Assam, Uttar Pradesh, Orissa, and Bihar. To this extent, the concern for regional inequality coincides with the concern for poverty. But any extra attention to inequality reduction across states independent of the concern for poverty can be counterproductive. For instance, diversion of infrastructure investment from richer states, on grounds of regional balance, is bound to undermine the growth objective.

Third, leaving poverty aside, inequality in growth rates across states, even when it results from richer states growing faster and the other states stagnating, may lead to beneficial demonstration effects on the latter. Thus, for instance, fast growth in Tamil Nadu and Karnataka may inspire other states, such as Bihar and Uttar Pradesh, to play catch-up, as has already been the case with Rajasthan and West Bengal. When it comes to rapid growth in South Korea or China, these latter states may be inclined to take the view that the Chinese are different or that the Indian conditions are different. But when some of the states *within* India begin to grow at the East Asian rates, lagging states may be more persuaded of their own potential. Additionally, the state leaders may feel greater pressure to deliver on better policies and infrastructure. To some degree, this has certainly happened in states such as Rajasthan, Madhya Pradesh, and West Bengal. The government in West Bengal has been particularly aggressive in shedding its Marxist credentials and courting foreign investment. This and the previous argument suggest that the focus of the government's policies has to remain on growth and poverty reduction. At least within limits, inequality can be tolerated.

Fourth, it bears remembering that the activist policies to promote regional balance during the investment licensing era did not yield particularly encouraging results. Under the licensing regime, the location of the manufacturing facility could be made a condition of the grant of the license. The central government used this power to distribute industries across states in order to achieve its regional balance objective. Likewise, freight equalization policies were adopted to deliver raw materials at the same cost to nearby and distant locations, so that the latter would not be disadvantaged. But measures such as these fostered inefficiency and hampered the growth of industry.

Finally, given interstate mobility of workers, migration is likely to help alleviate regional inequality at least to some degree. On the one hand, such movements reduce the pressure on land in regions of emigration and thus raise wages there, and on the other hand, they bring remittances to the families of emigrants. For instance, migrants from Bihar today work in significant numbers in richer states such as Delhi, Punjab, and Haryana, and repatriate a part of their earnings to their families. This evidently helps reduce inequality, though it is not captured in the per-capita state domestic product.

URBAN-RURAL INEQUALITY

The ratio of urban to rural per-capita consumption expenditure has risen steadily in India at least since the mid-1980s. According to the calculations done by Deaton and Drèze (1992, table 3), the average per-capita consumption expenditure between 1993–94 and 1999–2000 rose 8.7 percent in the rural areas and 16.6 percent in the urban areas in India. Thus, there is clear evidence of rising urban-rural divide.

From an economic standpoint, at least within limits, this form of increase in inequality should be least disturbing. In the traditional, labor-abundant economies, a key component of the process of economic transformation is the movement of workers from farm to nonfarm activities. While farm activities need not always be rural, and nonfarm activities urban, for the vast majority of workers such a correspondence exists. Therefore, it should be no surprise that rapid economic transformation is usually accompanied by increased urban-rural inequality. It is the faster growth in incomes in the urban areas that pulls rural workers into gainful employment there. Nevertheless, politicians tend to be more sensitive to this form of inequality than any other. For instance, in the aftermath of its surprise victory in the 2004 Parliament elections, the United Progressive Alliance (UPA) took the populist view that it was voted into power because the reforms under the outgoing government of the National Democratic Alliance (NDA) had increased the urban-rural divide. The inference was not only unsupported by evidence, but actually contradicted by it: There had been no rural-urban divide in the election results. As I (Panagariya, 2004d) document, there was a very strong state-level anti-incumbency element at play in the elections. Moreover, in the states where the NDA lost—for example, in Andhra Pradesh and Haryana—it lost in both rural and urban areas. Likewise, in the states where the Congress Party lost—for example, in Rajasthan and Madhya Pradesh—it lost not just in urban but also in rural constituencies.

The only hypothesis consistent with the observed pattern of the vote is the one offered by Bhagwati and Panagariya (2004), which has since been widely adopted by journalists and other analysts. According to this hypothesis, the anti-incumbent vote principally reflected the revolution of rising expectations. The view that the reforms had left the poor behind is convincingly contradicted by the extensive compilation of the evidence in the previous chapter. In Bhagwati and Panagariya's view, what accounted for the anti-incumbent sentiment that cut across the urban-rural divide was the belief by voters that the governments were failing to deliver on the reforms fast enough. In turn, they predicted that if the UPA government failed to deliver faster on the reforms, it might face the same fate as the NDA government in due course.

As with national and regional inequality, excessive preoccupation with the urban-rural inequality in a fast-growing economy runs the risk of diverting the government from pro-growth policies and toward wasteful populist policies. This has happened to some degree following the UPA victory, with the government redirecting its expenditures from urban toward rural projects. The redirection has led to deleterious effects on public investment in urban infrastructure in such growth centers as Bangalore, and in delays on such urgent projects as the renovation of airports.

CONCLUSIONS

According to the available evidence, rural inequality has remained unchanged or has declined marginally while urban inequality has at worst increased by 10 to 12 percent, depending on the index and methodology used. Evidence on the rise in the urban-rural inequality and regional inequality is more compelling. I have argued, however, that none of these developments warrant a shift in policies beyond what is desirable from the viewpoint of poverty alleviation. India's past experience shows that preoccupation with inequality can lead to the adoption of policies that are anti-growth and anti-poor. The policy regime during phase I and, especially, phase II was driven principally by concerns with inequality. The expansion of the public sector, strict industrial licensing, draconian restraints on investment by the MRTP firms, nationalization of banks, the amendments of the Industrial Disputes Act (IDA) to outlaw the firing of workers by firms with 100 or more workers under any circumstances, and the tight ceiling on urban landholdings had been motivated by equity considerations.

Regarding regional inequality, two points must be stressed. First, the increase in inequality has taken place in an environment of generally rising incomes. With two or three exceptions, even the states at the bottom of the distribution have experienced acceleration in growth in per-capita incomes in phase IV over phase III. Thus, fortunes have improved uniformly in contrast to the earlier times of general stagnation.

Second, from the future policy perspective, it is important to remember that direct measures that aim to address poverty must concentrate more heavily on the lagging states. Beyond this bias in favor of the lagging states, it will be imprudent for the government to embark upon activist policies to correct regional inequality. The ability of the government to change the distribution is generally very limited, and the risk of choking growth in the fast-growing states is great. Besides, some inequality among states may provide a healthy dose of competition. The fact that some Indian states can grow at the East Asian double-digit rates may be more effective in persuading the lagging states of their own potential than the East Asian growth itself.

The same set of points applies to increased urban-rural inequality. Growth has pulled up the living standards in both the rural and the urban sectors. More important, it is only through rapid increases in urban incomes that the rural population will be absorbed into gainful employment in the urban areas. Rather than slow the reform process for fear that the rural poor may be left behind, the experience so far favors accelerating it. As long as rural-urban migration offers an avenue for rural workers to compete for jobs in the urban sector, there is no reason to suppress growth in the latter to reverse the process.

PART III

Macroeconomics

9

DEFICITS AND DEBT

Is a Crisis around the Corner?

A key feature of the Indian economy since the early 1950s has been an exception-ally stable macroeconomic environment. To be sure, India has had its share of macroeconomic crises, but virtually all of them have been mild in comparison to those of their Latin American counterparts and have been quickly contained without major damage to the economy. Moreover, most of them had their origins in external shocks such as drought, oil price hikes, and microeconomic distortions rather than macroeconomic mismanagement.

For the vast majority of the period, the inflation rate in India has been in the single digits, and even when it has gone into double digits, it has rarely exceeded 15 percent. The Consumer Price Index for industrial workers has risen more than 20 percent during only two years: 21 percent in 1973–74 and 27 percent in 1974–75. These were years characterized by drought and a major oil price shock. Even these exceptional inflation rates were contained relatively quickly, with the Consumer Price Index actually declining in the following two years and the simple average of the inflation rates over the following four years being just 1.2 percent.

The unemployment rate, insofar as it can be accurately measured in an economy characterized by underemployment in the farm sector and in the informal services sector, has also been stable (chapter 7). Unemployment estimates based on the National Sample Surveys do not show periods of significant prolonged unemploy-ment in the economy. Likewise, India has had no banking crisis; indeed, even indi-vidual bank failures in the recent decades have been virtually absent.

Macroeconomic crises in India have almost always been dominated by balance of payments difficulties. The crisis in 1957–58 was entirely of this nature and led to the adoption of foreign exchange budgeting. The crisis during 1965–67 had its ori-gins in two consecutive droughts that necessitated increased food imports, and had an adverse impact on exports through reduced supplies of raw materials. Both fac-tors made the foreign exchange situation precarious, leading to a sizable devaluation of the rupee under pressure from the World Bank and the U.S. government. The crises in 1980–81 and 1991 were also primarily balance of payments crises, with the former leading to a substantial hike in borrowing from the IMF and the latter culminating in a substantial devaluation.

The only macroeconomic crisis that did not seem to have an overt balance of payments component was the inflation episode in the mid-1970s mentioned above. The domestic inflation at the time did not have a major impact on the competitiveness of Indian goods, and hence the balance of payments, partially because the switch in the peg from the U.S. dollar to the pound sterling following the breakdown of the Bretton Woods system, and the depreciation of the pound led to the depreciation of the rupee against the dollar and other currencies. According to Joshi and Little (1994, p. 56), depreciation of the pound sterling led to a 20 percent depreciation of the nominal effective exchange rate of the rupee.

In this part of the book, I discuss key macroeconomic features of the Indian economy and the major macroeconomic policy issues. The focus is primarily on the recent developments and policy issues facing the country. I begin with a consideration of the savings-investment identity and its relationship to the balance of payments accounts. The identity offers a useful logical framework for the discussion of various macroeconomic phenomena to be considered in the rest of part III.

THE INVESTMENT-SAVINGS AND BALANCE OF PAYMENTS IDENTITIES

According to the conventional accounting system, a country must finance its private investment (I_P) from private, government, or foreign savings (S_P, S_G, or S_F). Formally,

$$I_P \equiv S_P + S_G + S_F. \tag{9.1}$$

Private savings in this identity represent savings by households plus retained earnings of businesses.[1] Government savings equal budget surplus properly defined to include the central and state governments and public enterprises. If the government budget is in deficit, it absorbs a part of the private and foreign savings. Foreign savings equal the current account deficit, which in turn equals national expenditure minus national income. The current account can be in deficit (i.e., the national expenditure can exceed national income) only if foreigners lend the country a part of their savings. On the other hand, if the current account is in surplus (the national expenditure falls short of the national income), the country invests a part of its savings abroad.

Table 9.1 shows private investment, private savings, fiscal deficit (of the central and state governments), and the current account deficit as proportions of the GDP from 1980–81 to 2003–04. Column 6 shows the sum of the savings available to the private sector from the three sources: private, government, and foreign. Ideally, this sum should exactly equal private investment shown in column 2. But this rarely holds in the Indian data, principally due to the accounting anomalies resulting from the treatment of profits and losses of public enterprises in the government budget.

TABLE 9.1: The Investment-Savings Identity

Year	Gross Private Investment	Gross Private Savings	Gross Fiscal Deficit	Current Account Deficit	Savings Available to Private Investors	Capital Inflow	Reserves Accumulation	Gross Primary Deficit
1	*2*	*3*	*4*	*5*	*6(=3−4+5)*	*7*	*8*	*9*
1980–81	10.3	15.4	7.5	1.5	9.5	0.9	−0.6	5.4
1981–82	12.3	14.1	6.3	1.7	9.5	0.3	−1.3	4.1
1982–83	11.0	13.9	5.9	1.7	9.8	1.1	−0.7	3.4
1983–84	10.0	14.3	7.3	1.5	8.5	1.2	−0.3	4.8
1984–85	11.2	15.9	9.0	1.2	8.1	1.5	0.4	6.2
1985–86	12.9	16.3	8.0	2.1	10.4	2.0	−0.2	4.9
1986–87	12.0	16.2	9.9	1.9	8.2	1.9	0.0	6.5
1987–88	12.6	18.4	9.2	1.8	11.0	1.8	0.1	5.5
1988–89	14.2	18.8	8.5	2.7	13.0	2.8	0.0	4.6
1989–90	14.1	20.3	8.9	2.3	13.8	2.4	0.0	4.6
1990–91	14.7	22.0	9.4	3.1	15.6	2.3	−0.8	5.0
1991–92	13.1	20.1	7.0	0.3	13.4	1.5	1.1	2.3
1992–93	15.2	20.2	7.0	1.7	14.9	1.6	−0.1	2.1
1993–94	13.0	21.9	8.3	0.4	14.1	3.5	3.1	3.3
1994–95	14.7	23.2	7.1	1.0	17.1	2.8	1.8	1.9
1995–96	18.9	23.1	6.5	1.7	18.2	1.3	−0.3	1.6
1996–97	14.7	21.5	6.4	1.2	16.3	3.0	1.8	1.3
1997–98	16.0	21.8	7.3	1.4	15.9	2.5	1.1	2.1
1998–99	14.8	22.5	9.0	1.0	14.4	2.0	1.0	3.7
1999–2000	16.7	25.2	9.5	1.0	16.7	2.5	1.4	3.8
2000–01	16.3	25.8	9.6	0.6	16.8	1.9	1.3	3.6
2001–02	16.0	26.2	10.0	−0.7	15.5	1.8	2.5	3.7
2002–03P	17.3	27.2	9.5	−1.2	16.4	2.1	3.3	3.1
2003–04QE	17.4	28.5	8.4	−1.7	18.3	3.5	5.2	2.0

Note: "P" indicates "provisional" and "QE" "quick estimates."

Source: Author's calculations using data in RBI (2005a, table 1, col. 7; table 10, cols. 4 and 5; table 13, cols. 2 and 4; table 116, cols. 2, 3 and 4; table 145, item III, cols, 46–55.

Figure 9.1 plots the evolution of the key elements of the investment-savings identity from 1980–81 to 2003–04.

Perhaps the most notable feature of figure 9.1 is the steady rise in the private savings rate during the 24-year period covered. From an average of 14 percent in the early 1980s, the rate almost doubled to 28 percent in 2003–04. Rising private savings have pulled up private investment over the period covered, but not uniformly, due to differing behaviors of the fiscal and current account deficits.

In the 1980s, the larger fiscal deficits translated into larger current account deficits and only small crowding out of private investment. But following the 1991 crisis, as a part of the stabilization plan the government reduced both the fiscal deficit and the current account deficit by two to three percentage points. Insofar as savings are concerned, reductions in the twin deficits were essentially mutually canceling, so that the increases in private savings largely translated into increases in private investment. The fiscal deficit bottomed out in 1996–97, after which it began

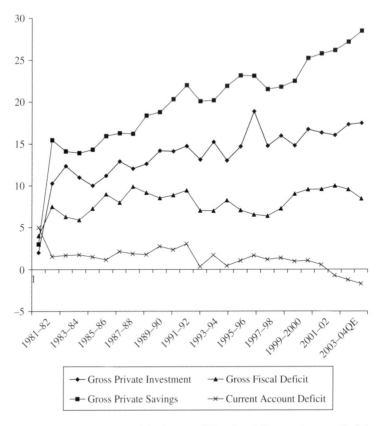

FIGURE 9.1: Private Investment and Savings, and Fiscal and Current Account Deficits

to climb again, peaking at 10 percent in 2001–02. But this time, the current account showed either modest deficits or even surpluses. The result was that the fiscal deficit absorbed a large chunk of the increased private savings. Once again, private investment got shortchanged.

Although we will consider the external account in detail in the next chapter, it is useful at this point to note that the current account surplus (negative of the current account deficit) is defined as the sum of net exports of goods and services, net factor income earned abroad, and net unilateral transfers received from abroad. In turn, net exports are defined as exports minus imports; net factor income earned abroad is income earned by domestically owned factors located abroad, minus income earned by foreign- owned factors located at home; and unilateral transfers principally include aid and remittances. In the Indian case, remittances make a large contribution to the current account balance. In addition, rising software exports have contributed significantly to the balance.

Denoting the current account surplus by CA, we can replace S_F by $-$ CA in (9.1). After a slight rearrangement, we can rewrite this identity as

$$I_P - (S_P + S_G) \equiv -CA. \tag{9.2}$$

In this form, the identity says that foreign savings (i.e., − CA) must cover the gap between total private investment and total domestic savings.

A remaining useful step in the discussion of the investment-savings identity is to relate it to the external capital account. The main transactions on the capital account include portfolio and direct foreign investment flows; short- and long-term private and public borrowing and lending abroad; and the change in the official reserves (mainly foreign exchange reserves of the central bank). For now, let us represent all net capital inflows other than the change in the official reserves in any given year by K, and the net increase in the official reserves by ΔR. The balance of payments identity implies

$$K + CA \equiv \Delta R. \tag{9.3}$$

This identity is most readily understood in the special case when the Reserve Bank of India (RBI) does not intervene in the foreign exchange market and therefore holds $\Delta R = 0$. In this case, inflows and outflows of foreign exchange associated with all international transactions must exactly balance. Positive net capital inflows worth, say, $10 billion generate a net supply of $10 billion on the market. Since we are assuming the RBI does not buy or sell foreign exchange in the market, this supply must be absorbed by an equal current account deficit. The exchange rate must adjust to ensure that some private agents are willing to absorb this supply. Only if the RBI decides to purchase or sell foreign exchange to influence the exchange rate can there be imbalance between net capital inflows and the current account deficit. For instance, if the RBI increases its reserves in any given year, such an increase must come from a net positive balance on K+CA.

It is useful to explain the balance of payments identity in (9.3) with the help of an explicit example. Suppose the only current account transaction in a given year happens to be the export of a machine worth $100 million by an Indian firm. Suppose further that the importer of the machine in, say, the United States pays for it with a check worth $100 million. In principle, the Indian firm has several options (though some of these may not be currently available due to capital controls). For example, it may choose to deposit the check in a New York bank where it holds an account. In this case, the current account surplus generated by the export is exactly offset by a capital outflow: CA = $100 million and K = − $100 million with K+CA = 0.

Alternatively, the firm may deposit the check in a bank in New Delhi and the New Delhi bank may deposit it in its New York bank and credit the firm's account with rupees worth $100 million. Again, we have a capital outflow with K = − $100 million, except that the owner of the dollar deposit in New York is the New Delhi bank instead of the firm.

Yet another alternative is that the New Delhi bank does not want to hold its assets in dollars and therefore takes the check to the Reserve Bank of India. The RBI "buys" the dollar check in return for equivalent rupees and then invests the $100 million in U.S. Treasury bills. In this case, CA = $100 million, K = 0, and $\Delta R = $100 million. The outflow of $100 million in this case takes place through the RBI purchase of the dollars that are then invested abroad (in U.S. Treasury bills). No matter what option various agents exercise, identity (9.3) necessarily holds.

Combining (9.2) and (9.3), we can obtain the following crucial identity:

$$I_P - (S_P + S_G) \equiv -CA \equiv K - \Delta R. \tag{9.4}$$

Thus, if combined domestic savings fall short of domestic investment, either capital inflows or decumulation of reserves or a combination thereof will have to fill the gap.

Two simple but powerful implications of this identity may be noted. First, unless it is offset by increased current account deficit, the fiscal deficit, which amounts to negative government saving, undercuts private investment. In India, this deficit has been 8 to 10 percent of the GDP since the mid-1990s. Given that the RBI has held the current account deficit strictly below 2 percent of the GDP, the deficit has translated into a sizable cut in potential private investment.

It must be acknowledged, however, that this crowding-out effect is often overstated for two reasons:

- A part of government spending finances public investment, such as that in infrastructure, so that private savings absorbed by the government do partially contribute to capital formation. But public investment as a proportion of the GDP fell from 8.7 percent in 1994–95 to 5.6 percent in 2003–04. Thus the fiscal deficit increasingly turned private savings into current public expenditures.
- Another qualification often ignored by even sophisticated analysts is that even leaving aside the Ricardian equivalence considerations, the reduction in the fiscal deficit is unlikely to leave the private savings entirely unchanged.[2] If the deficit is reduced through increased taxation, household and business incomes will fall, and therefore private savings will decline. If we cut the fiscal deficit by cutting current expenditure, private savings are likely to be affected less, but even in this case they will not remain entirely unaffected. Specifically, if the cut in government expenditure withdraws certain services that individuals must now buy privately, private consumption will rise and savings will fall.

The second implication of the identity in (9.4) concerns foreign capital inflows as a source of investment. It is tempting to view these inflows as a vast source of investment. Yet the reality is that only the part of net capital inflows that the RBI does not turn into foreign reserves, and thus allows it to be translated into the current account deficit, actually adds to the domestic savings. Given that large and persistent current account deficits often give rise to macroeconomic instability and crises, and that the appreciation of the exchange rate accompanying capital inflows can undercut exports, to date the RBI has chosen to turn a substantial part of the capital inflows into reserves. The maximum current account deficit India ran between 1994–95 and 2003–04 was 1.7 percent of the GDP. In 2002–03 and 2003–04, the current account was actually in surplus, implying that India invested a part of its savings abroad during these years.

Columns 7 and 8 in table 9.1 demonstrate the extent to which the RBI has chosen to neutralize capital inflows by the accumulation of reserves in recent years. During the last ten-year period shown, the RBI turned more than half of the capital inflows into reserves. In 2003–04, the reserve accumulation was a whopping 5.2 percent of the GDP, exceeding the total capital inflows of 3.5 percent of the GDP. Viewed differently, the stock of foreign exchange reserves of the RBI rose from $25 billion at the end of 1994–95 to $113 billion at the end of 2003–04, and reached $165 billion at the beginning of June 2006.

Given the concerns the RBI has with respect to the exchange rate and the current account, it is a mistake to expect capital inflows to contribute massively to capital formation. If the past experience is any guide, it is unlikely that this channel will annually contribute more than 2 percent of the GDP on a sustained basis. In the light of this fact, the benefits of capital inflows from abroad have to be viewed as much in terms of the links to the world markets, introduction of state-of-the-art management practices, and efficiency of the capital markets as in terms of additional funds for investment.

A BROAD FRAMEWORK OF ANALYSIS

The savings-investment and balance of payments identities offer a useful framework for a unified view of the macroeconomic analyses to be covered in part III. First, immediately below, we will study the implications of the fiscal deficit for the overall macroeconomic stability. In particular, we will analyze the relationship between the deficit and debt, and how persistent deficits can lead to such a large buildup of debt that it leads to a macroeconomic crisis. In the context of an open economy, deficits can also lead to the buildup of external debt, so that we must consider the possibility of domestic as well as external crisis.

Second, in the next chapter, we study the external imbalances on the current and capital accounts and their implications for the domestic economy, especially monetary policy. Insofar as the current account imbalances themselves depend on capital flows and the RBI policy toward reserves accumulation, the exchange rate, inflation, and regulations with respect to current account and capital account flows, these latter will form an integral part of our discussion.

Finally, savings by households, investment by businesses, fiscal deficits of the government, and foreign capital inflows and outflows all require financial interme-diation. These transactions bring us into the realm of the financial sector, whose development is crucial to the efficiency with which domestic and foreign savings are intermediated and invested. Therefore, in the last chapter in part III, we turn to a detailed discussion of the financial sector.

The savings-investment and balance of payments identities can also be helpful in gaining an overall perspective on various microeconomic issues considered in parts IV and V of the book. Broadly stated, the fiscal deficit is the difference between expenditures and revenues. On the revenue side, we must consider the efficiency of the tax system. This requires a look at the direct and indirect taxes; the for-mer include personal and corporate income taxes, and the latter, trade and domestic commodity taxes. The tax system must be designed and reformed to raise the requi-site volume of revenue while minimizing the efficiency cost of taxation.

The expenditures themselves are divided into public sector wages; various sub-sidies; spending on economic services such as telecommunications, electricity, and transportation; and social spending such as that on health, water supply, and safety and education. These raise issues of civil service reform, subsidy reform, and effi-cient delivery of economic and social services. These tax and expenditure reform issues occupy us in part V of the book.

Turning to the external account, trade and foreign investment policies facing var-ious sectors must promote efficiency. Trade policy, in particular, is a very important instrument of enforcing efficiency through competition and specialization in the goods of comparative advantage of the country. It raises issues of unilateral, bilateral, and multilateral liberalization in a natural way. Insofar as many services are tradable as well, it also brings into focus regulatory policies that must be adopted in order to facilitate the opening of services sectors.

Private savings consist of household and business savings. In turn, they depend on the ability of households and businesses to generate incomes and profits, respectively. Therefore, here we are confronted with the product and factor market policies and reforms in agriculture, industry, and services. We will take up the external trade policies and internal microeconomic policies relating to industry, services, and agriculture in part IV of the book.

DEFICITS, DEBT, AND CRISIS

We have already seen that, even taking into account public investments, fiscal deficits have had a detrimental effect on investment in India. But this is only one of the two important detrimental effects of the fiscal deficit. Persistent large deficits also lead to the accumulation of debt and, if left unchecked, can lead to a macroeconomic crisis. To see how persistent deficits can build up to a crisis, it is useful to briefly consider what macroeconomists call debt dynamics.

To finance the deficit, the government must borrow. It has three potential sources of borrowing: foreign, domestic households and firms, and the domestic monetary system. While the precise source of borrowing has important implications for the form the crisis takes, for now let us abstract from this issue. Instead, we will focus on the total borrowing.

A key variable on which macroeconomic stability depends is the ratio of the total public debt to the GDP. If this ratio is low, the government is seen as able to service the debt. It can pay the interest and principal due out of its revenues. If the revenues are insufficient, it can borrow additional funds to make the payments. With a low debt to GDP ratio, markets see the government as solvent and are willing to lend more to it. It is only when the debt to GDP ratio is high that the government may have difficulty borrowing more to pay the interest and principal. And if the economy is also doing poorly, revenues may fall short of the needs, and the government may be forced into a default.

To see how debt dynamics works, denote the government's total debt at current prices by D, GDP at market prices by Y, and the debt to GDP ratio by b. Thus, we have

$$b = \frac{D}{Y}.$$

(9.5)

We want to know how this ratio grows with budget deficits. A purely arithmetic point is that the ratio grows at the rate equal to the difference between the rates of growth of the numerator and the denominator. Therefore, using a circumflex (^) over a variable to denote the rate of growth of that variable, we have

$$\hat{b} = \hat{D} - \hat{Y}.$$

(9.6)

The rate of growth of D equals the fiscal deficit divided by the existing debt. We can divide the fiscal deficit into two components: interest on the existing debt and the rest. We refer to the latter as "primary deficit." Letting P denote the primary deficit in current rupees and R the nominal interest rate paid on the existing debt, we can represent the fiscal deficit by RD + P. The rate of increase in D is then R + (P/D). Representing the growth rate of the GDP at market prices by G, we can rewrite (9.6) as

$$\hat{b} = \left(R + \frac{P}{D}\right) - G \tag{9.7}$$

Writing P/D = (P/Y)/(D/Y) = ρ/b, where ρ = P/Y is the primary deficit as a proportion of the GDP, we can rewrite (9.7) as

$$\hat{b} = (R - G) + \frac{\rho}{b}. \tag{9.7'}$$

For a given interest rate, GDP growth rate, the primary deficit, and an initial level of the debt to GDP ratio, this equation allows us to plot the path of the debt to GDP ratio over time. Ceteris paribus, a high interest rate and a high primary deficit imply a high fiscal deficit, and therefore a rising debt to GDP ratio. A high GDP growth rate has the opposite implication.

Equation (9.7') allows us to do some interesting hypothetical experiments. For example, suppose the government wants to stabilize the debt to GDP ratio at its current level. Then, assuming the current growth rate and interest rate will persist in the future, we can calculate the primary deficit required to stabilize the debt at its current level by setting the right-hand side of (9.7') equal to zero and solving for ρ. Thus, we have

$$\rho = b(G - R). \tag{9.8}$$

For example, suppose G = .10, R = .08, and b = .8. According to (9.8), stabilization of b at its current level requires ρ = 0.8(.10 − .08) = .016, or 1.6 percent. If the current primary deficit is 4 percent, this means bringing it down by 2.4 percentage points. Otherwise, the debt to GDP ratio will rise further. The difference between the current primary deficit and the primary deficit that stabilizes the debt to GDP ratio is called the "primary gap." In our example, the primary gap is 2.4 percent.

Alternatively, we may ask what would happen if the current primary deficit is maintained. Again, assuming the current GDP growth rate and interest rate would persist, we can calculate the level at which the debt to GDP ratio would stabilize by setting the righthand side to zero and solving for b. Thus, we have

$$b = \left(\frac{\rho}{G - R}\right). \tag{9.9}$$

For example, assume, as before, that the nominal GDP is expected to grow at the rate G = .10 and the nominal interest rate is expected to stay at R = .08. With the primary deficit maintained at ρ = .04, according to (9.9) the debt to GDP ratio will continue to rise until it reaches .04/(.06 − .04) = 2, or 200 percent! Of course, markets are unlikely to tolerate such a high debt to GDP ratio. The interest rate will rise or the growth rate will fall well before the debt to GDP ratio rises to 200 percent.

An important point to remember is that as the debt as a proportion of the GDP grows, interest payments on it as a proportion of the GDP grow as well. In turn, the fiscal deficit as a proportion of the GDP grows even if the primary deficit is held constant. For instance, in our second example above, the debt to GDP ratio stabilizes at 2. If the economy does reach that point, interest payments alone will contribute $R \cdot b = (.08)(2) = .16$, or 16 percent of the GDP, to the fiscal deficit. With the primary deficit at 4 percent, this means a total fiscal deficit of 20 percent! That is too large a deficit for the markets to tolerate, and the government will find itself unable to borrow from the market at 8 percent nominal interest well before the debt and fiscal deficit reach such a high level.

It is useful to consider the evolution of India's gross total debt since the 1980s at this point. Figure 9.2 shows this for the years 1980–81 to 2003–04. Until 1981–82, the total debt was below 40 percent of the GDP. But it steadily rose throughout the 1980s until it more than doubled, reaching the peak level of 82.4 percent in 1991–92, just a decade later. This was the time India faced the 1991 balance of payments crisis.

According to table 9.1 (column 4), the steady upward climb in the debt was accompanied by very large fiscal deficits during the 1980s, indicating the centrality of fiscal deficit to debt accumulation. According to the calculations done by

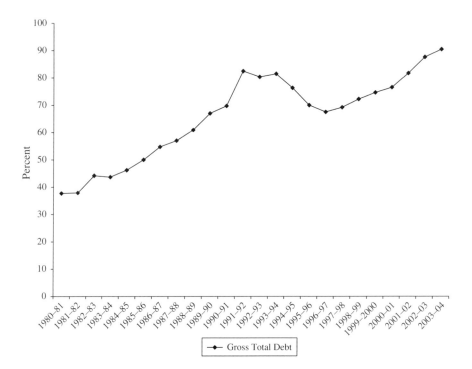

FIGURE 9.2: The Debt-to-GDP Ratio, 1980–81 to 2003–04

Rangarajan and Srivastava (2003) for the accumulation of the central government's debt, a key factor ameliorating the impact of the deficit was the large growth-interest rate differential throughout the 1980s. It exceeded five percentage points every year and was more than ten percentage points during four of the 11 years preceding 1991–92. The large differential resulted principally from financial repression that kept the nominal interest rates on the central government debt below the rate of inflation (implying negative real interest rates) throughout the 1980s. Therefore, the main driver of the debt in the 1980s, especially for the central government, was the high primary deficit. This is partially verified by column 9 of table 9.1, which shows the gross primary deficit for the central government, states, and union territories. During ten out of 11 years preceding the 1991 crisis, the primary deficit was more than 4 percent of the GDP.

The 1991 crisis was followed by efforts at macroeconomic stabilization and structural reforms. Because growth resumed relatively quickly and the primary deficit was substantially cut (see column 9 of table 9.1), the debt to GDP ratio declined during the first several years in the 1990s (figure 9.2). But toward the end of the 1990s, this trend reversed, with virtually all factors turning unfavorable: Real GDP growth rate fell, the primary deficit rose; and with the financial repression considerably reduced, the real interest rate climbed. According to the calculations by Rangarajan and Srivastava (2003, table A5), in 1995–96 the real interest rate on the central government debt became positive for the first time since 1978–79. In 2000–01, the real interest rate on the central government debt rose to 5.9 percent, with the growth-interest differential turning negative for the first time since 1954–55.

The debt to GDP ratio rose especially rapidly starting in 2001–02 and crossed the 90 percent mark in 2003–04. This level was substantially higher than the peak reached prior to the 1991 crisis. What is interesting, however, is that despite this fact, few economists are predicting a macroeconomic crisis in India today. For example, in their excellent paper on the budget deficits and debt, Buiter and Patel (2005–06) carry out some formal tests as well as an informal review of the developments, and conclude that the debt does not give reason for immediate alarm: Government solvency is not a serious concern. This contrast between the two situations calls for a closer look at other variables in the economy connected with the fiscal deficit and debt.

IS A REPEAT OF THE 1991 CRISIS IN THE OFFING?

In India, the gross total debt (as a proportion of the GDP) we have plotted in figure 9.2 is composed of four sources: internal (rupee) debt of the central government, rupee debt of the state governments (less debt to the central government), rupee debt of public enterprises not held by the government, and total foreign debt. The first three forms of debt carry rupee-denominated liabilities, and the last one, foreign-exchange-denominated liabilities.

The first difference between the late 1980s and the current debt situation is that the former was characterized by a much larger contribution of foreign debt. This can be seen from columns 5 and 6 of table 9.2, which respectively show the total domestic and foreign debts as proportions of the GDP. In 1991–92, the total debt was divided approximately equally between these two sources: Domestic debt was

42.4 percent of the GDP and foreign debt, 40 percent of the GDP. In 2003–04, foreign debt was only 15.2 percent of the GDP. During the 1980s, foreign debt as a proportion of the GDP had continuously risen, with the rate of expansion rising in the second half of the period. In contrast, in the postcrisis period, foreign debt as a proportion of the GDP has been declining.

Second, in the 1980s the composition of foreign debt turned progressively unfavorable. "Other" capital flows and errors and omissions moved from a large negative figure in the first half of the decade to a positive figure, indicating an increase in short-term borrowing in the latter period. The share of nonconcessional debt rose from 42 to 54 percent. The average maturity of debt declined from 27 to 20 years. In the postcrisis period, since foreign debt is relatively small, its composition is less of an issue.

TABLE 9.2: Debt-to-GDP Ratios

Year	CDD	SDD	PEDD	NTDD	TFD	GTD	R	NTFD	NTD
1	*2*	*3*	*4*	*5 (=2+3+4)*	*6*	*7 (=5+6)*	*8*	*9 (=6−8)*	*10 (=5+9)*
1980/81	20.5	4	1.6	26.1	11.6	37.7	3.8	7.8	33.9
1981/82	20	4.3	1.5	25.8	12.1	37.9	2.3	9.7	35.5
1982/83	23.9	4.4	1.9	30.2	14	44.2	2.5	11.5	41.7
1983/84	22	4.6	2.1	28.7	15	43.7	2.7	12.4	41
1984/85	23	4.6	2.2	29.8	16.5	46.2	2.9	13.6	43.4
1985/86	25.1	5.1	2.3	32.6	17.4	50	2.9	14.5	47.1
1986/87	27.7	5.1	2.6	35.4	19.3	54.7	2.7	16.6	52
1987/88	28.6	5.5	3.1	37.3	19.8	57	2.3	17.5	54.7
1988/89	29.6	5.5	3.9	39	21.9	60.9	1.6	20.2	59.2
1989/90	30.5	5.8	4.4	40.8	26.3	67	1.4	24.9	65.7
1990/91	30.7	6	4.8	41.4	28.3	69.7	1.8	26.5	67.9
1991/92	30.9	6.3	5.2	42.4	40	82.4	3.5	36.6	79
1992/93	32	6.4	4.8	43.2	37.1	80.3	4	33.1	76.3
1993/94	36	6.5	5.2	47.7	33.8	81.4	7	26.7	74.4
1994/95	35.5	6.4	4.5	46.5	29.8	76.3	7.8	22	68.5
1995/96	33.9	6.6	4.2	44.7	25.3	70	6.1	19.2	63.9
1996/97	33.8	6.7	4.6	45.1	22.4	67.5	6.9	15.6	60.7
1997/98	35.9	7	4.3	47.2	21.9	69.2	7.2	14.8	62
1998/99	37.2	7.5	5.8	50.5	21.7	72.2	7.9	13.8	64.3
1999/2000	40	8.7	5.5	54.3	20.3	74.6	8.5	11.8	66.1
2000/01	43	9.9	4.4	57.3	19.2	76.5	9.2	10	67.3
2001/02	47.6	10.8	4.9	63.3	18.4	81.7	11.4	7	70.3
2002/03	53	12.1	4.7	69.8	17.8	87.6	14.8	3	72.7
2003/04	56.6	13.8	4.7	75.1	15.2	90.4	18.6	−3.4	71.8
2004/05	57.4	14.1	NA	NA	NA	NA	20.1	NA	NA

CDD: Internal debt of the central government; less net credit outstanding from the Reserve Bank of India; plus liabilities on account of small savings fund and other accounts. SDD: Rupee-denominated market and other loans of state governments (excluding loans and advances from the central government); less net credit outstanding from the Reserve Bank of India; plus provident funds. PEDD: Long-term rupee-denominated debt of public enterprises not held by government. NTDD: Net total domestic debt (= CDD + SDD + PEDD). TFD: Foreign currency public and publicly guaranteed long-term debt; plus the use of IMF credit; plus imputed short-term public debt. GTD: Gross total debt (=NTDD + TFD). R: Official foreign exchange reserves, including gold and SDRs. NTFD: Net total foreign debt (= TFD − R). NTD: Net total debt (= NTDD + NTFD).

Source: Buiter and Patel (2005–06, Table A.1).

Third, high and rising foreign debt in the 1980s was accompanied by very low foreign reserves. In each of the last three years of the 1980s, foreign reserves (including foreign exchange reserves, gold reserves, and the IMF Special Drawing Rights) were below 2 percent of the GDP. In 2003–04, they were a hefty 20 percent of the GDP. In the 1980s, the decline in the foreign exchange reserves proved particularly fatal. From an average of 4.6 months' worth of imports during 1984–87, the reserves fell to 3.9 months' worth of imports in 1987–88. The trend continued with a drop in the reserves to 2.5 months' worth of imports in 1988–89, two months' in 1989–90, and just one month in 1990–91 (Joshi and Little 1994, table 7.10). The current level of foreign exchange reserves is sufficiently large to finance more than a year's worth of imports.

Column 9 of table 9.2 shows foreign debt net of foreign exchange reserves. Because reserves in the 1980s were low, net foreign debt remained high and grew over time. In the postcrisis period, with the rapid accumulation of reserves, limited external borrowing, and rapid growth, net foreign debt as a proportion of the GDP has been declining. Indeed, in 2003–04, net foreign debt turned negative, meaning that the reserves now exceeded India's total debt abroad.

Finally, India is currently far more open on its trade account than in the late 1980s. A high external debt to GDP ratio and a low exports to GDP ratio translate into a high debt service ratio (defined as the debt service payments as a proportion of exports). According to the RBI (*Handbook of Statistics on Indian Economy,* 2005a, table 159), the latter had reached 30 percent in 1989–90 and 35 percent in 1990–91. In 2003–04 and 2004–05, it stood at 16 and 6 percent, respectively.

Given these differences, despite a higher total debt to GDP ratio, the chances of a 1991-style balance of payments crisis in the near future are negligible. This still leaves the question of whether the high debt could lead to a different kind of crisis.

DEBT FINANCEABILITY AND ALTERNATIVE FORMS OF CRISES

Even though our analysis above leads to the conclusion that a repeat of 1991 in the near future is unlikely, is it possible that the large fiscal deficits and debt may trigger a different kind of crisis? In a paper originally written in 2004, Roubini and Hemming (2006) argue that India is as vulnerable to a financing crisis as it was in 1991 and as other economies that have experienced severe financial turmoil.

Roubini and Hemming rightly argue that debt sustainability and debt finaceability are separate issues. Even if a debt path is unsustainable in the long run, it is less of a problem in the short run as long as investors are willing to finance it. Symmetrically, a debt path may be sustainable but the economy may face serious problems in the short run if investors are unwilling to finance it.

Vulnerabilities in financeability may arise at three different points. First, large fiscal and current account deficits require the accumulation of new government and external liabilities, respectively. Persistently large primary deficits may signal the markets that the government is unable to undertake the necessary adjustment and make the markets less willing to lend to it. Second, the government must roll over the maturing debt. If the existing debt is large, markets may be willing to lend only short term or may expect excessively high interest rates on new loans. If the debt to be retired is in a foreign currency, the problem may be particularly serious. Finally, vulnerabilities may also arise from intersectoral linkages. Financial repression that forces commercial banks to hold government paper with low return may weaken the banking system. Conversely, contingent government liabilities arising from guarantees on bank deposits and bailing out of banks and other financial institutions can weaken the government's balance sheet.

In addition to the large fiscal deficit and debt to GDP ratio, Roubini and Hemming point to several vulnerabilities facing India. In particular:

- At less than 20 percent, the revenue to GDP ratio is low compared with that in similarly rated countries. This makes both the debt to revenue and interest payments to revenue ratios large. The former is 430 percent in India, in contrast to 289 percent in similarly rated countries, and the latter is 34 percent, compared with 20 percent in similarly rated countries.
- Contingent liabilities arising out of the potential cost of cleaning up nonperforming assets of the banking system, the losses of state-owned enterprises, central and state government guarantees, and arrears of state electricity boards are estimated as high a 20 percent of the GDP. Additionally, the government must deal with the unfunded pension liabilities of India's public employees.
- The banking system has a variety of vulnerabilities, including a high proportion of the government debt and nonperforming assets, in its portfolio. At 35 percent, the former exceeds the corresponding ratio for recent defaulters such as Russia (31 percent) and Argentina (21 percent).
- On the external front, a large part of foreign investment has been in the form of portfolio investment. According to the Government of India (2006), the total portfolio investment flow into India between August 1991 and December 2005 was $52.7 billion. If the markets come to expect a large depreciation of the rupee, this investment can turn into "hot money" and rapidly move out. In turn, this can cause the rupee to depreciate sharply.

My own assessment (Panagariya 2006e) of the case made by Hemming and Roubini is that they greatly overstate the risk of a financeability crisis in India. One way to assess their case is to ask precisely what form the crisis could take and then assess the prospects of that outcome. The discussion below takes this approach.

Capital Flight?

The currency crises in East Asia during 1997 and 1998, despite sound economic fundamentals, have led to fears that almost any developing country can be subject to a capital flight crisis triggered by the herd behavior and is vulnerable to a currency crisis. For instance, the large deficits and debt in India may make investors doubtful of the solvency of the government. Because the banks are heavily invested in government securities, investors may also lose confidence in the banking system. In turn, this may lead depositors to move their funds out of the rupee and into foreign currencies. Once this process gets under way, foreign investors may fear a large depreciation of the rupee and rapidly liquidate their investments. Foreign creditors may join by refusing to roll over the loans that become due.

Prospects for this scenario to play out are remote, however. For one thing, the government of India has had no history of default. India also has had few bank failures since the 1960s. Thus prospects that the public would lose confidence in the government's ability to honor its commitments or would fear that the banks would be subject to a systemic failure are low. Even if that were to happen, since the Indian rupee is not convertible on the capital account, the public has at best limited ability to move funds abroad. Current rules do permit individuals to hold foreign currency deposits up to a limit, but this facility is likely to be withdrawn at the first sign of large-scale movement of deposits abroad.

As for foreign lenders, India's short-run debt as a proportion of its foreign exchange reserves at the end of 2004–05 was a tiny 5.3 percent. As pointed out earlier, the ratio of debt service to exports, at 6.2 percent in 2004–05, is also quite low. Private debt incurred by both domestic and foreign firms is strictly controlled. Though direct foreign investment and portfolio investment have been rising and a sizable stock of them now exists, their ability to move out rapidly is limited by the fact that any massive movement would reduce the value of their assets dramatically. Finally, in contrast to the 1980s, high fiscal deficits since the mid-1990s have not manifested themselves in high current account deficits. Indeed, during some years in the 2000s, the current account has exhibited a surplus. Moreover, given the relatively muted response of imports, the RBI has had to purchase foreign exchange in large volumes to prevent the rupee from appreciating.

A Banking Crisis?

More than 80 percent of the assets of banks are in the public sector, which remains hugely inefficient. Commercial banks are also much more heavily invested in government securities than was the case in countries such as Russia and Argentina at the time they faced financial crises. Roubini and Hemming further note:

> The balance sheets of the Indian financial system are in worse shape than usually acknowledged. Banks not only hold large quantities of government debt that is of potentially lower quality than assumed, but also they are burdened with significant non-performing assets as a result of lending to state-owned enterprises and to the private sector. As discussed above, maturity mismatches leading to market risks and heavy reliance on government paper leading to large credit risk are crucial vulnerabilities of the financial system. Thus, the overall state of the banking and financial system is a concern. For example Moody's gives an overall very low grade/rating of "D" to the "weighted average bank financial strength"; this is as low or lower than in many other emerging market economies that suffered financial crises. It reflects concerns about supervision and regulation, capital adequacy ratios, disclosure and transparency, non-performing loans and exposure to the sovereign, to Indian states, and to inefficient state owned enterprises and other public entities. Moreover, some measures of foreign currency liquidity mismatches for the financial system suggest that the risk of a roll-off run should not be underestimated. In 1991, the external financing crisis was exacerbated by the roll-off of nonresident foreign currency deposits in the banking system. (2006, pp. 133–34)

From a long-term perspective, India must address all the weaknesses of the banking system noted by Roubini and Hemming. Indeed, it needs to go farther by privatizing the banks and establishing a sound regulatory system. But the weaknesses Roubini and Hemming point out do not add up to a banking crisis in the next few years. To begin with, given that deposits are held in the domestic currency, banks do have a lender of last resort in the RBI. Moreover, in the past, the government has refused to let any banks fail even when the cost of failure did not justify saving them. As a result, public confidence in the banking system remains high.

Some progress has also been made in cleaning up bank assets. Nonperforming assets (NPAs) as a proportion of total assets have been declining over the last several years even as the criteria for classifying assets as nonperforming have been tightened. Gross NPAs as a proportion of gross advances declined from 12.7 percent in 1999–2000 to 7.2 percent in 2003–04. As a proportion of gross assets, they fell from 4.4 to 3.3 percent over the same period. On a net basis, the NPAs were 2.9 percent of net advances and 1.2 percent of assets in 2003–04. On March 31, 2004, India began to classify an asset as nonperforming if the borrower failed to pay interest on it for 90 days. The earlier delinquency norm was 180 days.

TOWARD FISCAL CONSOLIDATION

Prospects of a macroeconomic crisis in the near future are, thus, negligible. Nevertheless, the need for a substantial reduction in the fiscal deficit can hardly be denied. As was noted above, even if the crowding-out effect is not dollar for dollar, the deficit has considerable serious consequences for private investment, and therefore for growth. Moreover, a crisis cannot be avoided indefinitely if the debt continues to rise. At some point, the public is bound to lose confidence in the government and flee the banks and the rupee, triggering a banking crisis and perhaps hyperinflation.

Expenditures and Revenues

Before considering where the government's efforts to contain the deficits stand, let us briefly consider the sources of the deficit. The first point to note is that both the central and state governments have contributed to the overall deficit over the years. In 2002–03, the fiscal deficit (taking into account receipts from disinvestments) of the central government was 6.3 percent of the GDP, and that of the state and union territory governments was 4.2 percent. Of the latter, 0.5 percent of the GDP was owed to the central government, so that the gross fiscal deficit was 10 percent. Both deficits have declined recently. According to the revised estimates for 2004–05, the central government deficit fell to 4.3 percent of the GDP, and that of the state and union territory governments to 3.6 percent of the GDP. Taking into account that 0.4 percent of the GDP was in loans owed by the states and union territories to the central government, the revised estimate for the combined deficit in 2004–05 was 7.5 percent of the GDP.

Next, figure 9.3 shows the evolution of the total expenditures, capital expenditures, and tax revenues of the central, state, and union territory governments. Table 9.3 additionally offers data on current revenues, defined to include tax revenues, interest receipts, dividends and profits, external grants, and other nontax revenues. Three features of figure 9.3 stand out. First, tax revenues in India have hovered around

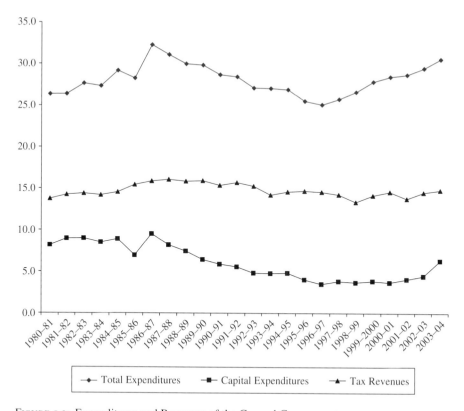

FIGURE 9.3: Expenditures and Revenues of the General Government

15 percent of the GDP since 1980–81. During 1986–90, they reached approximately 16 percent, but fell thereafter until bottoming out at 13.4 percent in 1998–99. As we will see in the chapter on taxation, the decline was largely due to a decline in tariff revenue and the failure to take a compensating action on domestic indirect taxes.

Second, total expenditures have shown greater volatility than tax revenues and have stayed at approximately twice the tax revenues throughout the period covered. The expenditures rose sharply in the 1980s, peaking at 31 percent of the GDP in 1987–88. They were clearly a major contributing factor to rising debt and the eventual crisis in 1991. Much of the fiscal consolidation that took place in the 1990s came from declining expenditures rather than an improvement in the revenues. After bottoming out at 25.1 percent of the GDP in 1996–97, expenditures began to climb again, and reached 30.6 percent of the GDP in 2003–04.

Finally, public investment (capital expenditures) took a very severe beating during the fiscal consolidation of the 1990s. In 1986–87, it had peaked at 9.6 percent of the GDP. It declined after that year, bottoming out at 3.5 percent in 1996–97. It began to recover in 1997–98, but very gradually, so that it remained below 4 percent until 2000–01. Only in 2003–04 did it show a significant jump, to 6.3 percent of the GDP.[3]

With the debt to GDP ratio being as high as it is, there is little surprise that interest payments account for the bulk of the fiscal deficit. This can be gleaned from

TABLE 9.3: Expenditures and Revenues of the Central Government

Year	Total Expenditures	Capital Expenditures	Total Current Revenues	Tax Revenues
1980–81	26.3	8.2	17.8	13.7
1981–82	26.4	9.0	18.0	14.3
1982–83	27.7	9.0	18.5	14.4
1983–84	27.3	8.5	17.8	14.2
1984–85	29.2	8.9	18.4	14.6
1985–86	28.3	7.0	19.4	15.5
1986–87	32.3	9.6	20.3	15.9
1987–88	31.1	8.2	20.0	16.1
1988–89	30.0	7.5	19.6	15.9
1989–90	29.9	6.5	20.2	15.9
1990–91	28.7	5.9	18.6	15.4
1991–92	28.5	5.6	19.5	15.7
1992–93	27.1	4.9	19.1	15.3
1993–94	27.1	4.8	18.0	14.2
1994–95	26.9	4.8	18.4	14.6
1995–96	25.6	4.1	18.3	14.7
1996–97	25.1	3.5	18.0	14.6
1997–98	25.8	3.9	17.8	14.3
1998–99	26.6	3.7	16.6	13.4
1999–2000	27.9	3.9	17.7	14.2
2000–01	28.5	3.7	18.1	14.6
2001–02	28.7	4.1	17.6	13.8
2002–03	29.5	4.5	18.4	14.5
2003–04	30.6	6.3	18.5	14.8

Source: Author's calculations, based data in RBI, (2005a, table 117 and table 1, col. 7).

columns 4 and 9 of table 9.1, which show the gross fiscal and gross primary deficits. In 2003–04, the gross fiscal deficit was 8.4 percent and the gross primary deficit was 2 percent of the GDP. This means interest payments accounted for as much as 6.4 percent of the GDP. This single fact underlines the urgency of debt retirement.

Efforts at Fiscal Consolidation

Large debt and fiscal deficits clearly pose a threat to macroeconomic stability by adding to the debt in the long run and to the growth rate by crowding out private investment in the short run. The government has recognized these problems for some time, though it has been slow to introduce corrective measures out of populism and a lack of political courage. For example, as trade liberalization in the 1990s predictably led to a fall in the tariff revenue, the government should have taken measures to boost domestic indirect tax revenues. Instead, it kept bringing the domestic indirect tax rates down without taking compensating measures to improve collection and broaden the tax base. Likewise, the government lacked the courage to bring down expenditures by cutting unproductive subsidies.

There is no doubt that the government needs to lower expenditures as well as improve tax collection on the road to bringing the deficit down. Equally important, it also needs to carry out many microeconomic reforms to improve the quality of public expenditures and the tax system. These reforms will form an integral part of our discussion in part V of the book. Presently, we focus on the government's effort to bring the deficit down at the aggregate level.

In August 2003, the Parliament passed the Fiscal Responsibility and Budget Management (FRBM) Act. In its original form, the act required the central government to balance the budget on the current account and bring the fiscal deficit down to 3 percent by 2007–08. It stipulated a minimum annual reduction of 0.5 percentage point in the revenue deficit and 0.3 percentage point in the fiscal deficit. The act also required the RBI not to subscribe to government paper after March 31, 2006.[4] After coming to power, the UPA government amended the FRBM Act in July 2004. The amendment moved the terminal date of the targets from 2007–08 to 2008–09, to align it with the last year of the UPA government. Though the 2005–06 budget pushed the Pause button on the annual targets in the act, ex post the targets have actually been met principally because of increased tax revenues made possible by the unexpectedly high rate of growth.

The FRBM Act sets targets for only the central government's budget. If the debt is to be brought down significantly within a reasonable time, however, it is equally important to contain the deficits in the state budgets. Luckily, some progress has been made here as well, with several states (including Kerala, Maharashtra, Karnataka, Tamil Nadu, Uttar Pradesh, and Punjab) adopting fiscal responsibility legislation. Buiter and Patel (2005–06) review this legislation in greater detail, and Rajaraman and Majumdar (2005) discuss it in the context of the recommendations of the Twelfth Finance Commission. Here it suffices to note that each of these laws sets targets similar to those the FRBM Act sets for the central government: elimination of the revenue deficit and cutting the state fiscal deficits to 3 percent of the Gross State Domestic Product within four to six years.

Buiter and Patel consider the short- and long-run implications of the FRBM Act for the debt and the conduct of policy. They compute that if the FRBM targets are met, the GDP grows at 6.2 percent in real terms, and the inflation rate is 3 percent, the central government's debt as a proportion of the GDP will stabilize at the comfortable level of just below 30 percent. They also conclude that the elimination of the revenue deficit would serve as the binding constraint: The fiscal deficit target of 3 percent of the GDP will be more than met if the revenue deficit is eliminated. For this reason, they rightly speculate that the government is likely to end up reclassifying many current account expenditures as capital account expenditures.

An important weakness in the FRBM Act that Buiter and Patel point out is that it does not give any incentive to the government to act countercyclically. Ideally, in a period of above-normal economic activity, as during 2004–06, the government should cut the deficit more, and when the activity falls below normal, it should cut it less. In the absence of incentives to act in this manner, the government may not overachieve the long-run target during the upswing, but will underachieve it during the downswing, and thus fail to meet the target overall. The EU has also suffered from this weakness in its Stability and Growth Pact, with its leadership failing to penalize the politically powerful members, such as France, Germany, and Italy, for a lack of fiscal restraint during upswings. The prospects for the government of

India's restraining itself in similar situations are likely to be even poorer. Buiter and Patel draw a rather pessimistic conclusion:

> A tentative picture that we can draw, albeit from a short history, is that non-compliance by governments is unlikely to be politically costly; there has been little attention by the electorate, the media, or even opposition parties to the subject matter! In fact it is widely felt that supplementary bills that boost expenditure from budgeted levels are unlikely to be rejected. Against this background, obtaining parliamentary waivers for missed targets should not be too difficult.
>
> Fiscal virtue cannot be legislated. It must be implemented and enforced—it must be incentive-compatible even for myopic and opportunistic governments. Unless India discovers a way of tying its fiscal Ulysses to the mast, the siren song of fiscal retrenchment tomorrow but fiscal expansion today will continue to lead the policy makers astray. (2005–06, pp. 33–34)

CONCLUDING REMARKS

In this chapter, I have introduced the overall macroeconomic framework within which our discussion in the following chapters will be conducted. I have also considered in detail the issue of a possible macroeconomic crisis in the near future, in view of the high debt and deficits. I concluded that a macroeconomic crisis in the near future is unlikely. Nevertheless, the need for continued reduction in the fiscal deficit can hardly be overemphasized. In recent years, India has made some progress in this direction, but that is no reason for complacency. A stable macroeconomic environment is a crucial condition for sustained growth. The pessimistic prognosis by Buiter and Patel notwithstanding, India must continue its efforts to achieve the goals set by the FRBM Act.

10

THE EXTERNAL SECTOR

On the Road to Capital Account Convertibility?

W e saw in the last chapter that the government budget is intimately linked to the external sector. For example, the government partially finances its expenditures by borrowing abroad. This fact directly links the government budget to the external sector. In turn, the external debt the government accumulates has important bearing on the conduct of its fiscal policy. The government's spending also impacts the current account in an essential way, which further links the budget and the external account.

In this chapter, we frontally focus on the external account. Specifically, we consider the current account and capital account transactions and their effects on the broad aggregates of the economy such as prices, exchange rate, and monetary policy. We begin by returning to the investment-savings and balance of payments identities introduced in the last chapter.

THE SAVINGS-INVESTMENT AND BALANCE OF PAYMENTS IDENTITIES ONCE AGAIN

To recapitulate, we saw in the last chapter that foreign savings must fill the gap between private domestic investment and private plus public domestic savings. Foreign savings themselves equal the current account deficit. In turn, the balance of payments identity dictates that the current account deficit be equal to the net external capital inflows minus the change in the volume of foreign exchange reserves held by the RBI.

As in the previous chapter, denoting private domestic investment by I_P, private domestic savings by S_P, fiscal surplus of the government by S_G, current account surplus by CA, net capital inflows by K, and the reserves accumulation of the RBI by ΔR, we can write

$$I_P - (S_P + S_G) \equiv -CA \equiv K - \Delta R. \qquad (10.1)$$

To elaborate upon the current account, let us further denote the exports and imports of goods and services by X and M, respectively; net factor income earned abroad by NFIA; and net transfers received from abroad by NFT. We then have

$$CA = (X - M) + NFIA + NFT. \qquad (10.2)$$

The NFIA equals the income earned by India's resources located abroad minus the income earned by foreign factors located in India. In the Indian balance of payments, this entry includes only the receipts on Indian investments abroad and payments on foreign investment in India. The NFT includes unilateral transfers such as foreign aid and remittances. The latter make a major contribution to the current account in India.

Capital inflows are divided into two main categories: foreign investment and foreign borrowing. In the Indian balance of payments, the former includes foreign direct investment and foreign portfolio investment. Foreign borrowing has three main components: concessional borrowing reported as "external assistance," commercial borrowing, and NRI deposits. The transactions defining the change in the reserve position of the RBI (ΔR in (10.1)) include the changes in the gold reserves, foreign exchange reserves, the Special Drawing Rights (SDRs), and the reserve position in the International Monetary Fund (IMF).

There is a tendency even among specialists to view capital inflows and unilateral transfers—overwhelmingly comprised of remittances, in the case of India—as being essentially identical. But there are important differences between them. Remittances generate no future obligations, and therefore they are a current account item. If the RBI does not intervene by accumulating extra reserves to neutralize the inflows of remittances, either an equivalent capital outflow or an import expansion (or a combination of the two) must take place to clear the foreign exchange market. In the former case, the current account surplus rises and effectively reduces foreign savings available to the country. Improved current account adds to the national income, however, which increases domestic private savings. In the latter case, unilateral transfers do not reduce foreign savings available, but they also do not increase the national income or private domestic savings. If the RBI does intervene by accumulating reserves to the extent of the remittances, the effect is similar to the first of the previous two cases.

In contrast to unilateral transfers, capital inflows bring future obligations, are a capital account item, and represent foreign savings available to the country. If the RBI does not take an offsetting action through equivalent reserves accumulation, the capital inflows generate a corresponding current account deficit, which is an increase in the available foreign savings. In this case, the national income and domestic savings are entirely unaffected, but the available foreign savings rise. If the RBI does take a countervailing action by accumulating equivalent foreign exchange reserves, the savings potential of capital inflows is neutralized.

Table 10.1 presents the balance of payments entries as proportions of the GDP from 1980–81 to 2003–04. Figure 10.1 shows the evolution of some of the key flows associated with the current and capital accounts. From the first entry in table 10.1 (top curve in figure 10.1), we gather that the exports to GDP ratio in India was quite low in the early 1980s and actually fell during the mid-1980s. It began to show an upward movement only in the late 1980s, then rose steadily throughout the 1990s and the early 2000s. At its lowest, the ratio was 5.6 percent in 1986–87; it rose to almost 15 percent in 2003–04. Despite this nearly threefold rise, the ratio remains approximately half that of China, suggesting substantial scope for further expansion. Transfers, which consist mainly of remittances, declined as a proportion of the GDP throughout the 1980s but showed a steady expansion after the 1990–91 crisis. From just 0.8 percent of the GDP in 1990–91, they expanded to almost 4 percent in 2003–04.

As we noted in the previous chapter, a large and rising current account deficit (i.e., declining current account surplus, depicted by the curve at the bottom of figure 10.1) characterized the 1980s. While the deficits helped push up the growth rate by providing additional savings to the economy, they also added to the external debt and, therefore, external vulnerability. In 1990–91, the year just prior to the crisis, the current account deficit had risen to 3.1 percent of the GDP. Since the crisis, the RBI has managed the current account conservatively, to the point that for each of the three years during 2001–04, India experienced a current account surplus. A key factor that has aided the RBI in this task is the expansion of remittances noted above and shown by the second curve from the top in figure 10.1.

Capital account flows have traditionally been small, reflecting the absence of capital account convertibility in India. In the 1980s, the policy regime discouraged foreign investment to the point that hardly any came into the country. The 1991 reform did away with most of the draconian provisions in the Foreign Exchange Regulation Act of 1973 and paved the way for phased liberalization of both foreign direct investment and portfolio investment. Currently, the policy regime with respect to foreign investment is on balance as open as in other economies of East and Southeast Asia, including China. The liberalization has led to an expansion of foreign investment, though the magnitude of the foreign direct investment remains tiny in relation to that going to China.[1] A key factor behind this muted response has been the virtual lack of pickup in labor-intensive manufacturing in India. Such manufacturing has accounted for the bulk of the direct foreign investment in China, especially in the early years of its opening up.

From a macroeconomic standpoint, perhaps the most important development in the balance of payments accounts has been the accumulation of a vast reserve of foreign exchange by the RBI. According to table 10.1, since 1991–92, with just two exceptions, the RBI has accumulated more than 1 percent of the GDP in foreign exchange reserves every year. During the last three years shown in the table, the accumulations were 2.5, 3.3, and 5.2 percent of the GDP, respectively. At the beginning of June 2006, the cumulative reserves had reached $165 billion. These movements contrast with negative or near zero reserves accumulation in all but two years during the 1980s. In no year during the 1980s did the reserves accumulation touch even 0.5 percent of the GDP.

This accumulation of reserves since the early 1990s is currently a major policy issue, and must be analyzed in the context of the monetary, exchange rate, and capital account convertibility policies. Before we turn to this task, however, let us consider two recent controversies relating to the reserves, one resulting from a policy proposal by the Planning Commission in 2004–05 and the other from an assertion made by a group of policy analysts.

TABLE 10.1: Balance of Payments as Proportion of GDP, 1980–81 to 2003–04

	Item	1980–81	1981–82	1982–83	1983–84	1984–85	1985–86	1986–87	1987–88
1	*2*	*3*	*4*	*5*	*6*	*7*	*8*	*9*	*10*
I	Exports of goods and services	6.2	6.1	6.3	6.2	6.5	5.6	5.6	5.9
II	Imports of goods and services	9.8	9.4	9.4	8.8	8.7	8.5	8.2	8.4
III	Investment income, net	0.2	0.1	-0.2	-0.2	-0.4	-0.3	-0.4	-0.5
IV	Transfers, net	1.9	1.5	1.5	1.4	1.4	1.1	1.1	1.1
V	Current account (I−II+III+IV)	-1.5	-1.7	-1.7	-1.5	-1.2	-2.1	-1.9	-1.8
VI	Total foreign investment							0.1	0.2
VII	Of which portfolio								
VIII	Borrowing abroad*	0.9	0.5	1.0	0.9	1.0	1.0	1.4	1.2
IX	NRI deposits, net	0.1	0.1	0.2	0.3	0.4	0.6	0.5	0.5
X	Debt service and other capital	-0.1	-0.3	-0.1	0.0	0.1	0.3	-0.1	0.0
XI	Capital account (VI+VII+VIII+IX)	0.9	0.3	1.1	1.2	1.5	2.0	1.9	1.8
XII	Reserves accumulation**	-0.6	-1.3	-0.7	-0.3	0.4	-0.2	0.0	0.1

		1988–89	1989–90	1990–91	1991–92	1992–93	1993–94	1994–95	1995–96
		11	*12*	*13*	*14*	*15*	*16*	*17*	*18*
I	Exports of goods and services	6.3	7.3	7.3	8.8	9.2	10.2	10.2	11.2
II	Imports of goods and services	9.2	9.6	9.9	9.3	11.1	11.5	12.8	14.5
III	Investment income, net	-0.9	-1.0	-1.2	-1.4	-1.4	-1.2	-1.1	-0.9
IV	Transfers, net	1.1	1.0	0.8	1.6	1.6	2.1	2.6	2.5
V	Current account (I−II+III+IV)	-2.7	-2.3	-3.1	-0.3	-1.7	-0.4	-1.0	-1.7
VI	Total foreign investment	0.1	0.1	0.0	0.1	0.2	1.5	1.5	1.4
VII	Of which portfolio			0.0	0.0	0.1	1.3	1.2	0.8
VIII	Borrowing abroad*	1.4	1.2	1.4	1.7	0.6	0.9	0.8	0.7
IX	NRI deposits, net	0.9	0.8	0.5	0.2	0.8	0.4	0.1	0.3
X	Debt service and other capital	0.4	0.2	0.3	-0.5	-0.1	0.6	0.5	-1.0
XI	Capital account (VI+VII+VIII+IX)	2.8	2.4	2.3	1.5	1.6	3.5	2.8	1.3
XII	Reserves accumulation**	0.0	0.0	-0.8	1.1	-0.1	3.1	1.8	-0.3

		1996–97	1997–98	1998–99	1999–2000	2000–01	2001–02	2002–03	2003–04
		19	*20*	*21*	*22*	*23*	*24*	*25*	*26*
I	Exports of goods and services	10.8	11.0	11.5	11.9	13.5	13.0	14.6	14.9
II	Imports of goods and services	14.4	14.5	14.1	15.0	15.9	14.7	16.0	16.4
III	Investment income, net	-0.9	-0.9	-0.9	-0.8	-1.1	-0.9	-0.7	-0.7
IV	Transfers, net	3.3	3.0	2.6	2.8	2.9	3.3	3.3	3.9
V	Current account (I–II+III+IV)	-1.2	-1.4	-1.0	-1.0	-0.6	0.7	1.2	1.7
VI	Total foreign investment	1.6	1.3	0.6	1.2	1.5	1.7	1.2	2.7
VII	Of which portfolio	0.9	0.4	0.0	0.7	0.6	0.4	0.2	1.9
VIII	Borrowing abroad*	1.0	1.2	1.3	0.3	1.1	-0.1	-0.9	-0.7
IX	NRI deposits, net	0.9	0.3	0.2	0.3	0.5	0.6	0.6	0.6
X	Debt service and other capital	-0.5	-0.3	-0.1	0.7	-1.2	-0.4	1.3	0.9
XI	Capital account (VI+VII+VIII+IX)	3.0	2.5	2.0	2.5	1.9	1.8	2.1	3.5
XII	Reserves accumulation**	1.8	1.1	1.0	1.4	1.3	2.5	3.3	5.2

* Includes concessional and commercial borrowing.

**Includes changes in foreign exchange reserves, IMF holdings, and SDRs.

Source: Author's calculations, using the data in RBI, (2005a, tables 1, 145, 147, and 157).

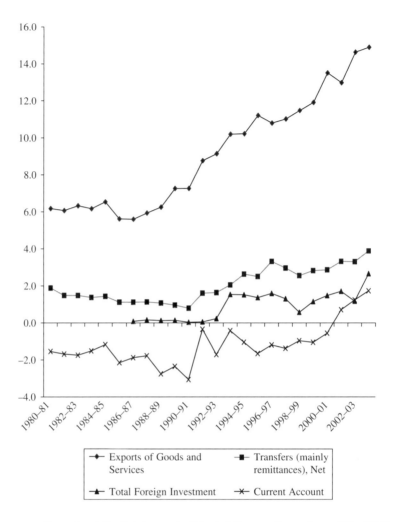

FIGURE 10.1: Current and Capital Accounts: Selected Items as Proportions of the GDP

TWO RECENT CONTROVERSIES

The first of the two controversies arose out of a policy proposal by the Planning Commission to use some of the foreign exchange reserves to build infrastructure, and the second, out of a claim by a group of policy analysts regarding the impact of the accumulation of the reserves on growth.

Infrastructure for Foreign Exchange Reserves

Since the 1991 reform, India has been rapidly accumulating foreign exchange reserves. At the beginning of June 2006, the reserves had reached $165 billion. They are potentially usable resources of the country, though they raise difficult macroeconomic issues. In 2004–05, the Planning Commission proposed that a part of these foreign exchange reserves be used to finance investment in infrastructure. It suggested that the RBI lend some reserves, say $5 billion, to a special-purpose vehicle (SPV) whose objective would be to finance infrastructure projects.[2] Given that the reserves are mainly invested in U.S. Treasury bills and earn the low rate of return of approximately 2 percent, their conversion into infrastructure would represent a much better use of them.

Several commentators in the Indian press, most notably Acharya (2004), criticized the Planning Commission's proposal on the ground that infrastructure required mostly nontraded factors of production, whereas foreign exchange reserves could be spent only on traded goods. As I explained in my own critique of the proposal (Panagariya 2005a), this was not a central issue. The SPV would simply sell the dollars in the market, acquire their equivalent in rupees, and use those rupees to acquire resources needed to build infrastructure. The net effect of this action would be a reduction in the resources available for the production of traded goods and an additional $5 billion in the hands of the agents selling rupees for dollars to the SPV. These latter would use the $5 billion for imports that could no longer be produced domestically. The ensuing current account deficit would have converted $5 billion into effective foreign savings.[3]

Therefore, the controversy surrounding the nontradability of infrastructure was largely a distraction. The critical question was whether the RBI was willing to follow an exchange rate policy that would allow injecting an extra $5 billion into the economy each year. For unless the RBI chose to accommodate an exchange rate policy that would increase the current account deficit by $5 billion, mere transfer of the reserves to the SPV would not lead to increased inflow of foreign savings. For example, while transferring $5 billion to the SPV, the RBI could simultaneously purchase an additional $5 billion from the market. The transfer to the SPV would increase imports by $5 billion, but the $5 billion purchased by the RBI would reduce imports by the same amount. No extra foreign savings would flow into the economy, and the burden of the extra investment in infrastructure would fall entirely on private domestic savings, and hence on private investment. The outcome would be equivalent to the government's financing the infrastructure projects though increased fiscal deficit.

Therefore, if the objective of the Planning Commission was to increase infrastructure spending without crowding out private investment, the most transparent approach would have been an increase in the fiscal deficit of $5 billion to finance the infrastructure projects and, simultaneously, an exchange rate policy that would accommodate an extra $5 billion in the current account deficit. An increased current account deficit would have ensured that increased fiscal spending on infrastructure would not crowd out private investment. It also would have automatically achieved the net reduction in the foreign reserves that the Planning Commission was seeking. Under the route it actually chose, the Planning Commission left the RBI the option to leave the current account unaffected and therefore allow private investment to be crowded out by infrastructure investment.

Growth Lost to the Reserves Accumulation

The second controversy has its origins in the assertion by Deepak Lal, Suman Bery, and Devendra Pant (2003) that if the RBI had not been accumulating the reserves it did in the 1990s, the additional inflow of foreign savings into India would have been sufficiently large to add 2.7 percentage points to India's annual growth. The conceptual argument is straightforward: The accumulation of the reserves held back potential foreign savings from being converted into actual savings and investment, and thus had a negative impact on growth.

But, as Joshi and Sanyal (2004) have persuasively argued, the analysis and the conclusion reached by Lal et al. are fraught with problems. For the moment, let us accept the argument that the only thing the reserve accumulation does is to withdraw potential savings from the economy. Even then, Lal et al. are in error because they grossly overestimate the impact of the RBI's accumulation of reserves on the savings. As we have seen, the maximum annual reduction in the annual foreign savings due to the RBI intervention is ΔR. But Lal et al. base their calculations on the erroneous assumption that the RBI intervention reduced the available foreign savings by capital inflows plus net foreign transfers that include large volumes of remittances.[4]

Joshi and Sanyal (2004) are right to point out that this is an error. They remind us that the reduction in potential savings is capped by the amount of reserves accumulated by the RBI. And since the reserves as a proportion of the GDP grew 1.2 percent annually during the 1990s, absent RBI intervention, investment as a proportion of the GDP would have been at most 1.2 percent higher than was actually observed. With the incremental net capital output ratio of 2.8 percent in the 1990s, the annual growth forgone was maximally 1.2/2.8, or approximately 0.4 percent.

Joshi and Sanyal further argue, correctly, that the actual negative effect of the reserves accumulation on the growth rate was much smaller, probably even positive. There are at least two reasons for this conclusion. First, there is no guarantee that under a "hands-off" RBI regime, the reserves would have fully translated into increased investment. For one thing, it is unlikely that at the exchange rate under a policy of nonintervention by the RBI, the current account deficit would have risen by the full amount of the reserves. But even assuming that to be the case, there is no guarantee that the appreciated rupee would not have led to increased expenditure rather than increased investment. It is likely that only a part of the increase in the foreign savings would have translated into increased investment.

Second, and more important, insofar as the RBI interventions supported a more undervalued rupee and helped create an environment of greater macroeconomic stability, the policy helped promote the outward orientation of the economy. An appreciation of the rupee in the early years of the reforms would have made exports less profitable and imports cheaper. The traded goods sector would have suffered in relation to the nontraded goods sector. In addition to the adverse productivity effects this would have brought, poor performance of the external sector would also have undermined support for the reforms.

EXTERNAL SECTOR POLICIES

Let us now turn to a systematic discussion of external sector policies of India during the 1980s and beyond, with particular attention to the 1990s and 2000s. These policies may be divided into four interrelated areas: the current account, the capital account, the exchange rate, and foreign exchange reserves and their implications for the monetary policy. I begin with the current account.

The Current Account

I have already discussed the trade policies during the 1980s and 1990s in chapters 4 and 5, respectively. During the 1980s, India gradually began to emerge from the near autarkic polices of the 1970s. Modest liberalization took place through the expansion of open general licensing, the reduced role of canalized imports, replenishment licenses, and a variety of pro-export measures that partially neutralized the large anti-trade bias of the import controls regime.

The 1990s and 2000s saw a much more significant and systematic liberalization. Virtually all licensing on intermediate inputs and capital goods was abolished in 1991–92, and tariff rates were progressively brought down. Starting in February 1994, India moved to permitting all current business transactions, education, medical expenses, and foreign travel at the market exchange rate.[5] These and other steps culminated in India's accepting the IMF Article VIII obligations on August 20, 1994, which made the rupee officially convertible on the current account. On April 1, 2001, India abolished licensing on consumer goods imports, including all agricultural goods. Tariff liberalization also continued. Setting aside a handful of exceptions, such as automobiles, the highest tariff rate on nonagricultural goods came down to 12.5 percent in 2006–07. Considerable liberalization also took place in services, but agricultural protection remains relatively high. The impact of this liberalization on the outward orientation of the economy is evident from the rise in the exports to GDP ratio discussed in the previous section.

The Capital Account

Traditionally, India has tightly controlled capital account transactions.Unlike trade and investment, capital flows experienced virtually no relaxation during the 1980s. All of the liberalization in this area to date took place in the 1990s.

Foreign Direct Investment

As discussed in chapter 3, the foreign direct investment regime until the mid-1960s was relatively liberal, but it became progressively restrictive from then on and culminated in the Foreign Exchange Regulation Act (FERA) of 1973. With some exceptions, FERA restricted the share of foreign investment to 40 percent and made investment in India wholly unattractive to foreign companies. This regime remained essentially intact throughout the 1980s, with the result that India received minimal foreign investment during the decade. As figure 10.1 shows, foreign investment as a proportion of the GDP was nearly zero until early 1990.

The 1991 reform opened the door to foreign direct investment in a major way by introducing the concept of automatic approval, whereby the government empowered the Reserve Bank of India to approve equity investment up to 51 percent in the 34 "priority" industries traditionally called "appendix I" industries. In the subsequent years, this policy was considerably liberalized. Currently, the regime operates on a "negative list" philosophy, meaning that unless there are specific restrictions spelled out in the foreign direct investment policy of the government of India, up to 100 percent foreign investment is permitted under the automatic route, subject to the sectoral rules and regulations. The policy lists only retail trading (except single-brand product retailing), atomic energy, the lottery business, and gambling and betting as the sectors in which foreign investment is prohibited. Moreover, the list of sectors subject to a cap on foreign investment below 100 percent is relatively short. Only broadcasting, print media and news channels, defense, insurance, petroleum refining, air transport services, asset reconstruction companies, and investment companies in infrastructure are subject to caps below 50 percent.[6]

Portfolio Investment

Until the 1990s, portfolio investment was tightly controlled. According to the data compiled by Athreye and Kapur (2001, table 2), portfolio investment accounted for 9 percent of the total stock of foreign investment in India in 1960. This percentage fell to 5.7 percent in 1970, 5.5 percent in 1980, and just 2.8 percent in 1992. As a part of the reforms, India opened its market in portfolio investment to foreign investors. On September 14, 1992, it permitted foreign institutional investors (FIIs), such as pension funds and mutual funds, to invest in primary and secondary markets for securities, as well as products sold by mutual funds, with a minimum 70 percent investment in equities. The equity share of a single FII in a single firm was limited to 5 percent, and of all FIIs together, to 24 percent.

Since 1992, several liberalizing steps have been taken. Precise chronology of these steps can be found in Shah and Patnaik (2006, table 4). The main features of the regime as of early 2006 are as follows. A single FII can own 10 percent of the total equity in a single firm. The ceiling upon the ownership by all FIIs in firms now equals the sectoral cap on foreign investment. In the large majority of these sectors, this cap is 100 percent, implying no restrictions on the ownership by the FII taken as a whole. The FIIs are also permitted to fully hedge the currency risk through the forward market. They also may invest in corporate as well as government bonds, with overall ceilings on ownership by all FIIs being $1.5 billion for corporate bonds and $2 billion for government bonds.

The FIIs are expected to operate as broad-based funds with at least 20 investors and no single investor having more than 10 percent of the total fund investment. Since February 2000, foreign firms and individuals have been given access to the Indian market as "subaccounts." Local fund managers are also allowed to manage funds for foreign firms and individuals through subaccounts.

Indian companies are permitted to raise equity capital abroad through American Depository Receipts and Global Depository Receipts sold in the United States and (mainly) in Europe, respectively.[7] There are currently no restrictions on companies wishing to raise equity capital through these instruments, other than the regulations applying to the activity for which funds are to be used. For example, companies must comply with the sectoral caps on foreign investment when financing their operations via ADRs or GDRs. Likewise, the Company Law regulations apply to mergers and acquisitions financed by these instruments. The companies currently listed on the foreign stock exchanges include Reliance, Infosys, Satyam Computer, Wipro, MTNL,

VSNL, the State Bank of India, Tata Motors, Dr. Reddy's Lab, Ranbaxy, Larsen & Toubro, ITC, the ICICI Bank, Hindalco, the HDFC Bank, and Bajaj Auto.

External Commercial Borrowing

A firm can borrow up to $20 million abroad when the maturity of the loan is three years or more. For loans exceeding $20 million, the minimum maturity requirement is five years. A firm can borrow up to $500 million without permission for certain end uses, including capital goods imports and the expansion of a factory. External borrowing by all firms together is capped at $9 billion. This limit is periodically revised. According to Shah and Patnaik (2006), firms are required to hedge their currency exposure, but there is no mechanism in place to enforce the regulation.

Bank borrowings abroad are mainly from nonresident Indians (NRIs) in the form of NRI deposits. Currently, the banks can set the interest rates on such deposits, subject to certain regulations. The exchange rate guarantee and the premium offered on this interest rate over the rate prevailing on the global markets during the 1990s and earlier are no longer available.[8]

Outward Flows

Individuals are allowed to put up to $25,000 per year in foreign currency accounts. Exporters of goods and services and other recipients of inward remittances in convertible foreign currency are authorized to hold up to 50 percent of the remittances in exchange earners foreign currency (EEFC) accounts maintained with authorized dealers in India. In the case of 100 percent export- oriented units and units located in export processing zones, software technology parks, or electronic hardware technology parks, the percentage rises to 70 percent. Under the automatic route, firms can invest abroad up to their net worth plus EEFC holdings as long as such investment does not exceed $100 million. Firms that raise foreign currency through ADR and GDR issues can invest abroad without any limit.

The Exchange Rate and Reserves Accumulation

With the exception of a few months during 1971 when it pegged the rupee to the dollar, India had pegged the rupee to the pound sterling until the mid-1970s. In September 1975, it decided to switch to pegging the rupee to an undisclosed basket of currencies but formally remained on the adjustable peg system. This system essentially remained intact until March 1993, when India formally adopted a "floating" exchange rate.

Under the system adopted in 1975, an effective nominal devaluation required either an explicit adjustment in the peg or a surreptitious shift in the weights of various currencies included in the basket. On the day-to-day basis, the exchange rate was kept within a specified band around the peg. According to Joshi and Little (1994, p. 268), the export-weighted nominal and real effective exchange rates (NEER and REER) appreciated slightly in the late 1970s and early 1980s, then stayed approximately unchanged until the mid-1980s. It was only in the second half of the 1980s that a policy of active depreciation was pursued.

Table 10.2 shows the rupee-dollar exchange rate, REER, and NEER in columns 2, 3, and 4, respectively, from 1984–85 to 2004–05. The REER and NEER use the exports to 36 major destination markets as weights. According to these measures, the real and nominal exchange rates depreciated 25 and 33 percent, respectively, between 1985–86 and 1990–91. This depreciation was crucial to the export growth in the second half of the 1980s.

As a part of the stabilization effort following the 1991 crisis, India devalued the rupee 18 percent in terms of the dollar. The devaluation also translated into a substantial decline in the NEER and REER. In February 1992, the government introduced a dual exchange rate whereby exporters were allowed to sell 60 percent of their foreign exchange earnings in the free market to authorized dealers and 40 percent to the government at the lower official rate. Importers were allowed to buy foreign exchange in the free market, which effectively put an end to the exchange control that had existed until then. These were transitional steps on the way to exiting the adjustable peg system and adopting a market exchange rate. The

TABLE 10.2: Exchange Rate Indexes and the Stock of Foreign Exchange Reserves

Year	Rupees per Dollar (annual average)	REER (export weighted, 1985 = 100)	NEER (export weighted, 1985 = 100)	Foreign Ex Reserves (end year)
1	2	3	4	5
1984–85	11.9	100.4	101.8	6.0
1985–86	12.2	97.9	98.5	6.5
1986–87	12.8	90.1	85.8	6.6
1987–88	13.0	85.4	81.2	6.2
1988–89	14.5	80.3	75.3	4.8
1989–90	16.6	77.3	71.6	4.0
1990–91	17.9	73.3	66.2	5.8
1991–92	24.5	61.4	51.1	9.2
1992–93	30.6	54.4	42.3	9.8
1993–94	31.4	59.1	43.5	19.3
1994–95	31.4	63.3	42.2	25.2
1995–96	33.4	60.9	38.7	21.7
1996–97	35.5	61.1	38.1	26.4
1997–98	37.2	63.8	38.9	29.4
1998–99	42.1	60.1	35.3	32.5
1999–2000	43.3	59.7	34.3	38.0
2000–01	45.7	62.5	34.2	42.3
2001–02	47.7	64.4	34.5	54.1
2002–03	48.4	67.9	35.4	76.1
2003–04	46.0	69.7	34.9	113.0
2004–05 P	44.9	72.5	34.4	141.5

Notes: Real and Nominal Effective Exchange rates (REER and NEER) are computed using the official exchange rates data up to 1991–92, and the FEDAI (Foreign Exchange Dealers' Association of India) indicative rates from 1992–93 onward.

REER and NEER indexes are estimated using the common price index and the exchange rate for the Euro (representing 31 countries) beginning March 1, 2002.

Source: RBI (2005a, tables 149, 151, 158).

shift was completed on March 19, 1993, with the official exchange rate unified with the market rate.

Though formally India has been on a market-determined exchange rate since March 1993, the RBI intervenes heavily in the foreign exchange market. Going by the observed behavior of the exchange rate, two factors have guided these interventions: stability of the rupee-dollar exchange rate in the short run and a competitive real exchange rate in the medium and long runs. The RBI has been more successful in achieving the former objective than the latter.

During most of the period since 1995, three factors have kept the rupee under upward pressure: large and rising inflows of remittances, significant inflows of foreign investment, and a muted response of imports to liberalization. These factors have meant that the RBI has had to virtually continuously buy large amounts of foreign currency with rupees to ensure that the rupee did not appreciate significantly and undermine the competitiveness of the producers of traded goods.

The short-run stability of the rupee-dollar exchange rate led Calvo and Reinhart (2002) to question the IMF classification of the Indian exchange rate regime as "floating." They calculated that during 1993–99, the probability of the rupee-dollar exchange rate staying 1 percent above or 1 percent below the mean monthly rate was 82.2 percent, well above the corresponding probability associated with many genuinely floating exchange rate regimes. For example, the probability of the same outcome for the dollar-deutsche mark rate between 1973 and 1999 was only 26.8.

Following the lead of Calvo and Reinhart, and recognizing that the short-term stability of the rupee-dollar rate has been punctuated by crawling depreciations, Joshi (2003) characterizes the Indian exchange-rate regime as "dirty crawl."[9] Patnaik (2003) goes a step further, labeling the regime as a de facto pegged system. Both characterizations have their limitations. "Dirty crawl" implies one-way movement in the exchange rate, which has not been the case with the rupee: There have been times that the rupee has appreciated. A pegged rate would imply relatively little movement in the exchange rate even over extended periods, but the rupee has depreciated significantly in terms of the dollar—34 percent between 1992–93 and 2001–02.

The importance of the upward pressure on the real value of the rupee in driving the reserves accumulation by the RBI is sharply brought out by figure 10.2. While the rupee has depreciated with respect to main export markets of India in nominal terms, the RBI has been at best partially successful in fighting its appreciation in real terms. The REER moved both upward and downward between 1992–93 and 1999–2000, but during 1999–2005, it moved upward only. The latter period also saw a major acceleration in the accumulation of foreign exchange reserves by the RBI, suggesting that it has leaned heavily against the appreciation. Relative to its trough level in 1992–93, the rupee had appreciated 33 percent in real terms by 2004–05.

Reserves, Money Supply, and Inflation

Closely connected to the question of ensuring a competitive exchange rate to producers of traded goods is the issue of inflation. Holding the line on the nominal effective exchange rate has meant that the RBI had to accumulate large volumes of foreign exchange reserves. But since the RBI must spend rupees to buy dollars so as

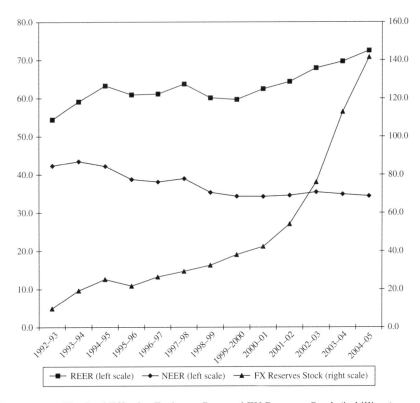

FIGURE 10.2: The Real Effective Exchange Rate and FX Reserves Stock (in billions)

to prevent depreciation of the dollar (and corresponding appreciation of the rupee), such accumulation necessarily results in the expansion of the money supply. The larger the magnitude of the foreign exchange reserves accumulated, the larger the volume of rupees released into the economy. In turn, the expansion of the money supply can lead to inflation and, hence, real appreciation of the rupee vis-à-vis other currencies through this alternative route.

To counteract this inflationary impact of the reserves accumulation, the natural course for the RBI is a policy of "sterilization": selling domestic assets, mainly government securities, in return for rupees in the open market. This is indeed the course the RBI has chosen since the early 1990s. This is seen in figure 10.3, which shows the level of reserve money and net foreign assets of the RBI in natural log of billion rupees.

The identity between RBI assets and liabilities ensures that the reserve money equals the sum of its net foreign assets and net domestic assets. If the RBI does not engage in sterilization, faster accumulation of foreign assets would imply faster growth in reserve money. Sterilization would imply that the RBI counteracts faster accumulation of foreign reserves by a slowdown in the accumulation (or outright decumulation) of domestic assets such that the growth in the reserve money is unaffected.

The slope of the top curve in figure 10.3 represents the growth rate of reserve money. The slope of the bottom curve represents the growth rate of net foreign

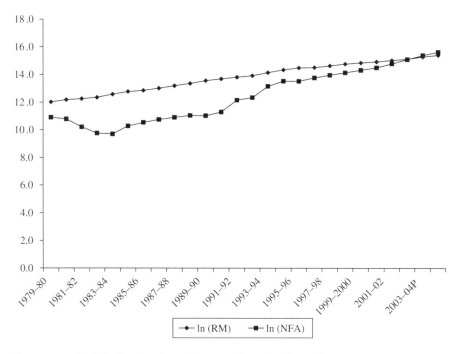

FIGURE 10.3: Net Foreign Assets and Reserve Money in Natural Log

assets. Whereas the growth rate of net foreign assets fluctuates substantially over the 25-year period shown, the growth rate of reserve money shows remarkable steadiness. If there is a shift in the growth rate of reserve money at all, it is in the direction of a decline in the 1990s and beyond, when much of the foreign asset accumulation took place. Indeed, as reported at the bottom of table 10.3, based on the average of the annual growth rates, reserve money grew 16.5 and 13.2 percent annually during 1980–91 and 1991–2005, respectively. The corresponding average annual growth rates of net foreign assets of the RBI were 8.7 and 40.5 percent, respectively. A safe conclusion from these movements is that the growth rate of reserve money did not rise during the 1990s and beyond relative to that in the 1980s, despite a large accumulation of foreign reserves. The RBI successfully sterilized the impact of the reserve accumulation on reserve money.

I may note two qualifications to this analysis, however. First, as we will see in the next chapter, monetary policy was conducted quite differently in the 1980s and early 1990s than since then. In the 1980s, the policy was entirely subservient to fiscal policy, with the RBI buying government securities to monetize the fiscal deficit. In recent years, the link between fiscal deficit and monetary policy has been severed, and the RBI conducts open market operations independently of the deficit. Second, as presented, the analysis focuses exclusively on sterilization and abstracts from important details with respect to alternative monetary policy instruments used to smooth out the effects of surges in capital inflows during specific episodes. For example, as Patnaik (2004) points out, during the capital inflow episode between June 1993 and November 1994, the RBI complemented its sterilization efforts with

TABLE 10.3: Annual Percent Change in Wholesale Prices, Foreign Reserves, and Money

Year	Wholesale Prices	Net Foreign Assets (RBI)	Reserve Money (M0)	Narrow Money (M1)	Broad Money (M3)
1	*2*	*3*	*4*	*5*	*6*
1980–81	18.2	–11.4	17.4	17.1	18.1
1981–82	9.3	–43.3	7.9	6.5	12.5
1982–83	4.9	–36.1	10.1	14.4	16.6
1983–84	7.5	–6.1	25.5	17.0	18.2
1984–85	6.5	78.5	21.5	19.5	19.0
1985–86	4.4	29.0	8.4	10.5	16.0
1986–87	5.8	23.5	17.4	16.8	18.6
1987–88	8.1	17.2	19.4	13.7	16.0
1988–89	7.5	14.5	17.7	14.1	17.8
1989–90	7.5	–2.1	23.2	21.4	19.4
1990–91	10.3	31.6	13.1	14.6	15.1
1991–92	13.7	136.0	13.4	23.2	19.3
1992–93	10.1	20.2	11.3	8.4	14.8
1993–94	8.4	127.1	25.2	21.5	18.4
1994–95	12.5	45.3	22.1	27.5	22.4
1995–96	8.1	–0.8	14.9	11.7	13.6
1996–97	4.6	28.0	2.8	12.0	16.2
1997–98	4.4	22.2	13.2	11.3	18.0
1998–99	5.9	19.0	14.5	15.4	19.4
1999–2000	3.3	20.2	8.2	10.6	14.6
2000–01	7.2	18.9	8.1	11.0	16.8
2001–02	3.6	33.9	11.4	11.4	14.1
2002–03	3.5	35.7	9.2	12.0	14.7
2003–04 P	5.4	35.2	18.3	22.2	16.7
2004–05 P	6.4	26.5	12.1	11.7	12.4
Average Rates					
1980–91	8.2	8.7	16.5	15.1	17.0
1991–05	6.9	40.5	13.2	15.0	16.5

Source: Author's calculations, using data in RBI (2005a, tables 38, 42, 43).

increases in the cash reserve ratio. In contrast, during the early- to mid-2000s, it relied nearly exclusively on sterilization.[10]

An interesting feature of figure 10.3 is that in the last two years, foreign assets cross the volume of reserve money. This would imply negative holdings of domestic assets, which is impossible. What happened is that in 2003–04, the RBI sterilization operations became constrained by its rapidly diminishing stock of government securities. Therefore, in April 2004, under the new Market Stabilization Scheme (MSS), the government of India introduced dated securities and Treasury bills that the RBI now uses to carry out its sterilization operations. Thus, in effect, the RBI now conducts its sterilization operations using "borrowed" assets.[11]

Table 10.3, to which I have already alluded, provides complementary evidence testifying to successful sterilization of monetary expansion attributable to the accumulation of foreign assets by the RBI. Column 2 of the table shows the annual percentage change in the Wholesale Price Index, and columns 3–5 show the annual growth rates of reserve, narrow money, and broad money (M0, M1, and M3), respectively. Growth rates of various measures of money supply have not shifted up on the average, and correspondingly, the Wholesale Price Index has not risen at higher rates since the mid-1990s, when reserves grew most. One exceptional year is 2003–04, when various measures of the money supply rose relatively rapidly; but this was the time when the RBI was temporarily out of the instrument necessary for sterilization.

LOOKING AHEAD: FULL CAPITAL ACCOUNT CONVERTIBILITY?

We saw in the previous chapter that the government gets a poor grade for its fiscal policy since the mid-1990s. The same is not true, however, of its management of the monetary and external sector policies.[12] Judgments will differ on whether the government went too far toward accumulating reserves and depriving the economy of some extra savings versus the possibility that it did not go far enough, thereby allowing the real exchange rate to appreciate. But few informed observers would advocate a policy mix drastically different from the one actually chosen. The judicious handling of the monetary and exchange rate policies must be largely credited with price stability in the domestic market and a broadly competitive exchange rate that facilitated a healthy growth of international trade.

Since the early 1990s, the Indian economy has made considerable progress toward integration into the global economy. The rupee is now fully convertible on the current account. While the currency is still some distance from full capital account convertibility, our discussion of the changes in the previous sections shows that substantial progress has been made in this direction as well. Foreign direct investment and portfolio investment are now virtually free, and firms are allowed to borrow abroad as long as the maturity of the loan is at least three years for loans below $20 million and at least five years for larger loans. All agents engaged in permitted international transactions—exporters, importers, and inward and outward foreign investors—are allowed to buy forward cover for their foreign exchange transactions.

The policy changes of the 1990s and 2000s have led to two key changes in the basket of capital inflows. First, the larger proportion of short-term borrowing in the second half of the 1980s has given way to longer-term inflows. For example, according to the RBI (2005b), short-term debt as a proportion of foreign exchange reserves fell from a whopping 146.5 percent at the end of 1990–91 to 5.3 percent at the end of 2004–05. Second, whereas foreign direct and portfolio investments had a tiny share in the total capital inflows in the 1980s, they now account for the lion's share of the inflows.

Nevertheless, India remains far from fully convertible on the capital account. Short-term borrowing and lending abroad are highly regulated; there remain strict caps on the investment in debt instruments by the FIIs; Indian citizens are not allowed to invest abroad; and correspondingly, foreign nationals are not allowed to invest directly in the Indian debt or equity market. Access to the forward exchange market is also off-limits to agents other than exporters, importers, and investors who have future receipts and payments due in currencies they do not wish to hold, and therefore need to cover the exchange rate risk through a forward transaction.

The key future policy question on the external account that we must address is whether the time is now ripe for India to move to full capital account convertibility within a short period, say, by 2010. If the answer to this question is in the affirmative, we must also confront a host of questions regarding the exchange rate regime India must adopt under full convertibility and the map leading to such a regime. If the answer is in the negative, we must still state what further policy measures must be taken toward future convertibility, and whether in the interim the current reserves accumulation and sterilization policies need to be adjusted.

My personal view is that though India is much better placed to embrace convertibility today than in 1997, when the RBI (1997) first recommended it, and though it must aim to eventually achieve it, it is still some distance away from committing to a specific timetable and milestones leading to full convertibility in three years' time.[13] Bhagwati (1998) makes the most eloquent case against a rush to convertibility, but others—including Williamson (1993) and Prasad, Rogoff, Wei, and Kose (2003)—have written in the same vein as well.

Briefly stated, the case against a rush to full convertibility in the case of India is as follows. First, as Bhagwati wrote forcefully, genuine empirical evidence on the benefits of capital account convertibility is lacking. Insofar as foreign savings are concerned, these can be exploited through foreign direct and portfolio investment, to which India has already opened. Besides, as I have noted before, the magnitude of foreign savings a country can absorb is constrained by its ability and willingness to tolerate current account deficits. On this consideration, it is unlikely that India would absorb any more foreign capital with full convertibility than it does without it.

Turning to the empirical evidence, most studies trying to quantify the benefits of convertibility rely on simulations rather than true empirical studies. The results of these studies largely reflect the assumed theoretical structure of the model, the functional forms, and the parameters.[14] Some attempts have been made to look for growth effects of convertibility, using cross-country regressions. Quite apart from the well-known shortcomings of such studies, the available evidence is at best mixed, and surely far less compelling than those in studies relating to the benefits of trade liberalization.

The most that the empirical studies are able to claim is that for countries with well-developed financial markets and stable macroeconomic environment, convertibility offers small positive growth effects. But for countries with weak financial sectors and macroeconomic vulnerabilities, convertibility leads to greater instability in the GDP growth without the benefit of higher average rates of growth (Mukerji, 2006).

Neither the simulation studies nor cross-country regressions distinguish between limited convertibility in terms of openness to foreign direct and portfolio investment and full-fledged capital account convertibility. In other words, we do not know the gains from a move from openness only to foreign investment to full convertibility, which is the relevant question for India at present. These facts about limited prospects of positive benefits from convertibility for India create a presumption in favor of great caution if convertibility brings risks in other forms.

Second, on the fiscal front, India faces far from satisfactory initial conditions for convertibility. As discussed in the previous chapter, the debt to GDP ratio and gross fiscal deficit remain very high. The average growth rate of almost 8 percent during 2003–04 to 2005–06 has led to increased tax revenues and some reduction in the deficit, but not nearly enough. Moreover, we can scarcely be sure that the deficit will not return to the higher level if the GDP growth rate (and therefore tax revenue growth) reverts to the previous trend, as happened after 1996–97. With interest payments on the debt amounting to more than 6 percent of the GDP, a gross fiscal deficit of 8 percent, and a debt to GDP ratio of more than 90 percent, convertibility is bound to leave India vulnerable to a crisis. One possible hazard is that the government itself would be tempted to turn to lower-interest short-term external debt to finance its deficits and to replace its existing higher-interest domestic debt.

Third, we will see in the next chapter that despite considerable progress, the financial sector is still insufficiently developed in India.[15] Banks are predominantly in the public sector, and credit markets are relatively shallow. Insurance has barely been opened to the private sector with the foreign investment capped at 26 percent. The debt and equity markets are thin and dominated by public sector financial institutions and the FIIs. Because the Indian equity market is tiny in relation to the worldwide stakes of the FIIs, any time the latter begin to exit the Indian market, the share prices plummet. Because few FIIs have the incentive to carefully gather detailed information on the future profitability of various firms, such exits are characterized by herd behavior.

Fourth, India is still far from fully integrated on the trade front. For this reason, ensuring a competitive exchange rate is a high priority. A move to capital account convertibility is initially bound to bring more capital inflows and force an appreciation of the rupee. If the appreciation ends up being large and persistent, it could put trade integration into jeopardy. Furthermore, even if the appreciation is only temporary, convertibility could hurt export growth by making the real exchange rate more volatile.

Finally, the embrace of full capital account convertibility, which raises the risk of a crisis, can place the reforms in other areas at grave risk. In the Indian political environment, building consensus for even the most straightforward reforms, such as privatization and trade liberalization, is an uphill task. Therefore, if capital account convertibility were to culminate in a crisis or even create greater volatility in growth, the cause of reforms could be set back. Given that India still has a long way to travel before it can complete its reform process, it will be unwise for it to expose itself to such a risk.

Two counterarguments made by the advocates of speedy convertibility are important to address here. First, the adoption of convertibility itself may serve as a means to speed up the reform, especially in the financial sector. For instance, giving individuals and firms access to the global markets may bring pressure on the domestic banks to become more competitive. Likewise, the possibility of a crisis may force the government to act more urgently on fiscal deficits and debt. Finally, capital account convertibility is an essential step toward building up the financial sector.

While these outcomes can indeed follow from the embrace of convertibility, as I argued above, the opposite may also happen. Both the government and firms may quickly proceed to accumulate short-term external debt and rapidly move the economy toward crisis. Therefore, the question is largely empirical. On balance, the weight of the empirical evidence favors erring on the side of caution: Whereas the countries that ended up in a crisis following the premature adoption of convertibility are many, those that reformed more speedily and smoothly on account of the premature embrace of convertibility are few and far between.

The second argument in favor of moving rapidly to convertibility is that this will help India turn into a major financial center in Asia. Given its vast pool of skilled labor and rapidly developing information technology industry, India certainly has the potential to become such a center. It is also true that full convertibility is a necessary condition for becoming a hub of financial activity. Yet, the argument is misleading. Currently, the financial sector in India is heavily dominated by the public sector in virtually all its aspects. According to Buiter and Patel (2005–06), 70 percent of the financial sector's assets are currently held by government-owned or -sponsored agencies.[16] It is highly implausible that without the reforms that give primacy to the private sector, including foreign players, India could turn into a major financial center in Asia. It is equally implausible that the government will overnight create a domestic policy regime in which the private sector would challenge its supremacy in the sector. The process leading to domestic and foreign private actors turning into substantial players in the banking, insurance, and capital markets has been, and will be, a slow one, and can proceed without full convertibility. Fast-tracking convertibility will bring the risk of a crisis and the prospects of consequent slowdown, even reversal, of reforms and growth.

FUTURE COURSE OF POLICY

Having ruled out the embrace of capital account convertibility in the immediate future, what should be the strategy of the government in the short to medium run? I will argue that we should stay the current course of gradual liberalization of both the financial sector and the capital account without committing to specific milestones toward full convertibility. We will consider the financial sector reforms in detail in the next chapter. On the capital account front, various caps currently in place on foreign equity investment and debt instruments can be eased and eventually removed. The government may also experiment on a limited scale with the relaxation of the limit on the length of maturity of external debt, which currently is a minimum of three years. It can also allow the citizens to invest their savings abroad on a limited scale. But all this should be done, as has been the practice to date, while retaining the option to reverse course in case of large outflows in the initial years.

This course of action still leaves the question of how the RBI should deal with the foreign exchange inflows that are likely to continue, and may even accelerate as growth accelerates and the government further liberalizes the financial sector and the external account. Two possible steps are faster liberalization of imports and early retirement of the external debt with a near moratorium on additional official external borrowing (Panagariya, 2002b). These steps would soak up at least part of the foreign exchange inflows, but they can be expected to play only a limited role in the adjustment. For one thing, if the past is any guide, the response of imports to liberalization in industrial goods is likely to be muted. Moreover, the current politics is unlikely to allow substantial liberalization in agriculture. As for the official external borrowing, as long as the interest rates abroad are lower, no government would forgo this option, since politically it offers the least costly means of bringing down the deficit.

Therefore, the RBI is left to choose between reserves accumulation with sterilization and real appreciation of the rupee. The latter would curtail exports and expand imports, thereby reducing the foreign exchange left for the RBI to absorb. But there are obvious limits to this course. India still needs its trade and traded goods sector to expand; substantial appreciation of the rupee would scuttle that process. Moreover, appreciation would raise the current account deficit and, if left unchecked, would bring the risk of macroeconomic instability. Therefore, the appreciation option is not available beyond the level that produces a current account deficit of 2 to 3 percent per year.

The inevitable conclusion is that unless the foreign exchange inflows themselves dry up, the RBI will have to continue to accumulate substantial reserves and sterilize their impact on the money supply in the years to come. Insofar as the reserves earn a much lower return than they would if productively invested, there is a definite cost of carrying them. But injecting them into the economy imposes an even bigger cost by causing real appreciation of the rupee and undermining the traded goods sector. Any gains in the growth rate through extra investment can be wiped out by the real appreciation and the consequent contraction of the traded goods sector. And to the extent that the reserves, when injected into the economy, will be partially used up in boosting consumption, it is not clear that they would boost investment dollar for dollar. As an example, the Chinese case is well known: China has accumulated reserves at a rate far higher than that of India and has sustained a very rapid growth. Increased domestic savings have more than made up any loss of savings through the reserves accumulation.

A final word needs to be said about the possibility of reserves accumulation without sterilization. Setting aside temporary flows that reverse themselves, should the RBI reduce slowdown on sterilization of the monetary expansion resulting from the reserves accumulation? More directly stated, the question here is whether the RBI should stay the course on reserve money or accelerate its expansion in response to reserves inflows. Once again, given the relatively low tolerance for inflation in India and the real appreciation of the rupee on the external account that accompanies inflation, the room for such acceleration is relatively limited. Both import liberalization and faster growth of reserve money offer at best limited scope for adjustment at the margin. The bulk of the adjustment will have to continue to fall on the accumulation of reserves and sterilization.

Unfortunately, this is not the end of the story. In the very long run, reserve accumulation and sterilization do have their limits. The difference between the interest paid on government securities and Treasury bills sold under the Market Stabilization Scheme, and the return on foreign exchange reserves must be covered by the government budget. As the stocks of the securities and reserves grow, so do the additional budgetary costs. Given a budget deficit that is already large, the ability of the government to add to the interest burden has limits. Therefore, unless imports expand dramatically in response to liberalization or capital inflows themselves reverse, eventually substantial appreciation of the rupee may be unavoidable.

CONCLUDING REMARKS

It this chapter, we have analyzed the macroeconomic implications of the movements in the external account, past policies relating to them, and their future course. The highlights of the chapter may be summarized as follows. First, India has made substantial progress in opening both the current and capital accounts since 1991. It became officially current account convertible in August 1994, and now allows foreign direct and portfolio investments freely into the economy. The FIIs are also allowed to invest, not just in equities but in corporate as well as government debt instruments. The opening up has led to considerable expansion of trade and investment flows, though the magnitudes are much smaller than in China.

Second, since the early 1990s, the RBI has managed the exchange rate such that it has allowed limited movements in the dollar-rupee rate in the short run, but substantial adjustments in it over the longer run, to hold the line on the real exchange rate. Monthly data show very limited movements in the rupee-dollar exchange rate, but the rupee nevertheless depreciated 34 percent against the dollar between 1992–93 and 2001–02.

Third, the biggest challenge the RBI has faced since the early 1990s is the large inflow of foreign exchange due to rapid expansion of remittances, software exports, foreign investment, and borrowing abroad. The RBI has met this challenge largely by accumulating reserves and sterilizing the accompanying monetary expansion. The latter is verified by the fact that the growth in the reserve money has been virtually unaffected by the reserve accumulation. Acceleration in the accumulation of reserves has been offset, on the average, by the deceleration of accumulation of domestic assets. While the reserve accumulation and sterilization have helped the RBI hold the line on inflation and the nominal effective exchange rate, the real effective exchange rate with respect to major destination markets has appreciated moderately in the last several years.

Fourth, I have discussed two recent controversies relating to the reserves. The first of these was opened by the Planning Commission, which proposed in 2004–05 that some of the RBI reserves be used to finance infrastructure projects. I have shown that the proposal is effectively equivalent to an increase in the budget deficit and an equivalent increase in the current account deficit over and above what the RBI would run otherwise. The second controversy relates to the assertion by Lal et al. (2003) that the reserve accumulation by the RBI in the 1990s cost India 2.7 percentage points in extra growth annually. Here I fully agree with Joshi and Sanyal (2004) that Lal et al. miscalculated the impact of the reserves accumulation on investment by wide margin, and that since the accumulation prevented a large appreciation of the rupee, and thus allowed exports to grow at a healthy pace, on balance it had a positive impact on growth.

Fifth, looking ahead, the most important external sector issue is whether India should embrace full capital account convertibility in a relatively short period, say by 2010. I have argued against such a move. I offer several reasons for this, the main one being that the expected benefits are substantially outweighed by the risks such convertibility will bring. By opening to foreign direct and portfolio investment and medium-to-long-term external borrowing, India already enjoys most of the benefits of capital account convertibility. The main remaining ingredients in full convertibility are borrowing abroad with the maturity of less than three years, the removal of caps on various forms of borrowing by domestic firms and inward investments in debt instruments by foreign firms and freedom to invest abroad to the citizens of India. These measures are associated with high risks of macroeconomic crisis. I have argued that rather than immediately expose itself to this risk, India should move toward capital account convertibility gradually, while simultaneously deepening its financial markets. In particular, it should not commit itself to a specific timetable and milestones.

Finally, I address the question of whether the RBI should modify its stance with respect to reserve accumulation and sterilization in the coming years. I argue that the options here are limited. On the margin, greater import liberalization, a slightly larger current account deficit, and some slowdown in sterilization can help, but the need to hold the line on the real exchange rate, inflation, and the current account deficit give the RBI very limited maneuvering room.

11

THE FINANCIAL SECTOR
Why Not Privatize the Banks?

In our discussion of the savings-investment identity, we saw that the entities that save are often distinct from the entities that invest. Households account for the bulk of the savings in India but invest only a little more than half of those savings in physical assets themselves. They channel the remaining savings through the financial system to other agents in the economy. Likewise, foreign savings need not always take the form of foreign direct investment, and may have to be intermediated by the financial system for investment by the domestic entrepreneurs or other foreign entrepreneurs. Even corporations in the declining sectors may choose to channel a part of their savings to the corporations in the expanding sectors, though the Indian accounting system so far does not record these flows explicitly.

Assets that help intermediate between savers and investors typically include currency, bank deposits, loans, bonds, mutual funds, stocks, life and general insurance policies, pension and provident funds, foreign exchange, and other intangible instruments. Institutions such as the central bank, commercial banks, nonbank financial institutions, stock exchanges, insurance companies, and regulatory agencies overseeing transactions in financial assets are all a part of the financial sector. They help encourage, mobilize, and allocate savings among investors and effectively link the household, corporate, government, and foreign sectors with one another.

In this chapter, I consider the developments in India's financial sector. For the purpose of policy discussion, I divide the financial sector into three subsectors: money and banking; capital markets; and insurance and retirement benefits that include pension and provident funds. But since the first of these subsectors accounts for the bulk of the financial sector transactions in India, a large part of the chapter is devoted to it. I begin immediately below with a general introductory section on the role of the financial sector in the expansion, mobilization, and efficient allocation of savings across different investment activities. I then turn to the working of the money and banking sector in India prior to the 1990s, followed by the developments during the 1990s and 2000s. I then take up the reforms that remain to be done, including the case for the privatization of the public sector banks. I discuss the developments and reforms in the capital markets and insurance and retirement benefits programs in the final two sections.

THE ROLE OF THE FINANCIAL SECTOR IN PROMOTING GROWTH

Faster accumulation and efficient allocation of capital are among the most important sources of growth. These in turn depend on the efficiency with which savings are converted into investment. In general, individuals who are good savers are not necessarily good entrepreneurs. For example, households that account for the bulk of the national income are typically the principal savers in the developing countries, but most of them are not likely to be consummate entrepreneurs. Therefore, the conversion of savings into investment requires financial intermediation, a process by which the savings of one set of individuals are transmitted to another set of individuals. This is where the financial markets and financial instruments come into play.

Three Avenues to the Accumulation and Efficient Allocation of Capital

In his lucid essay, Patrick (1966) distinguishes three mechanisms through which the financial system helps speed up the accumulation and efficient allocation of capital. First, appropriate financial instruments can help augment productive capital from the *existing* wealth that may be tied up in unproductive tangible assets. This is a one-time conversion of past wealth rather than the flow that is generated out of current production activity. For instance, suppose an individual holds a part of his wealth in a tangible but unproductive asset such as gold. Suppose further that we induce this individual to exchange gold for an intangible asset, such as money or bonds, which guarantees him the same or larger wealth in real terms as gold. We could then exchange gold for machines on the world market and augment productive capital stock. Likewise, if individuals hold their wealth in land and buildings that are not productively used, and can be induced to exchange them for an equivalent financial asset, those holdings are released for productive use.[1]

Second, financial intermediation can help the process of growth by efficiently allocating savings generated out of current production across entrepreneurs. As Gurley and Shaw (1956) noted in their pioneering work, this role of the financial markets arises on account of two plausible assumptions. First, not all savers are the most efficient investors in terms of the optimum allocation of investment. Second, savers are not willing to provide the full amount of their savings in excess of their own efficient investments directly to the most efficient investors.

The first assumption is reasonable in view of the fact that savings typically depend on income, but investment depends on entrepreneurial talent, knowledge, and willingness to take risk. The second assumption is justified on the ground that savers do not always want to invest directly in the primary securities (bonds or stocks) of the investors, since they desire a different mix of risk, return, and liquidity than is offered by those securities. Financial institutions can exploit this gap by selling savers indirect securities with characteristics they desire in return for their savings, and in turn investing those savings in the primary securities offered by investors. The financial system can create a wide variety of these indirect securities with varying mixes of risk, return, liquidity, maturity, and other characteristics. In turn, it can also invest the savings so acquired in the primary securities of the most efficient investors.

Finally, financial markets can help *increase* savings and investment from current production by raising the return available to the savers and lowering the cost of funds paid by investors. Improved intermediation produces cost savings that may be shared between savers and investors. Such savings allow financial institutions to offer financial instruments that pay higher returns and lower risk. This makes present consumption more expensive relative to future consumption and induces individuals to save more. Improved intermediation also induces investors to invest more by lowering the cost of borrowing through a variety of instruments, such as stocks and corporate bonds. Furthermore, the improved menu of financial assets matches more closely the savers who prefer certain asset characteristics in terms of return, risk, and liquidity with investors offering those same characteristics. This allows investments that would otherwise not be possible to take place. For example, some savers may be willing to undertake risky investments in the hope of high returns, as in the case of venture capitalists, and to make otherwise unlikely high-risk but innovative investments possible.

Demand- versus Supply-Driven Financial Development

How should financial development proceed? Patrick (1966) distinguishes between demand- and supply-driven development of the financial markets, which he calls "demand-following" and "supply-leading" phenomena, respectively. The demand-driven approach relies principally on economic growth to generate pressure for the financial instruments and for the market to supply them. The faster the growth rate, the larger is the demand by enterprises for the savings of other agents in the economy and the greater is the pressure for the supply of financial assets that facilitate the necessary intermediation. And for a given aggregate growth rate, the greater the variance in the growth rates among various sectors in the economy, the greater is the need for financial intermediation of savings from slow-growing sectors to fast-growing sectors. The larger and more complex the structure of the economy becomes, the greater is the mismatch between the needs of investors and their internally supplied savings. Empirically, household savings grow faster than household investments in physical assets as development proceeds. Therefore, the demand for financial assets grows proportionately faster than the GDP, leading to the deepening of the financial markets.

The success of a purely demand-driven approach depends critically on the elasticity of response of the markets to supply the demand for assets. In practice, government regulations and other impediments may limit this response. We will see that such impediments have surely played a role in the slow development of financial markets in India. Therefore, the success of the demand-driven approach often depends on the government's taking the necessary action to relieve the bottlenecks stifling the supply response.

The supply-driven or "supply-leading" approach assigns the government a more active role in building institutions and creating intermediation instruments ahead of the demand. Such an approach tries to actively encourage and transfer savings from the traditional sector to the modern sectors, and to stimulate entrepreneurial response in the latter. The expansion of bank branches and credit into the rural areas through active government intervention before banks are willing to go there in search of profits would be an example of supply-driven approach. Likewise, enticing the entrepreneurs to enter activities that they would not otherwise enter through the availability of credit at favorable terms is an example of supply-driven financial intermediation. India actively employed this approach during the second half of the 1970s and the 1980s with respect to both the expansion of rural bank branches and what came to be called the priority sector lending.

There are obvious limitations of the supply-driven approach. Insofar as the intermediation of this kind may not be privately profitable, and therefore may require the commitment of financial resources by the government, there remains the danger that it cannot be sustained. Any inducement offered to entrepreneurs through subsidized credit may also pose a moral hazard problem. For example, subsidized credit without collateral to small entrepreneurs, in the hope of stimulating entrepreneurial activity, has had a rather unhappy history in India. The entrepreneurs often channeled a part of the credit to build personal assets, declared the venture bankrupt after a few years, and defaulted on the loan. If the supply-driven approach is to be sustained and to succeed, it must have a large element of profit motive as, for example, has been the case with private venture capital that has financed many successful companies in the information technology sector in Bangalore in recent years.

Before turning to the financial sector in India, let me note that in an open economy, financial markets must intermediate foreign savings. This requires the development of instruments specifically targeted at foreign sources of savings. Also important in this context is the foreign exchange regime as it applies to the current and capital accounts. The issue of capital account convertibility, which I discussed in detail in the last chapter, is essentially a financial intermediation issue since it fundamentally affects the financial instruments available to foreign investors, as well as foreign financial instruments in which domestic savers can invest their savings. Since I have considered this sector in detail in the previous chapter, I will largely abstain from it in this one.

MONEY AND BANKING PRIOR TO THE 1990s

I have already described the early history of banking in India in chapter 3. To briefly recapitulate, the RBI commenced its operations as the central bank of India in 1935. In the post-independence era, it played an important role in building India's financial infrastructure. Recognizing the absence of institutions willing and able to fulfill the needs of development finance, it set up a variety of development finance institutions (DFIs). These institutions are all-India, state, or regional in character. All-India institutions themselves fall into four categories: term-lending institutions, specialized financial institutions, refinance institutions, and investment institutions.[2] In 2001, commercial banks accounted for 66 percent of the assets of financial intermediary

institutions, and the investment institutions for 18.1 percent. The remaining institutions accounted for the rest.[3]

Though the first state-owned commercial bank, the State Bank of India, came
into existence in 1955, it was the nationalization of the 14 largest banks in 1969 that
established the state as the dominant player in commercial banking. It brought the
share of deposits in the public sector from 31 to 86 percent in 1969. A second round
of nationalization in 1980 brought another six larges banks into the public sector.
This increased the share of deposits in the public sector in 1980 to 92 percent. A key
impact of nationalization was the expansion of rural banking: The proportion of the
bank branches in the rural areas jumped from 22 percent in 1969 to 35 percent in
1972 and 49 percent in 1981.

Credit market interventions aside, the banking sector was subject to liberal policies until at least the end of the 1960s. But starting in the early 1970s, a variety
of interventions were introduced. That process got intensified in the 1980s, with
substantial financial repression characterizing the decade. Though some financial
liberalization did take place in the second half of the 1980s, accelerating repression
by the government to mobilize savings at low interest to finance the deficit largely
overshadowed that liberalization.

Almost all monetary policy indicators point to liberal policies toward the banks
until at least the 1960s. For instance, the cash reserve ratio (CRR)—the minimum
share of the net demand and time deposits every scheduled commercial bank is
required to hold in cash reserves with the RBI—was just 2 percent from 1962 to
1973, when it was raised to 3 percent.[4] The statutory liquidity ratio—the minimum
proportion of the net demand and time deposits each commercial bank is required
to hold in approved public sector securities—was 20 percent until 1964, when it was
raised to 25 percent. It stayed at 25 percent until 1970. Foreign investment inflows
were relatively liberal until at least the mid-1960s. In the same vein, the deposit and
lending rates were not subject to intervention until late 1960s.

Though the 1970s were characterized by progressive expansion of interventionist policies, it was in the 1980s that the budget deficit expanded rapidly and the
government came to employ wholesale instruments of financial policy to mobilize
the savings of households to meet its fiscal needs. But not all interventions aimed at
mobilizing savings to finance the budget deficits. The government also intervened to
achieve other objectives, most notably the delivery of credit to the poor at low interest rates. In the following, I consider interventions aimed at mobilizing savings as
well as other objectives in detail.

Financial Repression

The first tool of financial repression was money supply, which became entirely subservient to the fiscal needs of the government. As Khatkhate (1990, pp. 1856–57)
points out, the net RBI claims on government, which coincided with the concept of
deficit financing at the time, came to constitute the most important factor affecting
reserve money in the 1980s. The Reserve Bank's extension of credit to the government accounted for as much as 85 percent of the variation in reserve money during the decade. As a result, the RBI's other credit operations involving banks were
rendered marginal to the functioning of monetary policy. This is in contrast to the

1990s and 2000s, when reserve money became effectively unlinked from the fiscal deficit and the RBI operated a more independent monetary policy. As we saw in the last chapter, the massive RBI purchases of foreign exchange necessitated that it employ monetary policy tools to sterilize the monetary expansion resulting from those purchases.

Second, the RBI steadily raised the CRR, which provided resources to the government at negligible interest cost. With one brief exception, the CRR had been held at or below 6 percent throughout the 1970s.[5] But as deficits grew in the 1980s, the CRR grew as well. It rose to 6.5 percent in 1981, 8.5 percent in 1983, 10 percent in 1987, and 15 percent in 1989. Thus, by 1989, the RBI was effectively confiscating 15 percent of the commercial bank deposits free of cost. This was a large tax on the latter. The CRR stayed at 15 percent until 1992 but was brought steadily down thereafter to reach 5 percent in 2004.

Third, the government steadily raised the statutory liquidity ratio (SLR)—the minimum proportion of the net demand and time deposits each commercial bank is required to hold in approved public sector securities—to raise resources required over and above those yielded by the CRR. Throughout the 1980s, the government fixed the return on these securities at a level well below what it would have had to pay in the open, competitive market. For example, the return it paid on short-term securities with maturity of one to five years ranged from 4.2 to 8.3 percent in 1984–85. In comparison, the interest rate on deposits with maturity of one to three years the same year ranged from 8 to 9 percent. Taking into account the operating costs, it is evident that for the banks, holding the government securities was a losing proposition.[6] The SLR steadily rose from 26 percent in 1970 to 32 percent in 1973, 34 percent in 1978, 35 percent in 1981, 36 percent in 1984, 38 percent in 1989, and 38.5 percent in 1990. As a part of the financial-sector reforms, the ratio was brought down to 31.5 percent in 1994 and 25 percent in 1997, where it currently stands.

Fourth, the low interest on the government securities that the commercial banks were required to hold under their SLR obligations was supported by restrictions on the deposit rates of the commercial banks. The interest rate on deposits with maturity of one to three years varied between 8 and 9 percent in the first half of the 1980s, and between 9 and 10 percent in the second half. Based on the wholesale price increases shown in table 10.3, the average inflation during 1980–91 was 8.2 percent. Therefore, the real interest rate on one-year deposits was barely positive. This fact had the obvious adverse implications for the amount of savings as well as their proportion intermediated through the banking system.

Fifth, the government exploited its access to other sources of funds to finance the deficit. It had the monopoly access to the funds in such savings instruments as the national savings certificates and employee provident funds. Though the administered real interest rate the government pays on these instruments currently is higher than what they would fetch in the market, the opposite was the case during the 1980s. Additionally, the Life Insurance Company, a public sector company with monopoly over life insurance until recently, was a heavy investor in government securities.

Finally, the strict capital controls during the 1980s that prevented savers from taking their savings abroad were a critical support to the financial repression by the government. If the economy had been fully convertible on the capital account, savers would have had the option to move their funds abroad in reaction to financial repression. This was especially likely in the 1980s, when the interest rates abroad were high and the rupee was expected to depreciate. Closing this option allowed the government to keep the deposit rates low, which in turn allowed the government to set the interest on its debt low as well.

Kletzer (2004, p. 247) estimates the average implicit annual subsidy (exclusive of seignorage) reaped by the government during 1980–2002 from financial repression. He calculates the average rupee interest rate the government would have had to pay in the world market and compares it to the average interest rate it actually paid on the domestically raised debt to arrive at a measure of the implicit subsidy it reaped from the financial repression.[7] He finds that on the average, the government collected as much as 8.2 percent of the GDP in revenue from the implicit subsidy during 1980–93. This revenue dramatically fell to 1.6 percent of the GDP during 1994–2002. Kletzer estimates an additional 2 percent of the GDP from seignorage measured by the change in the reserve-money-to-GDP ratio during 1980–2002. For the subperiod 1997–2002, this figure, at 1.4 percent, was lower, indicating larger seignorage during the prior period.

Other Policy Interventions

Quite apart from financial repression, the government intervened heavily in the financial market during the 1970s and 1980s through three additional instruments: credit allocation through priority sector lending and the Credit Authorization Scheme; controls on the deposit and lending rates; and building of bank infrastructure through the entitlement formula and the Branch Licensing Program.

Whereas the interventions aimed at financial repression can be reasonably described as "distortions," we cannot automatically attach the same label to these other interventions for two reasons. First, one may argue that the market itself was distorted initially, so that the interventions actually corrected those distortions. And second, the interventions were directed at certain goals that the market would not have fulfilled.

There is some truth in both of these arguments. Because of asymmetric information and moral hazard, financial markets fail more frequently than other markets, and thus produce suboptimal outcomes. Likewise, few would question the proposition that the above interventions were aimed at certain social goals that the market would not have fulfilled on its own. Nevertheless, the conclusion that the interventions did not produce distortions is not valid. With respect to the first argument, it is doubtful that the interventions were designed in any systematic way to alleviate the problems arising out of asymmetric information or moral hazard. For example, the interventions in favor of agriculture or small-scale industry units were done more for redistributive reasons than a recognition that the banks would fail to identify their productive potential. Therefore, it is the second argument that has greater validity. But here we must ask whether the chosen interventions targeted the objectives directly or indirectly, thereby generating by-product distortions. Insofar as the purpose of the interventions was redistribution in favor of certain sectors of the society, the instruments were expressly indirect. For example, one key by-product distortion generated by directed lending was the rapid expansion of nonperforming loans (NPLs) of the banks.

Credit Allocation: Priority Sector Lending

Turning to the interventions themselves, though priority sector lending is often associated with bank nationalization, a beginning in this direction had already been made in 1967–68. According to RBI (2005c), which offers an excellent discussion of priority sector lending from inception until today, priority sector prescriptions for the banks originated in the 1967–68 credit policy, which emphasized that the commercial banks should urgently increase their lending to priority sectors such as agriculture, exports, and small-scale industries. The concept of priority sector evolved over time, however, with a formal list of the items to be included under various categories issued for the first time in February 1972.

In November 1974, the RBI advised public sector banks to raise their priority sector lending to one-third or more of their outstanding credit by the end of 1978–79. Four years later, in November 1978, the RBI advised the private sector banks to achieve the same target by the end of 1979–80. These targets were achieved and, in 1980, the RBI raised the bar by advising all scheduled commercial banks to raise the proportion of priority sector credit to 40 percent of net bank credit (NBC) by the end of 1984–85.[8] Within this general limit, the RBI stipulated that agriculture receive 16 percent of the NBC by the end of 1984–85. It further stipulated that advances to small and marginal farmers and landless laborers should account for 50 percent of the advances to agriculture by 1983, and those to rural artisans, village craftsmen, and cottage industries, for 12.5 percent of the advances to the small-scale industries (SSI) by 1985.

In February 1983, the RBI issued a more elaborate classification of the priority sector, placing agriculture, SSI, small road- and water-transport operators, retail trade, small business, professional and self employed persons, statesponsored schemes for scheduled castes and tribes, education, housing, and consumption among priority sectors. Subsequently the target for agriculture was raised to 18 percent of the NBC, to be achieved by the end of 1989–90.

Priority sector lending was also extended to the foreign banks, though they were subject to somewhat different lending targets. They were first instructed to increase their advances to the priority sector borrowers to 15 percent of their NBC by the end of 1991–92. In April 1993, the RBI revised this ratio to 32 percent of the NBC and set the target date as the end of 1993–94. Within this overall target, the foreign banks were also required to lend 10 percent of the NBC to the SSI sector and 12 percent to exporters.

Another instrument deployed to exercise control over the allocation of credit was the Credit Authorization Scheme (CAS), under which individual loans larger than a specified limit required scrutiny and approval by the RBI. The threshold limit in the 1980s for these loans was a low 40 million rupees. In 1988–89, the CAS was replaced by a credit monitoring arrangement whereby banks were no longer required to obtain prior approval of the RBI for working capital advances and term loans, provided they were made according to certain norms.

Administered Interest Rates

The second major intervention by the RBI in the financial sector took the form of controls on various deposit and credit interest rates. The government and the

RBI intervened in the determination of virtually all interest rates by fixing ceilings, floors, or accrual levels. The following excerpt from Joshi and Little (1994, p. 34) gives the flavor of the complicated structure that the government implemented during the 1980s:

> We take 1982/83 figures for the purpose of description. Though nominal rates have changed (mainly increased) over the years, relativities have not changed much, so a single year is enough to bring out the main points. Deposit rates in commercial banks are in the region of 8 percent for one-year deposits, going up to 11 percent for five-year deposits. The general commercial bank short-term lending rate (applicable to the private sector generally) is around 19 percent, but there are a number of exceptions. Low rates of 4 percent are available under a scheme that directs banks to lend at least 1 percent of their loan portfolio to small businesses, small farmers, and activities in areas designated by the government of India as "backward regions." Intermediate rates of 9 to 13 percent are available for exports and food procurement. As far as term loans are concerned, the general rate is 14 percent, though there are exceptions in favor of small-scale industry and certain agricultural activities, which receive loans at around 12 percent. The government borrows cheaply. The Treasury Bill rate is 4.6 percent. Rates on government bonds are in the range of 5 to 9 percent, depending on maturity.

Bank Infrastructure

Kochar (2005) offers an excellent discussion of the interventions aimed at building the bank infrastructure.[9] According to her, the government strategy for branch expansion was multipronged and an integral part of its broader antipoverty program, especially during the 1980s. One of the instruments the RBI employed for the expansion of banking in the rural areas was the "entitlement formula" that required commercial banks to open a specified number of branches in rural or semiurban centers with no existing bank branches for every branch opened in a metropolitan or urban center. Precise history of the use of this instrument goes back to July 1962, when it was introduced. I provide the relevant details later, in my discussion of the controversy on the link between bank branch expansion and poverty reduction.

While the entitlement formula could influence the rural-urban mix of the bank branches, it was not designed to influence the total number of branches. Indeed, insofar as rural branches were unprofitable, the requirement could have deterred the banks from opening some new branches in the urban areas. Recognizing this fact, the government launched three separate but back-to-back branch licensing programs between 1979 and 1990. Once again, I relegate the details of these programs to the section on the controversy over bank branch expansion and poverty reduction.

The Efficiency Effects of the Intervention

Going by plausible assumptions, financial repression had adverse effects on savings as well as on the development of the financial markets. Lower deposit rates meant that savers got taxed, and therefore were discouraged from saving as much as they would have in the absence of the taxation. Some of them probably also shied away from putting their savings through the banking system, which discouraged financial deepening. Likewise, the high CRR and SLR curtailed the funds available to the banks for lending. and therefore had an adverse effect on the development of financial markets.

To a large degree, this hypothesis is confirmed by the econometric work by Demetriades and Luintel (1996), who studied the effects of various types of banking sector controls on financial deepening. They found that with the exception of the ceiling on lending rates, all other controls contributed negatively to financial deepening. They further found that financial deepening and growth are jointly determined, so that the controls also have an adverse effect on growth. .

The priority sector lending, including the low administered interest rates applicable to the borrowers in this sector, had been motivated by redistributive considerations. But as the report of Committee on the Financial System (Narasimham Committee I), issued in 1991, rightly pointed out, the pursuit of such objectives should use fiscal rather than credit instruments. Thus, even if the program moved the government closer to its desired social goals, it imposed extra cost on the economy through by-product distortions. Among other things, the diversion of the credit to these sectors adversely affected the availability of credit to "nonpriority" sectors. Moreover, insofar as the interest rate structure was tilted in favor of the priority sectors, the other sectors were subject to superhigh interest rates. Recognizing these problems, the Narasimham Committee I recommended phasing out the directed credit program, but the government rejected the recommendation.

One another costly by-product distortion of priority sector lending was the buildup of nonperforming assets (NPAs) of the banks. Loans to this sector, especially those to the weaker sections, are not backed by collateral, and therefore have a high default rate. According to the Committee on Banking Sector Reforms (Narasimham Committee II), which reported in 1998, 47 percent of all NPAs at the time originated in the priority sector. Perhaps keeping in view the fate of the recommendation by Narasimham Committee I and bowing to the political constraints, Narasimham Committee II did not repeat the prescription of fiscal rather than credit subsidies to the priority sectors. Instead, it argued against a sudden reduction in the priority sector targets while simultaneously recommending a phased move away from overall priority sector targets and subsector targets. But according to the data available in the RBI (2005c, annexure 6–8), priority sector targets of 40 percent of the NBC for domestic public and private banks and 32 percent of the NBC for foreign banks continued to be satisfied in virtually all years between 1996–97 and 2003–04.[10] The bank branch expansion program was successful in terms of the objectives it sought. But evidently it, too, had efficiency costs, in that it led to a waste of resources by opening branches with lower returns than could be reaped on the best alternative projects available. To some degree, this is confirmed by the fact that once the branch expansion program was discontinued, branch expansion came to a virtual standstill with the population per branch creeping back up (see below). The main defense given for the branch expansion, especially through the branch entitlement program, is its favorable impact on rural poverty reduction. But, as I discuss immediately below, the evidence provided in support of this hypothesis is highly suspect.

The Controversy over Bank Branch Expansion and
Poverty Reduction

In a recent paper, Burgess and Pande (2005, p. 781) offer the following conclusion:

> We show that between 1977 and 1990 rural branch expansion was relatively higher in
> financially less developed states. The reverse was true before 1977 and after 1990. The
> timing and nature of these trend reversals point to their being caused by the introduc-
> tion and removal of the 1:4 branch licensing policy...Our research design assumes
> that other state-specific economic and policy variables which affect poverty outcomes
> did not exhibit similarly timed trend reversals.

The authors (p. 781) further state, "This paper's main finding is that branch expansion into rural unbanked locations in India significantly reduced rural poverty. We
show that this effect was, at least partially, mediated through increased deposit
mobilization and credit disbursement by banks in rural areas." They calculate that
opening a bank branch in an additional rural location per 100,000 persons lowers
aggregate poverty by a hefty 4.1 percentage points.

This is an intriguing set of conclusions requiring careful scrutiny.

The History of the Ratio Rule of Rural Branch Expansion

It turns out that Burgess and Pande are incorrect both about the timing and the precise ratio rule. The link between rural unbanked and urban branches in India was
first introduced not in 1977 but in the early 1960s. The RBI began to require the
Indian commercial banks to observe a ratio of 2:1 between banked and unbanked
branches beginning in July 1962. Later, following its poor showing in the 1967 elections, the Congress Party adopted a ten-point program that included seizing the
"social control" of the banks. A key element of this policy was to ensure a more uniform expansion of the available credit over different areas and income strata of the
population. As a consequence, the branch licensing policy came up for discussion at
the first meeting of the National Credit Council in April 1968. The earlier norm of
2:1 between banked and unbanked center was modified to 1:1.

In February 1970, the RBI decided to adopt a rule of 1:2 between banked and
unbanked branches in the case of banks that had more than 60 percent of their
offices in rural and semiurban areas, and a ratio of 1:3 in the case of other banks.
In September 1971, it revised the norms yet again. Accordingly, a bank which had
60 percent or more of its branches in rural and semiurban areas became eligible to
open one branch each in an urban and a metropolitan or port town for every two
branches opened in rural and semiurban areas; other banks were required to have
three branches in rural and semiurban centers for one branch each in an urban and
in a metropolitan center.

On January 1, 1977, the RBI adopted the rule whereby a bank had to open four
branches in unbanked rural centers to get an entitlement to open one branch in a
metropolitan or port town *and* one branch in another banked center. The RBI was
open, however, to banks asking for an entitlement of a banked center in lieu of an
entitlement to a metropolitan or port town. Therefore, contrary to the assertion by
Burgess and Pande that the ratio rule was 1:4, it was actually 1:2. This was less
demanding than the rule in place between February 1970 and September 1971. If

the ratio rule was the key to branch expansion, one must confront the question why Burgess and Pande did not find even stronger poverty reduction effects of branch expansion during this period.

Actual Branch Expansion during 1972–2005

That the ratio rule by itself did not drive branch expansion in India is illustrated by the actual branch expansion. This observation by itself does not prove Burgess and Pande wrong since they employ difference-in-difference approach to the state level data. Nevertheless, it does bring into question a simple-minded connection from the ratio rule to branch expansion to poverty reduction. If the ratio rule drove branch expansion at the state level, by simple aggregation, it has to have done so at the national level as well.

The data on the branch expansion by the scheduled commercial banks, which account for 90 percent or more of the bank branches, are readily available from the RBI Web site for the period 1972–2005. Using these data, I compute the *incremental* ratio of rural plus semiurban branches to urban plus metropolitan branches for the years 1973–2005. These ratios are shown in figure 11.1.[11]

From the figure, the actual ratio of rural plus semiurban branches to urban and metropolitan branches bears virtually no relationship to the prescribed ratios in virtually any period except perhaps 1973–76. After the RBI switched to the 1:2 rule on January 1, 1977, the incremental ratio of rural to urban branches climbed steadily to 10 in 1980, fluctuated between 5 and 10 from 1980 to 1985, and then fluctuated even more wildly. During 1977–90, with the exception of 1986, when the ratio fell to 0.2, it remained above the prescribed limit throughout. Of course, the ratio collapsed in 1991 and rose above 1 only once (to 1.4 in 1994) during the period from 1992 to 2005.

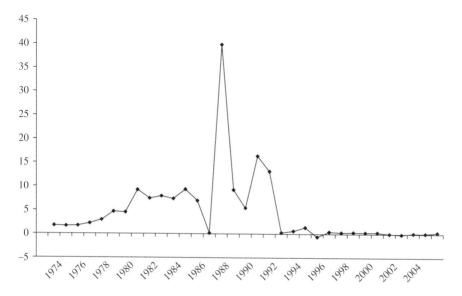

FIGURE 11.1: The Incremental Rural Plus Semi-Urban to Urban Plus Metropolitan Branches

It is thus evident that the bank branch expansion far exceeded the prescribed ratio of 1:2 during 1977–90. There are two possible explanations for this outcome. First, banks saw large profit opportunities in rural banking. and went after rural branch expansion well beyond what would have been required by the 1:2 ratio rule. But given that the ratio entirely collapsed after the RBI withdrew its interventions aimed at branch expansion in 1991, this explanation is unlikely to be valid. Additionally, the fact that the health of the banks in the early 1990s was quite poor undercuts this hypothesis. Second, the government and the RBI had additional objectives that required a far faster expansion of the rural and semiurban branches than the stipulated ratio would have yielded, and therefore they actively sought to expand the network. This is indeed a plausible explanation.

There is one further twist to the bank branch expansion story. Though the observed ratios of rural plus semiurban branches to urban plus metropolitan branches suggest something special about the 1980s (as opposed to 1977–90, the period Burgess and Pande regard as special), growth in the rural bank branches tells an altogether different story. This is shown in figure 11.2, which depicts the annual average growth rates of rural, semiurban, urban, and metropolitan bank branches during four periods: 1973–76, 1977–85, 1986–90, and 1991–2005. A quick look at this figure reveals that the 12.4 percent growth in the rural branches during 1973–76 more closely resembled the growth during 1977–85 than during 1991–2005. Moreover, the period 1986–90, which Burgess and Pande include in their period of rapid expansion of the rural branches, more closely resembles the period 1991–2005. In comparison to

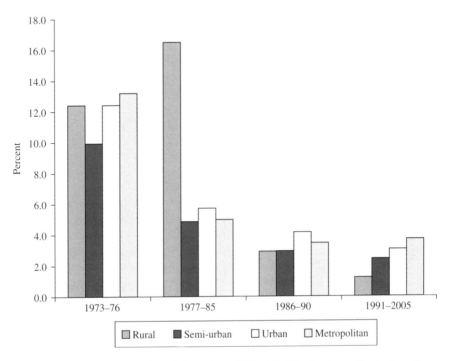

FIGURE 11.2: Growth Rates of Bank Branches of Scheduled Banks According to Location

16.5 percent annual growth during 1977–85, rural branches grew only 2.9 percent during 1986–90. This is not drastically different from the average annual growth of 1.2 percent during 1991–2005.

The Identification Issue

Given the state rather than the country as the unit of analysis, the results of Burgess and Pande would still be valid if 1977 and 1990 were the only candidates for break points in rural bank branch expansion and there were no other state-specific economic and policy variables affecting poverty outcomes that exhibited similarly timed trend reversals. Both these assumptions are problematic. A careful analysis of the data shows that 1979 is at least as good a candidate for a break in the trend as 1977. But here it turns out that the results of Burgess and Pande do not change dramatically if we replace 1977 by 1979 as the year of the first break point.[12]

But the second break point is more problematic. Other policies that impact poverty at the state level were changing around 1980. For one thing, quite apart from the deposit and credit expansion resulting from branch expansion, the government had increased the level of priority sector lending from one-third of the net bank credit in 1980 to 40 percent by 1984–85. The priority sector lending was targeted to help the poorer sections of the society.[13] It was also a policy measure separate from the expansion of deposits and credit that would have taken place purely from branch expansion.

But most important, as Kochar (2005, p. 2) points out in her compelling critique of Burgess and Pande, "the expansion of the banking network during this period went hand-in-hand with the government's broader anti-poverty programs, including the IRDP [Integrated Rural Development Program], making it impossible to distinguish the effect of the expansion of the banking network from that of government subsidies and other IRDP inputs." Kochar also presents evidence showing a close correlation between the real total expenditures on the IRDP and the expansion of the banking infrastructure between 1980 and 1990. Because of their very natures, both programs focused more heavily on the initially poor states. Kochar concludes that "it is almost impossible to separate the effect of the expansion of the banking infrastructure on outcomes such as poverty from that of the Government's anti-poverty programs, since the branch expansion program was designed to go hand-in-hand with the IRDP program." Surprisingly, Burgess and Pande make no mention of the IRDP.

Kochar adopts an alternative identification strategy and studies the relationship between poverty reduction and banking infrastructure at the level of the district, which is also the level at which the bank expansion strategy (as opposed to the rural-urban mix of the branches) was implemented under the Branch Licensing Program discussed previously. Contrary to Burgess and Pande, Kochar (2005, p. 2) reports her key results as follows:

> The IV [instrumental variable] and IV-FE [fixed effect] results are broadly consistent. They reveal that an increase in the number of banks benefited the non-poor, with little significant effect on the poor. This result remains robust across all the different classifications of the poor, with the sole exception of the positive and significant effect

of banks on scheduled castes in the IV regressions. The IV-FE regression, however, suggests no significant effect of the number of banks on scheduled castes, despite their significant effect on members of other castes.

Policy Implications

These arguments raise serious doubts about the validity of the positive link between bank branch expansion and poverty reduction. But even if we accept the link, there remains the issue of whether it offers an argument in favor of a return to the 1980s strategy of rural bank branch expansion to eradicate poverty. There are at least two reasons why such a conclusion is unwarranted.

First, we must still ask precisely what led to the growth in the number of bank branches. To be sure, the ratio rule was not behind it. It is also unlikely that the expansion was driven by profitability. Most likely, it was the Branch Licensing Program, itself a part of the Intensive Rural Development Program and other antipoverty programs, which drove the expansion. If so, we must take into account the extra cost of branch expansion beyond what would have been justified on grounds of profitability, and compare this cost to the cost of the best alternative policy available for the same poverty reduction in order to arrive at the optimal poverty reduction strategy.

In other words, we must still ask if an alternative strategy would have yielded the same poverty reduction at a lower cost. For example, would the same poverty reduction have been more sustainable and less costly if the bank branch expansion policies had been directed at maximizing growth, and the immediate relief to the poor had been brought through direct fiscal measures? Insofar as such reduction came from credits that were eventually defaulted, the eventual outcome was indeed a fiscal transfer. But branch expansion was surely a costly vehicle for affecting such transfers.

Second, even if we accept the unlikely conclusion that the bank branch expansion provided the least costly strategy for poverty reduction in the 1980s, it is highly doubtful that we can achieve the same outcome in the future. The returns to increased density of bank branches are bound to diminish rapidly. After a point, new branches would get business only by taking away customers from the existing branches, and raise costs without yielding extra poverty reduction. Now that a substantial network of bank branches in rural as well as urban areas already exists, it makes even more sense to let the bank branch expansion and credit respond to profit opportunities, and subsidize these activities only highly selectively when a clear need for them is identified.

The recognition of very low or negative returns to further branch expansion was probably the reason the government decided to abandon the supply-driven approach in 1990, discontinuing the branch expansion programs despite the continued policy of the priority sector lending program.

MONEY AND BANKING IN THE 1990s AND 2000s

Setting aside the financial repression that continued to rise until the end of the 1980s (Kletzer, 2004, Table 4), a process of phased liberalization in the financial sector had begun in the late 1980s. In 1988–89, the RBI abandoned the tight ceiling of 16.5 percent on the lending rate and replaced it by a floor rate of 16 percent. The annual gross redemption yield on the short-term (one to five years) government securities rose from the 6.5–11.7 percent range in 1987–88 to the 6.8–13.8 percent range in 1988–89 and to the 7.7–15.1 percent range in 1989–90. There were similar increases in the yields on medium- and long-term government securities. In 1988–89, the Credit Monitoring Arrangement replaced the Credit Authorization Scheme, thus freeing corporate loans from a lengthy approval process.

But admittedly, these reforms were limited in scope. More substantial reforms had to await the 1991 crisis.

Monetary Policy Reforms

I noted earlier that monetary policy in India in the 1980s had been hostage to the fiscal needs of the government. The 1990s saw a somewhat more independent monetary policy emerge. In part, this was the result of the reforms in other areas, especially banking but also the external sector, which brought very large foreign exchange inflows into the country and necessitated heavy interventions in the foreign exchange market to ensure exchange rate stability and the maintenance of a competitive exchange rate.

Several developments in the monetary area may be mentioned.[14] First, based on an agreement in 1994, the RBI gradually phased out the policy of automatic monetization of the fiscal deficit through the ad hoc Treasury bills by April 1997 (Mohan, 2006, p. 5 and box III). The RBI was thus freed from the direct link that had existed between fiscal deficit and monetary policy.

Second, the RBI gradually discontinued the use of direct instruments such as administered interest rates, CRR, and selective credit controls to regulate credit expansion, and came to rely on the open market operations for the conduct of monetary policy. The CRR steadily came down from 15 percent in 1994 to 5 percent in 2004. The SLR came down from 38.5 percent in 1990 to 25 percent in 1997, which remains its current level. The RBI also introduced the liquidity adjustment facility (LAF) as an instrument of short-term liquidity management. The LAF operates through the repo and reverse repo auctions. and serves as a useful signaling device for the overnight interest rate. Additionally, as noted in the last chapter, the RBI also introduced a separate instrument under the Market Stabilization Scheme to sterilize the impact of its foreign exchange interventions on money supply.

Third, the market in government securities is now free, with the interest on them determined on a competitive basis through regular auctions. The market in government securities is now deeper, and there is automated screen-based trading in them. Several new instruments, including 91-day Treasury bills, zero coupon bonds, floating rate bonds, and capital indexed bonds, have been introduced.

Finally, starting April 1, 2006, the RBI withdrew from the primary market in government securities. It now intervenes only in the secondary market for government securities. A decision has also been made for the RBI to stop raising resources for the state governments, which would have to rely on their own financial health to raise resources directly from the market in the future.

These measures have substantially reduced the financial repression that had existed in the 1980s. For example, as noted earlier, Kletzer (2004) estimates that the average revenue collected through repression by the government fell from 8.2 percent of the GDP in during 1980–93 to 1.6 percent during 1994–2002.

Banking Reforms

The post-1990 banking sector reforms are best discussed under three separate headings: liberalization; prudential regulation and supervision; and legal reforms. I will consider each of them in turn.[15]

Liberalization Measures

Liberalization has taken place along three main dimensions: interest rates, credit allocation, and entry of new banks. Most restrictions on the deposit and lending rates have been eliminated. On the deposit side, the remaining restrictions include floors on interest rates on the banks' short-term deposits and above-market administered rates on bank-deposit-like small savings instruments (most important, the Post Office Monthly Income Scheme and Kisan Vikas Patra) and provident funds.[16] These rates have been steadily brought down since 1992, but remain higher than would obtain in the market. They mainly serve the function of transfer of income to middle-class savers.

On the lending side, there are no restrictions on the interest rates except on loans of less than 200,000 rupees. The interest rate on the loans of less than 200,000 rupees must not exceed the bank's prime lending rate. The required share of priority sector lending remains unchanged at 40 percent. But even here some liberalization has taken place through two main channels. First, the list of priority sectors has been expanded. For example, lending to the information technology sector now qualifies as "priority sector" lending. Second, up to 4.5 percent of the net bank credit in indirect lending to agriculture qualifies as priority sector lending to agriculture. Indirect finance refers to finance provided to farmers indirectly. Examples of indirect finance include credit for financing the distribution of fertilizer and seeds, investment in certain bonds issued by the Rural Electrification Corporation, and deposits held by the banks in rural infrastructure development funds (RIDF) maintained with the National Bank for Agricultural and Rural Development.

Several measures have been introduced to increase competition among banks:

- The government has eased up on issuing licenses to new banks wishing to enter the market. In 1994–95 alone, six new private banks entered the market. Another four entered the following financial year (Hanson, 2001, p. 27).
- The entry of foreign bank branches was considerably liberalized. As a part of its Uruguay Round Agreement, India had committed to entry to 12 foreign bank branches per year. Foreign investment up to 74 percent of the paid-up capital has also been permitted in private banks.
- Public sector banks are permitted to raise 49 percent of the paid-up capital from the equity market. As a consequence, by the end of 2004–05, the equity share of the general public in the paid-up capital ranged between 40 and 49 percent in six banks and between 30 and 49 per cent in 12 banks. The government holding in four banks still exceeded 90 percent, however (Mohan, 2006, p. 11).

- In 1992, the access of the development financial institutions to government-guaranteed funds from the banking sector and long-term funds from the RBI was cut off, and they were expected to raise resources from the market or other commercial banks.
- Following the Narasimham Committee II recommendations, in 1999 the RBI adopted a policy whereby the development financial institutions were offered the option to transform into universal banks, provided they satisfied the prudential norms applicable to banks. This led the ICICI to reverse merge with its subsidiary, the ICICI Bank, in 2002. Subsequently, the IDBI reverse merged with the IDBI Bank. Currently, the conversion of the IFCI into a universal bank is under way. These conversions have brought relatively large players into the market and intensified competition in the banking sector.

Prudential Regulation and Supervision

Recognizing the moral hazard and adverse selection problems that characterize banking, the reforms in this sector have included the strengthening of the prudential regulation and supervision to complement the liberalization measures. In addition to recapitalization of the public sector banks, the following are some of the measures taken to strengthen the norms of prudential behavior:

- A minimum capital adequacy ratio—the proportion of the bank's capital to its risk-weighted credit exposure—of 8 percent was initially specified. This was raised to 9 percent at the end of 1999–2000.
- Norms for income recognition, asset classification, and provisioning were introduced, and have been gradually raised toward the international standards. Norms for the recognition of nonperforming assets were gradually tightened, so that by March 1995, assets with unpaid interest of more than two quarters (180 days) were considered nonperforming. The nonpayment criterion was upgraded to one quarter (90 days) in 2004, which is the international standard.
- Prudential exposure limits for individual borrowers and for interconnected groups of borrowers in terms of percentages of capital of the bank have been prescribed.
- Enhanced disclosure requirements have been prescribed on the maturity pattern of deposits, borrowings, investments, loans and advances, movements in nonperforming assets, and lending to market-sensitive sectors such as real estate, commodities, and the capital market.
- Starting in 2007–08, all banks must begin implementing Basel II norms, which are substantially stricter than the existing norms. This is in line with the government's strategy of bringing the prudential norms gradually up to the standards of the best international practices.

On the supervision side, efforts have been made to improve on-site inspections as well as off-site surveillance. In 1997, the RBI introduced the CAMELS system of annual supervision.[17] India supplements the traditional on-site supervision by a system of off-site supervision based on a regular flow of information from the banks on variables reflecting asset quality, capital adequacy, exposure, and connected lending.

Legal Reforms

On the legal front, two important developments may be noted. First, the Reconstruction of Financial Assets and Enforcement of Security Interest Act of 2002 allows banks to foreclose on collateral if borrowers are in default, without a lengthy legal process. Second, the Companies Amendment Act of 2002 establishes a national tribunal. Creditors, including banks, can refer companies in default on payments for 270 days to this tribunal. The referral in turn triggers a process whereby the companies must either present a restructuring plan acceptable to creditors or suffer liquidation. Unfortunately, this important reform has faced legal challenges and has not been implemented to date (see Bankruptcy Laws in chapter 13).

Performance of the Banking Sector

There is no doubt that considerable progress has been made in modernizing the banking sector. I will later consider many areas that require action, including the possibility of privatization of the banks. But presently, I focus on the overview of the outcomes in the key areas.

The Expansion of Banking

Table 11.1 presents the main indicators of banking expansion in five-year periods starting in 1969, the year the banks were nationalized. The number of banks expanded dramatically between 1975 and 1985, which was also the period of rapid branch expansion. The expansion was almost 175 percent over the ten-year period. Over the next ten-year period, 1985 to 1995, the expansion slowed to 21 percent, and during 1995–2000, to just 13 percent. The share of rural and semiurban branches in the total number of branches, which had expanded from 66.2 percent in 1975 to 77.8 percent in 1985, fell steadily during the 1990s and 2000s, reaching 68 percent in 2005. Correspondingly, the population per branch, which had fallen from 32,000 in 1975 to 14,000 in 1990, rose back to 16,000 in 2005. This change was clearly driven by a shift in the policy from subsidized branch expansion to profitability driven expansion.

The benefits from liberalizing measures during the 1990s and 2000s have come in the form of continued expansion of deposits and credits. Deposits as a proportion of the GDP have risen from 48.6 percent in 1990 to 60.4 percent in 2005. Credit has risen from 29.5 to 39.1 percent of the GDP. One disappointing aspect of this expansion has been the decline in the credit-deposit ratio in the 1990s, reflecting the accumulation of government securities by the banks that went well beyond the SLR. The banks have chosen to go for the safety of the government securities rather than seek profitable but risky investments. I will return to this issue later.

Finally, there has been some reduction in the proportion of the priority sector lending, but it remains within the specified targets. It is important to note that the targets are set in terms of the net bank credit. According to RBI (2005c, charts 3–5), public, private, and foreign banks taken as groups have satisfied these targets for virtually all recent years. The figures in table 11.1 are below 40 percent for the last three years shown, but this is because these figures represent priority sector lending as a proportion of the *total* credit.

TABLE 11.1: Performance Indicators of the Banking System

Indicator	June 1969	June 1971	June 1975	June 1980	June 1985	March 1990	March 1995	March 2000	March 2005
Number of commercial banks	89	85	83	153	267	274	284	298	289
Of which: Scheduled commercial banks	73	74	74	148	264	270	281	297	285
Scheduled regional rural banks	—	—	—	73	183	196	196	196	196
Number of bank offices in India	8,262	12,013	18,730	32,419	51,385	59,756	62,367	67,868	70,324
Rural as percent of total	22.2	35.6	36.3	46.6	58.7	58.2	52.9	48.4	45.7
Rural plus semi-urban as percent of total	62.6	69.3	66.2	71.6	77.8	77.2	74.3	70.3	67.9
Population per office (in thousands)	64	46	32	20	15	14	15	15	16
Scheduled commercial banks									
Aggregate deposits (Rs. billion)	46.5	62.2	125.5	333.8	770.8	1,735.2	3,868.6	8,515.9	17,002.0
Credit (Rs. billion)	36.0	47.6	89.6	220.7	509.2	1054.5	2115.6	4540.7	11004.3
Deposits as percent of nominal GNP	15.5	17.2	19.9	35.2	41.7	48.6	46.4	53.5	60.4
Credit as percent of nominal GNP	12.0	13.2	14.2	23.3	27.5	29.5	25.4	28.5	39.1
Credit-deposit ratio (percent)	77.5	76.6	71.4	66.1	66.1	60.8	54.7	53.3	64.7
Share of priority sector in nonfood credit*	15	23.2	27.5	37	44.9	41.5	35.8	35.4	35.5

*The share is in the total credit for the years 2000 and 2005.

Sources: Assembled from various volumes of *Reserve Bank of India, Banking Statistics and Statistical Tables Relating to the Banks of India* (RBI, 2005e).

General Health of the Banks

There are two key indicators of the general health of the banks: the capital to risk-weighted assets ratio (CRAR; also called the capital adequacy ratio) and nonperforming assets (NPAs). Both indicators suggest considerable improvement over the last several years. Table 11.2 reports the distribution of the scheduled commercial banks according to CRAR for three different years. The norm for CRAR was 8 percent until the end of 1998–99, and 9 percent from the end of 1999–2000. In 1996–97, 19 out of 92 scheduled commercial banks failed to satisfy the norm, and only 42 had a CRAR of more than 10 percent. By 2003–04, the picture had changed dramatically: Only 2 out of the 90 banks failed to satisfy the norm, and as many as 87 had CRAR in excess of 10 percent. Two factors account for the improvement. First, the government has undertaken massive infusion of funds to recapitalize the banks. By the end of March 2002, the government had already injected 223 billion rupees toward recapitalization of 19 nationalized banks. Second, the government has encouraged public sector banks to raise funds through disinvestments of up to 49 percent of the paid-up capital. As noted earlier, the vast majority of the banks have taken advantage of this provision.

The NPAs show a trend similar to that of the CRAR. Recall that since 2004, India has accepted the international standard of defining the assets on which interest or principal payment is overdue by 90 or more days as nonperforming. This tightening of the norm notwithstanding, the gross, as well as net, of provisioning NPAs has been declining. Table 11.3 reports the trend for public, old private, new private, and foreign banks, as well as scheduled banks taken together. In the Indian legal system, write-offs are difficult even for fully provisioned loans. This partially explains the proportionately greater progress in bringing down the net NPAs. At the aggregate level, net NPAs fell from 8.1 percent of the net advances in 1996–97 to 2.0 percent in 2004–05, and from 3.3 percent of the total assets to 0.9 percent over the same period. Unsurprisingly, it was the public sector and old private banks that had to undertake most of this reduction. The new private sector and foreign banks have had relatively low NPAs even in the mid-1990s.

There is some concern that the NPAs are actually much higher than reported. Ahluwalia (2002c) expresses this strongly, suggesting that under one scenario, uncovered NPAs could be as high as 11 percent of total advances. If true, this would wipe out virtually all capital in the banking sector (see table 11.3). But given the current practice of listing loans with overdue interest or principal for 90 days as nonperforming, this scenario seems rather extreme. It is quite unlikely that the NPAs could be more than twice those reported, which would place the gross NPAs at 10.4 percent of advances in 2004–05. Taking into account provisioning, uncovered NPAs would be much smaller than this number.

Productivity

The entry of foreign and new private banks has had a favorable impact on the overall productivity. For example, profit per employee rose from 10,000 rupees per employee in 1995–96 to 50,000 rupees in 1999–2000 and to 130,000 in 2004–05, at constant prices. Likewise, business per employee rose from 6 million rupees in

TABLE 11.2: Distribution of Banks by Capital to Risk-weighted Asset Ratio (CRAR)

Year	Bank Group	State Bank Group	Nationalized Banks	Other Public Sector Banks	Old Private Sector Banks	New Private Sector Banks	Foreign Banks	Scheduled Commercial Banks
1	2	3	4	5	6	7	8	9
1995–96	Below 4 percent	—	5		3	—	—	8
	4–8 percent	—	3		3	—	3	9
	8–10 percent	6	7		7	1	12	33
	Above 10 percent	2	4		12	8	16	42
1999–2000	Below 4 percent	—	1		2	—	—	3
	4–9 percent	—	—		2	—	—	2
	9–10 percent	—	4		2	1	5	12
	10 percent	8	14		18	7	37	84
2003–04	Below 4 percent	—	—		—	1	—	1
	4–9 percent	—	—		—	1	—	1
	9–10 percent	—	1		—	—	—	1
	Above 10 percent	8	18		20	8	33	87
2004–05	Below 4 percent				1		—	1
	4–9 percent				1		—	1
	9–10 percent		2		3	2	1	7
	Above 10 percent	8	17	1	15	7	30	78

Note: Scheduled commercial banks were required to maintain a minimum CRAR of 8 percent up to the end of 1998–99, and 9 percent from the end of 1999–2000.

Source: RBI (2005a).

TABLE 11.3: Gross and Net Nonperforming Assets (NPAs)

Year	Gross NPAs as Percent of Gross Advances	Gross NPAs as Percent of Total Assets	Net NPAs as Percent of Net Advances	Net NPAs as Percent of Total Assets
1	2	3	4	5
Scheduled Commercial Banks				
1996–97	15.7	7.0	8.1	3.3
1999–2000	12.7	5.5	6.8	2.7
2003–04	7.2	3.3	2.9	1.2
2004–05	5.2	2.6	2.0	0.9
Public Sector Banks				
1996–97	17.8	7.8	9.2	3.6
1999–2000	14.0	6.0	7.4	2.9
2003–04	7.8	3.5	3.0	1.3
2004–05	5.7	2.8	2.1	1.0
Old Private Sector Banks				
1996–97	10.7	5.2	6.6	3.1
1999–2000	10.8	5.2	7.1	3.3
2003–04	7.6	3.6	3.8	1.8
2004–05	6.0	3.2	2.7	1.4
New Private Sector Banks				
1996–97	2.6	1.3	2.0	1.0
1999–2000	4.1	1.6	2.9	1.1
2003–04	5.0	2.4	2.4	1.1
2004–05	3.6	1.6	1.9	0.8
Foreign Banks in India				
1996–97	4.3	2.1	1.9	0.9
1999–2000	7.0	3.2	2.4	1.0
2003–04	4.6	2.1	1.5	0.7
2004–05	2.8	1.4	0.9	0.4

Source: RBI (2005a) and *Report on Trends and Progress of Banking in India 2004–05* (RBI, 2005f).

1995–96 to 17.3 million rupees in 2004–05.[18] From table 11.1, we can also see that deposits per branch rose from 62 million rupees in 1994–95 to 242 million rupees in 2004–05. This is a 290 percent increase. The increase in the wholesale prices during the same period being only 66.4 percent, the deposits rose 223.6 percent in real terms. Thus, all indicators point to significant increase in productivity.

FUTURE REFORMS IN THE BANKING SECTOR

I noted earlier that reforms could improve growth performance by turning existing unproductive wealth into productive investment, intermediating the savings more efficiently and increasing the savings. In India a simple, though politically contentious, set of land and building reforms can help turn a very substantial amount of existing unproductive wealth into productive investment. Most farmers in India lack titles to their pieces of land, and cannot use them as collateral to borrow money or to invest. Giving them land titles will free up this resource for collateral. Likewise, though the center has passed the Urban Land (Ceiling and Regulation) Repeal Act, 1999 to facilitate the repeal of the ban on the sale of urban plots of land larger than a specified ceiling (under to Urban Land Ceilings Act, 1976), many states, including the important state of Maharashtra, which is home to Mumbai, the business capital of India, have yet to repeal the ceiling. Finally, many states, including Maharashtra, still have laws that are so heavily tilted in favor of the tenants that they undermine the ownership rights of the landlord. As a result, urban properties worth billions of rupees are unusable for collateral. Once again, the center has done its part by repealing the relevant central legislations, but many states have yet to introduce the necessary state-level legislation.

Though these reforms are themselves outside the banking sector, they can potentially make a large contribution to the latter's productivity. As for the reforms within the banking sector, they can be discussed under two broad headings. Under the first heading, I discuss the case for the privatization of the banks. Under the second, I consider possible reforms within the current ownership structure.

The Case for Privatization

The case for privatization must be addressed at two levels: efficiency and social objectives. Is there compelling evidence in favor of privately owned banks delivering a better *economic* outcome? And if there is, do social objectives such as lending to disadvantaged sections of the society make nationalized banks a necessary evil?

Growth and Productivity

There is now a growing body of evidence supporting the hypothesis that private sector bank performance is superior to that of public sector banks along a variety of dimensions. La Porta, Lopez de Silanes, and Shleifer (2002) study the link among ownership, financial development, and growth, and find government ownership of banks negatively correlated with financial development and growth in the cross-country regressions. This evidence would not be compelling by itself, in view of the well-known deficiencies of the cross-country regressions, but evidence from other sources corroborates it.

For example, Kumbhakar and Sarkar (2003) study productivity growth in the Indian banking sector over the period 1985–86 to 1996–97. The second half of this period is characterized by substantial financial deregulation. The authors find productivity growth of public sector banks to be slower, on the average, than productivity growth of private sector banks.[19] They also find that deregulation has virtually no effect on productivity growth in the public sector banks but has a positive effect on productivity growth in the private sector banks. Due to distortions in the relative input prices, public sector banks overemployed labor relative to capital throughout the period of the study. The overemployment declined over time, but only slowly. Private sector banks also overemploy labor in the initial years, but this distortion came down rapidly with deregulation.

Arun and Turner (2002) compare 27 public sector banks and 34 private sector banks in terms of five indicators of efficiency: business per employee, cost of intermediation as a proportion of the total assets, noninterest expenses as a proportion of total assets, staff costs as a proportion of the total assets, and staff costs as a proportion of noninterest expenses. All indicators uniformly show private sector banks operating substantially more efficiently than pubic sector banks. In each case, the authors also find the indicators to be statistically significantly different in the public and private sector banks. The authors also carry out regressions that control for the bank size, and find that privately owned banks perform more efficiently than the public sector banks along all five dimensions.

Banerjee, Cole, and Duflo (2004) study the question of whether nationalization speeded up the development of the financial sector. They find that in the period 1980–91, when the government tightly controlled the financial sector, nationalized and private banks of similar asset size grew at about the same rate. But in the more liberalized period 1992–2000, old private sector banks grew 8 percent more than public sector banks.[20] Banerjee et al. exclude the new private sector banks from the analysis because there are not enough observations on them to permit proper econometric testing. But according to all broad indicators available, these banks are in better health than the older private sector banks.

Khwaja and Mian (2004) use firm-level data to consider another dimension of private versus public ownership: manipulation of lending and the likelihood of default. They find that the public sector banks are more likely to lend to firms with directors or executives who have political ties, and are less likely to collect on these loans. Cole (2004) similarly finds that public sector banks in India are subject to political capture. Politicians manipulate the allocation of public credit to achieve electoral goals through lending booms just prior to elections and targeting of credit to the swing states. He further finds that the marginal political loan is less likely to be repaid.

Social Objectives

The second issue we must address in considering privatization is that of the social goals. Two key goals behind the government interventions in India have been the expansion of banking infrastructure in the rural areas and the expansion of lending to the "priority" sectors. A fundamental question we must ask in this context is whether these goals are necessarily the right ones. Insofar as the ultimate objective behind these policies is poverty alleviation, it may make more sense to let the banking sector develop so as to maximize growth, which generates sustained poverty reduction, and to bring immediate relief to the poor through direct fiscal transfers.

But even taking the twin goals of expanding rural banking and priority sector lending, we must ask whether bank nationalization was the more efficient means to achieving these goals. In view of the superior performance of private sector banks along most dimensions, would it not have been less costly to pursue these goals within the private sector ownership of the banks? For example, recall that the bank branch expansion policy had been put into place as early as 1962 by requiring that the banks open one rural branch for every two urban branches. Likewise, the priority sector lending had its beginning in the 1968–69 RBI credit policy, *before* banks were nationalized. Indeed, as described earlier, Prime Minister Indira Gandhi had used the 1969 nationalization as a political weapon to sack Finance Minister Morarji Desai, who happened to be from the rival group dominated by the organizational wing of the Congress Party. Absent this compulsion, the original plan was to promote the two goals within the existing ownership structure.

Under the 1949 Banking Regulation Act, banks in India must obtain a license from the RBI to open a new branch. Therefore, the RBI was in a position to enforce whatever proportion of rural to urban branches the government desired. Through the years, banks were indeed subject to the rural-urban branch ratio regulation. It is possible that due to lack of profitability of rural branches, private banks expanded less rapidly than public sector banks in both rural and urban areas, because the public sector banks could count on the government subsidy when opening loss-making rural branches. But here we must ask whether such subsidy would have been more productive if channeled through private sector banks.

In the area of priority sector lending, private sector banks have successfully met their overall obligations, as well as that in the small-scale industry subsector. But they have failed to meet their obligations in the agriculture subsector. Banerjee et al. (2004) use a regression discontinuity approach to compare the propensity of public and private banks to lend to borrowers in agriculture. They find that public sector banks lend substantially more to agricultural borrowers than private sector banks do.

But even this finding does not prove the inability of private sector banks to deliver on the social objectives. Instead, it reflects their profit-maximizing behavior. Until the 1990s, neither public nor private banks were subject to any penalty for failing to meet their priority sector targets. For obvious reasons, private banks were in a much better position to take advantage of the absence of the enforcement mechanism than the nationalized banks.[21]

Quite apart from the absence of a persuasive argument in favor of sacrificing the efficiency gains from privatization in order to achieve rapid expansion of rural branches and priority sector lending, the case for pursuing these objectives has itself been considerably weakened in recent years. The branch expansion policy was allowed to expire in 1990. The Narasimham Committee I also recommended phasing out the priority sector lending, though the government could not summon the political courage to accept this recommendation.

Governance

Although the case for privatization ultimately rests on the growth and productivity outcomes, it is useful to focus briefly on the governance problems posed by the public ownership of the banks and the inefficiencies that result from it. Under the current structure, the Appointment Committee of the Cabinet appoints the top management of public sector banks. Civil servants represent the government on the boards of the banks. Both factors impede the ability of the banks to behave as profit-maximizing entities. In addition, whereas the RBI has the authority to remove the chief executive officer and revoke the license of a private sector bank, it does not have the same authority over public sector banks.

The government ownership has had a detrimental effect on lending. Banerjee et al. (2004) find strong evidence of underlending. In a competitive setting, the banks will lend firms up to the point where the rate of return equals the interest rate. But Banerjee et al. find that the rate of return on capital facing the client firms at the margin is often far higher than the interest rate at which banks lend to them. In two-thirds of the cases in their sample, banks make no change in the nominal amount they lend to a firm from one year to another. When fresh loans are made, the beneficiaries are the firms experiencing growth in the turnover, regardless of the profitability.

The source of this underlending is the bureaucratic structure of the banks. Promotions and salaries have very little to do with the performance of the staff in lending and bringing profitable business. Bank employees are rewarded more for meeting the lending targets set by the government than for profitability. Indeed, failed loans can lead to investigation by the Central Vigilance Commission, and criminal punishment in case of successful prosecution. Prospects of such an outcome are probably even higher when the loan is outside the priority sector. Therefore, the safest strategy for the loan officers is to meet the credit targets set by the government and follow the procedures set by it rather than pursue profit opportunities.

Reforms within the Existing Ownership Structure

In my judgment, any reforms within the existing ownership structure would fall far short of what can be achieved by privatization. The idea that public sector banks can operate the same way as private sector banks may sound reasonable and plausible, but is false. Government ownership comes with soft budget constraint, near absence of performance-based promotions and salaries of the employees, inability to fire or even discipline employees except under very extreme circumstances, and continued interference by the government. As we have already seen, the existing evidence shows that the deregulation during the 1990s has produced at best limited gains in productivity in the public sector banks. Therefore, any reforms within the existing ownership structure would amount to no more than damage control.

The most important step the government can take to intensify competition is to facilitate greater and faster entry of both domestic private and foreign banks. The share of public sector banks in the total banking assets has declined from 84.4 percent in 1995–96 to 74.4 percent in 2004–05. The decline is even greater if we choose 1990–91 as the initial year. The share of new private sector banks has gone from1.5 percent to 12.9 percent between 1995–96 and 2004–05. Similar compositional shifts have taken place in the deposits and advances. If this process can be speeded up, over time, private domestic and foreign banks will grow in importance and public sector banks will decline. At some point along this path, enough transformation in public opinion would likely emerge to allow privatization of public sector banks.

Another obvious area of reform within the existing ownership structure is governance. Ahluwalia (2002c) makes some useful suggestions in this regard. He rightly points out that as the owner, the government would naturally have its appointees on the governing boards of the banks. But rather than appoint civil servants, it should opt for independent individuals who are not subject to a conflict between their roles as government servants and as board members. If the banks are to function as competitive entities, it is essential that their boards be independent.

Likewise, the government should discontinue the practice of the Appointments Committee of the Cabinet appointing the management of the banks. It should also delegate to the RBI the same powers with respect to public sector banks that it has with respect to private sector banks. Finally, the practice of industrywide wage negotiations should be replaced by bank-level negotiations to reflect productivity differences across banks. Workers lack incentive to improve efficiency if their wages are determined by industrywide rather than bank-level productivity.

The government must also reform its vigilance procedures. The current practice greatly discourages profit-driven lending. One option is to subject the public and private banks to the same regime with respect to priority sector credit, and then hold the bank managements more accountable to private sector profit levels over a three-to-five-year period. The pressure to earn private-sector-level profits will automatically force the public bank management to ensure that loans are driven by profitability considerations rather than a desire to favor relatives and friends or to extract bribes. In turn, the need for vigilance investigations will be considerably reduced.

A final set of reforms must address the issues of weak public and private sector banks. In India, the exit of large firms in general is difficult, and the exit of large public sector firms is exceptional. In the banking sector, no public sector bank has been closed to date. Even if the closure option is not exercised, the natural course for the government should be to privatize weak public sector banks, as long as a buyer can be found, but this is not done. Instead, the government almost always goes for restructuring without regard to the cost-benefit ratio.

The policy, at least in the case of insolvent banks, whether public or private, should be to close them down, with the deposits, up to a limit, protected fully through deposit insurance. Beyond a limit, depositors should bear some cost. An argument often made against this policy is that such closures may lead to increased risk of a systemic bank failure. This is a specious argument; closure of an insolvent bank is an indication of strict supervision and the ability of the regulatory agencies to take tough decisions. Such an action would actually discourage other banks from acting irresponsibly. If banks are never closed, it is a surefire invitation to all banks to act irresponsibly, and will make a systemic failure more, not less, likely.

THE CAPITAL MARKETS

Outside of the money and banking sector, the capital market is principally built on stocks and bonds, with the stocks being an equity instrument and the bonds a debt instrument. Owning a stock is like owning a piece of the company that issued it. The stock can bring its holder a share in the profits of the company through dividends. In addition, the price of the stock rises or falls as the valuation of the company by the market rises or falls. Therefore, a stockholder can experience a capital gain or loss when he sells the stock. A bond usually pays a fixed interest until maturity. If the interest rate on newly issued bonds subject to equivalent risk rises, the market price of the existing bonds falls. The changes in the valuation of a company by the market can also lead to changes in the prices of the bonds issued by it. Therefore, the bondholder may experience a capital gain or loss when he sells it.

Both private and public corporations may issue stocks and bonds, depending on their preferences for the equity or debt instrument. The government also issues bonds (but not stocks) to finance its fiscal deficit. Additional instruments in the capital market include mutual funds, hedge funds, venture capital funds, and a variety of derivatives. These are typically built on the stocks and bonds. For example, derivatives take the form of forward and futures contracts to buy and sell bonds, stocks, foreign currencies, or commodities. Options contracts give the holder the option to buy the specified asset by a certain date at a specified price that the holder may or may not choose to exercise. Mutual funds raise money from shareholders for investment in bonds, stocks, and derivatives issued by different companies and by governments. By holding shares in a mutual fund, even a small investor is able to access a highly diversified and professionally managed portfolio. A hedge fund is a special type of investment fund created by agreement among a few relatively rich investors and subject to minimal regulation. It is not open to the general public and uses more aggressive strategies.

Policy and Institutional Developments in the Capital Market

In India, the stock market is somewhat more developed than the bond market. There is now a relatively large market in the government bonds, but the corporate bond market remains very thin. Even the government bonds market is not very liquid, with several kinds of bonds not traded at all in any given year. A top priority currently is the development of the bond market, especially the corporate bond market.

Turning first to the stock market, it is interesting to note that the Bombay Stock Exchange (BSE) was founded as far back as 1875. But the stock market in India remained highly underdeveloped until the 1990s, when important policy changes were introduced to develop it. Until the 1980s, the government decided which companies could access the private capital market, in what volume, and at what prices of the shares. Ironically, while the government thus tightly controlled the volume and price of the stocks when they were issued, it left the subsequent trading in them almost entirely unregulated. This allowed small cliques of brokers to collusively manage the trades.

A halfhearted effort to develop the stock market was made in 1987 when the Securities and Exchange Board of India (SEBI) was established to evolve a framework for the regulation of the market along modern lines. But it was left as an advisory, rather than statutory, body with no real powers. Therefore, the development of the market did not begin in earnest until 1992, when the Securities and Exchange Board of India Act of 1992 gave the SEBI statutory status and abolished the government control over it.

Following its conversion into a statutory body, the SEBI has introduced several reforms. It got the Capital Issues (Control) Act of 1947 repealed, and the Office of Controller of Capital Issues abolished. This paved the way for giving the companies the freedom to raise funds from securities markets subject to meeting certain criteria, and to set the share prices based on market considerations. SEBI introduces regulations for primary and secondary market intermediaries, bringing them within the regulatory framework. New reforms by SEBI in the primary market include improved disclosure standards, introduction of prudential norms, and simplification of issue procedures. Companies are required to disclose all material facts and specific risk factors associated with their projects while making public issues. The SEBI Disclosure and Investor Protection (DIP) guidelines spell out the eligibility criteria for the issuance of the initial public offering (IPO) and further public offering (FPO). The key difference between these two issues, of course, is that companies not yet listed issue the IPO and those already listed issue the FPO.

Two technological innovations have helped speed up the buying and selling of the shares. First, established by the SEBI in 1994, the National Stock Exchange (NSE) introduced nationwide satellite-based electronic trading that matches the buyer and seller orders. In turn, this forced the BSE to modernize and introduce a similar system. Second, under the National Depositories Act of 1996, the SEBI introduced dematerialization of shares. Under the act, two depositories have now been set up: the National Securities Depository Ltd. and the Central Depository Services (India) Ltd. SEBI requires each issuing company to enter into an agreement with at least one of the two depository companies as an issuer company for dematerialization of its shares. The depository then maintains electronic records of ownership and completes buyer-seller contracts through electronic transfer of ownership. This change has eliminated the need for physical movement of paper securities and considerably speeded up the transactions. The presence of two depository companies introduces an element of competition in the provision of the depository services.

The SEBI permits foreign direct investment in stockbroking, asset management companies, merchant banking, and other nonbank finance companies. Foreign institutional investors (FIIs) are granted relatively free access to Indian equity markets. In the debt market, they are currently allowed to invest up to $2 billion in the government securities and up to $1.5 billion in private corporate bonds. Guidelines for offshore venture capital funds have also been spelled out. SEBI also has in place regulations governing mutual funds. Several private mutual funds (including some offered by foreign companies) now exist, and are allowed to apply for the allotment of shares in public issues. They are also allowed to invest in overseas instruments, with an overall ceiling of $2 billion. This last measure effectively gives the individual investors in India access to foreign stock markets.

In June 2000, India introduced trade in derivatives by launching index futures. This was followed by the introduction of index options, single stock options, and single stock futures in 2001. Interest rate futures were launched in June 2003. The NSE and BSE provide trading platforms for derivative transactions. Presently, the NSE dominates the derivatives market, accounting for 99 percent of the trades in them.

The SEBI (Central Database of Market Participants) Regulations of 2003 provides for the creation of a centralized database of market participants and investors (MAPIN database). It aims to register all the market participants in the Indian securities market by allotting a unique identification number (UIN). A key objective of the database is to establish an audit trail for each transaction. By March 2005, 294,925 participants had been allotted the UIN. But at that point, concerns with the cost of obtaining a UIN, coverage of various investor categories, biometric impression (such as electronic fingerprints, retina scans), and inadequate geographical coverage, expressed by many participants and investors, led the SEBI to appoint a committee. The committee recommended a compromise solution that the SEBI has accepted. Accordingly, for trade orders worth half a million rupees or more, a UIN with biometric impression would be required. For smaller transactions, the investor would be allowed to use the permanent account Number (PAN) issued by the Income Tax Department, though he also has the option of obtaining the UIN under the MAPIN.

While the development of the equity market in India is progressing well, the debt market lags behind. There is a large government securities market, but according to the Reserve Bank of India (2005d), the market suffers from three key problems. First, it is active and liquid when the interest rates are falling, but turns illiquid when interest rates rise. Second, the number of actively traded securities is low in relation to the total number of securities outstanding. For example, at the end of February 2005, there were 121 central government securities with an outstanding amount of 8,953 billion rupees. The ratio of turnover to total outstanding amount stood at 2 in 2003 and 1.5 in 2004, compared with 3 to 38 in developed countries. On a daily basis, no more than 10 to 12 securities are traded, and among these only four or five are actively traded. In December 2004, just five securities accounted for 73 percent of the total volume of trade in the government securities. Finally, the ownership of the government securities is concentrated heavily in the banks, which lends market power to a few large players who act as price makers rather than price takers. These shortcomings need to be addressed in the near future. The entry of FIIs should help generate some competition. But an effort may also be made to get the public at large to participate actively in the market.

A vibrant government securities market may also help in the development of the corporate bond market, which is essential for a healthy debt-equity mix of investment in the corporate sector. The government had constituted a high-level expert committee to make recommendations for a faster development of corporate bond market in July 2005. The committee made several recommendations in its report submitted in December 2005. A key recommendation was that the scope of investment in corporate bonds by banks, FIIs, insurance companies, and provident and gratuity (a cash sum paid to employees on leaving the service) funds be expanded. It also made a number of recommendations aimed at reducing the transaction costs of trading in corporate bonds. Many of these recommendations mirror the current practice in the equity market and can be readily implemented. The committee also suggested creating special debt funds, specifically in the infrastructure sector.

Developments in the Market

Considerable progress in policy and institutional development in the equity market notwithstanding, new capital issues by nongovernment public limited companies has had a rocky history. This partly reflects the "learning by doing" nature of the activity on the part of the investors, firms, and the government, especially the SEBI. But partly, it also reflects the ups and downs in the economy. Figure 11.3 depicts the volume of new capital issues (equity plus debt) by nongovernment companies in current billion rupees. Having grown modestly but steadily in the second half of the 1980s, these issues took off in a major way in the first half of the 1990s. But after reaching a relatively high peak in 1994–95, they began to decline sharply. The decline continued until the issues virtually collapsed in 1997–98. They did not rise again beyond the level (in current rupees) achieved in the late 1980s until 2004–05.

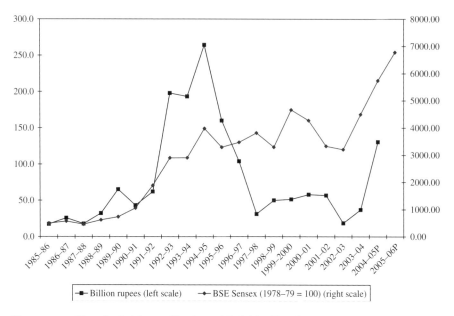

FIGURE 11.3: New Capital Issues (Equity and Debt) by Non-Governmental Companies and the BSE Sensex

Given the relatively underdeveloped corporate bond market, the graph of the new capital issues shown in figure 11.3 largely represents the movements in the equity issues. Thus they are related to the movements in the stock market index, which is also shown in the figure. Starting in the late 1980s, Sensex had shown a sharp increase, which drew investors into the market. But after peaking in 1994–95, Sensex oscillated without trend and began to recover decisively only in the last two years.

In part, the initial steady rise in Sensex reflected government's careful control of the public issues. This trend was probably sustained in the initial years of deregulation by the expectations created by the past performance. But as liberalization in the industrial sector began to lead to restructuring, and the excesses of many companies(including diversion of funds to activities other than the one for which they had been borrowed) came to the fore, the stock market performance deteriorated. A major scandal in 1992 further contributed to the weakening of public confidence in the stock market. Subsequently, the economy's performance also declined, adding to the woes of the stock market.

Table 11.4 provides more details on the evolution of the composition of the resources raised by the corporate sector. The second column shows the sharp and continued decline in the volume of resources raised through equity: in nominal terms; the amount fell from 148 billion rupees in 1995–96 to just 12.7 billion rupees in 2001–02. But resources raised through equity recovered dramatically, starting in 2003–04 and rising to 244 billion rupees in 2004–05. From the available, albeit incomplete information, the trend seems to have held up in 2005–06.

Table 11.4 also shows that the bulk of the resources raised by the corporate sector have come not from public issue but from private placements by public and private

TABLE 11.4: Resource Mobilization by Corporate Sector (billion rupees)

Year	Equity Issues*	Debt Issues		Total Resource Mobilization (2+3+4)	Total Resource Mobilization as Percent of GDP	Private Placement as Percent of Total Resource Mobilization
		Public Issues	Private Placements[†]			
1	*2*	*3*	*4*	*5*	*8*	*10*
1995–96	148.3	59.7	133.6	341.7	2.9	39.1
1996–97	79.2	63.6	150.7	293.4	2.1	51.3
1997–98	18.9	26.8	201.0	346.7	2.3	58.0
1998–99	9.4	46.5	496.8	552.7	3.2	89.9
1999–2000	45.7	32.5	612.6	690.8	3.6	88.7
2000–01	33.7	27.4	678.4	739.4	3.5	91.7
2001–02	12.7	62.7	648.8	724.2	3.2	89.6
2002–03	14.6	26.1	669.5	710.2	2.9	94.3
2003–04	189.5	43.2	639.0	871.7	3.2	73.3
2004–05	243.9	38.7	840.5	1,123.1	3.6	74.8

*Includes cumulative convertible preferences shares.

[†]Includes negligible amount of equity.

Source: Author's calculations, using data in Securities and Exchange Board of India, *Handbook of Statistics on the Indian Securities Market* (2005, table 8); and RBI, *Handbook of Statistics on Indian Economy* (table 1).

financial and nonfinancial institutions. While public issues had been declining between 1996–97 and 2002–03, private placements rose steadily. Their share in the total resource mobilization shot up from just 39 percent in 1995–96 to 94 percent in 2002–03. It is only since then that this share has declined. In 2004–05, it stood at 75 percent.

The last important observation from table 11.4 concerns the corporate debt market. Column 3 of the table illustrates the point previously made, that the corporate bond market remains relatively less developed. Based on the figures shown in the table, the share of debt in the total public issues in 2004–05 was only 14 percent. As a proportion of the total resources mobilized, debt issues by corporations were less than 4 percent in 2004–05.

The recent rapid expansion of new issues mirrors the large and increased volume of turnover in the equity market. During 2005–06, turnover of all stock exchanges in the cash segment, at 23,901 billion rupees, was 43.4 percent higher than in 2004–05 (SEBI, *Annual Report 2005–06,* p. 42). The NSE accounted for 66 percent of the turnover and the BSE for 33 percent. The market capitalization to GDP ratio of the BSE, which lists more shares than the NSE, rose from 23 percent in 2002–03 to 86 percent in 2005–06 (SEBI, *Annual Report, 2005–06,* table 2.15, p. 46).

Trade in the derivatives has grown exponentially since its introduction in 2000. The total turnover in this segment increased from 21,431 billion rupees in 2003–04 to 48,243 billion rupees in 2005–06. The turnover in the latter year was 307 percent of the cash market turnover at the NSE and 202 percent of the combined cash market turnover of the BSE and NSE in the same year (SEBI, *Annual Report 2005–06,* chart 2.8 and table 2.27). Mutual funds and FIIs are allowed to participate in the derivatives market subject to position limits.

TABLE 11.5: Mobilization of Resources by Mutual Funds (billion rupees)

Period	Gross Mobilization	Redemption	Net Inflow	Assets at End of Period
1	2	3	4	5
1999–2000	612.4	422.7	189.7	1,079.5
2000–01	929.6	838.3	91.3	905.9
2001–02	1,645.2	1,573.5	71.8	1,005.9
2002–03	3,147.1	3,105.1	42.0	1,093.0
2003–04	5,901.9	5,433.8	468.1	1,396.2
2004–05	8,397.1	8,375.1	22.0	1,496.0
2005–06	10,981.5	10,453.7	527.8	2,318.6

Source: Securities and Exchange Board of India, *Annual Report* (2005–06, table 2.35).

A final important development in recent years has been the emergence of private mutual funds. Until 1986–87, a single public sector mutual fund—Unit Trust of India (UTI)—had accounted for 100 percent of the resource mobilization through mutual funds. Though mutual funds sponsored by banks were granted entry in 1987–88, and those sponsored by financial institutions in 1989–90, UTI accounted for 85 percent of the net resource mobilization by mutual funds in 1992–93. It was only when private sector mutual funds were permitted in 1993–94 that the composition began to shift. The shift was later speeded up by the inability of the UTI to properly evaluate the quality of the equity issues, which led to huge losses to it and two major bailouts to protect the interests of influential middle-class investors in it. In 2005–06, the private sector mutual funds accounted for 81.4 percent of the net resources mobilized by all mutual funds. The share of public sector mutual funds was 12.1 percent, and that of the UTI mutual fund was 6.5 percent (SEBI, *Annual Report 2005–06*, table 2.36). Table 11.5 reports the volumes of resource mobilization by mutual funds in aggregate between 1999–2000 and 2005–06.

INSURANCE AND RETIREMENT BENEFITS

Insurance premiums and pension funds constitute important financial resources that can be mobilized for investment in productive activities. For example, according to the *IRDA Annual Report 2004–05*, gross financial savings of households was 14 percent of the GDP in 2003–04. Among other items, these savings included insurance funds equaling 1.9 percent of the GDP and provident and pension funds amounting to 2 percent of the GDP. Therefore, insurance and provident and pension funds together accounted for 28 percent of the financial savings of the households. It is evident that these sources are critical to the success of the financial markets, both in terms of the volume of funds they can bring to the markets and how these funds are invested.

Insurance

We saw in chapter 3 that life insurance was nationalized in India in 1956, and nonlife, general insurance in 1972. The Life Insurance Corporation (LIC) of India became the sole company issuing life insurance policies in India. Nonlife, general insurance was organized under the General Insurance Corporation (GIC) as a holding company with four subsidiaries: New India, Oriental, United India, and National Insurance. The original objective behind this setup was to generate competition among these companies, but in reality the GIC operated as a monopoly.

Over the years, being in the public sector and having complete monopoly over their respective businesses, LIC and GIC became highly inefficient, with the result that as late as 1990–91 insurance penetration, measured by insurance premiums as a percentage of the GDP, was less than 1 percent, well below the economy's true potential. The government regulation also required that the companies allocate 75 percent of their investments to government securities.

The need to reform the insurance sector had been recognized relatively early in the reform process. The government appointed the Malhotra Committee in 1993 to suggest changes necessary to make the insurance sector more efficient and competitive. The committee reported in 1994 and made extensive recommendations. To increase competition, it recommended the entry of private companies, including foreign ones as partners with local companies with up to 40 percent equity. To make the public sector companies more efficient, it suggested the dilution of the government stake to 50 percent, turning the GIC and its subsidiaries into independent corporations and allowing all companies greater freedom to operate. In the area of regulation, it recommended amendment of the Insurance Act to set up a regulatory body and give the controller of insurance independence from the Finance Ministry. Finally, it recommended a reduction in the mandatory investment of the LIC life fund in government securities from 75 to 50 percent.

Though the Congress Party government appointed a nonstatutory interim Insurance Regulatory Authority in January 1996 to initiate reforms in the sector, it was unable to make much progress due to its defeat in the 1996 general elections. The Janata Dal government that followed, tried to carry the reform forward but was unsuccessful, partly because it fell in less than 18 months. In the 1996–97 budget, it promised to introduce a bill to turn the interim Insurance Regulatory Authority into an appropriately empowered statutory body, but failed to deliver. In the following year, it granted the LIC and GIC some autonomy by giving them the power to make nonscheduled, nonconsortium investments, to determine the terms and conditions of service of their employees and agents, and to make regulations—but was unable to introduce genuine reforms.

In the end, it was left to the National Democratic Alliance (NDA), led by the Bhartiya Janata Party (BJP) that won the 1998 election, to implement many of the recommendations of the Malhotra Committee. When it had been in opposition, the BJP had opposed the entry of the private sector into the insurance sector. Nevertheless, overcoming opposition from the "swedeshi" lobby (a group favoring everything indigenous) within the BJP, the NDA government successfully introduced the Insurance Regulatory and Development Authority (IRDA) Bill, which passed the Parliament in December 1999. The resulting Insurance Regulatory and Development Authority (IRDA) Act, 1999 revised some of the key provisions of the three existing pieces of legislation: the Insurance Act of 1938 (as amended in 1968 and 1995), the Life Insurance Corporation Act of 1956, and the General Insurance Business (Nationalization) Act of 1972.

The IRDA Act opens the insurance sector to the private sector, including foreign firms as partners of Indian firms with 26 percent or less equity stake. To ensure that the companies are widely held, the act also provides for a phased reduction of equity of Indian promoters from 74 percent to 26 percent in ten years. The act establishes the IRDA as an independent statutory body with broad regulatory powers. It is entrusted with the power to issue licenses to new entrants after their rigorous evaluation; setting standards for insurance products; monitoring and modifying rates, terms, and conditions of the policies; and protecting the interests of policyholders. The IRDA is also expected to ensure that private companies take part in rural development on the lines of the nationalized companies. Under the Insurance Act, 1938, all insurance companies must maintain a required solvency margin (excess of assets over liabilities), which is to be set by the IRDA.

The IRDA (Assets, Liabilities, and Solvency Margins of Insurers) Regulations of 2000 sets the required solvency margin at the higher of 500 million rupees or a sum to be calculated according to a formula. The formula differs for life and general insurers. For the reinsurer, the required solvency margin is the higher of 1 billion rupees or a sum to be determined according to a given formula. The IRDA goes a step further, however, by setting a working solvency margin ratio, defined as the proportion of the actual solvency margin to the required solvency margin of 1.5.

The IRDA also lays down strict guidelines on the investments by the insurance companies. For example, insurance companies are required to allocate at least 50 percent of their investments to government securities or other approved securities. Of these, at least 25 percent must be in government securities. They must also allocate at least 15 percent of the investments in infrastructure. This leaves a maximum of 35 percent of the investments to be allocated to other instruments. But even here, investments outside of those listed as "approved investments" cannot exceed 15 percent. In other words, life insurers are entirely free to allocate only 15 percent of their total financial resources. The IRDA specifies similar (but not identical) allocation rules for investments by annuity and pension funds; and general insurance and reinsurance (IRDA, *Annual Report 2001–02*, tables 39–41, pp. 76–77).

The liberalization to date has produced encouraging results. The insurance penetration ratio (proportion of premiums to the GDP), which was below 1 percent in 1990–91 and between 1 and 2 percent in the 1990s, rose to 3.2 percent in 2004–05 (IRDA, *Annual Report 2004–05*, pp. 9 and 14). The total premiums on policies underwritten by life insurers rose from 666.5 billion rupees in 2003–04 to 828.5 billion rupees in 2004–05, representing a growth of 24.3 percent in nominal terms. Premiums on policies underwritten by nonlife insurers rose from 155.5 billion rupees in 2003–04 to 174.8 billion rupees in 2004–05, representing a nominal growth of 12.4 percent. As a proportion of the GDP, the life and nonlife insurance premiums amount to 2.7 and 0.5 percent, respectively.

Private companies have taken advantage of the removal of the entry barrier. In 2004–05, there were 12 private companies in the life and 8 in the nonlife insurance sector. The share of private companies in the total premiums in the life insurance segment rose from 4.7 percent in 2003–04 to 9.3 percent in 2004–05. If we focus on just first-year premiums, and thus exclude renewal premiums, the private sector share rose from 12.3 to 21.2 percent between the two years. The annual growth rates in the total premiums in the private sector were staggering: 178.8 and 147.7 percent in the two years, respectively.

These achievements notwithstanding, private sector companies have been uniformly unsuccessful in generating profits. This is not altogether surprising, however. Expenses of setting up operations, training costs of developing the workforce, the high rate of commissions in the first year, creating a niche for the products, low initial customer base, and maintaining the solvency margin make it difficult for the new entrants to earn profits in the initial five to seven years. Therefore, most of the new insurers had to inject capital to cover the losses during 2004–05. The cumulative losses of private insurers on March 31, 2005, were 25.9 billion rupees, which represented a 54 percent increase over the previous year. LIC, on the other hand, has regularly shown profits, which stood at 158.8 billion rupees in 2004–05.

The good news is that private sector companies have continued to stay in the market, and new ones have been entering as well. Moreover, despite losses, in 2004–05, companies declared bonuses in order to remain competitive. The bonuses were permitted by the IRDA on the condition that the companies comply with certain conditions.

Looking ahead, two specific reforms must be considered. First, the permitted share of foreign equity, at 26 percent, is extremely low. Insurance is an area in which Indian companies have virtually no experience in the state of the art products, sales, and management practices. Unsurprisingly, most private entrants have entered with a foreign partner. If the development of the industry is to be speeded up, it is essential to give a greater stake to foreign companies. This requires amendment to the IRDA Act of 1999, but this should be done. Unfortunately, the government has been unable to deliver on its recent promise to raise the share of foreign equity to 49 percent. The goal should be actually to raise this to at least 74 percent, as has been done in the banking sector.

Second, the IRDA should reassess the allocation of the company investments. The current rules have a clear element of financial repression, whereby almost 85 percent of the investment by the companies in the life insurance segment is allocated in the sectors or instruments chosen by the IRDA. The companies are left fully free to choose only 15 percent of their investments. From both the viewpoint of the company profitability and the efficiency of the financial markets, this is not an optimal policy.

Retirement Benefits: Pension Reform

Potentially, retirement benefits, including pension and provident funds, are a very large source of financial capital. But under the current system, retirement programs in India cover only a small proportion of the workforce. Old-age support comes principally from the younger family members. The Reserve Bank of India (2003) and Shah (2005) offer comprehensive treatments of the existing retirement benefits schemes in India, with the latter also discussing in detail various aspects of required reforms and describing the progress until 2005. Additionally, a discussion paper, "Pension Reform and the New Pension System," posted on the Web site of the Finance Ministry (http://finmin.nic.in/index.html), offers useful details. In the following, I draw on these sources.

The Current State of the Retirement Benefits Programs and Policies

The problem, in a nutshell, that India faces is that the current retirement schemes cover only 11 percent of the workforce; the government carries a large and rapidly rising burden of the pension benefits; and the regulatory regime with respect to both the management of the pension funds and delivery of the benefits is in virtually non-existent. Broadly, existing formal retirement benefits cover two distinct categories of employees: 26 million central and state government employees and 15 million workers in factories with 20 or more workers. This leaves approximately 325 million workers uncovered (Shah, 2005, table 2). The main option available to these latter are pension plans offered by life insurance companies, most notably the LIC.

The principal source of the government burden is the Civil Service Pension System (CSPS), which covers all employees of the central and state governments hired prior to January 1, 2004. This is an unfunded, defined benefits pension system that relies entirely on the budgetary revenues. The New Pension System (NPS), fully funded by defined contributions, covers employees hired on or after January 1, 2004. In addition to financing the pensions of employees hired before 2004, the government also bears a small burden of the benefits packages of the workers in the organized sector otherwise covered under the Employee Provident Fund Scheme (EPFS) and Employee Pension Scheme (EPS).

Under the CSPS, an employee becomes eligible for a pension after completing ten years of government service. The retirement age is 60 years in the central government and varies between 58 and 60 years in the states. The pension works out to approximately half the salary during the last ten months of employment. There is a one rank, one pension principle according to which employees of the same rank receive the same pension. Accordingly, the pension of a previous retiree is adjusted every six months to the level of the new retiree with the same rank.

Because the government salaries have risen sharply over the years and the stock of retired employees has been increasing, expenditures on pensions have risen sharply in recent years. According to the data provided in the Finance Ministry discussion paper mentioned above, pension expenditures by the central and state governments in 1993–94 were 52.06 and 51.07 billion rupees, or 0.6 percent of the GDP each. These expenditures rose to 247.3 billion rupees and 383.7 billion rupees, or 0.8 and 1.2 percent of the GDP, respectively, in 2004–05. These expenditures understate the true burden of the pensions on the government, since they do not include the pensions of the employees in autonomous bodies and grant-in-aid institutions.

The Employees' Provident Funds and Miscellaneous Provisions (EPFMP) Act of 1952 governs retirement schemes of employees of factories with 20 workers or more in 177 specified industries or classes of establishments. At present, two main schemes, statutorily set up under EPFMP Act of 1952 are in operation. First, the Employee Provident Fund Scheme (EPFS) covers those workers whose *initial* monthly basic salary and dearness allowances (allowance to compensate for inflation) do not exceed 6500 rupees. With rare exceptions, employees contribute 12 percent of their wages, and employers 3.67 percent. The contributions are credited to the personal account of each employee, with the benefit available in old age determined by the contributions plus the interest accrued. According to Shah (2005, p. 6), the flow of contributions in 2002–03 was 114 billion rupees, and the stock of assets was 1.03 trillion rupees. The mean pension wealth received by an average employee (36,000 rupees in 2002–03) was relatively low. According to Shah (2005, p. 6), if this money were used to buy an annuity, it would yield 230 rupees per month, which is less than 10 percent of the average per-capita income in India.

The second main scheme under the EPFMP Act of1952, covering the same set of employees as the EPFS, is the Employees' Pension System (EPS). The EPS was created in 1995 as a replacement for the Employees' Family Pension Scheme, which had provided survivor benefits. The employer and the central government contribute 8.33 and 1.16 percent, respectively, of the qualified employee wages of up to 6500 rupees per month, which fully fund the scheme. The employer contributions to the EPFS and EPS, at 3.67 and 8.33 percent, respectively, sum to 12 percent of the qualified employee wages. The pension benefit equals the worker's average salary in the 12 months preceding retirement, times the years of service, divided by 70. There is a ceiling on the pension of 6500 rupees per month.

This discussion reveals four major flaws of the existing regime that were noted at the beginning of this section, and may be reemphasized. First, the coverage of the workforce is extremely low. Almost 90 percent of the workforce is currently outside the formal retirement system. Neither is there any other form of social security provided to those employed in the informal sector. Second, the CSPS imposes a heavy burden on the government budget. With the population living longer, this burden has been increasing over time. Given the large fiscal deficits and the needs for government expenditures in areas such as infrastructure, education, and health, the budget can scarcely take on a greater burden in the future. Third, a key flaw of the EPFS is that for the magnitude of contributions, it has been yielding extremely low payoff at retirement. As Shah (2005) notes, under reasonable assumptions, a single contribution of 2500 rupees at age 20 can yield pension wealth of 35,000 rupees at 60 years of age. Thus, the average pension wealth of 36,000 rupees delivered by the EPFS in 2002–03 is truly tiny. Possible causes include premature withdrawals and closure of accounts during job movements. Finally, there appear to be serious problems with the management of the EPS funds. Shah (2005) notes that the ten-year interest rate fell dramatically from 13.4 percent on January 1, 1997, to 5.1 percent on October 18, 2003. Yet, the EPS managed to maintain the benefit at the previous level without any change in the rate of contribution. This suggests the existence of substantial underpayment in relation to the contributions in the earlier years. Annual actuarial reports, mandated by law, either have not been produced or have not been released to the public. The last two factors point to a generally poor regulatory oversight.

Reforms to Date

Thinking on the retirement system within the government in the postreform era has proceeded on two tracks, one relating to the informal sector and the other to the civil service. In 1998, the Ministry of Social Justice and Empowerment set up Project OASIS (Old Age Social and Income Security) to recommend initiatives for improved old age income security for informal sector workers. The committee submitted its report in 2000, and recommended an individual retirement accounts

(IRAs) scheme that would be unique to an individual and remain unchanged with employment. The accounts would be operated from a multiplicity of points of presence (POPs) located at banks and post offices. A centralized depository would be established to pool the funds received from the POPs and channel them to the relevant pension fund managers. Upon retirement, the account holder would be required to use a specified proportion of the proceeds to buy annuities. To date, no progress on implementing this proposal has been made.

The initiative on the second track came in the budget for 2001–02, which promised to launch a new pension scheme with a defined contribution basis for the new entrants in the government service. To give shape to this idea, the Ministry of Personnel, Pension and Public Grievances set up a high-level expert group. The group recommended a scheme that combines contributions from employees and the government on a matching basis, on the one hand, while committing to provide the employees a defined benefit as pension.

In the 2003–04 budget, the government announced a new pension system based on defined contribution, shared equally between the government and the employees. The government made the new pension system operational through a notification dated December 22, 2003, and applicable only to new recruits in the central government from January 1, 2004. The government also set up an interim Pension Fund Regulatory and Development Authority (PFRDA) that started functioning on January 1, 2004. In the 2004–05 budget, the government announced its intention to give the PFRDA statutory status, but has been unsuccessful in bringing a bill to the Parliament to this effect, due to opposition from trade unions. In December 2004, the government did give the PFRDA statutory status through an ordinance, but the latter expired after six months, as per the constitution, and the PFRDA has been functioning without legal status.

The new pension system (NPS) is implemented on all new central government employees hired on or after January 1, 2004, except those in the armed services on a mandatory basis. States can choose to join the scheme as well. Sixteen of them had done so by September 2006. As many as 500,000 employees were covered, and a corpus of 15 billion rupees existed under the NPS by the same date.

The scheme is also available to employees in the unorganized sector on a voluntary basis, with no contributions made by the government. Mandatory programs under the Employee Provident Fund and Miscellaneous Provisions Act of 1952 or other acts continue as before. The new scheme is not available to those already covered by these other schemes.

Under the NPS, all participants have individuals pension accounts that are portable in case of change of employment. The system is based on a defined contribution and uses post offices and banks to collect contributions, rather than create new infrastructure specific to the scheme. The employee contributes a certain percentage of the basic salary toward the pension, and the government makes a matching contribution. The contributions and accumulations are tax-exempt, but benefits are to be taxed as normal income.

On the benefits side, the employee would be required to convert 40 percent of the accumulated pension wealth into an annuity, so as to achieve a reasonable pension. The balance 60 percent would be paid as a lump sum, which he would be free to utilize in any manner, including the purchase of more annuities.

The NPS envisages four broad categories of pension schemes. At one extreme is the scheme that would invest all funds in government securities. At the other extreme is the scheme that invests a relatively high proportion of the funds in equity. The remaining two schemes propose to have smaller but different weights of equity. The participant would be allowed to move his funds from one scheme to the other, and possibly also to spread them over two or more schemes.

Looking Ahead

Though the NPS is already in place with more and more states joining, it is operating without a statutory PFRDA. The latter requires legislation which has been stalled due to opposition from trade unions that has translated into opposition by the Left parties in the Parliament. This is unfortunate, since a regulatory agency to oversee the collection and professional management of the funds is urgently required. In the interim, the government has decided to appoint a central recordkeeping agency to handle the pension corpus of the central government employees under the NPS.

One important desirable feature of the system would be to separate fund management from annuities. When the individual retires, he should have the full freedom to shop around for annuities in which the life insurance companies typically specialize. Under such an approach, the accumulation phase would be unbundled from the benefits phase.

A final point to note is that from the viewpoint of financial intermediation, the NPS represents a significant improvement over the existing system. It creates a new set of instruments through which individual savings can be channeled through the formal financial market, and may even help convert some of the physical savings into financial savings. Alternatively, the government currently uses more than 2 percent of the GDP in tax revenue to finance the pensions of its employees. Once the NPS is fully in place, this amount will be turned into financial savings that will flow through the financial markets to be prudently invested.

CONCLUDING REMARKS

In this chapter, I have covered the three most important components of the financial market: money and banking; the capital market; and insurance and retirement plans. Each of these subsectors constitutes a complex subject of analysis and is in need of reforms. We have seen that considerable progress in each sector has been made, but much also remains to be done.

Rather than summarize the vast number of issues covered in this chapter, I conclude with one final thought. We have seen that each subsector in India has or will soon have a regulatory authority of its own: banks are regulated by the RBI, the stock market by the SEBI, insurance by the IRDA, and pensions will eventually have the PFRDA. Given that these subsectors are ultimately a part of the same vast financial market, and many entities, such as universal banks, perform functions that fall under the jurisdiction of different regulatory authorities, will it not be wise to have a single regulatory authority overseeing the entire financial market, as is the practice in the United Kingdom? My own view on this is that India has taken the right course by decentralizing the regulatory functions across subsectors rather than concentrating it in a single entity. This poses some risks of some activities and transactions being left uncovered and others covered by two or more agencies. But it is better to resolve these problems as they arise rather than create a single and vast bureaucracy with multiple arms that do not communicate with each other. Specialized agencies are also likely to employ specialized staff, while a large bureaucracy is bound to fall into the usual trap of employing generalists who think they are capable of turning themselves into specialists of the functions delegated to them overnight.

PART IV

Transforming India

12

INTERNATIONAL TRADE
Carrying Liberalization Forward

India grew 6.3 percent per annum during 1988–2006. During 2003–07, the annual growth rate was 8.6 percent. The 2007–08 budget places the quick estimate for 2005–06 at 9 percent and the advance estimate for 2006–07 at 9.2 percent (the central Statistical Organization produces GDP estimates at various stages and revises them as better information becomes available. Advance Estimate is the most tentative and is followed by Quick Estimate.) The possibility that the long-run growth rate of India may have shifted to the levels achieved by the East Asian tigers in the 1960s and 1970s can no longer be ruled out.

Yet, even as the economy picks up pace and poverty continues to decrease, there remain doubts about the transformation of India from a primarily agricultural and rural economy to a modern one in the foreseeable future. This transformation has not progressed as far as one would expect, based on the experience of other Asian countries. For example, the proportion of the workforce employed in agriculture in the Republic of Korea fell from 68 percent in 1960 to 50 percent in 1970 and to 34 percent in 1980. In India, the decline has been far more attenuated: from 67 percent in 1991 to 58 percent in 2001. In terms of rural-urban split, the data give an even more pessimistic picture: Rural population fell from 79 percent of the total population in 1991 to just 77 percent in 2001.

In part IV of the book, I focus on the broad question of why the structural transformation of the economy in India has been slow, and what must be done to speed it up. A key theme running through this part of the book is that unskilled-labor-intensive manufacturing has done poorly in India, and that the future reform must focus on removing impediments facing its rapid growth.[1] In the present chapter, I focus on the impact of trade and foreign investment liberalization to date and on the future course of the policy in these areas. In chapter 13, I consider reforms aimed at rapid growth of industry and services, since these are the sectors that must draw ever increasing numbers of workers out of agriculture. In chapter 14, I turn to the reforms in agriculture. A very large proportion of workers will continue to be employed in this sector in the foreseeable future. Therefore, its modernization has to be an essential part of the strategy aimed at economic transformation. Finally, some key impediments to achieving the transition to a modern economy come from infrastructure bottlenecks in areas such as telecommunications, electricity, and transportation, on the one hand, and from the social sector services such as health, water supply and sanitation, and education on the other. The discussion of these subjects is taken up in part V, which treats the government sector in considerable detail.

In dealing with trade and investment policy, it is useful to compare them throughout with the policies in China. The latter is a highly populous country like India, and has been extremely successful in converting its inward-oriented economy into an outward-oriented one. Therefore, it holds the prospects of some useful lessons for India. I have undertaken the comparison in several recent papers (Panagariya, 2006a, 2006b, and 2006d). In the present chapter, I draw on these sources in addition to others cited at appropriate points.

TRADE AND FOREIGN INVESTMENT POLICY: COMPARING INDIA AND CHINA

I have discussed the changes in trade and foreign investment policies to date in greater detail in part I of the book, especially chapters 4 and 5. Rather than repeat them here, I offer brief comparative perspectives on India and China. Technically, trade liberalization in India and China began almost simultaneously in the late 1970s. But initially, China proceeded more rapidly and systematically. It achieved a much more liberal trade regime during the 1980s than India did. In foreign investment, China began much earlier than India. Whereas it started to open its regime in the late 1970s, India did not begin until the early 1990s.

Nevertheless, since the 1990s, India has nearly caught up with China on trade policy in industrial goods and services, as well as foreign investment policy. Setting aside some tariff peaks, India's top tariff rate on industrial goods stands at 10 percent. Customs revenue as a proportion of merchandise imports fell to 4.9 percent in 2005–06. On the foreign investment front, India is now just as open as China, except perhaps in the retail sector, though some backdoor entry has been permitted in this sector as well. Mainly, India remains more protected than China only in agriculture.

RESPONSE TO OUTWARD-ORIENTED POLICIES

The response of trade and foreign investment to the opening up of India has been muted relative to China except until recently. Figure 12.1 plots the ratio of exports of goods and services to the GDP between 1982 and 2003 in India and China. At the beginning of this period, the ratio was admittedly lower in India than in China. But during the subsequent years, it rose even more rapidly in China, and the gap between the two countries increased dramatically. By 2003, exports of goods and services were 30 percent of GDP in China and 14 percent in India.

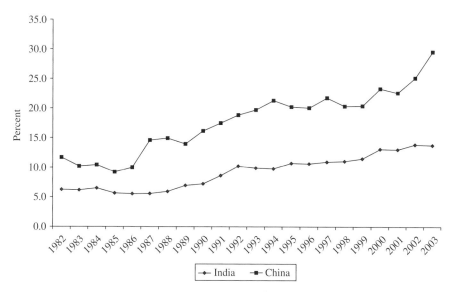

FIGURE 12.1: India and China: Exports of Goods and Services as Proportions of the GDP

Growth in India's trade has picked up recently, however. This is seen in figures 12.2 and 12.3, which show merchandise and services exports, respectively, at various points in time starting with 1991. Some notable facts are as follows:

- Merchandise exports in 1990–91 were $18.1 billion. In 2005–06, *growth* in exports over exports in 2004–05 exceeded this amount. Put another way, exports in 1990–91 doubled for the first time in 1999–2000. In the more recent period, they doubled in just three years: from $52.7 billion in 2002–03 to $102.7 billion in 2005–06.
- Services exports have grown even more rapidly in recent years: They doubled from $26.9 billion in 2003–04 to $60.6 billion in 2005–06.
- India's share in world merchandise exports grew from 0.5 percent in 1990–91 to 0.7 percent in 1999–2000 and to 1.0 percent in 2005–06. In services exports, the share had grown to a respectable 2.5 percent in 2005–06.
- These changes have greatly increased the integration of India into the world economy. The exports of goods and services as a proportion of the GDP, which grew rather gradually from 7.2 percent in 1990–91 to 11.6 percent in 1999–2000, shot up to 20.5 percent in 2005–06. The proportion of total trade (exports plus imports of goods and services) to the GDP rose from 15.9 percent in 1990–91 to 25.2 percent in 1999–2000 and to 43.1 percent in 2005–06.

While these changes clearly represent a major shift in the growth of India's trade, the contrast with China remains. In particular, the following facts may be noted:

- Trade in goods and services as a proportion of the GDP in China rose from 21 percent in 1982 to 65 percent in 2004.
- China's share in the world goods and services exports rose from 2.6 percent in 1994 to 5.8 percent in 2004.

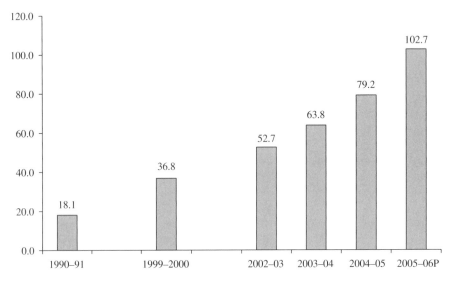

FIGURE 12.2: Merchandise Exports of India: Selected Years (in Billions) (*source*: Reserve Bank of India, *Annual Report*, various issues)

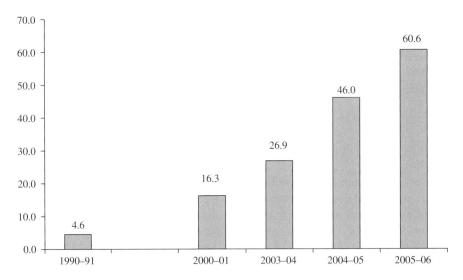

FIGURE 12.3: Services Exports of India: Selected Years (in Billions) (*source*: Reserve Bank of India, *Annual Report*, various issues)

- If we restrict ourselves to the world merchandise exports, China's share rose from 2.8 percent in 1984 to 6.5 percent in 2004.
- In 2004 and the two years preceding it, the *increase* in China's merchandise exports was larger than India's *absolute level* of exports.

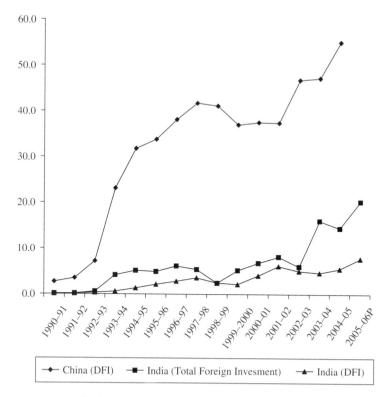

FIGURE 12.4: Direct Foreign Investment (DFI) in India and China (in Billions) (*source*: Prasad and Wei [2006, Table 6] for China and Government of India [2006] for India)

The contrast between India and China is even sharper in the area of direct foreign investment (DFI). In part, this is because India began opening its DFI sector more than a decade after China. But this is only a part of the explanation. As we will see below, much faster growth of China's manufactures has helped catalyze a higher growth of DFI as well. India seems to be catching up recently, especially if we include e portfolio investment ($12.5 billion 2005–06), but it has some distance to go. Figure 12.4 shows the growth in the DFI in the two countries and the growth of total foreign investment in India.

COMPOSITION OF TRADE

The evolution of the composition of exports of China and India offers an interesting contrast. Reflecting the dominance of central planning, whose primary objective was to generate foreign exchange, China opportunistically exported what was left after the domestic demand had been satisfied. As a result, its exports included a mix of highly capital-intensive products, such as petroleum products, and highly labor-intensive products, such as apparel. But as its liberalization progressed and comparative advantage began to guide its pattern, China's exports shifted toward light, labor-intensive manufactures.

In contrast, the pattern of trade in India has remained haphazard. India's exports consist of some very capital-intensive and skilled-labor-intensive products along-side unskilled-labor-intensive products even today. A variety of policy-imposed constraints we will discuss in the next chapter have barred India from exploiting its huge comparative advantage in unskilled-labor-intensive manufactures. This has meant slower growth of the Indian manufacturing sector, and since manufacturing tends to be more traded than services and also attracts more foreign investment, its slow growth has meant slow growth in trade and foreign investment.

Composition of Merchandise Exports

Table 12.1 presents all SITC (Standard International Trade Classification) two-digit products that accounted for 2 percent or more of total exports, on the average, during 2001–04 for India and for China. For each product, the table provides the average share in exports during three adjacent time periods: 1984–90, 1991–2000, and 2001–04. Among the top six exports of India, the only product that is unambiguously unskilled-labor-intensive is apparel. In addition, some of the products in the "miscellaneous manufactures" category may be unskilled-labor-intensive. Of the remaining four items, three (textiles; iron and steel; and petroleum) are capital-intensive and one (nonmetallic mineral manufactures), consisting principally of gems and jewelry, is semiskilled-labor-intensive. This is in sharp contrast to China, which exported products such as apparel, toys, footwear, travel goods, handbags, and sporting goods in large volumes during the 1980s and 1990s.

Table 12.1 also suggests much greater export dynamism in China than in India. Nonmetallic mineral manufactures have been the most important export from India since the mid-1980s. Based on factor endowments, apparel should have expanded far more rapidly and become the most important export from India, as happened in China in the 1990s. But the share of apparel in the total exports of India declined in the early 2000s. Instead, it was such capital-intensive products as petroleum and iron and steel that gained in share. In contrast, in China, as its labor force has become more skilled, it has shifted away from textiles, and to some degree even from apparel. Instead, office machinery and automatic data-processing machinery; telecommunications and sound recording equipment; and electrical machinery, apparatus, and appliances have gained in importance.

Figure 12.5, which plots the evolution of the top two exports of India and China on the same graph, further dramatizes the difference between the performances of exports in the two countries. The exports of office machinery and automatic data-processing machinery; and telecommunications and sound recording equipment, by China have risen at a breathtaking pace. Until as late as 2000, the exports of each group of products were below $20 billion. By 2004, exports of office machinery and automatic data-processing machinery had reached $87 billion, and telecommunications and sound recording, $68 billion. In contrast, India's top export, nonmetallic mineral manufactures, rose from $7 billion to just $11 billion over the same period. True, India's exports accelerated during the last two years, which are not included

TABLE 12.1: SITC Two-Digit Products with Export Shares Exceeding 2 Percent during 2001–04: India and China

SITC		1984–90	1991–2000	2001–04
India				
66	Nonmetallic mineral manufactures, n.e.s.	16.4	15.9	14.9
65	Textile yarn, fabrics, made-up articles, n.e.s.	12.0	14.0	10.6
84	Articles of apparel and clothing accessories	11.9	13.6	10.4
33	Petroleum, petroleum products, and related materials	4.7	1.7	6.3
89	Miscellaneous manufactured articles	2.0	3.7	5.2
67	Iron and steel	1.1	3.1	5.0
43	Animal or vegetable fats and oils, processed	0.0	0.1	3.6
53	Dyeing, tanning, and coloring material	1.1	1.3	3.1
28	Metalliferous ores and metal scrap	4.8	1.9	3.0
69	Manufactures of metal, n.e.s.	1.7	2.2	2.7
04	Cereals and cereal preparations	1.9	2.8	2.7
78	Road vehicles (incl. air cushion vehicles)	1.6	2.3	2.4
03	Fish, crustaceans, mollusks, and aquatic invertebrates	3.2	3.3	2.2
77	Electrical machinery, apparatus, and appliances	1.5	1.5	2.1
China				
75	Office machines and automatic data-processing machines	0.4	4.8	12.9
84	Articles of apparel and clothing accessories	14.3	16.8	11.8
76	Telecommunications, and sound recording and reproducing apparatus and equipment	2.9	6.1	10.4
77	Electrical machinery, apparatus, and appliances	1.2	7.2	10.1
89	Miscellaneous manufactured articles	4.9	9.3	7.3
65	Textile yarn, fabrics, made-up articles, n.e.s.	13.8	8.1	6.1
69	Manufactures of metal, n.e.s.	2.0	3.1	3.4
85	Footwear	2.0	4.4	2.9
74	General industrial machinery and equipment	0.6	1.4	2.7
78	Road vehicles (incl. air cushion vehicles)	4.0	2.1	2.6
82	Furniture and parts thereof; bedding, mattresses, mattress supports, cushions, and similar stuffed furnishings	0.5	1.4	2.1

Note: n.e.s. = "not elsewhere specified."

Source: U.N. Commodity Trade Statistics.

in the data in table 12.1 and figure 12.5. But the acceleration remained well below that observed in China.

Dimaranan, Ianchovichina, and Martin (2007) offer yet another perspective on the differences between the patterns of exports of India and China. Using the SITC six-digit export data for 2004, they compiled lists of the top 25 exports of the two countries. These 25 items accounted for 38.4 and 58.4 percent of the total merchandise exports of China and India, respectively. Given the similarity of the factor endowments of the two countries, we would predict a large overlap between their top 25 export items. But it turns out that except for one common item, these lists

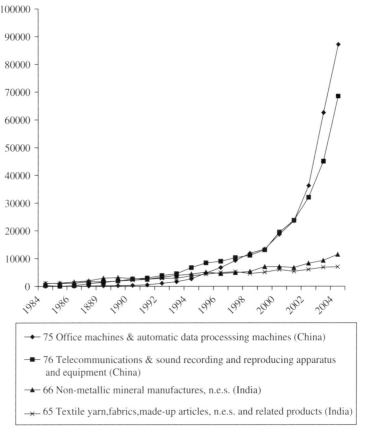

FIGURE 12.5: Top Two Exports of India and China

are entirely mutually exclusive. The only common item is petroleum oils (excluding crude) (SITC 271000), whose exports ands imports are not related to the factor endowments as conventionally defined.

Services Exports

Services account for a much larger share of the total exports in India than in China. In part this is because of the slow growth of merchandise exports from India. Figure 12.6 shows the evolution of services exports of India since 1990–91. The upper line represents the total services exports and the lower one, the "miscellaneous" category, which includes software exports. Two other major items included in the services exports are travel and transportation. Services exports showed a sharp expansion during 2003–06. From just $20 billion in 2002–03, they tripled to $60 billion in 2005–06.

Table 12.2 offers some details specific to software exports, which accounted for 39 percent of the total services exports in 2005–06. The growth rate of total software exports averaged 31 percent between 2001–02 and 2005–06. If we include the

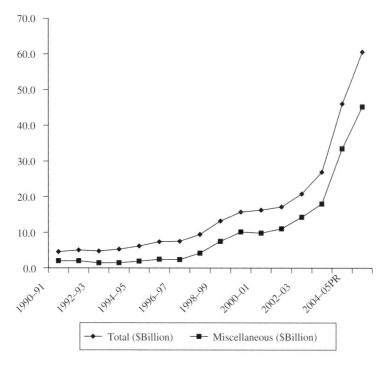

FIGURE 12.6: Services Exports of India (*source*: Reserve Bank of India, *Annual Report*, various issues)

TABLE 12.2: Software Exports of India

Year	IT Services	ITES-BPO	Total Software
1	*2*	*3*	*4 (= 2+3)*
1995–96	0.8		0.8
1996–97	1.1		1.1
1997–98	1.8		1.8
1998–99	2.6		2.6
1999–2000	3.4	0.6	4.0
2000–01	5.3	0.9	6.2
2001–02	6.2	1.5	7.6
2002–03	7.0	2.5	9.5
2003–04	9.2	3.6	12.8
2004–05	13.1	4.6	17.7
2005–06	17.3	6.3	23.6

Source: Reserve Bank of India, *Annual Report* (various issues).

earlier years, the growth rate was even higher. Likewise, the growth rate during the last three years spanning 2003–04 to 2005–06 averaged 35 percent. If the current growth rate is sustained for another five years, we will see this sector match the performance of the top two or three merchandise products of China. But there are some doubts as to whether this growth can be sustained. As I discuss in chapter 20, there remain questions regarding the ability of the Indian higher education system to keep pace with the demand for high quality graduates.

Merchandise Imports

Elsewhere, I offer a detailed comparison of import patterns of Indian and China (Panagariya, 2006c). Here I confine myself to pointing out one key difference between the patterns of the two countries. In 2004, the latest year for which comparable data are available, 46 percent of China's import expenditures were on machinery and transport equipment.[2] The corresponding expenditure by India was only 19 percent. This reinforces the point made earlier: For its needs, India is far more specialized in capital goods industries than China. The difference between India and China looks even more impressive when we consider the absolute levels of their expenditures on the imports of machinery and transport equipment: $253 billion by China versus just $22 billion by India. Purely in terms of accessing world-class machinery, China is very far ahead of India.

THE PATTERN OF DIRECT FOREIGN INVESTMENT

Data on the composition of DFI in India and China employ different classification schemes so that they are not directly comparable. Moreover, in the case of India, I have been able to obtain the composition for 1991–2005 only lumped together, while that for China is available on an annual basis. In India, the top six recipients of DFI between August 1991 and December 2005 were electrical equipment, including computer software and electronics (16.5 percent); transportation industry (10 percent); the services sector (10 percent); telecommunications (10 percent); power and oil refinery (8 percent); and chemicals 6 (percent). In China, manufacturing received approximately 70 percent of the DFI during 2002–04. Within manufacturing, electronics and communications equipment was the largest recipient.

This pattern suggests much greater harmony between exports and direct foreign investment in China than in India. In the case of China, Prased and Wei (2006) offer the following assessment of the flows between 1998 and 2004:

> Table 2 shows that about two-thirds of these flows have been going into manufacturing, with real estate accounting for about another 10 percent. Within manufacturing, the largest identifiable share has consistently gone to electronics and communication equipment. The share of manufacturing has risen by almost 15 percentage points since 1998, largely at the expense of the shares of utilities, construction, transport and telecommunication services, and real estate. Since the industries with declining FDI shares are largely focused on non-traded goods, the evolution of this pattern of FDI seems to be consistent with the notion that these inflows have been stimulated by China's increasing access (both actual and anticipated) to world export markets following its accession to the World Trade Organization (WTO) in 2001. (p. 4)

In contrast, foreign investment in India has largely come to take advantage of the domestic market in sectors such as transportation, telecommunications, services, and chemicals.

FUTURE POLICY DIRECTIONS

Major issues relating to trade policy include further unilateral liberalization and the removal of export subsidies; trade facilitation; the special economic zones (SEZs); anti-dumping and safeguard measures; preferential trade areas (PTAs); and multi-lateral trade negotiations. I consider each of these in turn.

Unilateral Liberalization of Tariffs and Ending Export Subsidies

A substantial part of India's trade liberalization since the mid-1980s has resulted from what economists call unilateral liberalization: Recognizing the benefits of outward orientation, India has proceeded to lower trade barriers on its own, without either reciprocal liberalization by its trading partners or an IMF or World Bank program. The elimination of import licensing for capital and intermediate goods carried some element of the IMF-World-Bank conditionality, though a consensus in this direction had been emerging among the country's leadership (as discussed in chapter 5). Likewise, the elimination of import licensing for consumer goods in April 2001 was triggered by the loss of a dispute settlement case at the World Trade Organization (WTO), but India had been moving in that direction. Absent the dispute settlement ruling, India was planning to phase out the licensing in two years' time on its own.

Tariff liberalization, which was confined largely to industrial goods, took place almost entirely on a unilateral basis. Even after reforms slowed down under the current UPA government, tariff liberalization continued. The 2004–05 budget brought the peak tariff down from 25 to 20 percent. The following three budgets reduced it to 15, 12.5, and 10 percent, respectively. This is very substantial progress.

But given that India is not vulnerable to a balance of payments crisis and has a flexible exchange rate in place, it must continue with liberalization by reducing the top tariff to no more than 5 percent by 2010. The eventual goal of the policy should be free trade in industrial goods in the near future. To get there, India also needs to tackle the problem of peak tariffs in some specific sectors, most notably automobiles and textiles. Automobiles are subject to customs duties nearing 100 percent. Even more important is to bring down the prohibitive duties on used cars. Used small cars, available at relatively low prices from countries such as Japan, offer cost-effective substitutes for the old, polluting cars currently on the road and for two-wheelers (scooters and motor cycles) that are highly risky for the transportation of a family of four. High duties on both new and used cars serve the singular purpose of protecting the domestic car and two-wheeler industries at the expense of the consumer. Likewise, peak customs duties on textiles must be brought within the discipline of the official top customs duty of 10 percent.

An important tariff-related issue concerns agriculture. India has had some success in expanding its agricultural exports. There are no clear reasons to believe that the benefits India reaped from the liberalization of industrial goods will not materialize in agriculture. In addition, if India is also able to get the OECD countries to liberalize their markets in agriculture, including a substantial reduction in their subsidies, prospects for India to raise its share in the world market for agricultural products to 2 to 3 percent are excellent. Therefore, it is important to begin building political support for liberalization in agriculture.

India also employs export subsidies of various kinds. Most prominently, profits earned on exports are not subject to the profit tax. Politically, export subsidies have salience since exporters want them, and politicians and bureaucrats love to distribute them. But from the standpoint of national welfare, they are worse than tariffs. Not only do they distort trade, they also turn into transfers to the importing countries in the form of reduced prices they pay.

Worse yet, under the WTO rules, the importing country can countervail export subsidies by an equivalent import duty. When faced with export subsidies, the United States has often resorted to this duty. It is easy to show that when the importing country countervails the export subsidy, the latter turns into an equivalent transfer to it. Consider, for example, a pair of Indian shoes sold in the U.S. market for $100. For ease of exposition, assume that Indian exporters are too small to influence the price in the U.S. market. Now let the Indian government introduce an export subsidy of $20 per pair. This raises the price (inclusive of the subsidy) received by exporters to $120. Indian shoe manufacturers expand shoe exports. Suppose this induces the U.S. government to impose a countervailing duty of $20 per pair. The Indian exporter is now left with only $80 plus the $20 in export subsidy for each pair of shoes exported. He is neither better off nor worse off than prior to the export subsidy. The only effect of the subsidy is to leave the Indian Treasury poorer by the amount of subsidy, and the U.S. Treasury is richer by an equivalent amount. Gradual dismantling of export subsidies is in India's own interest.

Trade Facilitation

Trade facilitation aims to improve the ability of countries to deliver imports and exports on time and at lower costs. As the formal barriers to trade such as licensing and tariffs come down, these delivery barriers assume increasing importance. Narrowly defined, trade facilitation relates to the movement of goods into and out of ports and airports. But broadly defined, it includes a host of factors such as customs procedures, internal transportation networks (roads, railways, waterways, and air transport), regulatory environment, product standards, and sanitary and phytosanitary measures.

On the bureaucratic front, Roy (2003) notes that an exporter in India must obtain 258 signatures and make 118 copies of the required information. Keypunching this information takes 22 hours. Importers face similar time-consuming and onerous procedures. Roy and Bagai (2005) further note that exports take 2.5 days to move out of, and imports 15 days to move into, India at the Delhi airport. This compares with the norm of less than 12 hours for both exports and imports at well-functioning airports around the world. For containerized sea freight, export dwell time at the Mumbai port is three to five days, in comparison to the international norm of less than 18 hours. For imports, the dwell time at Mumbai port is 7 to 14 days, compared to the international norm of less than 24 hours. Although in 1995 India began implementing electronic data interchange, which currently covers more than 90 percent of international trade transactions, delays at ports and airports remain a serious problem. Delays of this magnitude can entirely kill the ability of firms to export in certain sectors. This is especially true when firms are importing inputs to process and reexport—something at which China has been highly successful.

Infrastructure constitutes an additional major barrier to the swift movement of goods in India. Both railway and road connections from ports to manufacturing facilities remain deficient. The government recognizes this problem, but progress in improving the connections has been slow. I take up this subject in greater detail in chapter 17.

Special Economic Zones

The special economic zones (SEZs) have recently turned highly controversial in India. One aspect of the controversy relates to land acquisition, which is an important issue in its own right, and one that I will consider separately in the next chapter. Here I focus on the basic concept of the SEZ and its history, current form, and desirability in India independently of the land acquisition issue.[3]

Basic Concept and History

Conceptually, SEZs operate like foreign entities within the territory of a country. They are usually separated by physical barriers from each other and from the rest of the country. They have no trade barriers. The country's trade barriers apply strictly within the area excluding the SEZs, which is called the domestic tariff area (DTA). Any goods sold by agents within the DTA to agents inside the SEZ are treated as exports of the country, and those purchased by agents in the DTA from those in the SEZ, as imports subject to customs duty. Any trade between the SEZ and the outside world is allowed to bypass all customs requirements applicable to the DTA. That is, foreign goods enter the SEZ free of customs duty, and exit abroad without being subject to any domestic taxes or customs regulations. The main features distinguishing an SEZ from a foreign country are (1) its free-trade status, which may or may not be enjoyed by the foreign country; (2) free movement of factors of production between it and the DTA, which is usually not allowed between it and the foreign country and (3) the application of domestic laws, including those relating to law and order, taxation, investment, and labor to the agents located inside it.

In practice, countries temper this idealized conception of the SEZ by applying different labor, investment, and tax rules than in the DTA. Below, I will describe the policy regime applicable to the SEZs in India under the SEZ Act of 2005 and the rules notified under the act in February 2006. But first, it is useful to offer a brief historical background.

While the term SEZ entered the official Indian trade policy lexicon via the Foreign Trade Policy of 2000–01, something akin to it had existed in the past under the titles export promotion zone, export processing zone, and free trade zone. The first such entity was the Kandla Export Promotion Zone in Gujarat, established in 1965. Following the announcement of the Special Economic Zones Scheme in the Foreign Trade Policy of 2000–01, eight existing export processing zones were converted into SEZs. As of 2006, there were 11 functioning SEZs in all.

The SEZ Act of 2005 provides the overall legal framework within which the SEZs operate. States can have their own SEZ laws within the framework of the central law. For example, Gujarat has its own SEZ law. The rules notified in February 2006 offered several incentives (see below) to the SEZ operator as well as the units located in it. These incentives have led to a rush for SEZs, with more than 400 applications filed and more than 200 of them approved by the end of 2006. A hold on the approved proposals was placed amid the controversy over the acquisition of land for the SEZs, however. The government is currently seeking a satisfactory solution to this problem.

The Policy Framework

Any private, public, or joint sector enterprise, state government, and the central government can establish SEZs. The minimum stipulated area for a multiproduct SEZ is 1000 hectares, with at least 25 percent of the area earmarked for the development of processing. The minimum area is reduced to 100 hectares if the SEZ is devoted exclusively to services or is located near a port or airport. The limit is 200 hectares if the SEZ is located in a state listed in the rules or a union territory. The minimum stipulated area for an SEZ devoted to a single sector such as apparel is 100 hectares, with 50 percent of the area earmarked for the development of processing. The area limit is reduced to 10 hectares for certain products (electronic hardware and software, including information technology-enabled services; biotechnology; nonconventional energy; and gems and jewelry) and to 50 hectares if the SEZ is located in a state listed in the rules or a union territory.

The policy provides tax breaks to the SEZ developer as well as to units located in the SEZ. Among other things, the developer is granted a complete tax holiday for any ten consecutive years in the first 15 years, beginning with the year in which the SEZ is notified. Likewise, units located in the SEZ are given 100 percent exemption from profit tax in the first five years and 50 percent exemption for two additional years. These tax breaks have generated a major controversy to which I will briefly return below. Units located in the SEZs are required to achieve positive net foreign exchange earnings, calculated cumulatively beginning five years after commencement of production.

The SEZ Act has the status of a special rather than a general act. This means that in case of an inconsistency between this Act and any other, provisions of this Act apply. This special act status does not apply, however, with respect to laws relating to trade unions, industrial or labor disputes, labor welfare, provident funds, and workmen's compensation, pensions, and maternity benefits.

A potentially important feature of the SEZs is that the central government appoints a development commissioner to each SEZ who is in charge overall. He is also authorized to exercise any powers that the central and state governments may delegate to him. The SEZ rules advise the state government having jurisdiction over an SEZ to delegate the powers under the Industrial Disputes Act of 1947 and similar acts in relation to the units in the SEZ as well as to workers employed by the developer, to the development commissioner at the same time the government recommends the SEZ to the central government. If properly executed, this authority can go a long way toward depoliticizing labor disputes. Being a central government employee, the development commissioner may be able to exercise effective power to allow the units in the SEZ to reduce the number of workers, which is otherwise virtually impossible in the organized sector in India (see chapter 13 for details).

Under a related provision, the state governments can declare the SEZ a public utility. The public utility status prohibits worker strikes without due notice. While the right to strike is an important right conferred by democratic societies on workers, this right has been subject to undue abuse in India and has discouraged firms from entering large-scale production of labor-intensive products.

Evaluating the SEZs

From an economic standpoint, the first question we must ask is whether the SEZs would improve efficiency vis-à-vis the status quo. The answer is a qualified yes. There are two main reasons why they may lower efficiency. First, absent various tax breaks in the SEZs, the least-cost location of a unit may be outside the SEZ. But the tax breaks may induce the unit to locate inside the SEZ even though the real resource cost is higher there. Second, tax breaks in the SEZ that are not available elsewhere will result in the loss of revenue. This revenue loss will have to be recovered from alternative sources of taxation. Insofar as this alternative taxation imposes *additional* efficiency costs, the SEZ leads to further inefficiency.

Against these costs, we must consider the benefits the SEZ may bring. At least two sources of benefits must be considered. First, as discussed above, international trade in India remains subject to substantial bureaucratic red tape. Goods move into and out of the country at a slow pace. Faster movement is particularly important for exports that involve bringing components from abroad for assembly and reexport. Domestic indirect taxes that must be reimbursed when goods are exported, are not always fully reimbursed. The SEZs help overcome these inefficiencies. Second, the organized sector in India has been hamstrung by onerous labor market laws that have hampered the emergence of large-scale manufacturing in the labor-intensive sectors. If some states use the instrumentality of the SEZ to relax some of the most burdensome provisions in the labor regime, as is currently being tried by Gujarat, we may see the emergence of such firms.

There is no doubt that ideally, India should provide the same business environment and flexible labor market regime it is trying to create in the SEZs in the entire country. It should also refrain from the tax breaks it has offered, since they are distortionary. But absent this possibility, my own judgment is that the expected benefits of the SEZs as implemented still dominate the costs, and are worth promoting for this reason. The ultimate test of their success will be whether or not they help promote large-scale manufacturing of labor-intensive products. If success is achieved, it can even open the door to the extension of the policy throughout India.

I expect the efficiency costs of the SEZ discussed above to be low relative to the potential benefits. Entrepreneurs are likely to establish the SEZs precisely where they want to locate their processing units. Thus, the real resource cost of suboptimal location is likely to be small. Likewise, if India does move to the comprehensive goods and services tax as planned (see chapter 15), the excess burden resulting from the tax breaks in the SEZs will be contained. The real challenge facing the Finance Ministry is to avoid seizing on tax instruments, such as the fringe benefits tax and transactions tax, that deliver revenue but are highly distortionary.

Finally, let me briefly discuss the revenue-loss issue. Two points may be made. First, the debate on this issue has wrongly focused on the magnitude of the loss of revenue. The economically relevant issue is the inefficiency induced by the tax breaks. Revenue losses may also occur when inefficient sources of taxation, such as tariffs, are eliminated. But this is done, and alternative sources of revenue are sought, because tariffs are inefficient means of raising revenue.

Second, many of the tax breaks included in the calculation of the revenue loss by the opponents of the SEZs have existed independently of the SEZs. For example, duty-free status for imported inputs used in exports already exists through duty drawback and duty exemption schemes. The reimbursement of indirect taxes on domestically produced inputs used in exports is also a feature of the existing value-added tax system. Finally, exemption from profits tax on exports exists under current laws. Main new exemptions are two: the ten-year income tax holiday to the operator of the SEZ; and 100 percent profit-tax exemption for five years, and 50 percent profit-tax exemption for another two years for the units located in the SEZ even if the income is generated from domestic sales rather than exports.

Anti-Dumping and Safeguard Measures

India introduced anti-dumping and the traditional safeguard mechanism permitted under Article XIX (called the "escape clause") of the General Agreement on Tariffs and Trade (GATT) and the Uruguay Round Agreement on Safeguard Measures only in the early 1990s. Prior to the 1990s, India had strict import licensing and ultra-high tariffs, which eliminated the need for short-run relief from import surges. But once the country decided to embrace liberalization, political compulsions led to the creation of mechanisms permitting the system to respond to import surges that could injure otherwise viable domestic firms.

Under the traditional escape clause provisions of the GATT, a country can adopt domestic laws that permit it to temporarily roll back tariff reductions to give short-run relief, provided it is demonstrated that imports have been a substantial cause of the injury. An alternative, also permitted under the GATT/WTO, is anti-dumping. Under this provision, a country can selectively impose temporary anti-dumping duties on foreign firms that cause injury to its firms by selling the product at prices below what they charge in their home markets. A key difference between the traditional safeguard measures and anti-dumping duties is that the former are nondiscriminatory, while the latter are applied selectively to the firms charged with dumping. Economists generally consider the nondiscriminatory safeguard measures superior to anti-dumping because such an approach ensures that imports continue to come from the most efficient sources. Typically, anti-dumping targets the most efficient foreign firms, and therefore anti-dumping duties give inefficient firms an edge over the efficient ones.

Unfortunately, India introduced a provision in its safeguards law, not required by the GATT, stipulating that the domestic industry seeking such protection must demonstrate that it is capable of restructuring itself to survive in the long run. Since the anti-dumping law does not have a similar requirement, this provision has led to virtual nonuse of the superior, traditional safeguard measures for temporary relief. It is important for India to repeal this provision.

Setting aside the issue of the choice of the instrument for temporary protection, economists are generally skeptical of the use of temporary protection measures. This is because in practice these measures end up being used to blunt competition from some of the most efficient foreign suppliers. After India introduced the anti-dumping provisions in its laws, it quickly emerged as its top user in the world, displacing the United States. In recent years it has shown some restraint, but it is still among the heaviest users. Figure 12.7 depicts the total number of cases initiated by the major anti-dumping users between 1995 and 2005. With 425 cases initiated during these years, India tops the list, with the United States a distant second (366 initiations). An upward shift in the growth rate of the world economy has led to a sharp decline in the use of anti-dumping in the early 2000s. The total anti-dumping cases worldwide fell from the peak of 354 cases in 1999 to 191 in 2005.

Evidence provided by Aggarwal (2002) points to a strong protectionist motive behind many of the anti-dumping cases initiated by India. She analyzes the anti-dumping cases initiated between 1993 and 2001 and finds that in 76 of these cases, imports accounted for less than 25 percent of the total demand. Within these cases, 33 had less than 5 percent import share, and another 24 had less than 10 percent import share. While such low shares do not entirely preclude the possibility of injury, their preponderance does suggest a strong possibility of misuse of the instrument with protectionist motives.

An important institutional change India must make with respect to its anti-dumping procedures concerns investigations of the dumping duty and injury. The GATT rules require that the country imposing anti-dumping duties must establish two "facts": that the dumping margin, commonly measured by the difference between the prices charged by the foreign firm in its home market and in the market in which it dumps, is positive, and that the dumping has resulted in injury to domestic firms. To ensure independence of the two investigations, they must be conducted by separate agencies. For example, in the United States, the dumping margin is investigated by the Department of Commerce, and the injury charge by the International Trade Commission. In India, both investigations are done by a single agency, the

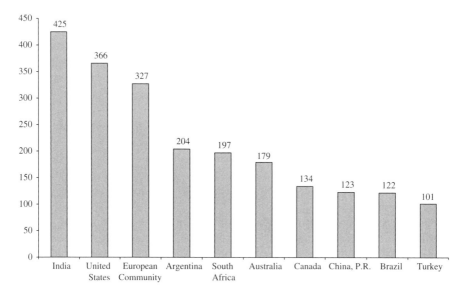

FIGURE 12.7: Anti-Dumping Initiations by the Major Users

Anti-dumping Directorate in the Ministry of Commerce. The natural agency to conduct the injury investigation in India would be the Tariff Commission.

Preferential Trade Area Arrangements

During the 1990s, while the United States and European Union aggressively negotiated the preferential trade area (PTA) arrangements that liberalize trade only with partner countries, and therefore discriminate against nonpartner countries, India chose the high road of unilateral liberalization, under which it lowered trade barriers against all trading partners on a nondiscriminatory basis. Unfortunately, this has now changed. Recognizing that trade blocs in North America and Europe discriminate against them, the countries in Asia, including India, have proceeded to embrace discriminatory PTA arrangements.

Under a PTA arrangement, two or more countries decide to lower trade barriers against imports from each other but keep them unchanged against other countries. If the arrangement involves the elimination of substantially all barriers among the partner countries, it is called a free trade area (FTA) arrangement.[4] In principle, a PTA can improve or worsen efficiency. If it increases trade between union members by eliminating inefficient within-union suppliers and allowing the efficient ones to expand, we call it a trade-creating union, and it is beneficial. But if it increases intra-union trade by diverting trade with outside countries that become less competitive due to tariff preference, despite being more efficient than within-union suppliers, we call the union trade-diverting. In general, trade-creating as well as trade-diverting effects are present, and the outcome depends on which effect dominates. Politics usually works in favor of predominantly trade-diverting unions since they allow inefficient within-union suppliers to survive at the expense of the more efficient outside-union suppliers. This is a key reason why most economists are opposed to liberalization via the PTA route.

An additional reason why economists advise against PTAs is that they fragment the trading system. Under nondiscrimination, each country has a single tariff rate applied to the import of a product, regardless of its origin. But with PTAs, the tariff depends on the specific PTA arrangement the country has with the country of origin of the good. Potentially, the country may apply as many tariff rates to a product as the number of trading partners. We can end up with what the economist Jagdish Bhagwati calls the "Spaghetti Bowl" of tariffs.

A final harmful effect of PTAs follows from the rules of origin that accompany them unless they happen to be customs unions, as is the case with the European Union. In this latter case, the member countries adopt a common external tariff on each product, which eliminates the incentive for them to import a product from outside and reexport it to another union member in order to take advantage of the tariff preference.

Most PTAs are not customs unions, however, and the external tariffs on a product differ across member countries. In this situation, a member with a low tariff on a product has the incentive to import that product from outside and reexport it to a member with a high external tariff. The rules of origin are ostensibly aimed at ensuring that only products produced within the union receive the tariff preference. Typically, they require a prespecified proportion of the value added in a product to originate within the union for the product to qualify for the tariff preference. The member countries can use these rules as protectionist devices, however, by imposing more stringent within-union value-added requirements on imports that threaten domestic producers than on those that threaten outside-union producers.

India has FTA agreements with Sri Lanka and Singapore in place. It also has in place agreements involving the exchange of partial trade preferences on a limited set of commodities with Chile, Mauritius, and the member countries of the South Asian Association for Regional Cooperation. India also expects to sign a comprehensive economic cooperation agreement with the Association of Southeast Asian Nations in July 2007. A South Asian Free Trade Agreement (SAFTA) has been signed, but the list of sectoral exceptions and the rules of origin remain to be negotiated. An agreement for partial trade preferences with the Southern Cone Customs Union, known by its Spanish acronym Mercosur and consisting of Argentina, Brazil, Uruguay, and Paraguay, also has been signed but not implemented. Finally, PTA agreements under consideration include those with China, the South African Customs Union, South Korea, and Japan.

India's agreements with Chile, Mauritius, and the member countries of the South Asian Association for Regional Cooperation are explicitly limited to the exchange of partial preferences on a handful of commodities. The agreement signed with Mercosur, but not yet implemented, falls into the same category. Even the agreements formally termed FTA agreements have long lists of sectoral exclusions and very strict rules of origin.

For example, the India-Sri Lanka FTA, which came into effect in March 2000, makes generous use of sectoral exceptions to minimize competition.[5] The top 20 exports of Sri Lanka to the world at the six-digit Harmonized System level accounted for 46 percent of its total exports in 1999. India subjects as many as 15 of these products to either a tariff rate quota (meaning the tariff preference applies only up to a prespecified quantity of imports) or negative-list exception.

The rules of origin further restrict the exports of Sri Lanka under the FTA arrangement. For example, apparel exports from Sri Lanka are not only subject to the tariff rate quota of eight million pieces, but at least six million of these pieces should be manufactured from fabrics of Indian origin exported to Sri Lanka from India. Likewise, exports of tea from Sri Lanka at the preferential tariff are not to exceed 12.5 million kilograms within a calendar year. Both products are also subject to a uniquely South Asian restriction we may call the rule of destination: The preference applies only if the products enter through specific Indian ports. Similar sectoral exceptions and rules of origin are applied by Sri Lanka to Indian exports.

The India-Singapore FTA likewise contains very stringent rules of origin. It requires that at least 40 percent of the value added be from within the union *and* that the four-digit SITC classification of the product receiving tariff preference be different from that of every intermediate input imported from outside the union contained in it. In many cases, the application of both of these criteria would likely result in a 100 percent within-union value added. India also placed 44 percent of the total tariff lines on the negative list.

These examples raise serious doubts about the wisdom of the PTAs being sought by India. Even when a clean approach is taken, as in the case of the North American Free Trade Agreement, which is a full-fledged FTA, such arrangements are problematic, as is now widely accepted. The partial PTA approach that India has taken is worse because such an approach allows trade diversion to dominate.

A final risk of the PTAs with developed countries such as the United States and European Union may be noted. Both these entities have promoted nontrade issues in their FTA agreements. The United States has been especially aggressive in building WTO plus intellectual property rights, labor and environmental standards, and restrictions on the use of capital controls into its agreements. The European Union has also built democracy and human rights provisions that have little to do with trade barriers into its PTAs. This is a very serious development, since it can eventually weaken the virtually united opposition the developing countries have offered to the inclusion of nontrade issues in the WTO to date.

In this context, India's prime minister and commerce minister are to be applauded for having been completely unequivocal in expressing their opposition to the inclusion of the democracy and human rights clause in the India-European Union trade and investment agreement currently under negotiation. Any weakening of the Indian position in the bilateral negotiations with powerful developed country partners on this front can be fatal to its ability to keep the nontrade issues out of the WTO. Therefore, it should stand firm in its insistence on signing an agreement with the European Union only if it is uncontaminated by trade-unrelated issues such as intellectual property and labor standards.

Multilateral Trade Negotiations

India was one of the 23 founding members of the GATT, which came into existence on January 1, 1948. It is also a founding member of the WTO, which subsumed and succeeded GATT on January 1, 1995. The Uruguay Round of negotiations establishing the WTO was the eighth and technically the last GATT round of multilateral trade negotiations. Along with Brazil, India has been at the forefront of the GATT and WTO as the advocate of the developing countries' interests that it has often found in conflict with the interests of developed countries.

Like most developing countries, India essentially opted out of reciprocal bargains in the negotiations until the Uruguay Round. It devoted its energies and goodwill to lobbying for unilateral concessions from the developed countries for the developing countries. These efforts led to the addition of Part IV, "Trade and Development," to the GATT in 1965. This part did not bring any concessions by itself, but paved the way for them. Specifically, it led to the adoption of a waiver, the Generalized System of Preferences, by the GATT membership on June 25, 1971. This waiver opened the door to one-way trade preferences by the developed to developing countries. In 1979, it was followed by the adoption of the Enabling Clause, which also allowed the developing countries to engage in the exchange of partial trade preferences.

In the run-up to the launch of the eighth GATT round, known as the Uruguay Round (UR), the United States insisted on the active participation of the developing countries in all reciprocal bargains. It proposed a wide-ranging agenda that included negotiations on intellectual property rights and trade in services. India and Brazil led the opposition to the inclusion of services on the agenda. India had feared that an agreement on services would automatically open the door to foreign investment for which it was not prepared at the time. In the end, services were placed on a separate negotiating track with the possibility that countries would be allowed to opt out of signing the agreement on them. But the remaining agenda, including intellectual property rights, agriculture, and the Multi-Fiber Arrangement, became a part of a "single undertaking," which each member was expected to accept or reject in totality.

In the ensuing negotiations, an agreement on intellectual property rights (IPRs) protection emerged as the most contentious issue. The language in the Punta del Este Declaration launching the round gave no indication that, led by the United States, the developed countries wanted to put in place a wide-ranging agreement covering IPRs in all areas. As negotiations progressed, India led the developing countries' demands for building various flexibilities into the draft Agreement on Trade Related Aspects of Intellectual Property Rights (TRIPS). The developing countries, with a comparative advantage in agriculture, also remained dissatisfied with the developed countries' offers in agriculture.

As it turned out, in the course of the negotiations, the developed countries decided to create a new institution, the WTO, which would supersede the GATT. The negotiating member countries were then left with the option either to join the WTO, accepting all its disciplines, or to opt out of it altogether. This was Hobson's choice. India remained opposed to the agreement until the end, but was left with no choice but to sign it after all others had done so.

Under the UR Agreement, India committed to replacing all border barriers on agricultural products with tariffs, and binding the latter.[6] It also undertook obligations for tariff reductions and binding them in both industry and agriculture. Other areas of commitment included liberalization in services and improved IPR standards as per the agreement on TRIPS. Since the end of the implementation period for the UR Agreement on January 1, 2005, India has fully complied with its obligations. The last important and controversial step was a new patent act for pharmaceuticals that provides both product and process patents in all areas for 20 years.

Soon after the conclusion of the UR Agreement, the United States began to push for the inclusion of labor and environmental standards on the WTO agenda. India lobbied particularly hard against this demand, especially labor standards. At the first WTO ministerial conference at Singapore in 1996, it was successful in keeping the labor standards out of the WTO in any form. The Singapore Ministerial Declaration explicitly delegated the issue of labor standards to the International Labor Organization. The issue did not disappear from the WTO agenda, however, and countries such as India and Brazil have had to fight against it at subsequent ministerial meetings, especially at the third WTO ministerial meeting at Seattle in 1999.

Developed countries were, however, successful in introducing four new issues for the WTO study agenda at Singapore: investment, competition policy, government procurement, and trade facilitation. The issues came to be known as the Singapore issues and, unsurprisingly, became a bone of contention between developed and developing countries during the launch of the Doha Round at the fourth WTO ministerial meeting in 2001. The European Union insisted upon turning these issues into negotiating issues.

India's Commerce Minister Murasoli Maran fought hard at Doha, and successfully negotiated sufficiently vague language on the Singapore issues that would allow the developing countries to fight for the eventual exclusion of the issues from

negotiations. Maran was widely criticized in the Western press for being obstruc-
tionist, and even took some heat in the domestic press (Panagariya, 2002f). But in
the end he prevailed: At the fifth WTO ministerial conference at Cancún in 2003,
the European Union agreed to take its demand for negotiations on three of the four
Singapore issues off the table. The only issue that remained on the agenda was trade
facilitation, on which India did not have serious reservations.

In the run-up to the Cancún meeting, the larger developing countries came
together to confront the developed countries through the instrumentality of the G-20
grouping. The formation of the grouping had a dramatic effect on the subsequent
dynamics of the negotiations. It became apparent to the developed countries that the
round could not be completed without bringing the larger developing countries to
the center stage of the negotiations. This led to the replacement of the Old Quad—
the United States, the European Union, Japan, and Canada—that had driven the
past negotiations by what I call the New Quad—the United States, the European
Union, India, and Brazil.

The elimination of the three contentious Singapore issues following the Cancún
ministerial meeting left the Doha Round focused principally on trade liberalization
in agriculture, industry, and services. Among these, agriculture remained the most
difficult area. At the sixth, and most recent, WTO ministerial conference, in Hong
Kong in 2005, the member countries agreed to eliminate the export subsidies in
agriculture by 2013, provided an eventual agreement is reached on the Doha Round
as a whole. The member countries also agreed to provide aid for trade to the least
developed countries, including duty-free access to the developed country markets in
97 percent of the products.

The negotiations between the United States and the EU are currently deadlocked.
The United States demands larger reductions in domestic subsidies and greater market access in agriculture from the European Union than the latter has offered, but
without symmetric concessions of its own. The situation is further complicated by
the fact that the Trade Promotion Authority (TPA) of the U.S. president is set to
expire at the end of June 2007. Without the TPA, it will be virtually impossible for
the United States to complete the round. Both the House and the Senate are currently controlled by Democrats, who are unlikely to renew the TPA without requiring the president to negotiate tougher provisions on labor standards in future trade
agreements, especially the bilateral ones.

The critical question, from India's viewpoint, concerns the stance it should take
in case the TPA is renewed and the United States and the European Union are able
to resolve their differences. At present, India's position is that it is willing to undertake liberalization in industrial products and services. But it has taken a much harder
line on agriculture. The commerce minister has essentially ruled out any significant
liberalization in this sector. In my judgment, this aspect of India's position must be
reassessed.

Despite the presence of large subsidies and high protection in the developed
countries and India's own near prohibitive trade barriers in agriculture, several
agricultural products have shown healthy expansion of exports. With appropriate
policies in place, India has the potential to emerge as a substantial exporter in agriculture. Not too long ago, the argument that Indian industry would fail to withstand
foreign competition was commonly made. Yet, once the exchange rate policy was

set correctly and the trade regime was opened, Indian industry not only survived foreign competition, it began to make its presence felt in the world markets. It will be surprising if this experience is not repeated in agriculture.

The experience of Chile, which has greatly expanded its agricultural exports while liberalizing that sector, reinforces this argument. The opening up will allow efficient agricultural sectors to expand and create high-wage employment opportunities for landless workers. In contrast, farms that provide employment at the margin are themselves barely profitable, and hence unable to pay decent wages. The pressure to become competitive in a more open economy will also speed up agricultural reforms in other areas that are long overdue (see chapter 14).

The implication of these arguments is that while negotiating hard to maximize market access for its exporters, India can benefit from taking a more flexible negotiating position in agriculture in the Doha Round. This is especially true since such liberalization can be leveraged to obtain major concessions from the developed countries in terms of lower agricultural tariffs and subsidies. Insofar as the fear of injury to farmers from imports is concerned, the Framework Agreement of 2004 that defines the broad parameters of the negotiations provides for a special safeguard for agriculture that can be activated relatively rapidly.

CONCLUDING REMARKS

I began by drawing attention to the fact that the unskilled-labor-intensive industry in India has not done as well as would be suggested by relative factor endowments. I then connected this feature to India's performance in the world markets. While liberalization has been followed by very substantial expansion of exports of both goods and services by India, the export growth has been an order of magnitude slower than in China. Likewise, while direct foreign investment has also shown healthy growth, it has been muted relative to China. I have argued that these features are intimately linked to the relatively poor performance of unskilled-labor-intensive manufacturing in India. In the next chapter, I will explore the reasons for the latter phenomenon and suggest policy reforms to stimulate the unskilled-labor-intensive industry.

I have also discussed in detail the key trade policy questions confronting India today. I have argued that India must keep moving forward unilaterally to liberalize trade in industrial products and services. In particular, India must keep lowering the tariffs, begin removing export subsidies, and take various trade facilitation measures to speed up the movement of goods into and out of the country. In agriculture, it may be politically more prudent to pursue liberalization as a part of the Doha Round negotiations. I have reviewed various aspects of the hotly debated special economic zones, concluding that on balance they are worthy of promotion. Finally, I have taken a critical view of the preferential trade area arrangements, favoring liberalization through unilateral and multilateral routes, which are both nondiscriminatory.

13

INDUSTRY AND SERVICES
Walking on Two Legs

I noted in chapter 7 that growth is the single most important instrument of poverty reduction. India's experience conforms to Bhagwati's (1988) hypothesis that rapid growth does not merely "trickle down," but "pulls up" the poor in large numbers into gainful employment. Nevertheless, as Bhagwati (2004, pp. 56–57) further argues, the type of growth matters for how much poverty reduction a given aggregate growth delivers. Rapid growth of unskilled-labor-intensive sectors is likely to create many more opportunities for the poor than rapid growth of capital- and skilled-labor-intensive Sectors.[1] It is here that India has been unsuccessful in taking full advantage of its rapid growth.

If India is to pull its vast workforce from agriculture into the formal economy, it must speed up the growth of its unskilled-labor-intensive industry. Trade liberalization, on which I focused in the previous chapter, is one component of the overall policy package required to achieve that transformation. Being an unskilled-labor-abundant economy, India has a comparative advantage in unskilled-labor-intensive products, and therefore has the potential for exploiting the vast international markets in them. But we saw in the previous chapter that opening up to trade has not been sufficient to achieve rapid growth of unskilled-labor-intensive exports. This suggests that there remain domestic policy constraints that hamper rapid growth of high-quality, unskilled-labor-intensive products that can effectively compete in the world markets. In this chapter, I focus on a set of domestic policy reforms aimed directly at unshackling unskilled-labor-intensive industry. Before I turn to these reforms, however, I present evidence supporting the need for the proposed reforms.

OUTPUT AND EMPLOYMENT PATTERNS

Five interrelated features of the pattern of output and employment have moderated the impact of growth on poverty reduction in India.[2] First, as I have already emphasized in part I of the book, India's growth process has been unique in that despite a very substantial reduction in the share of agricultural output in the GDP, the share of industry in general, and of manufacturing in particular, has not grown since 1990–91. Based on the national income data at 1993–94 prices, the share of agriculture in the Indian GDP fell from 46 percent in 1970–71 to 32 percent in 1990–91 and to 21 percent in 2004–05. Yet over this period, the share of industry moved very little. It rose from 22 percent in 1970–71 to 27 percent in 1990–91, and has stayed there. Correspondingly, the share of manufacturing rose from 13 percent in 1970–71 to 17 percent in 1990–91, and has remained at that level to date. The entire decline in the share of agriculture since 1990–91 has been absorbed by services, which have risen from 32 percent of the GDP in 1970–71 to 41 percent in 1990–91 and 52 percent in 2004–05.

Second, the organized sector, which consists of firms having ten or more workers and using power, and those having 20 or more workers and not using power, remains either capital-intensive or skilled-labor intensive. We saw in part I that from the beginning India wanted to be independent of the world markets, and therefore adopted the promotion of heavy industry as an explicit goal. In the early 1970s, the government confined the successful, large business houses to a group of 19 heavy investment sectors. This naturally created further bias in favor of capital-intensive industries and scuttled the growth of the labor-intensive industry. India also encouraged the engineering goods and chemical industries, which made intensive use of skilled labor.[3] The introduction of the Small-Scale Industries Reservation in April 1967 and its progressive expansion to include virtually all unskilled-labor-intensive products virtually guaranteed that these products would fail to compete on the world markets. Unfortunately, liberalization since the mid-1980s has not been able to correct the bias against unskilled-labor-intensive industry that this regime created.

Table 13.1, which shows the shares of various industry sectors in the GDP and in the total labor force in 1999–2000, sheds some light on the relative patterns of output and employment. The first point to note is that the share of agriculture and allied activities in the labor force in 1999–2000 was 60 percent, but in the GDP it was only 25 percent.[4] On the other hand, manufacturing accounted for 15 percent of the output but only 11 percent of employment in 1999–2000. It is also evident from this table that fast-growing sectors such as communications, construction, and business services (which include software services) are not big employers. Remarkably, finance, insurance, real estate, and business services, which accounted for 13 percent of the GDP in 1999–2000, employed only 1.2 percent of the labor force.

Third, as a consequence of the highly capital-intensive and skilled-labor-intensive character of the organized sector, transition of the labor force from agriculture to nonagricultural activities has been relatively slow. For example, according to the census data, farm workers (cultivators plus agricultural workers) accounted for 67.1 percent of the total workforce in 1991. This proportion fell to only 58.5 percent in 2001. Because the total workforce itself rose during the period, the absolute number of farm workers rose from 210 million to 233 million over this period.

TABLE 13.1: GDP and Employment Shares of Various Sectors, 1999–2000

Industrial Category	Output Share	Employment Share
1	*2*	*3*
1. Agriculture, forestry, & fishing	**25.3**	**60.3**
Nonagricultural	74.7	39.7
2. Mining & quarrying	2.3	0.6
3. Manufacturing	**14.7**	**11.0**
4. Electricity, gas, & water supply	2.5	0.3
5. Construction	5.9	4.4
6. Trade, hotels, & restaurants	14.2	10.3
7. Transport, storage, & communication	7.4	3.7
8. Finance, insurance, real estate, & business services	**13.0**	**1.2**
9. Community, social, & personal services	14.7	8.3
Gross Domestic Product at factor cost (1 to 9)	100.0	100.0

Source: Author's calculations using the GDP data (at 1999–2000 prices) from the CSO and employment data from the PowerPoint file "Informal Sector in India" at www.wageindicator.org/documents/wwwmeetingjune06/informalindia.

Fourth, while nonfarm employment has increased more rapidly than farm employment, as is reflected in the declining share of the latter, the bulk of this increase has been absorbed in the informal, unorganized sector.[5] Some indirect evidence supporting this assertion can be gleaned from the fact that the share of the rural labor force in the total labor force has grown by only a tiny amount. According to the census data, even though the share of the farm workforce fell by nine percentage points during 1990–2000, the share of the rural workforce in the total workforce fell by only two percentage points: from 79.3 percent in 1990–91 to 77.2 percent in 1999–2000. Therefore, the bulk of the shift away from the farm workforce was accounted for by rural industry or rural services, which are predominantly in the informal sector. More directly, according to the available data, employment in the private organized sector in India has been low and stagnant. It stood at 7.5 million (out of the total of 313 million workers) in 1991, peaked at 8.7 million in 1998, and fell back to 8.4 million in 2003.

Table 13.2, constructed from Saha, Kar, and Baskaran (2004, tables 1 and 2), shows the output and employment shares of the informal sector in various industry categories in the year 1999–2000. It is remarkable that outside of agriculture, as much as 88 percent of the labor force continued to be in the informal sector in 1999–2000 even though the output generated there was only 44 percent. Within manufacturing, 94 percent of the labor force was in the informal sector, though only 39 percent of the manufacturing output originated there. Indeed, except in public administration and defense, this pattern held across the board.

Yet one more piece of evidence that reinforces this picture comes from the Economic Census, which covers *all* entrepreneurial units located in India, regardless of size or sector (excluding crop production and plantations). According to the latest of these censuses, conducted in 2005, of the 42 million enterprises countrywide, only 1.4 percent employed ten or more workers.[6] The total number of workers employed in all enterprises was 99 million. Even under the conservative assumption

TABLE 13.2: Shares of Informal Sector Output and Employment by Industry, 1999–2000

Industry	Percentage Share in GDP, by Sector		Percent Share of Informal Employment
	Formal	Informal	
Agriculture	3.2	—	99.2
Forestry and logging	5.6	—	98.3
Fishing	0.1	—	98.5
Agriculture, forestry & logging, and fishing	3.1	—	99.1
Mining and quarrying	91.6	8.4	90.7
Manufacturing	60.8	39.2	94.9
Electricity, gas, & water supply	93.8	6.2	90.1
Construction	41.8	58.2	85.8
Trade	18.1	81.9	84.7
Hotels and restaurants	41.2	58.8	90.7
Transport & storage	35.2	64.8	79.3
Communication	91.4	8.6	92.8
Banking and insurance	90.5	9.5	88.7
Real estate, ownership of dwellings, and business services	18.6	81.4	89.9
Public administration & defense	100.0	0.0	0.4
Other services	69.5	30.5	87.4
Nonagricultural, other than paid domestic workers	56.0	44.0	88.3
Hired domestic workers	—	—	100.0
Total	42.0	32.4	95.6

Source: Saha, Kar, and Baskaran (2004, tables 1 and 2). This table reproduces table 2 with two modifications: (1) it eliminates the third column, and (2) it replaces the last column with the last column in table 1.

of two workers per enterprise, approximately 83 million workers would belong to the informal sector enterprises (enterprises with less than ten workers). All evidence points to a highly fragmented production structure of nonfarm activity in India, whether in industry or services.

Finally, the pattern of savings also points in this same direction. Corporate savings in China rose from the hefty 22 percent of GDP in 2000 to 29 percent in 2005. In contrast, private corporate savings in India are tiny: 8.1 percent in 2005–06. Dramatically, even the GDP share of the Indian corporate sector is less than 29 percent. Instead, it is household savings that supply the bulk of the investment funds in India. Astonishingly, household investment accounts for as much as 13 percent of GDP. Household investment of this magnitude is yet another indicator of a very substantial informal sector in the economy. Moreover, recognizing that the bulk of the financially intermediated household savings is absorbed by the fiscal deficit, corporate sector investment is relatively limited.

RESPONSE TO TWO OBJECTIONS

Two distinct objections may be raised to the rapid expansion of manufacturing, especially unskilled-labor-intensive manufacturing, as a centerpiece of the growth strategy: first, in view of the shift toward capital- and skilled-labor-intensive technologies, the traditional path to transformation through the expansion of manufacturing is no longer available; and, second, India can chart its own course by following a development path that relies on services rather than manufacturing.

According to the first argument, technology has so much shifted in favor of skilled-labor-intensive technology that countries transitioning out of agriculture today do not have the option to rely on unskilled-labor-intensive manufacturing that was available to the countries such as the Republic of Korea, Taiwan, and even China, which achieved a significant part of their transformation in the 1990s. According to this argument, today, robots have come to replace unskilled workers on the assembly lines.

This argument sounds plausible, but is flawed. While technologies in many industries have shifted toward greater skill requirements, those in apparel, footwear, toys, sports goods, and travel goods have not changed as dramatically. These sectors continue to employ vast numbers of unskilled workers around the world. But even granting this point, the proponents of the argument are wrong. For any *given* set of technologies, some products remain more unskilled-labor-intensive than others. Therefore, greater expansion of unskilled-labor-intensive sectors still offers greater scope for the employment of unskilled labor. How much greater depends on the *relative* differences in the factor intensities and the magnitude of expansion. No evidence is available showing that shifts in technologies have narrowed the relative differences between unskilled-labor intensities across sectors. As for the magnitude of expansion, the world markets offer huge scope for it. If policies are right, India could replace China as the manufacturing hub of unskilled-labor-intensive products of the world.

The proponents of the second argument against the development strategy centered on unskilled-labor-intensive products do not question the existence of such products, but argue that India need not follow the conventional growth path whereby the share of industry grows at the expense of agriculture in the early stages of development, but yields to services in the later stages. According to these analysts, given its vast stock of skilled labor and its lead in the information technology sector, it is natural for India to grow rapidly in services, skip industrialization, and leapfrog into the services stage. To put it dramatically, India need not become South Korea on the way to becoming the United States.

This is an enticing scenario, but it is hopelessly flawed. While software and communications services have shown rapid growth in recent years, given their tiny share in the economy, they have made only a minuscule contribution to the growth of services. Much of the growth in services has come from informal services such as trade, transport, and community services. More important, while it is feasible to move significant numbers of workers from agriculture into well-paid jobs in formal manufacturing activities, it is not feasible to move them to formal services sectors for two reasons. First, as table 13.2 shows, formal services sectors such as such as banking, insurance, finance, communications, and information technology have relatively low employment intensity. Second, and more important, employment in manufacturing requires only on-the-job training, whereas employment in the formal services requires at least a college-level education. A strategy that relies exclusively on services as the engine of growth must provide a minimum of fifteen years of education before workers are transferred out of agriculture. This is not feasible for the existing adult workers in agriculture.

But this is not all, since the chances of success of such a policy rest critically on the ability of the country to mobilize resources to achieve significant expansion of higher education. In 2002, the number of those (young or old) in college as a proportion of the population aged 19 to 24 was only 9 percent. Raising this proportion to even 20 percent within ten years is beyond the capacity of the current higher education system. The proportion of the GDP spent on higher education has progressively declined over the last several decades. And given the stringent fiscal constraints faced by the central and state governments, the prospects for a rapid expansion of public investment in higher education are quite bleak (see chapter 20).

This analysis leads to the conclusion that if India is to transition to a modern economy in less than two decades, it cannot escape the industrialization stage. This is not to suggest that the modern services sector, including software and telecommunications, should not be a centerpiece of the transition strategy. Given the strengths acquired recently in this sector and its importance to rapid industrialization, it will be nonsensical for anyone to advocate a transition in which this sector is relegated to the backseat. Instead, India must walk on two legs as it transitions to a modern economy: traditional industry, especially unskilled-labor-intensive manufacturing, and modern services such as software and telecommunications. Each leg needs to be strengthened through a set of policy initiatives.[7]

THE LABOR MARKET RIGIDITIES

Missing from the Indian manufacturing scene are the large-scale firms producing unskilled-labor-intensive products.[8] This is best illustrated by a comparison of the apparel firms in India with those in China, Bangladesh, and Sri Lanka. Whereas the firms in these latter countries often employ thousands of workers under a single roof, those in India remain tiny, frequently consisting of shops with less than 50 tailors. The composition of exports discussed in chapter 12 complements this story. India's leading exports are mostly capital- or skilled-labor-intensive. Apparel is among its leading exports, but the country's share in the important U.S. market is approximately the same as that of much smaller Bangladesh. To be sure, large firms do exist in India. But these are mainly concentrated in either capital-intensive industries such as steel, automobiles, petroleum, and power, or in skilled-labor-intensive sectors such as software, pharmaceuticals, and banking. In many cases, the large-scale firms are in the public sector.

Small-Scale-Industries Reservation No Longer the Culprit

The reforms undertaken to date have brought four important changes that open the door wider to the entry of large-scale firms and allow them to meet the quality standards expected in the world markets:

- Imports have been liberalized so that the lack of access to high-quality inputs is no longer a constraining factor.

- With the end of the investment-licensing regime, big business houses are no longer confined to heavy industry.
- The Foreign Exchange Regulation Act, 1973 has been repealed, and the door has been opened to foreign investors.
- The list of products reserved for production exclusively by small-scale enterprises has been progressively trimmed.

Unfortunately, however, these reforms have not yielded satisfactory outcomes in manufacturing. The latter has continued to grow at approximately the same rate as the overall GDP, so that its share in the GDP has remained virtually unchanged since the early 1990s. Judging from the export performance, unskilled-labor-intensive manufacturing has done even more poorly; its share in the total exports has declined.

It is tempting to attribute this outcome to the slow process of trimming the small-scale-industries (SSI) reservation list. This process got under way only in 1997 and is still incomplete, with the total number of products on the list declining from 821 in 1998–99 to 239 in January 2007. But this explanation fails to withstand closer scrutiny.

Many items, including toys, footwear, and several apparel products, have been off the reservation list for several years now. More important, even for products still on the SSI list, large-scale production has been permitted since at least March 2000, as long as the unit exports 50 percent or more of its output. This latter change means that firms predominantly interested in exporting their output have been free of the SSI reservation in all products since at least March 2000. While there remains a strong case for abolishing the SSI list and assisting smaller enterprises through fiscal measures within reasonable limits, it is a mistake to expect that dereservation by itself will lead to the emergence of large-scale manufacturing.

The Tyranny of the Labor Market Regulations

I have argued for some years now that the key barrier to the emergence of large-scale, unskilled-labor-intensive firms is the complex set of labor laws they face in India.[9] If a firm using power chooses to employ less than ten workers (20 if not using power), it stays in the unorganized sector and is subject to minimal labor market regulations.[10] Once a firm using power has ten or more employees (20 or more if not using power), it becomes a part of the organized sector. It is subject to the Factories Act of 1948, which brings the powerful labor inspector to its doorstep. Under the act, the firm is subject to a large number of regulations relating to the facilities on premises, safety of workers, overtime, and employment of women and children. At 20 or more workers, a firm operating in any of 177 specified industries or classes of establishments also becomes subject to the Employees Provident Funds and Miscellaneous Provisions (EPFMP) Act of 1952, which requires it to set up retirement funds (see the discussion of pension reforms in chapter 11). At 50 workers or more, the firm must offer mandatory health insurance under the Employee State Insurance Act of 1948 and be subject to the worker-management dispute resolution process under the Industrial Disputes Act (IDA) of 1947. Once the firm reaches 100 workers or more, it effectively loses the rights to fire workers or to reassign them to alternative tasks under the IDA.

Although Zagha (1998) mentions the existence of 45 different national and state-level labor legislations, it is the IDA of 1947 that has the most detrimental effect on the entry of large firms into unskilled-labor-intensive industries. The legislation applies to firms with 50 or more workers. It governs the relations between workers and management, and the settlement of disputes between them; rules relating to the reassignment of a worker to different tasks; and the conditions of layoff, retrenchment, and closure. In each area, the legislation stacks the deck disproportionately against the management.[11]

First, the legislation confers the power to regulate labor-management relations on the labor department with jurisdiction over the firm (usually the labor department of the state where the firm is located). The department first tries reconciling the two sides. If this process fails, it refers the matter to the labor judiciary. The latter predominantly rules in favor of the workers.[12] Labor unions like this system since it greatly increases their bargaining power over management. Indeed, an effort in 1950 to replace the IDA with alternative legislation that would have largely freed labor-management relations from state intervention was defeated by the trade unions.

Second, under section 9A of the IDA an employer must give three weeks' written notice to the worker of any change in working conditions. These changes include (a) changes in shift work, (b) changes in grade classification, (c) changes in rules of discipline, (d) a technological change that may affect the demand for labor, and (e) changes in employment, occupation, process, or department. The worker has the right to object to these changes, which may culminate in an industrial dispute and the associated cost in terms of time and financial resources. This provision makes it very difficult for the firm to respond quickly to technological changes or changes in demand conditions.

Finally, and most important, an amendment to the IDA in 1976 added chapter V.B, which made it mandatory for firms with 300 or more workers to seek the permission of the Labor Department for layoffs, retrenchment, or closure. The permission is seldom forthcoming, however. A further amendment in 1982 made this provision applicable to firms with 100 or more workers. Therefore, under the current provisions, a firm with 100 or more workers effectively has no right to retrench or lay off workers, or even to closure. Even when it is bankrupt, it must pay the workers out of profits in other operations.

Implications of the Labor Law Regime

The labor law regime in India has disproportionately strengthened the hand of the unions in the organized sector. This has resulted in wages in the organized sector that are substantially higher than those in the unorganized sector. For example, Glinskaya and Lokshin (2005) calculate that the wages in the public sector in 1999–2000 were on the average 2.1 times those in the private formal sector and 3.8 times those in the private informal sector. This makes the wages in the private formal sector 1.8 times those in the private informal sector. The authors also find that the proportionate wage differential between public and private formal sectors is larger at lower levels of skill. If this pattern also holds across private formal and informal sector wages, the proportionate differential across formal and informal sector unskilled wages would exceed 1.8.

This wage differential impacts unskilled-labor-intensive industry disproportionately more than capital-intensive industry. The reason is that labor costs are a tiny proportion of the total costs of the latter. Thus the wage differential has smaller impact on the overall cost structure of capital-intensive industries. This is one of the key explanations why large-scale manufacturing firms are concentrated in the capital-intensive sectors.

Quite apart form high wages, the absence of the option to exit at a reasonable cost discouraged the entry of large-scale firms into unskilled-labor-intensive sectors. Firms in these industries operate on relatively low profit margins. This makes them more vulnerable to price and cost fluctuations. Therefore, if they face the prospects of having to pay a vast labor force its wages even after the firm has become unprofitable, they choose not to enter the industry in the first place.

Responding to the Skeptics

While the vast majority of economists see the reform of labor market policies as crucial to stimulating manufacturing in general and unskilled-labor-intensive industry in particular, they are by no means unanimous on it. Skeptics of this view make several counterarguments requiring response.

First, some skeptics argue that when firms are interviewed for business environment surveys, they do not point to labor market rigidities as one of the most constraining factors. The problem with this argument, however, is that it is based on a biased sample in the first place. Small-scale-industries reservation and the stringency of labor laws have systematically kept large-scale firms out of unskilled-labor-intensive sectors. As for the large-scale firms operating in either capital-intensive or skilled-labor-intensive sectors which are present in these samples, labor laws probably do not constitute the most pressing problem. The very fact that they have chosen to enter the market suggests that these restrictions are not insurmountable for them. For instance, we should certainly not expect the CEO of Infosys, a software firm, to complain about labor laws as the most pressing problem facing his firm. For him, a high-quality labor force, airports, and urban infrastructure are likely to be more important. If we want to genuinely investigate the implications of labor market rigidities for unskilled-labor-intensive products, the right question to ask would be why the existing firms chose not to go into manufacturing toys, footwear, and apparel on a massive scale. Anecdotal evidence suggests that when the question is put this way, the CEOs of the existing firms are quick to point to labor market rigidities as the primary cause.[13]

Second, some skeptics argue that labor laws do not figure prominently as major constraints in the business environment surveys because firms are able to get around them by resorting to contract labor. Contract labor is not subject to the rigors of the IDA . There is no doubt that profit-maximizing firms look for ways around costly regulations, including bribes to the relevant officials to escape the regulations. Thus there is some merit in this argument. But it misses three crucial facts:

1. Only those firms which choose to enter the market have the option to hire contract labor to evade the IDA regulations. But the IDA turns away large-scale firms from entering unskilled-labor-intensive sectors in the first place. Prior to

liberalization, many advocates of investment and import licensing also argued that firms were able to work around them. But there were many firms that failed to enter the market in the first place.

2. Getting around the regulations is costly. Again, licensing offers an apt example. To be sure, many firms found ways to work around it, but this was costly.

3. Finally, the Contract Labor Regulation and Abolition Act of 1970 authorizes the government with jurisdiction over an establishment to prohibit the latter from employing contract labor if the work is perennial in nature, necessary for the functioning of the establishment, or being done by regular employees in other establishments. Many states do so.

The third argument made by skeptics of labor market reform is that only 10 percent of India's labor force is in the organized sector. The remaining 90 percent is employed in the unorganized sector, where labor laws have virtually no bite and the markets are more flexible than perhaps anywhere else in the world. I must say that the proponents of this argument are victims of elementary confusion. As much as 90 percent of the labor force remains in the unorganized sector precisely because labor market rigidities discourage firms from entering the organized sector. To dramatize the point, imagine increasing the rigidities in the organized sector further, to the point that 95 percent of the labor force is pushed into the unorganized sector. A naïve observer might conclude from this that labor markets have become even more flexible as a result. But such an inference would be absurd. If we are interested in the welfare of the workers, we should be creating conditions for increased job opportunities in the organized, not the unorganized, sector.

Finally, Bardhan (2006) offers a slight variation on the above argument, contending that low growth in the employment prospects of unskilled workers cannot be attributed to labor market rigidities in the organized sector since the bulk of the workforce is in the unorganized sector, where workers have virtually no rights. To quote him:

> In particular employment growth at the low-skill levels has been quite disappointing so far, and to blame this on the restrictive labor laws (applicable to the large factory sector) is asking the tail to wag too large a dog....

But this is an altogether misleading argument. Those of us advocating labor market reform do not blame labor market rigidities for the slow growth of unskilled employment *in aggregate*. That would indeed be nonsensical, since even 20 percent growth in 10 percent of the total jobs located in the organized sector will produce only 2 percent growth in aggregate jobs. Instead, we hold labor market rigidities responsible for the slow or no growth of unskilled employment *in the organized sector*, which has much greater potential for generating such employment than it has done so far. We also blame these rigidities for India's slow pace of *transition* from a traditional to a modern economy. The more favorable the environment for the growth of unskilled employment in the organized sector, the larger the base of well-paid unskilled jobs will be and the more it will be able to impact the overall growth in unskilled jobs in general. Recall that in 1991, exports of goods and services were only 7 percent of the GDP. Today they are in excess of 21 percent. If the organized sector jobs had been similarly growing since the early 1990s, they would today account for a much larger proportion of the total jobs than 10 percent.

What Can Be Done?

In reforming the labor laws, ideally we would want to return to the attempt made in 1950 to replace the IDA of 1947 with an entirely new legislation that would redefine the worker-management relations and rebalance the rights and obligations of workers in accordance with international best practice. But the current political realities rule out such far-reaching reform. Therefore, the reform process will have to be piecemeal. Three sets of reforms are worthy of immediate attention.

First, a minimalist reform would be to give the firms that are unprofitable for three consecutive years the right to exit smoothly after workers have been paid appropriate severance pay. To make the reform politically feasible, substantially more generous severance pay and unemployment and retraining benefits than are currently available may be offered. Under this reform, workers will retain the current rights of employment as long as the firm does not run at a loss for three consecutive years. The right to fire would become available to the firm only when it is left with no option but to exit.

An alternative approach would be to give the firms in the organized sector the right to fire newly hired workers, with the rights of the workers currently employed remaining unchanged. The reform would offer more generous unemployment and retraining benefits and severance pay than are currently available, in return for the restoration of the employer's right to retrench or lay off workers. Existing employees who choose to opt out of the old system can be given such an option.

The second area requiring reform concerns the conditions under which workers can be reassigned to other tasks. These conditions must be made more flexible. With technology and demand conditions shifting rapidly in today's global marketplace, flexibility in the reassignment of workers is an important condition of survival of a firm.

Finally, an avenue must be found to achieving speedy resolution of worker-management disputes. Under the current system, disputes automatically go to the labor department with jurisdiction over the firm. Consultation and conciliation conducted by the labor department are ineffective; workers do not participate, choosing instead to go to adjudication because labor courts almost always rule in their favor. In turn labor courts are slow, taking ten years to rule, on the average. Resolution takes even longer if we include appeals. There is a clear and urgent need to streamline the procedures so as to bring the disputes to speedy resolution in a timely fashion. The reform must make the conciliation more effective by providing that the failure to participate will result in the loss of the right to take the case to adjudication. The adjudication process itself needs to be speeded up, perhaps by setting up labor tribunals whose decisions can be appealed only in the High Court of the state with jurisdiction or in the Supreme Court.

As discussed in chapter 12, the Special Economic Zones Act of 2005 gives the states some flexibility for the relaxation of labor laws. But the true extent of this relaxation remains to be tested. Gujarat is said to have offered these flexibilities in its special economic zones, but it is not clear whether the firms have found it credible. If the experience in the SEZs does turn out to be successful, it may become politically easier to extend the policy nationwide.

At the other extreme, India needs to improve the protection of workers in the informal sector. Here the solutions have to be in the form of insurance (of which the employment guarantee scheme may be a part), funded pension schemes, medical insurance in case of hospitalization, and vocational training. The introduction of more labor laws aimed at increasing protection to labor will only expand the inspector raj further, and is likely to be counterproductive.

COMPLEMENTARY REFORMS

Firms in India operate in a world with virtually no exit doors. This is graphically illustrated by the data on bankruptcies. According to the World Bank (2005c, p. 7 and figure 2,6), India has a bankruptcy rate of 4 per 10,000 firms, compared with 14 in Thailand and more than 350 in the United States. Equally telling is the time it takes to complete bankruptcy proceedings in India. The initial decision to liquidate a firm often takes several years. Once that decision is made, the process of liquidation is extremely long. According to the Justice V. B. Eradi Committee (2000), as of December 31, 1999, 48 percent of the liquidation cases handled by the official liquidator (see below) had been in process for more than ten years, and 15 percent for more than 25 years.

If workers are to be laid off, it is important that payments due them be made expeditiously. Therefore, it is essential that the reform of the labor laws be balanced by the introduction of a transparent and time-bound bankruptcy procedure. In turn, this requires two further reforms: repeal of the Urban Land (Ceiling and Regulation) Act (ULCRA) of 1976 by the states that have not done so, and creation of a transparent bankruptcy law.

Repeal of the ULCRA of 1976

In chapter 3, I discussed the introduction of the ULCRA of 1976, which placed a tight ceiling on vacant land that individuals and firms could hold in an urban agglomeration. The ceiling varied from 500 to 2000 square meters, with the lower limit applying to the great cities. Holders of excess vacant land had either to sell it for a nominal price to the government or to develop it only for specified purposes. The ostensible objective behind the act was the prevention of the concentration of urban land in the hands of a few individuals or firms. But the result was the opposite. Often the most valuable asset of an unprofitable firm was land. Since the act prohibited the firm from selling it at the market price, the firm chose not to exit, and held on to the precious piece of land. This made urban land in the major cities extremely expensive. Until as late as 2002, the Planning Commission (2002) reported that only 19,020 hectares of urban land had been acquired under the ULCRA.

Recognizing the futility of the policy, the central government repealed ULCRA in 1999–2000. But under the Indian Constitution, the states have the power to legislate on urban land as well. Therefore, the repeal of the ULCRA by the central government meant only that the states were not obligated to retain the ceiling on urban land. To actually abolish the ceiling, the states needed to repeal their own laws. Some states—including Punjab, Uttar Pradesh, Madhya Pradesh, Rajasthan, Gujarat, and Haryana—have done this. But others—including Andhra Pradesh, Maharashtra, Kerala, and Orissa—have not.

Recently, the central government initiated a scheme for urban renewal known as the Jawaharlal Nehru National Urban Renewal Mission (JNNURM). Under the scheme, the central government provides very substantial funds for the modernization of more than 60 major cities to the states where these cities are located (see chapter 18). It has made the repeal of the urban land ceiling a precondition for the allocation of these funds. Unfortunately, despite the urgent need for such funds for a city like Mumbai, the state of Maharashtra has not acted to repeal the ceiling.

Bankruptcy Laws

In the United States, a firm in deep financial trouble may file (or be forced to file by its creditors) for bankruptcy in a federal court under chapter 7 of the U.S. Bankruptcy Code. The firm ceases all its functions as soon as it files the application. The court immediately appoints a trustee who expeditiously liquidates the company's assets and uses the proceeds to pay off its debts. Secured creditors, such as bondholders and mortgage lenders, get priority in debt repayment.

Alternatively, an ailing firm can file (or be forced to file by its creditors) for "reorganization" under chapter 11 of the same code. This is the preferred alternative of most firms, since it allows the management to continue to run the day-to-day business operations and influence the bankruptcy proceedings. Upon filing, the court appoints a trustee who in turn appoints one or more committees to represent the interests of creditors and stockholders. The committees negotiate a plan with the firm that usually forgives a part of its debt to help it get back on its feet. Once the creditors and the firm are agreed on the plan, the court reviews it to confirm that it complies with the Bankruptcy Code. The court takes a few months to complete the confirmation process, after which the plan can be implemented.

Nothing resembling chapters 7 and 11 bankruptcy procedures of the United States exists in India. What exists is a complex set of alternative procedures that are highly inefficient and take ten years, on the average, to bring the cases to a close. The government attempted a reform via the Companies (Amendment) Act of 2002, but legal challenges have so far precluded its implementation. I will return to this reform after completing the discussion of the existing procedures. There are four different avenues to bankruptcy currently in existence: three through the Companies Act, 1956 and one through the Sick Industrial Companies (Special Provisions) Act (SICA), 1985. In addition, banks have an alternative, direct recourse: claiming the assets of their debtors when the latter miss payments. This route was introduced in 1993 and considerably strengthened in 2002.

Bankruptcy under the Companies Act of 1956

Chapter VII of the Companies Act, 1956 offers three avenues to bankruptcy, which the act uniformly calls "winding up of the company":

- Winding up by the High Court on account of insolvency (sections 433 to 483).[14]
- Voluntary winding up by a solvent company (sections 484 to 497).
- Voluntary winding up by creditors of an insolvent company (sections 498 to 521).

Courts have the power to bring voluntary winding up by the company or creditors under their supervision as described in sections 522 to 527. Finally, sections 528 to 559 contain provisions that apply to all forms of winding up under the Companies Act. They describe, for example, who among employees and various creditors has priority in being paid in case of an insolvent company being wound up.

Under the first provision, the most common trigger is the inability of the company to pay its debts. If a creditor has served a notice to the company demanding payment of a debt of 500 rupees or more, and the company has not paid the debt within three weeks, the creditor can approach the court for an order to wind up the company. An application for winding up on the ground that the company is unable to pay its debt can also be made to the court by the company or its creditors and contributories.[15] Upon such application, if the court determines that the company is indeed unable to pay its debt, it can order winding up the company.

Between the application and the decision to wind up the company, the court may appoint a provisional liquidator, who acquires control of all assets and claims of the company. Otherwise, the debtors keep control of the company. Once the court reaches the decision to wind up, the control of all assets and claims of the company passes to the official liquidator (OL), an appointee of the central government attached to the court. The OL serves as the liquidator of the company and enjoys wide-ranging powers in that capacity (section 457).

Under the second provision in the Companies Act, 1956, a company can voluntarily wind up by passing a resolution to that effect, provided it is solvent. To fulfill the latter requirement, a majority of the directors must provide a declaration of solvency verified by an affidavit. The company ceases business once the resolution is passed. The company appoints one or more liquidators, after which the company board loses all its powers. The liquidator must dispose of the assets and liabilities as per the law.

Finally, under the third provision, creditors of a company can voluntarily wind up a company that is insolvent. They are also empowered to do this if in the course of the proceedings of a voluntary winding up by the company, the liquidator discovers that the assets of the company are insufficient to cover its liabilities, so that the company is insolvent. Under this provision, the creditors rather than the company board appoint the liquidator.

An important feature of the Companies Act, 1956 is that whatever avenue is chosen for winding up the company, workers and secured creditors have the highest priority for being paid what is due them. If the assets are insufficient to pay them fully, the proceeds are divided between them in equal proportions. The government and the wages and salaries of employees not classified as workers have the next priority. Unsecured creditors have the lowest priority.

Bankruptcy under the SICA of 1985

This avenue was created in response to industrial sickness in the early 1980s. The objective was to detect financially weak firms at an early stage so that they could be restructured. The act created the quasi-judicial body known as the Board of Industrial and Financial Restructuring (BIFR) for this purpose. It provides that *industrial companies that have been registered for five or more years, and have accumulated* losses at the end of any year in excess of net worth, are sick and must apply within 60 days to the BIFR for restructuring or winding up. As of December 31, 2004, 4940 private companies, 88 central government public sector units, and 119 state public sector units were registered with the BIFR. Together, they employed 1.77 million workers.[16]

Upon the completion of its review, the BIFR may come to the conclusion that the company cannot be revived, and send it to the relevant High Court for winding up. At the other extreme, it may find that the management filed a false case through accounting manipulation. In this case, it dismisses the case. In between, the BIFR can exercise one of two options: it can approve a plan for restructuring sponsored by the management and creditors of the company, but without any financial assistance; or it can declare the rehabilitation of the firm in the "public interest" and approve a plan requiring concessions from creditors and subsidies from the government. Any action taken by the BIFR can be challenged in the courts by the management or creditors. Under such circumstances, courts often return the case to the BIFR.

The Breakdown of Bankruptcy Procedures

Only the cases of voluntary windup of companies, which are a tiny proportion of the total number of cases, come to a swift conclusion. All other cases take an extremely long time, with the average being ten years or more. As previously noted, as of December 31, 1999, 48 percent of the cases handled by the OL had been in the works for more than ten years and 15 percent for more than 25 years. The vast majority of the cases go through BIFR, which itself takes a long time before making a decision in favor of restructuring or sending the case to the court for winding up. Kang and Nayar (2003–04, table 1) report data showing that the average life of the cases recommended for restructuring in 2002 was seven years, and of those recommended to the court for winding up, 6.5 years.

The Justice V. B. Eradi Committee (2000), appointed to examine the existing system with a view to reforming it, provides a horrifying account of the hurdles the OL faces in winding up the companies. At every stage from getting the initial statement of affairs from the ex-directors of the company to debt realization, settlement of the list of creditors and contributories, and the disposal of misfeasance proceedings, the OL must file court cases. And given the speed with which the Indian civil courts move, long delays in completing the proceedings are guaranteed.

Under the law, ex-directors are required to file a statement of affairs with the OL within 21 days of the winding-up order. But the norm is no filing for years. The Eradi Committee notes that the OL in Mumbai had received the statement of affairs in less than 5 percent of the cases. In the default cases, the OL must file prosecutions before the High Court and convince it that the default is "without reasonable cause." The statement of affairs is the main source of information on the assets, debts, and creditors of the company. Delays in receiving it or receiving it in incomplete form necessarily hampers progress at various stages of winding up.

At the next stage, the OL needs accounts books to verify the assets and liabilities, which are frequently either unavailable or incomplete. He may once again have to seek the help of the courts to obtain complete records from the ex-directors. Once the assets and liabilities are identified, the OL must recover funds from the company's reluctant debtors. In cases of nonpayment, he is required by law to file cases in the court, and, if directed by the judge, must do so even in cases involving a debt of as little as 150 rupees. The Justice Eradi Committee (2000, chap. 3) notes a case in which the Delhi OL had to file over 12,000 cases against the debtors.

After the OL has obtained a decree against the debtor, he must locate the asset and take possession of it. Given the resources of the OL and the functioning of the executive branch of the government at the local level, often both steps take a long time. Many times, the asset itself is in dispute due to clandestine transfer of rights by the debtor. Courts have to step in once again. In the case of industrial companies, the assets are often mortgaged with the secured creditors who remain outside the winding-up proceedings and will hand over the assets only to the court receiver. The Justice Eradi Committee (2000, chap. 3) reports that the Mumbai OL encountered four industrial companies that took 15 to 20 years to hand over the assets to the court receiver. The auction of assets itself is time-consuming, since the OL must seek court guidance at each stage.

The process of settlement with creditors is also involved. If the books are incomplete, the OL must first ascertain the list of legitimate creditors and their priority status under the Companies Act of 1956. Aggrieved creditors appeal to the court. Trade unions often file exaggerated claims on behalf of the workers, which lead to further court battles.

Finally, the OL has the right to file malfeasance proceedings against the delinquent ex-directors within five years from the order of winding up. The OL files these proceedings in virtually all cases, as a matter of routine. At the time the Justice Eradi Committee submitted its report, these cases had been pending in the courts for five to ten years.

The BIFR process, which precedes the liquidation proceedings in the case of sick companies, also takes a long time in the cases of companies for which the end outcome is either restructuring or winding up. The delays partially result from slow replies from secured creditors regarding concessions by them for the revival of the company. In the case of public sector undertakings, the relevant government responds slowly to inquiries related to revival. They are also slow to give consent to winding up when revival is not feasible. Finally, decisions by the BIFR can be challenged in the High Court, which usually sends such cases back to the BIFR.

A Major Bankruptcy Reform Held Hostage by the Judiciary

Based on the recommendations of the Justice Eradi Committee (2000), the central government introduced the Companies (Second Amendment) Act of 2002, which seeks far-reaching reform of both bankruptcy and restructuring laws. The amendment has many important features:

1. It takes High Courts entirely out of bankruptcy and restructuring proceedings by establishing the National Company Law Tribunals (NCLT) and the National Company Law Appellate Tribunal. All legal proceedings relating to the winding up and restructuring of companies are to be conducted the Law Tribunals, and their decisions can be appealed only in the Appellate Tribunal, which must give its decision within 60 days. In turn, the decisions of the

Appellate Tribunal can be appealed only in the Supreme Court. The amendment explicitly bars civil courts from entertaining any litigation under the jurisdiction of the Law Tribunal, which is empowered to create branches and special branches to discharge its functions.

2. The amendment replaces the SICA of 1985 and the BIFR with its part VIA, titled "Revival and Rehabilitation of Sick Industrial Companies," which gives complete jurisdiction over rehabilitation and restructuring to the Law Tribunal. The definition of sickness has been changed so that sickness is detected early. Accordingly, a company is sick if either (1) its accumulated losses in any financial year equal 50 percent or more of its average net worth during the immediately preceding four years or (2) it has failed to repay its debts, upon written demand by a creditor, within any three consecutive quarters.

3. In the case of a private company, the Law Tribunal can act on referral by the managers, petition by creditors, or on its own initiative. In the case of public sector enterprises, the enterprise must report upon approval by the relevant government. As soon as sickness is registered, the Law Tribunal appoints an operating agency, which must produce a preliminary report on whether the company should be restructured within one month. The Law Tribunal simultaneously appoints a director to the board of the company to safeguard the assets and to give a statement of affairs within two months. The operating agency and creditors are then given two months to submit their own restructuring schemes. The Law Tribunal then issues a restructuring plan within two months. Alternatively, if the decision is to wind up the company, the Law Tribunal appoints a liquidator, who must wind up the company in one year. Appeals to the Appellate Tribunal and the Supreme Court, and decisions by them, can take another 9.5 months.

4. To protect the interest of the workers, the amendment provides for a cess (tax) on all companies other than the sick companies at a rate up to 0.1 percent of the revenues. The proceeds go to the Rehabilitation and Revival Fund to be used by the Law Tribunal to make interim wage payments to the workers of sick firms, protect the assets of those firms, and revive and rehabilitate them.

There is no doubt that the amendment marks a very substantial improvement over the existing bankruptcy procedures. But it still allows for excessive centralization of authority in the hands of the Law Tribunal with respect to restructuring. Unlike chapter 11 proceedings, under which a restructuring plan acceptable to the debtors and creditors prevails, the amendment gives the final word to the Law Tribunal. This is likely to undermine the success of the restructuring plan.[17]

Unfortunately, the process of setting up the Law Tribunals and the Appellate Tribunal has been held up by successful challenges to the term and qualifications of their members in April 2004. The central government appealed the decision of the High Court in May 2004, and the matter has remained unresolved to date.

Securing the Loans of Banks and Financial Institutions

Banks and financial institutions are the major lenders in the system. Their health is also crucial to the health of the entire financial system. If their loans go unpaid and the system does not provide a speedy course of recovery, nonperforming assets accumulate rapidly and the financial system may face a crisis. Therefore, the recovery of loans of banks and financial institutions has special importance.

Until as late as 1993, banks and financial institutions had to seek redress for unpaid loans in the civil courts. The process of law in these courts was time-consuming and led to the accumulation of a very large number of cases. As of September 30, 1990, there were 1.5 million recovery cases pending in the courts. As a part of the financial sector reforms in the early 1990s, the government enacted the Recovery of Debts Due to Banks and Financial Institutions Act, 1993, which introduced the setting up of Debt Recovery Tribunals (DRTs) across India. Banks and financial institutions were authorized to pursue outstanding claims exceeding 1 million rupees through the DRTs, which gave speedy rulings.

While the DRT process did speed up the issuing of the decree for debt collection through liquidation of the assets, execution of the decree remained problematic due to the weakness of the executive branch of the government. As a result, actual recovery of debt following the DRT rulings remained limited. To address this problem, the government passed the Securitization and Reconstruction of Financial Assets and Enforcement of Security Interest Act (Securitization Act) of 2002. This act gave the banks and financial institutions the right to take possession of the secured asset if the borrower defaults on repayment and fails to respond to a notice within 60 days. The act was challenged in the Supreme Court, which upheld it with a modification that allows the defaulting debtor to appeal the seizure of the asset in the court more easily than provided in the original act. This act gives the banks and financial institutions considerable effective power to recover debts.

PRIVATIZATION

We have seen the massive reach of the public sector in part I of the book. The public sector in India has a massive presence not just in the social and infrastructure sectors, in which most economists see an important role for it (see part V of the book), but also in commercial activity spanning industry, services, and mining. According to the *Economic Survey 2005–06* (Government of India, 2006b, p. 148, box 7.5), central public sector enterprises (CPSEs) contributed a whopping 11.12 percent of the GDP at market prices in 2005–06. Their cumulative investment as of March 31, 2006, was 3930.6 billion rupees, with manufacturing, services, and mining sectors accounting for 51, 40, and 7 percent of this total, respectively.

According to Gupta (2005, p. 992), the CPSEs account for 85 percent of the total assets of all state-owned companies. Notably, they do not include either the departmental enterprises—railways, postal service, and broadcasting—or the state public sector enterprises (SPSEs). They engage in the production and supply of basic goods such as steel, cement, and chemicals; capital goods such as pressure vessels, boilers, and drilling rigs; and intermediate goods such as electricity and gas. They also render a large number of services such as telecommunications, tourism, and warehousing.

While a handful of analysts will always disagree, there is now general agreement that the government should refrain from engaging in what are commercial activities, whether they relate to manufacturing or to services. Monopoly operation or the advent of especially able leadership at the top may occasionally and temporarily lead to profitable outcomes, but this is insufficient to justify the provision of manufacturing and services by the government. The managers in state-run enterprises are not going to be guided by purely commercial considerations. Nor will they be answerable to their shareholders alone. And when running at losses, state-owned enterprises will find it much more difficult to exit than their private sector counterparts. We saw in the previous section that even the BIFR rules applicable to state enterprises are different from those applied to private enterprises. Unsurprisingly, according to the *Economic Survey 2005–06* (Government of India, 2006b, p. 148, box 7.5), accumulated losses of all CPSEs amounted to 731.5 billion rupees in 2005–06.

Privatization So Far

Privatization can take three broad forms: share issue privatization, asset sale privatization, and voucher privatization. The first method involves the sale of shares on the stock market; the second, the sale of the entire firm or a substantial part of it to a strategic partner; and the third, distribution of shares to the public, usually free of charge or at a nominal price. The last method has been deployed primarily in the countries of Central and Eastern Europe and the former Soviet Union.

Table 13.3 provides the target and actual values of disinvestment in different years from 1991–92 to 2005–06, and the method of disinvestment. At 492 billion rupees, the total disinvestment until 2005–06 was 12.5 percent of the remaining equity of 3930.6 billion rupees of the CPSEs in 2005–06. Therefore, privatization in India still has a very long way to go.[18]

Based on the policy toward privatization, the period from 1991–92 to the present can be divided into three phases: 1991–92 to 1997–2000, 2000–01 to 2003–04, and 2004–05 to the preset time.[19] I discuss each of these phases briefly below.

Phase I (1991–2000): Ad Hoc Sales of Shares

The government began by selling bundles of shares of multiple companies to institutional investors in 1991–92. It was expected that these investors would gradually offload the shares to the public. The sales took the form of auctions with a reservation price for each portfolio of shares that was based on a complex evaluation procedure. Subsequent sales, in 1992–93 to 1994–95, were of shares of individual companies. By the end of 1994–95, receipts from disinvestments had reached 98 billion rupees. The sales in the first two years were clearly motivated by a desire to reduce the fiscal deficit as a part of the initial structural adjustment. Subsequently, disinvestment itself began to find a place as an objective in policy discussions. The sales were gradually extended to foreign markets through global depository receipts and sales to nonresident Indians.

In 1992, the government appointed the Committee on Disinvestment of Shares in PSEs to formulate a proper policy. The committee recommended limiting disinvestment to below 49 percent in industries reserved for the public sector, which had been limited to just 8 percent by the Industrial Policy of 1991. In other industries,

TABLE 13.3: Disinvestment: Value and Methodology

Year	Number of Transactions	Target (billion rupees)	Actual (billion rupees)	Methodology
1991–92	47	25	30.4	Minority shares sold in Dec. 1991 and Feb. 1992 by auction in bundles of "very good," "good," and "average" companies
1992–93	29	25	19.1	Shares sold separately for each company by auction.
1993–94	—	35	0.0	Equity of 6 companies sold by open auction, but proceeds received in 94–95.
1994–95	17	40	48.4	Sale through auction, in which NRIs and other persons legally permitted to buy, hold, or sell equity, were allowed to participate.
1995–96	5	70	1.7	Equities of 4 companies auctioned
1996–97	1	50	3.8	GDR (VSNL) in international market.
1997–98	1	48	9.1	GDR (MTNL) in international market.
1998–99	5	50	53.7	GDR (VSNL)/domestic offerings with the participation of FIIs (CONCOR, GAIL). Cross-purchase by 3 oil sector companies (GAIL, ONGC, & IOC).
1999–2000	5	100	18.6	GDR-GAIL, VSNL-domestic issue, BALCO restructuring, MFIL's strategic sale, and others.
2000–01	5	100	18.7	Strategic sale of BALCO, LJMC; Takeover of KRL (CRL), CPCL (MRL), BRPL.
2001–02*	8	120	56.3	Strategic sale of CMC (51%), HTL (74%), VSNL (25%), IBP (33.58%), PPL (74%), and sale of hotel properties of ITDC & HCI; receipt from surplus cash reserves from STC and MMTC.
2002–03*	8	120	33.5	Strategic sale: HZL (26%), IPCL (25%), HCI, ITDC. Maruti: control premium from renunciation of rights issue, Put Option, MFIL (26%). Shares to employees of HZL, CMC, and VSNL.
2003–04	2	145	155.5	Jessop & Co. Ltd. (72% Strategic Sale), HZL (18.92% call option). Public Offering:Maruti (27.5%), ICI Ltd. (9.2%), IBP (26%), IPCL (28.945%), CMC (26.25%), DCI (20%), GAIL (10.%), and ONGC (9.96%).
2004–05	3	40	27.6	NTPC (5.25% offer for sale), IPCL (5% to employees), and ONGC (0.01%).
2005–06		0	15.7	Sale of shares to public sector financial institutions and public sector banks, "differential pricing method."
Total		968	492.1	

*Inclusive of control premium, dividend, dividend tax, restructuring, and transfer of surplus cash prior to disinvestment.

Source: Web site of the Department of Disinvestment, Ministry of Finance, India (http:// www.divest.nic.in).

the committee recommended disinvestment up to 74 percent. But in no case did the sales from 1991–92 to 1994–95 rise above 49 percent (Arun and Nixson 2000, table 2).

Though the government appointed the Disinvestment Commission in 1996 to give impetus to privatization, virtually no real progress toward that goal took place. Combined receipts from sales of shares from 1995–96 to 1997–98 were just 14.6 billion rupees (see table 13.3). This is not surprising, since 1995–96 was an election year and the following two years brought as many coalition governments (not counting the three-week run of the government headed by Vajpayee) supported by the Left Front parties. Fresh general elections, held in March 1998, brought Vajpayee as prime minister. His government fell after serving for a year and general elections had to be called again; the electorate returned the National Democratic Alliance in the October 1999 elections with enough seats to provide continuity until 2003–04.

Phase II (2000–04): An Activist Privatization Policy

The Vajpayee government was keen on privatization as a policy, especially after it won a clearer mandate in the October 1999 elections. In January 2000, it carried out the first "strategic" sale by selling Modern Food Industries Limited to Hindustan Lever. Beyond some worker protests, the sale went smoothly. This emboldened the government, and Finance Minister Yashwant Sinha formally announced the adoption of a new privatization policy in the 2000–01 budget speech to the Parliament on February 29, 2000:

> Government have recently established a new Department for Disinvestment to establish a systematic policy approach to disinvestment and privatization and to give a fresh impetus to this program, which will emphasize increasingly … strategic sales of identified PSUs [public sector units]. Government equity in all nonstrategic PSUs will be reduced to 26 percent or less and the interests of the workers will be fully protected.

The government also gave charge of the Department of Disinvestment to State Minister Arun Shourie, who was firmly committed to the cause of privatization (as opposed to the sale of minority shares for the purpose of raising revenue). On September 1, 2001, the government upgraded the Department of Disinvestment to the Ministry of Disinvestment to strengthen Shourie's hand vis-à-vis ministers in charge of enterprises, who invariably opposed the sales.

Including Modern Food Industries, the government undertook strategic sales of 13 enterprises, 3 hotels of the Hotel Corporation of India, and 19 hotels of the India Tourism Development Corporation by the end of 2001–02. The total receipts from these sales were 126 billion rupees.[20] Altogether, the receipts from disinvestment from 2000–01 to 2003–04 totaled 264 billion rupees (table 13.3). Some of the strategic sales proved highly controversial, but the government prevailed in each case.

In the end, the government lost out to the judiciary, which blocked the strategic sales of two major oil companies: Bharat Petroleum Corporation Limited (BPCL) and Hindustan Petroleum Corporation Limited (HPCL). In September 2003, the Supreme Court ruled that the language in the ESSO (Acquisition of Undertaking in India) Act of 1974 and the Burma Shell (Acquisition of Undertaking in India) Act of

1976, which created HPCL and BPCL, respectively, did not permit the government to privatize those firms without parliamentary approval.[21]

Phase III (2004–05 to the Present): Back to the Sale of Minority Shares

The United Progressive Alliance (UPA), which came to power in May 2004 under the leadership of the Congress Party and is supported by the Left Front parties in the Parliament, essentially shelved the privatization program. One of its first steps was to close down the Disinvestment Ministry and demote disinvestment back to a department within the Finance Ministry. Under its Common Minimum Program (CMP), the UPA committed to not privatizing profitable enterprises. It also committed to not privatizing the "navaratna" companies (nine jewels) , which included the leading CPSEs. The CMP also stated that every effort would be made to restructure and revive sick companies, with chronically loss-making companies to be either sold or closed down after all workers were given their legitimate dues.

Unsurprisingly, disinvestment has seen a dramatic slowdown. During 2004–05 and 2005–06, the total receipts from sales of shares were only 43 billion rupees. Perhaps the most notable "privatizations" under the current government have been the handing over of the Delhi and Mumbai airports to private management (see chapter 18). But these privatizations are not sales in the traditional sense, since they required the commitment of very substantial public resources.

Impact, Lessons, and Future Course

To my knowledge, so far there is only one econometric assessment of privatization efforts in India. This study, by Gupta (2005), relates to disinvestments in the 1990s that involved the sale of minority shares and did not transfer management to private hands. In her careful work, Gupta investigates the impact of equity sales on the firm's profitability, labor productivity, investment expenditures, and employment. Based on before-after summary statistics, she finds that firms experience a significant increase in profitability, labor productivity, R&D investment and intensity, asset size, and employment after partial privatization. Gupta goes on to estimate the effect of privatization, controlling for other variables including changes in the overall state of the economy and changes in the life cycle position of the firm before and after privatization. She finds that a ten percentage point increase in the level of private equity would increase annual sales and profits by about 13 percent and 10 percent, respectively. Gupta's results also suggest that partial privatization does not cause the government to abandon the political objective of maintaining employment.

Baijal (2002a) discusses the impact of strategic privatizations in 2000–01 and 2001–02, in which he had been an active player as the disinvestment secretary. His first point is that these sales brought in 72 billion rupees, leading to an equivalent reduction in borrowing by the government. Even if we use the low interest rate of 6 percent, this means a saving of 4.3 billion rupees per year in perpetuity. During the preceding eight years, the privatized CPSEs had yielded a net loss of 1 billion rupees per year. Therefore, the government made a net gain of 5.3 billion rupees per year in perpetuity.

Given that disinvestment itself is not controversial, the critical policy issue is whether the government should take the route of piecemeal sales of minority shares, as it currently does, or go to strategic sales that transfer the ownership, as during 2000–04. At least two considerations favor the latter strategy. First, the ultimate objective of disinvestment is to transfer ownership of the companies to private management that is invariably better equipped to make commercial decisions than government-appointed managers. The sooner the transfer of ownership takes place, the greater will be the benefits to the country from increased productivity.

The second reason for opting for the strategic sales route is that when shares are sold in small chunks with no clear mandate for the transfer of management to private hands, share prices fail to reflect their true long-term value. Baijal (2002b) makes this point emphatically. He notes that the price-earnings ratio on the basis of the sales value realized by the government on the sales of shares during the 1990s was 4 to 6 even for blue chip companies with a monopoly in the market, such as the Indian Oil Company, the Gas Authority of India Limited, and Videsh Sanchar Nigam Limited. In contrast, the price-earnings ratio for strategic sales of 33 CPSEs during 2000–01 to 2002–03 (until August 2003) was much higher—between 11 and 89. Baijal (2002b) goes on to conclude:

> The experience gained so far seems to justify the assumption that the strategic sale "discovers" the fundamental, long-term value of the company as opposed to the sale of small lots of shares in the market which get valued on short-term considerations linked to the current expectations of the market. The higher sales realizations through strategic sale reflect the control premium, which the investor is willing to pay for managing the company.[22]

A common criticism of strategic sales is that they threaten the employment prospects of workers in privatized units. This is an entirely misplaced criticism. Insofar as privatization increases productivity and profitability, it is likely to improve overall employment and wage prospects. It is only unproductive workers who enjoy large rents in public sector units who are likely to feel pressure to become productive. But that is as it should be if the production activity is to be run at commercial terms.

To date, evidence shows that strategic sales have improved rather than worsened employment and wage prospects of workers. According to Baijal (2002b), when rationalizing their workforces, privatized firms have offered voluntary retirement schemes that are more generous than those offered by the government. In the case of Modern Food Industries, wages were increased 1,600 rupees per month following privatization, notwithstanding the fact that within one month of privatization the firm had been referred to the BIFR. Likewise, in the highly difficult and contentious case of Bharat Aluminum Company, wages had stagnated prior to privatization. But despite a loss of 2 billion rupees due to the strike protesting the sale, the new owner quickly negotiated a new five-year wage agreement guaranteeing a benefit of 20 percent of basic pay to each employee.[23]

The argument is sometimes made that as long as the public enterprises are subject to competition from private sector firms, they would behave no differently than the latter. There is no doubt that the entry of private firms has an efficiency-enhancing effect on public enterprises, as is illustrated by the experience of the public sector telecommunications company Bharat Sanchar Nigam Limited (BSNL; see chapter 17). But it remains true that public sector enterprises still fail to achieve the efficiency exhibited by private firms. Shourie (2004, p. 234) states this forcefully, using the example of the BSNL in the post-private entry era of telecommunications:

> Everyone knows how swiftly things move in the telecom sector, how fierce competition is in it. Yet, it takes 8 to 19 months for the BSNL to process a tender. Equipment that began reaching the Northeast in May 2004 originated from a tender floated two *years* earlier. The equipment was woefully inadequate—for demand had exploded meanwhile; and also relatively obsolete—for technology had continued to advance by the day.

This analysis has the clear implication that India needs to put its privatization program back on its feet. Unfortunately, prospects for the change in the policy under the current government are quite bleak. With the reforms of the early 2000s having shifted the growth rate up to 8 percent, the government, already reluctant to privatize, faces even less pressure to move in this direction. This is unfortunate, since a very large part of manufacturing and services output remains in the public sector and will likely continue to drag down the overall performance of the economy.

INFRASTRUCTURE AND OTHER REFORMS

The discussion of reforms necessary for faster growth of industry and services is incomplete without the inclusion of the important subject of infrastructure. Electricity, telecommunications, and transportation are all crucial to the rapid growth of industry and services. Among these sectors, telecommunications has made dramatic progress since the mid-1990s. Road and air transportation, and recently railways, have also shown considerable improvements. But they remain inadequate when it comes to the swift movement of goods from the manufacturing site to the port or airport, and vice versa for exports and imports. In turn, this greatly hampers the ability of manufactures requiring timely delivery to penetrate the world markets. The electricity sector is also in urgent need of improved performance. This is a key input into most industrial products but remains expensive and poorly supplied.

In view of the great importance of infrastructure to industry and services, I will return to them in greater detail in part V, devoting chapter 17 to telecommunications and electricity, and chapter 18 to various transport services. There is also the important issue of efficient taxation, which I will consider in detail in chapter 15. Presently, I focus on some important areas of reforms bearing on industry and services not covered elsewhere in the book.

Urban Infrastructure

Poor urban infrastructure is a frequently occurring theme in the context of the software industry. Urban transportation in Bangalore is cited as a key factor constraining the software industry there, and possibly even forcing some IT firms to move to other cities. But urban infrastructure and real estate can turn into major constraints on the expansion of industry and services in general, since they determine the ability of the labor force to move between residence and workplace, and they are also crucial to the movement of domestic and foreign businessmen into and out of the city.

I discuss some aspects of the reforms in this area in chapter 18, in the sections dealing with urban transportation, airports, and water supply and sanitation. Many of the needed reforms in this area are a part of the central government's Jawaharlal Nehru National Urban Renewal Mission (JNNURM) that the 2005–06 budget launched. The JNNURM picks 35 cities with population exceeding one million each and another 28 smaller cities that are state capitals or cities of historic, religious, or tourist importance, and offers substantial funds for building urban infrastructure, provided the recipient states undertake some key reforms at the level of the state and targeted cities. Rather than discuss the JNNURM in detail, I discuss below some key reforms required for the smooth functioning of the cities in India.

Urban Land

The efficiency of land use crucially depends on the flexibility with which it can be converted from one use to another. A host of state and city laws and regulations have frozen land in some of the major cities into uses that no longer yield a high social return. Several constraints obstruct the emergence of a vibrant land market in the urban India:

- Many states have yet to repeal the ULCRA of 1976. This law not only hampers the exit of firms, as previously discussed, but also accounts for extremely high land prices in such cities as Mumbai and makes housing ultra-expensive.
- Rent control laws are still in place in such major and reform-minded states as Gujarat, Maharashtra, and Andhra Pradesh. These laws have a variety of harmful effects. First, many owners choose not to rent their unused apartments for fear that they might effectively lose them for good. Space goes unused at a time when it happens to be scarce. Second, apartments cannot be used as collateral, so they turn into unproductive assets. Third, owners have no incentive to renovate even the most dilapidated buildings with unsound structures. Finally, landlords cannot tear down buildings to build multilevel complexes in order to increase the supply of floor space.
- India lacks a system of clear, state-guaranteed property titles. As discussed painstakingly by Wadhwa (2002), this is a pervasive problem in cities and villages alike (see chapter 14 for further details). In the absence of such title to property, financial institutions are normally not willing to lend money against the property. Even if they do, the process of ensuring ownership is costly for the lenders and almost never devoid of uncertainty. The absence of titles also leads to perpetual litigation. Shourie (2004) highlights the problem when describing his experience in privatizing eight public sector hotels in Delhi operated by the Indian Tourism Development Corporation (ITDC). As the minister of disinvestment (i.e., privatization), he embarked upon the privatization of these hotels, only to discover the ITDC did not have titles to them.

To quote him (Shourie 2004, p. 25):

> On commencing the process for privatizing these properties in Delhi we discovered that:
>
> - Not one of them, *repeat not one of them* had the title deed or lease document in order—the documents were either just not available, or the lease was in dispute, and that in spite of the fact that hotels had been in operation for up to *forty-five years*;
> - Not one of them, *repeat not one of them* had a Completion Certificate—and that in spite of the fact that the buildings had been constructed *twenty to forty-five years* earlier; indeed, even the Building Plans on the basis of which Completion Certificates could be given—"with retrospective effect" so to say—were not available;
> - Not one of them, *repeat not one of them* had even the mandatory Certificate from the Fire Authorities. [All emphases in the original.]

- Public sector entities, most notably railways, often hold large pieces of land in the centers of the cities that are unused or suboptimally used. These entities are not allowed to sell this land at the market price for their own benefit. As a result, they continue to hold it, turning it into essentially an unproductive asset. The government must find ways to allow these entities to sell the land and keep the proceeds, so that land passes to agents who will use it productively.
- A major obstacle to the efficient use of land in the big cities is the low Floor Space Index (FSI). The FSI is defined as the proportion of living area in a building to the area of the plot on which it is built. For example, a building with four floors built on half of an 800 square meter plot would have 1600 square meters of living area, and therefore an FSI of 2. Land use regulations in some cities in India impose a very tight limit on the FSI, making land use highly inefficient. As Bertaud (2004) carefully documents, the most notorious case is that of Mumbai, which introduced such regulation for the first time in 1964. At the time, the FSI was fixed at 4.5 in the area that currently defines the central business district (CBD). In 1991, the FSI was reduced to 1.33 for the entire island city and to 1 for the suburbs. This pattern contrasts with those in comparable cities such as New York, Hong Kong, and Singapore: The FSI in these latter cities is much higher, varying between 5 and 15, and the FSI rises as we move closer to the center of the city. The higher FSI in the center of the city is a principal explanation for the development of a concentrated CBD in most of the world's major cities. In Mumbai, most buildings with a high FSI were built prior to the introduction of the regulation in 1964. They are old and dilapidated, but cannot be rebuilt since rebuilding would be subject to the 1.33 FSI.
- The efficiency of land use depends crucially on the ease of conversion from one use to another, such as from warehouse to office space and from factories to apartments. In many cities, laws governing the conversion of land from one use to another are rigid and make the conversion extremely costly. Some regulation of conversion is desirable, but excessive rigidity only leads to illegal conversion, which is costly and gives rise to corruption.
- Closely related to the previous point, the laws governing the conversion of agricultural land on the periphery of the cities into land usable for alternative

purposes also need to be more flexible than currently. A low FSI complemented by tough conversion laws is bound to create shortage of space for nonagricultural purposes, and illegal construction.

- Likewise, the law of eminent domain, which provides for the "taking" of land by the government for its own use or for delegation to third parties for public use, needs to be made transparent. Lack of clarity of this law has led to major delays in public projects such as road construction and building of city transit systems. Most recently, land acquisition by the government for special economic zones has resulted in violent protests culminating in deaths.
- Stamp duties charged on the sale of land are extremely high. This discourages land transactions, and when they do happen, the official price is grossly understated. Once again, this has implications for the use of land as collateral, since the value of the loan offered against land depends on the land's official value.

Real Estate

According to the Planning Commission (2006), the construction industry employs over 30 million workers and has been growing at 10 percent per year since the early 2000s. Being labor-intensive, its continued expansion promises to generate a large volume of jobs with decent pay. Several factors—including rising incomes, urbanization, smaller families, growth of businesses, the rush by foreign multinationals to open offices, and increased tourism—have led to a rapid expansion of demand for real estate in areas such as hotels, office space, and housing.

Decent hotels at reasonable prices in the major cities of India, in particular, remain in extremely short supply. During the peak season, occupancy rates in the major cities such as Delhi, Mumbai, and Bangalore shoot above 100 percent, with some rooms occupied by one guest part of the day and by a second guest after the first one departs to catch a night flight. The government urgently needs to help expand the hotel capacity.

Recently, the government has opened real estate to foreign direct investment. The current policy allows foreigners to own property in India. Foreign firms can develop housing estates of 10 hectares (25 acres) or more. They can also build commercial buildings with 50,000 square meters (538,200 square feet) or more floor space. Domestically, financial deregulation has helped make house loans accessible, and tax exemption on the interest paid on house mortgages provides an incentive to own a house. These are welcome developments, but the ultimate success of the policies in this area depends crucially on the reform of the land use laws discussed above.

Retail Trade

Retail trade contributed 14.1 percent of the GDP in 2004–05. Based on the data in table 13.1, it employs a little below 10 percent of the labor force.[24] A recent report by Crisil (2005) notes that the firms in the organized sector conduct only 2 percent of India's retail trade. This compares with the 50 percent share of organized sector firms in Malaysia, 40 percent in Thailand, 25 percent in Indonesia, and 20 percent in China. The sector remains highly fragmented in India, with most retail trade carried out by small shopkeepers, vendors, and hawkers. An earlier report by the McKinsey Global Institute (2001) had systematically analyzed the fragmented nature of the retail sector in India and had argued that opening it to foreign investment would bring very substantial gains to India. The experience in much of the rest of the world shows that through effective supply chain management, large retailers are better able to link manufacturers and consumers. By cutting the costs of intermediation, they are able to offer better prices to manufacturers, yet lower the prices to consumers. Allowing foreign retailers into the market has the advantage that they link the domestic consumer directly to the global supply chains.

In recent years, several Indian retail chains have emerged. These include Shopper's Stop, Tata-Trent Limited, RPG Enterprises, and Crossroads. The obvious resistance to the emergence of large retailers comes from small shopkeepers who may lose the market to the former. But these fears may be readily exaggerated. For one thing, large chains are likely to be concentrated in the large cities with populations exceeding half a million or so and will have to locate far away from the center of the city due to the shortage of land in the city center. The number of these large cities is small and the location of retail chains away from the city center would constrain their ability to undercut the small traders. The emergence of large chains would bring formal sector employment and an expanded market.

On balance, there is a good case for gradually lowering the barriers to the entry of retail suppliers, including foreign retailers. At present, India permits only up to 51 percent direct foreign investment in single-brand product retailing. There is a good case for allowing multiproduct foreign retailers such as Wal-Mart to intensify competition in this segment. There is no reason why consumers should be denied the benefit of lower prices in favor of protecting the interests of the local retail chains that have been granted entry.

Skill Formation

A final area that needs urgent attention of the government if the IT revolution is to be sustained is higher education. Wages of skilled workers in India have been rising during recent years faster than anywhere else in the world. At the same time, worker turnover rates in the IT firms are extremely high. Both factors point to a shortage of skilled workers. India's higher education system needs to be deregulated and greatly expanded. I return to this important issue in greater detail in chapter 20.

CONCLUDING REMARKS

In constrast to other countries that have successfully transitioned from the primarily rural and agricultural structure to the modern one, rapid growth in India has not been accompanied by a commensurate expansion of well-paid formal sector jobs. In large part, this has been due to a stagnant share of industry and manufacturing, especially unskilled-labor-intensive manufacturing, in the GDP. This pattern of growth has meant that the movement of the workforce out of agriculture and into the organized sector has been slow. Modernization of the economy requires the expansion of employment opportunities in the organized sector.

Since the mid-1990s, India has removed many of the barriers to the entry of medium and large firms into unskilled-labor-intensive sectors. Most important, the vast majority of the unskilled-labor-intensive products have been removed from the small-scale-industries reservation list. Even in the case of the products still on the list, medium and large firms have been allowed to enter production at least since March 2000, as long as they export more than 50 percent of their output.

The removal of these restrictions has not proved sufficient to speed up the transition of workers into the modern, organized sector, however. This inevitably points to the presence of yet more barriers to the entry of large firms into the unskilled-labor-intensive sectors. I have argued that various labor market rigidities, absence of a modern bankruptcy law, and infrastructure bottlenecks account for the continued muted response of unskilled-labor-intensive industries to the reforms undertaken to date. Unless the government brings some relief to the firms in these areas, the transformation will be slow and poverty reduction will be less than what is feasible. Also important is privatization of public sector enterprises. These enterprises account for a large proportion of the GDP and operate highly inefficiently.

I have also argued that unlike countries such as Korea, Taiwan, and China, which have relied principally on manufacturing to transform their economies, India has the prospect of walking on two legs: manufacturing and information technology. The reforms undertaken in the telecommunications industry have led to the expansion of phones at an astronomical pace. While systematic studies are yet to be conducted, one can reasonably hypothesize that this expansion has prepared the groundwork for even faster expansion of services in general and the IT sector in particular.

But the IT industry, too, faces two major constraints in the medium-to-long run: urban infrastructure and the supply of skilled labor. Because the IT industry mostly locates in large cities, urban infrastructure is crucial. Apart from Delhi, most cities have failed to respond adequately to the increased inflow of population and its housing and transportation needs. On the skills front, the shortage is reflected in the rapid increase of skilled workers' wages and high turnover rates. Therefore, India also needs to undertake major reforms in its higher education system to ensure a steady stream of qualified IT workers.

14

MODERNIZING AGRICULTURE

Approximately three-fifths of India's workforce is in agriculture. This workforce also accounts for a sizable proportion of India's poor. Therefore, it is not surprising that when asked what India should do to improve the lot of the poor, most analysts instinctively focus on productivity in agriculture. They differ on the precise policies to achieve productivity increases, but they agree on the centrality of the latter for improving the lot of the poor.

I do not share this view. By this I do not mean that productivity increases in agriculture should be a low priority item on the reform agenda, but that a sustainable solution to poverty largely lies outside agriculture. A populous country such as India cannot come out of poverty on a sustained basis with three-fifths of its workforce on the farm. It must generate gainful employment in industry and services, and move the bulk of the workforce out of agriculture. By lowering the labor-to-land ratio, this movement offers much greater potential for raising agricultural wages than any productivity-enhancing reform within agriculture. Even when a solution, such as food processing, has a direct link to agriculture, it involves the creation of employment opportunities outside farming. This is the reason I emphasized sustained, rapid expansion of unskilled-labor-intensive manufacturing in the last two chapters.

Argued differently, India is now more or less self-sufficient in cereals, so that increased output of cereals will have to be sold principally in the world markets or to the public distribution system (PDS). Absent the removal of rich country protection and subsidies, the world markets are unlikely to pay lucrative prices for cereals. And the PDS has limits on the purchase of excess grain at an artificially high price. Diversification into fruits, vegetables, and other commercial crops offers a way out, but only on a limited scale and only when combined with food processing. Therefore, in considering agriculture, it would be wrong to think that reforms inside this sector would solve the problem of poverty on a sustained basis. The most they can do is to bring relief to some farmers in the short run. But even here, faster relief requires direct measures such as cash transfers to the poor. Measures such as the National Employment Guarantee Scheme may accomplish the same goal, but they are suboptimal instruments since they are subject to large leakages, with only a tiny fraction of the funds that are spent, reaching the intended beneficiaries of the program. Various other subsidies, including those on food, fertilizer, electricity, and water, are actually regressive since the bigger a farm, the greater the utilization of these subsidies. In contrast, cash transfers can be effected electronically and be readily verified.

It is important to note at the outset that under the Indian Constitution, the states are given the bulk of the legislative and implementation authority for agriculture. Therefore, the ability of the central government to introduce reforms in this sector is limited. In part, this is the reason that even the most determined and influential leaders in the central government have had difficulty introducing major reforms in agriculture. A study of West Bengal by Franda (1968) graphically demonstrated that even Nehru, who enjoyed near universal confidence and support of the people, could not get the states to follow his lead when it came to agriculture. The state leaderships, often beholden to large farmers, usually did what they wanted.

We saw in chapter 1 that agriculture grew 2.1 percent during 1981–88 (phase III) and 3.4 percent during 1988–2006 (phase IV). Within the latter period, the average growth during 2000–06 (2.3 percent) was slower than during the earlier part of phase IV. This slowdown, accompanied by increased awareness of rising farmer suicides (see chapter 7), has led to serious concerns that productivity growth and incomes in agriculture have stagnated and it is urgent that something be done. While no single dramatic solution comparable to the Green Revolution is currently available, the prevailing incentives regime in agriculture has vast scope for improvement. Whereas the reforms in industry and services have made considerable progress since the 1980s, those in agriculture have barely begun. If the state governments introduce reforms, we may see improvements in agriculture and related activities in excess of those brought about by the Green Revolution. I begin with the discussion of reforms in product markets.

PRODUCT MARKET REFORMS

I have already argued, in chapter 12, the case for external trade liberalization in agricultural products. Through gradual but steady liberalization, India must bring the same benefits to agriculture that it has reaped in industry. By being exposed to trade, farmers can benefit from specializing toward the products of their comparative advantage and from technological improvements that accrue from competing against the world's most efficient producers. For instance, India has enormous scope for improvement in the area of fruits and vegetables both in terms of product variety and sanitary and phyto-sanitary standards. In addition to the external liberalization, India must introduce a wide variety of reforms in the domestic product markets. The vast majority of these distortions have resulted from government interventions that need to be systematically removed.

Food Subsidy and the Public Distribution System

The government is heavily involved in the pricing and distribution of grains through its public distribution system. Traditionally, the Commission for Agricultural Costs and Prices (CACP) sets the minimum support price (MSP) to ensure that the farmers are able to recover their costs on the average. But the commission nowadays sets the MSP at levels well above the market price. In turn the Food Corporation of India (FCI) uses the MSP as the procurement price, effectively subsidizing the farmers in the relatively rich states of Punjab, Haryana, and Andhra Pradesh, where it procures most of its supplies.[1]

Having procured large volumes of grain, the FCI stores it in its highly inefficient storage facilities and then sells it at concessional prices to consumers. In this way, the government subsidizes the consumers and the inefficiencies of the FCI. A significant percent of the stored grain is either washed away by the monsoon rains or eaten by rats. The FCI also maintains a workforce of approximately 400,000.

In chapter 16, where I consider the food subsidy in detail, I recommend the abolition of this system altogether beyond the maintenance of a small stock of food grains, say 20 million tons, procured at market prices, to meet food emergencies. All other food grain purchases, sales, and storage for normal times should be placed entirely in private hands. Imports and exports should be decanalized with recourse to the WTO legal safeguard measures in case import surges cause injury to the farmers (see chapter 12 for further details). The CACP must be abolished and the FCI drastically downsized both in terms of its workforce and its warehouse space. The government should replace the current inefficient and regressive food subsidies with a cash transfer to each family below the poverty line through a bank account in the name of the female in charge of the household (see chapter 16 for more details).

Interstate Movement of Grain and Related Distortions

The Essential Commodities Act (ECA), 1955, which enables states to impose restrictions on the storage, transport, price, distribution, and processing of agricultural produce, must be repealed.[2] The reach of the ECA is not limited to the agricultural commodities that have been judged "essential" at one time or another. Instead, it extends to coal; component parts and accessories of automobiles; cotton and woolen textiles; drugs; iron and steel, including manufactured products of iron and steel; paper, including newsprint, paperboard, and strawboard; and petroleum and petroleum products. Traditionally, states have maintained a host of regulations and controls on "essential" commodities, including restrictions on the movement of grains and other agricultural products within as well as between states. Under the powers of the ECA, the central government has recently threatened to resort to price controls to combat inflation.

The ECA was introduced prior to the Green Revolution and amid fears that traders would cause or exacerbate shortages through hoarding and speculative activities. But food shortages are no longer an issue. Moreover, given the FCI emergency stocks, the possibility of imports on short notice, and the renunciation of the controlled regime by India, there is little justification left for the ECA. It only tempts the politicians to resort to price controls the moment they see the inflation rate edging up. It is not clear how this act is compatible with India's recent embrace of the commodity futures trade.

The movement of grains and other agricultural products is so important that the reform in this area will need to go beyond the repeal of the ECA. States can currently restrict such movement under their own laws. Therefore, the central government will need to enact legislation that forbids state or local bodies from imposing these restrictions within or between states. In order to take full advantage of integration into the world economy, India must integrate internally and be a single market. Efficient farmers must be allowed the benefit of lucrative prices anywhere in the country, and consumers must have the option to buy cheaper grain wherever they can find it.

Agricultural Marketing

State-level Agricultural Produce Marketing Committee (APMC) Acts govern the marketing of agricultural produce in India. Traditionally, these laws provided for state-constituted APMCs that exercised a monopoly over the purchase of agricultural produce, especially fruits and vegetables but often also all kinds of grains, from farmers, and over its sale to wholesalers. Wholesalers were not permitted to buy produce directly from the farmers. This led to the farmers' receiving low prices and consumers paying high prices. Effectively, the laws gave the state-owned APMCs the monopoly right of intermediation between farmers and wholesalers. The state-appointed market commission agent sent village commission agents to the villages to collect the produce from the farmers. Farmers were required by law to sell their produce exclusively to them.

Once these agents brought the produce to the *mandi* (a market center for the purchase and sale of agricultural products), the market commission agent sold it to the wholesalers. In principle, this sale was to be effected through competitive auctions. But in practice, the agents negotiated the deals with the wholesalers in a highly nontransparent manner. The negotiated price became the market price. Out of this, the market commission agent and the village commission agents got their shares first, and the residual was passed on to the farmers. The produce was not graded before being sold, so farmers did not receive a premium on high-quality produce. This naturally encouraged them to target quantity rather than quality. Often the storage facilities at the *mandi*s were poor, and the produce would partially rot.

The state governments originally created this system to protect the farmers from exploitation by private monopoly buyers at the village level. But over time, the system degenerated, with the state-appointed commission agents themselves turning into monopsony buyers from farmers and monopoly sellers to wholesalers. Farmers continued to be exploited.

But more important, this model cannot adequately serve the farmers' interests for at least three reasons. First, with rising incomes, consumer tastes are shifting away from cereal and toward fruits, vegetables, processed foods, and milk and milk products. The volume of produce to be handled is expanding rapidly, and the current system is unable to cope with it effectively. A much more effective supply chain to

link the farmer and the consumer is required. Second, rising incomes are also shifting tastes toward higher quality and specialty produce. Under the traditional system,
the farmer has no incentive to opt for high-quality produce since the price does
not depend on the quality. Selling high-quality produce requires better coordination
with consumers than the traditional *mandi* system can provide. Given its perishable
nature, specialty produce is inherently more risky, and mechanisms are required
for risk sharing and risk diversification. Finally, exports and imports are becoming
increasingly important. If the farmer is required to sell his produce to the APMC-
sponsored commission agents, there is little chance that the produce can be exported.
This system gives the farmer no incentive to satisfy the sanitary and phytosanitary
standards of the importing countries. A potential exporter cannot hope to acquire
the produce from the APMC-run *mandi*s. Instead, he requires direct contact with
the farmer. Symmetrically, shifting tastes toward specialty produce, together with
trade liberalization, has brought imported fruits and vegetables to Indian soil. If the
domestic farmers are to effectively compete against these imports, they need a better marketing model.

Belatedly, the state governments have begun to replace the government monopoly marketing model with a more competitive, modern policy regime that promises
to transform Indian agriculture just as much as the Green Revolution did. As I will
briefly describe immediately below, some signs of this transformation can already
be seen. Although the APMC model still dominates India, states have begun to
replace the APMC Act with a model law titled State Agricultural Produce Marketing (Development and Regulation) Law, drafted and recommended by the central government. As of January 31, 2007, the vast majority of the states had either
adopted a version of this model law or undertaken partial reform through an ordinance or resolution. Among the major states still in the process of replacing the old
law with a new one are Assam, Uttaranchal, West Bengal, and Jharkhand.

Under the new state marketing laws being adopted or implemented, the *mandi*s
sponsored by the APMCs continue to operate, but growers are under no compulsion
to sell their produce through them. Likewise, new avenues have been opened up for
wholesale buyers. The new laws introduce three new avenues to the purchase and
sale of produce:

- In any marketing area, farmers, consumers, entrepreneurs, and local authorities can establish market yards. At these yards, farmers can sell their produce
  directly to consumers. Multiple market yards are allowed to exist in any marketing area. The traditional state-owned market committee must now compete
  with these and other buyers of the farmers' produce.
- The state government may grant a firm or individual license to purchase agricultural produce by establishing a private yard or dealing directly with farmers in one or more market areas for (1) processing of the agricultural produce
  notified through a government circular or press note; (2) trade of notified agricultural produce of particular specification; (3) export of notified agricultural
  produce; and (4) grading, packing, and any other type of transaction that adds
  value to notified agricultural produce.
- Farmers can contract to sell their produce directly to a contract farming spon-
  sor from their fields without routing the sale through notified markets.

In the states where the new laws are operative, signs of change can already be seen. In November 2006, Reliance Industries Limited (RIL) launched Reliance Fresh, a supermarket chain selling fruits, vegetables, groceries, and dairy products. The chain buys produce directly from farmers under the second provision above. RIL plans to invest 250 to 300 billion rupees (approximately $6 to $7 billion) by the end of 2011 in the chain and to open stores in 784 cities and 6400 towns across India. As of the end of March 2007, the chain had already opened more than 50 stores in Hyderabad, Chennai, Jaipur, Ranchi, and Bangalore. Under the traditional APMC model, farmers receive a very small proportion of the retail price due to multiple layers in the supply chain. Large retail chains, such as Reliance Fresh, that buy directly from the farmers are expected to double this share.

In the same vein, the eChoupal initiative of the Indian Tobacco Company (ITC) is revolutionizing agricultural marketing in not just fruits, vegetables, and dairy products but a host of other crops, including cereals and soybeans, as well. The central element in this initiative is a Web site that reports the prices of products and of inputs in different markets in real time. It also provides information on farming techniques and weather in the local language. The ITC has established numerous Internet kiosks, called eChoupal, through which the farmers can access the Website. The eChoupals allow them to instantly compare the prices in various markets and sell their specific product in the market that offers the most lucrative deal. This is not possible in the traditional APMC *mandi*s since their pricing does not distinguish between high- and low-grade varieties. Currently, the ITC program consists of 6500 eChoupals covering 3.5 million farmers in 38,000 villages in 9 states. The company plans to extend this to 20,000 eChoupals reaching 10 million farmers in 100,000 villages in 15 states by 2015.[3]

In specialty products, contract farming (third option above) has begun to emerge as a result of the implementation of the new marketing laws in many states. The arrangement involves a forward contract on the part of the buyer to buy, and on the part of the seller to sell, an agricultural commodity in a specified quantity at a specified time and price. The contract may also involve the buyer's providing seeds and other key inputs as well as technical know-how. This arrangement is ideal for specialty products for which the farmer needs an assured buyer and the buyer— typically an exporter or food-processing firm—an assured supplier. In homogeneous products for which thick markets exist, either the buyer or the seller has an incentive to break the contract, depending on the realized spot price at the time the contract is to be executed.

Additional advantages of contract farming arise from size. The buyer is typically a corporation needing the produce for further processing or for export in large volumes. This allows it to internalize the benefits of research and extension services. It is able to invest in R&D and offer technical advice and inputs, including implements, to its client farmers. One limitation, however, is that contract farming is unlikely to bring small and marginal farmers into its fold in large numbers. The reason is that enforcing a large number of small contracts is a costly affair. The experience of PepsiCo, the pioneer in contract farming in India, offers a nice illustration of a successful case of contract farming.[4] Currently, major corporations engaged in contract farming include FieldFresh of Bharti Enterprises, HLL, Tata,

DCM Shriram, and McDonald's. Retail chains such as Big Bazaar and Metro are likely to enter the field as well.

Small-Scale Industries Reservation

There still remain restrictions on the entry of large-scale firms in a handful of food-processing activities. These include pickles and chutneys, bread, rapeseed oil, mustard oil, sesame oil, peanut oil, and ground and processed spices. There is little rationale for these restrictions, and they must be eliminated so that the efficient firms may grow larger and other producers may enter the market on a larger scale.

Food Processing

Food processing is an unusually undeveloped industry in India. This is seen from the following striking observation by the Planning Commission (2001, p. 80) some years ago: "Less than 2% of fruit and vegetable production is processed compared with 30% in Thailand, 70% in Brazil, 78% in the Philippines and 80% in Malaysia!" The percentage in India has probably risen slightly since this report was done, but not by much. Therefore, food processing offers great scope for development and is directly beneficial to farmers.

The Planning Commission (2001) pointed to expensive power, poor rural-urban connectivity, small-scale industries' reservation, and the lack of suitability of the traditional produce for processing as among the reasons why this activity had fallen behind in India. But the most important reason it offered was the presence of an archaic legal framework "characterized by a multiplicity of laws and regulations related to food processing which are administered by different ministries and which are often inconsistent with each other" (Planning Commission, 2001, p. 82). Luckily, good news is on the way on virtually all fronts.

Infrastructure bottlenecks, including electricity and rural-urban connectivity, are being gradually addressed (see chapters 17 and 18). The small-scale industries' reservation has been ended on all agricultural products except those noted in the previous subsection. And the government has just put in place the Food Safety and Standards Act (FSSA) of 2006, which aims to modernize the legal framework for the food-processing industry.

The FSSA repeals eight existing laws relating to food safety and provides a unified food policy regime. It establishes the Food Safety and Standards Authority (FSSA) to regulate the food sector. The latter is to be aided by several scientific panels and a central advisory committee in laying down standards for food safety. These standards will include specifications for ingredients, contaminants, pesticide residue, biological hazards, and labels. State commissioners of food safety and local-level officials will enforce the law. Every distributor is required to be able to identify any food article by its manufacturer, and every seller by its distributor.

At this juncture, the government needs to expeditiously move forward with the implementation of the FSSA. Though the president signed the act in August 2006, so far no information is readily available on the appointment of the Food Safety and Standards Authority. Indeed, there still remains confusion as to whether the implementation will be delegated to the Ministry of Food Processing Industries or the Ministry of Health and Family Welfare. The matter remains with the prime minister.

Once the FSSA is fully implemented, food processing may also get a boost from the Companies (Amendment) Act, 2002, which added chapter IXA, on the conversion of cooperative societies into producer companies. Such conversion offers cooperative societies the opportunity to corporatize themselves and be governed by more liberal provisions of the Companies (Amendment) Act, 2002 rather than the usually more restrictive state laws that govern cooperative societies. As cooperative societies convert into producer companies, they are more likely to engage in food-processing activities.

Commercial/Corporate Farming

A final product market reform issue concerns the entry of commercial/corporate farmers through land leasing. With the continuing increase in the absolute number of farmers on limited land, farms in India are becoming smaller and smaller. According to the National Sample Survey Organization, the average size of a holding operated in rural India fell from 1.67 hectares (1 hectare equals 2.47 acres) in 1981–82 to 1.34 hectares in 1991–92 and to 1.06 hectares in 2002–03. In 2002–03, marginal holdings, defined as holdings of one hectare or less, accounted for 70 percent of all operational holdings. Smallholdings, defined as holdings between one and two hectares, accounted for another 16 percent of the operational holdings. The share of marginal holdings in the total operated area rose from 16 percent in 1991–92 to 22 to 23 percent in 2002–03.[5]

This fragmentation of landholdings is having a negative effect on productivity. One way to consolidate these holdings would be to permit commercial farming as is currently being practiced in Punjab. Farmers could lease their land to corporations for farming. Consolidation, combined with the ability of corporations to go for horticulture crops for export or food processing, can increase the returns sufficiently to allow a handsome rent on land along with attractive profit rates for corporations.

Punjab is one of the few states that currently permit land leasing. Bharti Enterprises has recently started organizing farmers, including many small and marginal farmers, in the state into land consortiums that enable farming on large contiguous tracts of land. According to Karunakaran (2006), one of Bharti's lead farmers has created a farm of 1620 hectares. The small farmers lease out their pieces of land for an annual rent. They also receive a salary for work done on the farm.

There are obvious fears that commercial farming will be capital-intensive and may lead to worker displacement. There are two possible responses to this problem. First, insofar as such farming is accompanied by the expansion of food processing and export activities, it may generate no net loss of jobs. Instead, it may actually give the holders of small units lucrative rent on the land and a job that pays well. Second, commercial farming is not about to spread overnight across India. The process is bound to be slow. This means that even when commercial farming leads to net displacement of workers, other sectors of the economy will be expanding to absorb them. Within the democratic politics of India, there are enough checks and balances to slow the process in order to avoid massive unemployment through such farming.

INPUT MARKET REFORMS

Input markets in agriculture suffer from many distortions. In the following, I discuss reforms required in the land, credit, fertilizer, electricity, and water markets.

Land

We have already encountered some issues related to land in the context of product market entry. But we may now consider this market more centrally. One fact worth reiterating is that the power to legislate on land issues is vested largely in the states. Therefore, the central government has had at best very limited leverage in promoting these reforms. Indeed, big landowners who happen to be politically powerful at the state level have had considerable influence on the policies relating to land.

Traditional Land Reforms

Land reforms launched immediately after independence constituted the first step toward the reorganization of land markets.[6] Land reforms in India have had three main components:

- Abolition of the absentee landlords popularly known as *zamindars*;
- The imposition of a ceiling on landholdings, with a view to redistribution of land;
- Securing the rights of tenant-cultivators.

Zamindars were originally appointed as revenue collectors by the Mughal emperors. The Permanent Settlement of 1793 by the East India Company conferred ownership rights to land on them in a number of provinces, including Bihar, Bengal, and Orissa. At independence, *zamindars* in these states enjoyed ownership rights but did not actually cultivate land. The postindependence land reform aimed to return the ownership rights to the cultivators. But since the *zamindars* were politically powerful in their respective states, they partially blocked the reform. States allowed the *zamindars* to retain large chunks of land for *khudkasht* (self-cultivation). Therefore, the effect of the reform was twofold: Some land got taken away from *zamindars* and redistributed to cultivators, and *zamindars* became owner-cultivators of large chunks of lands by evicting the original cultivators.

The singular objective behind the imposition of land ceilings was redistribution of land. The abolition of *zamindars* could redistribute land only in the states with the *zamindari* system. But large farmers existed even in states where the land tenure system was raiyatwari, under which the owner (raiyat) paid rent directly to the state. Thus the redistributive reach of land ceilings was wider. But as with the *zamindari* reform, the actual redistribution of land resulting from the imposition of land ceilings was quite limited. Initial land ceilings, enacted by 1961, were very high. Indira Gandhi persuaded the states to bring these down considerably in the early 1970s, but actual redistribution remained limited. As of October 1992, redistributed land represented only 1.25 percent of the operational holdings in the 18 major states (Appu, 1996, p. 175).

The central government made three key recommendations relating to tenancy reform through the instrumentality of the Five-Year Plans. First, the rent should be fixed at between one-fifth and one-fourth of the produce. Second, tenants should be given permanent occupancy rights on the land they cultivate. Finally, an effort should be made to confer ownership rights on the tenants. The government also recommended, however, that the states permit the owners to evict the existing tenants from a portion of their land in order to resume "personal cultivation" on it.

Following these recommendations, most states have fixed the rent at between one-fifth and one-fourth of the produce. But tenancy often goes unreported, so that the reform is sabotaged at the implementation level, with higher rents charged. Most states that allow tenancy have given permanent tenancy rights to long-term cultivators. Only limited success has been achieved, however, in transferring ownership rights to cultivators. Most states have adopted a rather liberal definition of "personal cultivation," allowing large landowners to continue leasing out their land. As of 1992, tenancy reform had led to the conferral of ownership rights on only 4 percent of the total operated area. Just seven states—Assam, Gujarat, Himachal Pradesh, Karnataka, Kerala, Maharashtra, and West Bengal—accounted for 97 percent of this transfer (Appu, 1996, p. 187).

In my judgment, the emphasis of the land reforms on redistribution was misplaced. It was akin to the tight restrictions placed on investments by big business houses by Mrs. Gandhi during the 1970s, to combat the concentration of wealth. From the perspective of poverty reduction, the concern in this case should not have been with big business houses accumulating too much wealth, but with ensuring that they plowed back profits into activities that would create jobs for the masses. Likewise, given the difficulties of redistributing land, the focus of the land reform should have been on the protection of the user rights of actual cultivators.[7] Excessive focus on the transfer of ownership rights—an extremely difficult task in a democratic society—distracted the government from ensuring adequate protection of the rights of the cultivators.

The focus on giving ownership rights to cultivators led many states, including Bihar, Himachal Pradesh, Karnataka, and Uttar Pradesh, to outlaw tenancy altogether. This worked against cultivators with tenancy based on oral contracts and the tenant typically paying 50 percent of the produce as rent. In contrast, West Bengal, which continued to recognize tenancy, was able to dramatically improve the lot of the sharecroppers known as *bargardars* in the 1970s. In 1979, under Operation Barga, it uncovered 1.3 million *bargardars* and successfully secured their tenancy rights.

Future land reforms should focus on the recognition and implementation of tenancy rights. States that do not permit land leasing and tenancy should be encouraged to amend their laws. Even the states that currently allow land leasing and tenancy should undertake reforms that permit the owner and the cultivator to write explicit contracts. This would require, among other things, the elimination of the current ceiling on rent of one-fourth of the produce, since few transactions actually take place at this price.

The Vexed Issue of Land Titles

I briefly touched on the poor state of legal titles to properties in the cities in chapter 13. This problem is even more acute in rural India. Wadhwa (2002), who has studied and written about the subject for almost two decades, discusses in great detail the precise nature and history of the problem India faces in this area.[8] Traditionally, land records were kept for the purpose of collecting revenue rather than ensuring ownership rights. This is the reason the land records, when they exist, contain details such as cultivable land, soil quality, sources of irrigation, and cropping pattern. It was assumed that the person responsible for the payment of land revenue was also the proprietor of the land. Wadhwa (2002, p. 4702) writes:

> Thus, the present records-of-rights in land in India are fiscal in nature and presumptive in character. The person shown in the record as responsible for paying land revenue for a particular piece of land is presumed to be the proprietor of that piece of land unless it is proved otherwise. … Whatever be the entry in the record-of-rights in land, it is permissible to challenge it in an appropriate court or tribunal. Therefore, the revenue laws of the states lay down that no suit shall lie against the state government or any officer of the state government in respect of a claim to have an entry made in any record or register that is maintained by the government or to have any entry omitted or amended.
>
> Similarly, the law relating to registration of documents (deeds) also lays down that while accepting a document for registration, the registering authority need not concern itself about the validity of the document. This position arises because in India property legislation and legislation relating to registration of documents were never framed with the objective of providing a state guarantee of title to land. The law provides for the registration of document only and not for the registration of title. Therefore, a deed does not in itself prove title, it is merely a record of an isolated transaction.

In addition to the fragility of the land records as instruments of establishing the right to property, the records themselves are very incomplete. Once again, Wadhwa (2002 p. 4702) states this succinctly:

> But in all parts of the country, records relating to land are in a very bad shape. In many cases the land is recorded in the name of a person who died long ago and whose legal successors are now the owners but their names are not entered in the record. A similar highly unsatisfactory feature exists in respect of situation of transfer of lands by acts of parties. Land goes on being transferred without consequential mutation in the records with the result that the records as they exist and continue to exist today hardly reflect the present day reality regarding ownership of land. Millions of cases of mutation and measurement are pending in the country.

In addition to being incomplete, in many cases there are no land records at all. Wadhwa gives the example of an Andhra Pradesh district in which the field measurement books were missing in 19.5 percent of the cases, and torn and brittle in another 30 percent of the cases in 1988. Successive Five-Year Plans have recognized the problem, and Wadhwa offers quotations to this effect from every one of them, starting with the First Five-Year Plan. A 1973 taskforce of the Planning Commission reviewing the progress on land reforms also pointed to the absence of up-to-date land records as a serious obstacle to implementing land reforms. But no progress has been made toward finding a solution that gives the farmer the legal right to his land.

In the report "Guaranteeing Title to Land," submitted to the Planning Commission on August 31, 1989, Wadhwa recommended replacing the current presumptive rights of farmers with legal rights guaranteed by the state. As in other well-functioning democracies, Indian states should create a system whereby these rights are documented in the records maintained by the government as conclusive proofs of ownership. The government took no action, however, and the matter stands where it was more or less at independence.

Currently, an effort is under way to digitize the existing land records. While this is a useful exercise to ensure that the records that exist are properly documented and preserved, it will not solve the fundamental problem of the absence of state-guaranteed titles. The latter requires legislative action. While politically complex, this reform has a very large payoff. Not only will it give millions of farmers peace of mind and avoid millions of lawsuits in the future, it will also give rise to a highly efficient rural land market in India. States that decide to take action will also need to establish special tribunals to resolve the existing disputes speedily.

Rural Credit

C. H. Hanumantha Rao (2003) notes that farmers currently meet 60 percent of their credit requirements from formal financial institutions and 40 percent from informal sources including moneylenders, traders who bundle the sales of inputs and credit, friends, and relatives. Marginal and small farmers depend on the informal sources of credit substantially more. Moneylenders and traders are known to charge exceptionally high interest rates. I noted in chapter 7 that farmers committing suicide systematically incurred larger debts and relied proportionately more on informal sources of credit. This does not imply a causal relationship but does point to the poor availability of credit to those in distress.

In part, imperfections in the credit market derive from imperfections in the land market. As just explained, few farmers can use land as collateral to obtain credit from financial institutions, for which ensuring ownership is costly. In contrast, the village moneylender is familiar with the ownership of land as generally understood within the village, and has the resources for litigation in case a dispute arises. Therefore, he is willing to accept land as collateral, provided he can extract an ultra-high interest rate in return. In states where land leasing is illegal, a sharecropper has virtually no access to institutional credit for the purchase of inputs. Therefore, the grant of state-guaranteed land titles and legalization of land leasing where it is not currently permitted would help relax the credit constraint to some degree.

Another route to relaxing the credit constraint noted by C. H. Hanumantha Rao (2003) is through contract farming. High-value agriculture requires more working capital and is riskier than the cultivation of traditional crops. Processors and NGOs that are vertically integrated with farmers can provide inputs on credit in return for their produce. Because they must work closely with the farmers to ensure the specific variety and quality of produce, their monitoring costs of such loans are low. They are also in a sound position to borrow from formal financial institutions, thereby acting as nonbanking intermediaries for farmers.

One further avenue to expanding rural credit is through the self-help groups (SHGs) of women that have had reasonable success in India. One advantage of the SHGs is that they give the womenfolk among marginal and small farmers entry into nonfarm activities such as housing, dairying, water harvesting, marketing of agricultural goods, and health and education programs.

C. H. Hanumantha Rao (2003) points out that despite a broadening of the definition of the "priority sector," *direct* agricultural advances by commercial banks have declined to 11–12 percent, versus the target of 18 percent, in recent years. This has resulted principally from the banks' desire to minimize defaults. It is not altogether clear that this is necessarily a bad development. In the current deregulated environment, the banks are paying greater attention to the commercial viability of loans. This is welcome. Subsidized bank loans are a poor substitute for social policy. If the objective is to assist the poor, the proper instrument is direct transfer.

Fertilizer

India has been giving massive subsidies on fertilizer for more than two decades. This subsidy goes partially to the farmers and partially to firms producing fertilizer. I deal with this issue in detail in chapter 16. I argue there that the fertilizer subsidy should be phased out altogether, and the domestic fertilizer price linked to the world price through decanalization of imports complemented by an appropriate customs duty. The reasons are that the subsidy is highly regressive as it applies to farmers; it distorts input usage; and it encourages huge inefficiency among fertilizer manufacturers. There is simply no excuse for the use of tax revenues to subsidize an inefficient industry rather than effecting transfers to the poor.

Electricity and Irrigation

Free electricity and water have remained popular with politicians during elections. As a result, reform in this area has been extremely difficult. This is unfortunate, since the subsidies are not only regressive but also highly distortionary. They are regressive because the bigger the farmer, the larger the amount of water and electricity he uses. The subsidies are distortionary because they lead to highly wasteful use of canal water, ecological degradation from waterlogging, and excessive use of electricity. Because groundwater in India automatically belongs to the owner of the land, free electricity has led to its overexploitation and caused the shortage of drinking water in many parts of the country. Simultaneously, the fiscal burden created by free water and electricity has led the states to neglect maintenance of electricity lines and canals. In this respect, the subsidies have been a lose-lose proposition.

From both the efficiency and the equity viewpoints, it is desirable to charge farmers for the electricity they use. This reform being a part of the overall reform in the electricity sector, I discuss it in greater detail in chapter 17. Here I may note that the Electricity Act, 2003 recognizes the need for metering electricity usage by all consumers and for requiring them to pay. Once the state electricity regulatory commissions (SERCs) begin to function truly independently, politicians are likely to find it increasingly difficult to promise free electricity. Recently, when the Maharashtra government announced free electricity to farmers, the Maharashtra SERC successfully insisted that the state government transfer cash to the electricity utility before the latter sends out "zero bills" to the farmers (Dubash, 2005). Such actions can deter politicians from making promises they may eventually fail to deliver.

Once electricity is properly priced, some restraint on groundwater use will be automatically exerted through reduced use of electric water pumps. But more needs to be done with respect to the use of water from other sources. C. H. Hanumantha Rao (2002) discusses this issue in detail and offers several useful suggestions. He notes, for example, that India is well behind other countries in Asia in the use of participatory irrigation management. According to the Planning Commission (2000), irrigated land transferred to water users associations in India is only 7 percent, compared with 45 percent in Indonesia, 22 percent in Thailand, and 66 percent in the Philippines.

PUBLIC INVESTMENT IN AGRICULTURE AND RURAL INFRASTRUCTURE

Critics of reforms have often pointed out that public investment in agriculture in India has been declining steadily since the early 1980s. While this is evidently an unwelcome development in view of the importance of public investment in agriculture, this development must be evaluated in the context of three accompanying facts.

First, as the Planning commission (2001, p. 74, footnote 4) points out, public investment in agriculture in the national accounts does not include "investment in rural roads or development of markets, which are extremely important for agricultural production." and "It is possible that if these investments are included the decline in total investment may be less than it appears otherwise." Second, while public investment in agriculture has been declining, private investment in it has been rising and has partially compensated for the former. Finally and most important, as Gulati and Narayanan (2003, chap. 6) emphasize, the expansion of agricultural subsidies since the early 1980s has far outstripped the decline in public investment in agriculture. If we add public investment in agriculture and agricultural subsidies as a proportion of the GDP, they show a sharply rising trend during the 1980s and 1990s. If the government can bring the subsidies down—a desirable policy in itself—plentiful resources can be released for investment in rural India. Unfortunately, through the electoral process, farmers themselves seem to have shown a preference for privately beneficial subsidies over public investment.

In formulating future policy toward public investment in agriculture and rural development, three areas should get priority: rural roads, electricity (including rural electrification), and major and medium irrigation projects. Rural roads that feed into major highways connect farmers to the marketplace, and electricity is the critical input in both agricultural and nonagricultural economic activities. The provision of these two critical amenities can go a long way toward allowing farmers to exploit their private entrepreneurial talents. Major and medium irrigation projects provide a key public input into agriculture. Luckily, all three items are on the agenda of Bharat Nirman, a four-year business plan of the central government for rural infrastructure extending from 2005–06 to 2008–09.

I briefly discuss rural roads in chapter 18 and rural electrification in chapter 17. Therefore, here I focus on rural on irrigation. C. H. Hanumantha Rao (2003) notes that India has an irrigation potential of 58.5 million hectares from major and medium irrigation projects. The existing schemes exploit only 60 percent of this potential. The Bharat Nirman program proposes to create 10 million hectares of additional assured irrigation. The Planning Commission (2006) notes that achieving this goal would require accelerating the pace of 1.42 million hectares per year in recent years to 2.5 million hectares per year. A large number of major and medium irrigation projects launched in the Ninth and Tenth Five-Year Plans are incomplete. According to the Ministry of Water Resources, 4.2 million hectares of irrigation capacity can be added by simply completing these projects.[9]

Unfortunately, the progress to date on irrigation under the Bharat Nirman is not encouraging. The Ministry of Water Resources reports that the achievement during 2005–06 was approximately 1.55 million hectares, which is well below the average pace of 2.5 million hectares per year required to achieve the overall target, and much closer to the pace of 1.42 million hectares per year achieved in recent years. The achievement during the first six months of 2006–07 (353,000 hectares) is even more worrisome. One measure the government can take to speed up the completion of irrigation schemes is to use the instrumentality of public-private partnership that has been successful in road construction.

CONCLUDING REMARKS

I began by arguing that the solution to poverty even among farmers is to be found outside farming. Acceleration of growth in industry and services must pull increasingly larger numbers of marginal farmers and landless laborers in agriculture into gainful employment. This will not only improve the well-being of the migrating workers but also will raise the wages of those left behind by increasing land-labor ratio.

Nevertheless, the process of this transformation can easily take two decades. This calls for immediate relief to the farm population. In part, this relief must come from direct transfers to those below the poverty line. But importantly, it should come through increased productivity in agriculture. In this chapter, I have identified several distortions in product and factor markets that constrain productivity in agriculture. Removal of these constraints can bring rapid relief to the farm population.

Some of the recent reforms have already triggered a process that promises to begin the transformation of agriculture. Most important among these is the reform of agricultural marketing in a large number of states. In addition to giving farmers direct access to buyers, this reform opens the door to contract farming. Contract farming can bring a major shift in the pattern of cultivation toward horticulture that contributes to the development of the food-processing industry. If rapidly implemented, the recent Food Safety and Standards Act, 2006 would complement the marketing reform and accelerate the expansion of food processing.

Among the reforms that remain are the replacement of food, fertilizer, and electricity subsidies by cash subsidies to the poor, and improved provision of rural roads, electricity, and irrigation. In the medium run, the government must also tackle three difficult but most crucial reforms: creation of state-guaranteed land titles; legalization of tenancy rights where they do not currently exist; and giving the owner and the tenant the right to freely negotiate the terms of their contract. It is time that markets are allowed to function competitively not just in industry and services but also in agriculture.

PART V

The Government

15

TAX REFORM

Toward a Uniform Goods and Services Tax

In part III, we considered taxes and revenues at the aggregate level in relation to the fiscal deficit. In doing so, we restricted ourselves to macroeconomic issues such as how gaps between total taxes and expenditures contribute to budget deficits, and how they should be adjusted over time on the way to reducing the latter. We now turn to microeconomic aspects of taxes and expenditures, focusing in particular on the efficiency implications of their overall level and allocation across different sectors.

In principle, we must determine the taxes and expenditures on various items simultaneously through an optimization exercise that maximizes the real income of the country with respect to these variables. But the data necessary to solve such a gigantic maximization problem are seldom available. Moreover, in practice, considerations other than real income that are not readily incorporated into a formal maximization exercise usually influence the choices of taxes and expenditures. For example, past taxes and expenditures, pressures from interest groups, and electoral politics influence the current tax and expenditure choices at the margin. Therefore, the common practice is to determine the expenditures and taxes separately and to apply the key principles of taxation and expenditures informally and at best approximately. The discussion of tax policies in this chapter and of expenditure policies in the next several chapters reflects this reality. I begin immediately below with a brief introduction to some conceptual issues in the choice of taxes.

TAXATION: SOME CONCEPTUAL CONSIDERATIONS

The conventional optimal taxation theory seeks to determine the tax rates so as to yield the required revenue at the minimum efficiency cost. A central message of this theory is that in a small open economy, which cannot influence world prices, the government must rely solely on taxes on final consumption of goods to raise the revenue it needs. In other words, optimal taxation rules out direct taxes such as the personal income tax and the corporate profits tax, and trade taxes. The intuitive reasoning behind this prescription is that it is best to first maximize the value of the production basket at world prices and then distort prices to raise the necessary revenue. Taxes on inputs, the personal income tax, the corporate profits tax, and trade taxes adversely affect the value of the production basket at world prices, and are therefore ruled out.

Under some simplifying assumptions, the optimal taxation theory yields the well-known Ramsey Rule, which states that the optimal ad valorem tax on the consumption of a good is higher, the lower the (compensated) elasticity of demand for it. Intuitively, if the elasticity of demand is low, a given tax on the product leads to a relatively small deviation from the initial distortion-free optimal quantity and, thus, imposes a relatively small efficiency cost. Taxing this product more highly than those with high demand elasticities minimizes the efficiency cost of taxation.

Despite its dominance in the academic literature, the theory of optimal taxation has played at best a limited role in the actual design of the tax systems. There are at least five reasons for this fact. First, governments are often driven by both efficiency and equity considerations. The prescriptions derived from the conventional optimal tax theory may be in conflict with equity considerations. At the broadest level, the rich save a much larger proportion of their income than the poor. Therefore, the tax on consumption is in general regressive. At the micro level, the Ramsey Rule states that we tax the products with low demand elasticity at high rates and vice versa. But the poor often spend their incomes disproportionately on products, such as food, that exhibit low demand elasticity. If the government wishes to target equity through indirect taxes, it will tax the products consumed by the rich at high rates and products consumed by the poor at low rates, regardless of their demand elasticity. Additionally, it will resort to progressive direct taxes.

The second reason why the core optimal taxation theory has played a very limited role in the actual design of the tax policy is that the detailed information required to compute precise optimal tax rates is seldom available. Even the implementation of the Ramsey Rule, which relies on a very strict and unrealistic set of assumptions, requires information that is not readily available. Moreover, the elasticities shift over time, so that having their values at any one point in time is insufficient.

Third and more important, even if we had the necessary information on the relevant elasticities, the presence of political economy pressures would be likely to rob the actual tax structure of the optimality sought by the government. Specifically, once producer lobbies recognize that the government is willing to tax different products at different rates, they become active in seeking lower taxes for their specific products. Insofar as the government is susceptible to these pressures, the actual structure that emerges has no resemblance to what had been initially thought to be the optimal structure. In the presence of strong self-interested lobbies, the government has a better chance of minimizing the efficiency cost by taxing all products at a uniform rate. As Panagariya and Rodrik (1993) demonstrate in the context of tariffs, such a policy introduces a free-rider problem in lobbying: The tax applied to a given product is the same as that applied to all other products, regardless of the lobbying effort by the producers of that product. This virtually eliminates the incentive to lobby.

Fourth, taxation of some products at high rates and others at low rates leads to tax avoidance. Producers subject to high rates try to misclassify their products as those subject to low rates. Therefore, even if the tax system is ex ante optimal, it may turn out to be nonoptimal ex post. Additionally, the attempts to misclassify the products give rise to tax disputes that are very costly in a country where dispute resolution moves at a snail's pace.

Finally, at least in the early stages of development, administrative barriers may make it difficult for a country to raise the necessary revenue solely from a consumption tax. Trade taxes are administratively the easiest to collect and often form a significant part of tax revenues in the early stages of development. Likewise, domestic indirect taxes take the form of easier-to-collect excise duties in the organized sector, with little provision for rebates on the taxes paid on inputs. Other sources of revenue, such as personal income tax and corporate profits tax in the formal sector of the economy, are tapped as well.

The task of tax reform is to gradually replace this hybrid system with one that better targets the twin objectives of efficiency and equity while raising the necessary tax revenue. Our discussion above suggests that one element of this reform has to be reduced reliance on trade taxes. As for domestic indirect taxes, they must be replaced by a genuine consumption tax at a uniform rate on all commodities, with the poor protected against the burden of such taxes through cash subsidies. In practice, the governments find it politically more expedient to exempt food from taxation rather than opt for cash subsidies. Indeed, even when cash subsidies to the poor are offered, they shy away from taxing food. Therefore, uniformity in indirect tax rates is unlikely to be absolute. In terms of further advancing the equity objective, the focus should be on poverty reduction rather than promotion of equity at all levels. In turn, antipoverty expenditure programs, rather than an overly progressive direct tax system, best address poverty reduction. Therefore, direct taxes should aim at raising sufficient revenue to finance antipoverty measures. This points to a modestly progressive orientation of direct taxes, with the bulk of the redistribution in favor of the poor achieved through expenditures, mainly cash transfers. An aggressively progressive direct tax system, such as that prevailing in India in the early 1970s, has an adverse impact on the incentives to create wealth, and therefore growth, which is the primary tool of poverty reduction.

For future reference, it may be noted that a major task of the tax reform in India has been to replace myriad domestic indirect taxes with the so-called value-added tax (VAT). It is important to note in this context that if it is properly designed, the VAT effectively mimics the consumption tax. Under it, the producer is rebated the taxes paid on inputs. This feature of the VAT eliminates the taxes on production at all stages, with the burden of taxation falling entirely on the final consumption. The VAT enjoys a key administrative advantage over a tax levied on consumption directly: It provides the authorities a tool to better enforce tax payments. Thus, for example, the rebate claim filed by a shirt producer provides tax authorities information on the tax he has paid to his supplier of fabric. If the tax paid by the fabric supplier (net of his own rebates on inputs such as fiber) does not match this rebate claim, the tax authorities immediately know that one of the two parties has committed tax fraud.

THE TAX SYSTEM AND TAX REVENUES IN INDIA

The Constitution of India explicitly spells out the tax powers of the central and state governments. It assigns the major broad-based taxes, including nonagricultural personal income and wealth taxes; corporate profits taxes; customs duties; and excise duties on manufactured products (other than alcoholic products) to the central government. In recent times, excise duties have largely been converted into the manufacturers' VAT.[1] The constitution assigns agricultural personal income and wealth taxes; sales taxes; excise taxes on alcoholic beverages; taxes on motor vehicles and passengers traveling in commercial vehicles such as taxis and buses; stamp duties and registration fees on the transfer of property; and taxes on electricity to the states. The state list also includes the taxes on property and on the entry of goods into a local area for consumption, use, or sale, but these are assigned to local bodies. Originally, taxes on certain specific services, such as entertainment and trade, were explicitly assigned to the states; those on the remaining services got assigned to the central government by default, under residual taxation powers given to it by the constitution. But in 2003, the 88th constitutional amendment assigned the power to tax all services to the central government, with the tax proceeds collected and appropriated by the latter and the states according to the principles formulated by the Parliament.

Recognizing that the revenue proceeds of the states will be inadequate to meet their expenditure needs, the Indian Constitution provides for the sharing of some of the central government's tax revenues with them. For example, in 2002–03, the states raised 38 percent of the overall government revenues but accounted for 58 percent of the expenditures (M. G. Rao and Singh, 2004). The constitution originally provided for the compulsory sharing of the personal income tax proceeds and the central government (union) excise duties. Trade taxes and corporate profits taxes were not subject to sharing. The 80th Constitutional Amendment changed these provisions by making all but a few narrowly defined central tax revenues subject to sharing. This change became effective in fiscal year 2000–01. The Finance Commission, which the president appoints every five years, determines the shares of the central government and the states in these taxes and the allocation of the share of the latter across different states.

For clarity in discussion, it is customary to divide the total taxes into direct and indirect taxes at the central and state levels. Personal income and corporate profits taxes account for virtually all of the direct taxes at the central level. Excise and customs duties likewise account for more than 90 percent of the indirect taxes at the center.[2] At the level of the state, indirect taxes account for more than 95 percent of the tax revenue. And as for indirect taxes, sales taxes account for 60 percent of the revenues.

Table 15.1 shows the direct and indirect taxes collected as proportions of the GDP by the central government, the states, and the country as a whole at ten-year intervals until 1970–71, at five-year intervals from 1970–71 to 1990–91, and every year since 1990–91. Figure 15.1 correspondingly shows all-India tax collections as proportions of the GDP for all years starting in 1980–81. Three features of all-India tax-GDP ratios in table 15.1 and figure 15.1 stand out:

- The total tax revenues as proportions of the GDP rose steadily until 1987–88, stagnated briefly, and then exhibited a declining trend before turning upward again in the 2000s. Virtually all of the increase in the tax-GDP ratio until 1987–88 came from indirect tax revenues, which rose from just 4 percent of the GDP in 1950–51 to 14 percent in 1987–88.
- Direct taxes as a proportion of the GDP stagnated during the 1980s but showed a mildly rising trend during the 1990s and a sharper rise in the 2000s. The share of direct taxes in the total revenues had dropped to just 13 percent by 1987–88. This trend reversed subsequently, with the budgetary estimates of this share rising to almost 28 percent in 2004–05.
- Decline in indirect taxes at the center largely accounted for the decline in the all-India tax-GDP ratio during the 1990s. We will later see that contrary to some predictions, trade liberalization in the 1990s led to a decline in trade

TABLE 15.1: Direct and Indirect Tax Revenues as Proportion of GDP

Year	Total (All India)			Center			States		
	Direct	Indirect	Total	Direct	Indirect	Total	Direct	Indirect	Total
1	*2*	*3*	*4*	*5*	*6*	*7*	*8*	*9*	*10*
1950–51	2.3	4.0	6.3	1.8	2.3	4.1	0.6	1.7	2.2
1960–61	2.3	5.5	7.9	1.7	3.5	5.2	0.6	2.0	2.7
1970–71	2.2	8.2	10.4	1.9	5.1	7.0	0.3	3.1	3.4
1975–76	3.0	10.4	13.4	2.7	6.5	9.1	0.4	4.0	4.3
1980–81	2.3	11.5	13.8	2.1	7.1	9.2	0.2	4.5	4.6
1985–86	2.3	13.3	15.6	2.0	8.3	10.3	0.2	5.0	5.3
1987–88	2.1	14.0	16.1	1.9	8.7	10.6	0.2	5.2	5.5
1990–91	2.2	13.3	15.4	1.9	8.2	10.1	0.2	5.1	5.3
1991–92	2.6	13.3	15.8	2.4	8.0	10.3	0.2	5.3	5.5
1992–93	2.6	12.7	15.3	2.4	7.6	10.0	0.2	5.1	5.3
1993–94	2.5	11.7	14.2	2.4	6.5	8.8	0.2	5.2	5.4
1994–95	2.9	11.8	14.6	2.7	6.5	9.1	0.2	5.3	5.5
1995–96	3.0	11.7	14.8	2.8	6.5	9.4	0.2	5.2	5.4
1996–97	3.0	11.7	14.7	2.8	6.6	9.5	0.2	5.1	5.2
1997–98	3.3	11.2	14.5	3.2	6.0	9.1	0.2	5.2	5.4
1998–99	2.8	10.6	13.4	2.7	5.6	8.3	0.1	5.0	5.1
1999–2000	3.1	11.0	14.2	3.0	5.9	8.9	0.2	5.2	5.3
2000–01	3.4	11.2	14.6	3.3	5.8	9.0	0.2	5.4	5.6
2001–02	3.2	10.6	13.8	3.1	5.2	8.2	0.2	5.4	5.6
2002–03	3.6	10.9	14.5	3.4	5.4	8.8	0.2	5.5	5.7
2003–04 (R.E.)	3.9	11.2	15.2	3.8	5.5	9.2	0.2	5.8	5.9
2004–05 (B.E.)	4.7	11.6	16.2	4.5	5.7	10.2	0.2	5.8	6.0

Note: R.E. and B.E. stand for "revised estimate" and "budget estimate," respectively.

Source: Ministry of Finance, Government of India, *Public Finance Statistics* (2004–05).

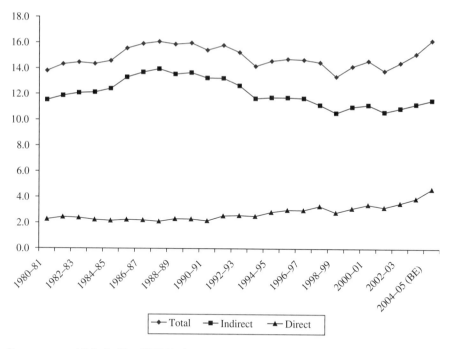

FIGURE 15.1: All-India Tax-GDP Ratios

taxes as a proportion of the GDP. Import response to liberalization was rather muted, so that increased imports failed to offset the decline in the revenues resulting purely from the decline in the tariff rates. Rationalization of the excise duties was accompanied by a substantial reduction in them, with a concomitant decline in the excise tax revenues as a proportion of the GDP. What prevented the complete collapse of the tax-GDP ratio was significant improvement in the performance of the central direct taxes, which rose from barely 1.9 percent of the GDP in 1990–91 to 4.5 percent in 2004–05.[3] Both personal income taxes and corporate profits taxes rose sharply during the 1990s and early 2000s. We will discuss these changes in greater detail later.

I next turn to a discussion of tax reforms in India. As in other areas, reforms in this area were piecemeal in the pre-1990s era, with some acceleration during the second half of the 1980s. They turned more systematic and systemic in the 1990s and 2000s.

TAX REFORMS PRIOR TO THE 1990s

Tax reform in India has taken the existing tax system as given. Moreover, the reforms of direct and indirect taxes have been undertaken independently of each other. Given persistent shortfall in the tax revenues, even the issue of how tax revenues should be divided between these two categories or across more detailed subcategories has rarely been discussed. Instead, the objective in each area has been to raise more revenues.

The issue of whether the country should simply eliminate direct taxes and rely exclusively on indirect taxes, as suggested by the optimal taxation theory, has never been a subject of serious debate in India. Even in the late 1980s, when direct taxes contributed less than 15 percent of the total tax revenues, personal income taxation was a major source of harassment of taxpayers by tax authorities, and the populism of the 1970s having somewhat receded and given way to pragmatism in policy, the issue of the abolition of direct taxes never surfaced. In the 1990s and 2000s, the situation changed considerably. Indirect tax revenues declined in importance, and the share of direct taxes in the total revenues rose to almost 30 percent by 2004–05. Moreover, fiscal deficits remained relatively large. Therefore, the option to abolish direct taxes, even if politically feasible, became entirely unavailable on fiscal grounds.

Prior to the 1990s, two key reports guided the piecemeal reforms in direct and indirect taxation. As the 1970s unfolded, the desire to raise resources for planned development and obsession with income distribution had given rise to marginal tax rates on personal incomes in excess of 90 percent. The inability of tax authorities to control the resulting tax evasion led the government to set up the Direct Taxes Enquiry Committee (Government of India, 1971) under the chairmanship of K. N. Wanchoo, which recommended significant reductions in the marginal tax rates.[4] On the indirect taxes, the Indirect Taxes Inquiry Committee (Government of India, 1977), under the chairmanship of L. K. Jha, undertook a similar exercise. It recommended replacing the central excise duties with a modified value-added tax. A half-hearted attempt to implement this recommendation was made in 1986.

Direct Taxes

An overly progressive personal income tax regime was yet another element in the set of populist policies Prime Minister Indira Gandhi introduced following the 1969 split in the Congress Party. She had ousted Morarji Desai from the Finance Ministry just prior to the announcement of the bank nationalization and had retained the portfolio herself. As finance minister, in March 1970, she presented the 1970–71 budget and announced the redistributive role of taxation policy in no uncertain terms: "Taxation is also a major instrument in all modern societies to achieve greater equality of incomes and wealth. It is, therefore, proposed to make our direct tax system serve this purpose by increasing income taxation at higher levels as well as by substantially enhancing the present rates of taxation on wealth and gifts."[5]

In her budget, Gandhi raised the top marginal tax rate from its already high level of 82.5 percent to 85 percent, and lowered the threshold defining the highest income bracket from 250,000 rupees to 200,000 rupees. In addition, she imposed a 10 percent surcharge on the tax. This meant that anyone with an annual income of 200,000 rupees ($25,674 at the prevailing exchange rate) or more faced an effective marginal tax rate of 93.50 percent. In the 1971–72 budget, Y. B. Chavan, the newly appointed finance minister, raised the surcharge to 15 percent, bringing the top marginal tax rate to 97.75 percent.

Reporting in December 1971, the Direct Taxes Enquiry Committee (Government of India, 1971), popularly called the Wanchoo Committee after its chairman, took a critical view of the high marginal tax rates. It held the high rates responsible for widespread tax evasion and recommended bringing the effective top marginal rate down to 70 percent. But its recommendations were not immediately heeded and the system continued to get worse, at least for a short while. By 1973–74, the system came to have 11 tax brackets, ranging from 10 to 85 percent. The exemption limit was set at 5,000 rupees, which meant that anyone earning more than 5,000 rupees per year was subject to positive personal income tax. There was a surcharge on top of the regular tax of 10 percent for individuals with incomes below 15,000 rupees, and of 15 percent for those with higher incomes. This brought the top effective tax rate to 97.75 percent.[6]

Luckily, the 1974–75 budget saw the return of some sanity to the tax system.[7] In line with the recommendation of the Wanchoo Committee, Finance Minister Chavan brought the top marginal tax rate down to 70 percent, though with a twist: He kept a 10 percent surcharge on the regular tax, which made the effective marginal tax rate 77 percent. In the 1976–77 budget, C. Subramanium, who succeeded Chavan as finance minister, continued this process by reducing the top marginal tax rate to 60 percent plus the 10 percent surcharge. Subramaniam also lowered the wealth tax from 5 percent to 2.5 percent.

Under the Janata government, which lasted from March 1977 to January 1980, the income tax surcharge rose to 20 percent, taking the top effective marginal income tax rate to 72 percent in 1979–80. The top wealth tax also rose back to 5 percent. Interestingly, however, Gandhi returned to power in January 1980 and resumed the process of compressing the top tax rates. She lowered the tax surcharge back to 10 percent in the 1980–81 budget. Though this rose marginally to 12.5 percent in the 1982–83 budget, the 1983–84 budget brought the top marginal tax rate down to 55 percent from 60 percent. This lowered the top effective marginal tax rate from 67.50 percent to 61.875 percent.

The last major reform of personal income tax prior to 1991 took place in 1985–86. The assassination of Gandhi in December 1984 had brought her son Rajiv Gandhi to the helm. The latter appointed pro-reform V. P. Singh as finance minister. In his 1985–86 budget, Singh slashed the effective top marginal tax rate to 50 percent and cut the number of tax brackets from eight to four. He also reduced the top wealth tax rate from 5 percent to 2 percent.

Very little was done prior to the 1990s in the area of corporate profits tax. Singh took the main action in his 1985–86 budget. He brought down the basic rate for widely held companies to 50 percent. He also unified the several rates applicable to different categories of closely held companies at 55 percent.

Indirect Taxes

In the postindependence era, the government levied excise duties to raise revenue on a small number of selected items. This list grew over time with the increase in revenue needs. Initially, the duties were levied on raw materials and intermediate inputs, but eventually consumer goods were included as well. The government extended the tax to all manufactures in 1975–76.

The structure of excise duties was highly variegated, with some commodities subject to per-unit (specific) duties and others to ad valorem duties. By the mid-1970s, there were as many as 24 different ad valorem rates, varying from 2 to 100 percent. The Indirect Tax Enquiry Report (Government of India, 1977), presented by the Jha Committee (named for its chairman), offered a detailed analysis of the efficiency and distributive effects of this complex tax system and recommended the conversion of the specific duties into ad valorem rates, unification of rates, and introduction of an input tax credit to replace the cascading excise tax with a manufacturing stage value-added tax (MANVAT).

No action was taken on the Jha Committee recommendations until Singh became finance minister. In the 1986–87 budget, he proceeded to introduce the so-called modified VAT (MODVAT) in 37 chapters of the Central Excise Tariff. The MODVAT promised rebates on input taxes paid by producers up to the manufacturing stage; such rebates could not be extended to the final sales of goods since sales taxes fell under the purview of the states and not the central government. Acharya (2005), who served in the Finance Ministry during this period, describes this reform as a "huge" step forward. Indeed, noting that Singh addressed the reform of both direct and indirect taxes in a "reasonably integrated manner" and paid due attention to efficiency in the design of the reforms, he credits Singh with having launched the modern tax reform in India.

M. G. Rao and R. K. Rao (2005–06) take a critical view of the MODVAT reform, however, arguing that the government introduced the change virtually without any preparation, with the result that the implementation became an exercise in "learning by doing." To quote them:

> This was a strange combination of taxation based on physical verification of goods with provision of input tax credit. The coverage of the credit mechanism too evolved over time—it started with items from select chapters on both the inputs side and the output side, where the credit mechanism was based on a one-to-one correspondence between inputs and outputs. It was only by 1996–97, however, that it covered majority of commodities in the excise tariff and incorporated comprehensive credit. Nowhere else in the world can one find VAT introduction so complicated in its structure and so difficult in its operations and so incomplete in its coverage. In fact, the revenue from the tax as a ratio of GDP showed a decline after the introduction of MODVAT. (pp. 72–73)

As usual, truth perhaps lies somewhere in between these two extremes. The direct tax reform by Singh did go farther than that under any previous finance minister. A good case can be made that this reform brought significant efficiency gains. This is particularly valid since we know that the larger the existing distortion, the greater the gain from unit reduction in it. But regarding the MODVAT, the criticisms of M. G. Rao and R. K. Rao are valid in that tax rebates were determined by physical verification of products rather than through matching of the rebate claim by the input buyer and the tax paid by the input seller. Moreover, the highly partial coverage of products and the inputs used in them left it unclear whether efficiency was gained or lost. As subsequent efforts to put a genuine VAT in place in the 1990s and 2000s revealed, this was a rather complex reform requiring sustained effort over a long period of time, which the Singh reform did not seem to anticipate.

On trade taxes, the 1980s largely saw an increase in the duty rates. Some authors view this as a sign of increased protection, but as I have noted in chapter 4, this is an erroneous assessment. Increases in the tariff rates were largely applied to products subject to strict import licensing, and merely converted the quota rents accruing to importers into government revenues. Products subject to delicensing through the

OGL actually saw their duty rates decline. The net effect of the change (including the expansion of the OGL) was a decline in protection and improved fiscal position.

REFORMS IN THE 1990s AND 2000s

The door to systematic tax reform was opened by the 1991 crisis. The reform followed the recommendations of the Tax Reform Committee (TRC) headed by Raja Chelliah. The TRC submitted its interim report in December 1991, and its two-part final report in August 1992 and January 1993 (Government of India, 1992, 1993). Part I of the final report dealt with domestic taxes, and part II with trade taxes. The next milestone in the reform process was the Expert Group on Taxation of Services (Government of India, 2001), headed by Govinda Rao, which outlined the program for bringing services centrally into the tax net. Finally, the Task Forces on Direct and Indirect Taxes (Government of India, 2002a, 2002b), headed by Vijay Kelkar, initiated a second round of reform of the conventional direct and indirect taxes, frontally attacking the "exemption raj" and emphasizing the importance of improving tax administration to bring down the transaction costs. The recommendations of these Kelkar task forces were later subsumed into or superseded by those of the Task Force on the Implementation of the Fiscal Responsibility and Budget Management Act (Government of India, 2004), also headed by Kelkar. I discuss below the reforms flowing from these and other key reports.

Direct Taxes Imposed by the Central Government

In this subsection, I discuss the reforms of the personal and corporate income tax policies, steps taken to improve the tax administration in these areas, the introduction of some ad hoc measures going against the spirit of the reforms, and the impact of the reform on the revenues and progressiveness of the tax system.

The Personal Income Tax

The 1992–93 budget of Manmohan Singh implemented the key reforms recommended by the Chelliah Committee for personal income taxation. Singh reduced the number of tax rates to three: 20, 30, and 40 percent. He also exempted all financial assets from the wealth tax and reduced the wealth tax rate on other assets to 1 percent, with an exemption of up to 1.5 million rupees. These changes represented major reductions and rationalization of the direct taxes. After these changes, the next major set of changes in direct taxation came with the 1997–98 budget, which reduced the personal income tax rates to 10, 20, and 30 percent; these remain in force to date, with some adjustments made over time to the income brackets to which these rates apply. Per the 2005–06 budget, incomes between 100,000 and 150,000 rupees are subject to 10 percent tax; those between 150,000 and 250,000, to 20 percent; and those above 250,000, to 30 percent. Additionally, a 10 percent surcharge applies to incomes exceeding 1 million rupees, and a 2 percent education cess (tax) applies to all taxpayers. The exemption limit, which had been 50,000 rupees since 1998–99, was raised to 100,000 rupees by the 2005–06 budget. This budget also raised the exemption limit for women and senior citizens to 125,000 and 150,000 rupees, respectively. Additionally, savings up to 100,000 rupees were made deductible from the taxable income, and many instrument-specific exemptions were eliminated.

The Corporate Income Tax

Turning to the corporate income tax, per the recommendations of the Chelliah Committee report, the 1993–94 budget eliminated the distinction between widely held and closely held companies, and reduced the common tax rate on them to 40 percent from 50 percent for the former, and from 55 percent for the latter. The 1997–98 budget reduced this rate further, to 35 percent for domestic companies and 48 percent for foreign companies. The 2005–06 budget reduced the rate for domestic companies to 30 percent, with a surcharge of 10 percent. Thus, the corporate income tax and the top personal income tax rates have now been aligned, and the reform has progressed far beyond the recommendations of the Chelliah Committee.

Tax Administration

Important improvements have also been made in the area of tax administration. The scope of tax deduction at the source has been gradually expanded to cover hard-to-tax groups. Progress has also been made in expanding the permanent account number, which is equivalent to the Social Security number in the United States and allows easy tracking of the returns over time. The Tax Information Network, aimed at the verification of tax information filed by individuals, has been expanded as well, and was recently outsourced to the National Securities Depository Ltd. Finally, from 1997–98 to April 2006, a one-by-six scheme was operated to expand the personal income tax base. Under the scheme, every individual living in a large city and satisfying any one of six specified conditions—ownership of a house, a car, a credit card, a telephone connection, or a membership in a club, or undertaking foreign travel—was required to file a tax return. This requirement was abolished by the 2006–07 budget.

New Distortionary Taxes

While these changes represent considerable simplifications and rationalization of the direct tax system, the period since the mid-1990s has also seen the emergence of several ad hoc measures that violate the spirit of the reforms. First, successive budgets have shown a great deal of instability with respect to the taxation of dividends. Originally, India had taxed dividends first as company profits and then as income in the hands of the respective recipients at the marginal rates applicable to them. The Chelliah Committee wrestled with this "double taxation" issue at length but eventually came out in favor of letting the existing system stay in place. In 1997–98, Finance Minister Chidambaram decided to abandon this system, however, and freed dividends in the hands of the recipients from taxation. Instead, he introduced a 10 percent tax on the distributions at the company stage, in addition to the usual corporate income tax on them. Finance Minister Yashwant Sinha raised this rate to 20 percent in the 2000–01 budget, but brought it back down to 10 percent in the

2001–02 budget. In his 2002–03 budget, Sinha reverted to the original "double tax-ation" system, but his successor, Jaswant Singh, reversed that decision yet again by switching to a 12.5 percent tax at the company stage and no taxation on dividends in the hands of the recipients.

Second, the 1996–97 budget also introduced the so-called minimum alternate tax (MAT). Through taking advantage of the generous investment and deprecia-tion allowances, there had come to exist "zero-tax" companies that paid no corpo-rate income tax. The MAT stipulated that if, after all eligible deductions, the total income of a company fell below 30 percent of the book profit, its total income would be deemed to be 30 percent of the book profit. At the time, this led to an effective MAT of 12 percent of book profits.

Third, in April 2004, the government introduced the securities transactions tax, and in April 2005 it introduced the cash withdrawal tax.[8] The former is a tax on the purchases and sales of equity-based instruments, and the latter is a 0.1 percent charge on all cash withdrawals above 25,000 rupees from current accounts of com-mercial banks. Both measures are contrary to the spirit of economic reforms in that they discourage financial intermediation. The former additionally discriminates against equity instruments relative to debt instruments. The latter falls dispropor-tionately on small and medium-sized firms, which have to withdraw large amounts of cash from bank accounts to pay their employees.

Finally, the 2005–06 budget introduced a rather anomalous tax on certain legiti-mate expenses of companies as perquisites. The Income Tax Act allows the govern-ment to tax identifiable perquisites received by employees from their companies as ordinary personal income. But the 2005–06 budget goes a step further and classi-fies a range of other expenses by the company not directly assignable to any single employee as taxable perquisites. These benefits—including entertainment, confer-ences, gifts, use of club facilities, maintenance of guest house, hotel boarding and lodging, company car and telephone provided to employees, and travel (including foreign travel expenses)—are now taxed through the so-called Fringe Benefits Tax, payable by the employer at 30 percent.

Impact on the Revenue and Progressiveness of the Tax System

Table 15.2 shows the evolution of the shares of various central taxes and of total central tax revenues in the GDP. As we saw earlier, direct taxes had declined in importance during the 1980s. This is true of both corporation and personal income taxes, according to table 15.2. But with the reform and improved administration, the share of these taxes in the total central government revenues rose from less than 20 percent in 1989–90 to almost 44 percent in 2004–05. The expansion of corporation taxes has been particularly impressive, with their share in the total tax revenue ris-ing from just 9.4 percent in 1989–90 to 27.2 percent in 2004–05.

Bhalla (2004) credits tax cuts with the rise in the personal income tax revenues. To quote him (Bhalla, 2004, p.3), "Thus, the total effect of tax cuts [in 1997–98] on tax compliance on 'adjusted' tax revenues (after controlling for the fact that there was growth in the economy and inflation, both factors which moved people into higher tax groups and therefore higher tax revenue) is a 43 percent *increase* in rev-enues i.e. the revenue elasticity of tax cuts is a high—1.43." This claim goes farther

TABLE 15.2: Gross Tax Revenues of the Central Government (as percent of GDP)

Year	Corporation	Personal Income	Customs	Union Excise	Service	Others	Total
1	*2*	*3*	*4*	*5*	*6*	*7*	*8*
1969–70	0.8	1.1	1.0	3.6	0.0	0.0	6.5
1974–75	0.9	1.1	1.7	4.2	0.0	0.0	8.0
1979–80	1.2	1.1	2.4	5.0	0.0	0.0	9.7
1984–85	1.0	0.8	2.9	4.5	0.0	0.0	9.3
1989–90	1.0	1.0	3.7	4.6	0.0	0.1	10.4
1994–95	1.4	1.2	2.7	3.7	0.0	0.1	9.0
1995–96	1.4	1.3	3.0	3.4	0.1	0.1	9.2
1996–97	1.4	1.3	3.1	3.3	0.1	0.1	9.2
1997–98	1.3	1.1	2.6	3.2	0.1	0.1	8.4
1998–99	1.4	1.2	2.3	3.1	0.1	0.1	8.1
1999–2000	1.6	1.3	2.5	3.2	0.1	0.1	8.8
2000–01	1.7	1.5	2.3	3.3	0.1	0.0	9.0
2001–02	1.6	1.4	1.8	3.2	0.1	0.0	8.1
2002–03	1.9	1.5	1.8	3.3	0.2	0.1	8.8
2003–04	2.3	1.5	1.8	3.3	0.3	0.0	9.2
2004–05 (R.E.)	2.7	1.6	1.8	3.2	0.5	0.0	9.8

Source: Acharya (2005, table 2), which in turn cites *Indian Public Finance Statistics* (various issues); Ministry of Finance, *Economic Survey* (2004–05); and Budget Papers (2004–05, 2005–06).

than the Laffer curve hypothesis. During the 1980s, the supplyside economists in the United States, most prominently Arthur Laffer, had argued that the personal income tax cuts proposed by President Ronald Reagan would lead to such a large increase in income that the tax revenues would actually rise. Bhalla finds an extremely large increase in the tax revenue even holding the incomes constant!

But, as M. G. Rao and R. K. Rao (2006) point out, there are not only technical problems with the way Bhalla derives this result, but he also ignores one crucial factor behind the rise in the tax revenue: improved enforcement. As already discussed, the reforms in India throughout the 1990s, and especially during 1996–98, had been accompanied by a major effort to improve the tax administration. But Rao and Rao (2006, p. 90) make the point more concretely:

> The information presented in Table 4 shows that the main reason for the increase in revenues is the administrative arrangement extending the scope of tax deduction at source. The proportion of tax deducted at source (TDS) to total revenue collections actually declined from 42 per cent in 1990–91 to 22 per cent in 1994–95. It increased to 50 per cent following the expansion in the scope of TDS in 1996–97 and further to 67 per cent in 2001–02 before declining marginally to 64 per cent in 2003–04. As a proportion of GDP, the ratio of collections from TDS increased by 0.67 percentage points over the period considered. When compared with the increase of 0.56 percentage points in ratio of personal income tax collections to GDP, this suggests that the improved compliance is largely if not solely due to improved coverage or greater effectiveness of TDS as a tool for collecting taxes.

The experience with indirect taxes reinforces the point made by M. G. Rao and R. K. Rao (2006). As we will see immediately below, during the 1990s, India also cut the excise duties considerably. But the efforts at enforcement and the expansion of the tax base in this area lagged behind those in the direct tax area. Unsurprisingly, the excise tax revenue as a proportion of the GDP fell. The same happened even more dramatically in the case of the customs duties, which fell dramatically in the 1990s.

Assertions that a mere reduction in the tax rates can lead to increased tax revenues, buttressed by faulty studies, carry the danger of encouraging the policymakers to drop the tax rates as revenue-raising measures, with devastating implications for the fiscal deficit. This is particularly relevant for the indirect tax rates since business lobbies are constantly seeking such reductions. Indeed, the argument that taxpayers become more compliant at lower tax rates, without any change in the degree of enforcement, is less than compelling. Tax evasion at the marginal rate of 90 percent is certainly more attractive than at 30 percent, but if enforcement is lax, the latter is still quite attractive. Holding both income and enforcement constant, prospects for a large increase in the tax revenue are extremely poor.

Some may be tempted to argue that the tax reform has made the tax system less progressive. If one merely looks at personal and corporate income tax *rates*, which have undisputedly declined at the top level, this would seem to be a correct claim. For example, the top marginal personal income tax rate has come down from more than 90 percent to 30 percent. Yet the inference is hugely misleading, and indeed incorrect. It is entirely possible that some of the superrich who honestly paid their taxes in the past now pay less to the exchequer. But many of the superrich, including corporations, substantially or wholly evaded taxes in the past due to high tax rates and poor enforcement. The current tax system has brought these and many other entities, including the former zero-tax companies, into the tax net. This has meant that the corporations and the top 3 to 4 percent of the population pay far more taxes today than prior to the reform.

The claim that the tax system as a whole has turned regressive thus would be patently false. As just noted, the share of corporation and personal income taxes, which apply almost exclusively to the relatively rich and corporations, has risen dramatically, and that of indirect taxes, which tend to be regressive for reasons explained earlier, has declined. Additionally, it is worth recalling the related point, made earlier, that we should rely principally on expenditures to redistribute income in favor of the poor, and place greater emphasis on efficiency and revenue buoyancy when designing the tax system.

Indirect Taxes Imposed by the Central Government

The Chelliah Committee recommended a major restructuring of central government excise taxes, including extension of coverage to all manufactures; reduction of the tax rates to three in the 10 to 20 percent range; MODVAT credit on all inputs, including machinery; conversion from specific to ad valorem rates; and an end to myriad exemptions. The 1994–95 budget made some progress in implementing these recommendations by extending the MODVAT to capital goods and petroleum products, replacing a large number of specific rates by ad valorem rates, remov ing many exemptions, and reducing the number of excise rates.

A much greater impetus to the reform in this area came with the 1999–2000 budget, which merged 11 different rates, ranging from 5 to 40 percent, into three

MODVAT rates of 8, 16, and 24 percent, with a handful of "luxury" items subject to two nonvatable additional excise duties at rates of 6 and 16 percent. "Nonvatable" in this context meant that in the unlikely event a product subject to the additional excise duty was used as input into another product, the producer of the latter would not be entitled to the reimbursement of that additional excise duty.[9] The nonvatable rates on the luxury goods were applied to the select group of products at the top of the MODVAT. The 2000–01 budget achieved further unification of the tax rates by replacing the three basic rates with a central VAT (CENVAT) rate of 16 percent, with three special additional nonvatable excise duties at rates of 8, 16, and 24 percent for a few luxury consumer items. This structure has remained more or less intact, though some recent budgets have tended to treat the exceptional additional excise rates as MODVAT rates and have switched some products from the 16 percent CENVAT to the 8 percent MODVAT rate. As Acharya (2005) forcefully argues, such deviations violate the spirit of a single MODVAT rate and openly invite other producers to lobby for the lower MODVAT rates for their products.

Customs Duties

I have discussed the changes in customs duties in detail in chapters 4 and 5, and also touched upon them in chapter 12. Therefore, I shall treat the subject only briefly here. The 1991 reform abolished licensing on all but a few intermediate and capital goods, which made tariffs the binding constraint on the imports of these products. Therefore, subsequent liberalization focused on tariffs.

In 1990, less than 4 percent of the 5000 positions in the harmonized system of tariffs were subject to rates below 60 percent, and as many as 60 percent were characterized by rates between 110 and 150 percent. The top tariff rate was 355 percent. The reform compressed the tariffs at the top and the number of tariff lines. Starting in 1992–93, four successive budgets capped the tariff rates at 110, 85, 65, and 50 percent, respectively. That is to say, by 1995–96, the top tariff rate on nonagricultural goods (with some exceptions) had come down to 50 percent.

Though there were some reversals along the way through the introduction of special duties, first under Chidambaram and then under Sinha, as well as through rationalization of tariff rates whereby two successive tariff rates were unified into the higher one, the long-term trend has been toward liberalization. Four budgets, beginning with the 2004–05 budget, brought the top rate down to 20, 15, 12.5 and 10 percent, respectively. Leaving aside some tariff peaks, such as the 100 percent duty applicable to motor vehicles, there are currently four tariff rates in existence: 2, 5, 7.5, and 10 percent. Even though many analysts continue to assert that India is among the most protected countries, its tariff regime for nonagricultural products is now only marginally more protective than that of China. The customs duty as a proportion of merchandise imports was just 4.9 percent in 2005–06.

The story is quite different in agriculture, however. Here India took the same essential approach as the OECD countries, and chose excessively high tariff bindings ranging from 100 to 300 percent to replace border measures under the Uruguay Round Agreement on Agriculture. For such agricultural products as skimmed milk powder, rice, corn, wheat, and millet, India traditionally had zero or very low bound rates. These were renegotiated under GATT, article XXXVIII, in December 1999, in return for concessions on other products.[10] According to the WTO (2002, table III.1), India's average bound rate in agriculture is 115.2 percent. In comparison, the applied most favored nation (MFN) tariff rate was 35.1 percent in 1997–98 and 41.7 percent in 2001–02.

Services Tax

I previously noted that originally the Indian Constitution assigned the taxation of a handful of services, including electricity, entertainment, and transportation of goods and passengers to the states but was silent about the rest, which placed the latter automatically in the hands of the central government under the residual powers it enjoys. The 88th Amendment has corrected this anomaly, giving the taxation of all services to the central government, with the tax proceeds collected and appropriated by the center and states according to the principles formulated by the Parliament.

If the objective is to implement a uniform VAT on consumption, it is essential to tax services, and to have a rebate on taxes paid on goods and services used in the production of all final goods and services. From this perspective, the 88th Amendment was an important development. The 1994–95 budget had first introduced a central services tax on general insurance, stock brokerage, and telecommunications. The scope of this tax has now been expanded to nearly 100 items. Moreover, from 5 percent initially, the tax rate has been raised to 8 percent in 2003–04, 10 percent in 2004–05, and 12 percent in 2006–07.

The M. Govinda Rao Expert Group on Taxation of Services (Government of India, 2001) had recommended the extension of the services tax to virtually all services, with rebates given on virtually all services used in the production of both goods and services. The group suggested two short negative lists: one containing services that would not be subject to the services tax and another containing services on whose use tax rebates would not be given. The group also recommended the harmonization of the services tax with the CENVAT to achieve a uniform VAT across goods and services.

At present, the government is following the strategy of expanding the services tax through a positive approach. But the recommendation to introduce rebates on the services used in the production of goods and services has been implemented. Likewise, the services tax rate is being gradually moved toward the CENVAT on goods. Harmonization with the CENVAT is expected by 2010, the target date for a national goods and services tax.

Revenue Impact of the Reforms

Columns 4–6 in table 15.2 trace the evolution of various central government indirect taxes as proportions of the GDP. The key observation following from these columns is that both customs and excise revenues saw a sharp decline during the 1990s. Customs revenues fell from the peak of 3.7 percent of the GDP in 1989–90 to barely 1.8 percent in the 2000s. Excise duties steadily fell from the high of 4.6 percent of the GDP in 1989–90 to the low of 3.1 percent in 1998–99, and recovered only marginally to 3.2 to 3.3 percent of the GDP in the subsequent years. Among indirect taxes, only the services tax has risen since its introduction, going from no contribution to 0.5 percent of the GDP in 2004–05.

Rajaraman (2005) is highly critical of trade liberalization by India on account of the revenue loss. She effectively holds the rapid decline in the customs revenue responsible for the rising fiscal deficit, which arguably has had an adverse impact on public investment. But two points must be made in response to this criticism. First, trade liberalization is perhaps the most critical and politically feasible reform. Sacrificing this reform for revenue reasons could have easily stalled most other reforms as well. Thus the solution to the revenue problem lay not in the sacrifice of the trade reform but in building up alternative sources of revenue. While the government achieved some success in this task with respect to direct taxes, it failed miserably in the area of excise duties. Successive finance ministers were eager to lower the excise tax rates without capping the exemptions, erosion of the tax base through the proliferation of exempted products, and the abuse of MODVAT rebates.

The second point that has been uniformly ignored in the literature and policy analyses is that, as commonly reported, the customs revenue in India includes not just the true customs duty (officially called "basic customs duty") but also the countervailing duty, which equals domestic taxes applied to similar domestically produced goods. A part of the decline in the customs revenue during the reform era has come not from trade liberalization, but from cuts in the excise duties. Thus it is wrong to attribute the entire decline in the customs duties to trade liberalization. The good news, of course, is that the share of basic customs duty in customs revenue is rather low now, and future trade liberalization carries relatively minor revenue implications.

A Critical Comment on the Tariff Reform

From the efficiency standpoint, successive tax committees have recommended tariff structures entirely contrary to what economists normally recommend. Both the Chelliah Committee and the Kelkar Task Force on Indirect Taxes recommended raising tariffs with the stage of production: low tariffs on raw materials, higher ones on intermediate inputs, and even higher ones on final products. Such a structure results in much higher protection to final products than is indicated by the nominal rates of tariffs on them. This is because the inputs they use are subject to low duties, so that the higher nominal tariff gives much higher protection to value added at the final stage of manufacturing. For this reason, and also to neutralize protectionist lobbies, economists favor uniform tariffs across products. But repeated pleas by economists to abandon the cascaded structure of tariffs and adopt a uniform tariff have been ignored.

State Tax Reform: Converting the Sales Tax into a State VAT

There were no serious reforms at the state level for a considerable period even after beginning of the systematic reform of the tax system in the early 1990s. Any changes that were attempted were driven by the need to boost revenues rather than a desire to improve the efficiency of the system (M. G. Rao and R. K. Rao, 2006). The sales tax was not subject to any rebate, varied considerably across commodities and states, and was levied even by many local jurisdictions in many states.

This system has a number of shortcomings that called for its replacement by some form of coordinated VAT at the state level. First, the sales tax was applied in a haphazard manner, with different states choosing not only different rates but also different tax bases. In some states, this was a retail tax, and thus did not apply to wholesale transactions. In other states, it was the first point tax applying to the manufacture or import of a good into the state and was topped by turnover taxes or surcharges. These across-state variations were clearly detrimental to efficiency in production.

Second, closely related to the previous point, the sales tax applied to all purchases, including machinery, raw materials, and final goods. In the absence of rebates, it inevitably involved the taxation of inputs, and therefore distorted production and distribution.

Third, insofar as interstate sales are concerned, the system included a central sales tax (CST), collected and appropriated by the "exporting" state. As M.G. Rao (2003) discusses in detail, this had at least two undesirable implications. One, it segmented the national markets by introducing an effective border tax on interstate trade. And two, insofar as the "exporting" states tended to be richer and the ultimate burden of the tax fell on the consumer in the importing state, the tax became regressive at the state level.

Finally, under the sales tax regime, local jurisdictions *within* many states levied taxes called *octroi* on the entry of goods for consumption, use, or sale. This feature of the state tax systems segments even the intrastate markets. The tax imposed very substantial transaction costs by slowing the movement of goods between jurisdictions. The transportation of goods on the Indian highways has been known to be notoriously slow. *Octroi* is a principal cause of this slow speed.

The Chelliah Committee, which had recognized some of these problems, had recommended the extension of the central VAT to the wholesale stage and the conversion of the state sales taxes into a retail-stage VAT. At the urging of the government, the issue was analyzed in detail by the National Institute for Public Finance and Policy (NIPFP; 1994) in a study led by Amaresh Bagchi. The study considered three options to introduce a coordinated consumption tax on a nationwide basis:

- A centralized sales tax that unifies the state and central government duties, with full rebate on taxes paid at each stage;
- Grant of the powers to levy all domestic indirect taxes to the states, with a corresponding reduction in tax devolution;
- An independent dual VAT at central government and state levels, with no credit for the payment of the central government taxes by the states and vice versa.

The study favored the last of these options, on the ground that it gave states fiscal autonomy without preventing the central government from undertaking interstate redistributions of the tax proceeds. Therefore, it recommended the levy of a separate destination-based, consumption-type retail stage VAT in place of the existing sales taxes by the states.

Achieving consensus among the states in favor of this option took a very long time, however. After prolonged negotiations among the central government, the states, and the union territories, all but two states—Uttar Pradesh and Tamil Nadu—have chosen to implement the state VAT. In most states, the implementation began on April 1, 2005, though Haryana, for example, began a year earlier.

Four features of the state VAT may be noted. First, the state VAT works entirely in parallel with the central VAT, with no interaction in terms of the rebate system. Any central VAT paid at a prior stage of production is reimbursed under the central VAT system, and any state VAT at the prior stage of production (for example, on the purchase of machinery or inputs) is reimbursed under the state VAT. This means that in the production and distribution stages, when a manufacturer sells the product to a wholesaler or retailer, there is no reimbursement of the CENVAT to the purchaser.

Second, the standard rate for the state VAT is 12.5 percent, but it is buttressed by a lower 4 percent rate and a zero rate on approximately 75 necessities. Most items of common consumption, inputs, and capital goods (approximately 275 items) are taxed at 4 percent, and the remaining ones at 12.5 percent. Major exceptions are gasoline and diesel, which are kept outside the VAT regime and are subject to a floor rate of 20 percent in sales tax. Currently, these items contribute almost 40 percent of the states' sales tax revenues. Also excluded from the state VAT are sugar, textiles, and tobacco. The authority to impose the sales tax on these latter items has been traditionally assigned to the central government, which imposes the "additional duty of excise" on them.

Third, the credit on the state VAT paid at a prior stage operates in full only on intrastate sales. With regard to interstate sales, an exporting state is to continue to collect the CST for two years, after which it will expire. During the transition period of two years, the exporting state is to give rebates to the exporting firms on the tax paid on local purchases against the CST . The latter is not rebated, however, on the sales in the importing state.[11] Once the CST is phased out, there are plans to rebate the taxes paid on the purchases in the exporting state on products sold in the importing state. ICICI Info Tech has been contracted to build the information base on interstate trade for this purpose.

Finally, to smooth out the transition, the central government has guaranteed to cover any revenue losses not exceeding 100, 75, and 60 percent in the first, second, and third years, respectively. The losses are to be calculated by projecting revenues through applying the average of the three best annual growth rates during the last five years and comparing them to the accrued revenues collected.

CONCLUDING REMARKS: THE ROAD AHEAD

The tax reform, though still not complete, has come a long way in virtually all areas in India. The direct taxes on both personal and corporate incomes have been considerably simplified and tax administration has substantially improved. Because the indirect tax system was in a far more chaotic state when the reform began, even though much more has been done in this area, much still remains to be done. I conclude with the discussion of a few key reforms waiting to be done in both areas.

Future Reforms of Direct Taxes

There are three principal areas in which further reform of direct taxes is desirable.

First, both personal and corporate income taxes remain subject to far too many exemptions. Notwithstanding populist pressures and political opposition, the Kelkar

Task Force on Direct Taxes valiantly pushed forward in this direction. But its success has been only partial to date. For instance, on the personal income taxation front, considerable horizontal equity has been achieved across savings instruments through the exemption of savings up to 100,000 rupees that is not instrument-specific. But many other exemptions still remain in place. Progress on capping exemptions on corporate income taxes has been far more limited; indeed, there may even have been backsliding through the tax holidays given in the context of the rapidly proliferating special economic zones (SEZs). Examples of exemptions include those on profits on exports by 100 percent export-oriented units and units located in SEZs, export processing zones, and technology parks; shipping and tea industries; and profits on infrastructure projects.

Second, as mandated by the Indian Constitution, income earned from agriculture remains entirely outside the income tax net. This exemption probably made some sense in the 1950s, when virtually all farmers were poor. But the situation has changed, with well-to-do farmers emerging in many states such as Punjab and Haryana. Horizontal equity in taxation requires that taxes be collected regardless of how the income is generated. Insofar as poor farmers are concerned, they would be excluded from taxation under the exemption limit of 100,000 rupees.

An important side effect of the exclusion of agricultural income is that many urban rich evade taxes on income by claiming the income from other sources as being agricultural. This evasion has been taking place for several decades, with individuals making claims of huge agricultural incomes from farmhouses. The Kelkar Task Force on Direct Taxes even reported taxpayers in Bombay claiming large agricultural incomes from land that is unfit for agriculture.

Finally, there is continued need for improved tax administration along all dimensions. Tax forms must continue to be simplified, harassment of those paying taxes must be avoided, and the focus of the enforcement authorities should be on those not filing returns. The expansion of the allotment of permanent account numbers, the equivalents of Social Security numbers in the United States, must continue, and eventually must cover all individuals, at least in the urban areas. Likewise, the scope of the Tax Information Network and tax deduction at the source must be expanded.

Future Reforms of Indirect Taxes at the Center and in the States

Beginning with the customs duty, India must aim to undertake three further reforms in the coming years. First, the rates on industrial goods must be brought farther down and made uniform. The goal should be to achieve a uniform customs duty of 5 percent by 2009–10. Given the current ceiling rate of 10 percent, this would require only a sustained reduction of 2.5 percentage points in each of the next two years—an entirely attainable goal. It is also important to eliminate the existing tariff peaks that lie outside the current ceiling rate, such as the 100 percent customs duty on motor vehicles of various kinds. It makes no sense to grant this industry such high protection and deprive the consumer of the benefits resulting from increased competition from abroad. Tariffs on secondhand car imports must be lowered for the same reason. This may lead to large improvements in road safety for individuals who currently carry a spouse and two children on a scooter but can afford to buy cheap secondhand automobiles. Uniformity in the tariff rate would probably also require raising tariff rates on some products currently subject to the zero rate, though it may be ruled out by India's WTO commitments in some cases.

The second area of reform in customs duties is the containment of exemptions. Myriad user-based duty exemptions still plague the Indian customs system. According to the WTO (2002), India has more than 100 kinds of exemptions related to customs duties, each running to several pages. The general notification for exemptions has 378 entries. WTO (2002, p. 35) notes, "The use of such exemptions not only increases the complexity of the tariff, it also reduces transparency and hampers efficiency-increasing tools such as computerization of customs." The problem will be considerably alleviated if the customs duty itself is brought down to 5 percent, as has been recommended. Nevertheless, exemptions not only have adverse efficiency effects, they also impose unnecessary administrative costs and make the system nontransparent.

Finally, it is time that India began to consider and build support for some liberalization in agriculture. Customs duties in this sector remain excessively high despite good prospects for substantially improved export performance.

This leaves us with the central and state VAT systems. Despite very substantial reforms since the mid-1990s, this area still remains somewhat of a mess. While there is considerable merit in giving states freedom to impose their own taxes, since the needs for local public goods may vary widely across jurisdictions, given the messiness of separate, dual-track central and state VAT systems, I am persuaded in favor of the recommendation by the Kelkar Task Force on Fiscal Responsibility and Budget Management Act for a comprehensive goods and services tax (GST) of the value-added variety that unifies the current central and state VATs.

The task force recommends replacing all current indirect taxes except the customs duty with a unified value-added tax on all goods and services, with full rebates at all stages of manufacturing and distribution. It recommends three rates of 10, 20, and 34 percent, with the central government's share in these rates being 6, 12, and 20 percent, respectively. In my judgment, even this structure remains complex, and it will be best to have just a single rate of 20 percent with the center and the states having shares of 12 and 8 percent, respectively. If absolutely essential for political reasons, a handful of the necessities can be exempted from the tax.

A key advantage of the GST is that it fully mimics a consumption tax. Under the current dual-track VAT, this is still not true, since the VAT collected by the manufacturer from the wholesaler is not rebated back to the latter. For example, suppose the production cost of an air conditioner, after all central tax rebates to a manufacturer, is $100. When a distributor buys this air conditioner, he pays $16 in CENVAT and $14.50 in state VAT (at 12.5 percent on the CENVAT inclusive price of $116), resulting in a total cost of $130.50. When the distributor sells the air conditioner to the consumer, he is reimbursed $14.50 for the state VAT, and the $16 in CENVAT is left unreimbursed. This leaves a large tax on the distribution activity in place. This problem will be alleviated by the GST, since the tax will be charged at 20 percent at each stage and reimbursed at 20 percent as well. In the above example, the distributor will pay $20 in GST and will be reimbursed $20 when he sells the air conditioner to the consumer.

The single rate may be criticized on the ground of a lack of progressiveness. Acharya (2005), in particular, repeatedly opts for additional taxation of luxury goods. My view on this issue is that the administrative and efficiency advantages of a single rate greatly outweigh any benefits resulting from hitting the products consumed by the well-to-do harder. As I have argued earlier in this chapter, it makes more sense to achieve progressivity through two alternative instruments: income tax and expenditures. Given that the rich save a large proportion of their income, indirect taxes are bound to fail to reach a substantial part of their income in any case. Moreover, insofar as the objective of redistributive policy is to assist the poor, it is best to let the tax system target efficiency in production and achieve redistribution through expenditures targeted at the poor.

16

TACKLING SUBSIDIES AND REFORMING
THE CIVIL SERVICE

In considering government expenditures and their reform, the conceptual question we must ask is why the government should either influence the market outcome through subsidies or itself become the provider of certain goods and services. The broad rationale economists give for such involvement is the underprovision of certain goods and services by the market relative to their optimal level. In the Indian context, four factors accounting for the underprovision may be distinguished.

First, the market fails to supply the goods and services with "public" good properties in optimal quantities. Two key properties distinguish public goods from private ones: non-exclusion and non-rivalry in consumption. Non-exclusion means that once a good is provided, citizens cannot be excluded from enjoying it even if they choose not to pay for it. Non-rivalry in consumption means that once the good is made available, adding another consumer does not reduce its availability to other consumers. This property means that all costs are fixed, so that per-unit costs fall as the number of consumers rises. Non-exclusion implies that the supplier cannot recover the cost of production, which deters private suppliers from providing the product. Non-rivalry means that letting a single producer provide the good minimizes the cost. It is generally agreed that the government is justified in being the monopoly supplier of these goods, financing them from general revenues. General administration, defense, and local roads fall in this category of pure public goods.

The second set of circumstances arises when exclusion is possible but production is subject to substantial fixed costs that, once incurred, are sunk. Because a single producer minimizes the cost of supplying such a good, it is called a "natural" monopoly. Examples in this category of goods include electricity, water, highways, and telecommunications. The traditional approach to the provision of these goods has been a government monopoly, though there are user charges to cover the costs. But over time, it has been found that the government is not an efficient producer of these services, which has paved the way for bringing in private producers, with a regulator setting the prices and overseeing the quality of the service to avoid the exercise of monopoly power. In telecommunications, the introduction of cell phones has largely eliminated scale economies, allowing private producers to compete relatively freely.

The third set of circumstances in which government intervention is justified occurs when the social benefit from a product differs from its private benefit, often due to the presence of an externality on the demand side. For example, vaccination benefits not just the child receiving it but also the rest of the population, whose chances of catching a disease from the child decline. In such cases, a partial subsidy on the purchase of the service is justified. Alternatively, the subsidy may be provided through public provision of the service below cost or a subsidy to private providers of the service.

One final justification specific to India is the poor access of the private sector to credit on a large scale. In such a situation, private sector may fail to supply a product requiring large investments. The Indian government applied this justification to its entry into a number of heavy industry sectors in the 1950s and 1960s. It argued that these sectors required investment on a scale beyond the capacity of the private sector. Therefore, the state needed to enter them. The conclusion was questionable, since ensuring access to credit to private firms would have been a superior solution. In today's context, the justification is invalid altogether: The Indian private sector is able to access financial resources from around the world, and large foreign investors are now present in the economy.

A separate consideration that drives many governments into the provision of health, education, and infrastructure is their desire to bring these services free of charge to the poor. I will argue throughout this chapter and in chapters 19 and 20 that this is a poor justification for the government to enter the provision of health and education. Unless the government enjoys a particular advantage in providing them more efficiently than private providers, which turns out to be untrue in India, the poor can be better served through cash transfers, vouchers that allow them to purchase the specific service from the provider of their choice, or free health insurance.

Against this background, let us now turn to a consideration of the government expenditures and its involvement in various sectors in India. Given the government's wide participation in economic activity, my discussion extends to five chapters. In this chapter, I focus on explicit subsidies and civil service. In chapters 17 and 18, I discuss economic services: telecommunications and electricity in the former and various transportation services in the latter. In chapters 19 and 20, I turn to social services, including health; water supply and sanitation; elementary education; and higher education. I begin with an overview of the composition of government expenditures across various items in India.

GOVERNMENT EXPENDITURES: AN OVERVIEW

I briefly touched on the aggregate government expenditures in chapter 9. I now consider them more frontally, offering the details of their composition. Despite some repetition, this is useful for setting the stage for a discussion of the necessary microeconomic reforms in the government sector that will occupy us in this and the next several chapters. I begin by depicting the expenditures as a percent of the GDP of the central and state governments separately and combined since 1980–81 in figure 16.1.[1] With some exceptions, the expenditures have been between 25 and 30 percent of the GDP since the early 1980s.

In 1980–81, the total expenditures of the central and state governments stood at 26.3 percent of GDP. They then rose steadily, peaking at 32.3 percent in 1986–87. Though the expenditures fell as a proportion of the GDP thereafter, the absolute levels remained high, especially with the superhigh growth of 7.6 percent during 1988–91, and greatly contributed to the crisis of June 1991. As a part of the stabilization effort in the postcrisis era, there was a genuine effort to compress the expenditures, principally at the central level. This compression continued until 1996–97, after which expenditures began to rise again, peaking at 31 percent in 2003–04. The key difference this time around was that the expenditures rose more sharply at the level of the states, though they rose at the center as well. Only since 2004–05 have the expenditures reversed

Precisely how these adjustments took place requires a look at the components of the expenditures. As noted in chapter 9, there is a broad division of the expenditures in India between the current or "revenue" expenditures and capital expenditures. The latter are highly correlated with public investment and contain expenditures on infrastructure. Figure 16.2 shows the revenue and capital components of combined expenditures of the center and the states. It is apparent from this figure that the bulk of the compression in the 1990s took place via a reduction in capital expenditures. This is not surprising since politically current expenditures, which predominantly include such items as salaries and pensions of government employees, subsidies of various kinds, and many social and economic services, are harder to cut. A major

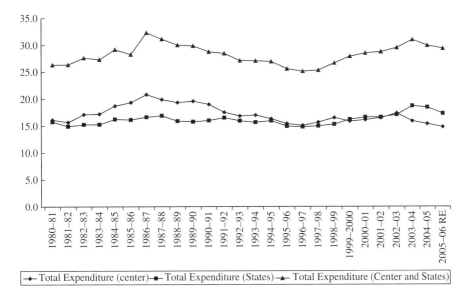

FIGURE 16.1: Expenditures of the Central and State Governments

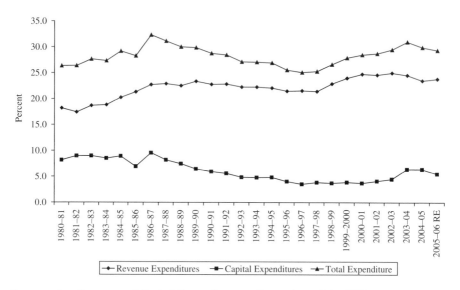

FIGURE 16.2: Revenue and Capital Expenditures as Proportions of the GDP

item in capital expenditures is infrastructure, which is critically important for development but does not have a well-organized constituency. After peaking at 9.6 percent in 1986–87, capital expenditures fell steadily, bottoming out at 3.7 in 1998–99. Capital expenditures picked up again starting 2001–02 with the massive road construction projects under the National Democratic Alliance government.

Unsurprisingly, once again the significant upward turn in total expenditures in 1998–99 did not result from an upward turn in capital expenditures, which were still moving downward. Instead, this turn originated in the revenue expenditures, which rose from 21.4 percent of the GDP in 1997–98 to 22.9 in 1998–99. The shift in the revenue expenditures in turn was rooted in the implementation of the salary and pension increases for government employees recommended by the Fifth Pay Commission. The increases were phased, with the states typically following the center after one year, which is the reason the full effect of the change was felt in 2000–01.

The available data on revenue and capital expenditures of the central and state governments are subdivided into developmental and nondevelopmental expenditures. Rather than report these details for each category, I show the division of the total expenditures between developmental and nondevelopmental expenditures in figure 16.3. These details reinforce the picture emerging from figure 16.2. The compression of expenditures relative to the GDP during the 1990s until 1996–97 is accompanied by a compression of developmental expenditures with nondevelopmental expenditures rising continuously until they reversed slightly in 2004–06. The former predominantly include many of the capital expenditures, whereas nondevelopmental expenditures have a large component of revenue expenditures.

For our discussion of microeconomic reforms, it is useful at this point to introduce some of the major headings under developmental and nondevelopment expenditures. This is done in table 16.1, which shows the allocation of the total nondevelopmental

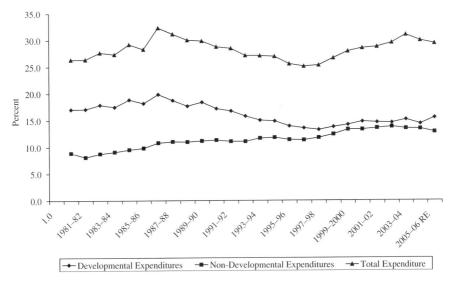

FIGURE 16.3: Total Developmental and Non-Developmental Expenditures

and developmental expenditures of the center and the states among a number of subcategories for 1990–91, 1996–97, 1999–2000, 2004–05, and 2005–06.[2] Based on the table and using the allocations in the 2005–06 budget, we can make the following observations on some of the key categories of expenditures:

- Nondevelopmental expenditures: Expenditures on five items in this category— interest payments; defense; administrative services; pension benefits; and food subsidy—amounted to 12.8 percent of the GDP in 2004–05 and 12.4 percent in 2005–06. These amounts compare with the total nondevelopmental expenditures of 14.7 and 14.2 percent of the GDP in the two respective years.
- Developmental expenditures on social and community services: Expenditures in this category—principally on health, water supply and sanitation, and education—account for a little less than half of the developmental expenditures. They amounted to 5.6 percent of the GDP in 2004–05 and in 2005–06.
- Developmental expenditures on economic services: Within the economic services category, three sectors—agriculture and allied services; power, irrigation, and flood control; and transport and communications—account for more than one third of the developmental expenditures. They amounted to 4.9 percent of the GDP in 2004–05 and 4.7 percent in 2005–06.
- Subsidies: Explicit subsidies in the budgets apply only to food and fertilizer. Together they currently amount to a little more than 1 percent of the GDP. This greatly understates the true magnitude of the subsidies, since many social and economic services have a large element of subsidy from an economic standpoint.

We have already seen in chapter 9 that the elimination of the fiscal deficit would require a reduction in government expenditure alongside an increase in revenues. In this and the next several chapters, we will see that in most cases, expenditure cuts

TABLE 16.1: Expenditures of the Center and States as Proportions of GDP

Item	1990–91	1996–97	1999–2000	2004–05RE	2005–06BE
A. Non-developmental expenditure	12.2	12.2	14.1	14.7	14.2
1. Defense services	2.7	2.2	2.4	2.5	2.4
2. Border roads	0.0	0.0	0.0	0.0	0.0
3. Interest payments	4.4	5.1	5.6	6.0	5.9
4. Fiscal services	0.6	0.4	0.5	0.4	0.4
5. Administrative services	1.6	1.5	1.7	1.6	1.7
6. Organs of state	0.2	0.2	0.3	0.3	0.2
7. Pension & other retirement benefits	0.9	1.1	1.9	1.8	1.7
8. Relief on account of natural calamities	0.2	0.1	0.1	0.2	0.1
9. Technical & economic cooperation with other countries	0.0	0.0	0.0	0.0	0.0
10. Compensation & assignment to local bodies	0.1	0.1	0.2	0.3	0.2
11. Food subsidy	0.4	0.5	0.5	0.9	0.8
12. Social security & welfare	0.4	0.4	0.5	0.3	0.3
13. Others	0.5	0.6	0.4	0.5	0.6
B. Developmental expenitures	13.0	10.5	11.2	12.3	12.0
1. Railways	0.3	0.1	0.1	0.3	0.2
2. Posts & Telecommunications	0.1	0.0	0.0	0.0	0.0
3. Social & Community Services	5.4	5.0	5.6	5.6	5.6
a) Education, art, & culture	3.1	2.7	3.2	2.9	2.8
b) Medical & public health, and water supply & sanitation	1.2	1.0	1.2	1.2	1.2
c) Others	1.2	1.3	1.2	1.6	1.6
4. General economic services	0.9	0.2	0.2	0.5	0.6
5. Agriculture & allied services	2.1	1.7	1.9	1.8	1.8
a) Rural development	0.9	0.9	0.8	0.9	0.9
b) Others	1.2	0.8	1.0	0.8	0.8
6. Industry & minerals	0.7	0.5	0.4	0.5	0.5
7. Fertilizer subsidy	0.8	0.4	0.5	0.3	0.3
8. Power, irrigation, & flood control	1.8	1.7	1.4	2.0	1.6
9. Transport & communications	0.8	0.8	1.0	1.1	1.3
a) Roads & bridges	0.6	0.6	0.8	0.8	1.1
b) Others	0.2	0.2	0.2	0.3	0.2
10. Public works	0.2	0.2	0.2	0.2	0.2
C. Loans and advances	2.1	1.1	1.1	0.9	0.6
Total (A+B+C)	27.3	23.8	26.4	27.9	26.8

Note: RE and BE = "revised estimate" and "budget estimate," respectively.

Source: Author's calculations, using the expenditure data in Government of India, Ministry of Finance, *Indian Public Finance Statistics* (2005–06, table 1.1).

would accompany microeconomic reform of the government sectors. In this chapter, I consider two items of explicit subsidy—fertilizer and food—identified in the *Indian Public Finance Statistics 2005–06* (see table 16.1) and the expenditures on civil service. In each case, my focus is on reform rather than on expenditure cutting for its own sake. Other major items of public expenditure—telecommunications, electricity, transportation, health, water supply and sanitation, and education—are taken up in the following chapters.

FERTILIZER SUBSIDY

Although conceptually subsidies can be said to exist whenever the price of a service provided by the government falls short of the marginal social benefit—an observation that will directly or indirectly influence our discussion throughout this and the next chapter—the *Indian Public Finance Statistics 2005–06* (see table 16.1) explicitly reports their existence in only two sectors: fertilizer and food. India also employs some explicit export subsidies to which I referred in chapter 12 on trade policy.[3] I will argue below that, as administered, food and fertilizer subsidies fail to attack the desired objective directly, and create by-product distortions detrimental to efficiency. The eventual goal of the policy should be not just the elimination of the subsidies from the fiscal viewpoint, but of the associated distortion as well. For example, if more efficient fertilizer plants are taxed to give cross-subsidies to the less efficient ones, the policy may not impose a net fiscal burden on the budget, but it remains distorted.

Fertilizer Pricing Policy and Subsidy: A Critical Examination

Fertilizer subsidy has declined from 0.8 percent of the GDP in 1990–91 to 0.3 percent in 2004–06 (table 16.1), but at approximately $2.5 billion in the 2005–06 budget, it remains large in absolute terms. Much of this subsidy applies to urea, the principal fertilizer used by the farmers. The subsidy has been administered under the Retention Price Scheme (RPS), introduced at the recommendation of the Fertilizer Prices Committee (popularly called the Marathe Committee, after its chairman) in 1977.[4] While some changes have been made starting in 2003, it is useful to first describe the system as it operated until then.

The system guaranteed a uniform price of urea to farmers and a 12 percent after-tax return on the net worth to urea producers. Under the scheme, each urea-producing unit was required to sell all its fertilizer to the farmers at an administered price, which was usually below its production cost.[5] The government then used a combination of industry norms and actual parameters of the unit to estimate its total cost of production. To this cost, it added 12 percent return on the net worth, and gave the unit the difference between the resulting amount and the revenues received from sales to farmers as a subsidy.

Imports and exports of fertilizer were prevented from subverting the system by "canalizing" (giving the government the monopoly rights over them). This meant that if the import price happened to be below the administered price, farmers could not resort to imports. Likewise, if the export price was above the administered price, fertilizer producers could not divert sales abroad.

The system was grossly inefficient for many reasons:

- By fixing the urea price for farmers below the social opportunity cost, the system encouraged excessive use of fertilizer in relation to other inputs.

- By guaranteeing the 12 percent return on net worth, the system encouraged extreme inefficiency in the production of urea. In particular:

  - Some of the plants that would have closed down under free-market competition remained in operation.
  - Producers had no incentive whatsoever to improve efficiency. For example, even when it was cheaper for them to import the feedstock, they continued to rely on the more expensive domestic sources since the central government covered such costs without penalty for the higher price paid.
  - States found it convenient to impose hefty sales taxes on feedstock since such taxes became a part of the producer's cost to be covered by the central government's subsidy.
  - Producers took no initiative whatsoever to improve energy efficiency of their plants, despite their extremely poor record.
  - A symptom of the inefficiency in the system was that the costs of urea varied from 4,851 rupees per metric ton for the most efficient plant to 15,175 rupees per metric ton for the least efficient one in operation at the time the Expenditure Reforms Commission issued its second report. (ERC Report, September 20, 2000, para. 37)

- The manufacturers had an incentive to inflate their capital costs, thereby increasing the amount of the subsidy.

There is some debate in the literature on who has benefited from the fertilizer subsidy: farmers or the industry? The answer to this question depends on the import and export prices.[6] The price of urea in the world market fluctuates wildly. As a result, there have been times, especially during the 1990s, that farmers paid prices higher than the import price inclusive of internal delivery costs. For these years, it is clear that the industry benefited not only from the subsidy but also from the difference between the administered price and the import price.[7] But even in the years that this was not the case, a part of the subsidy accrued to the industry. Only when the difference between the export price and the administered price paid by the farmer exceeded the subsidy per unit of urea did the industry stand to lose under the system.[8]

Regardless of this distributional question, the discussion above makes it clear that the RPS was a most inefficient system. Yet, the government rejected the recommendations of committee after committee to reform it even at the margin. For example, a high-powered committee of secretaries on the RPS recommended replacing the unit-by-unit system with a groupwise scheme in 1986, but the government rejected it. The same was the fate of the recommendations for marginal improvements by the High Powered Committee on Fertilizer Consumer Prices (1987); The Bureau of Industrial Costs and Pricing study (1992); and the High-Powered Review Committee (HPRC) on Fertilizer Pricing Policy (1998).

On September 20, 2000, the ERC presented another set of recommendations to make the fertilizer industry more competitive. It recommended dismantling the control system in four stages, beginning with the conversion of the plantwise RPS into a complex groupwise RPS starting on February 1, 2001. Action was at last taken on January 30, 2003, with the announcement of a new groupwise pricing policy that would take effect on April 1, 2003. The policy identified three stages of implementation but specified clear modalities for only the first two stages: stage I, lasting until March 31, 2004; and stage II, lasting until March 31, 2006. It stated that the Department of Fertilizers would decide the modalities for stage III after review of the implementation of stages I and II.

The key element of the policy was to adopt a complex groupwise pricing scheme. It divided the existing units into six groups based on the type of feedstock and the age of the plant. It then outlined a two-step methodology for the calculation of the subsidy. In the first step, an overall average retention price was computed. Units within the group with an individual retention price 20 percent lower or higher than this overall average were defined as "outliers." In the second step, a new average retention price was computed after excluding the outliers. For units with a unit-level retention price below the second-step average retention price, the unit-level retention price determined the subsidy. For the nonoutlier units with a unit-level retention price at or above the second-step average price, the latter determined the subsidy. For outlier units with a unit-level retention price above the group average price, an additional subsidy was applied, but only in stage I. In stage II, six groups were retained with the same pricing formula, except that no additional subsidy was given to outliers with above-average unit-level retention price.

The new policy also provided for decontrol of distribution. It stipulated that in the first and second halves of stage I, only 75 and 50 percent of the installed capacity, respectively, would be allocated under the Essential Commodities Act (1955). Units would be free to sell the remaining urea at the government-set maximum retail price (MRP) to farmers or other buyers. In stage II, distribution of urea would be entirely decontrolled after an evaluation of the experience in stage I.

According to available information, the new policy has been implemented and the stage II regime is currently in force. The new policy partially accounts for the decline in the subsidy from 0.5 percent of the GDP in 1999–2000 to 0.3 percent in 2004–06. It is also reported that the policy has led to a virtual halt on new investments in the sector, with some urea plants actually closing down.[9] Imports of fertilizer have risen steadily from $503 million in 2003–04 to $962 million in 2004–05 and $1.7 billion in 2005–06.

Future Policy Reform

While the new policy represents a major step forward, it falls considerably short of a reform that would bring the fertilizer sector under the same market discipline as other sectors. The principal motivation behind the new policy appears to be the compression of subsidy rather than promotion of efficiency. Specifically, while it does penalize the inefficient units in comparison to the old unit-by-unit RPS, it falls well short of giving proper incentives to the relatively efficient units. For instance, if the world price far exceeds the production cost of these units, they are not free to take advantage of it. They must still sell all fertilizer at the administered price domestically.

In reforming the sector, the government needs to recognize that there is no economic case for subsidizing either the user or the producer of fertilizer. In the 1960s and 1970s, when farmers did not fully appreciate the benefits of fertilizer use and the government knew better from the scientific evidence, a case could be made for subsidizing the users. But today the benefits of fertilizer use are fully appreciated by the farmers. A subsidy on it only encourages its overuse and results in environmental degradation. As for producers, the case for the subsidy has never been persuasive. Fertilizer is a traded commodity and, moreover, reliance on its importation does not compromise India's food output, let alone its national security. Indeed, India already relies wholly on imports of potash-based fertilizers and partly on imports of phosphate- and nitrogen-based fertilizers.

Once these principles are recognized, the goal of the reform has to be freeing up trade, complete deregulation of production, and withdrawal of all subsidies (whether given to farmers or fertilizer producers, including cross-subsidies from more efficient to less efficient plants).[10] Since there is widespread belief that India has market power in the world fertilizer market, a tariff duty at the current peak rate of 10 percent may be imposed. Once a fully deregulated, subsidy-free regime is in place, farmers would pay the import price adjusted for the customs duty if India is a net importer of fertilizer, and the FOB export price if the opposite is the case. Inefficient plants unable to compete with imports or with the efficient Indian plants would shut down.

While this reform would have to be phased in over a period of five years to smooth out the adjustment, and to be complemented by adjustment assistance as necessary, it is unconscionable to use the scarce tax revenue to encourage either excessive use of fertilizer in relation to other inputs or its production at excessive cost. On the production side, even fertilizer industry captains seem to desire complete deregulation. This is evidenced by the following statement by Viren Kaushik, director-general of the Fertilizer Association of India, which represents all fertilizer manufacturers in the public, private, joint, and cooperative sectors.[11]

> The fertilizer industry has made repeated pleas to the Government that it should be freed from all controls and given the freedom as enjoyed by other sectors of the economy. In its zeal to contain the fertilizer subsidy bill, the Government has not addressed the real causes behind the rising subsidy bill but has instead tightened the subsidy parameters to such an extent that profitability of the industry is badly eroded.
>
> It is for this reason that, when all other sectors of the economy are booming, the fertilizer sector has not attracted any FDI or FII investment and is not a favorite of domestic investors.

FOOD SUBSIDY

Explicit food subsidy in India has risen from 0.4 percent of the GDP in 1990–91 to 0.9 and 0.8 percent in 2004–05 and 2005–06, respectively (table 16.1). In absolute terms, the subsidy was approximately $6 billion in the 2005–06 budget. Like the fertilizer subsidy, the food subsidy is highly inefficient. Its ostensible objective is to help the poor, but no more than a tiny fraction of the subsidy reaches them.

The Current Policy: A Critical Examination

Since the creation of the Agricultural Prices Commission (APC) and Food Corporation of India (FCI) in the mid-1960s (see chapter 3), India has evolved an extensive system of food grain procurement, storage, and distribution. The APC determines the procurement prices at which the FCI buys food grain from farmers. The latter, with its 400,000-strong workforce, maintains an extensive network of storage facilities and "fair" price shops that sell food grain at subsidized prices. The difference between the costs of operation of the FCI, which include procurement, storage, and distribution; maintenance of its huge bureaucracy; and the revenues from sales of food grains, are covered by the food subsidy.

My back-of-the-envelope calculations (Panagariya, 2002c) for the year 2000–01 led me to the startling conclusion that at most 3.7 percent of the subsidy that year actually reached the poor. The calculation is straightforward: In 2000–01, the FCI sold approximately 3 million metric tons of wheat to below-poverty-line (BPL) households. With the subsidy per metric ton being 415 rupees, this sale resulted in a transfer of 1.25 billion rupees to the BPL families. A similar calculation for rice, based on sales of 3.1 million metric tons to BPL households and a subsidy of 565 rupees per metric ton yielded a transfer of an additional 1.75 billion rupees. The sum of the two subsidies (3 billion rupees) turns out to be a tiny 2.5 percent of the total food subsidy of 12 billion rupees in 2000–01. This calculation slightly understates the benefit to the poor since the element of subsidy was higher in the grain sold under the Antyodaya Anna Yojana (AAY), a food distribution scheme for the poorest of the poor. But even after we apply the higher AAY subsidy rates of 630 rupees per metric ton for wheat and 830 rupees per metric ton for rice to all the BPL purchases, the subsidy to the poor rises to only 4.45 billion rupees (3.7 percent of the total budgeted subsidy).

Some may be tempted to argue that the high procurement price paid to farmers also contributes to poverty alleviation. But this turns out to be largely misleading since the bulk of the procurement is done in the relatively rich states. For example, as I have noted (Panagariya, 2002c), Punjab and Haryana accounted for over 80 percent of the wheat procurement, and Punjab and Andhra Pradesh for more than 70 percent of the rice procurement in 2001–02.[12] The proportions of the poor in the total population in Punjab, Haryana, and Andhra Pradesh in 1999–2000 were only 6.16, 8.74, and 15.77 percent, respectively, versus the national average of 26.10 percent. Moreover, it is unlikely that the poor, who are either landless laborers or marginal farmers, generated significant amounts of food grain for sale to the FCI.

Admittedly, the calculation is still very crude, and may understate the transfer to the poor for other reasons. For example, to the extent that some of the subsidy may have gone to accumulate food grain stocks for future sales at subsidized prices, the estimate above would understate the true transfer to the poor. But while we should not take the specific estimate seriously, it does signal a very small transfer to the poor resulting from the subsidy. For example, even if the true estimate is five times that calculated above, we would conclude that 82 percent of the subsidy goes to entities other than the poor.

Future Reform of the Policy

To eliminate the inefficiency from which the current system suffers and to place the bulk of the subsidies into the hands of the poor, a number of reforms must be undertaken. Given the political difficulties in carrying out many of these reforms, it is unrealistic to expect that they will be implemented in the near future. Nevertheless, it is useful to list them and spell out the rationale for them.

Beginning with the food subsidies to the poor, India must gradually move to a system of direct cash transfers. There are at least three reasons why this instrument is superior to the alternatives. First, given that all states have now identified the BPL families, cash transfers can place the money directly into the hands of the poor. India can cut virtually all costs of intermediation present in the current system. To appreciate the effectiveness of this policy, we only need note that the budgeted food subsidy of 212 billion rupees for the year 2002–03 could have placed a handsome 3250 rupees (at 2002–03 prices) annually in the hands of each of the 65.2 million BPL families in existence at the time. This amount would have been sufficient to buy approximately half of the family's ration for the entire year. Today, with the subsidy amount having gone up in real terms and the number of households below the poverty line having declined, possible per-capita transfer would be even larger. Moreover, if several of the other explicit and implicit subsidies are tightened up as argued in this section, the magnitude of transfers can be vastly increased without increases in the taxes.

Second, in today's electronic age, direct cash transfers have a much greater chance of containing corruption. The government can simply open an electronic account for each BPL family (possibly in the name of the most senior female member, to ensure responsible use) and transfer the funds to it. In turn the families can be authorized to operate the account, using biometric authentication (thumbprint or retinal scan), from the nearest post office or bank branch. The clerk in the government office making the transfer will never see the recipient and will be in a weak position to extract a bribe from the latter. Money can be withdrawn electronically, with no intermediation by a human being. If necessary, independent auditors can be employed to oversee whether the transfers have been made in the right amounts or not. This is in contrast to the current distribution system, under which an army of government employees is involved in delivering the food grain at subsidized prices to the final recipient, with potential for theft and corruption at a number of stages.

Finally, cash subsides are transparent, and therefore more amenable to public scrutiny. If the recipients do not receive the transfer on time, the responsible office is clearly identified and the NGOs can press it for answers. In contrast, under the current system, there are numerous fair price shops spread across the landscape and the points of delivery are diffused. Moreover, any specific owner of the shop can blame his source of delivery of food grain for any delays or shortage.

A shift to direct transfers to the poor is only a part of the overall reform in the food sector. Once direct transfers are accepted as the means to assist the poor, there is no need for the elaborate public distribution system in existence today.[13] Aided by the transfers, the poor will buy food grain in the private market just like the non-poor. The only reason for the FCI to hold food stocks will be emergency shortages. These stocks need not be more than 20 million metric tons, since imports can be and should be mobilized to meet shortages beyond this volume. Therefore, in one stroke, the shift to direct transfer will eliminate the need for the hugely inefficient network of fair price shops and many of the highly inefficient storage facilities. It will also allow the government to greatly downsize the FCI.

I. this regime, the need for government procurement, storage, and distribution will b. limited to food emergencies. Such procurement should be done in the open market at market prices. This means that no need is left for the Agricultural Prices Commission, which should be disbanded.

Critics will no doubt argue that such a system would greatly harm the farmers and agricultural output. There are two reasons why this is a specious argument. First, under the current system, only the farmers in a handful of the rich states are able to sell their food grains to the FCI at the lucrative procurement prices. Absence of guaranteed lucrative procurement prices could have an adverse effect on the output of only these farmers. But it is simply not clear why the country should subsidize these richer farmers, thereby effectively lowering the amount of cash transfers available to the truly poor and needy. Second, once appropriate direct income transfers put sufficient purchasing power in the hands of the poor, the market would generate enough demand to provide remunerative prices to the farmers.

There remains the issue of the role of imports and exports. Critics of a liberal trade policy in food grains argue that India cannot adopt such a policy while other countries subsidize their producers. At the conceptual level, the answer to this criticism is that these subsidies are no reason for India to forgo the benefits of trade. If the subsidies allow India to import needed food grains more cheaply, it is good for India. But even if the target of the policy is the protection of domestic producers of food grains against possible injury from subsidized imports, the solution is countervailing duty on the latter, rather than outright protection. Indeed, once we consider the competitiveness of Indian farmers, existing high duties on food grain imports, and the possibility of countervailing duty in case of injury from subsidized imports, the case for the current set of policies is without firm basis.

CIVIL SERVICE: SIZE, SALARIES, AND PENSIONS

I divide the discussion of the civil service into two parts: issues relating to the size, salaries, and pensions of public sector employees overall, and those relating to the role of the top civil service, the Indian Administrative Services (IAS). I consider the former in this section and the latter in the next one. More then half of the public sector employees are in the social services, principally health and education. Therefore, we will encounter many productivity- and reform-related issues bearing on this part of the labor force when we explicitly discuss the health and education sectors in later chapters.

Table 16.2 shows the evolution of the public sector labor force in India since 1981, divided according to the branch of the government and the industry. Three major facts emerge from this table. First, the 1980s were characterized by a very large expansion of the public sector. The total public sector employment in 1991 was 23 percent higher than that in 1981. This expansion is consistent with the highly expansionary policies pursued during the 1980s. During the 1990s, all branches of the government exercised restraint and held the employment levels more or less unchanged. Indeed, quasi-government and local bodies' branches experienced marginal declines in the early 2000s. Second, the bulk of the expansion in the 1980s took place in the branches other than the central government. The largest expansion took place at the level of the state governments. Finally, and unsurprisingly, a large proportion of the public sector labor force is employed in community, social, and

TABLE 16.2: Employment in the Public Sector: Total and Composition

	1981	1991	1995	2000	2003
Total (million employees on March 31)	15.5	19.1	19.5	19.3	18.6
By branch					
Central government	20.6	17.9	17.4	16.9	16.9
State governments	36.7	37.3	37.8	38.6	39.7
Quasi-governments	29.6	32.6	33.5	32.8	31.8
Local bodies	13.2	12.1	11.3	11.7	11.7
By industry					
Agriculture, hunting, etc.	3.0	2.9	2.8	2.7	2.7
Mining and quarrying	5.3	5.2	5.2	4.8	4.6
Manufacturing	9.7	9.7	9.0	7.9	6.8
Electricity, gas, and water	4.4	4.7	4.8	4.9	4.9
Construction	7.0	6.0	6.0	5.7	5.1
Wholesale and retail trade	0.8	0.8	0.8	0.8	1.0
Transport, storage, communications	17.5	15.9	16.0	15.9	15.8
Finance, insurance, real estate, etc.	4.8	6.3	6.6	6.7	7.4
Community, Social, & personal services	47.5	48.4	48.8	50.6	51.7

Source: Government of India, Ministry of Finance, *Economic Survey* (2005–06, table 3.1).

personal services. Altogether, these services have consistently accounted for almost half of the public sector employment. This is not surprising since they include the health and education sectors, both big employers.

An important question is whether India has too many civil servants. There is no easy answer to this question. Howes and Murgai (2006) compare civil servants per 100 individuals internationally and conclude in the negative. They cite a figure of 1.2 employees per 100 population in India versus 2.8 in China and 7.7 in the OECD countries. If we take the total number of civil service employees in table 16.2 and divide it by the population, we obtain 1.8 per 100 individuals in 2002–03 in India. Though this is higher than the figure reported in Howes and Murgai, it remains below that in China.

But as M. G. Rao (2006) points out, such comparisons can be quite misleading. For example, in China, the employees of state enterprises, which are numerous, are counted among public sector employees. But more important, an assessment of whether there are too many or too few employees must be done in relation to the optimum number of employees, which itself depends on the size of the country, the income level, and, above all, productivity in state employment. With its superior organizing capacity and discipline, perhaps the Chinese public sector enjoys high productivity and can deliver handsome outcomes. The same may not be true of India, where a significant number of public sector employees treat high salaries as an entitlement and want to be paid bribes for performing the service they are hired to deliver in the first place. Given these differences, the optimal proportion of the civil service employees to the population cannot be identical across countries.

One economically meaningful way of framing the question is to ask whether the reallocation of a marginal state employee to the most productive alternative employment in the private sector would raise or lower social welfare. The answer to this question is almost sure to suggest that India has too many civil servants. At least in the area of support and logistical personnel, there is general agreement that India is overstaffed. We will later see that absenteeism among health workers and teachers is extremely high, which brings into question the use of the state's scarce resources in hiring more health workers and teachers. I will argue instead that a better use of the state's resources is cash subsidies and education vouchers to the bottom 30 percent of the population, which can use them to buy services from private providers.

But more than the number of total employees, it is the high level of public sector wages in relation to private sector counterparts in the unorganized sector that is most detrimental to the efficient allocation of resources in India. Not only is the productivity of the employees in the public sector well below the wages they receive, but the latter also serve as the signal to trade unions that seek similarly high wages in the organized public and private sectors. But such high wages price out many of the labor-intensive products in which India has a comparative advantage.

The government sets public sector wages through the pay commissions in the civil service and the wage boards in the public enterprises. These institutions have set public sector wages at levels well above those of their private sector counterparts. Glinskaya and Lokshin (2005) report that in 1999–2000, the average real wage in the public sector was 2.1 times that in the organized private sector and 3.8 times that in the unorganized private sector. Even after the authors control for differences in education and experience, the differences remain large. Estimates based on different approaches show the human-capital-adjusted wages in the public sector to be 1.62 to 2.01 times those in the organized private sector and 2.64 to 3.59 times those in unorganized private sector.

I have already mentioned the detrimental effect of the recommendations of the Fifth Pay Commission on the fiscal deficit in the late 1990s and beyond. This fact, combined with the superhigh level of public sector salaries and the continued low productivity of public sector employees would argue for holding the line on public sector salaries. But, unfortunately, the government has appointed the Sixth Pay Commission, which is bound to bring about yet one more round of escalation of public sector salaries. This is most unfortunate.

Pensions and retirement benefits constitute another major item in the budget. As shown in table 16.1, they accounted for as much as 1.7 percent of the GDP in 2005–06. I discussed the reform of the pension system in greater detail in chapter 11. Here I may note that from the fiscal standpoint, it is important to complete this reform. It is important to reform the existing defined benefits scheme as well as to replace it with a defined contributions scheme for future employees.

REFORMING THE TOP CIVIL SERVICE

Far more damaging than the fiscal consequences of the overpaid Indian bureaucracy is the damage its inefficiency inflicts on the functioning of the economy. In his brilliant book *Governance,* Shourie (2004) offers a graphic account of how senior officers spend vast amounts of time seriously deliberating the most inconsequential matters, and how bureaucratic delays in decision-making on account of literal interpretation of the often silly rules imposes disproportionately large costs on the taxpayer.[14] In the concluding chapter of the book, Shourie (2004, pp. 234–35) offers this grim description of how the system functions:

> The cases we have considered above document how administration is entangled in Red Tape, how it entangles others in it, they show that administration entangles them in that tape whatever their field, and howsoever vital the function they have to discharge is for the country.
>
> It does so in many ways, and for a variety of reasons:
>
> 1. Ministries function as silos: from another silo a question arrives in a file; the file travels down to lower and lower forms of life; it comes to rest at the desk of the long-suffering officer somewhere near the bottom; he looks up files on this or similar questions, and prepares a draft response; the file now begins its journey up the ladder in this particular silo—at each step the preceding noting is summarized. Sometimes a marginal addition of substance is made; eventually it reaches the top; the imprimatur of the appropriately high authority having been affixed, the file is sent to the silo from which the question emanated.
>
> 2. A consequence of even this first bit of the sequence should be noted: while the draft will notionally be deliberated upon as the file travels up the silo, often what has been drafted by the official low down in the silo, survives intact; that official is one who is liable to have the narrowest perspective, he is liable to feel most constrained by precedent, he is liable to be the most "literalist."
>
> 3. Every decision has to be referred to half a dozen other silos: thus, having returned from one silo, the file now begins its journey to a third silo.... The question would have been processed for months—I can at short notice cite half a dozen examples from my own experience; various officials would have pored over it; inter-ministerial meetings would have taken place; the draft would have been circulated among different "stakeholders"—a much favored expression these days; and yet, when the file comes up to you, the officers would have recorded, "May be sent to Law Ministry for vetting."
>
> 4. As a consequence, a case gets to be "processed" for periods that are incomprehensible to those outside government....
>
> 6. The core competence of many a civil servant, and the reason he is so indispensable is that he knows the successive turns of this maze, he knows the sign-posts along it, and the way-side inns in which one can safely put the matter to rest.
>
> 7. The system is such that it swiftly entangles in the same faded-tape every effort to reform it.

At the core of this Byzantine bureaucracy is India's top civil service—the Indian Administrative Services (IAS). Because ministers are constantly changing, the system grants the IAS virtual monopoly over power that it guards zealously. Sadar Vallabhbhai Patel, India's first home minister and deputy prime minister, who had championed the creation of the IAS, described it as the "steel frame" that would hold the country together. But over time, the service has turned into steel armor that protects its own members. The enormous power, combined with near complete absence of competition, punishment, or accountability, has made many officers arrogant and self-indulgent.

Two countries with political systems and civil services very similar to those of India that have tried civil service reforms are New Zealand and the United Kingdom.[15] Traditionally, sacking and lateral entry were extremely difficult and unusual in both countries, and the salary was unrelated to the performance. New Zealand carried out a wholesale reform in the late 1980s by breaking up its homogeneous civil service into a set of separate departments and state-owned enterprises. It placed a chief executive, appointed on a fixed-term, renewable contract, in charge of each of these corporate units. The chief executive was made the legal employer of all staff in his unit, with responsibility for hiring, firing, salaries, and discipline. Symmetrically, he was required to enter a performance agreement with his minister for the output he was expected to produce.

The U.K. reform has been less drastic in that it did not disband the career civil service. The key change there, introduced beginning 1989, was to break up the civil service into core departments and executive agencies. The departments were entrusted with policy setting, resource allocation, and regulation responsibilities; and executive agencies, with service delivery under conditions specified in the framework agreements they signed with the departments. The agencies' chief executives (and some other professionals) came to be appointed on fixed-term contracts and could be from either the regular civil service or outside. Their salaries were delinked from the regular civil service salaries at levels substantially higher than the latter. The departmental civil servants retained the traditional tenure-type contracts.

In India, it is unrealistic to expect a drastic, New Zealand–style civil service reform. But experimentation with some changes at the top is highly desirable. One minimalist approach would be to convert all secretary and equivalent positions (except perhaps those related to the maintenance of law and order and basic administration) in the central and state governments into fixed-term positions with negotiable salaries and explicit contractual obligations. The positions could then be opened to both insiders and outsiders, based on a set of specified criteria. Such a change will attract talented outsiders in the academic, business, and financial fields to the top government positions. If properly administered, it will also allow the most talented officers within the civil service to move to the top faster, and thus infuse greater dynamism into policymaking. Based on performance, contracts may be renewed. Those appointed from any of the civil services to these positions may be given the option to return to their regular civil service job upon completion of the contract.

As I have argued for some years now, my own preference is for a more ambitious approach that opens all positions at the joint secretary and higher levels at the center (and equivalently in the states) to competitive recruitment.[16] The key additional advantage of this more ambitious reform is that it would encourage the most talented young men and women to move back and forth between the government and outside employment.

Currently, since there are no lateral entry points, the decision to enter the top civil service must be made at an early age. If lateral entry is available at the senior level, an individual can take a position outside the government in the early parts of his or her career and enter the government later. Under the current system, once an individual has entered the civil service, the cost of exit is prohibitive since he or she will not be able to return to a top position in the government.

It is important to understand that the reform in the civil service cannot be piecemeal in the sense that an entry here and an entry there to outsiders cannot produce a change in the system. On the contrary, it will give the reform a bad name. The civil service functions like a monopoly, and it is relatively easy for it to isolate solitary outsiders so that they are effectively reduced to spending their time reading the newspapers or writing research papers.

The entry of outsiders will have to be complemented by two additional steps. First, even when the positions are not opened to outsiders because IAS officers have the right qualifications, it will be desirable to formally spell out the duties of officers at the joint secretary and higher levels at the center, and the secretary and higher levels in the states, and make this information public. This will make the senior officers more accountable to the public. Second, it is highly desirable to start pruning the civil service through a more rapid exit in the case of irresponsible officers and reduced entry at all levels. The pruning should be accompanied by the phasing out of many superfluous positions.

At the local levels of administration, there is no reason for the IAS or other civil servants to be the effective rulers. For example, the collector, who is an IAS officer, currently rules at the district level. The IAS officer is known to commonly complain that the local members of the Legislative Assembly (MLAs) constantly interfere in the affairs of the district. On the one hand, one can be sympathetic to the view that the officer cannot run the administration smoothly if the local MLAs from different parties pull him in opposite directions, but on the other hand, the MLAs are the elected representatives of the people. The point is that in a democracy, the elected representatives should head the administration, and it is time to consider making that transition at the district and block levels.

The specific suggestions I have made are not panaceas, and the government will need to do a great deal of homework before it proceeds to undertake the reform. Yet, one thing that is certain is that reforms which subject the civil service to greater outside competition and give an increased role to those with specialized talent are required. Few outside of the IAS would disagree with this prescription.

CONCLUDING REMARKS

The government plays an extensive role in the Indian economy. It not only runs the general administration and provides security, as all governments do, but it also redistributes incomes through subsidies; provides economic services such as telecommunications, electricity, and transportation; plays a central role in the provision of social services such as health and education; and even directly engages in manufacturing activity. This set of roles needs a closer examination.

In this chapter, I have focused on the broad patterns of the government expenditures and considered in greater detail the reforms of fertilizer and food subsidies and of the civil service. I have argued for the total elimination of the two sets of subsidies as they currently exist, and their replacement by cash transfers to the bottom 30 percent of the population. I have discussed several benefits of such transfers in assisting the poor over the current system.

In the area of civil service, I have argued that India needs to contain the salaries of public sector employees except at the top level. These employees are already substantially better paid than their private sector counterparts, not just in the unorganized sector but also in the organized sector. The high level of salaries is justified even less when we consider the productivity of these employees. I have also presented a case for introducing greater competition at the top level of the civil service through lateral entry of specialized individuals. This is essential to break the current monopoly over power exercised by the members of the Indian Administrative Services. At the top level, the salaries will have to be substantially raised, however, to attract talented individuals from business and other walks of life. Indeed, even within the current structure, salaries at the top level would require substantial upward revision to be competitive with the private sector.

17

TELECOMMUNICATIONS AND ELECTRICITY
Contrasting Experiences

Telecommunications and electricity both generate benefits that are largely private. Moreover, the exclusion of consumers unwilling to pay for them is entirely feasible. Therefore, the case for their provision by the government must rest on the natural monopoly argument. Traditionally, this is the argument most countries have invoked, but the experience of the last several decades casts serious doubt on its validity in modern times.

In India, public sector monopolies have served the consumers so poorly that their replacement by a regulated private sector monopoly looks considerably more attractive. In telecommunications, this view has been strongly reinforced by technological changes that greatly undermine the argument for a monopoly supplier in order to achieve efficiency. Benefits of competition and the resulting rapid adoption of the newest technologies in this sector far outweigh any benefits scale economies may confer. Even in electricity, it is now increasingly recognized that its various components can be unbundled, which considerably expands the scope for private sector participation. For example, in principle, electricity generation can be separated from transmission and distribution, and left to private companies that are able to carry out production activity more efficiently. There is also considerable scope for giving the private sector play in the distribution of electricity without losing the benefits of large-scale operation.

India has already introduced private sector participation in both telecommunications and electricity. But the progress and benefits have been far greater in telecommunications than in electricity. Indeed, progress in telecommunications is perhaps the biggest success story of India's reforms—arguably bigger than that of the software industry. In contrast, India is still struggling for a workable solution in electricity. There have been modest successes in some parts of the country, but none that would measure up to the success in the telecommunications sector nationwide. The reasons for the differences in the achievements will become clear as we proceed to consider the evolution of the reforms in the two sectors in detail.

TELECOMMUNICATIONS: A SUCCESS STORY

Telecommunications offers a fascinating example of the persistence and determination the government must have if it is to bring private players into a sector that has functioned as a public sector monopoly for more than a century. It also graphically illustrates the power of a public sector incumbent, its ability to continuously find new ways to grab—even create—tax revenues, and the fight it puts up to bankrupt private entrants in order to reestablish its monopoly over the sector. The experience also offers a glimpse of how private entrants, once granted entry, can fight their way forward, provided the judicial process functions reasonably and the political leadership is responsive to the public interest.[1]

To offer some sense of the magnitude of the success India has achieved in the telecommunications sector, consider the following facts. India had barely 5.1 million telephones *in aggregate* in 1991. In contrast, it added 5.2 million telephones *per month* during the year ending on November 30, 2006. Even at this high average rate, growth had been accelerating at the margin, with the number of new telephones during the month of November 2006, at 6.75 million, exceeding the monthly average in the preceding year by a wide margin.[2]

In aggregate, India had 183.5 million telephones as of November 30, 2006, with the nationwide tele-density reaching 16.3 percent. Between 1998 and 2005, urban tele-density rose from 5.8 to 33 percent, and rural tele-density from 0.4 to 2 percent. In terms of price, as of March 1, 2006, customers could call anywhere in India for one rupee (2 cents) per minute, using fixed-line service offered by Bharat Sanchar Nigam Limited (BSNL), the public sector telephone company. Private sector companies such as Reliance offer similar, even cheaper, services though their networks.

Table 17.1 reports the evolution of telephone lines in India since 1980–81. In addition, figure 17.1 shows the growth rates of these lines for each five-year period since 1981–82. These growth rates reveal an accelerating pattern, with a major shift occurring after the introduction of cellular technology in 1996–97. Tele-density in 1995–96 was only 1.3 percent. In just ten years, it rose to almost ten times that level, to 12.6 percent in 2005–06. While the latest figure on tele-density, at 16.3 percent in November 2006, was still low by international standards, the rate of increase has been nothing less than spectacular.

The 1980s: A Modest Beginning

As the 1980s opened, the telecommunications sector suffered from proverbial inefficiencies in India. Loud criticisms of the poor phone service could be heard in the halls of the Parliament and were clearly written in the newspapers. Tele-density in 1980–81 was a paltry 0.3 percent. As for the quality, the running joke was that half the time you could not get the dial tone, and the other half of the time you would get a wrong number upon dialing. G. Das (2000, p. 208) describes the state of the service and the official attitude toward it in the following words:

> The telephones that existed were not dependable—it was rare to get a number on the first attempt. The employees of the telephone department were arrogant and corrupt. If the lines were down, it could take months to fix unless one bribed the linesman. When an MP [member of Parliament] complained in Parliament of these breakdowns,

TABLE 17.1: Growth in Telephones

Year	Fixed Lines (million)	Mobile (million)	Total Telephones (million)	Growth Rate (mobile)	Growth Rate (total)	Population (in millions)	Tele-Density
1980–81	2.15		2.15			679	0.3
1981–82	2.3		2.30		7.0	692	0.3
1982–83	2.47		2.47		7.4	708	0.3
1983–84	2.67		2.67		8.1	723	0.4
1984–85	2.9		2.90		8.6	739	0.4
1985–86	3.17		3.17		9.3	755	0.4
1986–87	3.49		3.49		10.1	771	0.5
1986–87	3.8		3.80		8.9	788	0.5
1987–88	4.17		4.17		9.7	805	0.5
1988–89	4.59		4.59		10.1	822	0.6
1989–90	5.07		5.07		10.5	839	0.6
1990–91	5.81		5.81		14.6	856	0.7
1991–92	6.8		6.80		17.0	872	0.8
1992–93	8.03		8.03		18.1	892	0.9
1993–94	9.8		9.80		22.0	910	1.1
1994–95	11.98		11.98		22.2	928	1.3
1995–96	14.54	0.34	14.88		24.2	946	1.6
1996–97	17.8	0.88	18.68	158.8	25.5	964	1.9
1997–98	21.59	1.2	22.79	36.4	22.0	983	2.3
1998–99	26.51	1.88	28.39	56.7	24.6	1,001	2.8
1999–2000	32.44	3.58	36.02	90.4	26.9	1,019	3.5
2000–01	37.94	6.43	44.37	79.6	23.2	1,037	4.3
2001–02	40.62	12.69	53.31	97.4	20.1	1,055	5.1
2002–03	42.84	33.69	76.53	165.5	43.6	1,073	7.1
2004–05	45.9	52.21	98.11	55.0	28.2	1,091	9.0
2005–06	49.75	89.92	139.67	72.2	42.4	1,107	12.6

Source: Noll and Wallsten (2004, 2005–06) and author's calculations.

C. M. Stephens, Mrs. Gandhi's communications minister, replied that telephones were a luxury, not right, and that anyone who was dissatisfied could return the telephone, because there was an eight-year waiting list for this "broken-down product."

Responding to the criticisms, in 1981 the government appointed a committee (the Sarin Committee), which recommended splitting the Post and Telegraph (P&T) Department into two and importing 100,000 telephones.[3] But the communications bureaucracy could not be moved. The signs of change began to emerge only in the mid-1980s, when telecommunications services were separated from the P&T Department. This brought the Department of Telecommunications (DoT) and the Telecommunication Board (upgraded to the Telecom Commission in 1989) into existence in 1985. The following year, the DoT was reorganized, with telecommunications services divided into three parts. The services in Delhi and Bombay were assigned to the newly created, state-owned corporate entity Mahanagar Telephone Nigam Limited (MTNL); services in the rest of the country remained with the DoT; and international telephone service was assigned to the Videsh Sanchar Nigam Limited (VSNL), a newly created state-owned corporate entity.[4]

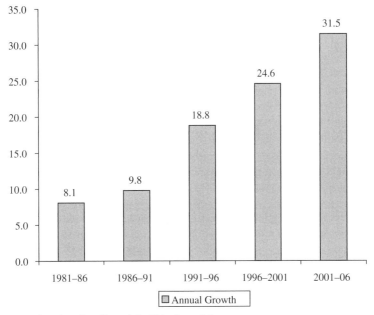

FIGURE 17.1: Accelerating Growth in Telephone Lines

Earlier, in August 1984, the government had created the Center for Development of Telematics (C-DoT) with the mandate to design and develop digital exchanges and to facilitate their large-scale manufacture by Indian industry. This had been done largely at the initiative of Sam (Satyen) Pitroda, a successful nonresident Indian, who had returned to India and persuaded Indira Gandhi and Rajiv Gandhi that he could design an indigenous digital technology to build small rural exchanges within three years. These exchanges would bring telephones to the vast rural economy of India. Pitroda argued that, having no use for such technology, rich countries would not develop it, which necessitated local research effort by India.[5]

Alongside these changes, Prime Minister Rajiv Gandhi, who was keen to launch India into the twenty-first century, put an end to the monopoly of the government on the manufacture of telecommunications equipment, and allowed the private sector into it in the mid-1980s. The DoT selected the technology and negotiated the terms of the transfer of technology from among several bidders.[6] Gandhi also opened the first technology park in Bangalore and liberalized imports of electronic equipment. These measures helped accelerate the expansion of the telephone network to some degree in the second half of the 1980s (see figure 17.1).

The most important achievement of this period, however, was a relatively minor innovation that greatly expanded the access to "public" pay phones by the common man. In India, coin-operated pay phones had suffered from frequent mechanical failures for environmental or other reasons, and had never been successful. In 1988, the government introduced a scheme that led to a rapid expansion of the so-called STD booths across the country. Under the scheme, small "entrepreneurs" could get a phone with a device that would meter the local and long-distance calls and produce a bill at the end of each call. On the one hand, the entrepreneur made a commission on each call, and on the other hand, he faced competition from other booths nearby. This provided an incentive to maintain the phones and service.[7] The STD booths proliferated rapidly, and the public experienced vastly improved access to phones.

An attempt was made in the 1980s to introduce the cellular technology at the initiative of the DoT, but it failed due to opposition from C-Dot and, more directly, Pitroda. This episode offers an interesting example of the turf battles that arise in response to policy changes. Chakravarti (2004, p. 241) offers an interesting description of the episode:

> In 1987, the department announced a pilot project funded by the World Bank to introduce a cellular network in Bombay. The deal was awarded to Ericsson, and the DoT officers argued that they would be able to gain technological and organizational experience from this collaborative project. Pitroda, who had no official power within the DoT at this time, went straight to the press arguing that "luxury car phones" were "obscene" in a country where "people were starving." He claimed that this was a duplicitous strategy by a transnational company trying to get "backdoor" entry into the Indian market (*Times of India,* February 15, 1987). Although the plan had already received permission, Pitroda's objections went straight to the Prime Minister's Office, and the project was immediately scrapped. Journalists, keen to expose corruption associated with Rajiv Gandhi's administration, pointed out that Pitroda had, through his own company based in the US, introduced cellular technology to countries like Brazil in the early 1980s. And it was not long before sections of the media claimed that Pitroda's opposition to the Ericsson deal had to do with his allegiance to other corporate players, raising the issue of corruption for the first time in this missionary era of reforms.

In the end, the strategy centered on the development of indigenous technology, championed by Pitroda, failed to deliver sufficiently rapid expansion of telecommunications. The demand continued to outstrip supply by a wide margin. Engulfed in the charges of corruption, Rajiv Gandhi lost the office of prime minister to V. P. Singh in the 1989 elections. Subsequently, unproven corruption charges led to the resignation of Pitroda as well.

The 1990s: A Messy Road to Private Entry

Rajiv Gandhi was assassinated on May 21, 1991, during an election campaign. This led to the ascendancy of P. Narasimha Rao as prime minister in June 1991. As already stated in previous chapters, the event coincided with a macroeconomic crisis that set India on the path to systematic reforms. A key plank of the reform was fiscal discipline, with the immediate implication that rapid expansion of the telecommunications network could not be achieved without the participation of the private sector. In addition, the need to bring the state-of-the-art technology meant that foreign investors must be offered entry alongside domestic entrepreneurs. But this policy faced serious opposition from approximately half a million employees of the DoT. Supported by all major trade unions, the DoT employees viewed the entry of the private sector as a direct threat to their employment prospects.

Discussions for reforms had been under way, even before the macroeconomic crisis unfolded, with the Telecom Restructure Committee (Athreya Committee) issuing its report as early as March 1991. Additional committees were appointed, and reported in 1992, 1993, and 1995.[8] Based on the ongoing discussions, the government opened the "value added" services to the private sector in July 1992, and invited bids for the grant of licenses to two cellular operators per city in the metro cities of Mumbai, Delhi, Chennai, and Calcutta.[9] But before licenses could be issued, aggrieved bidders successfully challenged the evaluation and award process of the DoT in the courts. This delayed the actual entry of the private sector by two years. In the meantime, the telecom policy, 1994 additionally opened basic (meaning fixed-line) phone service to the private companies registered in India. Simultaneously, 49 percent foreign equity in the telecommunications sector was introduced.

To implement the telecom policy, the government divided the nation into four metropolitan cities and 20 territorial telecom circles in 1994. The circles more or less corresponded to the states, and were classified into categories A, B, and C, according to the expected value of licenses; category A consisted of licenses with the highest expected value; category B, the next highest value, and category C, the lowest value. The plan was to allow two cellular mobile operators and one basic fixed-line operator for local service in each circle. The DoT and MTNL were barred from bidding for cellular licenses, on the ground that investment in the wireless technology was to come solely from the private sector. As for the basic service, they were the incumbents.

Ideally, an independent authority should have conducted the auctions. But at this stage in the game, with the policymaking as well as regulatory functions vested in the Ministry of Telecommunications, the task was assigned to the DoT.[10] While the DoT accomplished the task reasonably promptly for the cellular mobile service in the four metropolitan cities, it did everything it could to delay the entry of private operators in all other areas and services.

Auctions for cellular mobile service in the four metropolitan cities took place in November 1994, and eight licensees began operation in August 1995. Auctions for cellular mobile services in the state circles took much longer. Eventually, the DoT issued 34 licenses for 18 territorial telecom circles to 14 private companies between 1995 and 1998. During this period a maximum of two licenses were granted in each service area. The licensees were to pay fixed license fees annually, based on the agreed amount determined during the bidding process.[11]

The auctions for licenses for basic service began in August 1995. But the process was messy and long, with the DoT changing the terms of the auctions midstream multiple times. After several failed attempts, the DoT made a final attempt at auctions in 13 circles. But even then it set the reservation prices of the licenses so high that bids were received for only six circles. In the end, as late as 1999, only two of the six recipients of the licenses were able to offer basic service, and they could mobilize only a few subscribers. It is reasonable to conjecture that the DoT saw private sector operators in basic service as direct competitors to its own monopoly operation, and tried to delay them as much as possible.

The DoT went on to abuse the powers it enjoyed as the public sector entity in three other ways. First, it gave itself and the MTNL licenses to operate cellular mobile service in their respective areas at no fee. This naturally placed the carriers that had paid huge license fees at great disadvantage. Second, the DoT set very high usage charges for cellular service: 16.80 and 8.40 rupees (37 cents and 18 cents) per minute during peak and off-peak hours, respectively. In the same vein, it charged 1.40 rupees per minute in access charges for calls from cellular phones to its fixed-line network. In comparison, it charged only one rupee per minute for calls within its own network. Finally, the DoT required all interconnections to go through the DoT or MTNL. This meant that two cellular providers could not call directly into each other's network; instead, they had to go through the DoT or MTNL fixed-line network. The DoT also denied cellular carriers access to the VSNL, and hence to all outgoing or incoming international services.

Unsurprisingly, private operators incurred large losses and could recruit only a small number of customers during this period. For example, at the end of 1998–99, there were only 1.2 million cellular customers (see table 17.1). In basic service, private operators had entered only two circles, and had only a small number of customers as late as 1999. Both cellular and basic service operators in the private sector were unable to pay the large licensing fees to which they had committed. By 1999, they had accumulated several hundred million dollars' worth of unpaid fees to the DoT.

Initially, this situation was caused by the failure of the Parliament to create an independent regulatory authority with powers to set tariffs and decide who should be given a license. Later, after the Parliament did create such an authority, courts complicated matters by ruling that Parliament did not have the power to regulate the DoT. Using its enormous clout as a public sector agency with half a million employees and the cover of the archaic Indian Telegraph Policy Act, 1885, which still governed the telecommunications sector, the DoT could de facto escape being subject to the regulatory authority.

After several failed attempts, the government was successful in enacting the Telecom Regulatory Authority of India (TRAI) Act in March 1997.[12] It gave the TRAI the authority to set the tariffs and resolve disputes. But in the area of licenses, it limited the TRAI's power to make recommendations to the DoT. Consistent with the Indian Telegraph Policy Act, 1885, the actual authority to issue or revoke licenses and to make policies remained with the DoT.

Ordinarily, the establishment of the TRAI should have paved the way for healthy competition between the DoT and private cellular operators. But it soon turned out that the TRAI Act had fallen short of giving the TRAI the powers to regulate the DoT in a way that would allow such competition. Soon after commencing operation, the TRAI was confronted with a number of disputes between new entrants and the DoT on issues of interconnection charges and issuance of licenses. To rebalance the interests of the two sides, it invariably ruled against the DoT. Each time, the DoT took the matter to the Delhi High Court, challenging the authority of the TRAI over it. Each time, the High Court ruled in its favor.

For example, in one important case, the new entrants challenged the grant of a cellular license by the DoT to MTNL without prior recommendation by the TRAI. The TRAI ruled against the DoT. The DoT took the matter to the Delhi High Court, which argued that "it is unimaginable that the power to grant license rests with the government but would be subject to the discretion of another Authority."[13] It ruled that the DoT was within its rights to issue the license.

Thus, by early 1999, the court rulings against the TRAI and mounting losses of private entrants, resulting from ultrahigh licensing fees and various hostile actions of the DoT, had left the reform process and the telecommunications industry in grim shape. The TRAI had effectively lost jurisdiction over the pricing and licensing actions of the DoT. The threat of foreign investors exiting the industry loomed large.

The New Millennium: Cleaning up the Mess, and Takeoff

At this critical juncture, the government acted. It introduced the New Telecommunications Policy (NTP), 1999 and then proceeded to systematically implement it. The process was greatly helped by the return of Prime Minister Atal Bihari Vajpayee, with a clear mandate to the National Democratic Alliance, following the 1999 elections. Since the 1996 elections, in which the Congress Party failed to return to power, a series of short-lived coalition governments had ruled India. The last of these had been led by Prime Minister Vajpayee, and was responsible for the NTP. With a clear mandate from the electorate, the Vajpayee government could now move the reform process forward with resolve. Indeed, given the power of the DoT, it took direct involvement of the prime minister's office to even partially implement the agenda set out in the NTP.

Breakup of the TRAI and the Creation of an Independent Tribunal

A key change effected as a result of the NTP, 1999 was the TRAI (Amendment) Act, 2000, which split regulatory and dispute settlement roles of the original TRAI. The latter role was assigned exclusively to the newly created independent Telecom Dispute Settlement and Appellate Tribunal (TDSAT). Under the new regime, all disputes involving consumers and providers (including public sector providers) must go to the TDSAT. The TDSAT also hears any challenges to TRAI decisions. This regime excludes civil courts from ruling on disputes arising out of TRAI decisions, or any others involving consumers and service providers in the telecommunications sector. Decisions of the TDSAT can be challenged only in the Supreme Court.

Powers of the New TRAI

The TRAI (Amendment) Act, 2000 defined more precisely and strengthened the regulatory powers of the TRAI. The TRAI is now responsible for recommending the introduction of new service providers, technological improvements, quality standards, and fixing the terms and conditions of licenses. It is mandatory for the DoT or other governmental agencies to seek recommendations from the TRAI for the purpose of issuing licenses, although they are not bound by the recommendations.

Breakup of the DoT and the Birth of the BSNL

In order to separate the policymaking (including licensing) and service provision roles of the DoT, the government created the Department of Telecom Service (DTS), which was then turned into the corporate entity known as the Bharat Sanchar Nigam Limited (BSNL) on October 1, 2000. The road to the conversion of the DTS into the BSNL was a rough one: 400,000 DoT employees went on a long strike, demanding retention of the salaries, pensions, and perks of government employees even after they were transferred to the new corporate entity. The government conceded virtually all demands, including free phone installation, no rental charge up to a specified date, and a fixed number of free local calls.[14]

MTNL, BSNL, and Another Provider Enter the Cellular Mobile Market

On the policy front, the MTNL was allowed to enter cellular mobile service in Delhi and Bombay, and the BSNL, in the rest of the country. This brought to three the number of operators in the cellular mobile sector. The government then proceeded to open the door to a fourth cellular mobile operator in 21 circles. It asked for bids in March 2001 and completed the process in August 2001, awarding license to a fourth operator in each of 17 circles (no bids were tendered in the remaining four circles).

The Revenue-Sharing Regime

Under the NTP, 1999, all new cellular mobile service providers are to pay a modest fixed fee upon entry, and then pay a portion of their revenues to the government. The existing providers, who owed millions of dollars to the government in unpaid licensing fees, were offered a bailout package. They were asked to pay a fixed amount to the government, and then moved to the revenue-sharing arrangement. In return, they agreed to withdraw cases against the government and to the entry of the fourth cellular service provider. The revenue-sharing arrangement came into effect August 1, 1999.

Open Entry into the Domestic and International Long-Distance Service

On August 15, 2000, the government opened unlimited competition in domestic long-distance service. This quickly brought Bharati and Reliance as competitors against BSNL in this important market. On April 1, 2002, the government ended the monopoly of the VSNL on international telephony, two years ahead of the WTO deadline India faced. As compensation, the government gave the VSNL a license to operate domestic long-distance service free of charge. The end to the monopoly quickly brought Reliance and Bharati into the market. The government also released 25 percent of its equity in the VSNL, bringing its share in the company to 26 percent in February 2002. Tata Indicom bought the equity, and now manages the company.

Private Entry into the Basic Service

The first-round reforms to allow private entry into the basic service had been a failure. Given an ambitious (at the time) target to achieve a tele-density of 7 percent, the NTP sought to bring private players into basic service. At the implementation level, the TRAI included the wireless local loop (WLL) technology as an admissible basic service technology. This led to a prolonged legal battle that, nonetheless, helped bring important pro-competitive changes in the industry.

Because the WLL technology had some resemblance to the cellular mobile service due to the limited mobility it allowed within the service area, and basic service providers were not subject to a license fee, cellular mobile operators saw its introduction as placing them at a disadvantage and a change of the rules midstream. They made a plea against the inclusion of the WLL to the TRAI, but the latter rejected it, arguing that exclusion of the technology would be against the interests of the consumers.

On its part, the DoT accepted the TRAI recommendations; began taking applications for licenses on a first come, first served basis; and issued 40 letters of intent on March 26, 2001 (15 to Tata, 18 to Reliance, and 7 to HFCL).[15] At this point, the cellular mobile operators petitioned the TDSAT, but the latter ruled against them on March 15, 2002, stating that the matter was outside its jurisdiction. The cellular mobile operators then took the matter to the Supreme Court, which in its December 12, 2003, verdict took the view that the matter was well within the jurisdiction of the TDSAT, and asked the latter to reconsider the petition.

Nevertheless, the Supreme Court refused the request of the cellular mobile providers to stay the rollout of the WLL-based basic service. The license holders moved aggressively, and by August 8, 2003, when the TDSAT gave its final verdict, had signed up approximately 3 million customers. The TDSAT essentially rejected the plea by the cellular mobile operators, but instructed the DoT to look at the issue of providing a level playing field to cellular operators after consultation with the TRAI.

A Unified License

In response to the TDSAT ruling and in consultation with the TRAI, the DoT decided to eliminate the distinction between licenses based on basic and cellular service. On November 11, 2003, it introduced a unified access service (UAS) license that allows its holder to provide wire-line as well as wireless services in a service area. Wireless services include full mobile, limited mobile, and fixed wireless services. The licensee can also provide various value-added services. Existing providers were given the option to stay on their original license or change to the UAS license. This single policy change considerably limited the scope for litigation, since no provider can now complain about the absence of a level playing field. It also facilitated communications convergence by allowing the provision of the value-added services on the same license.

Progress under the New Regime

As a result of these changes, growth in the telecommunications industry in India exploded, as I have documented above. But some more details may be offered here, particularly emphasizing the role of the private sector in this growth. As of March 31, 2006, a total of 73 UAS and 38 cellular mobile licenses issued to private entities were in service. Each license gives its holder the right to provide the service in one telecom circle.

In basic service (including WLL), there were five private operators at the end of 2005–06. Two of them served in 20 circles, and a third in 16 circles. In addition,

BSNL and MTNL together provided basic service throughout the country. The total expansion of basic line telephones during 2005–06 was from 46.2 million to 50.2 million. Interestingly, private basic service operators increased their subscribers by 92 percent, whereas BSNL increased them marginally and MTNL experienced a decline. The market share of private operators in the basic service rose from 11 to 18 percent during 2005–06.[16]

The dominance of the private sector is much greater in the cellular mobile service, though its share remained approximately unchanged during 2005–06. The total expansion of telephones in this sector during 2005–06 was from 52.2 million to 90.1 million. BSNL and MTNL together expanded from 11 million to 19.7 million. This places their share at 21.1 and 21.9 percent at the end of 2004–05 and 2005–06, respectively.

The Universal Service Obligation

The philosophy underlying the universal service obligation (USO) is that certain basic services should be available to all citizens. The National Telecom Policy,1994 introduced the USO, noting that the policy would aim to "achieve universal service, covering all villages, as early as possible." It went on to note, "What is meant by the expression universal service is the provision of access to all people for certain basic telecom services at affordable and reasonable prices."

The NTP of 1999 reiterated this objective, and laid down specific targets for the expansion of telecommunications in the rural areas:

- Provide voice and low-speed data service to the balance of 290,000 uncovered villages in the country by 2002
- Achieve Internet access to all district headquarters by 2000
- Achieve telephone on demand in urban and rural areas by 2002.

The NTP 1999 stipulated, "The resources for meeting the USO would be raised through a 'universal access levy' which would be a percentage of the revenue earned by all the operators under various licenses." The tax rate was subsequently set at 5 percent of the revenues. The NPT of 1999 further stated, "The implementation of the USO obligation for rural/remote areas would be undertaken by all fixed service providers who shall be reimbursed from the funds from the universal access levy." A second tax levied to promote the USO is an "access deficit charge," which is incorporated into interconnection charges and is paid directly to the BSNL to compensate it for providing below-cost service in rural areas.

The pursuit of the USO can be criticized at two levels. First, there is no clear social or economic rationale for it. The idea of bridging the digital divide, which is another way the USO is often expressed, sounds good but lacks a firm basis upon close examination. Second, even taking the objective as given, the manner in which it is currently being implemented is patently wrong. The principal beneficiary of it is the state enterprise, BSNL.[17]

The argument against the USO as a desirable social objective is that if given a choice, recipients of the service would prefer a cash subsidy. And it is highly unlikely that they would spend this subsidy on the acquisition of a telephone. Therefore, any policy targeting the expansion of rural telephony through subsidy must rest on the assumption that such expansion generates an external social benefit beyond the benefit to the actual users of the service. In principle, one could argue that other, non-subsidized users may benefit from the expansion of the network, but the evidence for such benefits has not been provided. Indeed, the government has never based its case for the USO on the externality it may generate for the existing users.

But even taking the objective as given, the manner in which the USO has been implemented has serious problems. From the income distribution point of view, it is somewhat perverse. The bulk of the subsidy is used to cover the cost of access to the rural households. But virtually no low-income rural households subscribe to access service. Instead, they make calls from pay phones, and insofar as telephone usage is subject to taxation to provide subsidy on access, the poor end up subsidizing the well-to-do who subscribe to access service.

Finally, the decision to fulfill the USO through the expansion of the fixed-line network has been a most terrible mistake. To begin with, it makes no economic sense to promote one form of delivery over another: Instead, the subsidy should be based on the provision of the service to the rural households, regardless of the medium of delivery (including technologies that may be discovered in the future). The decision turns out to be even more damaging, since the fixed-line mode of delivery is far more costly than cellular mobile technology. It is not an accident that even in urban areas, where the density of population is much higher, it is cellular mobile service that is expanding vastly more rapidly than the fixed-line service. The only justification for the government's decision would seem to be to favor the BSNL, which greatly dominates in the fixed-line service.

Future Course of the Policy

While the most important reforms of telecommunications are in the past in India, scope for further action remains. First, as I have just argued, from a social welfare perspective, the government must rethink its decision to promote the USO in telecommunications. Should India spend scarce resources on expanding rural telephony or rural electrification and roads? If given a choice, the rural poor will not spend the resources allocated to the USO on providing themselves telephones. In this context, the view taken by the Planning Commission in its "Towards Faster and More Inclusive Growth: An Approach to the 11th Plan" (2006) is disturbing. The paper essentially proposes to expand, rather than roll back, the USO when it states, "We need to make special intervention to connect rural areas and develop a strategic plan to carry text, data and video to make rural telephony a viable proposition." Such intervention cannot possibly serve the poor, since few of them are likely to make use of video technology.

But even taking the USO as given, the government should focus on the end—expanding access of the poor to communications—not the means. The service can be brought to the rural poor at much lower cost through the cellular technology than through the basic service.[18] The policy should be to give the USO subsidy for the expansion of rural service, not for expanding the fixed-line phones.

Second, the access deficit charges impose a very large efficiency cost. The reason is that the price elasticity of demand for usage of telephone service is very high. The charge is a subsidy to the BSNL for operating its rural lines that supposedly run at a loss. In reality, the BSNL has never provided separate accounts for rural and urban operations to allow verification that rural operations indeed run at a loss, and that the subsidy matches such losses. Presently, the access deficit charge is slated to expire in 2009, but it could be speeded up.

Third, down the road the government will need to confront the issue of privatization of the MTNL and BSNL. The experience since the 1990s has demonstrated that the private sector is entirely capable of supplying this sector efficiently and, therefore, has undermined the argument for provision by public sector companies. Indeed, their presence only leads to policy distortions, since the DoT always has to ensure their good health. This is evident from the adoption of the USO and the decision to promote it through the expansion of the basic service, in which the BSNL enjoyed an advantage, without regard to the cost-effectiveness of this service or the benefits of the USO relative to alternative uses of the revenue.

Fourth, related to the previous point, in view of the developments since the 1990s, the government should reassess the need for the C-DoT. It must ask whether, at a time when the initiative has passed into the hands of the private sector and it is responsible for virtually all the recent advances, there is a need to maintain a center for research in telecommunications at the taxpayers' expense. The government should do a cost-benefit analysis of the center, and if the costs exceed the benefits, the government should close the center down.

Finally, an important provision of the NTP of 1999 that remains to be implemented is the replacement of the Indian Telegraph Act, 1885 by a new law that takes into account changes in technology and market conditions, especially since the 1980s. The Communication Convergence Bill was introduced for this purpose in August 2001, but has not been passed to date. The bill aims to establish an independent commission, known as the Communications Commission of India, consisting of a chairperson and seven members from specialized fields such as broadcasting, telecommunications, information technology, finance, management, and law. The latest development on this front has been a recommendation by a parliamentary committee to enact the bill as the Communications Act, on the ground that convergence is already a reality, making the qualification "convergence" redundant. Before the government proceeds in this direction, it should reassess the need for such a bill. Given that the current system is working reasonably smoothly, there may not be a need to enact another piece of legislation that may end up adding more bureaucratic red tape.

ELECTRICITY

On the surface, the problem of reforming the electricity sector may seem similar to that of telecommunications. But upon closer examination, it turns out to be vastly different for at least four reasons. First, whereas telecommunication is entirely under the jurisdiction of the center, electricity distribution is a state subject. At the national level, it is easier to muster technical and legal talent necessary to build independent regulatory and dispute settlement institutions. At the state level, the vast majority of the employees of the regulatory body come from the agency (often on deputation) they are supposed to regulate. There is also greater scrutiny by the media and NGOs at the national level, which forces the regulatory agency and the government to act broadly in the interest of the consumer, and strengthens its hand vis-à-vis public sector players in the market that constantly try to manipulate the process through the government.

Second, recent technological advances in telecommunications have made it relatively easy to let multiple providers compete against one another without loss of efficiency. Similar advances have not taken place in the provision of electricity. While electricity generation can be decentralized to some degree, transmission and distribution must still go through a common grid. Thus, the key section of the industry remains a natural monopoly.

Third, telecommunications and electricity have had very different initial conditions. In the former, only a tiny elite in the population was covered by the service, calls were metered for all, and nonpayment quickly resulted in the discontinuation of the service. Therefore, virtually all customers paid their bills and bankruptcy of the public monopoly was not an issue—instead, it contributed handsomely to the revenue kitty of the government. The issue facing the reformers was the poor service and its very slow expansion. The electricity sector suffers not only from huge inefficiencies but also from financial ruin. The sector covers a very large proportion of the population that includes poor and middle-class, as well as rich, sections of the society. While India remains far from providing electricity to all, a large part of the sector serves rural areas. Many customers are not even metered, and many among those who are metered do not pay the bills. Theft in both rural and urban areas is a common problem. Politicians frequently promise free electricity in the rural areas to win votes. For all these reasons, most state electricity boards are nearly bankrupt.

Finally, the electricity industry is inherently more complex than telecommunications. In the latter, each cellular service provider has its own spectrum, and each basic service provider can lay down its wire. This allows different providers to compete effectively against one another. In the electricity sector, with rare exceptions, all electricity must flow through a common transmission and distribution grid. This makes the introduction of competing providers more difficult.

Progress in Generation and Rural Electrification

To be sure, India has made considerable progress in the expansions of generation and delivery of electricity since independence. Table 17.2 shows the evolution of installed capacity and electricity generation from 1947 to 2006–07. In addition, figure 17.2 shows per-capita consumption of electricity. All measures show substantial growth, but given the low initial level, India does poorly when compared with other countries. For example, per-capita consumption of electricity in China and in the world in 2001 was 2326 and 1093 kilowatt-hours per year, respectively. In contrast, the same figure for India was 408 kilowatt-hours in 2000–01.

As of February 1, 2007, 65.6 percent of the installed capacity was thermal, 26.6 percent hydro, 3 percent nuclear, and 4.8 percent renewable. Within thermal, 54.2 percent of the total installed capacity was coal, 10.6 percent was gas, and 0.9 percent was oil. In terms of supplying entities, 55.3 percent of the installed capacity was owned by the states, 32.6 percent by the center, and 12.1 percent by private companies. The share of private companies in the total installed capacity was less than 4 percent in 1990–91. Therefore, some progress has taken place in the entry of private companies into generation, but not nearly enough.

TABLE 17.2: Electricity: Installed Capacity and Generation

Year	Installed Capacity (1,000 megawatts)*	Electricity Generated (billion units)
1947	1.4	4.1
1960–61	4.7	16.9
1970–71	14.7	55.8
1980–81	30.2	110.8
1990–91	66.1	264.3
2000–01	101.6	499.5
2006–07**	128.4	652.2

*Represents capacity at the end of the year shown.

**Installed capacity is as of February 1, 2007, and electricity generation is for the calendar year 2006.

Source: Ministry of Power, *Annual Report 1992–93* (1993, p. 56; 2000–01, p. 3); *Performance Report* (2006).

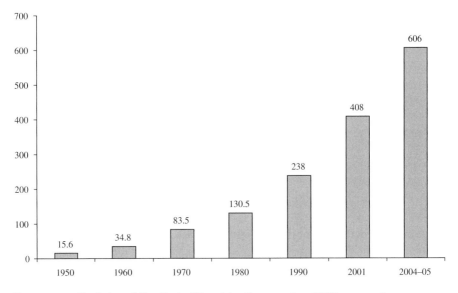

FIGURE 17.2: Evolution of Per-Capita Electricity Consumption (KWh per year)

After rapid progress until the mid-1980s, rural electrification slowed down. The current proportion of villages electrified is placed at 84 percent. But the definition of electrification is undemanding, in that any presence of electricity in a village qualifies it as being electrified. Therefore, the proportion of rural households electrified is a better measure. On this score, India does much worse, with only 44 percent of the households having been electrified, according to the 2001 census. There is large variation in progress across states. In West Bengal, Northeast Region, Uttar Pradesh, Orissa, Jharkhand, and Bihar, the proportion of rural households with electricity is below 40 percent. In the last three of these states, the proportion is below 30 percent, with Jharkhand having only 10.3 percent of the rural households having electricity.[19]

Industry Structure and Evolution of the Policy Regime

The electricity sector has three key components: generation, transmission, and distribution. Generation refers to actual production of electricity, using a variety of fuels including coal, natural gas, nuclear energy, oil, hydroelectric power, wind, and biofuel. Transmission refers to the delivery of electricity from a generation plant to the distribution point over high voltage towers and lines. Distribution refers to the delivery of electricity received on the transmission lines at the distribution center to the retail consumer's home or business through the system of poles, wires, conduits, or other fixtures along public highways or streets.

In principle, different companies can carry out generation, transmission, and distribution activities. There is room for a fourth set of players to be active in the sector: retail suppliers. The latter are intermediaries who buy electricity from generation companies and sell it to retail customers, wheeling (i.e., transferring) it on the transmission and distribution system leased at an access charge set by the regulatory agency. When permitted by law, some large customers can operate so-called captive plants that generate and supply electricity principally to them. If permitted, they can sell any excess electricity to a local distribution company.

In India, the constitution empowers both the central and the state governments to legislate in the electricity sector, with distribution being exclusively in the domain of the states. The Indian Electricity Act, 1910 provided the original framework for the electricity supply industry in India. It empowered the state governments to issue licenses authorizing the licensees to supply electricity in specified areas, and spelled out the legal framework for laying wires and other work. It also specified the rules governing the relationship between licensee and consumers. This act allowed private agents in both generation and distribution.

The Electricity (Supply) Act, 1948 laid the foundation of the policy and institutional framework that remained in force until the recent reforms began. It mandated the creation of the Central Electricity Authority to develop a sound and uniform national power policy. It also mandated the creation of the State Electricity Board (SEB) in each state. By the 1960s, the electricity sector had become a vertically integrated monopoly in each state, with generation, transmission, and distribution coming under a single umbrella.[20] The 1948 act also called upon the SEBs to expand the delivery of electricity to areas not yet receiving it.

An important amendment of the 1948 act in 1975 opened electricity generation to the central government. This led to the creation of the National Thermal Power Corporation (NTPC) and the National Hydroelectric Power Corporation Limited (NHPC) as wholly owned companies of the government of India the same year. NTPC is now a major player in electricity generation in India: It contributed approximately 28 percent of the total generation during 2005–06, and accounted for 20 percent of the installed capacity at the end of that year. In 1989, the Power Grid Corporation of India Limited was incorporated under central government auspices, and has the responsibility for all existing and future transmission projects.

Electricity generation was reopened to the private sector through an amendment of the 1948 act in 1991. In the early 1990s, the government actively courted the U.S. based Enron Corporation to establish a major power plant in Maharashtra, which eventually cost the country (and Enron) dearly. The Electricity Laws (Amendment)

Act, 1998 recognized transmission as a separate activity for the first time. It also provided for private participation in transmission.

Orissa laid the foundation of the modern reforms through the Orissa Electricity Reform Act, 1995. Though the reform itself was immediately unsuccessful, it inspired other states and the central government to begin legislating changes. Two of the most important developments at the center since the late 1990s have been the Electricity Regulatory Commission Act, 1998 and the Electricity Act, 2003. I will return to these developments in greater detail below. Presently, let me explain further why achieving positive results in electricity has proven to be difficult.

The Complexity of the Reform

The SEBs and their successor transmission and distribution companies in the states where they have been unbundled have been financially sick.[21] They incur losses amounting to well above 1 percent of the GDP every year. These losses are partially covered by the government subsidy and partially by accumulating arrears. For example, at the end of 2002, they cumulatively owed 410 billion rupees (approximately $9 billion) to the central power sector undertakings (CPSUs), railways, and coal suppliers. Though a bailout package to wipe out this debt was implemented in March 2003, with the CPSUs and state governments sharing the burden, SEBs or their successor companies now face increasingly harder budget constraints.[22] In turn, this situation makes it difficult for the state power utilities to invest further in generation, despite a large electricity shortage reflected in regular power cuts and the vast regions of the country that still remain to be electrified.

The problem could be considerably alleviated if the private sector would enter electricity generation in a big way. But this solution cannot work as long as the SEBs or their successor companies are in poor financial health. Generation plants require very large investments, and recover their costs over a very long period of time. To be viable, they require credible long-term purchase contracts. Presently, the SEBs or their successor companies are the only possible long-term bulk buyers, but they are not credible on account of their dismal financial condition.

One option in this situation would be to hand over electricity distribution to credible private companies and allow them to buy electricity directly from the companies of their choice. If this is done, private generation companies will be selling electricity to these distribution companies. But for this solution to work, the distribution companies must themselves be seen as profitable, and thus viable in the long run.

Therefore, the ultimate problem the reform faces is that of making electricity supply a profitable business. The starting point to address this problem is to examine the sources of the losses. These fall into several categories:

- The SEBs and their successor transmission and distribution companies suffer from the usual inefficiencies of government-run operations. They are overstaffed, and their technical operations are highly inefficient. In the area of generation, the average plant load factor (PLF), which represents electricity generated as a proportion of the capacity at peak, remains low in the plants owned by the states. Though the average PLF in thermal plants owned by the states rose from 58.1 percent in 1995–96 to 68.2 percent in 2002–03, it remains well below the average PLF in the plants owned by the central government within India (76.6 percent in 2002–03), which is itself below the international norm of 80 percent.

- It is estimated that 15 to 20 percent of the electricity is lost in transmission for technical reasons. The technical losses are due to energy dissipated in the conductors and equipment used for transmission, transformation, subtransmission, and distribution of power. While some technical losses will always be present, they are unusually large in India, even after we take into account the remoteness of many of its villages. For example, in the United Kingdom, these losses are only 7 percent.
- Commercial losses amount to another 20 to 25 percent of the electricity generated. These losses include theft of electricity from distribution lines and nonpayment of bills. The latter may result from lack of meters, faulty meters, deliberate underbilling of household and business customers on account of bribery, and decisions by politicians to grant free electricity to farmers.
- Tariffs for farmers and households are set at below average costs, with some cross-subsidy from industrial users, who pay tariffs exceeding the average cost.

Any reform of the electricity sector must find solutions to these problems. This in turn requires reforms on two fronts: rational tariff setting and turning various players in the sector into commercial entities subject to competitive pressures. The reforms since the 1990s have centrally focused on these objectives, though the success to date has been limited.

The Reforms to Date

As noted previously, the modern electricity reforms in India originated not at the center but in the state of Orissa in the mid-1990s. Around this time, with the macroeconomic stabilization program firmly in place, the government of India had drastically cut its loans from the World Bank. Therefore, the Bank was looking for new ways to lend money in India, and had begun to focus on the states. Because electricity distribution is exclusively a state subject in the constitution, and states have been deeply involved in transmission and generation as well, electricity was the obvious sector to target. By 1993, the World Bank was offering substantial financial resources to states that would "buy" its reform package.[23] The package consisted of unbundling the SEBs into their components (generation, transmission, and distribution), privatizing them, and letting an independent commission set electricity tariffs.

The chief minister of Orissa at the time had been keen to clean up the sector, and decided to court the World Bank. Overcoming strong opposition from the central government, his government passed the Orissa Electricity Reform Act, 1995, which unbundled the SEB into its components with the intent to privatize them.[24] The act also provided for the creation of the Orissa Electricity Regulatory Commission. The key function of the latter was to independently set the tariffs so as to ensure profitability in the provision of electricity. In the event, the Regulatory Commission raised the tariff only moderately, arguing that the utilities, and not the consumers, should bear the high costs of generation, transmission, and distribution. This stance naturally put a hole in the reform program, whose key objective was to reduce the losses incurred by the SEB. Though Orissa did go ahead and privatize distribution in 1999, the results were not encouraging, and undermined the privatization of distribution in other states.

Recognizing the need for reforms in the electricity sector nationwide, and in order to assert its lead, the central government moved forward to enact the Electricity Regulatory Commissions Act, 1998, which mandated the creation of the Central Electricity Regulation Commission, with the charge to set the tariff of centrally owned or controlled generation companies. The act also introduced a provision for the states to create state electricity regulatory commissions with powers to set tariffs without having to enact separate state-level laws. But this was optional, and states still had the right to set up the commissions under their respective laws, as in Orissa. They also had the option to continue business as usual, and not create state regulatory commissions at all. Gujarat in 1998, and West Bengal and Maharashtra in 1999, chose to set up regulatory commissions under the central act. In contrast, Madhya Pradesh, Haryana, and Uttar Pradesh, in that order, went on to create the regulatory commissions via their own laws in 1998.

A key step toward reforms was taken by the central government in 2002–03 with the launch of the Accelerated Power Development and Reform Program, under which it signed memorandums of understanding (MOU) with states, promising financial support in return for satisfying certain performance criteria. The MOU milestones included metering of all 11 KV feeders, 100 percent consumer metering, reduction in technical and commercial losses, energy audits, control of theft, and timely payment of subsidies. By the end of 2002–03, 24 states had signed such MOUs.

While this process was under way, the government introduced the landmark Electricity Act, 2003, which replaced the 1910, 1948, and 1998 electricity laws. This act has brought about far-reaching changes in the policy regime. In the following, I discuss some of the highlights of the regime that has come to exist on account of it.

The Central Government and Central Electricity Authority

The central government prepares the national electricity policy, tariff policy, and rural electrification policy in consultation with the state governments and the Central Electricity Authority. In turn, the Central Electricity Authority, originally created by the Electricity Act, 1948, advises the central government on the national electricity policy and formulates short-term and perspective plans for development of the electricity system. It also specifies the technical standards for construction of electrical plants and electric lines; the safety requirements for construction, operation, and maintenance of electrical plants and electric lines; the grid standards for operation and maintenance of transmission lines; and the conditions for installation of meters for transmission and supply of electricity.

The central government recently issued a comprehensive National Electricity Policy (February 12, 2005), Tariff Policy (January 6, 2006), and Rural Electrification Policy (August 23, 2006). The National Electricity Policy spells out some of the details in order to implement the Electricity Act, 2003. The Tariff Policy gives direction to the states in formulating tariff policy. The Rural Electrification Policy sets access to electricity by every household by 2009, and the consumption of at least one unit per household per day as merit (i.e., socially desirable) good by 2012, as the key goals of the future rural electrification programs.

The Regulatory Commissions at the Center and in the States

The regulatory regime consists of a mandatory Central Electricity Regulatory Commission (CERC) and of a State Electricity Regulatory Commission (SERC) in each state. The commissions are statutory bodies with quasi-judicial status. The following are among the most important functions of the CERC:

- Regulation of the tariff of generating companies owned or controlled by the central government and other generating companies that sell electricity in more than one state
- Regulation of the interstate transmission of electricity
- Determination of tariff for interstate transmission of electricity
- Issuing licenses for transmission and trading of electricity for operations between states
- Adjudication of disputes involving generating companies or transmission licensees in regard to the above matters, and reference of any dispute for arbitration.

The SERCs have parallel functions within the states. In addition, they play an important role in regulating the distribution activity. Thus, their functions include

- Determination of the tariff for generation, supply, transmission, and wheeling of electricity—wholesale, bulk, or retail—within the state
- Regulation of the electricity purchase and the procurement process of distribution licensees, including the price at which electricity is procured from the generating companies within the state
- Issuing licenses for transmission, distribution, and trade in electricity for operations within the state
- Adjudication of disputes between the licensees and generating companies, and referral of any dispute for arbitration.

By the end of 2005–06, 24 states had formed an SERC, and 20 of them had issued orders to rationalize the tariff structure.

The Appellate Tribunal

Appointed by the central government on July 21, 2005, the Appellate Tribunal for Electricity is empowered to hear appeals against the orders of an adjudicating officer of the CERC or SERC. The tribunal is normally expected to bring the cases to conclusion within 180 days of the appeal, failing which it must give reasons. The decisions by the tribunal can be appealed only in the Supreme Court.

Unbundling of the SEBs and Privatization

The new policy requires each state to break up the SEB into a state transmission utility, generation companies, transmission licensees, and distribution licensees within a year of the Electricity Act, 2003. States may extend this deadline, however, with the consent of the central government. An important objective behind the breakup is transparency: The separation will help pinpoint the source of the financial losses, and place responsibility on the appropriate entity. The state governments are free to privatize the new entities. By the end of 2005–06, 13 states had unbundled their SEBs, with Orissa and Delhi also privatizing distribution. Eleven states postponed the unbundling with the permission of the central government.

Transmission

The central government has the responsibility to keep developing the national grid for interstate transmission of power. The central transmission utility (CTU) and the state transmission utilities (STU) have the responsibility of network planning. The CTU is responsible for the national and regional transmission system planning and development. The STU is responsible for planning and development of the intrastate transmission systems.

The Electricity Act, 2003 mandates nondiscriminatory open access in transmission from the beginning. This is expected to promote competition among the generation companies, which are free to sell to different distribution licensees across the country. In due course, the act also requires the states to give bulk consumers open access to distribution networks (see below). This provision, combined with the open access in transmission, is intended to intensify competition on both the demand and the supply side. The Electricity Act, 2003 prohibits the state transmission utilities and transmission licensees from engaging in trading in electricity. This means that the generation companies will have to write power purchase agreements with the distribution companies or licensees.

To create an integrated power system countrywide, the central government has established five regional load dispatch centers. It also plans to establish a national load dispatch center by May 2008. Correspondingly, each state has established or is in the process of establishing a state load dispatch center. The dispatch centers at various levels are to function in unison, ensuring optimum scheduling and dispatch at the national, regional, and state levels.

Competition in Generation and Distribution

The Electricity Act, 2003 has several provisions to create a competitive market in electricity. It abolishes all licensing requirements in generation, except that for hydroelectric plants with capital expenditure exceeding a specified limit. Captive generation has been freed from all controls to allow firms access to secure, reliable, quality, and cost-effective power. Captive generation plants have access to distribution licensees and will also be granted access to consumers who are allowed open access (see below).

The National Electricity Policy, 2005 sees the distribution segment of the electricity business chain as key to promoting competition in the sector. Accordingly, multiple licensees in the same area of supply are permitted. State governments have full flexibility in carving out distribution zones while restructuring the government utilities. The second and subsequent distribution licenses within the area of an incumbent distribution licensee are to minimally cover a revenue district, a munici-pal council for a smaller urban area, or a municipal corporation for a larger urban area. The second and subsequent licensees for distribution in the same area would have the obligation to supply to all consumers. The SERCs are required to regulate the tariff, including connection charges to be recovered by a distribution licensee. This is to ensure that a second distribution licensee does not resort to "cherry pick-ing" by demanding unreasonable connection charges from consumers.

The Electricity (Amendment) Act, 2003 provides that all states must allow open access to all (mainly industrial or commercial) consumers drawing one megawatt or more of power per year by January 27, 2009. These consumers may enter into agree-ment with any person for supply of electricity on mutually agreeable terms, includ-ing tariff. While making regulations for open access in distribution, the SERCs determine wheeling charges and a cross-subsidy surcharge. The latter is to be even-tually eliminated. In its recent tariff order, the Maharashtra Electricity Regulatory Commission has already eliminated this cross-subsidy surcharge.

Tackling the Commercial Losses

At least four important provisions aimed at brining the commercial losses down can be identified. First, all consumers are to be metered by law. The SERCs are empowered to obtain the metering plans of distributors and monitor their imple-mentation. The SERCs are also advised to arrange for third-party meter-testing arrangements. The coverage of feeder meters has risen from 81 percent in 2001 to 96 percent in 2006 and of consumer meters from 77.6 percent to 92 percent over the same period.

Second, stealing electricity by tapping electric wires, tampering with meter and damaging meter or wiring to falsify meter reading are punishable with up to three years of imprisonment and hefty fine. Authorized officers are also given broad pow-ers to enter the premises and conduct searches if they suspect electricity theft.

Third, special emphasis is placed on consumer indexing and mapping in a time-bound manner. Support is being provided for information technologybased systems under the Accelerated Power Development and Reforms Program.

Finally, energy accounting and declaration of its results in each defined unit, as determined by SERCs, is to be mandatory by the end of 2006–07. Each unit is required to draw an action plan for reduction of the losses, with adequate invest-ments and suitable improvements in governance.

Cross-Subsidy and the Poor

Cross-subsidies are to be largely eliminated, except that to the poor. Consumers below the poverty line who consume below a specified level, say 30 units per month, may be charged a tariff that is 50 percent of the overall average cost of supply. The tariff on other domestic consumers is to be gradually raised to levels sufficient to cover the cost. By the same token, the tariff on industrial consumers will have to come down. This last change is likely to be forced in any case by the open access provision that allows customers consuming one megawatt or more of electricity per year to seek their own suppliers. The state governments are now expected to give subsidies to the state-owned units in advance and to make provision for them in the budget.

Impact of Reforms: A Mixed Scorecard

There is no denying that the Electricity Act, 2003 is a landmark development in the history of electricity policy in India. It dramatically alters the organization and governance in the sector. The SEBs have been replaced by state transmission units, generation companies, and distribution licensees, with the independent regulator given broad powers to set tariffs and issue licenses. Yet, so far, the success in improving the service, attracting private sector entry into generation, and bringing down commercial losses has been limited. The direction of change is right, but progress has been slow.

As I noted earlier, the electricity industry is fundamentally different from telecommunications. For example, consider the provision of multiple distribution licensees and open access. Most generation companies are bound by long-term power purchase agreements. This makes it difficult for distribution licensees and consumers with open access to find alternative sources of electricity unless there is massive new entry, which has not happened. In addition, interstate transmission corridors are heavily congested. This means that even if surplus electricity can be found in another state, its delivery to the consumer is not automatic.

What is needed is the emergence of profitable distribution companies that will provide incentive to generation companies to increase the electricity supply in a major way. Success on this front has been modest at best. Given that reductions in costs in the absence of commercial pressures are difficult, and even then they take time, the only avenue to improving the financial health of the distribution companies or SEBs is increased revenue. In the short term, this means improving collection. But three factors have impeded the progress in improving the revenue collection.

First, the political resolve to get the farmers to pay for electricity, which was already weak, has weakened further. During or immediately following the elections in 2004, Andhra Pradesh, Maharashtra, Punjab, and Tamil Nadu introduced free electricity for the farmers. Subsequently, virtually no other state has had the courage to increase the tariff on farmers, even though it was either zero or very low.

Second, in many states, the regulatory agencies have failed to act independently of the government in moving the tariff toward the cost for household consumers. Drawing on Mahalingam (2005) and Electricity Governance Initiative-India (2005), Dubash (2005) explains why. Sometimes, state governments tell state-controlled utilities not to file for tariff revision at politically inconvenient moments. At other times, they direct state-owned generation companies to sell power cheap to the distribution companies in order to eliminate the basis for tariff revision. At still other times, regulators internalize the motives of their political masters. For example, following the decision to provide free power to farmers in Tamil Nadu in 2005, the state utility chose not to file a statement of annual revenue requirement and did not seek a tariff increase.

Finally, except in Delhi, where privatization of distribution has resulted in improved collection (see below), the SEBs or their successor companies still do not have an incentive to operate as commercial entities. As a result, progress toward reduced leakages from the power lines and improved bill collection has been at best slow. The breakup of the SEBs has no doubt improved the overall transparency. But the problem of commercial losses had been well known for years. Thus very little has changed in that regard. Unless the distribution companies are forced to face hard budget constraints, they have little incentive to aggressively fight the leakages of electricity from power lines or nonpayment of bills.

The modest success achieved by Delhi with privatization of distribution, which increased incentives for the companies to act as commercial entities, offers some hope in this regard. The NGO Prayas (2006) has produced an excellent study of this experience during the first three years, ending with 2004–05. The Delhi government handed over distribution to three companies—two owned by the Reliance Group and one by Tata—in July 2002. The companies were given a five-year transition period, during which they were to cut commercial losses by 17 percentage points relative to the base-level loss of 50.7 percent in 2001–02. They were promised 34.5 billion rupees (approximately $750 million) in subsidy from the government. At the end of five years, they must become self-sufficient.

According to Prayas (2006), with one exception, the three companies have met or exceeded their targets in each of the three years studied. Only one of the two Reliance-owned companies missed the target in 2002–03. The Tata-owned company exceeded its target in the third year (2004–05) by seven percentage points. The Prayas report predicts that the company is likely to accomplish the same in 2005–06. The tariff increases during the three years were 0, 5, and 10 percent, in that order. In the fourth year, the increase was 6.66 percent. These increases work out to approximately 5.3 percent per year, which is comparable to the increases in the past. Prayas (2006) concludes that privatization has resulted in a saving of 8 billion rupees (approximately $175 million) relative to what it would have cost Delhi taxpayers if technical and commercial losses had stayed at their base level of 50.7 percent. But it also notes that the quality of service has not improved. Additionally, it points to some glaring deficiencies in the work of the regulatory commission.

It can be hypothesized that the Delhi experience will open the door to more privatizations in the future. When Delhi privatized, there was no experience, other than the anomalous case of Orissa, on which either the seller or a potential buyer could draw. The experience with the regulatory process was also limited, making the future price increases uncertain. Therefore, both the government and the potential bidders faced considerable uncertainty. The result was that no bids met the minimum demands of the government. The government then decided to enter into negotiation with the two companies that had offered bids below the minimum demanded by the Delhi government. Luckily, the two sides could come to an agreement and privatization could proceed. The Delhi experience has now provided some information on the parameters of the problem the potential buyers face and the profitability of the venture.

Future Course of the Policy

Two interrelated areas in which progress is necessary are regulatory independence and privatization of distribution. Going by the evidence collected to date, unlike the TRAI in telecommunications, state regulatory commissions in many states have not shown the kind of independence necessary to make the distribution companies financially solvent. At present, as state arms, the distribution companies do not have a truly independent voice in aggressively seeking high tariffs. Consumers are obviously happy to see their tariffs left low. This situation leads to the maintenance of the status quo. Privatization of distribution companies offers a way out of this conundrum. Private companies will have a vested interest in seeking high tariffs, and consumers will oppose them through the regulatory commission, the tribunal, and the political process. In such a situation, if the government does want to intervene on behalf of the consumer, it will have to be entirely transparent and foot the necessary subsidy up front, as happened in Delhi in 2005.[25]

The generation companies need to be subject to more competition. For example, the relevant regulatory commissions continue to set the tariff of the central and state generation companies on a cost-plus basis. This pricing eliminates the pressure on the companies to minimize their costs. The absence of proper incentives remains the central problem. Not only is the profit motive missing, but improvements in efficiency are not expected to result in increased salaries for the employees.

Another important reform is to end the cross-subsidy regime with the subsidy to the poor covered from tax revenues. At present, the industry pays an excessively high tariff and subsidizes household consumers. As in the case of cross-subsidies on telephone calls, cross-subsidies on the use of power are highly distortionary. They also asymmetrically impede growth of industries intensive in the use of power. In principle, open access (with the cross-subsidy surcharge eliminated as planned) should eventually eliminate this distortion, but this will not happen if surplus power is not available or transmission corridors are congested. Therefore, the regulatory commissions must directly move to eliminate the cross-subsidy.

If the government were to largely privatize generation and distribution, it could focus more centrally on the two activities in which it is needed the most: building the transmission network and rural electrification. The existing transmission grid is woefully inadequate. The central and state governments need to add new transmission capacity as well as modernize the existing grid in order to plug the large technical losses. The focus of much of the public debate has been on the commercial losses, but India also incurs very large technical losses relative to most countries. This reflects a transmission grid in desperate need of modernization.

In India, rural electrification has moved slowly, with nearly 55 percent of the rural households still without electricity at the time of the 2001 census. Given the critical importance of electricity in promoting development and improving the well-being of the people, the government is likely to do greatest public good by bringing electricity to the rural areas rapidly. Though the government does have a rural electrification program under the Rajiv Gandhi Grameen Vidyutikaran Yojana, a part of the four-year business plan called Bharat Nirman, at the current level of generation capacity, it can scarcely achieve its objectives. One dramatic statistic is that in 2006 alone, China created additional capacity of more than 100,000 megawatts. In comparison, utility-based generation capacity is expected to rise by less than 30,000 megawatts during the entire Tenth Five-Year Plan (2002–07) in India. It is perhaps fair to say that the current differences between India and China in the area of electricity are comparable to those in the telecommunications sector in the mid 1990s. India has much catching up to do.

CONCLUDING REMARKS

India has made very substantial progress in putting in place modern policy regimes in telecommunications and electricity. Helped by important technological advances, it has achieved striking success in telecommunications, raising the tele-density from less than 3 percent in 1999–2000 to more than 16 percent by the end of 2006. A recent measure of the success of the industry is the valuation of the fourth largest mobile operator, Hutchison Essar, at $19 billion in a takeover bid. The success in electricity has been modest so far, but the Electricity Act, 2003 and subsequent policy changes offer a good start. The modest success of privatization of distribution in Delhi holds some hope. In my detailed discussion of each sector, I have provided detailed recommendations for future policy changes necessary to make further progress.

18

TRANSPORTATION

A Solvable Problem

There are four modes of transportation: roads, railways, air, and water. In each case, we must deal with issues related to the building of infrastructure: airports, ports, roads, and railway tracks. In addition, we must consider issues related to the organizational structure of the commercial vehicles industries that move the traffic on each mode: trucks and buses on the roads, passenger and freight trains on the railway tracks, passenger and cargo planes at the airports, and vessels of various sizes moving into and out of ports. In this chapter, I will consider both aspects of infrastructure, though the emphasis will vary from mode to mode. For example, I will consider the airline industry in detail, but not shipping.

Virtually all forms of transport infrastructure—roads, railway tracks, airports, and ports—have the property of natural monopoly. Occasionally, adjacent airports or ports and parallel roads and railway lines may compete, but this is not significant enough to detract from the fact that efficiency dictates monopoly provision of infrastructure, which may be done either by the government or by a regulated monopoly. Competition is possible, however, in the commercial vehicle industries such as the airlines, trucking, buses, and even freight and passenger trains.

By now it must be clear that natural monopoly does not justify financing through taxation. In most cases, exclusion is possible so that user charges can be imposed to recover costs at least partially. This is true of highways, airports, ports, and even railway tracks. Rural roads are intended to promote the social goal of linking the poor to the marketplace, and therefore qualify for financing exclusively through public revenues. As for urban transportation, it is mostly subject to nonexclusion, so that the only practical way to recover costs is through taxes on vehicles and fuel.

Traditionally, India had relied on the government agencies to build and maintain various components of infrastructure. This resulted in very slow progress and poor quality of infrastructure. In the early 2000s, the government decided to move wholesale toward contracting the building and maintenance activity to the private sector, except in the case of railway tracks. The government now pays private contractors outright for projects with no potential user charges such as tolls on the roads (e.g., rural roads) and gives concessions on a build, operate, and transfer (BOT) basis for projects generating future revenues via user charges (e.g., national highways). In the latter case, private builders recover a part of their costs through user charges they are authorized to collect for an agreed-upon period of time. The government pays the costs not covered by the user charges in the form of either an up-front lump-sum payment or an annuity.

In the discussion below, we will come across several issues that are common to all modes of transportation. Of these, three may be mentioned up front. First, building and maintenance of infrastructure raise issues of financing. Here the government has relied on a variety of sources, including user charges as a part of the BOT concessions, tax revenues, special duties on gasoline and diesel in the case of roads, and borrowing from multilateral institutions. Second, tolls on roads and tariffs on the use of airports and port facilities raise the important issue of whether an independent regulatory agency is needed. Such an agency has the advantage of enforcing the user charges transparently and with certainty. If political considerations lead the government to insist on lowering tolls or tariffs set by the regulatory agency, it must compensate the recipient through an explicit subsidy. This makes the government commitments on tolls and tariffs in the BOT concessions more credible and also subjects the government to greater economic discipline. Finally, the government often has social objectives whereby it wants to supply transportation services to certain segments of the society at below cost. For example, it may offer low fares to certain sections of the society or run air service on routes that are unprofitable for private firms. In such cases, we must deal with issues of cross-subsidy.

In the following, I consider the broad developments within each mode of transportation and the analytic issues related to it. My discussion is deliberately brief. The interested reader may find additional details in N. K. Singh and Wallack (2005), the World Bank (2002), and the Web sites of the relevant ministries, departments, and specific initiatives such as the Pradhan Mantri Gram Sadak Yojna (PMGSY, the Prime Minister's Rural Road Plan), the Jawaharlal Nehru National Urban Renewal Mission (JNNURM), and Bharat Nirman (Building India). I begin with air transportation, where the changes during the reform era have been most far-reaching.

AIR TRANSPORTATION

The functioning of air transportation depends on the organization of the airline industry as well as the availability of infrastructure (airports). I discuss the existing policies in each area and then offer suggestions for future reforms.

Civil Aviation

The Air Corporations Act of 1953 merged all existing airlines other than Air India International Ltd. into a new public sector corporation called Indian Airlines (renamed simply "Indian" in December 2005), which was then given monopoly over scheduled domestic flights.[1] The act also converted Air India International Ltd. into another public sector corporation called Air India, which became the sole Indian carrier permitted to operate international flights. The Directorate General of Civil Aviation was set up to oversee regulatory matters such as pilot licenses, safety certification, and procedures for airports and airspace.

Although genuine liberalization in the airline industry began only in 1994 with the repeal of the 1953 Air Corporations Act, the government had introduced the entry of nonscheduled air taxis in 1986. The conditions for the operation of these taxis were liberalized in 1990–91 and again in 1992. The latter liberalization paved the way for the entry of Jet Airways, which began "unscheduled" flights with a fleet of four leased Boeing 737 aircraft on May 5, 1993.[2] Sahara Airlines (later rebranded Air Sahara) followed with its nonscheduled flights on December 3, 1993, with a fleet of two Boeing 737 aircraft. In February 1993, the government also permitted 40 percent foreign equity under the Air Taxi Scheme, on a case-by-case basis. After the repeal of the Air Corporations Act in 1994, these airlines were permitted to operate scheduled services, and foreign equity investment up to 40 percent (recently raised to 49 percent) was extended to the scheduled air transport services the same year.

In 1997, the government introduced another set of important liberalizing steps. Barriers to entry into and exit from domestic airline operation were removed. The government now required only preentry scrutiny of applications. It eliminated the ceiling on the number of seats that had been set at 50 in 1996 (and was only 30 prior to that date). The 1997 liberalization gave the new entrants the freedom to choose any type and size of aircraft, and the nonresident Indian investment limit was set at 100 percent.

The opening up of international routes is of more recent origin and has proceeded along two lines. First, domestic private airlines and Indian Airlines have been permitted to fly abroad, thereby breaking the Air India monopoly. Indian, Jet, and Sahara are the three carriers now operating flights to and from foreign destinations. Second, the so-called open skies policy has been implemented through more liberal bilateral agreements with the major destination countries. Of particular significance is the agreement with the United States, signed in April 2005, that replaced the highly restrictive and antiquated Air Services Agreement of 1956. The new accord allows the two countries' carriers to operate as many flights as they want between each other's cities. The agreement also allows all-cargo carriers to operate in either country without directly connecting to their homeland. Other countries with which new, more liberal bilateral agreements have been signed include the United Kingdom, Germany, the United Arab Emirates, China, and Australia.

Several domestic airlines—including Jet, Sahara, Air Deccan, Spice Jet, GoAir, Indian (previously Indian Airlines), IndiGo, and Kingfisher—compete for domestic air passengers.[3] During the early 2000s, domestic air traffic has grown rapidly, which in part accounts for the entry of many new airlines. This is shown in figure 18.1. The total number of passengers carried domestically by air grew relatively gradually in the 1990s, rising from 8.1 million in 1991 to 13.3 million in 2000. But it shot up to 22.7 million in 2005. Annual growth in passenger travel during 2004 and 2005 has touched 25 percent. This growth has been accompanied by a major shift in the share of passengers in favor of private airlines. From the paltry figure of 0.4 percent in 1991, this share rose to 52.8 percent in 2000 and to 68.5 percent

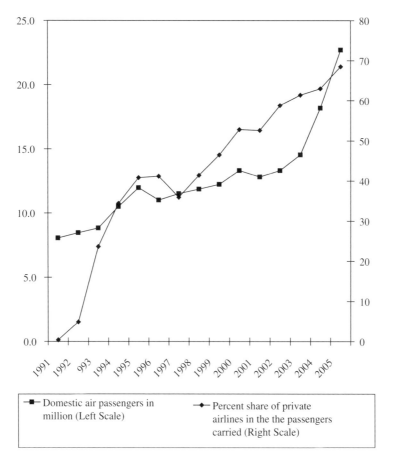

FIGURE 18.1: Growth in Domestic Passenger Air Traffic and in the Share of Private Airlines (*source*: Gohain 2005 and Ministry of Civil Aviations 2005–2006)

in 2005. Based on the data for January-September 2006, the share further rose to 77.5 percent. The shares of Jet and Deccan Airways, the two largest private airlines, during this period were 32.8 and 17.9 percent, respectively, and the share of Indian was 22.5 percent.

Until recently, the growth of international travel had been greatly hampered by restrictions on the number of flights. The number of passengers flying internationally on the domestic carriers rose from 3.1 million in 1995–96 to 5.3 million in 2004–05. But with the opens skies agreements with key destination countries in place, this constraint has been removed. Relaxation of the constraints imposed by airports will take some more years, however, as I discuss immediately below.

Airports

India has 125 airports in total, of which 11 are designated as international airports. In 2004–05, the airports handled 60 million passengers and 1.3 million metric tons of cargo. Until recently, all airports were owned and operated by the Airport Authority of India (AAI). But the AAI Act of 1994 was amended in 2003 to provide for restructuring of airports through leasing, and exclusion of private airports from its jurisdiction except for security and air traffic control functions that the AAI would continue to discharge at all airports. The amendment has paved the way for privatization of airports and for the construction of new private airports.

Delhi and Mumbai airports were recently turned into public-private partnerships (PPPs) between the AAI and consortiums of private companies including foreign companies.[4] The AAI has equity shares of 26 and 27 percent in Delhi and Mumbai airports, respectively. Under the Operations, Maintenance, and Development Agreement, the two airports were handed over to the Delhi International Airport Ltd. (DIAL) and Mumbai International Airport Ltd (MIAL) in May 2006. The concession is for 30 years with an option for extension for another 30 years. Both DIAL and MIAL are to share revenues with the AAI at previously agreed rates. The DIAL is to complete enhanced facilities at the existing airport, including development of new terminals and runways, by March 2010, in time for the 2010 Commonwealth Games to be held in Delhi.

Two greenfield airports (i.e., entirely new rather than renovation of the existing airports), Bangalore International Airport Ltd. and Hyderabad International Airport Ltd., are under construction via the PPP under the build, own, operate, and transfer model. The host state government and the AAI each have 13 percent equity shares in these projects, with the rest invested by private companies. These airports are expected to become operational by 2008.

The government is also looking into the privatization of the remaining two metro airports: those in Kolkata and Chennai. Five other greenfield airports in Goa, Nagpur, Pune, Navi Mumbai, and Greater Noida are planned. In addition, the AAI has decided to modernize 35 nonmetro airports to world-class standards in three separate phases of ten, fifteen, and ten airports, respectively. In all, the Infrastructure Committee, chaired by the prime minister, estimates approximately $9 billion worth of investment in airports during 2006–10.

Future Course of Air Transportation Policy

There are four important issues to consider with respect to the future policy. First, and perhaps the most important, the need for independent authorities for the regulation of civil aviation and airports requires careful study. Currently, the Directorate General of Civil Aviation oversees aviation-related regulatory issues such as pilot licenses, safety certification, entry and exit of airlines, and procedures for airports and airspace. In parallel, the AAI manages all national and international airports (except those just privatized) and administers air traffic control.

My own tentative view is that a new regulatory agency for civil aviation is unnecessary. Given the generally competitive structure of the airline business, there is no need to burden the industry with a regulator. What the government does need to do is allow relatively free entry and exit of airlines and maintain open skies. Leaving regulation in the hands of the government when two major airlines are in the public sector carries some moral hazard, but it is preferred to the alternative for two reasons: (1) putting in a whole new bureaucracy devoted to regulating civil aviation may end up impeding competition, and (2) the solution to the moral hazard is privatization of Air India and Indian.

As regards airports, my tentative view is the opposite: They are local monopolies, and absent regulation, may try to exploit their market power. But even here, any regulatory regime should take account of potential competition among the airports that are near each other, especially if they happen to be in the same city. Currently, an independent Airports Economic Regulatory Authority Bill is under consideration by the government. Before this bill is turned into law, some more thought must be given to the precise problem the regulatory agency is intended to solve.

Second, for the purpose of providing service on routes that are uneconomical but socially desirable, cross-subsidy is an inefficient solution. Two distortions arise. First, taxing the usage in profitable sectors has the usual detrimental effect on efficiency. Second, the airlines that end up serving the uneconomical but socially desirable routes do not necessarily have a comparative advantage in serving those routes. The optimal solution to the problem, which is also transparent, is to create a subsidy pot from general revenues and let the airlines willing to serve the route at the lowest subsidy, do so.

Third, the composition of revenues of airports in India suggests inefficiencies in the pricing of services. In most countries, airports earn the bulk of their revenues from nonaeronautical services such as duty-free shops, land and space rental, and car parking. Aeronautical services such as landing and parking fees paid by the airlines, passenger service fees, terminal charges, and X-ray charges usually contribute less than 40 percent of the total airport revenues. In India, the opposite is true: As much as 70 percent of the airport revenues come from aeronautical services (KPMG, 2006). This is inefficient, since the imposition of high fees on aeronautical services discourages passenger travel and cargo traffic.

Finally, there remain major bottlenecks at the Indian airports, leading to inordinate delays in inward movement of imports and outward movement of exports. A study by Roy and Bagai (2005) documents that in most countries it takes airports 12 hours to clear exports and imports. In India, the average time is 15 days for imports and 2.5 days for exports. This is highly detrimental to the growth of international trade.

MARITIME TRANSPORT

India has 12 major ports and 187 minor ports, but only one-third of the latter are able to handle cargo. Of the 12 major ports, 11 are run by port trusts and the remaining one is a corporation under the central government. These ports handled 384 million metric tons out of the total of 519 million metric tons of cargo handled by all ports in 2004–05. According to the Draft Policy (Modified) for the Maritime Sector, maritime transport carries 95 percent of India's trade in volume terms and 70 percent in value terms. Port capacity has responded to the increasing demand generated by the rapid expansion of international trade, especially in the early 2000s. The most important problem remains the slow clearing of goods. According to the Roy and Bagai (2005) study mentioned above, ship waiting time in India is three to five days, export dwell time is three to five days, and import dwell time is

7 to 14 days. The international norms for these activities are less than 6, 18, and 24 hours, respectively.

The Current Policy Regime

India allows 100 percent FDI in port development projects under the automatic route that does not require lengthy approval process. There is also 100 percent income tax exemption. India has had considerable success in operating berths through PPPs on the build, operate, and transfer basis at some of the major ports. Therefore, the government has decided to allocate the construction of new berths through PPPs. State governments in Gujarat, Orissa, Tamil Nadu, and Andhra Pradesh have adopted this essential model and have been actively building minor ports.

According to N. K. Singh and Wallack (2005), the policy toward entry into port servicing in India is extremely liberal. Most of the port services are open to domestic and foreign private sector participants. Private companies are involved in port maintenance, construction of new berths and terminals, warehousing and storage, container freight stations and tank farms, and dry docking and ship repair facilities. State governments have generally followed the central government in adopting these liberal policies, with the domestic and foreign private companies playing an important role in the development of minor ports.

Of the 12 major ports, 11 are managed by port trust boards created under the Major Port Trusts Act, 1963. The remaining port, Ennore, is the newest and has been set up as a company under the Companies Act, 1956. The 1963 Port Trusts Act was amended by the Port Laws (Amendment) Act, 1997 to create the Tariff Authority for Major Ports (TAMP). The TAMP regulates tariffs for all services related to vessels and cargo, as well as rates for lease of properties in the major port trusts and private terminals. The decisions of the TAMP are final and must be appealed to the High Court. The government can override any decisions made by the TAMP. Minor ports, which have competed effectively with the major ports in recent years, are regulated by their respective states. Some states have set up autonomous maritime boards for the purpose.

Future Course of the Maritime Transport Policy

The Draft (Modified) Policy for the Maritime Sector, dated February 10, 2005, is posted on the Web site of the Department of Shipping. This draft policy will probably form the basis of the comprehensive national maritime policy currently being formulated, according to the Web site of the Infrastructure Committee of the Planning Commission. The draft policy offers a comprehensive discussion of the issues related to both port development and shipping. In port development, it covers issues such as modernization and expansion of port capacity, connectivity, dredging, land policy, private sector participation, special economic zones, and electronic data interchange. . In the area of shipping, the policy covers issues related to the development of infrastructure, manpower, trade interests, and international cooperation.

Next, I selectively touch on four key issues. First, the central problem the government has been unable to solve effectively is the slow pace with which imports and exports are cleared at the Indian ports. An important source of the delays at the major ports is the low productivity of workers, which is rooted in the Dock Workers (Regulation and Employment) Act, 1948. This act gives the workers such a high level of job security and rights that they have little incentive to improve efficiency. Some reform of this law will be key to improving performance at the major ports. Unfortunately, the draft policy essentially ducks this issue. Improvements in customs procedures, effective use of information technology, and streamlining security procedures will also help reduce the dwell time.

Second, related to the previous point, there is a need to better connect the ports to the hinterland. A key barrier to the development of manufactures exports in India has been the inability of entrepreneurs to move goods expeditiously from factories to the ports. While building road links and the development of the trucking industry would also help, the key to solving this problem is improvement in the railway links. This requires both building railway tracks and ensuring that freight trains run with the necessary frequency between ports and manufacturing centers. The end to the monopoly of the state-owned Container Corporation of India on inland container transport in January 2007 is an important step in this direction. It is remarkable that though the door to containers supplied by companies other than Container Corporation of India had been opened in 1994, no railway minister took advantage of it until just now.

Third, the need for an appropriate form of regulatory regime must be carefully studied. One question we may ask is whether there is sufficient scope for competition among various ports that only light regulation is required. Or are the ports local monopolies that need more aggressive regulation than is currently in place? If the latter, is there need to give the TAMP independent statutory status and eliminate the final authority in all matters the government currently enjoys? If yes, should the regulatory authority be complemented by a tribunal that would hear appeals on the decisions made by the regulatory authority and rule on other disputes involving parties engaged in maritime transport? A related issue concerns the existence of separate regulatory regimes of the center and states governing the major and minor ports, respectively. Do these separate regimes promote greater competition, or would replacing them with a single nationwide regulator enhance efficiency? The current draft policy pays inadequate attention to this set of issues.

Finally, the government must proceed with corporatization of the major ports. This will allow the ports to function as proper companies rather than arms of the central government. As profit-making entities, they are more likely to introduce cost-effective measures and compete against one another for traffic. The issue has been widely discussed since the mid-1990s, and the Major Port Trust (Amendment) Bill was even introduced in the Parliament in 2001 to provide the legal basis for the change. But the issue seems to have been moved to the back burner.

ROAD TRANSPORT

India has a total road network of 3.3 million km. Of this, approximately 66,600 km. are national highway, 131,900 km. are state highway, 467,800 km. are district-level roads, and 2.65 million km. are rural roads. As of January 31, 2007, 10 percent of the national highways had four or more lanes, another 55 percent had two lanes, and the remaining 35 percent had one lane. Approximately 65 percent of freight and 80 percent of passenger traffic internally is carried by road. The number of vehicles increased at an average annual rate of slightly above 10 percent during the five years spanning 2002–03 to 2006–07.

Under the NDA government, road development received very high priority. In recognition of the urgent need for improving connectivity, this priority has been maintained under the UPA government. Both governments have brought the private sector into play in a big way to construct roads. This strategy has paid handsomely in the building of a modern network of roads. The transformation of the road network is visible: Roads and bridges that seemed beyond the capability of India to build are now being built in a relatively short period of time, just as in the developed countries.

The National Highway Development Project

The key institutional innovation in recent times was the creation of the National Highway Authority of India (NHAI) in 1998. The government launched a major program of modernizing the national highways under it. Phases I and II of the National Highway Development Project (NHDP) consisted of widening the Golden Quadrilateral (GQ) and north-south and east-west (NS-EW) highways to four lanes. The GQ highway connects the metropolitan cities of Delhi, Mumbai, Chennai, and Kolkata, and NS-EW highways connect Srinagar and Kanyakumari along the north-south dimension and Silchar and Porbandar along the east-west dimension.

The government approved NHDP-I in December 2000 and had awarded all contracts except one under it by February 2002. As shown in table 18.1, of the 5846 km. covered by the GQ highway, 5,521 km.had already been converted to four lanes as of January 31, 2007. The NS-EW highway, which spans NHDP-I and II, has also made considerable progress, with 964 km. already converted to four lanes and another 5,266 under implementation. This only leaves 908 km. for which contracts are yet to be awarded. The NHAI estimates that it will complete NHDP-II by the end of 2008.

In January 2005, the government adopted an ambitious plan consisting of NHDP-I to VII at the cost of 2200 billion rupees (approximately $50 billion), to

TABLE 18.1: National Highway Development Project (NHDP) as of January 31, 2007

	GQ	NS-EW (phases I & II)*	NHP (phase IIIA)	NHDP (phase V)	Total
Total length (km.)	5,846	7,300	4,000	6,500	23,646
Already 4 lanes (km.)	5,521	964	30	—	6,515
Under implementation (km.)	325	5,266	1,296	148	7,035
Contracts under implementation (number)	35	146	20	2	203
Balance of length for award (km.)**	—	908	2,674	6,352	9,934

*Out of 7,300 km. 981 km. is included in phase I and the rest in phase II. Against 981 km. in phase 1,853 km. was turned into 4 lanes. With respect to phase II, 111 km. has been turned into 4 lanes as of January 31, 2007. Excluding 442 km. common length with GQ, net length to be constructed under NS-EW project is 7,274 km.

**The difference in length in the third and fourth columns is because of change in length after award of works.

Source: Web site of National Highway Development Authority, http://www.nhai.org/WHATITIS.asp.

be completed by 2012. NHDP I and II were already well under way at the time the plan was adopted. NHDP-III proposes to convert another 10,000 km. of national highway to four lanes. The project covers portions of the national highways carrying high volumes of traffic, stretches connecting state capitals with the NHDP phases I and II network, and roads providing connectivity to places of economic, commercial, and tourist importance. Phase III is to be implemented in two stages: phase IIIA, consisting of 4000 km., by December 2009 and phase IIIB, accounting for the remaining 6000 km., to be completed by December 2012. NHDP-IV proposes to widen 20,000 km. of national highways to two lanes; NHDP-V would widen 6500 km. of GQ and other high-density national highways to six lanes; NHDP-VI would develop 1000 km. of national highways into expressways; and NHDP-VII would construct ring roads, bypasses, grade separators, and service roads necessary for the efficient utilization of highway capacity.

The government has been making extensive use of private companies to complete these highway projects. The principal instruments employed are straight construction contracts and "build, operate, and transfer" contracts based on either the lowest annuity or the lowest lump-sum payment from the government for some stretches of road. In the latter case, the builder is allowed to recover a part of his cost through toll collection for a specified period of time. To expedite contracting, the government has formulated a model concession agreement.

To meet the funding requirement for all categories of roads in the country, the central government has created a central road fund. The financing for the fund came from a 1 rupee per liter duty on gasoline in the 1998–99 budget. In the 1999–2000 budget, a 1 rupee per liter duty was also levied on high-speed diesel. In the 2003–04 budget, the government raised both duties to 1.50 rupees per liter. The government gave the fund a statutory status through the Central Road Fund Act, enacted in December 2000. The government allocates 50 percent of the duty on high-speed diesel to the rural roads (see below), and the rest to the national highways and other roads.

Rural Roads

Roads and electricity are the two most important public services that a government can bring to its rural population. They enable the rural population to access other public services such as education and health, and to be connected to the mainstream economy. Both the NDA and the UPA governments gave high priority to rural road construction, but to date the achievements have been less than spectacular.

The principal vehicle for the development of rural roads is the Pradhan Mantri Gram Sadak Yojna (PMGSY, or Prime Minister's Rural Road Program), which has been folded into the multidimensional rural development program launched by the UPA and known as the Bharat Nirman. The PMGSY was launched in December 2000 with the objective of connecting the eligible communities by means of all-weather roads with necessary culverts and cross-drainage structures operable throughout the year. The aim was to cover all unconnected communities with a population of 500 and above (250 and above in hilly regions) by the end of 2006–07.

The Bharat Nirman is a four-year scheme spanning 2005–06 to 2008–09 that aims to connect 66,802 habitats with all-weather roads. The scheme involves the construction of 146,185 km. of new rural roads and the upgrading of 194,132 km. of existing rural roads. It envisages an investment of 480 billion rupees (approximately $10 billion) in total. By the end of December 2006, approximately 30,000 km. of new roads had been constructed and 7000 km. had been upgraded. The total number of communities covered during 2005–06 and in 2006–07 (until December 2006) was 3200.[5] These achievements are far short of the targets, and considerably more work remains to be done toward improving rural connectivity.

Though the PMGSY is a centrally sponsored scheme, rural roads are a state responsibility; thus the execution responsibility for the program is entirely on the states. The state-level standing committee, in cooperation with the intermediate *panchayat* (a village council) and the district *panchayat,* is required to draw up detailed programs on the basis of the guidelines issued by the central government to get funding. Based on the approved plans, construction is tendered, with each project ranging between 10 and 50 million rupees (approximately $225,000 to $1.1 million). Financing comes largely from the central road fund.

Urban Transportation

It is useful to briefly touch here on urban transportation. Major manufacturing and service industries concentrate in and around urban areas. An efficient urban transportation system is crucial to the movement of the workforce between the places of work and residence, and of intermediate inputs used and final goods produced by these industries. In this respect, India's major cities such as Bangalore and Chennai, which are home to a significant part of the Indian software industry and have experienced very rapid growth of economic activity since the mid-1990s, have been facing severe transportation problems. It is reported that many workers in Bangalore take up to two hours to get to work in the morning and another two hours to return home. Chennai has made some progress in building the mass rapid transit system to complement its suburban railway network that dates back to 1931, but progress has been slow. Likewise, Mumbai has invested in urban roads, ring roads, and suburban railroads, but its transportation problems remain acute.

Among the major cities, only Delhi has made significant progress in building an efficient transportation system in recent years. Numerous overpasses have been constructed, public transportation has been converted to the CNG (compressed natural gas), and major investment has been made in the development of the Delhi metro system. The latter opened in December 2002 and currently covers 65 km. and has 59 stations. Another 85 km. are to be added in phase II, slated for completion by 2010.

Future Course of the Policy

It is useful to divide this discussion into the policies relating to rural roads, highway transportation, and urban transportation.

Rural Roads

The rural road construction data under PMGSY reported on the PMGSY Web site are incomplete and opaque, making an assessment of progress difficult. But going by the data under Bharat Nirman, which was launched in 2005–06, progress seems slow. At the current pace, it may be more than a decade before all rural habitats with 500 persons (250 in the hilly areas) are connected. If the poor are to be served well, this process must be speeded up.

One important weakness of the current strategy is the exclusive reliance on small contracts ranging between 10 and 50 million rupees for road construction. This essentially excludes all large companies, both domestic and foreign, that are often much more efficient, from bidding. The government's strategy is reminiscent of the small-scale industries reservation policy that entirely excluded large-scale producers from manufacturing many products. The government must experiment with contracting the building of the entire network of rural roads within a district to a single reliable builder. The overall cost under this approach will likely be lower, and the quality of the roads higher, than are realized with many small contracts. Giving small contracts to many entrepreneurs may seem more equitable, but the poor living in the villages will pay the cost of the resulting slow progress and the poor quality of the roads. Under the current model, the gains in equity in contracting are more than offset by the delayed and poor-quality connectivity. A side benefit of bundling the rural road contracts is that it would allow the government to monitor the quality of roads more effectively and hold the larger companies responsible for poor delivery in terms of timing and other parameters.

Highway Transportation

By all accounts, the strategy of relying on private sector builders via outright contracts or "build, operate, and transfer" concessions, pursued since the early 2000s, has been successful. For decades, the government departments of roads at the central and state levels had built poor-quality roads with one or two lanes that got washed away as soon as the monsoons came. In contrast, the roads, bridges, and overpasses that even smaller cities have built in recent years were unthinkable prior to the 1990s. The creation of the central road fund through the gasoline and diesel duty has proved very effective in mobilizing the necessary resources. There was some slowdown in the award of the contracts for the NHDP II after the UPA government took over, but the latter is now moving forward more aggressively.

There are two issues that deserve particular attention with respect to the highways. First, there is need to turn the NHAI into an independent entity with powers to set tolls and enforce safety regulations. This is essential to ensure that the tolls are set on the basis of economic rather than political considerations. If the government then chooses to lower the tolls on the basis of political considerations, it may do so through a transparent subsidy out of the budget. As noted in the introduction, the independence of the regulatory agency will also lend credibility to the government's BOT concessions, since the holder of the concession will be assured that the regulator will ensure that its receipts are not reduced on account of political pressure.

The second issue worthy of attention with respect to highway transportation concerns the organization of the trucking industry and intercity bus travel. For roads to be used effectively, it is important that the trucking industry and bus service be efficient. In India, truck companies are often tiny. According to a 1998 study by the Central Institute of Road Transport, as many as 77 percent of the trucks in India belong to operators who own five trucks or less. At the other extreme, only 6 percent of the trucks belong to operators with 20 or more trucks. Even operators with more than 10 trucks account for only 13 percent of the trucks.[6] In contrast, according to a World Bank (2005b) study, the operators with more than 10 trucks account for 49 percent of the trucks in Great Britain, 81 percent in the United States, and 89 percent in Japan. Operators with more than 100 trucks account for 12 percent of the trucks in Great Britain, 45 percent in the United States, and 19 percent in Japan. India's almost complete absence of large truck companies on which large manufacturers can rely is puzzling.

The presence of numerous tiny operators in the industry has certainly resulted in intense competition, leading to freight rates that are among the lowest in the world (World Bank, 2005b). But the quality of service is extremely poor. The World Bank (2005b, para 1.21, p. 13) puts the matter succinctly: "The service may be adequate for much of the present traffic comprising low-value bulk products—much of which would normally be served more economically by railway or coastal shipping. It is not adequate for the higher-value manufactures or the time-sensitive export trade that comprises a growing share of the Indian economy." Given that the railways are likely to stay a public sector monopoly in the foreseeable future, and the prospects of huge improvements in their efficiency remain poor despite some recent successes, it is extremely important that steps be taken to develop a world-class trucking industry capable of providing high-quality service to corporate customers.

Delays in the movement of goods by road are endemic. An important and well-known source of these delays is the presence of multiple checkpoints on the highway. Various departments of the state governments, such as police, revenue, forest, and local municipalities, erect barriers at different locations without even consulting or informing the local public works departments in charge of the national highways. State governments clearly need to undertake a comprehensive review so that these barriers are at locations such as the interstate borders and processing is speedy.

But the delays also result from the fragmented structure of the Indian trucking industry. For instance, small operators are reluctant to use tractor-trailers. This means the truck must sit idle at the loading station as the goods are loaded. Likewise, individual truck operators receive goods to be transported in small packages from multiple sources, and they must wait until they have a full truckload of goods. In contrast, large truck companies with good reputations have sufficient business to run daily service to all the important destinations.

Future reforms must remedy the causes of the fragmentation in the trucking industry and provide an enabling environment for the growth of trucking firms in the organized sector. There does seem to be something in the current policy regime that keeps firms small despite some obvious scale economies. Possibly, stringent labor laws discourage potential large operators from entering the business. But there could be other factors.

Another important area of reform is the intercity bus service. The World Bank (2005b) discusses this subject in detail and offers several suggestions for reforms. Briefly, the State Transport Undertakings (STUs) currently monopolize virtually all the major intercity routes. These entities are hugely overstaffed (an average of seven employees per bus, according to the World Bank, 2005b) and either run at losses or charge fares that are not justified by the service they provide. Although unauthorized private operators have entered many of these routes to challenge the monopoly of the state carriers, the public will be better served by reforms that give the private operators proper legal status and subject them to proper regulation. The long-term goal should be to corporatize and privatize the STUs and subject them and private operators to a common regulatory regime.

Other issues worthy of consideration include commercial motor insurance, technology upgrading in trucks and buses, rationalization of motor vehicle taxation, highway safety, and environmental pollution. They are covered briefly in the draft National Road Transport Policy, but must be taken up for reform in the coming years.

Urban Transportation

The problem of urban transportation is well identified. The real issue is how best to solve it. Construction of roads and overpasses, development of commuter rail systems, improved design of traffic flow, rationalization of fares on public transport systems, and improved maintenance of existing roads all have to be part of the solution. But there is scope for improved performance through other urban infrastructure related reforms as well.

For example, one important avenue to containing the pressure on urban transportation is to improve the availability of urban housing. In June 2003, the NDA government had introduced the Urban Reform Incentive Fund (URIF), which provided financial assistance to states willing to undertake seven key reforms that included repeal of the Urban Land Ceiling and Regulation Act (ULCRA) of 1976; reform of rent control laws; rationalization of the stamp duty; reform of property taxes; and computerized processes of registration. The total of the funds allocated to the program was a modest 5 billion rupees (approximately $110 million).

All these reforms are required in order to allow the development of a healthy housing market within cities. This is particularly true of the ULCRA, which gives the state the right to buy any land available on the market for a tiny fraction of the market price. As a result, a large proportion of urban land is sitting idle. Likewise, rental laws in many states de facto transfer the ownership rights to the renters, thereby deterring property owners from putting their properties for rent even though the latter are unused. Lack of a proper registration system and high stamp duties pose similar barriers to the development of the urban housing market.

Some states, including Punjab, Uttar Pradesh, Madhya Pradesh, Rajasthan, Gujarat, and Haryana, have repealed the ULCRA under the URIF. But others, including Maharashtra, Karnataka, Kerala, and Orissa, have chosen not to do so. In December 2005, the UPA government replaced the URIF with the Jawaharlal Nehru National Urban Renewal Mission (JNNURM). The JNNURM has two parts: one focusing on urban infrastructure and governance, and the other on basic services to the urban poor. Urban transportation is taken up as a part of the former.

In comparison with the URIF, which was focused exclusively on reforms, the JNNURM envisages expenditures summing to 1205 billion rupees (approximately $27 billion) over a period of seven years beginning with 2005–06. But it also includes a major reform package at the state as well as the local level. It selects 63 cities and divides them into three categories: category A, consisting of seven cities with populations of four million or more; category B, consisting of 28 cities with populations of one to four million; and category C, consisting 28 selected cities of historic and cultural importance with populations of less than one million. Recipient cities are expected to leverage the resources provided by the central government to mobilize private resources through PPPs.

In terms of urban transportation, JNNURM provides the cities with resources for building roads, highways, expressways, mass rapid transit systems, and metro projects. The scheme also makes several reforms at the state and local levels mandatory to qualify for the funds. State-level reforms include repeal of the ULCRA; reform of rent control laws so as to balance the interests of landlords and tenants; and rationalization of the stamp duty to bring it down to no more than 5 percent within seven years. Insofar as these reforms will help ease the housing problem, they will also aid in alleviating the urban transportation problem.

The JNNURM is an ambitious scheme aimed at modernizing the major Indian cities. In principle, the promised expenditures require the recipient states and cities to undertake far-reaching reforms. But the risk is that the government will not have the means to monitor the program, and substantial amounts of resources will end up being wasted. In this respect, the more modest scheme of the NDA government to induce reforms was a safer bet.

RAILWAYS

Indian Railways (IR) constitutes the world's second largest rail network under a single management. At approximately 1.5 million, it has more employees than any other organization in the world. Potentially, railway transport is by far the most cost-effective and environmentally friendly means of carrying freight long distances on land. But IR suffers from serious inefficiencies and has lost share in the total freight traffic, from more than 80 percent in 1970 to less than 50 percent currently (N. K. Singh and Wallack, 2005).

Much is wrong with IR and much has been written about it. But being an extremely large and unwieldy public sector monopoly that has to compete at most indirectly against road transportation, it has remained immune to virtually any efficiency-enhancing measures except since about 2005. The expert group set up by the Ministry of Railways (2001) to recommend reforms under the chairmanship of Rakesh Mohan graphically described this lack of responsiveness in its report:

> Indian Railways is one of the most studied institutions on the planet. For almost every conceivable question that can be asked there already exists a comprehensive and rigorous report that lays out the facts and indicates the answers. What is striking, however, is that there has been little action on the many reports IR has commissioned, both internal and external.

Organizational changes such as corporatization or significant privatization in the operation of IR in the near future are unlikely. For this reason, and because so much ink has already been spilled over it, I will not attempt to outline detailed reforms of IR here. Instead, I will briefly discuss the recent turnaround in its fortunes that has received a great deal of press attention, and additional steps that may be taken on the margin to enhance efficiency. Personally, I remain skeptical that this gigantic bureaucracy will deliver efficient transportation at a reasonable cost on a sustained basis. If it is to become efficient, it will have to be broken up into smaller units, corporatized, and privatized. Short of that, despite its high costs, road transportation is likely to continue to capture the market share. This is particularly likely if the conditions for the emergence of an organized trucking industry are put in place.

Recent "Turnaround" of the Railways

The 2001 Rakesh Mohan report had stated that IR was "on the verge of a financial crisis.... and operationally in a terminal debt trap." It went on to predict that business as usual would lead IR to bankruptcy and saddle the government with an additional fiscal liability of 610 billion rupees (approximately $14 billion) over the following 16 years. This has not happened, however, and the net revenues (before dividends to the central government) of IR have shown a steadily rising trend since 2001–02. Net revenues increased from the low of 10.7 billion rupees (approximately $235 million) in 2000–01 to 44.8 billion rupees ($975 million) in 2003–04, and to 80 billon rupees ($1.8 billion) in 2005–06.[7]

While the initiatives taken by Lalu Prasad Yadav, the current railways minister (see below), have deservedly received the most attention in explaining the turnaround story, it is important to recognize the role of other factors as well. In this context, it may be noted that the performance of IR, as measured by net revenues, has been improving steadily since 2000–01, well before Yadav took charge of the Railways Ministry in May 2004.

At least four major factors have combined to produce the improved outcome for the railways. First, as Mathur (2006) points out, the average annual industrial growth of 8.3 percent between 2002–03 and 2005–06 led to an average annual growth in freight of 11.3 percent over the same period. This meant increased freight demand for all modes of transportation, including railways. But two factors worked asymmetrically in favor of IR. One, increased prices of diesel led to an increase in the cost of road transport that was three to four times greater than that of railway transport. And two, a ruling by the Supreme Court banned overloading of trucks, which further increased per-unit cost of road transport. Mathur notes that partially as a result of these factors, road freight rates in August 2006 were 8 percent higher than those in October 2005.

In contrast, with rare exceptions, railways were able to keep their freight rates virtually unchanged. The last significant increase in the freight rates that IR made was in 2001–02. Any subsequent changes took place only through reclassification resulting from the compression of the freight classes. The number of freight classes came down from 59 in 2001–02 to 27 in 2003–04 and 18 in 2006–07 (Raghuram, 2007, exhibit 6).

Second, Yadav took some key steps to contain the costs, which in turn allowed the railways to hold the line on the freight rates. At his initiative, IR added four to eight metric tons of load per freight car to the existing 55 metric tons per freight car, depending on the product. This not only helped reduce the cost per metric ton but also immediately increased the carrying capacity by 7 to 15 percent. Another innovation put in place by Yadav was the reduction in the freight car turnaround time from seven to five days, through 24-hour loading and reduced train inspection.

Third, as Raghuram (2007) points out, IR has introduced a number of measures to attract freight customers since July 2005. These measures include mini rates for the small customer, volume discounts for the large customer, a long-term freight incentive scheme, and discounts for providing traffic in trains that would normally run empty. These schemes have allowed IR to increase its share in the total freight.

Finally, Yadav has taken a number of steps to improve the revenues from passenger travel. He has introduced several new trains and added coaches to trains with high occupancy. He has also either held the line on passenger fares or brought them down in nominal terms in the successive railway budgets. In the most recent (2006–07) budget, he cut the fares in the first- and second-class air-conditioned coaches by 18 and 10 percent, respectively. Yadav has introduced several measures directly aimed at increasing passenger volume. For example, passengers in second class can be upgraded to first class if the latter is running empty and the former has a waiting list.

The Course of the Future Railway Policy

Initiatives taken by Yadav and their success offer an excellent example of the improvements a determined and innovative politician can bring to the functioning and profitability of public sector undertakings. To be sure, entrenched bureaucracy is no match for a political master who knows what he wants and is not hesitant to use the power given by the voters to achieve it.

From this, it is tempting to conclude that India need not give increased play to the markets—public-sector undertakings can deliver the goods just as well as private sector undertakings, and perhaps even promote equity in the process. But this would be a wrong conclusion to draw: Yadav has been an exception, not the rule. And even then, IR remains a gross underachiever today. What Yadav has been able to do is exploit the huge potential for improvement that existed on account of the inefficiencies that had been accumulating over the years. Moreover, he has been helped by an upward shift in the growth rate of industrial output and the diesel price increase that gave IR an extra advantage over road transportation. If the momentum achieved under Yadav is to be sustained over a long period and after he leaves the Railways Ministry, there is no alternative to reforms. In this respect, while one may quibble with its specific recommendations, in broad terms the analysis and recommendations of the expert group headed by Rakesh Mohan remain valid.

As already stated, I do not offer a full-scale road map of the needed reforms in the sector. Instead, I limit myself to several specific reforms that are entirely politically feasible in today's context. First, within the existing structure of IR, Yadav has adopted what is clearly a winning strategy. Given the cost advantage IR enjoys over the alternative modes of transportation, his decision to go after larger *volume* rather than higher *prices* is entirely on the mark. As long as the price is higher than marginal cost, social welfare maximization dictates focusing on increased volume rather than price hikes. The focus on the volume has, moreover, led to initiatives that have actually resulted in reduced per-unit costs.

This strategy needs to be sustained and refined. Over the years, railways have massively lost market share to roads. This trend has seen some reversal recently, which must be sustained. Railway freight rates and high-end passenger fares in India are still on the high side. Holding the line or even bringing them down in nominal terms would be desirable. Such a strategy will not only rebalance the fares vis-à-vis road transportation as well as low-end railways passenger fares, which currently are considerably subsidized, but also keep the pressure on the management for further cost-cutting measures such as those applied by Yadav since 2004–05. This is justified by the fact that there remains considerable scope for cost-cutting in the sector.

Second, even within the public ownership structure, it is possible to take advantage of competitive private sector services in a variety of areas. Yadav himself has taken a major initiative in this direction by effectively breaking the monopoly of IR's own subsidiary, Container Corporation of India, and signing concession agreements with 14 private container operators in January 2007. The companies are expected to invest 4 billion rupees (approximately $90 million) for manufacturing 2000 freight cars. The companies would buy containers from manufacturers, build inland container depots, and find customers, while railways would run the freight trains. A similar initiative had been taken earlier with respect to food service on the trains and at the stations.

There is considerable scope for extending these PPPs to other areas. One important area is the laying of railway track. IR not only needs to expand its network but also must replace a substantial part of the existing tracks to ensure safety. IR has already decided to build dedicated freight corridors on the Delhi-Mumbai and Delhi-Kolkata corridors. This is expected to require investments worth 220 billion rupees (approximately $5 billion). In view of the success achieved in building the national highways, a good case exists for taking advantage of privatesector financial resources and technical expertise in such projects. Under the current law, only IR can lay the track, but this law should be changed.

Similarly, private companies may be given concessions for running passenger trains on the tracks owned by IR. This will be consistent with the recent entry granted to private container operators in carrying freight. Based on past experience, IR has done a relatively poor job of maintaining high-end passenger trains. Allowing private companies will introduce the necessary competition to hold both private and public service providers to a higher standard.

Third, if private entry is granted along these lines, two additional natural steps will be corporatization of IR and establishment of an independent regulatory agency. Corporatization will place the public and private sectors on equal footing and also separate the service provision and policy-making functions of the government, as in the telecommunications sector. In turn, the regulator will have greater independence in setting tariffs and enforcing the standards of service provided by both public and private providers.

Finally, a more controversial but necessary reform is the rationalization of the labor force. With more than 1.5 million employees, IR is saddled with a massive labor force whose members are paid wages that are well above the marginal product. At some point, the government will need to confront the issue of cutting the labor force through appropriate voluntary retirement schemes.

CONCLUDING REMARKS

Progress in the transportations sector to date has been variable across modes. In air transportation, major success has been achieved in breaking the monopoly of public-sector airlines and granting entry to private carriers. In domestic air travel, the largest carrier is now private, with the share of Indian (formerly Indian Airlines) declining to approximately one-fifth. In turn, private entry has been accompanied by massive expansion of both passenger and freight traffic. On the negative side, airports in India remain an embarrassment, as anyone taking a trip from Shanghai to Delhi or Mumbai would testify. Here the government has at last been able to bring the private sector into the game with concessions given for revamping of the Delhi and Mumbai airports and for building those in Bangalore and Hyderabad on the BOT basis. But the impact of these changes on the service is yet to be felt.

In maritime transportation, while port capacity has responded flexibly to increased demand resulting from the rapid expansion of foreign trade, export and import dwell times remain extremely high in relation to the international standards. For example, import dwell time in India varies from 7 to 14 days, compared with the international norm of less than 24 hours.

There has been some breakthrough in road transportation with the completion of the GQ project, consisting of the widening of the national highways connecting the metropolitan cities of Delhi, Mumbai, Chennai, and Kolkata to four lanes. Contracts have also been awarded for the conversion of the NS-EW national highways to four lanes, and this project is slated for completion by the end of 2008. Additional projects to convert the national highways connecting the capital cities and major centers of economic, commercial, and tourist importance to four lanes are under way. An ambitious scheme called the Prime Minster's Rural Road Scheme is under way to connect habitations of 500 persons (250 in the hilly areas) via all-weather roads to the major highways, but progress to date appears less than satisfactory. Likewise, the success in building the urban transportation system, in most cities except Delhi, has been less than satisfactory. In 2005–06, the government launched the massive seven-year Jawaharlal Nehru National Urban Renewal Mission, but it is too early to assess its results.

Indian Railways has been well known for its massive inefficiencies. Nevertheless, it has seen some turnaround in the early 2000s, partially due to increased freight demand in general and increases in the relative cost of road transportation, but more significantly due to the efficiency-enhancing measures introduced by the dynamic minister Lalu Prasad Yadav, who came to the helm in May 2004. Yadav's strategy has been to hold the line on fares and increase the volume of freight and passengers carried on the railways. This has worked like a charm, with net revenues rising rapidly since about 2005.

Overall, the transportation sector is well behind the telecommunications sector in the progress achieved so far, but it is well ahead of the electricity sector. I have suggested further reforms specific to different modes of transportation in the text. The common theme running across these suggestions is that while the government needs to remain involved in planning infrastructure development and mobilizing financial resources, it should progressively rely on private providers for the delivery. In addition, the government needs to strengthen the regulatory authorities and judicial mechanisms for several modes of transportation. Maritime transportation also needs a major labor reform, and IR needs a cutback in its massive labor force.

19

HEALTH AND WATER SUPPLY AND SANITATION

Can the Government Deliver?

Social services include health, water supply and sanitation, education, family welfare, housing, urban development, broadcasting, labor and employment, and relief on account of natural calamities. Of these, health, water supply and sanitation, and education are the most important. Expenditures on them amounted to 4 percent of the GDP in 2005–06, versus 5.6 percent on all social services taken together. I discuss health and water supply and sanitation in this chapter, and education in chapter 20.

Most economists recognize that the government must play an active role in the financing as well as the provision of social services. This recognition, and the concern for bringing health and education to the masses in a short period of time, led the government to become deeply involved in the provision of virtually all social services. It created an elaborate system of primary health centers across rural India, opened rural schools, and assumed a virtual monopoly of higher education.

Unfortunately, however, a close examination of the performance of the public sector since the early 1950s in this and the next chapter persuades me to the view that the government in India is largely incapable of delivering critical social services to the public. Despite continuous assertions of commitment to serve the poor through free health care centers, elementary schools, and colleges and universities, the government has simply failed to deliver the services adequately to either the poor or the rich. A measure of the government's failure is that the private sector provides as much as 80 percent of outpatient care in both rural and urban areas today. And this is not because private providers offer top-quality service—virtually all rural medical practitioners and some in the urban areas lack the necessary qualifications—but because public providers are either absent or unable to provide even minimal service.

In principle, reform of the system is possible if the state governments, which have the principal responsibility for health and education, will shift the supervisory authority, backed by the ability, to fire incompetent employees to the levels (village, block, or district) at which the service is provided. But in practice this reform is unlikely in view of the power the employees enjoy in the current system. My pessimism flows from the fact that the virtues of this reform have been well known for a long time, and yet it has not happened to date.

Therefore, the argument I develop in this and the next chapter is that for services that the private sector can provide at a price, the government should gradually scale back its operations. In these services, the government should eventually limit its role to financial assistance to the poor in the form of cash transfers or vouchers that allow them to "buy" the services in the marketplace. In terms of direct provision, the government should concentrate on services with public good properties that private agents would fail to supply optimally. These include, for example, regulatory oversight of the health and education systems, water supply and sanitation infrastructure, and public health needs of national importance, such as family planning and treatment of malaria and HIV/AIDS.[1]

HEALTH

Expenditures on health alone were 0.9 percent of the GDP in 2005–06. When it comes to international comparison of public expenditures on health as a proportion of the GDP, India is near the bottom. This is seen from table 19.1, which provides the relevant data in 2003, the latest year for which such data are available across countries.[2] Luckily, the private sector has helped fill some of the vacuum left by the public sector. In 2003, private sector expenditures on health care in India were three times public sector expenditures. As a result, if we combine public and private expenditures, India's position begins to look more favorable, at least among countries with similar levels of income.

TABLE 19.1: Private and Public Health Expenditures in Various Countries, 2003

Country	Per Capita (current dollars)	Private (% of GDP)	Public (% of GDP)	Total (% of GDP)
Argentina	305	4.6	4.3	8.9
Bangladesh	14	2.3	1.1	3.4
Brazil	212	4.2	3.4	7.6
Chile	282	3.1	3.0	6.1
China	61	3.6	2.0	5.6
Costa Rica	305	1.5	5.8	7.3
Cuba	211	1.0	6.3	7.3
Ghana	16	3.1	1.4	4.5
India	27	3.6	1.2	4.8
Korea	705	2.8	2.8	5.6
Mexico	372	3.3	2.9	6.2
Poland	354	2.0	4.5	6.5
South Africa	295	5.2	3.2	8.4
Sri Lanka	31	1.9	1.6	3.5
United States	5,711	8.4	6.8	15.2

Source: World Bank, *World Development Indicators* (2006).

Health Care Infrastructure: Public and Private Sectors

Rural India consists of more than 740 million Indians and approximately 638,000 villages. In the public sector, a network of subcenters, primary health centers (PHCs), and community health centers (CHCs) provides primary health care services in rural India. In addition, the private sector plays an important role.

The subcenter is the first contact point between the community and the primary health care system. It employs one female and one male health worker, with the female worker being an auxiliary nurse midwife (ANM). Subcenters have the responsibility for tasks relating to maternal and child health, nutrition, immunization, diarrhea control, and programs aimed at the control of communicable diseases. They are equipped with basic drugs for minor ailments and essential health needs of women and children. Current norms require one subcenter per 3000 people in the tribal and hilly areas and one per 5000 people in the plains. In September 2004, there were 142,655 subcenters in all.

One PHC is required for each 30,000 people in the plains and for each 20,000 people in the tribal and hilly areas. Each PHC serves as a referral unit for six subcenters. It has four to six beds for patients and performs curative, preventive, and family welfare services. As of September 2004, there were 23,109 PHCs in all.

The current norms also require one CHC per 120,000 people in the plains and per 80,000 people in the tribal and hilly areas. The CHC has four specialists—one each of physician, surgeon, gynecologist, and pediatrician—supported by 21 paramedical and other staff members. It has 30 beds, one operating theater, X-ray and labor rooms, and laboratory facilities. It serves four PHCs as a referral unit and provides emergency obstetrics care and specialist consultation. As of September 2004, there were 3222 CHCs in operation.[3]

In addition to this basic rural infrastructure, there are also government-run hospitals in rural areas. The Government of India (2005a, table 6.2.2) places this number (inclusive of CHCs) at 3964, and of hospital beds at 111,872. The private sector contributes significantly to rural health care principally through inpatient care in private hospitals and outpatient care by rural medical providers (see below). According to one estimate, the private sector serves 46 percent of hospital inpatients and 81 percent of outpatients in rural India.[4]

Despite this relatively extensive public health care system in the rural areas, the private sector has increasingly come to dominate the delivery of health services. According to the most recent comprehensive report on the health system in India by the World Bank (2001), official sources report the total number of private hospitals as rising from 3000 in 1981 to 10,300 in 1995, and of private hospital beds from 133,000 to 225,000 over the same period. The report goes on to note that a census of private facilities in Andhra Pradesh in 1993 revealed that the official data understated the number of hospitals by 3.8 times and the number of hospital beds by 10.5 times. It places the more recent figure for the number of private hospitals at 67,000, accounting for 93 percent of all hospitals. According to the numbers cited by Radwan (2005), the proportion of patients seeking ambulatory care in the public sector fell from 32 percent in 1985–86 to 26 percent in 1995–96 in rural areas and from 30 percent to 17 percent over the same period in urban areas. Similarly, by 1996 the private sector accounted for 54 percent of rural hospitalization and 70 percent of urban hospitalization.

Radwan (2005), who offers a systematic discussion of private sector providers, divides them into three categories: rural medical providers (RMPs), the not-for-profit sector, and the for-profit sector.[5] RMPs are unqualified medical practitioners offering curative services in rural and semi-urban areas. The vast majority of them are male and have no more than a high-school education. They operate principally on an outpatient basis and charge 10 to 50 rupees per consultation, depending on the ailment and the income level in the area where they operate. In the absence of regulation, RMPs have flourished since they often provide the only available care in the rural areas. They are present in virtually every village. At two per village, their number is conservatively estimated at 1.25 million.

The not-for-profit sector, consisting mainly of NGOs and religion-based organizations, provides only a tiny proportion of medical care in India. Radwan (2005) places this proportion at less than 1 percent. Facilities in this sector generally take the form of charitable clinics and larger hospitals. The quality of service is higher than the average and the price is lower. NGOs funded by international agencies typically operate in poorer states.

Small operations consisting of clinics and nursing homes dominate the private for-profit sector. Facilities with fewer than 30 beds account for the vast majority of the establishments. It is estimated, however, that approximately one-third of the beds in the private sector are in larger hospitals with 100 beds or more. A recent development in the private sector has been the entry of nonresident Indians and multinationals in building hospitals offering a broad range of services as well as those focusing on specialty services.

Table 19.2 provides a comparison of some broad indicators of the availability of medical manpower and hospital beds between India and the rest of the world. The indicators relate to various years from 1990 to 1998, and do not reflect some of the acceleration in the pace of expansion of medical personnel. Nevertheless, they do indicate rather poor availability of facilities and services until the late 1990s. Except in terms of the number of physicians per 1000 persons, India does worse than the average of the low-income countries along virtually all dimensions.

TABLE 19.2: International Comparison of Health Manpower and Hospital Beds per 1,000 Persons, 1990–98

Country	Physicians	Nurses	Midwives	Hospital Beds
India				
Public sector	0.2	—	0.2	0.4
Total	1	0.9	0.2	0.7
All countries, by income				
Low income	0.7	1.6	0.3	1.5
Middle income	1.8	1.9	0.6	4.3
High income	1.8	7.5	0.5	7.4
All	1.5	3.3	0.4	3.3

Source: *World Bank* (2001, table 2.1).

A final important part of health care infrastructure is the institutions imparting medical education and training. The number of medical colleges rose from 146 in 1991–92 to 242 in 2005–06, with the number of firstyear students in the bachelor's degree programs rising from 12,199 to 26, 449 over the same period. The number of dental colleges rose from 77 in 1994–95 to 205 in 2005–06, with the number of students admitted to the first year of the Bachelor of Dental Surgery course rising from 1987 to 14,700 over the same period. According to the detailed data, there has been acceleration in the growth rate of colleges and numbers of students in the 2000s.[6]

As of March 31, 2004, there existed 747 general nursing and midwifery schools, 235 auxiliary nurse midwife training schools, 254 nursing colleges conducting gradute courses, and 40 colleges conducting postgraduate courses. India also had 358 approved institutions awarding diplomas in pharmacy to 21,200 students per annum and 212 approved institutions awarding degrees in pharmacy to 11,670 students per annum. The AYUSH system has about 437 colleges, with an annual admission capacity of nearly 87,130.[7] At the end of 2003–04, 622,576 doctors were registered with the Medical Council of India.[8]

A Critique of the Public Health System

Demographic indicators have uniformly improved since 1990. Life expectancy at birth rose from 59.7 years during 1991–95 to 61.6 years during 1998–2002 for males, and from 60.9 years to 63.3 years for females over the same period. Infant mortality fell from 74 per thousand in 1994 to 58 in 2004. All indicators of mortality—crude death rate, infant mortality rate, neonatal mortality rate, postnatal mortality rate, and stillbirth rate—declined in the rural and urban areas between 1993 and 2003.[9] Progress was also made in eradicating or containing certain diseases. For example, as the National Health Policy (NHP) of 2002 notes, smallpox and Guinea worm disease have been eradicated entirely, and polio is on the verge of being eradicated.

From these achievements, it is tempting to conclude that all is well with the health system in India. The reality, however, is that these are relatively modest achievements, with India still lagging behind otherwise comparable countries. Moreover, this progress is partially the result of progress in other important dimensions, such as increased incomes and improved education levels. Public health care in India is in such a dire state that it would not receive even a passing grade from its users. The *Report of the National Commission on Macroeconomics and Health* states it bluntly: "The existing system of primary health care has collapsed in several parts of the country, for reasons other than under-funding."[10] Earlier, the National Health Policy of 2002, which succeeded the one issued in 1983, had acknowledged this as well, though it seemed to place much greater blame on funding:[11]

> For the outdoor medical facilities in existence, funding is generally insufficient; the presence of medical and para-medical personnel is often much less than that required by prescribed norms; the availability of consumables is frequently negligible; the equipment in many public hospitals is often obsolescent and unusable; and, the buildings are in a dilapidated state. In the indoor treatment facilities, again, the equipment is often obsolescent; the availability of essential drugs is minimal; the capacity of the facilities is grossly inadequate, which leads to over-crowding, and consequentially to

a steep deterioration in the quality of the services. As a result of such inadequate public health facilities, it has been estimated that less than 20 percent of the population which seek OPD [Outpatient Department] services, and less than 45 percent of that which seek indoor treatment, avail of such services in public hospitals. This is despite the fact that most of these patients do not have the means to make out-of pocket payments for private health services except at the cost of other essential expenditure for items such as basic nutrition. (Government of India, 2002c, paragraph 2.4.1)

Radwan (2005) offers a more systematic critique of the public health system, pointing to three broad categories of problems: bureaucratic approach; lack of accountability; and inadequate funding in relation to commitments. Under bureaucratic approach, he points out that the PHCs have a rigid structure. Regardless of the local conditions, this structure remains uniform across all parts of India. For instance, the number of ANMs per PHC and subcenter is the same, regardless of the fertility rate in the region. The bureaucratic approach leads to the measurement of performance in terms inputs rather than output. Doctors who serve as medical officers and manage the system often lack skills in the management of a public health care system.

Lack of accountability brings with it an even more serious set of problems. The employees are paid by the state, and the local authorities have no powers to supervise them. As a result, many medical officers visit the PHCs infrequently and run parallel private practices in the nearby town. Chaudhury et al. (2006) estimate the countrywide absenteeism rate in the public health care system in India at 40 percent. ANMs are frequently unavailable for childbirths even if the mother is willing to come to the PHC. In Karnataka, the *dai*, the hereditary informal midwife, attends as many deliveries as the ANM. In one-third of the cases in which women had made prior arrangements with the ANM, they had to turn to a *dai* because the ANM did not keep the commitment. Most PHCs charge a fee informally, even though they are supposed to provide their services free. When adjusted for the inconvenience and quality of service, such fees often make the private sector more attractive even to poor patients, especially for outpatient care that does not involve large absolute expenses or a threat to life.

Finally, PHCs are strapped for resources, with public health expenditures in many states falling well short of what is necessary to provide the promised services. Medicines and medical equipment are lacking, vehicles are in disrepair, salaries are low, and infrastructure is a shambles. This state of affairs robs even the sincere staff of the motivation to serve, and the patients of motivation to seek their services.

To these problems noted by Radwan (2005), I may add that public health services have done poorly along the income distribution dimension. A study by Mahal et al. (2001) has shown that the poorest 20 percent of the population captures only 10 percent of the public health subsidy, compared with 30 percent by the richest 20 percent. Indeed, the share in the subsidy rises monotonically as we move from the bottom 20 percent to the next 20 percent to the next 20 percent, and so on. The argument, commonly made, that the government must actively engage in the delivery of medical service to the poor because it has an obligation to provide this service to them has its limitations. As in the case of the food subsidy, it can do a lot better by putting the money directly in the hands of the poor and letting them buy the services from the private sector.

Table 19.3 provides information on the use of public and private sector services by patients in 1986–87 and 1995–96. All indicators uniformly show a steady shift of the patients from the public to the private sector in both rural and urban areas. By 1995–96, the public sector presence in outpatient treatment had fallen to 20 percent or less in both rural and urban areas. Its presence also fell dramatically in inpatient treatment, though the large absolute expenses involved in such care kept the proportion at the significant level of 44 percent in rural areas and 43 percent in urban areas.

Anecdotal evidence points to serious flaws in private-sector service. The World Bank (2001) reports a study of a district in Maharashtra by Nandraj and Duggal (1996) that found a large number of unqualified practitioners practicing modern medicine. It also found many hospitals that were operating without license or registration, and were lacking the basic infrastructure and personnel. Other studies point to similar problems in the Bombay and Calcutta hospitals. But studies on how the services by public and private sectors compare when they function side by side are lacking.

From a policy perspective, an important question is the quality of private sector service *relative* to public sector service. I have been able to find only one study to date that indirectly sheds some light on this question. Das and Hammer (2006) employ tests whereby a battery of questions about hypothetical cases is administered to doctors, and their responses are evaluated to measure the quality of their medical expertise. The study is administered to medical practitioners in Delhi. The authors find that doctors with the M.B.B.S. degree in the private sector perform better than their counterparts in the public sector. However, private sector practitioners without the M.B.B.S. degree do worse than public sector doctors, who all have the degree. Doctors operating in the poor areas, whether in the public or the private sector, are distinctly worse than those in the rich areas.

To place the implications of these results in perspective, it may be noted that superior medical expertise need not translate into superior treatment. In this respect, the issue of absenteeism in public health facilities remains central. A test would probably

TABLE 19.3: Distribution of Outpatient and Inpatient Health Services across the Public and Private Sectors in India, 1986–87 and 1995–96

Treatment of Ailing Persons	1986–87		1995–96	
	Rural	Urban	Rural	Urban
Not treated	18	11	17	9
Treated as outpatients				
Public	26	28	19	20
Private	74	72	81	80
Treated as inpatients				
Public	60	60	44	43
Private	40	40	56	57

Source: World Bank (2001, table 2.4). The World Bank cites the National Sample Survey Organization as the source.

reveal the PHC staff to be better qualified than the RMPs, but the superior qualification is not of much value if the staff is not present to treat the patients.

Future Policy Directions

In thinking about the future policy, an important point to remember is that the Indian Constitution assigns the primary responsibility for health care to the states. Counting the financing received for the centrally sponsored schemes, state budgets account for 75 to 90 percent of the public health care expenditures in India (World Bank, 2001). The rest is spent directly by the central government. This means that the quality and effectiveness of the delivery of public health services vary according to the income levels and administrative capacity of the states. This calls for focusing the reforms at the state level, as the World Bank (2001) rightly emphasizes.

A detailed discussion of the policy reform at the state level is beyond the scope of this book.[12] Instead, I limit my discussion to broad issues that the center and the states must attempt to address. The key point I make is that given its poor track record in the delivery of health care to date, the government should concentrate its efforts on light oversight of the private sector to protect patients from quacks; combating major threats to health and life such as malaria, tuberculosis, and HIV/AIDS; and the provision of financial resources for inpatient care for the poor. As far as the actual delivery of inpatient and outpatient care is concerned, the government should be highly selective, concentrating its efforts in areas where the private sector lacks the incentive to go. It must also seek cooperation of and partnership with private operators.

For an orderly discussion of the policy reform, I follow the World Bank (2001) in classifying the functions that the health care system must perform into four categories: oversight of the health system; public health service delivery; ambulatory service delivery; and inpatient care and financing options.

Oversight of the Health System

Areas where improved oversight can potentially improve the delivery of service to the patients include medicines, personnel, and hospitals. In the press, there are widespread complaints of fake medicines being supplied not just in the market but also in government hospitals. Rural medical providers and many practitioners of medicine in the cities lack the necessary qualifications. Private hospitals are reported to operate without license or registration, and diagnostic facilities offer substandard services.

There is no doubt that improved surveillance in these areas can lead to better outcomes. But the critical question is how best to achieve such improvement. Resort to formal regulation through the appointment of a statutory regulatory agency is an option, but it is likely to turn counterproductive. One reason private sector health services have grown rapidly in India is the largely regulation-free environment, just as in the information technology industry. The introduction of a formal system of regulation runs the major risk of putting the equivalent of the "license raj" in the health services sector and stifling its growth. Until such time as the sector is substantially more mature and a critical minimum of large-scale units emerges, it would make more sense to continue to deal with egregious practices based on complaints.

Additionally, informal mechanisms relying on oversight by the NGOs and committees consisting of medical professionals and representatives of citizens at various levels—village, district, block, and city—that provide information and give voice to the concerns of both providers and patients would be worth developing. In the rural areas, the government should pay greater attention to measuring output (service delivery) rather than inputs.

India has had a good track record of providing medicines at relatively low price. This resulted largely from the growth of a low-cost generic medicine industry under a relaxed patent regime that protected only process and not product. But under the WTO agreement on trade-related aspects of intellectual property rights (TRIPS), India now provides both product and process protection. This is likely to raise the prices of newly patented drugs. The government will have to be vigilant, however, that the pharmaceutical industry, which is becoming increasingly organized, does not misuse the patent regime to raise the prices of drugs without patents in India. It will also have to be vigilant that the large firms do not push out low-cost producers of generic drugs in the hope of raising the prices. Finally, the TRIPS agreement offers a number of flexibilities in terms of compulsory licensing and price ceilings, which the government should not shy away from invoking if the circumstances so demand.

Public Health Services

The objective of public health services is to address health problems and issues that are national in scope and require the involvement of national as well as local (including state) governments. These include family planning; immunization against communicable diseases; water, sanitation, and hygiene; treatment of diseases such as malaria, typhoid, and HIV/AIDS; and informing the public of harmful consequences of smoking and other addictions. In the past, India has successfully eradicated smallpox and Guinea worm disease, and is close to eradicating polio. Similar efforts are under way to combat malaria, typhoid, kala-azar, diarrhea, whooping cough, measles, and diphtheria.

Recently, the government launched the "National Rural Health Mission: 2005–2012" (NRHM) with the objective to "improve the availability of and access to quality health care by people, especially for those residing in rural areas, the poor, women and children."[13] The mission proposes to raise public expenditure from 0.9 percent to 2 to 3 percent of the GDP. Insofar as the mission focuses on the promotion of public health—reduction in infant and maternal mortality rates; universal access to public health services such as women's health, child health, water, sanitation and hygiene, immunization, and nutrition; and prevention and control of communicable and noncommunicable diseases—it is a welcome initiative. But it also expands the role of the government in the delivery of primary health care, a task not easily justified on economic grounds (see below). There is also the issue of whether some of these resources will be better spent on providing insurance for inpatient services for the poor than on expanding the health bureaucracy in the public sector. And, of course, there is the question of fiscal implications of the increase in the expenditures: Unless subsidies are cut, as advocated in the previous section, a hike of this order in health expenditures is bound to put a hole in the deficit reduction program of the government.

One public health issue that has not received its deserved share of attention is HIV/AIDS.[14] The first case of HIV in India was identified in 1986. By December 2005, as many as 5.2 million Indians were infected by the virus. This constitutes approximately 0.9 percent of the adult population between ages 15 and 49. Though the prevalence rate in India is low, due to its large size, it is second only to South Africa in absolute numbers. The infected population is concentrated in six states—Maharashtra, Tamil Nadu, Andhra Pradesh, Karnataka, Nagaland, and Manipur—with the first four accounting for 75 percent of the cases. It is estimated that 85 percent of the cases have resulted from heterosexual transmission, with the male-female ratio of the infected patients being 3 to 1.

Belatedly, in April 2004, the central government launched a program of providing antiretroviral therapies (ART) to persons accessing government hospitals in selected high prevalence areas and, in New Delhi, to HIV-infected women enrolled in government prenatal clinic transmission prevention programs, and children below 15 years of age. As of April 2006, 28,664 patients were enrolled at 54 ART clinics, well below the target of 100,000 by 2007 set by the government.

While this beginning is commendable, it falls well short of the effort necessary to contain the epidemic. Gupta (2006, p. 10) offers the following sobering assessment of the knowledge and use of ART:

> Currently, little is known about how patients are accessing HIV care or using ART, how adherent patients have been to their ART, how physicians are managing their HIV infected patients on ART, and what the prevalence of ART resistance is among patients being treated in the Indian private health care sector. Preliminary data from our group show that of 1,667 HIV-patients surveyed, only 36% had ever heard of ART. Twenty-four percent were on ART of some form, but only 32% had ever had a CD4 count and only 11% had ever had a viral load; 15% of patients who thought they were on ART were determined not to be on ART by their physician.

There is acute and urgent need for the government to multiply its efforts to bring treatment to the currently infected population as well as to contain the spread of the virus. For this, it must go well beyond public sector provision of ART. It must forge partnerships of various kind with private sector providers in disseminating ART and seek the active help of the NGOs in raising awareness about the dangers of HIV, how best to avoid contracting the infection, and where to seek help if one suspects having contracted the infection. Because India faced HIV several years after its spread in many other countries, it has had the benefit of being able to draw on their experience. It also has had the advantage that its pharmaceutical firms are among the leading producers of inexpensive generic versions of ART. Finally, many major international public and private aid agencies are keen to offer financial as well as human resources to combat the epidemic. What is needed is a focused coordination effort by the central and state governments, especially in the six major states with high prevalence.

Delivery of Outpatient Care

The case for the public provision of ambulatory care is rather weak. Benefits of such care are largely private, and there are no scale economies in their provision. In the early years of development, a case could have been made on the ground that private sector operators would not step in to provide these services, especially in the rural areas, but that argument is invalid today. Private providers account for 80 percent of the outpatient care in both rural and urban areas.

Another possible argument is that the private market serves the patients poorly due to asymmetric information: Patients cannot assess whether they are getting quality service at the right price. Once again, insofar as outpatient care is concerned, repeated interactions do allow patients to observe the quality of the service, and the information on fees is public knowledge. Moreover, the last fifty years of experience does not indicate that the public sector is better able to serve the patients. The flight of patients from subcenters and PHCs to private providers has resulted precisely from the inability of the former to do better than the latter.

Finally, we have the argument that many patients are too poor to afford outpatient care, and the government has an obligation to provide them with such services. But this argument only dictates the provision of the necessary financial resources for the poor, and not public provision of health care services. Moreover, since the 1950s, the government has utterly failed to provide universal health care despite repeated promises, and there is no reason to expect that it can do better now.

I noted above that the government recently launched the NRHM. One component of this mission is to provide access to "comprehensive primary health care." In view of the arguments just made, justification for public delivery of such care is lacking. Yet, if revitalization of public provision is insisted upon, it should be strictly limited to areas that private care is failing to reach. It would be irresponsible to throw good money after bad by going after revitalization of *all* facilities indiscriminately. Given that the health care employees are employed and paid by the state governments, and that they cannot easily be fired despite shirking their duties, no amount of resources can make a dent in the rate of absenteeism. The solution to this latter problem, which constitutes the key to reforming the public health care system, is not more money but the delegation of full authority to hire and fire to the relevant local administrations. Unfortunately, given the political clout of the health workers, the government lacks the courage to make this key change.

Therefore, in the vast majority of the areas, the emphasis of the policy should be on decentralized heath care that allows the patient to choose the provider. One option worth exploring is the allocation of health care vouchers or cash electronic transfers to the poor that the latter can use to purchase health services from public or private providers according to their preference. Simultaneously, a formal fee sufficient to cover the marginal cost of the service must be introduced at the public facilities. This would allow both poor and nonpoor patients to choose between private and public services based on the fee and quality of service. Currently, publicly provided service is subsidized and therefore offered free to patients, which allows it to compete against private service even when its quality is lower.

Between cash transfers and vouchers, I lean in favor of the former, principally because they are less prone to corruption in today's electronic age. The states have identified the BPL (below poverty line) families and have even issued them the BPL cards. As a part of the ongoing National e-Governance Plan, the government can open a bank account for each of these families that can be accessed via biometric authentication (thumbprint or retina scan) at the nearest bank or post office. The government can make cash transfers to these accounts. Independent auditors (possibly including NGOs) can be appointed to verify that this has been done. If a BPL household finds it has not been given its due, it can challenge and produce evidence of non-transfer.

In contrast to cash transfers, vouchers will have to be collected from a district-level office. The clerk issuing them will undoubtedly demand baksheesh, thereby depriving the family of a part of its entitlement. Then there will be the issue of unused vouchers by families that do not fall sick. They will probably sell them at a discount to the health care provider. Also, the rural health care providers are not qualified personnel. Therefore, some enterprising individuals will simply declare themselves providers to collect on the unused vouchers.

It is also important to begin creating a class of qualified practitioners who can treat patients with routine illnesses. This would be in line with the National Health Policy of 2002, which envisages a role for paramedics along the lines of nurse practitioners in the developed countries.[15] The eventual goal should be to replace the current RMPs and unqualified practitioners in the urban areas with these qualified "nurse practitioners."

Inpatient Care and Financing Options

A key difference between outpatient and inpatient care is that the latter is associated with greater uncertainty and large expenses per episode in relation to the wealth of many individuals. Therefore, when such episodes occur, individuals often experience financial ruin. This characteristic makes inpatient care an ideal candidate for risk pooling through health insurance.

A common problem with insurance, of course, is adverse selection. Individuals seeking insurance know more about their own health than the insurer does. Therefore, those in poor health are the ones likely to buy insurance, with those in good health staying out of it. The solution to the problem is prior screening, group insurance, or excessively high price. Prior screening would often exclude precisely the illnesses against which insurance is sought. Excessively high price can make insurance unattractive. Therefore, group insurance, which covers, for example, everyone living in a given area or all employees of a large firm or the members of an association with large membership, is usually the ideal solution to the problem.

Governments try to solve this problem by offering inpatient care at prices below cost and covering the loss through budgetary expenditures. But as the World Bank (2001) documents, even then many individuals find themselves in heavy debt and financial ruin as a result of hospital expenses. Moreover, the poorest individuals are still priced out of these facilities and, thus, are unable to access the benefits of public expenditures.

There are no easy solutions to this set of problems. Efforts will have to be made on multiple fronts. In the organized sector, group insurance is clearly a viable option. In addition, a part of the population in the urban areas can afford to buy insurance even at a relatively high price or to pay directly for services at private hospitals. But this still leaves a large chunk of the population without clear options.

One scheme that has some potential is publicly provided insurance for those below the poverty line (BPL). Assuming 250 million BPL individuals and recognizing that approximately 6 percent of them fall sufficiently ill in any given year to require hospitalization, such insurance will need to pay for the hospitalization of 15 million individuals annually. Allowing for an average of 2000 rupees per hospitalization in coverage, the total insurance cost would be 30 billion rupees or 0.08 percent of the GDP in 2005–06. This is less than one-tenth of the current public health expenditures.

Evidently, 2000 rupees cannot pay for very many inpatient services in most private hospitals. Therefore, the need for low cost public hospitals and CHCs will still remain, and even then insurance will cover only a part of the cost, with patients required to pay the balance. The main function of the insurance would be to allow the poor to access these facilities for at least some of their ailments. It will also help encourage entry of some low-cost private hospitals that would provide credible competitive pressure on public sector hospitals to shape up.

WATER SUPPLY AND SANITATION

At one level, it would seem that consensus on policies necessary to ensure adequate water supply will be easiest achieve: This is an everyday necessity for all, whether they be rich or poor. Yet, the provision of waster supply and sanitation (WSS) has emerged as one of the most intractable problems in both rural and urban India in recent years. In health and education, there are no significant economies of scale. Therefore, private entrepreneurs can supply these services optimally as long as the law permits them to operate. In water supply and sanitation, this option is not as obvious. Given substantial scale economies at least within each local jurisdiction, this activity constitutes a natural monopoly.

Therefore, a government wishing to bring private players into the sector has the option either to run the sector as a regulated private monopoly or to forge public-private partnerships, with specific activities within the sector contracted out to private entrepreneurs. Within the Indian political context, no local government is likely to risk experimenting with handing over the entire WSS system to a private operator. Therefore, at least at the current state of political play, the only realistic choice is between complete public sector monopoly and contracting of selected activities to private operators, often described under the rubric of private-public partnerships.

Water supply and sanitation are state responsibilities within the Indian Constitution. The central government has a very limited role in these areas. Its authority is confined to measures necessary to ensure integrated development of interstate rivers, adjudication of disputes between riparian states, and interventions in the interest of environmental protection. In addition, it can intervene through its powers for national economic and social planning, hydropower development, and management of international rivers. In practice, the central government has played an extremely limited role in the sector. This means that the quality of state administration in this area is even more important than in health care.

The WSS Services and Their Poor Status

Substantial progress has been made in terms of both urban and rural infrastructure in water supply and sanitation. This can be seen from table 19.4, which reports some

TABLE 19.4: Access to Water Supply and Sanitation

Item	1991	2001
Total population (million)	850	1030
Urban population (million)	210	290
Rural population (million)	640	740
Percent of the urban population with WSS access		
Access to "safe" water	82.4	97.9
Access to "piped" water	64.8	75.2
Individual connections	42.9	51.0
Public standpipes	21.9	24.1
Access to "improved" sanitation	72.4	82.1
Access to sewers	25.2	35.9
Access to septic tanks	21.0	27.2
Access to latrines	26.2	19.0
Percent of rural population with WSS access		
Access to "safe" water	65.6	92.4
Access to "improved" sanitation	5.8	20.3

Source: Author's calculations, using data in World Bank (2006, table 1).

broad indicators of WSS availability in the urban and rural areas, based on 1991 and 2001 censuses. Despite substantial increase in the population between 1991 and 2001, the proportion of the population with access to "safe" water and "improved" sanitation rose in both urban and rural areas. Access to safe water went up from 82 to 98 percent in the urban areas, and from 66 to 92 percent in the rural areas over the two censuses. Access to piped water also went up from 65 to 75 percent. Access to "improved" sanitation rose from 72 to 82 percent in the urban areas and from 6 to 20 percent in the rural areas.

But beyond these very broad trends, the picture is far less encouraging. In the developing country context, a 24-hour supply of water is a good indicator of water quality. Though reaching the developed country quality standard whereby one can drink water straight from the tap without risk to health is a distant goal in the developing countries, intermittent supply greatly adds to the risk of water contamination. Irregularity in the supply is also associated with very high cost to the customers in terms of solutions they must find. The latter include installation of booster pumps, storage tanks, and water purification equipment; alternative water sources such as a tube well in the yard; and purchasing water.

Most cities in India score poorly when it comes to reliable and safe drinking water in adequate volumes. According to the World Bank (2006), water supply is available less than two hours per day in Chennai; between two and three hours per day in Ahmadabad and Bangalore; four hours per day in Delhi; and between five and six hours per day in Mumbai. The World Bank report notes, "Indeed, there is even evidence that the quality of service is deteriorating. In many cities, for example, the number of hours during which water is available has recently decreased. Regardless of the quantity of water available, piped water is never distributed for more than a few hours a day, whether in small towns, in multi-village schemes, or even class 1 cities and mega-cities." Regarding rural areas, the report adds, "Hand pumps, which still serve half the rural population, can remain out of order for months before being repaired by state agencies."

Sewage and drainage infrastructure suffer from similar deficiencies. With the waste output rapidly rising with consumption levels, drainage systems have begun to get clogged, and raw sewage often overflows into open drains in the cities. Ramachandriah (2005, p. 4115) offers a graphic account of the woes of Hyderabad, capital of Andhra Pradesh, even in the face of relatively minor rainfalls: "The city sinks with as little as 5–6 cm of rain. Traffic comes to a standstill for hours. Tanks breach. Several colonies get inundated. Hundreds of families are shifted to safer places.... It has become common every year for a few children in poor localities to get washed away in swirling waters of open drains or manholes and this is small news." Hyderabad is not an exception: Other major cities, including Mumbai, have found themselves unable to cope with rains, especially when they are heavy. The problem in rural areas is different but not less severe: Few villagers have access to proper latrines, and open defecation remains widespread.

Future Course of Policy

In India, WSS decisions in most states remain centralized at the level of the state administration. The same agency or department often performs all functions related to the provision of the service: policymaking, regulation, financing, building of infrastructure, and delivery. Within the work culture of the Indian bureaucracy, this bundling virtually guarantees poor performance. Jagannathan (2006, p. 926) makes this point succinctly in the context of the Delhi Jal Board (DJB), which does rather poorly when compared to its counterparts in other major Asian capital cities from Singapore to Phnom Penh in terms of efficient, accountable, or reliable services. He argues that this poor performance is the result of the concentration of virtually all the major functions related to water supply in all of Delhi in the hands of the DJB:

- The chairperson of the DJB is the chief minister.
- The DJB sets and approves the tariffs in Delhi.
- If tariffs are below operating costs, the Delhi government is always at hand to cover the deficit.
- Tariffs are heavily influenced by the highly political nature of the DJB's governance structure and are never sufficient to cover operating and maintenance costs.
- The DJB is able to access substantial public funds to finance extension of its WSS infrastructure, rather than designing these investments in response to customer demand.
- The number of workers per 1000 house connections is sufficient to fill a Delhi minibus (as opposed to a lone employee per 1000 house connections in Singapore). These employees are not known to be particularly proactive in the event of damage to a pipe, leading to the disruption of service to an entire neighborhood.

Jagannathan (2006, p. 926) further notes that "This depressing story is repeated in most metro cities in India—utility managers are not accountable to users for service quality, equity in service and least of all for efficiency."

The current system is replete with the "free-rider" problem whereby one arm of the central authority, such as the DJB, can blame another arm for failures in service delivery. The only solution to the free-rider problem is to unbundle various functions of the authority and assign them to different autonomous agencies. Beginning at the bottom of the pyramid, where the customers are, an autonomous local body with separate financial accounts should be delegated the responsibility of providing the service. This body should also have the responsibility to identify the demand for new infrastructure projects and to build and maintain the projects within its area of jurisdiction. For any projects it wishes to undertake in the public interest, it should be required to submit applications complete with a cost recovery plan. A statelevel agency or a bank responsible for financing the project should then review the application. The approval process should be time bound.

Transferring the operational authority to the local level will also help alleviate the mismatch between the service demanded and the service provided. For example, distant state authorities sometimes refuse to recognize the existence of consumers willing to pay for the regular supply of water. For example, in rural communities the willingness to pay for a convenient house tap is quite high. Yet, many standard public health engineering department designs assume that a hand pump or a communal tap should serve rural communities. But if such modes of delivery do not match user demand, they are not maintained. A locally responsible body is more likely to pay attention to the local needs.

Tariffs should be set by a state-level, independent regulatory agency, based on the financial statements of revenues and costs submitted by the local autonomous bodies responsible for delivery of the service to customers. In turn, the regulatory agency should operate within the pricing policy set by the state. This separation of the policy and actual tariffs would minimize the scope for political interference. Of course, success will depend critically on ensuring that the regulatory agency is staffed and headed by competent, independent individuals who do not depend on the state government for future employment or other favors.

The success of this model depends on two key factors. First, the top leadership in the state must be committed to the reform. A halfhearted effort is likely to be readily defeated by the vested interests at the state level that currently run the entire show from the decision to build the infrastructure to its maintenance and setting the tariffs. To build confidence, the authority can begin the process with pilot projects, but must ensure that the latter are protected against interference from the existing water bureaucracy.

Second, to discourage wastage of water that is currently common, it is critical that all, including the poor, are required to pay for water at least at the margin.[16] As Jagannathan (2006) notes, the experience in city after city has been that the poor readily pay for water, provided it meets the basic quality standards and is supplied regularly. It may come as a surprise to many readers that China has the policy of full cost recovery in the WSS projects: Even customers in villages are provided house connections, and they pay for water usage. Many among the poor see the water bill as a symbol of official recognition of their existence. Looked at another way, by and large the poor do pay for food they buy. The government may provide a subsidy on food, but it does not provide the food for free. If some subsidy on water is a political necessity, the government could provide a minimal amount of water per connection free of charge and apply the standard tariff on any additional consumption. This will ensure that customers do not waste water.

With minor tweaking, this essential model could be applied to the rural areas and to waste management in the urban areas as well. The ultimate success of the model would depend on the ability of the state government to ensure the autonomy of various agencies and the courage to set the tariff at the right level. A determined government is likely to find that the provision of water can be successfully managed like any other commodity.

CONCLUDING REMARKS

Under the "National Rural Health Mission: 2005–2012" the government proposes to raise public expenditure on health from 0.9 percent to 2 to 3 percent of the GDP. The analysis in this chapter raises serious doubts about the wisdom of allocating this increase in the expenditures to further expand the provision of public health services. If such an increase in the expenditures is undertaken, it should be used to place the purchasing power in the hands of the bottom 30 percent of the population, with the option to choose between public and private health providers. The resources can go a long way toward the provision of universal health insurance for the poorest 30 percent of the population. A small part of the additional resources may be used to improve the existing health care facilities in the public sector, mainly in the provision of medicines and equipment necessary for inpatient care and for the expansion of the network in areas that the private sector is unable to reach. But even in these areas, an effort must be made to draw the private sector. For example, it may be worth experimenting with private management in the community health centers.

Potentially, water supply and sanitation constitute the most difficult areas of reform. Progress in this area will crucially depend on the state governments, since this sector is almost entirely in their hands. The prospects largely depend on a handful of the states taking the initiative and demonstrating the determination necessary to produce success. A few successes can set the examples for the lagging states and build the needed public pressure for change.

20

EDUCATION

Expenditures or Transfers?

The government is deeply involved at all levels of education in India. Education is a concurrent subject in the Indian Constitution, which means that both the states and the central government can legislate in this area. Under the directive principles of state policy, the Indian Constitution set the goal of free compulsory education for all children aged 14 or less by 1960. Given the inability of a very large proportion of the population to afford privately provided education, and the expectation that private schools would not expand fast enough, the states naturally assumed the primary responsibility for the provision of elementary education. But it missed the goal set out in the constitution by a long shot. India is still some years away from bringing all children 14 years and below into the ambit of education. According to the careful and extensive survey by the NGO Pratham (2006), 8.9 percent of the children between ages 6 and 14 in rural areas remain out of school.

In higher education, India did better than most countries. Because a key objective in the early years was to build the entire spectrum of industries, including heavy industry, the planners recognized the need for well-trained personnel, especially engineers. India also has had a long-standing intellectual tradition going back to ancient times. This tradition got formalized under the British, with British-style universities established by the nineteenth century. At independence, India already had 20 universities and approximately 500 colleges. The planners built upon this tradition. Today, India has 335 universities and almost 18,000 colleges. It also has some of the world's best-known teaching institutions, such as the Indian Institutes of Technology and Indian Institutes of Management.

In the following, I present a detailed analysis of elementary and higher education. In elementary education, the essential argument is no different from the one I made in the context of health. The government has created an extensive system of public education, but it is highly ineffective. Teacher absenteeism is endemic, and achievement levels, based on the test scores, are worse than even those in the low-end private schools. Unless the government can give the local administrative units, where the teachers serve, the power to fire them for incompetence and repeated absences, it is unlikely that the absenteeism can be brought under control. But given the enormous power of the teachers' unions, this is highly unlikely. Therefore, the best course for the government is to give private schools greater play. I argue that the resources at the margin should be used to give education vouchers to the bottom 30 percent of the population, with the choice of school left to the parents of the students.

In higher education, India needs wholesale reform. The current central monopoly over the system is stifling creativity at the local level. The system provides virtually no incentive to promote excellence, which is so essential for a well-functioning higher education system. Private colleges exist, but they must affiliate to some government university in order to issue degrees. Until recently, private universities did not exist. States now have found a way to establish them, but the University Grants Commission still keeps tight control over them. Without an overhaul of the system, India runs the risk of the flight of its IT industry to a country, such as China, that has made much greater progress in modernizing its higher education system and has gross enrollment ratios approaching twice those of India.

For clarity of analysis, I divide the discussion of education between school and college levels. The former includes primary (grades 1 to 5 and children aged 6 to 10), middle (grades 6 to 8 and children aged 11 to 14), and secondary (grades 9 to 12 and children aged 15 to 18) levels. The latter includes both colleges and universities, and students typically aged 19 to 24. Table 20.1 offers a broad overview of the enrollments at various levels, and expenditures on education, in the years 1993 and 2002.

ELEMENTARY EDUCATION

In this section I focus mainly on primary and middle schools, which taken together are referred to as elementary schools. Under the directive principles of state policy, the Indian Constitution had set the goal of free compulsory education by 1960 for all children until they reached the age of 14 years. Though purely private and government-aided private schools had existed in India under the British, it was reasonable to assume at the time that private or government-aided schools would not expand rapidly enough to meet the goal set by the constitution. Therefore, the government rightly placed heavy emphasis on the expansion of state-run (government) schools.

In the event, India failed to achieve universal elementary education by 1960. Indeed, two national policy statements in 1968 and 1986 (revised in 1992) still left India some distance away from the goal. In 2001, the country launched the Sarva Shiksha Abhiyan (SSA), the National Movement for Universal (Elementary) Education. To give teeth to the movement, the government adopted the 86th constitutional amendment of 2002 that elevated the right to education from a directive principle of state policy to a fundamental right. Recently, the government was set to bring the necessary implementing legislation, called the Right to Education Bill of 2005, to the Parliament, but it decided to shelve the bill in July 2006, citing insufficient funds. Nevertheless, the momentum and drive for achieving universal elementary education has been maintained, with many influential NGOs joining in the cause.

TABLE 20.1: Enrollment Ratios and Expenditures on Education

Item	1993	2002
Gross Enrollment Ratios (%)*		
Primary education (grades 1–5, ages 6–10)		
All students	82	95
Male	90	98
Female	73	93
Upper primary education (grades 6–8, ages 11–14)		
All students	54	61
Male	62	65
Female	45	56
Secondary education (grades 9–12, ages 15–18)		
All students	32	36
Male	39	39
Female	24	30
Tertiary education (postsecondary to postgraduate, ages 19–24)		
All students	5.3	9
Male	6.8	10.3
Female	3.6	7.5
Expenditures		
Total public spending on education and training (% of GDP)	3.6	4.1
Total public spending on elementary education and training (% of GDP)	1.7	2.1
Public spending per elementary student (constant 2002 dollars)	25	44

*Gross enrollment is the ratio of the number of children enrolled in primary education, regardless of age, to the population of the age group. In general, it can exceed 100 percent, since enrolled students can include underage as well as overage children.

Source: Wu, Kaul, and Sankar (2005).

A key policy question in the context of promoting universal elementary education concerns the role of private schools in the changed circumstances. Today, circumstances are vastly different from those in 1950, when the constitution was adopted. As discussed below, private schools have shown excellent response to the market opportunities, providing better education than their counterparts in the public sector. The government schools have increasingly become dysfunctional, with no easy fixes in sight. Thus, the case for continued expansion of the government schools is considerably weaker today than in the 1950s and 1960s.

Moreover, those with the capacity to pay place enough value on elementary education that they are willing to pay the price charged by the private schools. Thus, even the case for a subsidy for elementary education is weak except in the case of the bottom quarter or third of the population, which lacks resources beyond those necessary for food and shelter. I argue below that assistance to this section of the population is eminently sensible, but it should be provided through education vouchers rather than further expansion of free but dysfunctional government education.

The Current Status: Government versus Private Schools

Responding to social concerns, much of the recent research has focused on the spread of elementary education in the rural areas. The issues relate to the extent to which children aged 14 or less are in elementary schools, the quality of the education they receive, and how best to improve it.

According to the extensive nationwide sample surveys done by Pratham (2006), an NGO devoted to the promotion of universal primary education, 95.3 percent of the children aged seven to ten, and 91.1 percent of those aged 11 to 14, in rural India were in school in 2006.[1] Of the children in each age group, 18.6 percent were in private schools. Pratham does not compile comparable figures for urban areas, but we can safely assume that they are higher. Assuming this to be the case, for the age group 11 to 14, the low aggregate figure in 2002 in table 20.1 suggests that the increase in the proportion of children in school captured by Pratham (2006) may be of more recent origin. Overall, these figures now place India within striking distance of universal elementary education.

Nevertheless, the quality of education in India remains poor. According to the results reported by Pratham (2006), only 6.6 percent of the students in first grade are able to read level 1 text, defined as small paragraphs with small sentences of grade 1 level of difficulty. Likewise, only 8.3 percent of the second grade students are able to read level 2 text, defined as "story" text with some long sentences of grade 2 level of difficulty. Of all fifth grade students, 53 percent are able to read level 2 text, and an additional 28.1 percent can read level 1 text. Achievements in arithmetic show a similar pattern. The low achievement level is intimately linked to teacher absenteeism, which is especially rampant in the rural government schools. Chaudhury et al. (2006) estimate an overall rate of teacher absence in India at 25 percent, compared with 16 percent in Bangladesh and 29 percent in Uganda.

A study by Muralidharan and Kremer (2006) offers systematic comparison of government and private schools to shed light on what ails elementary education in rural India. Using nationally representative samples collected in 2003, the authors estimate that 28 percent of the rural children in India have access to fee-charging private primary schools in the village where they live. Children in private schools exhibit higher attendance rates and test scores than those in government schools, even after controlling for family and school characteristics.

A key distinguishing feature of private schools is the lower teacher absence rate. Private-school teachers are two to eight percentage points less likely to be absent, and six to nine percentage points more likely to be teaching than government-school teachers. They are significantly younger and more likely to come from the same area as the location of the school than their counterparts in the government schools. They are also more likely to hold a college degree than the latter, though they are less likely to be formally certified as teachers.[2]

Muralidharan and Kremer (2006) also report that private-school teachers receive salaries that are typically one-fifth, and sometimes as low as one-tenth, of those received by government-school teachers. Private schools also hire more teachers and have lower pupil-to-teacher ratios than government schools. The authors find that one important reason why absenteeism in private schools is lower is the ability of the head teacher to discipline the teachers under him. Out of 3000 government schools surveyed, they found only one head teacher who had dismissed a teacher for repeated absences. In the private sector, they found 35 such cases in just 600 schools.

A final important finding of Muralidharan and Kremer (2006) is that private schools are more likely to be established in villages where teacher absenteeism is higher in government schools, rather than in richer areas. In richer areas where government schools function satisfactorily, private schools have not emerged. Therefore, it stands to reason that it is the dysfunctional nature of government schools rather than increased incomes that are providing impetus to progressive privatization of elementary education in India.

Evidence from urban areas, though less systematic and comprehensive, points in the same direction. Tooley and Dixon (undated) carried out a census of primary and secondary schools in one of the poorest areas of Delhi, Shahdara, in 2004–05. They found private schools to be vastly superior to their government counterparts along virtually all dimensions even in this poor area. There were 275 schools in the area, of which 27 percent were government-owned; 7 percent private but government-aided; 38 percent private, unaided, and recognized; and 28 percent private, unaided, and unrecognized.[3] Taking the last two categories together, private unaided (or just private for brevity) schools accounted for 66 percent of the total number of schools.

Tooley and Dixon found that when their researchers visited the schools unannounced, 38 percent of the teachers were teaching in government schools, against 70 percent in private schools. Tests administered by them to 3,500 students revealed that on average, students in unrecognized private schools scored 72 percent higher than their counterparts in government schools in mathematics, 83 perecent higher in Hindi, and 246 percent higher in English. Students in the recognized private schools did even better. The private school advantage was maintained after controlling for background variables.

On salaries, Tooley and Dixon found that the government teachers earned seven times as much as teachers in private, unrecognized schools. Class sizes were larger in the government schools, but this still left the salary per pupil in those schools two and a half times that in private, unrecognized schools. Yet, teachers in unaided schools are no less satisfied than their public sector counterparts in terms of salaries, holidays, or social standing. Only on issues such as work environment, infrastructure, and the leadership of the head teacher do the government teachers show greater satisfaction than their private school counterparts.

Many of the findings by Muralidharan and Kremer (2006) and Tooley and Dixon (undated) reinforce those documented in the comprehensive report by the PROBE Team (1999). They also mirror several of the prior micro studies by other researchers focusing on specific states or regions. Kingdon (2005) provides a comprehensive survey of these earlier studies.

In assessing the finding of superior performance of private schools, skeptics may point to the sample selection problem: Private schools may be attracting brighter and more motivated students who also receive greater attention at home. But the totality of the evidence, including that on teacher absenteeism, makes it rather unlikely that the sample selection problem, if any, would make the basic finding of the superior performance of private schools go away.

Future Policy Directions

I divide this discussion into three sections: the case for an enhanced role of the private sector in elementary education; the role of parateacher schemes; and policies regarding secondary education.

Enhanced Role of the Private Sector

The official view in India is that funding is the key problem ailing elementary education in India. Officials acknowledge the existence of teacher absenteeism, but see increased expenditures as the most important key to solving the problem. This is entirely misguided. Under the current system, the state government pays salaries to the teachers, but the administrations at the village, block, district, and city levels where they serve have no supervisory authority over them. Under such a system, throwing good money after bad cannot solve absenteeism. The solution—transfer of power to hire, supervise, and fire the teachers to the jurisdictions in which they serve—has been well known for some time, but the government lacks the political courage to implement it.[4]

The most efficient practical solution to the problem is to open the door wider to the private sector and subject the public sector to competition. This solution not only promises better-quality education, it also requires minimal resources. Specifically, the government should give education vouchers worth 2000 rupees per child, on average, to children aged 5 to 14 years whose parents are in the bottom 30 percent of the income distribution.[5] The precise amount could vary depending on the location, since the costs of running schools vary with location. The voucher would suffice to cover one year's tuition and expenses on textbooks in an average private or public school.[6] Parents wishing and capable of more would be free to add to this amount to send the child to a more expensive school of their choosing.[7]

This alternative has many advantages. First, the expense involved is rather modest. Using the demographic data for 2003 and population projections for 2007 (Government of India, 2005, tables 1.1.2 and 1.1.5), there are currently 242 million children aged 5 to 14. Assuming uniform distribution of children across age groups, the bottom 30 percent would include 72.6 million children. At 2000 rupees per child, this would imply vouchers worth 145.2 billion rupees. This represents only 0.4 percent of the GDP in 2005–06.

Second, the measure is clearly pro-poor. Currently, the poor have no choice but to send their children to a government school, irrespective of the quality of education the school offers. With vouchers, they would have the means to send the children to a decent public school. This would also partially reverse the sorting of children by the income levels of their parents that is currently under way. Indeed, if the government wanted to push farther in this direction, it could choose to give vouchers in even higher amounts.

Finally, the vouchers would place private and government schools on an equal footing. Currently, the poor are captive to the government schools since they provide free education, while private schools do so only on a limited scale. Once government schools have to compete for students, they are bound to feel the heat of competition, forcing reluctant teachers to begin delivering the services expected of them. But there is another, more subtle force at work. Public schools that do not shape up will lose students and face the prospect of being closed down. On the other hand, those that do shape up will attract poor students and be able to collect the revenue associated with vouchers.

Some would argue that the voucher scheme would lead to corruption. This is entirely possible, but the right question to ask is whether it would reduce or increase the scope for corruption in relation to the current system or another practical alternative. Given that vouchers are to be issued to no more than a fixed proportion of the population (bottom 30 percent, as per my proposal), there would be a check on the maximum number of vouchers. The main issue then would be corruption in who gets the vouchers. Here the local NGOs that champion the cause of the poor can provide the necessary oversight, particularly in ensuring that no one below the poverty line is left out. Given the current poverty ratio of approximately 27 percent, the worst-case scenario is that three percentage points of the vouchers would end up in the hands of those above the bottom 30 percent of the population. This would be a vastly superior outcome to virtually every existing antipoverty program.

An alternative to the voucher is cash transfer based on the number of schoolgoing children in a family designated as below the poverty line. This is the option I have advocated in the case of direct assistance to combat poverty and to assist the poor to meet expenses on outpatient care. In the present case, the goal is to ensure that the assistance results in the children actually attending school. In the case of direct cash transfers, some families may choose to use the proceeds to meet other expenses, which would conflict with the social goal of universal primary education.

The Role of Parateachers

The National Policy on Education of 1986 provided for a large-scale, nonformal education (NFE) centers program "for school dropouts, for children from habitations without schools, working children and girls who cannot attend whole-day schools" (National Policy on Education, 1986, para. 5.8). Under this program, talented and dedicated young men and women from the local community are chosen as instructors and are often called parateachers. The policy also states (para. 5.11) that "Much of the work of running NFE centers will be done through voluntary agencies and *panchayati raj* (village council) institutions." The central government provides 100 percent of the assistance to the NFE centers operated by voluntary agencies. For the centers operated by the states, the assistance is 60 percent for coeducational and 90 percent for female-only centers.

The Seventh All-India Education Survey, dated September 20, 2002, estimated 12 million students at these centers and expected the number to grow to 19 million in 2004–05 (Planning Commission, 2005, p. 53). State governments run the vast majority of the centers. States with sizable enrollments in the NFE centers include Uttar Pradesh, Bihar, Andhra Pradesh, Madhya Pradesh, Orissa, and Rajasthan. The most prominent program is the Education Guarantee Scheme in Madhya Pradesh.

The findings of the studies on the effectiveness of various parateacher programs have been controversial. But there is agreement on three important points: these programs bring education to children in areas where no other alternative is available; they cost much less than the regular public schools; and students in them do not perform any worse than those in the regular public schools.[8] While raising the quality of education remains a major issue in all schools, rapid expansion of NFE centers employing parateachers is clearly a welcome development on account of these facts. Nevertheless, teacher absenteeism at the NFE centers is at least as serious a problem as at the regular public schools.

Raising Quality, Reducing Absenteeism

As previously discussed, low quality of education and the related issue of teacher absenteeism remain major concerns. Various programs are being tried by influential NGOs with the assistance of the government, and randomized experiments have attempted to study their impact. Perhaps the most extensive such program is the Balsakhi program for remedial education operated by Pratham, which is aimed at third and fourth grade students identified as falling behind their peers. A paper by Banerjee et al. (2006) studies the impact of this program on student achievements, using the currently popular technique of randomized experiments.

The Balsakhi program has been in place in municipal schools in many cities across India. Pratham started the program in 1998 in Mumbai. Subsequently, many state governments joined in the initiative, so that the program now reaches hundreds of thousands of students. The program recruits young women from the local community, who have themselves finished secondary education, to work as Balsakhi instructors. It gives them two weeks of training and provides a standardized curriculum that Pratham developed. Balsakhi classes meet in groups of approximately 15 to 20 students who have been lagging behind their peers for two hours a day during school hours (the school day is usually four hours long). Balsakhi teachers focus on the core competencies normally taught in the first and second grades. She is paid 500 to 750 rupees ($10–$15) per month.

Banerjee et al. study the achievements, based on test scores of the children in the Balsakhi program, against control groups, and find strong positive effects, at least in the short run. The longer-run effects turn out to be less encouraging, however. One year after the program, the gains decline dramatically, though they remain statistically significant for the targeted children. It remains open to interpretation whether the residual positive gains observed a year after the program are permanent or are likely to dissipate entirely over the years.

Given the limited success of other programs in raising the achievement levels and the continuing poor achievement levels, the Balsakhi program would seem to be worth promoting despite the qualifications suggested by the long-run results of Banerjee et al. If the residual effect observed a year after the program does turn out to be permanent, the low cost of the program and the fact that it is easy to replicate make it an attractive instrument of improving the achievement levels of the children at the bottom of the class.

As previously discussed, one important source of poor performance of the schools in India is teacher absenteeism. This problem afflicts even the NFE centers, despite the transfer of hiring and firing authority to the local level. This is largely due to the difficulties in monitoring teacher attendance. A randomized experiment study by Duflo and Hanna (2005) finds, however, that placing a camera in the classroom that takes pictures of the teacher with at least eight students at the beginning and end of the class, coupled with 50 rupees per day bonus for teaching more than the norm (20 days) and 50 rupees per day penalty for teaching less than the norm, substantially brings down teacher absenteeism and improves the students' test scores. The study finds that monitoring, combined with appropriate incentives (bonus for teaching more and penalty for teaching less than the norm), not only brings the teachers to the classroom, but once the teachers choose to be present, they teach the students.

While the camera, with appropriate incentives, thus offers an effective instrument of monitoring, its applicability on a large scale seems doubtful. For example, it is unlikely that the governments will have the ability to overcome the opposition from the teachers' unions to such monitoring in the regular public schools. Indeed, Duflo and Hanna conducted their experiment in schools operated by a single NGO near a single city. It is not clear what the feasibility of camera monitoring would be in other NFE centers. It is especially doubtful that this would be politically feasible in the vast majority of the NFE centers, since the state governments run them. Therefore, a shift in favor of private schools through the vouchers offers a more viable alternative.

The central government has been operating other schemes to improve attendance of students, most prominently the midday meal scheme. Under the scheme, schools can get free food grain from the nearest Food Corporation of India (FCI) storage facility at the rate of 100 grams per student per day, plus the cost of transportation and cooking costs. Starting September 1, 2004, this program has been made universal at the primary level. While the scheme can be expected to have a positive impact not just on attendance of the students, but also on their health and ability to learn, its administration can be made more cost-effective by letting the schools buy their own food grain rather than its being distributed through the FCI. The latter is known to be a highly inefficient institution, and the midday meal program is likely to become yet another instrument of giving disguised subsidy to it.

Secondary School Education and Vouchers

A final question concerns secondary education. Is there a role for the subsidy through vouchers or other means at this level of education? Given that universal secondary education is not a part of the social goals in the way elementary education is, the case for subsidizing it is weaker. Nevertheless, it may still be socially desirable to ensure that qualified poor students have access to such education.

The current system does provide such access in the form of nearly free education in government schools. Had budgetary resources been plentiful, it would have been desirable to extend the voucher scheme discussed above to secondary education, to allow the poor access to better secondary schools as well. But under the current fiscal constraints, this is possible only if the government eliminates some of the existing subsidies, such as those on food and fertilizer. Another option is to begin recovering a part of the cost of secondary education in government schools through the introduction of a modest tuition fee. In turn, the proceeds can be used to finance the vouchers for the poor. This would give the poor the option to access at least some private schools and give further impetus to competition between government and private schools. An alternative to free vouchers is the provision of loans at generous terms. An advantage of loans is that they can be made accessible to all, regardless of the income level of the parents.

HIGHER EDUCATION

India has an extensive network of higher education institutions. Table 20.2 displays the evolution of the total number of colleges, universities, and students since 1857–58. In 2005–06, India had 20 central government universities, 215 state government universities, 100 "deemed" (defined below) universities, and 17,625 colleges.[9] The same year, student enrollment in higher education was 10.5 million. The gross enrollment ratio in higher education, as reported by UNESCO, rose from 10 percent in 2000 to 12 percent in 2004 in India.[10] In China, this ratio rose from 6 percent in 1999 to 13 percent in 2002, and to 19 percent in 2004. This single comparison dramatically illustrates the difference in dynamism between the higher education sectors in India and China.[11] In 2003–04, India spent 0.6 percent of the GDP on higher education. In absolute terms, this was approximately $3.7 billion at the average exchange rate of 45.95 rupees per dollar that year.

A Highly Centralized System

Following independence, India opted for a highly centralized system of higher education.[12] The key legislation governing the higher education system is the University Grants Commission (UGC) Act, 1956. Among other things, the act gave statutory status to the UGC, a body created in 1952. Complemented by 13 professional councils at the national level and several others at the state level, the UGC centrally controls the entire higher education system as no other institution in any sector in India does. The UGC Act assigned the right to confer degrees exclusively to a university established by an act of Parliament or a state legislative assembly; an institution "deemed" to be a university under the UGC Act; or an institution specially empowered to grant degrees by an act of Parliament. As a consequence, until recently, degree-awarding

TABLE 20.2: Number of Colleges, Universities, and Students

Year	Colleges	Universities	Students (million)
1857–58	27	3	0.00025
1947–48	496	20	0.2
1950–51	578	28	0.2
1960–61	1819	45	0.6
1970–71	3277	93	2.0
1980–81	4577	123	2.8
1990–91	6627	184	4.4
2001–02	11,146	272	8.8
2005–06	17,625	335	10.5

Sources: Central Advisory Board of Education (2005, table 1); Government of India (2005–06b, chap. 10).

institutions in India fell into one of the following three categories:[13]

- Central universities established by acts of Parliament or state universities estab-lished by acts of state legislative assemblies
- Institutions "deemed" to be universities by the UGC, and thus given university status under the UGC Act, 1956
- Degree-awarding institutions of national importance, such as the Indian insti-tutes of technology (IIT), established by acts of Parliament and outside the purview of the UGC.

Institutions such as the Indian institutes of management (IIM), which are also outside the purview of the UGC, are neither established by legislation nor deemed to be universities, and therefore can award only diplomas, not degrees. The same holds true for many private management institutes. All colleges, whether private or public, wishing to award degrees must affiliate themselves to a university. The latter in turn not only confers degrees on the students of its affiliated colleges, but also tightly controls the colleges' curriculums as per the UGC rules.

Two broad factors justified the state-run centralized system India adopted in the 1950s. First, on the supply side, it was not unrealistic to assume that few private uni-versities would emerge, and therefore the states needed to take the initiative in this area. With the economy still small, administrative resources scarce, and the curricu-lum in most disciplines relatively standardized, it also made sense for a central body such as the UGC to oversee the entire higher education system. The UGC could prepare more or less standardized curriculums in disciplines that reflected the state of the art, uniformly implement them in universities, lay down qualifications for the faculty, determine the structure of departments and of the university, and ensure quality. It was also feasible for it to ensure that the scarce resources were allocated efficiently and equitably. Furthermore, at the beginning, the system was relatively free of vested interests, so that the UGC could function in the social interest without being captured by external or internal lobbies.

Second, on the demand side, the vast majority of potential students lacked resources as well as knowledge of what benefits higher education might bring them. Thus they would have been unable or unwilling to pay the full cost of higher educa-tion. It can further be argued that social benefits in terms of nation building were large relative to private benefits of higher education to the recipients. Therefore, leaving matters to the market would have likely resulted in underprovision of higher education. Therefore, subsidy for higher education was justified.

But like many other areas which the government chose to enter in the 1950s and 1960s, it went too far in higher education. Specifically, except at the level of the college or diploma-granting institution, it shut the door to the private sector. The central and state governments passed acts to create universities exclusively in the public sector. Likewise, until recently, the UGC conferred the "deemed" university status on private institutions of higher education sparingly.

A Changed World Today

Today, the landscape has dramatically changed from the 1950s, when the higher education policy in India was enunciated. On the supply side, with hundreds of universities and thousands of colleges, the network of higher education institutions is too large and complex for a single institution such as the UGC to remote-control. In addition, driven by rapid technological change and globalization, new areas of study have been mushrooming in virtually all disciplines. As a result, universities in countries such as the United States, that are on the cutting edge of modern education, are continuously reinventing themselves. They are also of diverse forms and not clones of one another. In contrast, the static, cookie-cutter approach of the UGC gives faculty members on the campuses no stake whatsoever in their institutions, other than receiving guaranteed salaries. The result has been rapidly deteriorating quality of education and absenteeism among faculty and students at unprecedented rates. On any particular day, students must guess whether the professor will show up, and the professor must form an estimate of the number of students who will attend the class. The equilibrium outcome is either no lecture or a lecture with only a small proportion of the students present.

The higher education world has changed equally dramatically on the demand side. Students now fully appreciate the private value of education. They have access to information to judge which universities offer good education and which courses are valued in the marketplace. One measure of their ability to access and process information is that there are currently 150,000 Indian students studying in the United States, Canada, the United Kingdom, and Australia, spending close to $2 billion.[14] In comparison, the entire annual expense of the central and state governments on higher education in India in 2003–04 was $3.7 billion. So confident and aware are the students of the value of education, that many of them borrow large sums of money to finance their education abroad.

Brilliant Graduates and a Dysfunctional System: A Paradox?

It may seem paradoxical that a dysfunctional system such as the one India currently has can produce so many students able to compete with the best in the world. Such students come not merely out of the top, well-run institutions outside the ambit of the UGC, such as the IITs and IIMs, but also lesser universities and colleges. The paradox is readily explained, however, in three steps.

First, with a preponderantly young population of more than a billion individuals and a long-standing tradition that places the highest value on intellectual pursuits, India has a large number of young men and women interested in education.[15] Second, thanks to the entry of a large number of excellent private schools in the urban areas and a well-functioning secondary school system, many students are well prepared for higher education when they reach college age. Finally, despite their inability to impart education, universities and colleges in India continue to do an adequate job of quality control. They have a standardized curriculum. The centralized examinations the universities administer are able to adequately and credibly sort out at least the very best 5 to 7 percent of the students from the rest. As a result, good performance in the examinations continues to have a signaling value in the marketplace for the students who distinguish themselves among the top students. Knowledge of this fact provides the necessary incentive to brighter students to study hard to master the curriculum, and even to spend large sums of money on coaching institutes if required.

Continued outflow of excellent students from the universities is, thus, consistent with the low value added inside classrooms at the universities and colleges.[16] A parallel outcome of this process is that the market ignores the vast majority of the graduates the system produces. It knows that students who are in the top quarter of the class can excel. But the degree has very little value for the bottom half of the students. Prospective employers know that these students learned very little in the classroom and that they learned very little on their own initiative as well. It is precisely because of this fact that so many graduates find their degrees no help in the marketplace even at a time when the market is facing an unprecedented shortage of skills. It is also the reason why private rural schools have been able to find teachers with college degrees.

A related relevant fact indicating poor academic standards in the Indian institutions is the near absence of cutting-edge research by their faculty. With rare exceptions, even the top Indian institutions, such as the IITs and IIMs, do not produce research matching that by faculty at the top U.S. universities. There are virtually no instances of a scholar who has been continuously at these institutions for ten or more years and is wooed by the top U.S. universities for a tenured faculty position.

The Advent of Private Universities through Acts of State Legislatures

For a long time, it had been assumed that only the central government in India had the power to create private universities by having the UGC confer the "deemed university" status on an existing institution. Indeed, in August 1995, the government presented a private universities bill in the Parliament to create an alternative route to the creation of private universities. The Lok Sabha (the upper house) passed the bill, but the Rajya Sabha rejected it.[17]

Interestingly, however, in 2002 the state of Chhattisgarh took advantage of a constitutional provision allowing states to enact laws in the area of higher education and passed a law granting entry to private universities. The Chhattisgarh government rapidly approved entry to private universities, with their number rising above 100 within two years. But in 2004, Professor Yashpal, a former chairman of the UGC, filed a writ of petition in the public interest in the Supreme Court, challenging the key sections 5 and 6 of the law. In its verdict on the writ, the Supreme Court struck down the two sections and ordered 97 universities opened under those sections closed.[18]

While the Supreme Court did not question the right of the states to allow private universities, it forcefully restored the power of the UGC to regulate the latter with a heavy hand. To give an idea of the extent to which the Supreme Court brought private universities under the UGC umbrella, it is useful to quote from paragraphs 20 and 24 of its judgment. I reproduce paragraph 20 in its entirety:

> The consistent and settled view of this Court, therefore, is that in spite of incorporation of University as a legislative head being in the State List [of the Constitution], the whole gamut of the University which will include teaching, quality of education being imparted, curriculum, standard of examination and evaluation and also research activity being carried on will not come within the purview of the State legislature on account of a specific Entry on co-ordination and determination of standards in

institutions for higher education or research and scientific and technical education being in the Union List [of the Constitution] for which the Parliament alone is competent. It is the responsibility of the Parliament to ensure that proper standards are maintained in institutions for higher education or research throughout the country and also uniformity in standards is maintained.

In paragraph 24, the Supreme Court makes clear that any degree issued by an institution of higher education has to be "recognized," and that only the UGC is empowered to confer such recognition. To quote from this paragraph:

> Mere conferment of degree is not enough. What is necessary is that the degree should be recognized.... Sub-section (3) of this Section [Section 22 of the UGC Act, 1956] provides that "degree" means any such degree as may, with the previous approval of the Central Government, be specified in this behalf by the Commission by notification in the Official Gazette.

The broad implication of this ruling is that whereas the states can establish private universities, such universities cannot escape regulations and norms of the UGC. It turns out that following the passage of the Private Universities Act by Chhattisgarh in 2002, the UGC had realized that the constitution gave the states the power to grant entry to private universities. Therefore, it issued a notification titled UGC (Establishment and Maintenance of Standards in Private Universities) Regulations in 2003, providing detailed rules the private universities would have to follow. These regulations came into effect on December 27, 2003, and brought the existing, as well as future, private universities under the tight control of the UGC. By the end of 2005–06, the UGC had given approval to seven private universities under these regulations.[19]

Under the UGC (Establsihment & Maintenance of Standards in Private Universities) Regulations, 2003, each private university must be established through a central or state act by a sponsoring body. The sponsoring body can be a society registered under the Societies Registration Act, 1860 or any other corresponding law in force in the relevant state at the time, or a public trust, or a company registered under the Companies Act, 1956. The university must conform to the relevant provisions of the UGC Act, 1956. It is required to have a unitary structure (meaning that it is not to have any affiliated colleges). The university must also fulfill the minimum criteria in terms of programs, faculty, infrastructure facilities, and financial viability, as laid down from time to time by the UGC and other relevant statutory bodies. Its programs of study leading to a degree or diploma must conform to the relevant regulations and norms of the UGC or other relevant statutory bodies. Finally, the admission procedures and fees must be in accordance with the norms and guidelines prescribed by the UGC and other concerned statutory bodies.

Future Policy Direction

At a time when India is embarking upon the most unusual experiment of building a knowledge economy despite being at a relatively low level of income, such tight control of higher education is most unfortunate. According to all available sources, skilled wages in India have been rising faster than anywhere else in the world, and the employee turnover rates in the IT industry are exceptionally high. Both factors indicate a shortage of skilled workers.

There are no magical solutions that will solve the current shortage of skilled manpower in India overnight. But delays in the reforms threaten to considerably slow the growth of skilled-labor-intensive sectors, most notably the IT industry. There is a real risk that this latter industry will begin to migrate to countries such as China, in search of more plentiful skilled labor. Reforms are required in four areas: autonomy to colleges and universities, greater freedom to private colleges and universities, sources of finance, and barriers to research by foreign scholars.

At the outset, let me note that the reforms I advocate below are far-reaching. Most of them cannot be carried out within the existing legal structure. They will require new laws, perhaps even constitutional amendments. It is my view that the institutional structure of the higher education system built in the 1950s can no longer serve the modern-day educational needs of India. As incomes rise, the brightest Indians will choose to go abroad in search of better education, even if it means borrowing large sums of money. Only a wholesale restructuring of the system can stem this outflow.

Decentralization

The UGC Act, 1956 assigns the UGC the functions of coordination, determination, and maintenance of standards in the universities. Under this provision, the UGC lays down the admission criteria; disciplines and curriculums at all levels; qualifications of teachers at the universities and colleges; degrees to be awarded by the universities and criteria for them throughout the system. It exercises this power directly on the universities and indirectly on the colleges through the affiliating universities. The UGC requires universities to implement its standards and curriculums in their affiliated colleges.

The UGC determines what the legitimate disciplines for universities and colleges are, how departments are to be staffed, and how fees are to be determined. It provides detailed model curriculums with the list of compulsory and optional courses (equivalent to core requirements and electives in the American system), and the list of recommended textbooks. If a university wants to introduce a new discipline, the UGC must not only recognize it as a legitimate discipline but also give the university permission to introduce it. The process of approval can often be lengthy.

Whatever the logic of such a centralized system in the 1950s and 1960s, it makes little sense in today's complex world. In practical terms, a system consisting of more than 300 universities and 18,000 colleges is beyond the capacity of a single body to administer. Even if we take the view that colleges are overseen entirely by their affiliating universities, overseeing virtually all aspects of more than 300 universities is beyond the capacity of the UGC. Equally, on the average, there are now more than 50 affiliated colleges per university, a number which is beyond the capacity of any university to administer.

Additionally, centralization stifles creativity and initiative at the local level. A vast body such as the UGC suffers from all the usual diseconomies of management that afflict large-scale organizations. When new disciplines open up—something that happens with high frequency in today's rapidly advancing globalized world—the slow-reacting UGC is unable to incorporate them into the curriculum. Likewise, there may be potential for introducing new courses appropriate to satisfy local needs, but colleges and universities cannot introduce them unless they are first recognized by the UGC.

Centralization also destroys the incentive to compete. Given the strict salary guidelines, colleges and universities cannot compete to hire the best faculty, which makes it difficult to improve quality and attract good students. Effectively, the quality of the institution is determined by history and geography—if an institution such as the Delhi School of Economics has been known to be a leading institution in the past and has an attractive location in a major city, it continues to attract better faculty and students, and to show better results. Homogenization of the curriculum takes away the ability to compete even on the menu of courses and curriculums offered.

Two examples illustrate the incapacity of the current centrally controlled system to move forward in a timely fashion. First, as early as the mid-1960s, the Education Commission (1964–66) had recommended college autonomy, arguing that the exercise of academic freedom by teachers was a crucial requirement for development of the intellectual climate in the country. But it was not until 1978 that the first set of colleges—eight in all—was granted autonomy. Progress subsequently was slow as well. To jump-start the process, the National Education Policy (NEP) of 1986 (revised in 1992) offered detailed guidelines on college autonomy. It stipulated that autonomous colleges be granted freedom to determine and prescribe their own courses of study and syllabi, and to restructure and redesign the courses to suit local needs. The NEP also called upon autonomous colleges to evolve methods of assessing student performance, the conduct of examinations, and notification of results. It provided that the affiliating university would continue to confer the degree, but with the name of the college appearing on it.

This policy should have greatly accelerated the process of college autonomy. But that did not happen: In 2005–06, there were still only 214 autonomous colleges, spread over 47 universities and 13 states. The UGC has very elaborate and onerous requirements for completing the process of autonomy, which discourages colleges from applying for it in the first place. The college must fulfill a host of conditions to prove readiness, bring the affiliating university on board, and get the approval of the UGC. At the same time, positive incentives to the existing faculty resulting from autonomy are scarce and, with ever-tighter government budgets, are getting scarcer. Therefore, even the current modest goal of the UGC to grant autonomy to 10 percent of the colleges is unlikely to be met in the foreseeable future.

The second example of the utter failure of the centralized system to move ahead in timely fashion relates to the quality assurance system. The NEP of 1986 recommended putting such a system in place. But it was not until 1994 that the accreditation body, the National Assessment and Accreditation Council (NAAC), came into existence. It took another four years to accredit the first institution. The process has picked up in the last few years, but in June 2005, NAAC had accredited only 105 universities and 2311 colleges. Worse yet, along the way, the UGC adopted the policy that accreditation will have no implications for funding and salaries, robbing it of any substantive value.[20]

There is a good case for granting autonomy to both colleges and universities. For reasons already discussed and from the evidence just provided, the UGC lacks the capacity to centrally control these institutions. Moreover, after more than 50 years of UGC control, colleges and universities should now be mature enough to make their own decisions. It is simply too paternalistic of the central government to think that these institutions or the local jurisdictions to which they belong cannot make decisions in their self-interest or that it alone can enforce high standards. The latter premise turns especially hollow when we consider the recent highly irresponsible act of the UGC to recognize astrology as a legitimate discipline, and even allocate public resources to its study. The UGC now allows selected Indian universities to award Ph.D. degrees in Vedic astrology!

China, which was as highly centralized in its higher education policy prior to the mid-1980s as India has been since the 1950s, has decentralized in a big way. Starting in 1985, the central government relinquished many decision-making powers to the provincial and municipal administrations. This decentralization progressed further in 1998.[21] Even the United Kingdom, which served as the model for India in the 1950s, disbanded its University Grants Commission years ago and replaced it with the Higher Education Funding Council for England and the Quality Assurance Agency.[22]

If the government wants genuine progress toward autonomy, it must adopt a far more aggressive policy than the current piecemeal process of autonomy to colleges. The focal point of the grant of autonomy has to be the university. It is the universities that need freedom from the yoke of the UGC. Academic freedom has no meaning if universities have to regularly take orders from the bureaucrats at the UGC, even if these latter happen to be former academics. It is an oddity that the reform committees that passionately argued for college autonomy have remained comfortable with the universities under central control.

An important part of university autonomy has to be the freedom to offer merit-based salary increases. Unless mechanisms are introduced to recognize and reward excellence, the culture of absenteeism will continue, with professors spending an ever-increasing part of their time in coaching institutes to earn a second, even third, salary. Autonomy must also allow universities to raise their own supplementary financial resources, including through tuition fees, creation of endowed professorships, and even naming buildings and halls after major donors.

At the college level, the process of autonomy must be simplified. One obvious step would be to give the universities full freedom to make the decision regarding autonomy to its affiliate colleges. This outcome would, of course, be automatically achieved if the UGC were to relinquish control of the universities to the local level. Incentives for the faculty to perform in the interest of the students, including merit-based pay, have to be a part of autonomy in the colleges.

Alongside autonomy to the universities and a large number of colleges, the government should encourage the formation of unitary universities that will give both undergraduate and graduate education on the same campus, as in the United States. The current rules already require private universities to be unitary. But the UGC can go further by converting many colleges into unitary universities. These institutions are likely to intensify competition for good students as well as good faculty.

The process of granting autonomy will naturally have to be gradual, with currently well-run universities given priority. For example, Delhi University would be a good starting point. But the process has to be much faster than the rate at which the UGC has moved on granting autonomy to colleges since the 1970s. A major reform such as this requires the government to give up the principle that every university or college that is granted autonomy must be an unequivocal success. Some colleges will perhaps not improve after autonomy, but as long as half or so do, the change will have been worthwhile.

Unshackling Private Colleges and Universities

The single most important positive feature of the higher education sector in recent years has been the rapid growth of private colleges and nondegree postsecondary educational institutions. With private universities given entry first through the "deemed" university route, and now acts of state legislative assemblies, their numbers are climbing rapidly. Table 20.3, constructed using the data provided in Agarwal (2006, table A3), illustrates the extent to which the private sector has expanded in recent years. Private sector universities and colleges are divided into aided and unaided, with the former receiving partial funding from public funds. Aided colleges and universities function virtually identically to their public counterparts. The genuinely private colleges and universities are entirely unaided.

The number of students in private (unaided) colleges and universities rose sharply from 21.7 percent in 2000–01 to 30.7 percent in 2005–06. In parallel, the share of the private sector in colleges rose from 26 percent to 43.4 percent over the same period. These years also saw the entry of private universities on an unprecedented scale. Their absolute number rose from 21 to 70. Of the latter, 63 were "deemed" universities and seven were set up under state acts.[23]

Kapur and Mehta (2004) studied the growth of engineering and medical colleges in 19 states and provide more long-term data on their growth. They report that the share of the private sector in the total number of seats available in engineering rose from just 15 percent in 1960 to 86.4 percent in 2003, and in medical colleges, from 6.8 to 40.9 percent over the same period. Four states with the most private sector participation in engineering in 2003 were Tamil Nadu, Andhra Pradesh, Maharashtra, and Karnataka, with 234, 213, 133, and 99 private colleges, respectively. The two largest states in the medical field are Karnataka and Maharashtra, with 22 and 18 private colleges, respectively.

Insofar as the curriculums, examinations, and degrees are concerned, private colleges and universities in India are controlled almost as tightly by the UGC as

TABLE 20.3: Private Versus Public Universities and Colleges

	Universities		Colleges		Students (million)	
	2000–01	2005–06	2000–01	2005–06	2000–01	2005–06
Total	276	348	12,296	17,625	8.4	10.5
Composition (percent)						
Government	88.8	77.0	33.3	24.0	41.0	35.8
Private aided	3.6	2.9	40.6	32.6	37.3	33.5
Private unaided	7.6	20.1	26.0	43.4	21.7	30.7

Source: Author's calculations, using data in Agarwal (2006, table A3).

their counterparts in the public sector. The colleges must affiliate to some public university (since private universities are unitary) that will give the degrees. States where the colleges are located get to dictate the admissions of the majority of the students. Because the executive branch of the government has been utterly incapable of giving policy direction, litigation has been common, with the judiciary actively framing the rules on admissions, fees, and profits, giving equity the greatest consideration, which often leads to contradictory outcomes.[24]

Perhaps the single most important reform in higher education would be to give the private sector genuine freedom to compete. Such competition, accompanied by autonomy, not only will help India produce first-rate universities and colleges in the private sector, but also will bring pressure on government universities to excel. The U.S. experience in this regard is instructive. Public universities sponsored and partially financed by state governments not only impart a decent education; many of them figure prominently in the national rankings as research universities. The University of California-Berkeley, the University of California-Los Angeles, the University of Michigan, the University of Wisconsin-Madison, and the University of Minnesota are all public institutions.

There are three complementary reasons why public universities have flourished in the United States while their counterparts in the rest of the world, including even Great Britain and continental Europe, have declined. First, the United States has an excellent collection of private universities. The top U.S. universities such as Harvard, Princeton, Yale, Stanford, MIT, and Chicago are all private. These universities compete against each other for top rankings and set the standards to which public universities must aspire in order to achieve distinction.

Second, like private universities, public universities in the United States have full autonomy. There is no body even remotely resembling the UGC in India that controls public (or private) universities from afar. Consequently, public universities are not hamstrung in their ability to compete against their rivals, whether private or other public universities.

Finally, public universities have considerable flexibility in setting fees. In view of the subsidy from the state government, the fees are not as high as those charged by private universities, but they are substantial. In-state students pay anywhere between 30 and 50 percent of the total fees charged by private universities, while out-of-state students may pay as much as 75 percent. The fees ensure that the universities have the resources necessary to attract first-rate scholars for appointments to their staff and to establish labs and other infrastructure.

If India is to take full advantage of the benefits the private sector can potentially confer, three major reforms are needed. First, entry of private universities must be simplified. The current route of a state act and prior approval by the UGC is far too restrictive. Just as no license is required to enter an industry today, so no approval from an agency such as the UGC should be required in higher education. States should have the right to issue a set of guidelines within which universities can be established without further legislative approval. If foreign universities wish to enter, they should have the right to do so as well, under the guidelines established by the state in which they locate. This will free states to compete against one another to attract the best potential universities. It will also allow those able to establish excellent universities in one state to bring their expertise to other states.

Second, financially, both private universities and colleges should be allowed to operate as either profit-making institutions, subject to taxation like any other private enterprise, or as tax-exempt, nonprofit institutions that are free to set their own fees based on market conditions, but use the profits to augment their endowment to be used for future expansion or quality improvements. In turn, these institutions should be required to purchase land at market prices. The current system, whereby land is given free or at highly concessional prices, and fees are set by a UGC-sanctioned committee at levels just enough to recover costs, distorts incentives. On the one hand, entrepreneurs are attracted by prospects of acquiring land virtually free, and on the other hand, they shy away from raising the quality of education, since it would bring no more profits for the institution. Fixing the fees at levels necessary to recover costs also encourages inefficiency in the use of resources, since such use has no negative implications for profits.

Finally, while autonomy is desirable for both public and private universities and colleges, it is far more crucial for the latter. This is because private institutions can mobilize resources necessary to provide high-quality education, whereas public institutions cannot do so, at least in the short term. Once the principle of letting the institutions operate as profit-maximizing entities is accepted (even if these profits are to remain the property of the institution), it is essential that they be allowed to choose the mix of product, the disciplines and degrees they offer.

Since equity is always at the center of any reform of education in India, and especially in the context of private educational institutions, let me briefly address it here. The interests of qualified but poor students can be readily protected through the provision of loans to be repaid with interest upon employment. The payment can be collected, for example, at a fixed percentage of the salary along with the income tax.

There are two reasons why the current system is more inequitable than the one proposed here. First, higher education generates sufficient private value to the recipient that having the recipient repay the loan does not compromise equity. There is nothing sacrosanct about redistributing income in favor of those acquiring higher education. Second, with no incentives to offer high-quality education in the present system, top-quality education is not available in India except perhaps at the IITs and IIMs. As a result, those who can afford education abroad have effectively exited the Indian education system, and are now spending billions of dollars on education abroad. Indeed, many of those studying abroad now borrow vast sums of money. Surely, a system that offers quality education within India, keeps its talented young men and women at home, and offers opportunity to all through the availability of loans is more, not less, equitable than this system.

Augmenting Financial Resources

Institutions of higher education have three main sources of funding: public funds, fees, and income from other sources including charitable contributions, project grants from industry and government, sales of publications, and income from renting land and other facilities on the campus. It can be safely asserted that funding from all sources has been declining in real terms in recent years. The share of government expenditures on higher education in the GDP rose steadily from

0.2 percent in 1950–51 to 1 percent in 1980–81, but fell thereafter.[25] In 2003–04, it stood at 0.6 percent. Public expenditure per student at 1993–94 prices fell from 7676 rupees in 1990–91 to 5522 in 2002–03.[26] Likewise, during the 1950s, the tuition fees accounted for 15 to 20 percent of the recurring expenses of the institutions of higher education. By the early 1990s, they had declined to only 2 to 3 percent of recurring expenses.[27]

Given the tight fiscal constraints facing the economy, it is unlikely that the government expenditure on higher education will rise either as a proportion of the GDP or per student. At the same time, universities suffer from an extreme shortage of funds, as a visit to virtually any university, including Delhi University, makes obvious. Infrastructure is falling apart, and the number of students per class has grown very large. There is little option but to raise the tuition to bring its share in recurring expenditures to the original level of 15 to 20 percent. Higher education brings large private gains to its recipients, so that it is more inequitable if its recipients are entirely exempt from paying for it while taxpayers, many of whom reap no direct benefits, foot the bill. Qualified students with no financial resources of their own should be offered credit, as argued above. This is the route the United Kingdom took recently in reforming its own fee structure.[28]

Universities and colleges also need to make themselves more relevant to industry, in order to attract resources from it. In turn, this is possible only if they are granted autonomy. In this sense, autonomy and efforts to mobilize private resources are intimately linked. Universities can mobilize resources by carrying out projects for the government. Charitable contributions for libraries, computers, or other specific purposes, and rental income from university or college land, constitute additional sources of income. If the UGC would show flexibility, endowed professorships and the naming of rooms and buildings after major donors are yet other ways to raise resources.

Prospects that public universities and colleges will be able to mobilize resources to achieve a significant increase in expenditures per student remain bleak. This is the reason it is extremely important to strengthen and expand private sector higher education. The only effective way to ease the burden of public institutions within the resources likely to be available to them is to shift students increasingly to private institutions of higher education.

Bringing Down the Barriers to Foreign Scholars

Currently, India subjects the research projects and visits of foreign scholars to Indian universities or institutions of higher learning to close scrutiny. The Web site of the Department of Higher Education under the Ministry of Human Resource Development (HRD) offers detailed guidelines on visits by foreign scholars to institutions of higher learning. The guidelines state, "In case a foreign scholar proposes to undertake a research project in a university/institution of higher learning in India, he is required to make an application in the prescribed form to the Ministry of Human Resource Development (Department of Higher Education) and get his research project approved by the Government before he is allowed to undertake any research in a university/institution." Universities and institutions of higher learning hosting an international conference must get prior permission from the HRD Ministry on virtually all aspects of the conference, including foreign scholars likely to participate. In the same vein, a university wishing to host a foreign scholar as a visiting professor must get clearance from the HRD Ministry.

When we consider India's long-standing tradition of welcoming foreign scholars with open arms and the potential benefits from it to India, these restrictions seem out of place. In his monumental work *Discovery of India,* Prime Minister Jawaharlal Nehru offers a fascinating account of the two-way exchange of scholars that took place between India and China throughout the first millennium. Following the missionaries of Emperor Ashoka, who blazed the trail in the third century B.C., thousands of Indian and Chinese scholars crossed the Gobi Desert to reach one another for scholarly exchanges. It is said that in the sixth century A.D., there were 3000 Buddhist monks and 10,000 Indian families living in the Lo Yang province of China alone.

Among many Chinese scholars who visited India was Hsuan Tsang, who came in the seventh century, during the reign of Emperor Harshavardhana. He spent many years at the great Nalanda University, taking the degree of master of law and eventually becoming its vice principal. His book *Si-Yu-Ki* (Record of the Western Kingdom [India]) gives the most valuable account of the Indian education system at the time.

Subsequently, from the eighteenth century onward, European scholars took the center stage and made pioneering contributions to the understanding of Indian history, culture, and society. They put together the grammar of Sanskrit in Latin, translated ancient Indian scriptures into French and English, and played a key role in the discovery of the Indus Valley civilization. Max Mueller, after whom India has named the beautiful Max Mueller Bhavan (house), produced the classic translations of the Rig Veda, and Sir Richard Burton brought to the world's attention the Indian classic *Kama Sutra.*

In more recent times, during the 1950s and 1960s, India became the darling of U.S. scholars. Attracted by its future importance, strong intellectual tradition, diversity, and, above all, its openness and hospitality toward outsiders, U.S. scholars of history, culture, sociology, and economics flocked to India. In the area of economics, particularly development economics, the study of India quickly acquired central importance. In turn, India extended a warm welcome to visiting economists, with the important ones invariably getting an audience with Prime Minister Nehru.

Unfortunately, the Cold War era politics placed India on the side of the Soviet Union, and Prime Minister Indira Gandhi essentially shut the door to foreign scholars. Visas for them, especially Americans, became scarce, and their research projects came under heavy official scrutiny. India's progressive movement toward autarky in trade brought with it a rapid movement toward autarky in ideas. These developments hastened the decline of the interest in India among foreign scholars that was already under way on account of the country's poor economic performance. The result has been that today there are few top-class scholars of India in the United States who started their careers in the 1970s or later.

The end of the Cold War, the embrace of liberal trade policies by India, and the renewed promise of its economy have combined to produce an unexpected benefit by reigniting scholarly interest in India in the United States. Scholars of Indian origin, serving as professors at leading U.S. universities, are among those leading the charge through their own research, as well as generating interest in India among their young graduate students. This is not unlike the Indian scholars in ancient China, who not only promoted scholarship on India in that country, but also sent their disciples to India to gain first-hand experience.

Benefits to India from reinforcing this turn of events are enormous. In contrast to India, scholars in the United States exert major influence on policies. Not only do top policymakers frequently consult them, but they themselves are often appointed to important policymaking positions. They also influence the decisions of business-men on where to invest and which markets to enter as exporters and importers.

Therefore, India's persistence in obstructing foreign scholars and scholarship in India is unfortunate. It is time India did a thorough reform of the regulations fac-ing foreign scholars and capitalized on the newly kindled interest in India among them. In areas that are not related directly to national security, all regulations must be lifted. Scrutiny of research projects should be limited to a short negative list of subjects related to national security. As regards visits by scholars and international conferences, the HRD Ministry should have full faith in the ability of the universi-ties to do the necessary screening.

CONCLUDING REMARKS

In its public statements, the government has asserted that if India is to adequately serve the public in the area of education, it must raise public expenditures on it to 6 percent of the GDP. The expenditure on education in 2005–06 being 2.8 percent of the GDP, the government effectively seeks to more than double it.

Even setting aside the issue of fiscal resources, the analysis in this chapter raises serious doubts about the wisdom of this strategy. The bottom line conclusion from my analysis is that substituting public expenditures for genuine reforms will not solve the problem of adequate provision of education in India. It would amount to throwing good money after bad. Both elementary and higher education can be provided efficiently by the private sector, which must operate on the principle of full cost recovery. The government needs to concentrate its efforts and resources in elementary education in areas that are hard for private providers to reach. In other areas, it should devote its scarce resources to protecting the interests of the poor. In particular, it should offer education vouchers for elementary education to the bottom 30 percent of the population, and loans to qualified students for higher education.

Potentially, higher education constitutes the most difficult area of reform. Given the need for new central legislation that decentralizes higher education and provides smooth channels for the entry of private universities, which in turn may require a constitutional amendment, it is difficult to be optimistic. At present, there are no signs that the Human Resource Development Ministry in India is in any mood to give up its monopoly.

APPENDIX 1: INDUSTRIAL POLICY 1990

POLICY MEASURE FOR THE PROMOTION OF
SMALL-SCALE AND AGRO-BASED INDUSTRIES
AND CHANGES IN PROCEDURES FOR
INDUSTRIAL APPROVALS

1. Government have been considering the need to take measures for promotion of small-scale and agro-based industries and to change procedures for grant of industrial approvals.
2. In pursuance of our policy to reorient industrial growth to serve the objective of employment generation, dispersal of industry in the rural areas, and to enhance the contribution of small-scale industries to exports, it has been decided to take the measures enumerated below.
3. The investment ceiling in plant and machinery for small-scale industries (fixed in 1985) would be raised from the present Rs. 35 lakhs to Rs. 60 lakhs [10 lakhs equal 1 million], and correspondingly, for ancillary units from Rs. 45 lakhs to Rs. 75 lakhs. In order to enable small-scale industries to play an important role in the total export effort, such of the small-scale units which undertake to export at least 30 percent of the annual production by the third year will be permitted to step up their investment in plant and machinery to Rs. 75 lakhs.
4. Investment ceiling in respect of tiny units would also be increased from the present Rs. 2 lakhs to Rs. 5 lakhs. However, with regard to their location, the population limit of 50,000 as per the 1981 census would continue to apply. Steps will be taken to ensure better inflow of credit and other vital inputs and to improve the infrastructure support to the constituents of the tiny sector.
5. Presently, 836 items have been reserved for exclusive manufacture in the small-scale sector. Efforts would be made to identify more items amenable

to similar reservation. Encroachment and violation by large-scale units into areas reserved for small-scale sector will be effectively dealt with.

. . .

(ii)   A new scheme of Central investment subsidy exclusively for the small-scale sector in rural and backward areas capable of generating higher level of employment at lower capital cost would be implemented.

(iii)   With a view to improving the competitiveness of the products manufactured in the small-scale sector, programs for modernization and upgradation of technology would be implemented. A number of technology centers, tool rooms, process and product development centers, testing centers, etc. will be set up under the umbrella of an apex Technology Development Center in Small Industries Development Organization.

(iv)   To ensure adequate and timely flow of credit of the small-scale industries, a new apex bank known as SIDBI has already been established. One of the major tasks of SIDBI and other commercial banks/financial institutions would be to channelize need-based, higher flow of credit, both by way of term loan and working capital, to the tiny and rural industries. A targeted approach will be adopted to ensure implementation and to facilitate monitoring this objective.

(v)   The existing regime of fiscal concessions will be reviewed both to provide sustained support to the units in the small-scale sector and to remove the disincentives for their graduation [to grow out of the small-scale-unit status] and further growth.

(vi)   An exercise will be undertaken to identify locations in rural areas endowed with adequate power supply and intensive campaigns will be launched to attract suitable entrepreneurs, provide all other inputs and foster small-scale and tiny industries. Similarly industries which are not energy-intensive will be identified for proliferation in rural areas where power supply is presently a constraint.

(vii)   In order to widen the entrepreneurial bases the Government would lay particular emphasis on training of women and youth under the Entrepreneurial Development Program. A special cell would be established in SIDO and State Directorates of Industries to assist women entrepreneurs.

(viii) One of the persistent complaints of the small-scale units is their being subjected to a large number of Acts/Laws, being required to maintain a number of registers, submit plethora of returns and face an army of inspectors, particularly in the field of labor legislation. These bureaucracy controls will be reduced so that unnecessary interference is eliminated. Further, procedure will be simplified and paperwork cut down.

6. In order to assist the large number of artisans engaged in the rural and cottage industries, the activities of the KVIC and KVI boards will be expanded, and these organizations will be strengthened to discharge the responsibility more effectively. Special marketing organizations at the Center and State levels shall be created to assist rural artisans in marketing their products and also in supply of raw materials. Besides, concessional credit, training facilities and free consultancy to groups of artisans will be provided.

7. In agro-processing industries greater success has been achieved where growers and processors have been integrated, as in the case of sugar. For the success of other agro-based industries also, close links must be forged between the growers and processor units. Industrial policy will, therefore, especially promote projects which are organized in close co-operation on the basis of joint ownership. Growers will be encouraged to set up processing units within the framework of co-operative societies or similar institutional framework. This will also ensure the transmission of better technology for enhanced agricultural production.

8. In sectors where units require licensing, the policy will also encourage location of processing units in rural areas where growers are concentrated. Apart from economic benefits of proximity to raw materials it will help in dispersal of industry and increasing employment in rural areas.

9. Agro-processing industry will receive high priority in credit allocation from the financial institutions. In appointment of working capital, bank will give higher priority to such industries as compared to the rest of the industrial sector.

10. In order to bring best technology available to these industries, technology approvals will be given [within] 30 days of presentation to the Secretariat for Industrial Approvals in the Department of Industrial Development. Government will actively promote the generation, adaptation and adoption of new technologies in the field.

Procedures for Industrial Approvals

11. Indian industry must be made more competitive internationally. It also is to be released from unnecessary bureaucratic shackles by reducing the number of clearances required from the Government. While the Government will continue to examine large projects in view of resource constraints, decisions in respect of medium sized investments will be left to the entrepreneurs. To achieve these objectives, the following decisions have been taken.

Delicensing

12. All new units up to an investment of Rs. 25 crores [one crore equals 10 million] in fixed assets in nonbackward areas and Rs. 75 crores in centrally notified backward areas will be exempt from requirement of obtaining license/registration.

13. For the import of capital goods, the entrepreneur would have entitlement to import up to a landed value of 30 percent of the total value of plant and machinery required for the unit.

Raw Materials and Components

14. For imports of raw materials and components, imports will be permissible up to a landed value of 30 percent of the ex-factory value of annual production. The ex-factory value of production will exclude the excise duty on the item

of production. Raw materials and components on OGL will not be included within this 30 percent limit. For all licensable items of raw materials and components, import licensing procedures will continue to operate.

Foreign Collaboration

15. In respect of transfer of technology, if import of technology is considered necessary by the entrepreneur, he can conclude an agreement with the collaborator, without obtaining any clearance from the Government, provided that royalty payment does not exceed 5 percent on domestic sales and 8 percent on exports. If, however, lump-sum payment is involved in the import of technology, the proposal will require Government clearance, but a decision will be communicated to the entrepreneur within a period of 30 days.

Foreign Investment

16. Keeping in view the need to attract effective inflow of technology, investment up to 40 percent of equity will be allowed on an automatic basis. In such proposals also, the landed value of imported C.G. [capital goods] shall not exceed 30 percent of value of plant and machinery.

Minimum Economic Size

17. In order to ensure that investment leads to production of goods that attain international competitiveness and that maximum efficiency is ensured, the unit would have to conform to the minimum economic size in cases where such a size has been prescribed.

Expansion

18. The deregulation suggested above would cover all cases of expansion and would not be restricted only to new units.

Broad-banding

19. The existing broad-banding scheme would continue to be in force. In addition, if no extra investment is required, no clearance from the Government would be necessary for production and sale of any new item by existing unit. This would not include those items which are reserved for small-scale industries.

Location Policy and Environmental Clearances

20. The location policy would not be applied to such industries by the Center except for location in and around metropolitan cities with population above 4 million. For these cities location will not be permissible within 20 km calculated from the periphery of the metropolitan area, except in prior designated

industrial areas and for nonpolluting industries such as electronics, computer software and printing. It will be up to State Government to regulate industrial locations, keeping in mind local conditions and requirements and their respective special development plans, and zoning and town planning laws. Similarly environmental clearance would have to be obtained from the prescribed authority at the State level. If further central legislation should introduce new provisions, that law would automatically apply to these units as well.

Export-oriented Units

21. 100 percent export-oriented units (EOUs) and units to be set up in export-processing zones (EPZs) are also being delicensed under the scheme up to an investment limit of Rs. 75 crores.

Convertibility Clause

22. Such investment shall be exempt from the "convertibility clause" applicable to financing the Indian financial institutions.
23. It may be clarified that in the application of the proposals listed above, 836 items which are reserved for production in the small-scale sector will continue to be excluded.
24. The above proposals will be applicable to all manufacturing items in a specified list. The list shall follow the nomenclature of the Indian Trade Classification based on the Harmonized System. In such section of the classification, apart from positive mention of approved items, those not permissible shall be specifically excluded from the benefit of the proposals list above. Approval for excluded items will be as per the existing industrial policy regime and procedures.
25. Units set up by MRTP/FERA companies will be covered by the procedures set out above, but they will continue to need clearances under the provisions and regulations of these two Acts.
26. The existing De-licensed Industries Scheme, Exempted Industries Scheme and DGTD Registration System will stand abolished.

APPENDIX 2: DERIVING THE
SAVINGS-INVESTMENT IDENTITY

The GDP is composed of private consumption (C_p), government spending (C_g), private investment (I_p), and exports (X) net of imports (M) of goods and services. The standard GDP identity is written

$$GDP \equiv C_p + I_p + C_g + (X - M). \tag{A2.1}$$

The gross national product (GNP) equals the GDP plus the net factor income earned abroad (NFIA). In turn, the latter equals income earned by the factors owned by the country but located abroad, minus the income earned by factors owned by foreigners but located at home. We can write

$$GNP \equiv GDP + NFIA$$
$$\equiv C_p + I_p + C_g + (X - M + NFIA). \tag{A2.2}$$

For simplicity, let us ignore depreciation. The National income (NI) represents the income received by households and firms as returns to the factors of production, such as land, labor, and capital, that they supply. It differs from the GNP in two respects. First, the factor income comes out of the revenues earned by producers, net of indirect taxes (T_I). Put differently, the NI is income measured at producer prices, while GNP is income measured at consumer or market prices. And second, the NI includes net foreign transfer (NFT) receipts, such as aid and remittances. The NFT is not income of the factors of production of the country, but it is a part of the income of the households and firms. Thus,

$$NI \equiv GNP - T_I + NFT$$
$$\equiv C_p + I + C_g + (X - M + NFIA + NFT) - T_I$$
$$\equiv C_p + I + C_g + CA - T_I. \tag{A2.3}$$

In the last identity, CA ($\equiv$ X $-$ M $+$ NFIA $+$ NFT) stands for the current account surplus.

The NI is allocated among consumption, private savings (S_p), and direct taxes (T_D):

$$NI \equiv C_p + S_p + T_D. \tag{A2.4}$$

Private savings can be further split into household savings and business savings (retained earnings). Likewise, direct taxes can be split between personal income taxes and corporate profit taxes. But we do not need to introduce these complications here. Instead, we use (A2.3) and (A2.4) to deduce

$$I_P \equiv S_P + (T_D + T_I - C_g) - CA$$
$$\equiv S_P + S_G + S_F. \tag{A2.5}$$

Here S_G ($\equiv T_D + T_I - G$) and S_F ($\equiv - CA$) represent government and foreign savings invested at home, respectively. This is the investment-savings identity reported in the text. It is easy to show that if we allow for depreciation, (A2.5) still holds, with investment and savings both interpreted as either gross or net.

NOTES

CHAPTER I

1. India's fiscal year begins on April 1 and ends on March 31. Thus, 2003–04 refers to the period beginning April 1, 2003, and ending March 31, 2004.

2. In 1951, India had adopted planning as the principal instrument of launching rapid growth. The strategy took the form of five-year plans that laid out a detailed map of policies and sectoral investments for periods of five years. The first three plans covered 1951–52 to 1955–56, 1956–57 to 1960–61, and 1961–62 to 1965–66. Two consecutive droughts forced a three-year "plan holiday" in the mid-1960s, with the Fourth and Fifth Five-Year Plans launched in 1969–70 and 1974–75, respectively. At the time of writing, India was in the last year of the Tenth Five-Year Plan, covering 2002–03 to 2006–07.

3. The remaining three countries, Sri Lanka, Costa Rica, and Jamaica, are all relatively tiny. The brief period of emergency rule—from June 26, 1975, to March 21, 1977—in India may be viewed as representing a break in its democratic tradition, but even this aberration left all political and economic institutions intact and had virtually no impact on the economic policies.

4. Throughout the book, a period such as 1951–65 in relation to India would refer to the period from 1951–52 to 1964–65, with end point years included.

5. The average growth rate during 1988–06 has been calculated using the growth rates between 1988–89 and 2004–05 at 1993–94 prices, and that for 2005–06 at 1999–2000 prices. This is because the Central Statistical Organization recently shifted the base year for the GDP calculations to 1999–2000 and does not provide the GDP figure for the year 2005–06 at 1993–94 prices. If we wish to maintain full consistency in terms of the base year, we must limit the calculation to the years 1988–89 to 2004–05. For this period, the growth rate at 1993–94 prices is 6.1 percent.

6. Panagariya (2004a). I also produce a plot of the GDP and GNP growth rate series on the same graph to make the point that they are indistinguishable from one another.

7. Taking the GDP series from 1950–51 to 1980–81, the trend line during 1965–81 lies below that during 1950–51 to 1964–65 with 95 percent or higher probability.

8. My teacher Raj Krishna at Rajasthan University, who later also taught at the Delhi School of Economics, popularized the catchy phrase "Hindu rate of growth." The term had its origins in Najinyanupi (1973), who argued that the growth rate of 3 to 4 percent conformed to a development process that suited the Hindu way of living; a higher rate would lead to a breakdown of that form of living. "Thus, those areas of our country or those sections of our population whose own condition has improved at faster than 3–4 percent rate of growth have not been protected by the Hindu outlook from the evils of temptations of the Western way of life. The older among them have already yielded to wife swapping and the younger to delinquency and drugs" (Najinyanupi, 1973, p. 141). This description later led Raj Krishna to term the 3 to 4 percent annual growth "the Hindu rate of growth."

9. An alternative to phases II and III in my scheme would be to include the year 1980–81 in phase III instead of phase II. If this were done, the superhigh growth rate of 7.7 percent in 1980–81 would pushp the growth in the newly defined phase III (1980–88) up to 5.1 percent and that in phase II (1965–80) down to 2.9 percent. Undoubtedly, these rates differ more sharply than those in my scheme. Yet, I chose to reject this alternative because the 7.7 percent growth in 1980–81 came on the heels of a 5.5 percent *decline* in the GDP in 1979–80. We must either include both 1979–80 and 1980–81 in phase III or neither. Putting them both in phase III results in growth rates of 3.5 and 4.0 percent in phases II (1965–79) and III (1979–88), respectively, which offers a less sharp distinction than the scheme I have chosen.

10. This is a point I had made forcefully (Panagariya, 2004a) in response to initial assertions by Rodrik (2003) that the 1990s reforms did not contribute to growth in India. Contrary to the common impression in the literature, Rodrik and Subramanian (2005) wrote in response to the original version of my paper, which was then available under the title "India in the 1980s: Weak Reforms, Fragile Growth" and was presented at the conference "A Tale of Two Giants: India's and China's Experience with Reform and Growth" (organized jointly by the International Monetary Fund and the National Council of Applied Economic Research, November 14–16, 2003, at the Taj Mahal Hotel, New Delhi).

11. This section draws heavily on Panagariya (2006a).

12. While the 2007–08 budget, presented on February 28, 2007, gives the advance estimate of the growth rate for 2006–07, most other data were available only until 2005–06 at the time of writing. Therefore, much of the analysis in the book ends in 2005–06.

13. The average exchange rate in the year 2002–03 was 48.4 rupees per dollar. It changed to 46, 44.9, and 44.3 rupees per dollar in the subsequent three years.

14. I have taken a cautiously optimistic view on India for some time. In an article titled "India: A New Tiger on the Block?" (Panagariya, 1994), I had predicted a 6 to 7 percent growth at a time when few observers thought this was possible. Later, in an article titled "My Millennium Wish: Double-Digit Growth" and published in January 2000 (Panagariya, 2000a), I had concluded that though the reforms were getting into rough territory, double-digit growth was "within the grasp of the country."

15. Growth rate for 2005–06 used to compute the phase IV growth rate is based on the GDP data at 1999–2000 prices. All other GDP data used are at 1993–94 prices.

16. For phase IV, the last year for which comparable data are available is 2004–05. The shares for 2005–06 are available, but they are not directly comparable to those for the earlier years. This is because the GDP series at 1993–94 prices goes up to 2004–05 only.

17. Bosworth, Collins, and Virmani (2007) forcefully bring out the deficiencies of these series, especially that on employment.

18. Bhagwati (1993) provides a lucid discussion of the developments until the end of the 1980s. In particular, he offers a compelling analysis of why the Indian economy failed to perform well in the first three decades following independence.

19. The fascinating book by Shourie (2004) offers several striking examples of how the process of setting up committees contributes to poor governance in India. I will return to this theme later in the book, in my discussion of the civil service reform.

20. Singh (2006) offers a lucid discussion of this debate.

21. The fear of being seen as doing an about-face to Nehru's essential policy framework remained with the leadership as the 1990s unfolded. As I noted (Panagariya, 1994), "Even the July 1991 budget speech by Finance Minister Manmohan Singh, which ushered in the current era of reforms, had to balance the announcements of reforms by a constant reiteration of the usefulness of past policies. The minister made repeated references to India's first Prime Minister Jawaharlal Nehru's contributions to development, while recalling the just-assassinated Rajiv Gandhi's vision of taking India into the 21st century."

22. "Broad bending" meant that even if the initial license had been issued for a specific product, say automobiles, the firm could now use that capacity to produce related products, such as vans or trucks.

CHAPTER 2

1. Quoted in Bhagwati and Desai (1970, p. 65).

2. As shown in table 1.1, it is the 3.7 percent decline in the GDP in the last year of the Third Plan (1965–66) which pulled the growth rate during the entire plan period down to 2.8 percent.

3. The following section is largely drawn from Panagariya (2006b).

4. Bhagwati and Srinivasan (1975), who classify trade policy regimes into five "phases" ranging from the most restrictive "Phase I" to the most liberal "Phase V," characterize the period 1951–56 as "Phase IV" and 1956–62 as "Phase I." My own evaluation is that the entire 1950s qualify to be labeled as "Phase IV." The policy began to turn restrictive after the introduction of foreign exchange budgeting in August 1958, but remained liberal until the end of the 1950s.

5. See Panagariya (2006b) for details.

6. This translation is by Nayar (1972, pp. 127–28), who also provides the source of the original speech in Hindi in his footnote 114.

7. Both previous quotations are as quoted in Nayar (1972, pp. 108–09).

8. See Bhagwati and Desai (1970).

9. Under open general licensing, goods placed on the OGL list could be imported without a license.

10. For many of the details of foreign exchange budgeting here and below, I have relied on the autobiography of B. K. Nehru (1997), which is not specific on some of the dates. As a result, I have had to guess the date of the introduction of foreign exchange budgeting.

11. See Nehru (1997, p. 261). Unfortunately, Nehru provides no details on the circumstances leading to the abandonment of foreign exchange budgeting.

12. Planning Commission (1956, chap. 4, para. 48).

13. For example, until 1959, imports of cereals into India were strictly below 4 million tons except in 1951, when they amounted to 4.08 million tons. These imports steadily climbed in the 1960s, reaching 10.34 million tons in 1966 and averaging 8.2 million tons between 1964 and 1967 (Sarma, 1978, table 1). Even in 1965–66, food imports as a proportion of the GDP were only 1.3 percent (Fourth Five-Year Plan, chap. 5, para. 27).

14. If the ratio is taken with respect to the GDP at factor cost, as is often done, the ratios will be higher.

15. In his autobiography, Nehru leaves the distinct impression that he never considered discussing alternative solutions to the problem with experts on the subject.

16. Charges of corruption forced TTK out of office in 1958.

17. It is doubtful that B. K. Nehru understood the far-reaching implications of his action. This is suggested by the fact that while repeatedly complimenting himself for having introduced foreign exchange budgeting, he was very critical of TTK for having authored "the Industrial Policy Resolution 1956 which put Indian industry into a complete straitjacket.... Nobody could start or continue any kind of industrial enterprise without getting an industrial license and an industrial license was granted only for the manufacture of specific goods up to a certain capacity." Nehru did not seem to see that foreign exchange budgeting made this regime far worse by making the grant of the investment license dependent on the allocation of foreign exchange.

18. This paragraph is based on the information available on the Web site "The World Bank in India" at http://www.ieo.org/world-c2-p1.html. A detailed discussion of the events leading up to the statement and its contents can also be found in the classic work by Kidron (1965, chap. 3) on foreign investment in India. In addition, see Bhagwati and Desai (1970, pp. 216–19).

19. The Mahalanobis model showed that the higher the proportion of machinery output devoted to the machinery sector, the higher the long-run growth of the GDP and consumption. A crucial feature of this model was the total absence of foreign trade.

20. This provision proved useful when the state sought the participation of the private sector in the telecommunications sector in the mid-1980s.

21. For example, in 1960, undertakings with up to 1 million rupees in investment in fixed assets (land, building, and machinery) and fewer than 100 workers were exempt from licensing. In 1962, the requirement on the number of workers was dropped. In 1964, the investment limit of undertakings exempt from licensing was raised to 2.5 million rupees, with the exception of some industries (see Sharma, 1974, p. 26). At various times, the government also announced industries that were not subject to licensing requirements, though this exemption usually came with additional conditions.

22. The small-scale industries (SSI) reservation, whereby the government would reserve certain products for production exclusively by small-scale enterprises, appeared later in 1967.

23. Marathe (1989, p. 51) goes on to note that a committee under the chairmanship of T. Swaminathan did the first appraisal of the licensing system in 1964. He suggests that until then, the system functioned relatively smoothly and did not generate major complaints.

24. DGTD was located in the Ministry of Industry and had the responsibility for giving clearance on the domestic availability of products before import licenses could be issued.

25. An interesting example cited by Sengupta (1985) is that of Kilachands and Nanu Bhai Jewelers, who were given preference over established large Indian business houses in setting up basic chemical capacity in nylon and synthetic rubber.

26. According to Sengupta, the Birlas generally got licenses in almost all industries in which the Tatas operated. In turn, the Tatas got licenses in industries dominated by foreign firms. For instance, the government gave them entry into the tire industry, which had traditionally been dominated by Dunlop and Firestone.

27. The evidence is only suggestive, since in principle the same outcome can also arise in the absence of any market interventions. In practice, it is not very likely that on their own, the resources would have gone into the machinery sector in preference to more labor-intensive sectors in a labor-abundant country such as India.

28. As previously noted, this hypothesis is reinforced by the fact that the first appraisal of the licensing system was undertaken in 1964 by a committee under the chairmanship of T. Swaminathan.

29. For example, the Third Plan saw room for the private sector in sectors such as fertilizer and pig iron, in which the public sector had already assumed a dominant role.

30. In their extensive critique of the licensing system, Bhagwati and Desai (1970) draw extensively on the information in the Ninth Report of the Lok Sabha Committee on Industrial

Licensing of 1967 (which they often refer to as the Ninth Report of the Estimates Committee) and the Hazari Committee Report.

31. For a detailed discussion of the distribution and price controls, see Bhagwati and Desai (1970, chap. 14).

32. Varshney (1995, chap. 2), on which I draw liberally in this section, provides an excellent treatment of the evolution of agricultural policy under Nehru.

33. See Varshney (1995, p. 35).

34. Narain (1977) has made this point more systematically.

CHAPTER 3

1. This is in comparison to 6 million tons during the entire First Plan and only 840,000 tons and 755,000 tons during the calendar years 1954 and 1955, respectively.

2. In 1965–66, India's total food production was 72.3 million tons, four fifths of the level in the previous year. The output remained nearly the same in 1966–67 before bouncing back in 1967–68.

3. Cohen attributes Johnson's strategy to keep India "ship to mouth" to a desire to persuade India to adopt a pro-agriculture policy. But this is at odds with the fact that under Shastri, India was already keen to move in that direction, and C. Subramaniam was doing everything he could to make the Green Revolution a reality. Varshney (1995) makes a compelling case against the theory that Johnson was motivated by a desire to push India to adopt a pro-agriculture policy. His ire at India's refusal to endorse his Vietnam policy offers a more compelling explanation for his "ship to mouth" policy.

4. The World Bank organized the Aid to India Consortium in August 1958. The Consortium consisted of the World Bank Group and thirteen countries: Austria, Belgium, Britain, Canada, Denmark, the Federal Republic of Germany (at that time, West Germany), France, Italy, Japan, the Netherlands, Norway, Sweden, and the United States.

5. See Joshi and Little (1994, p. 76) and Nayar (2003, p. 10) for details.

6. The letter "O" in Congress (O) stands for "organization."

7. In the meantime, the Supreme Court had overturned the conviction of Mrs. Gandhi by the Allahabad High Court.

8. Around this time, Singh (1964) had made a persuasive case for the devaluation of the rupee to correct the imbalance in external payments. But I can find no evidence that the policymakers paid any attention to this important and timely piece of work. Had they done so, devaluation might have come sometime in the early 1960s, when the economy was growing at more than 4 percent and was not faced with external shocks. As we will shortly see, when devaluation was eventually carried out in June 1966, circumstances had turned against its success.

9. The first Swaminathan Committee on Industries Development Procedures was appointed in September 1963 and reported in May 1964. The second was appointed in August 1965 and reported in February 1966 (Bhagwati and Desai, 1970, p. 255, footnote 1).

10. The following discussion of the crisis is partially based on its excellent description by Joshi and Little (1994).

11. The definition of interconnection has been controversial over the years. Originally, the MRTP Act of 1969 took the definition from the Monopolies Inquiry Commission of 1964 and the Dutt Committee report that was based on management control exercised by the Managing Agency System. After the Managing Agency System was abolished, the definition became more restrictive: Two companies with common directors or directors who were related by blood or marriage came to be defined as interconnected.

12. See Kumar (1994, p. 26), who cites a Government of India press note as the source of this information.

13. Under the Companies Act of 1956, a foreign subsidiary is defined as an enterprise or undertaking with more than 50 percent of its shares held by a single foreign company. The management of a company can be controlled with the ownership of a much smaller proportion of the shares. According to Kumar (1994, p. 28), both MRTP and RBI consider 25 percent equity holding to be sufficient for the exercise of effective control of an enterprise.

14. See Desai (1994, p. 46).

15. At the time, 114 British tea companies dominated tea plantations. In the post-FERA regime, 45 companies incorporated in India, with up to 74 percent foreign equity share, took over the business of these companies. See Kumar (1994, p. 26).

16. This section relies heavily on G. D. Sharma (1974).

17. The list included agricultural inputs such as fertilizers, pesticides, and tractors and power tillers; iron and steel, including iron ore, pig iron, and steel; nonferrous metals; petroleum; heavy industrial machinery; newsprint; and electronics.

18. Foreign firms included all undertakings owned by foreign companies, by their branches or subsidiaries, or by companies whose paid-up equity share capital in excess of 50 percent was held directly or indirectly by foreign companies, foreign nationals, or nonresident Indians.

19. Schedule II of this note listed undertakings to which the exemption did not apply: the MRTP and foreign firms.

20. In 1978 the reservation list was recast in terms of classification adopted in the NIC. This led to the list of reserved items expanding from 504 to 807, with no actual additions to the list. Post-1978 data on small-scale units are in terms of the NIC classification, and therefore comparable to 807 items in 1978.

21. In part, this may have been driven politically. Previously, India had pegged the rupee to the U.S. dollar, but with the relations with the United States at an all-time low in December 1971, India may have taken the opportunity provided by the breakdown of the international monetary system to unlink the rupee from the dollar.

22. The regulations discussed in this section were introduced in 1976, and thus did not impact growth in phase II. I nevertheless include them here since they are an integral part of the march toward socialism that characterized this period.

23. For the history of the Reserve Bank of India and State Bank of India, I have drawn heavily on the information available on the respective Web sites of the two institutions.

24. In 1809, the Bank of Calcutta was redesignated as the Bank of Bengal, which has the distinction of being the first joint stock bank of British India sponsored by the government of Bengal. The Bank of Bombay and the Bank of Madras were created in 1840 and 1843, respectively. The three banks remained the apex of modern banking in India until their amalgamation as the Imperial Bank in 1921.

25. Scheduled commercial banks are those banks included in the second schedule of the RBI Act (1934). To be included in the schedule, a bank must satisfy the criteria laid down in section 42 (6) (a) of the RBI Act.

26. The act was passed in July 1969. But on February 10, 1970, the Supreme Court declared it void. On February 14, 1970, the president of India issued an ordinance that allowed the government to retain control of the nationalized banks. The ordinance was later replaced by the Banking Companies (Acquisition and Transfer of Undertakings) Act of 1970.

27. I draw heavily on T. Sinha (2002) for the historical details in the section.

28. General insurance companies provide nonlife insurance services such as property and casualty insurance and reinsurance.

29. My account of the Green Revolution draws heavily on Gulati (2000) and S. Sinha (2001).

30. The Left parties argued that the new technology would mainly benefit well-to-do farmers. Moreover, since increased output would lower prices, poorer farmers who would not have access to the new technology would be hurt.

31. In table 3.3, production data relate to the crop year such that 1962 refers to 1961–62. Hence, the period 1961–65 is defined by 1962 and 1965.

32. The Seed Corporation of India, charged with promoting the development of a seed industry in India and producing and supplying the foundation seeds of various crops, was initiated in 1961 under the ICAR, and was converted into a public sector limited company in 1963.

33. According to Joshi and Little (1994, pp. 109–10), the government policy contributed to the mess created by the droughts.

34. For example, see Rodrik (1999).

CHAPTER 4

1. Among other things, an attempt was made to nationalize the wholesale trade in food grains in the early 1970s, in order to eliminate the intermediaries who were thought to profit at the expense of the farmers. The attempt led to a complete disruption of the supply chain, and the government was forced to retreat entirely.

2. See Desai (1994, p. 15).

3. Marathe (1986, p. 100) attributes the use of the term "by stealth" to qualify the modest liberalization measures in 1975 and 1976 to an unnamed civil servant. Subsequently, the term "liberalization by stealth" came to be used to describe the policy changes during the 1980s as well, since policymakers still saw political risks in explicitly renouncing the old policy framework, and instead preferred to shed it surreptitiously. To quote Marathe (p. 100): "By far the most important reason why this phase [in 1975 and 1976] of liberalization did not add up to much was that there was an unwillingness at the political level to recognize or accept that a change in direction was needed....In the words of a distinguished civil servant who had retired by then, the attempt was 'to go by stealth' and necessarily, therefore, the amount of good that could be done had to be modest."

4. This section draws heavily on Sengupta's excellent and indispensable account of the industrial policy changes in India from 1951 to 1985. In addition, I draw selectively on chapter 3 of Marathe (1986).

5. Since 1966, actual production had been allowed to exceed licensed capacity by 25 percent. See Biswajit Dhar, "State Regulation of Private Foreign Capital in India," at http://isidev.nic.in/pdf/statreg.pdf.

6. These measures are described in World Bank (1985, pp. 12–16; 1987, pp. 39–79; 1988, pp. 34–36; and 1990, pp. 47–52).

7. For example, in the auto sector, licenses were divided into two categories: those for vehicles with two or three wheels and for those with four or more wheels. A license holder in the first category could then switch production across scooters, mopeds, motorcycles, and three-wheelers. Likewise, a holder of a license in the second category could switch among cars, trucks, buses, and any other commercial vehicles with four or more wheels.

8. In this section, I draw heavily on the excellent discussion of trade policies during the period under review in Pursell (1992).

9. The limited permissible category, not suggested by the Alexander Committee, was a later development.

CHAPTER 5

1. Given my own involvement in the early stages of the negotiations for this loan, I may offer some details on the state of the play on the policy reform between the World Bank and the government of India at the time. The Bank mission for the trade and investment

liberalization loan made its first visit to India in late March 1993. As a Bank staff member working in the Research Department at the time, I participated in this mission. Senior officials in the India Department of the Bank had told the mission team that if the Bank were to offer this loan, the government of India would have to take action on the liberalization of consumer goods imports. Soon after the mission arrived, India announced its new export-import policy, which took no action toward the liberalization of consumer goods. The mission leader discussed the matter with the officials in the Finance Ministry and was told that the prime minister had decided against further liberalization until the elections in some key states, due in June 1993, were over. The following evening, the chief of the India Country Operations Division arrived and told the mission that if there was no action on consumer goods, it was "no go" on the loan. The next morning, the chief went to the Finance Ministry and spoke with the senior officials there. Upon returning to the hotel, he informed the mission that the loan could perhaps still go forward on the basis of the actions already taken by the government of India. In the event, that is just what the Bank did—the $300 million loan was based entirely on the actions the government had already taken. As a postscript, India liberalized consumer goods imports almost a decade later, on April 1, 2001, upon losing a World Trade Organization dispute settlement case brought by the United States. In the meantime, the World Bank continued to loan money to India without so much as a hiccup!

2. State-level votes in February 2007 in Punjab and Uttarakhand followed the same pattern.

3. In one respect, the policy statement need not surprise us. V. P. Singh had served as finance minister in the Rajiv Gandhi government during 1984–87 when it announced its most significant reforms. Expelled from the Gandhi Congress Party in 1989, Singh formed the Janata Dal, which managed to defeat the Gandhi Congress Party in the parliamentary elections in December that year. But in the end Singh's government failed to survive the coalition politics.

4. The Chandra Sekhar government was asked to stay as a caretaker government until June 1991, when elections brought P. V. Narsimha Rao as the new prime minister. Despite its minority status, the Rao government served its full term until 1996 and firmly set the course of the economy toward a progressively liberal regime.

5. Thus, the policy statement opened with the politically correct rhetoric of the time: "[The] Government have been considering the need to take measures for promotion of small scale and agro-based industries and to change procedures for grant of industrial approvals." In the second paragraph, it went on to state, "In pursuance of our policy to re-orient industrial growth to serve the objective of employment generation, dispersal of industry in the rural areas, and to enhance the contribution of small scale industries to exports it has been decided to take the measures enumerated below."

6. From a political economy standpoint, it is interesting to note that the intellectual environment in India was still generally unfriendly to liberalization. Intellectuals including the members of the press and economists, as well as entrenched economic interests in India, displayed hostility to liberalization, so that even the piecemeal reforms during the 1980s had to be carried out by stealth. As I noted (Panagariya, 1994), "Even the July 1991 budget speech by Finance Minister Manmohan Singh, which ushered in the current era of reforms, had to balance the announcements of reforms by a constant reiteration of the usefulness of past policies. The minister made repeated references to India's first Prime Minister Jawaharlal Nehru's contributions to development, while recalling the just-assassinated Rajiv Gandhi's vision of taking India into the 21st century."

7. For example, in its negotiations with the United States, India gave market access to apples.

8. I base the discussion of foreign investment policy on the Government of India (2006a).

CHAPTER 6

1. Under the World Bank classification, a country with per-capita income between $3125 and $9655 at 1996 prices is classified as an upper-middle-income country. Korea's per-capita income in 1987 had reached $3248 at current prices (Harvie and Lee, 2003).

2. Leaving aside Turkey, which has been a member of the OECD since 1961, Mexico is the only other developing country to have been invited (in 1994) to join the OECD.

3. See Yoo (1997, p. 8).

4. Harvie and Lee (2003, p. 266) place the rate of growth of the Korean economy during the entire colonial period (1910–45) at 4 percent. They note, however, that the principal beneficiaries of this growth were Japan and Japanese settlers in Korea.

5. See Lim (2000, p. 18).

6. This comparison is based on the real per-capita incomes of Korea and Haiti reported in the data set posted on the World Bank Website under the title "Global Development Network Growth Database." In turn, the database cites Penn World table 5.6 as the source.

7. All data on Korea in this chapter relate to the calendar year. Periods such as 1963–73 are inclusive of the beginning and ending years. This means that 1963–73 refers to the 11-year period that includes both 1963 and 1973.

8. During the1980s, the manufacturing share saw a slight downturn, declining to 29 percent in 1990.

9. Among other sources, this section draws on Panagariya (2004c).

10. These indicators are based on the data in the "Global Development Network Growth Database" of the World Bank mentioned in note 6.

11. See Yoo (1997, pp. 4–5).

12. See Harvie and Lee (2003, p. 269).

13. This paragraph draws on Yoo (1997).

14. The World Bank (1993) goes to the extreme when it argues that there is no conclusive evidence that sectoral patterns were any different from what a factor endowments model would predict. Little (1996) is closer to reality on this point when he counters, "Common sense tells one that the timing, scale and pattern of investment in heavy industry—especially cars, shipbuilding, and petrochemicals—was markedly different from what would have occurred under laissez faire (or under some non-selective industrial promotion)."

15. Exceptions included cement, fertilizer, and petroleum refining in the early 1960s and steel and petrochemicals in the late 1960s (Westphal 1990, p. 47).

16. For example, see Bhagwati (1999) and Little (1996).

17. For the discussion of the critique by Little, I rely on Bhagwati (1999).

18. The won was devalued from 398 won per dollar in 1973 to 484 won per dollar and was held fixed at that exchange rate until the beginning of 1980.

19. See Harvie and Lee (2003, p. 272).

20. Ibid. (table 1).

CHAPTER 7

1. Disguised unemployment is said to exist when a routine reorganization of a task would allow a part of the labor force to be released without a fall in output. If a part of disguised unemployment turns into open unemployment, the measured rate of unemployment would rise even though the true level of unemployment had not changed. Conversely, if open unemployment turns into disguised unemployment, the unemployment rate would appear to have declined when no such decline actually took place.

2. For sources predating independence, see Srinivasan (2000, chap. 3).

3. The following discussion relies on T. N. Srinivasan (1999), an unpublished manuscript, which cites Srinivasan and Bardhan (1974, chap. 1).

4. Maran (2002) places this growth rate at 7.5 percent.

5. Systematic measurement of poverty in India originated in Dandekar and Rath (1971). Many of the studies on the subject or references to them can be found in Srinivasan and Bardhan (1974, 1988), Fields (1980), Tendulkar (1998), and Bhalla (2002).

6. The expert group deemed these amounts adequate to enable an individual to consume enough food to satisfy a basic calorie intake of 2400 calories per day in rural areas and 2100 calories per day in urban areas, and to meet other needs, such as clothing and shelter. The amounts are exclusive of expenditures on health and education, on the assumption that the state would provide these public goods. To convert the 1973–74 poverty lines to equivalent poverty lines in the other years, Datt (1998, footnote 7) uses the Consumer Price Index for Agricultural Laborers (CPIAL) for the rural sector and the Consumer Price Index for Industrial Workers (CPIIW) for the urban sector.

7. See Planning Commission (1993).

8. But starting with 1986–87, an annual survey with a "thin" sample to complement the quinquennial "thick" survey was reintroduced.

9. For reasons not explained in his paper, Datt (1998) does not report the results for the 26th NSS round, relating to 1971–72. On the other hand, though Datt does report the results for the 4th, 6th, 9th, and 12th rounds, I have deleted them to retain no more than one survey per fiscal year and to achieve the greatest comparability across the surveys.

10. The choice of the division is dictated by the fact that the poverty ratio is missing for the year 1962–63 in table 7.1.

11. Observe that the official estimates in table 7.2 do not necessarily match those in table 7.1 by Datt. The difference is likely due to differences between the precise price indexes applied in the two methodologies.

12. Sen and Himanshu (2004b) also derive "corrected" estimates, but virtually no scholar has come forward to endorse them. In their careful survey, Deaton and Kozel (2005, p. 188) offer the following evaluation of the estimates by Himanshu and Sen: "Their estimates are in line with Sen's (2000) original view that there was little decline in headcount poverty in India in the 1990s.... Although there is no way to know with certainty what the results of Round 55 would have been had the questionnaire been unchanged, this small a drop in poverty during the 1990s seems implausible. There is considerable evidence from other sources than the consumption surveys, such as information on wage rates, ownership of durable goods, and incomes from other surveys, which, though imperfect indicators on their own, taken together are extremely difficult to reconcile with an India in which poverty rates are not declining."

13. For the most part, Deaton and Drèze (2002) rely on the work of Deaton and Tarozzi (Deaton, 2001a, 2001b; Deaton and Tarozzi, 2000). But since the Deaton and Drèze paper brings these contributions together in a coherent whole, I rely exclusively on it in this chapter.

14. Subsequently, Sen and Himanshu (2004a) have claimed that the Deaton and Drèze adjustment results in an upward rather than a downward shift in the expenditures on food. This suggests that the relationship between food expenditure and total expenditure did shift upward in the 55th round, undermining the second of these identifying assumptions. Deaton and Kozel (2005, pp. 187–88) seem to acknowledge this as a problem but do not give an idea of its implications for their poverty figures, except that they are understated. On the other hand, the calculations by Deaton (2005), based on the thin samples from the 56th to 59th rounds, show a sharp declining trend in the poverty ratio.

15. Sundaram and Tendulkar (2001, p. 129).

16. The gross primary school enrollment ratio is the ratio of all primary school attendees (regardless of their age) to the total number of those in the primary school age group.

Because the numerator of this ratio can be larger than denominator, the ratio can be larger than 100 percent.

17. See Mishra (2007, p. 11).

CHAPTER 8

1. For details on step 1 and step 2 corrections, see chapter 7. Step 2 correction involves applying a different price index to all nominal expenditures so that it has no impact on the distribution of income.

2. For example, Forbes (2000) finds that greater equality of incomes leads to slower growth.

3. Regressions aimed at testing for conditional convergence control for other variables relevant to explaining growth, whereas those testing for unconditional convergence estimate the growth rate as a function of the initial level of income only. From the viewpoint of inequality, the latter is more appropriate.

4. See M. S. Ahluwalia (2001) on this issue.

5. Due to a recent switch in the base period, State Domestic Product data at constant prices are available at 1980–81 prices for 1980–99, and at 1993–94 prices for 1993–2004. In table 8.2, the growth rates for 1981–88 and 1988–94 are calculated using the series at 1980–81 constant prices, and those for 1994–2004 using the series at 1993–94 prices. Strictly speaking, the change in the base influences the growth rate calculations and makes the growth rates for the first two periods noncomparable with those for the third period. Going by calculations for 1994–98 at both 1980–81 and 1993–94 prices, which are possible due to the overlap between the two series, the difference is not large and can go either way.

CHAPTER 9

1. I provide a formal derivation of the investment-savings identity in appendix 2.

2. According to the Ricadian equivalence, the actions of the government are fully neutralized by offsetting actions of private agents. In this case, increased public savings through the reduction in the fiscal deficit will be offset dollar for dollar by reduced private savings.

3. Kochhar (2006, tables 2.4 and 2.5) provides international comparison of expenditures and tax revenues. Expenditures as a proportion of the GDP in India (28.4 percent) exceed those in Chile (23.6 percent), Ecuador (24 percent), and Indonesia (18.8 percent), but are exceeded by those in Brazil (48.3 percent), Turkey (42.9 percent), and Russia (36.5 percent). On the tax side, India remains on the low side with its tax to GDP ratio being well below those of Brazil, Chile, Argentina, Turkey, and Russia.

4. The act permits the ways and means advances from the RBI, which allow the government to cover "temporary excess of cash disbursement over cash receipts during any financial year." It also allows the RBI to buy and sell government securities in the secondary market.

CHAPTER 10

1. Gordon and Gupta (2004) provide an econometric analysis of the determinants of portfolio investment in India.

2. Of course, the RBI lending directly to the government of India could have achieved the same objective. But that would have explicitly raised the budget deficit, which is what the Planning Commission tried to avoid by going the SPV route. In this latter case, the government was merely to provide the loan guarantee on behalf of the SPV to the RBI.

3. Insofar as some of the resources necessary for the infrastructure projects are specific to the production of other nontraded goods, the price of these resources, and hence the prices of the nontraded goods, would rise. This adds a complication to the argument in the text but does not invalidate it.

4. Lal et al. include unilateral transfers in the capital account rather than the current account and treat them like capital inflows. As I have already discussed, the two inflows are fundamentally different.

5. According to Shah and Patnaik (2006), the only remaining current account restriction is the $10,000 ceiling on the expenses on foreign travel permitted annually.

6. See Government of India (2006).

7. ADRs are securities a non-U.S. company wishing a listing on any of the U.S. stock exchanges offers. Each ADR is backed by a certain number of the company's regular shares, which are deposited in a custodial account in the United States. ADRs allow U.S. investors to buy shares of these companies without the costs of investing directly in a foreign stock exchange. ADRs are issued by an approved New York bank or trust company against the deposit of the original shares. GDRs constitute a similar financial instrument.

8. Gordon and Gupta (2004) offer an analysis of the determinants of the NRI deposits.

9. Joshi and Sanyal, who adopt this terminology as well, point out that the rupee-dollar exchange rate barely moved between mid-1993 and mid-1995, mid-1996 and mid-1997, mid-1998 and mid-1999, and December 2000 and September 2001.

10. Also see Srinivasan and Tendulkar (2003, pp. 63–66).

11. These securities and bills are identical to those the government issues for its normal borrowing operations to avoid segmentation of the market. The government of India pays the interest on the securities or Treasury bills under the MSS out of its budgetary expenditures. See Mohan (2006) for further details.

12. Thus, I fundamentally agree with Joshi and Sanyal (2004, p. 171) who note, "India's policymakers score high marks for their conduct of the external aspects of macroeconomic policy in the 1990s."

13. The RBI Committee on Capital Account Convertibility, headed by former Deputy Governor S. S. Tarapore, which submitted its report in June 1997, recommended full convertibility within three years: 1997–98 to 1999–2000. Given the state of the Indian financial markets, this was a hugely ambitious goal. As luck would have it, simultaneously the Asian currency crisis broke out, sealing the fate of the committee's recommendations. At the urging of the prime minister, the RBI appointed another committee under Tarapore to revisit the convertibility issue in March 2006.

14. See Kletzer (2005) for a discussion of some of these studies.

15. Mukherji (2006), among others, emphasizes the importance of the financial sector development for the timing of capital account convertibility.

16. The role of the government is much more extensive than this ownership would indicate. Thus, as Buiter and Patel state, "The scope ranges across appointment of management, regulation, mobilization of resources, providing 'comfort and support' to depositors, as well as influencing lending practices of all intermediaries and the investment incentives of private corporations. An array of instruments (formal and informal) are deployed, which comprise treating banks as quasi-fiscal instruments...."

CHAPTER II

1. The economist Hernando de Soto (2000) of Peru has popularized a related but different point relating to what he calls "dead capital" in many developing countries. This concerns the absence of formal ownership rights to land, buildings, and other assets, which makes them unsuitable as collateral against a loan that can be productively invested in a

business. In this case, the problem is not the absence of an appropriate financial asset, but the absence of rights to the savings (the asset) to be intermediated. Of course, as I discuss in chapters 13 and 14 in greater dtail, the problem of dead capital noted by de Soto is pervasive in India: With virtually no land titles on farms in the rural areas (chapter 14), and rent laws that effectively rob the owner of the property right in the urban areas (chapter 13), there remains a large, untapped source of savings.

2. See RBI (2004). Some examples in these categories of institutions include (1) term-lending institutions: the Industrial Development Bank of India, the Industrial Finance Corporation of India, and the Industrial Credit and Investment Corporation of India; (2) specialized financial institutions: the EXIM Bank and the Infrastructure Development Finance Corporation; (3) refinance institutions: the National Bank of Agriculture and Rural Development, the Small Industries Development Bank of India, and the National Housing Bank (NHB); and (4) investment institutions: the Unit Trust of India (UTI), the Life Insurance Corporation of India (LIC) and the General Insurance Corporation of India (GLC), and ICICI Venture Capital Funds Ltd.

3. See Bhattacharya and Patel (2002).

4. The data on CRR and the statutory liquidity ratio (SLR) in this chapter are taken from the RBI, *Handbook of the Indian Economy* (2005a, table 45).

5. During a ten-month period beginning in September 1973, the CRR was 7 percent.

6. Various interest rate data in this chapter come from the RBI *Handbook of the Indian Economy* (2005a, table 70). The repression through this instrument seems to have declined to some degree by the end of the 1980s. For example, in 1989–90, the average annual yield on the short-term government securities with one to five years' maturity ranged from 7.6 to 18.4 percent, and the interest rate on deposits with one to three years' maturity, from 9 to 10 percent. Inflation in the second half of the 1980s being less than that in the first half, this shift represented a move toward liberalization.

7. Kletzer estimates the interest rate abroad by first dividing external interest payments on nonconcessional long-term debt by the sum of nonconcessional long-term debt and new disbursements. This gives him the interest rate facing the government for borrowing in dollar terms. Assuming that the uncovered interest rate parity holds ex post, he adds the percentage depreciation of the rupee during the year to this interest rate, to convert the latter into the rupee-equivalent interest rate. Kletzer calculates the interest rate on domestic government debt by dividing current-year interest payments by current-year outstanding government debt.

8. Net bank credit is approximately equal to bank deposits minus CRR and SLR holdings.

9. My discussion in this subsection is based almost entirely on Kochar (2005).

10. This is in contradiction to the priority sector data underlying figure 1 in Burgess, Pande, and Wong (2005), which show a declining trend in priority sector lending since 1988, with its share dropping to well below 25 percent in 1997.

11. Strictly speaking, I must look at the incremental ratio of rural and semiurban branches *in previously unbanked areas* to the branches in the urban and metropolitan areas. Unfortunately, my source does not provide the data to separate out the rural and semiurban branches in previously banked areas from the total rural and semiurban branches. But the number of these branches is likely to be relatively too small to overturn the gigantic deviations of the actual ratio from the ratio rule observed in figure 11.1.

12. I owe this point to the generosity of the economist Kishore Gwande, who has subjected the data used by Burgess and Pande to further econometric scrutiny and informally shared this preliminary finding with me.

13. In 1980, the government nationalized six additional banks. The operations of these banks were spread unevenly across states.

14. For more details, see Mohan (2006).

15. Papers by Ahluwalia (2002c), Hanson (2001), and Mohan (2006) list many of these reforms in boxes.

16. Buiter and Patel (2005–06, table A.2) provide a detailed list of the savings instruments still subject to administered rates.

17. CAMEL is a standard acronym referring to capital adequacy, asset quality, management quality, earnings, and liquidity. India added "S," for systems evaluation, to this acronym.

18. See Mohan (2006, table 5).

19. The sample includes only those banks that were in existence for the entire period covered by the study.

20. Banerjee et al. exclude the new private sector banks from the analysis because there are not enough observations on them to permit proper econometric testing.

21. Following an announcement in the 1995–96 budget, the government created a Rural Infrastructure Development Fund (RIDF) with the National Bank of Agriculture and Rural Development, and required both private and public banks to deposit an amount equal to the shortfall in the subsector lending target for agriculture in it at less than competitive interest rates.

CHAPTER 12

1. I had originally written about the poorer performance of the Indian industry as the key factor explaining why India was lagging behind China in an op-ed piece in the *Economic Times* (Panagariya 2002a). I developed this theme further (Panagariya 2004a, 2004b) in terms of the poor performance of unskilled-labor-intensive exports by India, documenting the fact that on average India had been experiencing faster growth of skilled-labor-intensive and capital-intensive goods than of unskilled-labor-intensive goods. Subsequently, Joshi (2004) embraced my idea, noting that countries such as the Republic of Korea and Thailand underwent a transformation similar to that of China. More recently, Kochhar et al. (2006) extended the idea in terms of the overall industrial structure of India being tilted toward skilled-labor-intensive and capital-intensive goods.

2. The figure relates to the one-digit SITC category 7.

3. My students Pande (2006) and Savant (2006) provide detailed accounts of the provisions and controversies surrounding the SEZs in India.

4. For a comprehensive survey of the theoretical literature on PTA arrangements, see Panagariya (2000c).

5. I base the following discussion of the India-Sri Lanka agreement on Baysan, Panagariya, and Pitigala (2006).

6. In the WTO parlance, binding a tariff implies that the country cannot raise the customs duty above its bound rate without renegotiation with its trading partners who would be adversely impacted by the increase.

CHAPTER 13

1. The pattern of growth will in general interact with the aggregate rate of growth. Here I would argue, however, that a shift in favor of unskilled-labor-intensive products in a labor-abundant country would reinforce rather than impede aggregate growth.

2. This section is based almost entirely on Panagariya (2006a).

3. Kochhar et al. (2006) provide systematic empirical evidence demonstrating the high capital and skilled-labor intensity of the Indian production structure.

4. Employment data in table 13.1 are from the Employment-Unemployment Survey of the National Sample Survey from the 55th Round. These data do not identically match those from the census quoted immediately below. Likewise, the shares in the GDP are based on the GDP data at 1999–2000 prices, and need not match those cited earlier, based on the GDP data at 1993–94 prices.

5. In the Indian context, "informal sector" refers to unincorporated household units engaged in the production of goods and services with the primary objective of generating employment and income for the household concerned. These units do not have legal status independently of the household and lack a complete set of accounts that will distinguish their income and expenditures from those of the households owning them. The nearest term to "informal sector" officially used in India, including in the national accounts statistics, is "unorganized sector" (as contrasted with the organized sector). The unorganized sector includes unincorporated household enterprises or partnership enterprises as well as enterprises run by cooperative societies, trusts, and private and limited companies. Therefore, the informal sector is a subset of the unorganized sector.

6. This census has been conducted five times so far, on an intermittent basis: in 1977, 1980, 1990, 1998, and 2005.

7. I had originally advocated this "walking on two legs" strategy in Panagariya (2005d).

8. In some parts of this section, I draw on Panagariya (2006a).

9. See Panagariya (2000b).

10. Even then, under the Trade Unions Act of 1926, seven or more workers are allowed to form a trade union.

11. I rely heavily, though not exclusively, on Datta Chaudhari (1996) for the discussion of the IDA.

12. In this context, Datta Chaudhari (1996, p. 16) offers the following insightful quotation from the High Court judge Mehta (1994): "Some judges are overwhelmed by the view that the only object and purpose of the Industrial Disputes Act is to take a view favorable only to labor, ignoring other facts and circumstances as also the necessity of preserving industrial peace. It is sometimes forgotten that the problem confronting industrial adjudication is to promote twofold objectives: (1) security of employment of the workers; and (2) preservation of industrial peace and harmony so that industry can prosper and employment can increase. Any lopsided view, that to favor labor is the only goal of the statute, is counterproductive inasmuch as it ultimately harms the cause of labor itself."

13. Several econometric studies, including Fallon and Lucas (1991, 1993), Dutta Roy (2004), Besley and Burgess (2004), and Ahsan and Pages (2005), evaluate the effects of labor laws on employment in the organized sector. Bhattacharjea (2006) provides a comprehensive and critical review of many of these studies. In my view, all these studies suffer from the problem pointed out in the text: Large-scale firms producing unskilled-labor-intensive products are missing from the sample. Some of the studies rely on data from the period when investment licensing was in full force. The principal effect of labor laws during that period was to redistribute the rents in favor of workers, with entry largely governed by licensing. These studies cannot tell us how labor laws impact entry and employment decisions in today's license-free regime. Even studies relying on more recent data suffer from the absence of large-scale firms in the unskilled-labor-intensive sectors due to both small-scale-industries reservation and the IDA of 1947. Some studies rely on differences in labor laws across states, but do so using rather crude indexes of labor market regimes. But more important, they cannot capture the effect of the stringent national laws within which state laws must be enacted.

14. The High Court is the highest court of a state in India. Its decisions can be appealed only to the Supreme Court.

15. The term "contributory" is defined in the Companies Act of 1956 as a person liable to contribute to the assets of a company in the event of its being wound up. Under this definition, the holder of any shares that are fully paid up is considered a contributory.

16. These data are taken from the BIFR Website at http://bifr.nic.in/.

17. Virtually concurrently with the Justice Eradi Committee (2000), a committee appointed by the Reserve Bank of India (2001) had recommended a separate bankruptcy code that was much closer to chapter 11 of the U.S. Bankruptcy Code.

18. I do not consider here privatization of the state public sector enterprises that account for approximately 15 percent of the total assets of all state-owned companies. According to Gupta (2006, table 3), of 1036 state public sector enterprises, only 36 had been privatized between 1991 and 2004. Of these, 13 were in Andhra Pradesh and 9 in Orissa.

19. Arun and Nixson (2000) offer a detailed account of the policy during the first phase, and Baijal (2002a, 2002b), of that during the second phase. Gupta (2006) presents an overview of the entire period, including the third phase. In the following, I draw on all these sources.

20. See Ram Mohan (2003, table 1).

21. See "Supreme Court halts privatization of HPCL, BPCL," in the newspaper *Hindu*, September 17, 2003, p. 1.

22. Ram Mohan (2002) offers some counterarguments, but they fail to persuade me.

23. Kapur and Ramamurti (2003) offer further details in the BALCO case and also discuss several others in greater detail.

24. Hotels and restaurants, which are included in the category "Trade, Hotels, andRestaurants," contributed less than 1 percent to the GDP. The bulk of the employment reported under "Trade, Hotels, and Restaurants" in the table is in trade.

CHAPTER 14

1. According to Goyal (2002), a senior civil servant, it is the rich farmers and traders who have cornered the FCI purchases. Small, poor farmers lack access to the FCI and are sometimes forced into distress selling.

2. The task force on employment opportunities, which was appointed by the Planning Commission and reported in 2001 (Planning Commission 2001, chapter 4), discusses the Essential Commodities Act, 1955, and several other policies impeding agricultural growth. It also offers suggestions for a series of reforms that may help raise agricultural productivity. It particularly emphasizes the need for the development of the food processing industry that I discuss below.

3. Visit http://www.itcportal.com/ruraldevp_philosophy/echoupal.htm to access the current information on the status of the program. The information reported in the text was taken from the Website on March 26, 2007.

4. See National Institute of Agricultural Extension Management (2003) for details. When PepsiCo established a plant for tomato processing in 1989 in Punjab, the entire supply of tomatoes in the state was insufficient to run it efficiently. The company used contract farming to ensure the necessary supply, and subsequently moved into Basmati rice for exports as well.

5. See the NSSO press note dated August 31, 2006.

6. In the following, I partially draw on Blakeslee (2006).

7. In their econometric work on India, Besley and Burgess (2000) find that it is the protection of *cultivation* rights rather than redistribution of *ownership* rights that has been more conducive to poverty reduction.

8. In 1987, Dr. Manmohan Singh, then the deputy chairman of the Planning Commission, invited Wadhwa to study the problem of the record-of-rights in land in the country and to recommend measures for improvement.

9. See http://mowr.gov.in/bharatnirman/index.htm.

CHAPTER 15

1. Since the central government is empowered to tax commodities only up to the final stage of manufacturing, it can implement tax rebates on inputs only up to that stage. The sales tax, levied on the final sale to the consumer, falls under the jurisdiction of the states. Therefore, a genuine VAT can be imposed only with the cooperation of the states. We will later see that this has been a major issue in implementing the full-scale VAT.

2. This proportion used to be higher, but has declined recently, in part due to the rising importance of the services tax, which is not included in the excise duties.

3. The figure for 2004–05 is "budget estimate."

4. Acharya (2005) and M. G. Rao and R. K. Rao (2006) briefly recount the history of tax reform in independent India going back to the 1950s. This section draws heavily on both sources.

5. The quotation is from Acharya (2005, p. 2062).

6. See Government of India (2002a, chap. 3.2).

7. As Acharya hints, this may have been partially facilitated by the switch from the dogmatic Ashok Mitra to the pragmatic Manmohan Singh as chief economic adviser in the Finance Ministry.

8. Conceptually, these are both indirect taxes, but following the practice in the Indian budget, I discuss them here.

9. In all likelihood this provision was intended to cap the evasion of additional excise duty. In principle, producers could claim products such as air conditioners, refrigerators, or glazed tiles, used in their offices, as inputs and seek a rebate on them. While this would be a legitimate and economically sensible rebate, it could also be abused. Moreover, within the Indian political setting, the use of these "luxury" items, even in offices, without paying the "sin tax" (additional excise duty) may not be acceptable.

10. For example, in its negotiations with the United States, India gave market access in apples.

11. No CST is paid on within-firm movements of consignments across states. In this case, the firm is allowed a rebate on the state VAT paid in the state of origin beyond 4 percent of the value of the consignment. This practice places within-firm consignments at par with other interstate sales. Either way, the 4 percent state tax on interstate sales remains unreimbursed.

CHAPTER 16

1. Observe that the sum of the central and state expenditures exceeds the combined expenditures because central expenditures include substantial transfers to the states that are netted out when the two sets of expenditures are combined.

2. Figures in table 16.1 are taken from the *Indian Public Finance Statistics 2005–06.* These do not exactly match those put together from budgetary figures in the RBI *Handbook of Statistics on Indian Economy,* on which figures 16.1 to 16.3 are based. The discrepancy arises from a number of adjustments the Indian Public Finance Statistics make to the budgetary figures. For example, the budget data report some pure transfers to certain funds as expenditures. Indian Public Finance Statistics drop them from expenditures. The advantage of the budgetary figures put together by the RBI *Handbook* is that they are more up-to-date, but they do not give the detailed composition available in the Indian Public Finance Statistics.

3. In the Indian context, Mundle and Rao (1991) first drew attention to the fact that actual subsidies in this sense far exceed the explicitly reported subsidies. They offered detailed sector-by-sector estimates of the implicit subsidies for the center and states for the

year 1987–88. M. G. Rao and Mundle (1992) and Srivastava and Sen (1997) have replicated this work for other years.

4. Until 1992, this scheme also applied to potash and phosphate fertilizers. In 1992, these fertilizers were decontrolled and the subsidies were removed. But sharp increases in their prices led to the reintroduction of price controls sustained through subsidy. While potash fertilizer is wholly imported, phosphate fertilizer is partially domestically produced. The subsidy is applied to keep the price to the farmer low.

5. In fairness to the Marathe Committee, it may be noted that it had recommended a groupwise rather than a unit-by-unit scheme to calculate the production cost and subsidy. It explicitly warned against the dangers of adopting the unit-by-unit approach.

6. Here the relevant import price is inclusive of the cost of delivery to the farmer and the export price is the net price the exporter receives.

7. See Gulati and Narayanan (2003, chap. 3) in this context.

8. The argument made in this paragraph is slightly modified if we assume that, as is likely, India has market power in the world market; that is to say, the world price itself depends on how much India exports or imports.

9. See the editorial "Fertilizer Famine," *Business Standard,* December 14, 2006.

10. I made this case originally in Panagariya (2001a).

11. See Viren Kaushik, "Fertilizer Subsidy Demystified," *Business Line,* September 1, 2004.

12. See Government of India, Ministry of Finance, *Economic Survey 2001–02.*

13. I discussed some of the reforms relating to the public distribution system in Panagariya (2002d).

14. Regarding the former, Shourie describes in detail an instance in which senior officers in several ministries wrote numerous memos and participated in many meetings to decide what should be the color of the ink used in the files by officers of different ranks. Regarding the latter, Shourie reports the case of a tree falling on the residence of the Indian high commissioner in Singapore and the inability of the officers involved to reach a decision on what repairs should be made, how they should be made, and by whom they should be made for *nine years.* In the meantime, the government spent 650,000 rupees per month on rent on "temporary" accommodation.

15. The rest of this section is largely drawn from Panagariya (2005c).

16. See Panagariya (2000d).

CHAPTER 17

1. In addition to the sources cited at appropriate points, my discussion in this section draws on Noll and Bagchi (2000), Chakravarti (2004), R. Gupta (2001), and Noll and Wallsten (2004, 2005–06). Two book-length treatments of the sector are McDowell (1997) and Desai (2006).

2. These data are taken from the Web site of the Department of Telecommunications, India.

3. See Bagchi (2000, p. 12).

4. McDowell (1997) provides further details on both the evolution of the sector and the political economy underlying it.

5. See Chakravarti (2004, p. 237).

6. See Mody (1995, p. 115).

7. According to Chakravarti (2004, p. 242), the government picked the entrepreneurs from among the handicapped, war widows, "backward" classes, and retired DoT officials.

8. These were the Nanda Committee, the ICICI Committee, and the Gupta Committee, respectively.

9. Value-added services included e-mail, voice mail, data services, video conferencing, radio paging, and cellular telephone. See the Telecom Policy of 1994.

10. Quite amazingly, the main governing legislation, the Indian Telegraph Policy Act of 1885, has not been replaced by a more modern law.

11. This information is taken from the Web site of the DoT. As we will see below, subsequently the licensees were permitted to move to the New Telecom Policy of 1999 regime, wherein they are required to pay a license fee based on revenue share, which became effective August 1, 1999.

12. The authority had been set up in January 1997, but did not have statutory status until the Parliament passed the TRAI Bill. It had been held up for at least two sessions in the Rajya Sabha, where the opposition dominated.

13. See R. Gupta (2001, p. 12).

14. See R. Gupta (2001, p. 20).

15. See R. Gupta (2001, pp. 24–28) for details.

16. Data in this paragraph are from Telecom Regulatory Authority of India (2005–06, pp. 35–38).

17. The paper by Noll and Wallsten (2005–06) provides an excellent, detailed critique of the USO. My discussion below draws on it.

18. Pradip Baijal, who served as the chairman of the TRAI from 2003 to 2006, has forcefully made this point in a variety of forums.

19. See Planning Commission (2005, table 10.5).

20. According to the Ministry of Power (1993, p. 24), five private companies existed in the early 1990s. Of these, two—the Tata Electricity Company and CESC—had existed since at least the early 1900s and accounted for 75 percent of the total private sector installed capacity reported by the Ministry of Power (1993). The Gujarat and Andhra Pradesh state governments promoted two other companies, Gujarat Industrial Power Company Limited and Andhra Pradesh Gas Power Corporation, during the 1980s. I have been unable to trace the origins of the remaining company, known as the A.E. Company. The implication is that there was virtually no genuine private sector entry in electricity generation after the Electricity Act of 1948.

21. Recent reforms, described below in detail, have begun to unbundle the traditionally vertically integrated SEBs into their components—generation, transmission, and distribution—and have constituted them as independent companies.

22. The states issued bonds worth 315.8 billion rupees (approximately $7 billion) to securitize their share of the debt burden.

23. See Dubash (2005, pp. 3–4).

24. Dubash (2005, p. 5) notes that the Home Ministry argued that the act was unconstitutional, and the Ministry of Power and the Central Electricity Authority were hostile to see their powers erode.

25. In July 2005, the Delhi Electricity Regulatory Commission announced a 10 percent hike in the tariff. This led to widespread public protests, forcing the government and the companies to roll back the tariff increase and work out an arrangement whereby they equally shared the cost of the rollback.

CHAPTER 18

1. The airlines in existence at the time included Air India Ltd., Air Services of India Ltd., Airways (India) Ltd., Bharat Airways Ltd., Deccan Airways Ltd., Himalayan Aviation Ltd., Indian National Airways Ltd., Kalinga Airlines, Air India International Ltd. and "existing air

2. Under the law, these carriers could operate only nonscheduled flights. But the flights actually operated like scheduled flights.

3. East-West Airlines and Modi-Luft Airlines, which had entered the industry in the 1990s, are no longer in existence.

4. DFI up to 100 percent of the equity in airports is permitted through the automatic route. Additionally, there is complete exemption from taxation on airport projects for ten years.

5. The Web site of the PMGSY is unclear about the precise relationship of the PMGSY as launched under the NDA and the rural road construction under Bharat Nirman. Even more problematic are the data on rural road construction reported on the Web site. It seemingly offers detailed data on contracted and completed projects by states and by year under PMGSY. But the data on completion remain the same for all years. The data reported under Bharat Nirman being clearer, I have chosen to report them in the text.

6. I was unable to obtain a copy of the study by the Central Institute of Road Transport and the have relied on Sriraman (2006) for the information reported in the text.

7. See Raghuram (2007).

CHAPTER 19

1. See Devarajan and Shah (2004) for an overview of the issues in the delivery of social services and World Bank (2004) for detailed discussion of the lessons of international experience in this area.

2. In all likelihood the WDI data report the combined expenditures on health and on water supply and sanitation as expenditures on health. Expenditures on health alone have hovered around 0.9 percent in India in recent years.

3. I have taken all information on subcenters, PHCs, and CHCs up to this point from the Government of India (2005–06a).

4. See Satpathy and Venkatesh (2006).

5. The following discussion of the private sector is based on Radwan (2005).

6. See Government of India (2005a, tables 6.1.1 and 6.1.3).

7. AYUSH refers to the system of traditional medicine in India that covers *ayurveda,* yoga-naturopathy, *unani, sidha,* and homeopathy.

8. Information in this paragraph is taken from Satpathy and Venkatesh (2006).

9. The statistics in this paragraph are from the Government of India (2005a, chapter 1.2).

10. See Government of India (2005b).

11. See Ministry of Health and Family Welfare, Government of India, "National Health Policy 2002," paragraph 2.4.1.

12. For this, a good starting point is the World Bank report, which remains relevant today.

13. See the mission document of the NRHM at the Web site of the Ministry of Health, Government of India (http://mohfw.nic.in/nrhm.html).

14. My discussion of HIV/AIDS relies exclusively on the excellent paper by Gupta (2006), who carefully documents the sources of the data cited below.

15. See para. 4.5.1.1 of the policy.

16. Interestingly, as noted below, China has the policy of full cost recovery in the WSS projects. Customers in villages are provided house connections, but they pay.

CHAPTER 20

1. The survey covered 549 out of 575 districts in all.

2. Private-school teachers are typically young men from the village who have acquired a college degree and are looking for better opportunities. Teaching in the village private school gives them some income and the flexibility necessary to scout around for alternative jobs.

3. The central, state, or local governments may run the government schools. Private management runs the government-aided schools, but they are largely funded by grants-in-aid from the state governments. As Kingdon (2005) notes, these schools were independent in the 1950s and 1960s, but have increasingly come to be controlled by the government and are run like government schools. In most states, their teachers are now paid directly by the state government, at the same rate as the teachers in the government schools. Independent private management runs private unaided schools without interference from the government. When the government authorities do not formally recognize a school, it is called "unrecognized." The practical implication of a school's being unrecognized is that students may sometimes encounter difficulty in transferring to a recognized school.

4. As A. Kochar (2005b, 2006) points out, there is a serious limitation of this avenue as well. Wealthier households often opt out of public schools by sending their children to private schools, and do not have a stake in monitoring the teacher performance in the public schools. Therefore, even passing the supervisory control to the local level may not yield the desired result.

5. Two recent contributions advocating education vouchers are Kelkar (2006) and Muralidharan (2006). The former favors vouchers to all, and the latter to the poor only.

6. This is not unrealistic, given the 125 rupees per month fee in the unrecognized private schools in the Shahdara, reported by Tooley and Dixon (undated).

7. It may be noted that the original model of aided schools was equivalent to a voucher system, with every student (rather than just the poor ones) entitled to the voucher. Administratively, the government transferred the value of the voucher directly to the school in the form of aid per student. But this way of administering the system gave the teachers a sense of entitlement that led them to demand salaries directly from the state and at rates applicable to their government school counterparts. It also led the schools to exaggerate their enrollments in order to claim larger aid. A voucher scheme exclusively for the poor does not suffer from this problem, since it makes clear that the entitlement is to the poor rather than to the school.

8. For example, see Gopalkrishnan and Sharma (1998), Leclerq (2003), Sharma and Gopalkrishnan (2003), and Clarke (2003). My discussion in this paragraph is based on the summary of these studies in Howes and Murgai (2006, box 8.1).

9. See Government of India (2005–06b, chap. 10).

10. These figures are taken from the UIS (UNESCO Institute of Statistics) database. Generically, gross enrollment ratio is defined as the ratio of the pupils enrolled in a given level of education (regardless of age) to the theoretical age group for the same level of education. For the indicators reported in the text, UIS uses the five-year age group following the secondary school leaving age as the denominator. This age group is different from the (larger) six-year age group used to compute the gross enrollment ratio in higher education in table 13.5.

11. For a comprehensive and up-to-date overview of the Indian higher education system, see Agarwal (2006).

12. In addition to the sources cited, I draw on Panagariya (2001b, 2001c, and 2002e) in this section.

13. As I describe later, dramatic changes have taken place in the 2000s, with the number of deemed private universities expanding rapidly as the route to private universities through acts of state legislative assemblies has opened up.

14. Kripalani (2006) places this figure at $4.5 billion. This would mean $30,000 per student, which is on the higher side, since many students come on scholarships and the fees in Canada and Australia are substantially below those in the United States, where they average $30,000.

15. In ancient India, it was Brahmins, the intellectual class, who occupied the highest status in the society, and not Kshatriyas, the warrior class, from whom kings and queens were drawn, or the Vaishyas, the trader class, that produced wealth.

16. Some of my friends who graduated from IITs tell me that in retrospect, the value added in the classrooms there fades in comparison with what they got in the U.S. universities.

17. See Naik (2001).

18. See the Supreme Court judgment dated February 11, 2005, on writ of petition 19 of 2004.

19. See Agarwal (2006, p. 9).

20. See Agarwal (2006) for further details.

21. See Xue (2006) for details on the evolution of higher education and policies toward it in China.

22. See Agarwal (2006).

23. See Agarwal (2006).

24. See Kapur and Mehta (2004, sec. V).

25. See Varghese (2000, tables 1 and 3).

26. See Central Advisory Board of Education (2005, table 9).

27. See Government of India (1992–93, para. 2.16).

28. See Barr (2005).

REFERENCES

Acharya, Shankar. (2004). "Forex for Infrastructure, Anyone?" *Business Standard*, October 24.
———. (2005). "Thirty Years of Tax reform in India," *Economic and Political Weekly* 40(20), May 14–20: 2061–69.
———, Isher Ahluwalia, K. L. Krishna, and Ila Patnaik. (2003). "India: Economic Growth: 1950–2000." Global Research Project on Growth, Indian Council for Research on International Economic Relations. Mimeo.
Agarwal, Pawan. (2006). "Higher Education in India: The Need for Change" Working Paper no. 180. New Delhi: Indian Council for Research on International Economic Relations.
Aggarwal, Aradhna. (2002). "Antidumping Law and Practice: An Indian Perspective." ICRIER working paper 85.
Ahluwalia, Isher J. (1991). *Productivity and Growth in Indian Manufacturing*. Delhi: Oxford University Press.
———. (1994). "TFPG in Manufacturing Industry." *Economic and Political Weekly*, October 22, 2836.
Ahluwalia, M. S. (2001). "State Level Performance Under Economic Reforms in India." Working Paper no. 96, Center for Research on Economic Development and Policy Reform, Stanford University (March).
———. (2002a). "Economic Reforms in India Since 1991: Has Gradualism Worked?" *Journal of Economic Perspectives*, 16 (3), 67–88.
———. (2002b). "India's Vulnerability to External Crises." In M. Ahluwalia, Y. V. Reddy, and S. S. Tarapore (eds.), *Macroeconomics and Monetary Policy: Issues for a Reforming Economy* (pp. 183–214). New Delhi: Oxford University Press.
———. (2002c). "Financial Sector Reforms in India: An Assessment." Paper presented at the conference "Financial Sector Reform Across Asia: Facts, Analyses, Solutions." Kennedy School of Government, Harvard University, December 10–11.
Ahsan, Ahmad, and Carmen Pages. (2005). "Helping or Hurting Workers?: Assessing the Effects of *De Jure* and *De Facto* Labor Regulation in India." Washington, DC: World Bank. Mimeo.

Amsdan, Alice. (1989). *Asia's Next Giant: South Korea and Late Industrialization.* Oxford: Oxford University Press.

Appu, P. S. (1996). *Land Reforms in India: A Survey of Policy Legislation and Implementation.* New Delhi: Vikas.

Arun, T. G., and F. I. Nixson. (2000). "The Disinvestment of Public Sector Enterprises: The Indian Experience." *Oxford Development Studies,* 28 (1), 19–32.

———, and J. D. Turner. (2002). "Public Sector Banks in India: Rationale and Prerequisites for Reform." *Annals of Public and Cooperative Economics,* 73 (1), 89–109.

Athreye, Suma, and Sandeep Kapur. (2001). "Private Foreign Investment in India: Pain or Panacea?" *World Economy,* 24 (3), 399–424.

Austin, Granville. (2000). *Working a Democratic Constitution: A History of the Indian Experience.* New Delhi: Oxford University Press.

Bagchi, Pradipta. (2000). "Telecommunications Reform and the State in India: The Contradiction of Private Control and Government Competition." CASI Occasional Working Paper 13, Center for the Advanced Study of India (December).

Baijal, Pradip. (2002a). "Privatization: Gains to Taxpayers and Employees." *Economic and Political Weekly* 37(17), April 27–May 03, 1595–98.

———. (2002b). "Privatisation: Compulsions and Options for Economic Reform." *Economic and Political Weekly* 37(41), October 12–18, pp. 4189–95.

Balakrishnan, P., and K. Pushpangandan. (1994). "Total Factor Productivity Growth in Manufacturing Industry: A Fresh Look." *Economic and Political Weekly,* July 30, 2028–35.

Banerjee, Abhijit V., Shawn Cole, and Esther Duflo. (2004). "Banking Reform in India." *India Policy Forum,* 1, 277–332.

———, Shawn Cole, Esther Duflo, and Leigh Linden. (2006). "Remedying Education: Evidence from Two Randomized Experiments in India." Mimeo. Forthcoming in the *Quarterly Journal of Economics.*

Bardhan, Pranab. (2006). "Globalization Hits Road Bumps in India." *Yale Global Online,* October 3. Available at http://yaleglobal.yale.edu/display.article?id=8246.

Barr, Nicholas. (2005). "Financing Higher Education." *Finance and Development,* 42 (5).

Baysan, Tercan, Arvind Panagariya, and Nihal Pitigala. (2006). "Preferential Trading in South Asia." WPS 3813. Washington, DC: World Bank.

Bertaud, Alain. (2004). "Mumbai FSI Conundrum: The Perfect Storm. The Four Factors Restricting the Construction of New Floor Space in Mumbai." Available at http://alain-bertaud.com/AB_Files/AB_Mumbai_FSI_conundrum.pdf.

Besley, Timothy, and Robin Burgess. (2000). Land Reform, Poverty Reduction, and Growth: Evidence from India." *Quarterly Journal of Economics,* 115 (2), 389–430.

———. (2004). "Can Regulation Hinder Economic Performance? Evidence from India." *Quarterly Journal of Economics,* 119, 91–134.

Bhagwati, Jagdish. (1988). "Poverty and Public Policy." *World Development,* 16 (5), 539–55.

———. (1993). *India in Transition: Freeing the Economy.* Oxford: Clarendon Press.

———. (1998). "The Capital Myth: The Difference Between Trade in Widgets and Dollars." *Foreign Affairs,* 77 (3), 7–12.

———. (1999). "The 'Miracle' That Did Happen: Understanding East Asia in Comparative Perspective." Available at http://www.columbia.edu/~jb38/East_asian_miracle.pdf. Published version in Eric Thorbecke and Henry Wan, Jr. (eds.), *Taiwan's Development Experience: Lessons on Roles of Government and Market.* Boston: Kluwer Academic.

———. (2004). *In Defense of Globalization.* New York: Oxford University Press.

———, and Padma Desai. (1970). *India: Planning for Industrialization.* Oxford: Oxford University Press.

———, and Arvind Panagariya. (2004). "Great Expectations." *Wall Street Journal,* May 24.

Bhagwati, Jagdish, and T. N. Srinivasan. (1975). *Foreign Trade Regimes and Economic Development: India*. New York: National Bureau of Economic Research.

Bhalla, Surjit. (2002). *Imagine There's No Country*. Washington, DC: Institute for International Economics.

———. (2004). "Tax Rates, Tax Compliance and Tax Revenues: India, 1988–2004." Available at http://www.oxusresearch.com/downloads/ce070704.pdf.

———, and Tirthatanmoy Das. (2006). "Pre- and Post-reform India: A Revised Look at Employment, Wages and Inequality." *India Policy Forum,* 2, 182–253.

Bhargava, Sandeep, and Vijay Joshi. (1990). "Faster Growth in India: Facts and a Tentative Explanation." *Economic and Political Weekly*, 25 (48–49), 2657–62.

Bhattacharjea, Aditya. (2006). "Labor Market Regulation and Industrial Performance in India: A Critical Review of the Empirical Evidence." Working Paper no. 141, Center for Development Economics, Delhi School of Economics.

Bhattacharya, Saugata, and Urjit Patel. (2002). "Financial Intermediation in India: A Case of Aggravated Moral Hazard?." Working Paper no. 145, CREDPR, Stanford University (July).

Blakeslee, David Samuel. (2006). "Land Reform in India." Paper written for the course "Indian Economy in Transition," Columbia University (December).

Bosworth, Barry, Susan Collins, and Arvind Virmani. (2007). "Sources of Growth in the Indian Economy." *India Policy Forum*, 3, forthcoming.

Buiter, Willem, and Urjit Patel. (2005–06). "Excessive Budget Deficits, a Government-abused Financial System and Fiscal Rules." *India Policy Forum*, 2, 1–38.

Burgess, Robin, and Rohini Pande. (2005). "Can Rural Banks Reduce Poverty? Evidence from the Indian Social Banking Experiment." *American Economic Review*, 95 (3), 780–95.

———, Rohini Pande, and Grace Wong. (2005). "Banking for the Poor: Evidence from India." *Journal of the European Economic Association*, 3(2–3), 268–278.

Calvo, Guillermo, and Carmen Reinhart. (2002). "Fear of Floating." *Quarterly Journal of Economics*, 117 (2), 379–408.

Central Advisory Board of Education. (2005). *Financing of Higher and Technical Education*. New Delhi: National Institute of Educational Planning and Administration (June).

Cha, Myung Soo. (2004). "Facts and Myths about Korea's Economic Past." *Australian Economic History Review*, 44 (3), 278–93.

Chakravarti, Paula. (2004). "Telecom, National Development and the Indian State: A Postcolonial Critique." *Media, Culture & Society*, 26 (2), 227–49.

Chand, Satish, and Kunal Sen. (2002). "Trade Liberalization and Productivity Growth: Evidence from Indian Manufacturing." *Review of Development Economics*, 6 (1), 120–32.

Chaudhury, Namzul, Jeffrey Hammer, Michael Kremer, Karthik Muralidharan, and H. Rogers. (2006). "Missing in Action: Teacher and Health Care Worker Absence in Developing Countries." *Journal of Economic Perspectives*, 20 (1), 91–116.

Chaudhury, Praveen K., Vijay L. Kelkar, and Vikash Yadav. (2004). "The Evolution of 'Homegrown Conditionality' in India: IMF Relations." *Journal of Development Studies,* 40 (6), 59–81.

Clarke, Prema. (2003). "Education Reform in the Education Guarantee Scheme in Madhya Pradesh, India, and the Fundescola Program in Brazil." Background paper prepared for the *World Development Report 2004*. New Delhi: World Bank.

Cohen, Stephen P. (2000). "India and America: An Emerging Relationship." Paper presented to the Conference on the Nation-State System and Transnational Forces in South Asia, Kyoto, Japan.

Cole, Shawn. (2004). "Fixing Market Failures or Fixing Elections? Agricultural Credit in India." MIT, mimeo.

Crisil Research. (2005). *Retailing*. Crisil Research Annual Review (September). Available at http://www.crisil.com/research/research-industry-information-report-retailing-contents.pdf.

Dandekar, V. M., and N. Rath. (1971). *Poverty in India*. Pune: Indian School of Political Economy.

Das, Gurcharan. (2000). *India Unbound: A Personal Account of a Social and Economic Revolution*. New York: Knopf.

Das, Jishnu, and Jeffrey Hammer. (2006). "Which Doctor? Combining Vignettes and Item-Response to Measure Doctor Quality." WPS 3301. Washington, DC: World Bank.

Datt, Gaurav. (1998). "Poverty in India and Indian States: An Update." Discussion Paper no. 47, International Food Policy Research Institute (July).

———. (1999). "Has Poverty in India Declined During the Post Reform Period?" International Food Policy Research Institute (February). Mimeo.

Datta Chaudhari, Mrinal. (1996). "Labor Markets as Social Institutions in India." IRIS-India Working Paper no. 10, Center on the Institutional Reform and Informal Sector, University of Maryland at College Park.

Deaton, Angus. (2001a). "Adjusted Indian Poverty Estimates for 1999–2000." Research Program in Development Studies, Princeton University. Available at http://www.wws.princeton.edu/~rpds.

———. (2001b). "Computing Prices and Poverty Rates in India, 1999–2000." Research Program in Development Studies, Princeton University. Available at http://www.wws.princeton.edu/~rpds.

———. (2005). "Poverty Trends in India Since 1999–2000." Princeton University, mimeo.

———, and Jean Drèze. (2002). "Poverty and Inequality in India: A Reexamination." *Economic and Political Weekly*, September 7, 3729–48.

Deaton, Angus, and Valerie Kozel. (2005). "Data and Dogma: The Great Indian Poverty Debate." *World Bank Research Observer*, 20 (2), 177–99.

Deaton, Angus, and Alessandro Tarozzi. (2000). "Prices and Poverty in India." Research Program in Development Studies, Princeton University. Available at http://www.wws.princeton.edu/~rpds.

DeLong, J. Bradford. (2003). "India Since Independence: An Analytic Growth Narrative." In Dani Rodrik (ed.), *In Search of Prosperity: Analytic Narratives of Economic Growth*. Princeton, NJ: Princeton University Press.

Demetriades, Panicos O., and Kul B. Luintel. (1996). "Financial Development, Economic Growth and Banking Sector Controls: Evidence from India." *Economic Journal*, 106, 359–74.

Deshpande, R. S. (2002). "Suicide by Farmers in Karnataka: Agrarian Distress and Possible Alleviatory Steps." *Economic and Political Weekly*, 37 (25), 2601–10.

Desai, Ashok. (1994). *My Economic Affair*, 2nd ed. New Delhi: Wiley Eastern Limited.

———. (1999). "The Economics and Politics of Transition to an Open Market Economy: India." OECD Working Paper 7/100.

———. (2006). *India's Telecommunications Industry: History, Analysis, Diagnosis*. New Delhi: Sage Publications India.

De Soto, Hernando. (2000). *The Mystery of Capital: Why Capitalism Triumphs in the West and Fails Everywhere Else*. New York: Basic Books.

Devarajan, Shanta, and Shekhar Shah. (2004). "Making Services Work for India's Poor." *Economic and Political Weekly*, February 28, 907–19.

Dhar, Biswajit. "State Regulation of Private Foreign Capital in India." http://isidev.nic.in/pdf/statreg.pdf.

Dholakia, B. H., and R. H. Dholakia. (1994). "Total Factor Productivity Growth in Manufacturing Industry." *Economic and Political Weekly*, December 31, 3342–44.

Dimaranan, Betina, Elena Ianchovichina, and Will Martin. (2007). "Competing with Giants: Who Wins, Who Loses?" In Alan Winters and Shahid Yusuf (eds.), *Dancing with Giants: China, India, and the Global Economy*. Singapore: Institute of Policy Studies.

Dubash, Navroz K. (2005). "The New Regulatory Policies of the Electricity of India: Independent, Embedded or Transcendent?" Paper presented at the workshop "The Politics of Necessity," Oxford University, September 9–10.

Duflo, Esther, and Rema Hanna. (2005). "Monitoring Works: Getting Teachers to Come to School." NBER Working Paper no. 11880. Forthcoming in the *American Economic Review.*

Dutt, S. (1969) *Report of the Industrial Licensing Policy Enquiry Committee.* New Delhi: Government of India.

Dutta Roy, S. (2004). "Employment Dynamics in Indian Industry: Adjustment Lags and the Impact of Job Security Regulations." *Journal of Development Economics,* 73, 233–56.

Electricity Governance Initiative-India (2005). "Electricity Governance Initiative-India: Draft Indicators." Cited in Dubash (2005).

Fallon, P., and R. E. B. Lucas. (1991). "The Impact of Changes in Job Security Regulations in India and Zimbabwe." *World Bank Economic Review,* 5, 295–413.

———. (1993). "Job Security Regulations and the Dynamic Demand for Labor in India and Zimbabwe." *Journal of Development Economics,* 40, 241–75.

Fields, Gary. (1980). *Poverty, Inequality and Development.* Cambridge: Cambridge University Press.

Forbes, Kristin. (2000). "A Reassessment of the Relationship Between Inequality and Growth." *American Economic Review,* 90 (4), 869–87.

Franda, Marcus F. (1968). *West Bengal and the Federalizing Process in India.* Princeton, NJ: Princeton University Press.

Glinskaya, Elena, and Michael Lokshin. (2005). "Wage Differentials Between Public and Private Sector in India." WPS 3574. Washington, DC: World Bank.

Gohain, K. (2005). "Airline Operations: Regulatory Issues in India." PowerPoint file posted on the Web site of the Ministry of Civil Aviation (http://civilaviation.nic.in/).

Goldar, B., and V. S. Renganathan. (1990). "Liberalization of Capital Goods Imports in India." Working Paper no. 8, National Institute of Public Finance and Policy, New Delhi.

Gopalkrishnan, R., and Amita Sharma. (1998). "Education Guarantee Scheme in Madhya Pradesh: Innovative Step to Universalize Education." *Economic and Political Weekly,* September 26.

Gordon, Jim, and Poonam Gupta. (2003a). "Understanding India's Services Revolution." Paper presented at the IMF-NCAER conference "A Tale of Two Giants: India's and China's Experience with Reform." New Delhi, November 14–16.

———. (2003b). "Portfolio Flows in India: Do Domestic Fundamentals Matter?" IMF Working Paper no. 03/20. Washington, DC: IMF.

———. (2004). "Nonresident Deposits in India: In Search of Return?" IMF Working Paper no. 04/48. Washington, DC: IMF.

Government of India. (1971). *Direct Taxes Enquiry Committee: Final Report.* New Delhi: Ministry of Finance.

———. (1977). *Report of the Indirect Taxation Enquiry Committee.* New Delhi: Ministry of Finance.

———. (1992). *Tax Reforms Committee, Interim Report.* New Delhi: Ministry of Finance.

———. (1992–93). *UGC Funding of Institutions of Higher Education. Report of Justice Dr. K. Punayya Committee.* New Delhi: University Grants Commission.

———. (1993). *Report of the Tax Reforms Committee.* New Delhi: Ministry of Finance.

———. (2001). *Report of the Expert Group on Taxation of Services.* New Delhi: Ministry of Finance.

———. (2002a). *Report of the Task Force on Direct Taxes.* New Delhi: Ministry of Finance (December). http://finmin.nic.in/kelkar/final_dt.htm.

———. (2002b). *Report of the Task Force on Indirect Taxes.* New Delhi: Ministry of Finance (December). http://finmin.nic.in/kelkar/final_idt.htm.

———. (2002c). "National Health Policy 2002," New Delhi: Ministry of Health and Family Welfare.

———. (2004). *Report of the Task Force on the Implementation of the Fiscal Responsibility and Budget Management Act*, New Delhi: Ministry of Finance.

———. (2005a). *National Health Profile 2005.* New Delhi: Central Bureau of Health Intelligence, Ministry of Health and Family Welfare.

———. (2005b). *Report of the National Commission on Macroeconomics and Health.* New Delhi: Ministry of Health and Family Welfare.

———. (2005–06a). *Annual Report 2005–06.* New Delhi: Ministry of Health and Family Welfare.

———. (2005–06b). *Annual Report 2005–06.* New Delhi: Ministry of Human Resource Development.

———. (2006a). *Foreign Direct Investment Policy.* New Delhi: Department of Industrial Policy and Promotion, Ministry of Commerce and Industry.

———. (2006b). *Economic Survey 2006–07*, New Delhi: Ministry of Finance.

———. (2007). *Economic Survey 2006–07*, New Delhi: Ministry of Finance.

Goyal, Prashant. (2002). "Food Security in India." *Hindu*, January 10.

Gulati, Ashok. (2000). "Grain of Truth." *India Today* (25th anniversary issue), 102–03.

———, and Sudha Narayanan. (2003). *The Subsidy Syndrome.* New Delhi: Oxford University Press.

Gupta, Amita. (2006). "Combating HIV/AIDS in India: Public-Private Partnerships Are Necessary for Success." Paper presented at the conference "Challenges of Economic Policy Reform in Asia," Stanford Center for International Development, June 1–3.

Gupta, Nandini. (2005). "Partial Privatization and Firm Performance." *Journal of Finance,* 60 (2), 987–1015.

———. (2006). "Privatization in South Asia." Kelley School of Business, Indiana University. Mimeo.

Gupta, Rajni. (2001). "India Attempts to Give a Jump-start to Its Derailed Telecommunications Liberalization Process." Paper presented at the 29th Telecommunications Policy and Research Conference, Alexandria, VA, October 27–29.

Gupta, S. P (2002a), Chairman, Planning Commission "Report of the Steering Committee on Labour & Employment for the 10th Five Year Plan (2002–2007)." New Delhi: Planning Commission.

———. (2002b). "Report of the Special Group on targeting Ten Million Employment Opportunities per Year over the 10th Plan Period." New Delhi: Planning Commission.

Gurley, John G., and E. S. Shaw. (1956). "Financial Intermediaries and the Savings-Investment Process." *Journal of Finance*, 11 (2), 257–76.

Hanson, James. (2001). "Indian Banking: Market Liberalization and the Pressures for Institutional and Market Framework Reform." Working Paper no. 104, Stanford Center for International Development, Stanford University.

Harvie, Charles, and Hyun-Hoon Lee. (2003). "Export Led Industrialization and Growth: Korea's Economic Miracle 1962–1989." *Australian Economic History Review*, 43 (3), 256–86.

Hasan, Rana, Devashish Mitra, and Beyza Ural. (2007). "Trade Liberalization, Labor Market Institutions and Poverty Reduction: Evidence from Indian States." *India Policy Forum 3*, forthcoming.

Hathi Committee on the Indian Drug Industry. (1975). *Report of the Committee on Drugs and Pharmaceutical Industry.* New Delhi: Government of India.

Hazari, R. K. (1967) *Industrial Planning and Licensing Policy in India*. New Delhi: Planning Commission.

Howes, Stephen, and Rinku Murgai. (2006). "Subsidies and Salaries: Issues in the Restructuring of Government Expenditure in India." In Peter Heller and Govinda Rao (eds.), *Sustainable Fiscal Policy for India* (pp. 216–71). New Delhi: Oxford University Press.

Hulten, Charles R. (1975). "Technical Change and the Reproducibility of Capital." *American Economic Review*, 65 (5), 956–65.

———, and Syleja Srinivasan. (1999). "Indian Manufacturing Industry: Elephant or Tiger? New Evidence on the Asian Miracle." NBER Working Paper 7441.

Jagannathan, N. Vijay. (2006). "Story of a Hiss: Water Scarcity and the Need for Reform." *Economic and Political Weekly*, March 11, 925–27.

Joshi, V. (2003). "India and the Impossible Trinity." *World Economy*, 26 (4), 555–83.

———. (2004). "Myth of India's Outsourcing Boom." *Financial Times*, November 16.

———, and I. M. D. Little. (1994). *India: Macroeconomics and Political Economy: 1961–91*. Washington, DC: World Bank.

Joshi, V., and Sanjeev Saanyal. (2004). "Foreign Inflows and Macroeconomic Policy in India." *India Policy Forum*, 1, 135–87.

Justice V. B. Eradi Committee. (2000). *Report on Law Relating to Insolvency of Companies*. Department of Company Affairs (July). http://www.dca.nic.in/comp/insolv-comp.html.

Kang, Nimrit, and Nitin Nayar. (2003–04). "The Evolution of Corporate Bankruptcy Law in India." *Money & Finance*, October 2003–March 2004, 37–58.

Kapur, Devesh, and Pratap Mehta. (2004). "Indian Higher Education Reform: From Half-Baked Socialism to Half-Baked Capitalism." Working Paper no. 108, Center for International Development, Harvard University (September).

Karunakaran, Naren. (2006). "Growth for All." *India Abroad,* special supplement (December), 40–41.

Kelkar, Vijay. (2004). "India on the Growth Turnpike." K. R. Narayanan Oration, Australian National University, April 27.

———. (2006). "Educating the Government." *India Today*, January 16.

Khatkhate, Deena. (1990). "Monetary Policy in India: A Command Approach." *Economic and Political Weekly*, August 18, 1856–58.

———. (2006). "Indian Economic Reform: A Philosopher's Stone." *Economic and Political Weekly*, June 3, 2203–05.

Khwaja, Asim, and Atif Mian. (2004). "Corruption and Politicians: Rent-seeking in an Emerging Financial Market." Harvard University. Mimeo.

Kidron, Michael. (1965). *Foreign Investment in India*. London: Oxford University Press.

Kingdon, Geeta Gandhi. (2005). "Private and Public Schooling: The Indian Experience." Paper presented at the conference "Mobilizing the Private Sector for Public Education." Kennedy School of Government, Harvard University, October 5–6.

Kletzer, Kenneth. (2005). "Liberalizing Capital Flows in India: Financial Repression, Macroeconomic Policy and Gradual Reforms." *India Policy Forum*, 1, 227–75.

Kochar, Anjini. (2005). "Social Banking and Poverty: A Micro-empirical Analysis of the Indian Experience." Stanford Center for International Development, Stanford University. Mimeo.

———. (2006). "Comments on the Subsidies and Salaries: Issues in Restructuring of Government Expenditures in India." In Peter Heller and Govinda Rao (eds.), *Sustainable Fiscal Policy for India* (pp. 272–77). New Delhi: Oxford University Press.

Kochhar, Kalpana. (2006). "Macroeconomic Implications of the Fiscal Imbalances." In Peter Heller and Govinda Rao (eds.), *Sustainable Fiscal Policy for India*. New Delhi: Oxford University Press.

———, Raghuram Rajan, Arvind Subramanian, and Ioannis Tokatlidis. (2006). "India's Pattern of Development: What Happened, What Follows." NBER Working Paper no. 12023.

Kohli, A. (2006). "Politics of Economic Growth in India, 1980–2005. Part I, The 1980s." *Economic and Political Weekly* 41(13), April 1–7, 1251–59.

KPMG. (2006). *Now Boarding: Indian Airports.* New Delhi: KPMG.

Kripalani, Manjeet. (2006). "India's Affirmative Action Rocks the Boat." *Business Week*, May 15.

Krishna, Pravin, and Arvind Panagariya. (2001). "A Unification of the Second Best Results in International Trade." *Journal of International Economics,* 52 (2), 235–57.

Krugman, Paul. (1994). "The Myth of Asia's Miracle." *Foreign Affairs,* November/December.

Kumar, Nagesh. (1994). *Multinational Enterprises and Industrial Organization: The Case of India.* New Delhi: Sage Publications.

Kumbhakar, Subal C., and Subrata Sarkar. (2003). "Deregulation, Ownership, and Productivity Growth in the Banking Industry: Evidence from India." *Journal of Money, Credit and Banking*, 35 (3), 403–24.

Kurian, M. K. (1966). *Impact of Foreign Capital on Indian Economy.* New Delhi: People's Publishing House.

Lal, Deepak, Suman Bery, and Devendra Pant. (2003). "The Real Exchange Rate, Fiscal Deficits, and Capital Flows: India, 1981–2000." *Economic and Political Weekly*, 38 (47), November 22–28, 4965–76.

La Porta, Rafael, Florencio Lopez de Silanes, and Andrei Shleifer. (2002). "Government Ownership of Banks." *Journal of Finance*, 57, 265–301.

Leclerq, Francois. (2003). "Education Guarantee Scheme and Primary Schooling in Madhya Pradesh." *Economic and Political Weekly* 38(19), May 10–16, 1855–69.

Lewis, John P. (1962). "Quiet Crisis in India: Economic Development and Amercian Policy." Washingotn, DC: Brookings Institution.

Lim, Phillip Wonhyuk. (2000). "Path Dependence in Action: The Rise and Fall of the Korean Model of Economic Development." Seoul: Korean Development Institute.

Little, Ian. (1996). "Picking Winners: The East Asian Experience." Social Market Foundation Occasional Paper. London.

Lok Sabha Secretariat (1967). *Ninth Report of the Committee on Industrial Licensing*, New Delhi.

Maddison, Angus (1971). "Reasons for the Acceleration of Economic Growth Since Independence." In Maddison's *Class Structure and Economic Growth: India and Pakistan Since the Moghuls* (pp. 76–85). London: George Allen and Unwin. Reprinted by Routledge on November 11, 2005 under its Economic History series.

Mahal, Ajay, Janmejaya Singh, Farzana Afridi, Vikram Lamba, Anil Gumber, and V. Selvaraju. (2001). "Who Benefits from Public Health Spending in India?" New Delhi: National Council of Applied Economic Research.

Mahalingam, Sudha. (2005). "Regulatory Experiments in the Indian Power Sector: Missing the Wood for the Trees." In Amita Singh (ed.), *Administration in the Perspective of Reforms.* New Delhi: Sage Publications.

Mahalonobis, P. C. (1955/62). "Draft Recommendations for the Formulation of the Second Five Year Plan 1956–61." In Planning Commission, *Papers Relating to the Formulation of the Second Five Year Plan 1955.* Delhi: Manager of Publications.

———. (1963). *The Approaches of Operations Research to Planning in India.* London: Asia Publishing House.

Malhotra, R. N. (1992). "Economic Reforms: Retrospect and Prospects." ASCI Foundation Day Lecture. Administrative Staff College of India, Hyderabad.

Maran, Murasoli. (2002). "Keynote Address." Annual Bank Conference on Development Economics, Oslo, Norway, June 24.

Marathe, S. S. (1986). *Regulation and Development: India's Policy Experience of Controls over Industry.* New Delhi: Sage Publications.

Mathur, Sachin. (2006). "Indian Railways: Changing Tracks." Crisil Research, http://www. sbf.org.sg/download/docs/home/indianrailways.pdf.

McDowell, Stephen D. (1997). *Globalization, Liberalization and Policy Change: A Political Economy of India's Communications Sector.* New York: St. Martin's Press.

McKinsey Global Institute. (2001). *India: the Growth Imperative.* http://www.mckinsey. com/mgi/publications/india.asp.

Mehta, T. U. (1994). "Contribution of Judiciary to Industrial Equity." In D. S. Saini (ed.), *Labor Judiciary, Adjudication and Industrial Justice.* New Delhi: Oxford University Press and International Book House.

Ministry of Agriculture. (2004). *Agricultural Statistics at a Glance.* New Delhi: Government of India.

Ministry of Civil Aviation. (2005–06). *Annual Report 2005–06.* New Delhi: Government of India.

Ministry of Power. (1993). *Annual Report 1992–93.* New Delhi: Government of India.

———. (2001). *Annual Report 2000–01.* New Delhi: Government of India.

———. (2006). *Performance Report.* New Delhi: Government of India.

Ministry of Railways. (2001). *Indian Railways Report on Policy Imperatives for Reinvention and Growth by Expert Group on Indian Railways,* vols. 1 and 2. New Delhi: Government of India.

Mishra, Srijit. (2006a). "Suicide Mortality Rates Across States of India, 1975–2001: A Statistical Note." *Economic and Political Weekly* 41(16), April 22–28, 1566–69.

———. (2006b). "Farmers' Suicides in Maharashtra." *Economic and Political Weekly* 41(16), April 22–28, 1538–45.

———. (2007). "Agrarian Scenario in Post-reform India: A Story of Distress, Despair and Death." WP 2007–001. Mumbai: Indira Gandhi Institute of Development Research.

Mody, Bella. (1995). "State Consolidation Through Liberalization of Telecom." *Journal of Communication,* 45 (4).

Mohan, Rakesh. (2000). "Small Scale Industry Policy in India: A Critical Evluation," presented at the conference "Indian Economic Prospects: Advancing Policy Reforms" held on May 31–June 1, 2000 at the Center for Research on Economic Developmentand Policy Reform, Stanford University.

———. (2006). "Financial Sector Reforms and Monetary Policy: The Indian Experience." Paper presented at the Pan Asia Conference, Stanford Center for International Development, June 1–3.

Monopolies Enquiry Commission. (1964). *Report of the Monopolies Enquiry Commission.* New Delhi: Government of India.

Mukerji, Purba. (2006). "Ready for Capital Account Convertibility?" University of San Francisco (September). Mimeo.

Mundle, Sudipto, and M. Govinda Rao. (1991). "Volume and Composition of Government Subsidies in India: 1987–88." *Economic and Political Weekly,* May 4, 1157–72.

Muralidharan, Karthik. (2006). "Public-Private Partnerships for Quality Education in India." *Seminar,* no.565 (September).

———, and Michael Kremer. (2006). "Public and Private Schools in Rural India." Department of Economics, Harvard University. Mimeo.

Naik, B. M. (2001). "Positive Aspects of Privatization." *Hindu,* July 3.

Najinyanupi. (1973). "Some Philosophic Aspects of the Approach." *Economic and Political Weekly,* 8 (annual no.; February), 141–43.

Nandraj, S., and R. Duggal. (1996). "Physical Standards in the Private Health Sector." *Radical Journal of Health,* 2 (2–3), 141–84.

Narain, Dharam. (1977). "Growth of Productivity in Indian Agriculture." *Indian Journal of Agricultural Economics,* 32 (1), 1–44.

National Institute of Agricultural Extension Management. (2003). "Contract Farming Ventures in India: A Few Successful Cases." *Spice* 1 (4), 1–6.

National Institute of Public Finance and Policy. (1994). *Reform of Domestic Trade Taxes in India: Issues and Options*. New Delhi: National Institute of Public Finance and Policy.

National Sample Survey Organization. (2006). *Employment and Unemployment Situation in India, 2004–05,* part I. Report no. 515, New Delhi: National Sample Survey Organization.

Nayar, Baldev Raj. (1972). *The Modernization Imperative and Indian Planning*. Delhi: Vikas.

———. (2003). "Globalization and India's National Autonomy." *Journal of Commonwealth and Comparative Politics*, 41 (2), 1–34.

Nayyar, D. (2006). "Economic Growth in Independent India: Lumbering Elephant or Running Tiger?" *Economic and Political Weekly* 41(15), April 15–21, 1451–58.

Nehru, B. K. (1997). *Nice Guys Finish Second*. New Delhi: Viking.

Nehru, Jawaharlal. (1946). *The Discovery of India*. New York: John Day.

———. (undated). *Planning and Development: Speeches of Jawaharlal Nehru 1952–56*. New Delhi: Publications Division, Government of India.

Noll, Roger G., and Scott Wallsten. (2004). "Telecommunications Policy in India." Preliminary draft, Stanford Center for International Development and AEI Joint Center on Regulation (June 1).

———. (2005–06). "The Universal Telecommunications Service in India." *India Policy Forum*, 2, 254–87.

Panagariya, Arvind. (1990). "Indicative Planning in India: Discussion." *Journal of Comparative Economics*, 14, 736–42.

———. (1994). "India: A New Tiger on the Block?" *Journal of International Affairs*, 48 (1), 193–221.

———. (2000a). "My Millennium Wish: Double-Digit Growth." *Economic Times*, January 12.

———. (2000b). "And Now to Enter the Exit Policy." *Economic Times*, July 19.

———. (2000c). "Preferential Trade Liberalization: The Traditional Theory and New Developments." *Journal of Economic Literature*, 38, 287–331.

———. (2000d). "Bringing Competition to Bureaucracy." *Economic Times*, September 27.

———. (2001a). "Fertilizer Subsidy." *Economic Times*, February 28.

———. (2001b). "End the State Monopoly in Higher Education." *Economic Times*, March 28.

———. (2001c). "Trading Freely in Ideas." *Economic Times*, December 19.

———. (2002a). "Why India Lags Behind China." *Economic Times*, May 22.

———. (2002b). "Resolving the RBI Dilemma." *Economic Times*, August 28.

———. (2002c). "Stamping in Nutrition." *Economic Times*, April 24.

———. (2002d). "The Right Recipe." *Economic Times*, March 27.

———. (2002e). "Tackling the Crisis in Higher Education." *Economic Times*, October 23.

———. (2002f). "India at Doha: Retrospect and Prospect." *Economic and Political Weekly* 37(04), January 26–February 01, 279–84.

———. (2004a). "Growth and Reforms During 1980s and 1990s." *Economic and Political Weekly* 39(25), June 19–25, 2581–94.

———. (2004b). "India's Trade Reform." *India Policy Forum*, 1, 1–57.

———. (2004c). "Miracles and Debacles: In Defense of Trade Openness." *The World Economy*, 27 (8), 1149–71.

———. (2004d). "Vote Against Reforms?" *Economic and Political Weekly* 39(21), May 22–28, 2079–81.

———. (2004e). "Miracles and Debacles: Do Free Trade Skeptics Have a Case?" Columbia University. Mimeo.

———. (2005a). "Muddles on Forex for Infrastructure." *Economic Times*, January 12.

Panagariya, Arvind. (2005b). "Is a Crisis Around the Corner?" In Peter Heller and Govinda Rao (eds.), *Sustainable Fiscal Policy for India* (pp. 143–49). New Delhi: Oxford University Press.

———. (2005c). "Bringing Competition to the Top Civil Service." *Yojana*. New Delhi: Planning Commission (August).

———. (2005d). "A Passage to Prosperity." *Wall Street Journal*, July 14.

———. (2006a). "Transforming India." Paper presented at the conference "India: An Emerging Giant." School of International and Public Affairs and Columbia Business School, Columbia University, October 13–15.

———. (2006b). "The Political Economy of Trade and Foreign Investment Policies in India: 1950–2006." Paper presented at the conference "Applied Economic Research in Independent India: The Way Forward." National Council on Applied Economic Research, December 17.

———. (2006c). "India and China: Trade and Foreign Investment." Paper presented at the conference "Challenges of Economic Policy Reform in Asia." Stanford Center for International Development, June 1–3.

———. (2006d). "External Liberalization by India and China: Recent Experience and Future Challenges." Paper presented at Macroeconomy Research Conference of the Tokyo Club Foundation for Global Studies, December 6–7.

———. (2006e). "Is a Crisis Around the Corner?" (comment on "A Balance Sheet Crisis in India," by Nouriel Roubini and Richard Hemming) in Peter S. Heller and Govinda Rao, *A Sustainable Fiscal Policy for India: An International Perspective*. New Delhi: Oxford University Press.

———, and Dani Rodrik (1993). "Political Economy Arguments for a Uniform Tariff." *International Economic Review*, August, 685–703.

Pande, Anuja Joshi. (2006). "So What Is So Special About Special Economic Zones?" Paper written for the course "Indian Economy in Transition" at Columbia University (December).

Pant, Pitambar. (1962). *Perspectives of Development 1961–76: Implications of Planning for a Minimum Level of Living*. New Delhi: Planning Commission.

Patel, I. G. (1987). "On Taking India into the Twenty-first Century (New Economic Policy in India)." *Modern Asian Studies,* 21 (2), 209–31.

———. (2002). *Glimpses of Indian Economic Policy: An Insider's View*. New Delhi: Oxford University Press.

Patnaik, Ila. (2003). "India's Policy Stance on Reserves and the Currency." ICRIER Working Paper no. 108.

———. (2004). "India's Experience with a Pegged Exchange Rate." *India Policy Forum*, 1, 189–216.

———, and Ajay Shah. (2006). "The Interplay Between Capital Flows and the Domestic Indian Financial System." June 19 draft. Mimeo.

Patrick, Hugh T. (1966). "Financial Development and Economic Growth in Under-developed Countries." *Economic Development and Cultural Change*, 14 (2), 174–89.

Planning Commission. (1951). *First Five Year Plan*. New Delhi: Government of India.

———. (1955/1962). *Papers Relating to the Formulation of the Second Five Year Plan 1955*. Delhi: Manager of Publications.

———. (1956). *Second Five Year Plan*. New Delhi: Government of India.

———. (1993). *Report of the Expert Group on Estimation of Proportion and Number of Poor*. New Delhi: Government of India.

———. (2000). *Mid-Term Appraisal of Ninth Five Year Plan (1997–2002)*. New Delhi: Government of India.

———. (2001). *Report of the Task Force on Employment Opportunities*. New Delhi: Government of India.

———. (2002). *Tenth Five Year Plan (2002–07)*. New Delhi: Government of India.

———. (2005). *Midterm Appraisal of the Tenth Five Year Plan (2002–07)*. New Delhi: Government of India.

———. (2006). *Towards Faster and More Inclusive Growth: An Approach to the 11th Five Year Plan*. New Delhi: Government of India.

Prasad, Eswar, Kenneth Rogoff, Shang-jin Wei, and Ayhan Kose. (2003). "Effects of Financial Globalisation on Developing Countries: Some Empirical Evidence." IMF Occasional Paper 220. Washington, DC: International Monetary Fund.

——— and Shang-Jin Wei. (2006). "Understanding the Structure of Cross-border Capital Flows: The Case of China." Presented at the the the conference "China at Crossroads: FX and Capital Markets Policies for the Coming Decade," held at Columbia University on February 2–3, 2006.

Prasad, Eswar S., Kenneth Rogoff, Shang-Jin Wei, and M. Ayhan Kose. (2003). "Effects of Financial Globalization on Developing Countries: Some Empirical Evidence." IMF Occasional Paper 220. Washington: International Monetary Fund.

Prasad, H. A. C. (2003). "Services Exports: Opportunities and Barriers." *Business Line*, August 23.

Pratham. (2006). *Annual Status of Education Report (Rural)*. http://www.pratham.org/aser2006.php.

Prayas. (2003). *A Good Beginning but Challenges Galore: A Survey Based Study of Resources, Transparency, and Public Participation in Electricity Regulatory Commissions in India*. Pune: Prayas.

———. (2006). *A Critical Review of the Performance of Delhi's Privatized Distribution Companies and Regulatory Process*. Pune: Prayas.

PROBE Team. (1999). *Public Report on Basic Education in India*. New Delhi: Oxford University Press.

Purohit, Brijesh. (2001). "Private Initiatives and Policy Options: Recent Health Care Experience in India." *Health Policy and Planning*, 16 (1), 87–97.

Pursell, Garry. (1992). "Trade Policy in India." In Dominick Salvatore (ed.), *National Trade Policies* (pp. 423–58). New York: Greenwood Press.

Radwan, Ismail. (2005). "India: Private Health Service for the Poor." Health, Nutrition and Population (HNP) Discussion Paper 33579, World Bank (May).

Raghuram, G. (2007). "'Turnaround' of Indian Railways: A Critical Appraisal of Strategies and Processes." Working Paper no. 2007-03-03, Indian Institute of Management, Ahmadabad.

Raj, K. N. (1965). *Indian Economic Growth: Performance and Prospects*. New Delhi: Allied Publishers.

Rajaraman, Indira. (2005). "Fiscal Developments and Outlook in India." In Peter Heller and Govinda Rao (eds.), *Sustainable Fiscal Policy for India*. New Delhi: Oxford University Press.

———, and Debdatta Majumdar. (2005). "Equity and Consistency Properties of TFC Recommendations." *Economic and Political Weekly* 40(31), July 30–August 5, 3413–20.

Ram Mohan, T. T. (2003). "Strategic Sale Versus Public Offer: Dispelling Myths." *Economic and Political Weekly* 38(28), July 12–18, 2969–76.

Ramachandriah, C. (2005) "Hyderabad's Floods: Nature's Revenge." *Economic and Political Weekly* 40(38), September 17–23, 4115–16.

Rangarajan, C., and D. K. Srivastava. (2003). "Dynamics of Debt Accumulation in India: Impact of Primary Deficit, Growth and Interest Rate." *Economic and Political Weekly,* November 15–21, 4851–58.

Rao, C. H. Hanumantha. (2002). "Sustainable Use of Water for Irrigation in Indian Agriculture." *Economic and Political Weekly* 37(18), May 4–10, 1742–45.

Rao, C. H. Hanumantha. (2003). "Reform Agenda for Agriculture." *Economic and Political Weekly* 38(07), February 15–21, 615–20.

Rao, J. Mohan (1996). "Manufacturing Productivity Growth, Method and Measurement." *Economic and Political Weekly*, November 2–8, 2927–36.

Rao, M. Govinda. (2003). "Reform in the Central Sales Tax in the Context of VAT." *Economic and Political Weekly*, February 15.

———. (2006). *Mid-Year Review of the Indian Economy 2005–06*. Delhi: Shipra.

———, and Sudipto Mundle. (1992). "An Analysis of Changes in State Government Subsidies: 1977–87." In A. Bagchi, J. L. Bajaj, and W. A. Byrd (eds.), *State Finances in India*. New Delhi: National Institute of Public Finance and Policy.

———, and R. Kavita Rao. (2005–06). "Trends and Issues in Tax Policy and Reform in India." *India Policy Forum*, 2, 55–107.

———, and Nirvikar Singh. (2004). "The Political Economy of India's Federal System and Its Reform." University of California at Santa Cruz. Mimeo.

Reserve Bank of India. (1969). Reported by Bhagwati and Desai (1970, chap. 11).

———. (1985). *Report of the Committee to Review the Working of the Monetary System*. Mumbai: Reserve Bank of India.

———. (1997). *Report of the Committee on Capital Account Convertibility*, Mumbai.

———. (2001). *Report of the Advisory Group on Bankruptcy Laws*. Mumbai: Reserve Bank of India (May 9).

———. (2003). *Report of the Group to Study the Pension Liabilities of the State Governments* October, Mumbai.

———. (2004). *Report of Working Group on Development Financial Institutions*. Mumbai: Reserve Bank of India.

———. (2005a). *Handbook of Statistics on Indian Economy*. Mumbai: Reserve Bank of India (September).

———. (2005b). *Report on Foreign Exchange Reserves*. Mumbai: Reserve Bank of India (July 6).

———. (2005c). *Draft Technical Paper by the Internal Working Group on Priority Sector Lending*. Mumbai: Reserve Bank of India (September).

———. (2005d). *Report of the Internal Technical Group on Central Government Securities Market*. Mumbai: Reserve Bank of India (July).

———. (2005e). *Statistical Tables Relating to the Banks of India*. Mumbai.

———. (2005f). *Report on Trends and Progress of Banking in India 2004–05*.

———. (2006). Handbook of Statistics of Indian Economy, Mumbai: Reserve Bank of India.

———. Various Volumes. *Banking Statistics*. Mumbai.

Rodrik, Dani (1995). "Getting Interventions Right: How South Korea and Taiwan Grew Rich." *Economic Policy*, 20, 55–107.

———. (1999). *The New Global Economy and Developing Countries: Making Openness Work*. Washington, DC: Overseas Development Council.

———. (2003). "Institutions, Integration, and Geography: In Search of the Deep Determinants of Economic Growth." In Dani Rodrik (ed.), *In Search of Prosperity: Analytic Narratives of Economic Growth*. Princeton, NJ: Princeton University Press.

———, and Arvind Subramanian. (2005). "From 'Hindu Growth' to Productivity Surge: The Mystery of the Indian Growth Transition." *IMF Staff Papers*, 52 (2).

Roubini, Nouriel, and Richard Hemming. "Balance Sheet Crises." In Peter Heller and Govinda Rao (eds.), *Sustainable Fiscal Policy for India* (pp. 114–42). New Delhi: Oxford University Press.

Roy, Jayanta. (2003). "Feeling Good, but Vision Still Needed." *The Financial Express*, October 20.

————, and Shweta Bagai. (2005). "Key Issues in Trade Facilitation: Summary of World Bank/EU Workshops in Dhaka and Shanghai in 2004." World Bank Policy Research Working Paper no. 3703.

Saha, V., A. Kar, and T. Baskaran. (2004). "Contribution of Informal Sector and Informal Employment in Indian Economy." Paper presented at 7th Meeting of the Expert Group on Informal Sector Statistics, New Delhi (February).

Sarma, J. S. (1978). "India—A Drive Towards Self-Sufficiency in Food Grains." *American Journal of Agricultural Economics*, 60 (5), 859–64.

Satpathy, S. K., and S. Venkatesh. (2006). "Human Resources for Health in India's National Rural Health Mission: Dimensions and Challenges." *Regional Health Forum,* 10 (1), 29–37.

Savant, Tejas. (2006). "India's Special Economic Zones: The Next Big Thing?" Paper written for the course "Indian Economy in Transition" at Columbia University (December).

Sen, Abhijit. (2000). "Estimates of Consumer Expenditure and Its Distribution: Statistical Priorities after NSS 55th Round." *Economic and Political Weekly*, December 16–22.

————, and Himanshu. (2004a). "Poverty and Inequality in India—I." *Economic and Political Weekly* 39(38), September 18–24, 4247–63.

————. (2004b). "Poverty and Inequality in India—II: Widening Disparities During the 1990s." *Economic and Political Weekly* 39(39), September 24–30, 4361–75.

Sengupta, Sunanda. (1985). "Review of Industrial Licensing Policy." Working Paper VII. In World Bank, *India: Structural Change and Development Perspectives,* report no. 5593-IN.

Shah, Ajay (2005). "A Sustainable and Scalable Approach in Indian Pension Reform." December 5, mimeo. Available at http://www.mayin.org/ajayshah/PDFDOCS/Shah2005_sustainable_pension_reform.pdf. Revised version published in David A. Kelly, Ramkishen S. Rajan, and Gillian H. L. Goh, editors, *Managing Globalisation: Lessons from China and India*, chapter 7. Singapore: World Scientific, 2006

Shah, Ajay, and Ila Patnaik. (2006). India's Experience with Capital Flows: The Elusive Quest for a Sustainable Current Account Deficit." Mimeo. Revised version published in Sebastian Edwards, ed., *Capital Controls and Capital Flows in Emerging Economies: Policies, Practices and Consequences*, chapter 13, pages 609–643. Chicago, IL: The University of Chicago Press, 2007

Sharma, Amita, and R. Gopalkrishnan. (2003). "Opinion or Facts? EGS in Madhya Pradesh." *Economic and Political Weekly* 38(49), December 6–12, 5210–15.

Sharma, G. D. (1974). *Streamlined Procedures of Industrial Licensing, Law & Regulations.* Delhi: Press Publications Agency.

Sharma, Gunjan. (2006). "Competing or Collaborating Siblings? Industrial and Trade Policies in India." Department of Economics, University of Missouri at Columbia (May 29).

Shetty, S. L. (2003). "Growth of SDP and Structural Changes in the State Economies: Inter-state Comparisons." *Economic and Political Economy*, December 6, 5189–5200.

Shourie, Arun. (2004). *Governance and the Sclerosis That Has Set In.* New Delhi: Rupa.

Singh, Nirvikar. (2006). "Services-led Industrialization in India: Prospects and Challenges." Working Paper no. 290, Stanford Center for International Development, Stanford University.

————, Lavesh Bhandari, Aoyu Chen, and Aarti Khare. (2003). "Regional Inequality in India: A Fresh Look." *Economic and Political Economy*, March 15, 1069–73.

Singh, Nirvikar, and T. N. Srinivasan. (2002). "Indian Federalism, Economic Reform and Globalization." Paper prepared for CREDPR Project on Globalization and Comparative Federalism.

Singh, N. K., and Jessica Wallack. (2005). "Moving India: Policy Strategies for Transport Sector Reform." Paper presented at the Stanford Center for International Development Annual Conference on Indian Economic Reforms (June).

Sinha, Suresh K. (2001). "Architect of the Green Revolution." *The Hindu*, magazine section, November 4.

Sinha, Tapan. (2002). "Privatization of the Insurance Market in India: From the British Raj to Monopoly Raj to Swaraj." CRIS Discussion Paper Series, 2002. Center for Risk and Insurance Studies, University of Nottingham.

Sivasubramonian, S. (2004). *The Sources of Economic Growth in India: 1950–51 to 1999–2000*. New Delhi: Oxford University Press.

Srinavasan, T. N. (1999). "Poverty and Reforms in India." Yale University (December). Mimeo.

———. (2000). *Eight Lectures on Indian Economic Reforms*. New Delhi: Oxford University Press.

———. (2005). "Comments on 'From Hindu Growth to Productivity Surge': The Mystery of the Indian Growth Transition." *IMF Staff Papers*, 52 (2).

———, and P. K. Bardhan. (1974). *Poverty and Income Distribution in India*. Calcutta: Statistical Publishing Society.

———, and P. K. Bardhan (eds.). (1988). *Rural Poverty in South Asia*. New York: Columbia University Press.

———, and S. Tendulkar. (2003). *Reintegrating India with the World Economy*. Washington, DC: Institute for International Economics.

Sriraman, S. (2006). "Cartelization in the Trucking Industry in India." PowerPoint presentation posted at http://www.competition-commission-india.nic.in.

Srivastava, D. K., and Tapas K. Sen. (1997). *Government Subsidies in India*. New Delhi: National Institute of Public Finance and Policy.

Sundaram, K., and S. Tendulkar. (2001). "NAS-NSS Estimates of Private Consumption for Poverty Estimation: A Disaggregated Comparison for 1993–94." *Economic and Political Weekly* 36(02), January 13–19, 119–29.

———. (2002). "Recent Debates on Data Base for Measurement of Poverty in India." Delhi School of Economics. Word-processed. Presented at joint GOI/World Bank poverty workshop, Delhi (January). Available at http://www.worldbank.org/indiapovertyworkshop.

———. (2003a). "Poverty *Has* Declined in the 1990s: A Resolution of Comparability Problems in NSS Consumer Expenditure Data." *Economic and Political Weekly* 38(04), January 25–31, 376–84.

———. (2003b). "Poverty in India in the 1990s: Revised Results for All-India and 15 Major States for 1993–94." *Economic and Political Weekly* 38(46), November 15–22, 4865–72.

Swaminathan, T. (1964). *Report of the Industrial Development Proceures Committee*, New Delhi: Government of India.

Telecom Regulatory Authority of India (TRAI). (2005–06). *Annual Report 2005–06*. New Delhi: TRAI.

Tendulkar, Suresh. (1998). "Indian Economic Policy Reforms and Poverty: An Assessment." In Isher Judge Ahluwalia and I. M. D. Little (eds.), *India's Economic Reforms and Development: Essays in Honor of Manmohan Singh* (pp. 280–309). Delhi: Oxford University Press.

———, and T. A. Bhavani. (2003). "Understanding the Post-1991 Indian Economic Policy Reform." Global Development Network, second draft (undated).

Tooley, James, and Pauline Dixon. (undated). "Private Schools Serving the Poor: A Study from Delhi, India." Working Paper, Viewpoint 8, Center for Civil Society, New Delhi.

Topalova, Petia. (2005). "Trade Liberalization, Poverty and Inequality: Evidence from Indian Districts." NBER Working Paper no. 11614.

Varghese, N. V. (2000). "Reforming Education Financing." *Seminar* October, No. 494, Available at http://www.india-seminar.com/2000/494/494%20n.v.%20varghese.htm.

Varshney, Ashutosh. (1995). *Democracy, Development, and the Countryside: Urban-Rural Struggle in India*. New York: Cambridge University Press.

Virmani, Arvind. (1997). "Economic Development and Transition in India." Paper presented at the Tokyo Dialogue on Alternatives to the World Bank-IMF Approach to Reforms and Growth. Economic Planning Agency, Tokyo, November 7.

Wade, Robert. (1990). *Governing the Market: Theory and the Role of Government in East Asian Industrialization*. Princeton, NJ: Princeton University Press.

Wadhwa, D. C. (2002). "Guaranteeing Titles to Land." *Economic and Political Weekly* 37(47), November 23–29, 4699–722.

Wallack, Jessica. (2003). "Structural Breaks in Indian Macroeconomic Data." *Economic and Political Economy*, October 11–17, 4312–15.

Westphal, Larry E. (1990). "Industrial Policy in an Export-Propelled Economy: Lessons from South Korea's Experience." *Journal of Economic Perspectives*, 4 (3), 41–59.

———, and Kwang Suk Kim. (1982). "Korea: Incentive Policies for Exports and Import Substitution." In Bela Balassa (ed.), *Development Strategies in Semi-industrialized Economies* (pp. 212–79). Baltimore: Johns Hopkins University Press.

Williamson, John. 1993. "A Cost-Benefit Analysis of Capital Account Liberalisation." In B. Fischer and H. Reisen, eds. *Financial Opening: Policy Issues and Experiences in Developing Countries*. Paris: OECD

World Bank. (1985). *Structural Change and Development Perspectives*. Report no. 5593-IN. Washington, DC: World Bank.

———. (1987). *India: An Industrializing Economy in Transition*. Report no. 6633-IN. Washington, DC: World Bank.

———. (1988). *India: Recent Developments and Medium Term Issues*. Report no. 7185-IN. Washington, DC: World Bank.

———. (1990). *India: Trends, Issues and Options*. Report no. 8360-IN. Washington, DC: World Bank.

———. (2001). *Better Health Systems for India's Poor: Analysis, Findings and Options*. Report no. 24124. Washington, DC: World Bank.

———. (2002). *India's Transport Sector: The Challenges Ahead*. Energy and Infrastructure Sector Unit, South Asia Region (May 10).

———. (2003). *Global Economic Prospects: 2003*. Washington, DC: World Bank.

———. (2004). *World Development Report 2004: Making Services Work for the Poor*. Washington, DC: World Bank.

———. (2005a). *World Development Report 2006: Equity and Development*. Washington, DC: World Bank.

———. (2005b). *India: Road Transport Service Efficiency Study*. Report no. 34220-IN. Energy and Infrastructure Operations Division, South Asia Regional Office. Washington DC: World Bank.

———. (2005c). *Improving the Investment Climate in India* South Asia Region and Investment Climate Unit, Washington, DC.: World Bank

———. (2005d). *World Development Indicators*, Washington, DC.

———. (2006a). "India Water Supply and Sanitation: Bridging the Gap Between Infrastructure and Service." South Asia Region Working Paper 35834. Washington, DC: World Bank.

———. (2006b). *World Development Indicators*. Washington, DC: World Bank.

World Trade Organization. (1998). *Trade Policy Review: India*. Geneva: WTO Secretariat.

———. (2002). *Trade Policy Review: India*. Geneva: WTO Secretariat.

Wu, Kin Bing, Vanita Kaul, and Deepa Sankar. (2005). "The Quiet Revolution." *Finance and Development*, 42 (2).

Xue, Lan. (2006). "The Role of Universities in China's Economic Development: A National Innovation System Perspective." Paper presented at the conference Challenges of Economic Policy Reform in Asia." Stanford Center for International Development, June 1–3.

Yoo, Jungho. (1997). "Neoclassical Versus Revisionist View of Korean Economic Growth." Development Discussion Paper no. 588, Harvard Institute for International Development, Harvard University.

Zagha, Roberto (1998). "Labor and India's Economic Reform." *Journal of Policy Reform* 2(4), 403–26.

INDEX